EDWARD MUSSEY HARTWELL (1850-1922)

A GUIDE TO
THE HISTORY OF
PHYSICAL EDUCATION

BY

FRED EUGENE LEONARD, A.M., M.D.

LATE PROFESSOR OF HYGIENE AND PHYSICAL EDUCATION IN OBERLIN COLLEGE
OBERLIN, OHIO

THIRD EDITION, REVISED AND ENLARGED BY

GEORGE B. AFFLECK, A.M., M.P.E.

FORMERLY DIRECTOR, HEALTH AND PHYSICAL EDUCATION DIVISION,
SPRINGFIELD COLLEGE, SPRINGFIELD, MASS.

Illustrated with 121 engravings

GREENWOOD PRESS, PUBLISHERS
WESTPORT, CONNECTICUT

The Library of Congress cataloged this book as follows:

Leonard, Fred Eugene, 1866–1922.
  A guide to the history of physical education. 3d ed., rev. and enl. by George B. Affleck. Illustrated with 121 engravings. Westport, Conn., Greenwood Press [1971, °1947]

  480 p. illus., ports. 23 cm.

  Includes bibliographical references.

  1. Physical education and training—History. I. Affleck, George Baird, 1876–   II. Title.

GV1211.L35 1971	613.7	73–138593
ISBN 0–8371–5794–3		MARC
Library of Congress	71 [4]	

TO

THE MEMORY OF

DR. EDWARD MUSSEY HARTWELL

WHO FIRST IN AMERICA BLAZED THE TRAIL

WHICH I HAVE TRIED TO FOLLOW

PREFACE TO THE THIRD EDITION.

THE publication of a third edition of Dr. Fred Leonard's text has been decided upon because of many urgent requests, chiefly from teacher training institutions.

Present chaotic conditions render it difficult to secure authoritative information, especially from abroad, so this edition makes no claim to completeness, but simply aims to bring up to date significant facts concerning the development of the subject through selected organizations in various countries and to indicate the main contributions to the profession of certain leaders and of their successors during the last twenty years.

Acknowledgement and appreciation of the splendid coöperation of others appears in connection with the various articles.

GEORGE B. AFFLECK.

SPRINGFIELD, MASS.

PREFACE TO THE FIRST EDITION.

THIRTY years ago, when the writer of these lines was called to a professorship in physical education, there existed no comprehensive survey of the field he was entering. The reports of Dr. Hartwell contained excellent summaries which suggested our debt to the past and to foreign lands, and fuller treatment of certain earlier periods in the United States; but the English language offered little else of value. Suitable preparation of courses in the principles and methods of physical education required more ample knowledge of what others had done and were doing, and the task of finding out and gathering together the best of the European literature bearing on the subject was at once begun and has been continued ever since. A summer trip to Germany in 1896 whetted an appetite which later found satisfaction in an entire year (1900–1901) on the Continent, where the large special collections at the Stockholm Central Institute of Gymnastics and the Berlin *Turnlehrerbildungsanstalt* supplied for the first time an opportunity to become familiar with the older books and periodicals. The year also contributed to the linguistic knowledge and experience needed for the handling of such material. The direct contact with historic spots and significant aspects of physical education in Europe which it brought was afterward renewed and broadened by five months (February to June, 1913) spent at important centers in Switzerland, Germany, the three Scandinavian countries and Great Britain.

Meanwhile the collection of material had progressed at a rapid rate, and from time to time as circumstances permitted chapters of a book-to-be were prepared and published, in irregular order, and biographical sketches which might later be incorporated in such a work as the present one. Thus it happens that only five of the twenty-eight chapters in this volume are altogether new, though all have been carefully revised and many of them largely rewritten within the last year and a half. The selection of topics, order of arrangement and manner of presentation have been determined experimentally in courses given to students in Oberlin College since the spring of 1894, and for thirteen years (1899, 1902, and 1908–1919) at the Harvard University Summer School. The illustrations are chosen from nearly six hundred which have been employed in the form of lantern slides in these courses. With few exceptions the references in the text and footnotes are based on first-hand examination of the originals.

(9)

If we except Viktor Heikel's *Gymnastikens Historia* (issued at Helsingfors in four parts, 1905–1909), comprehensive in plan but quite erratic in its treatment of the United States, no work undertaking to trace the history of physical education in Europe and America and to describe the chief present-day movements has appeared hitherto in any language.   Euler's standard *Geschichte des Turnunterrichts* and the lesser German manuals, while they are in general excellent guides so far as ancient and medieval Europe are concerned, and for the recent history in that particular country, have little or nothing to say of the rest of modern Europe, except as it has influenced Germany herself.   This is less true of Euler's monumental *Encyklopädisches Handbuch des gesamten Turnwesens* and the more recent *Handbuch des gesamten Turnwesens* of Dr. Rudolf Gasch, but in these, too, the space allotted to non-German subjects is altogether insufficient.   Similarly Illeris and Trap's brief *Grundtræk af Gymnastikkens Historie* covers chiefly Danish experience. For each country one must consult its own literature, and particularly the periodical publications, and he needs also to supplement his reading by personal observation and investigation on the ground in order to avoid distorted views and arrive at sound conclusions.

If this attempt to set forth clearly the characteristics of the different stages and phases through which physical education has passed, to introduce the persons who have contributed to its advancement, and to guide the reader to the best that has been written on the subject, shall lead to deeper and more general appreciation of the place which physical education should win and hold in general education, and to the adoption of wiser measures where it is introduced, the labor expended upon the volume will be well rewarded. Much has been omitted which might have been included.   If inaccuracies are discovered the author will be glad to have his attention called to them.   F. E. L.

CONTENTS.

CHAPTER I.

THE GREEKS.

CHAPTER II.

THE ROMANS.

CHAPTER III.

THE TEUTONIC INVADERS OF THE ROMAN EMPIRE

CHAPTER IV.

ASCETICISM IN THE EARLY CHRISTIAN CHURCH.

CHAPTER V.

MONASTERY AND CATHEDRAL SCHOOLS

CHAPTER VI.

CHIVALRY

CHAPTER VII.

THE UNIVERSITIES OF THE MIDDLE AGES 47

CHAPTER VIII.

THE PERIOD OF THE RENAISSANCE AND THE REFORMATION.

CHAPTER IX.

LOCKE AND ROUSSEAU.

CHAPTER X.

THE BEGINNINGS OF MODERN PHYSICAL EDUCATION IN GERMANY.

CHAPTER XI.

FRIEDRICH LUDWIG JAHN, AND POPULAR GYMNASTICS IN GERMANY.

CHAPTER XII.

ADOLF SPIESS, THE FATHER OF GERMAN SCHOOL GYMNASTICS.

CHAPTER XIII.

PHYSICAL TRAINING IN THE PRUSSIAN SCHOOLS.

CHAPTER XIV.

THE PLAYGROUND MOVEMENT IN GERMANY.

CHAPTER XV.

PER HENRIK LING, FATHER OF PHYSICAL EDUCATION IN SWEDEN.

CHAPTER XVI.

LING'S SUCCESSORS AT THE CENTRAL INSTITUTE IN STOCKHOLM.

CHAPTER XVII.

PHYSICAL EDUCATION IN THE SCHOOLS OF SWEDEN.

CHAPTER XVIII.

PHYSICAL EDUCATION IN DENMARK.

CHAPTER XIX.

GREAT BRITAIN.

CHAPTER XX.

INTERNATIONAL GATHERINGS.

CHAPTER XXI.

THE FIRST INTRODUCTION OF THE JAHN GYMNASTICS INTO AMERICA.

CHAPTER XXII.

THE "NEW GYMNASTICS" OF DIO LEWIS.

CHAPTER XXIII.

PHYSICAL EDUCATION IN AMERICAN COLLEGES AND UNIVERSITIES.

CHAPTER XXIV.

GERMAN-AMERICAN GYMNASTIC SOCIETIES AND THE NORTH AMERICAN TURNERBUND.

CHAPTER XXV.

PHYSICAL TRAINING IN THE YOUNG MEN'S CHRISTIAN ASSOCIATION.

CHAPTER XXVI.

SWEDISH SCHOOL GYMNASTICS IN THE UNITED STATES.

CHAPTER XXVII.

THE PLAYGROUND MOVEMENT IN AMERICA. STATEWIDE PHYSICAL EDUCATION.

CHAPTER XXVIII.
THE TRAINING OF TEACHERS.

CHAPTER XXIX.
PREWAR CONDITIONS IN EUROPE.

CHAPTER XXX.

CHAPTER XXXI.

CHAPTER XXXII.

CHAPTER XXXIII.

CHAPTER XXXIV.

CHAPTER XXXV.

CHAPTER XXXVI.
BIOGRAPHIES.

HISTORY OF
PHYSICAL EDUCATION.

CHAPTER I.

THE GREEKS.

MAN's earliest endeavor to perfect the body, discipline the mind and mold the character of the young by means of selected forms of physical activity and special regimen could doubtless be traced back to a prehistoric age. The study of ancient customs of China and India, Egypt, Babylonia and Assyria, the Phœnicians and Carthaginians, the Persians and the Hebrews might also yield some curious facts. But if one's purpose is to follow the evolution of modern forms of physical education in Europe and America and to note the significant contributions and modifications introduced at various stages, it is sufficient to begin with Greece as it was in the century and a half whose middle point is the year of Salamis and Thermopylæ (480 B.C.). There we find "gymnastics" generally adopted as a necessary part of education, provision everywhere made for the exercise of youths and grown men in establishments supported and administered by the state, great national festivals at which the chief attractions were contests in physical prowess, and at a later day sculptors able to reproduce from the type presented to them in the gymnasia ideal human figures which have never been excelled in beauty.

Several things must be borne in mind when one thinks of Greece in the period of the Persian Wars. It was not a nation in the modern sense of a political unit with a central government and circumscribed territory, but a group of independent states and cities in European Greece, on the islands of the Egean Sea, along the west coast of Asia Minor, and wherever else the Greek language was spoken by persons who felt the tie of a common descent, common religious beliefs and common customs.

(17)

These customs, furthermore, were not uniform. For example, education embraced two subjects of instruction and training, gymnastics and "music." The former reached primarily the body and the will; the latter, which included literary studies as well as music in the narrower sense, affected the intellect and the emotions. Sparta, surrounded by an unfriendly and subject people, was little more than an organized camp, in which self-preservation required a form of training designed to mold every citizen into the best possible weapon of defense. Individual welfare was therefore strictly subordinated to that of the community. Education was viewed as a function of the state, and physical hardihood, skilful use of weapons, self-reliant courage and iron discipline were developed by a type of education which was chiefly gymnastic and military. Literary training was neglected, and music, in the form of religious and patriotic hymns, war songs and ballads recounting the deeds of heroes, was valued solely for its stimulating effects. At Athens, on the other hand, we find a much broader type of education, which came more and more to dominate the practice of her sister states and cities. Complete and harmonious development of the individual was the object sought, and the schools were private affairs, over which the state exercised nothing more than police supervision. Gymnastics was hardly less essential than at Sparta, but literary training occupied a prominent place, and music was esteemed for its refining influence on character and its contribution to social enjoyment.

A third point to be noted is that whatever may be said of Greek education applies to free citizens only, and hence takes no account of slaves and the foreign-born, who made up possibly as much as three-fourths of the total population—at least in the case of the larger cities. And even within these limits it was usually boys alone for whom provision was made.

Turning first to physical education at Sparta, the earlier type, we find that the state began its efforts to secure a sound body of citizens by carefully regulating the life of the women, and formed an exception to the statement just made in that it prescribed for girls a course of gymnastic exercise. There was need of vigorous mothers for the sturdy race which public welfare demanded. As a further precaution, the new-born infant was brought before a council of old men, whose decision whether or not he should be raised was based upon his physical condition and promise, and was final. The first six years were passed in the home, but at the age of seven the boy was taken away from his parents, to be placed in public quarters. Here he slept and ate in company with a large number of other boys, and shared with them a common discipline at the hands of state officials who shaped every detail with reference to his future career as a citizen-warrior. He spent the night in a room open to the sky, without the luxury of bedclothes, on a pallet of hay or straw, exchanged when he was older for one of rushes which he had gathered himself along the river banks. He went summer and winter clad in a single scanty garment, unshod, bareheaded and with close-cropped hair. The food, of the plainest sort, was hardly sufficient to satisfy the cravings of hunger. The amount might be eked out by theft, however, but with the understanding that anyone so indiscreet or maladroit as to be detected in the act would receive prompt and severe punishment. Indeed, the rod and lash were freely applied, by public officers or by any offended citizen, upon the least provocation, and as a necessary part of the regular discipline, since it accustomed the future soldier to the endurance of pain. There were even what might be considered periodical tests of this capacity to endure, for at one of the annual festivals the flogging of youths was an essential feature, often carried to the drawing of blood, it is said. Like the Indian under torture, the victim was expected to give no signs of suffering.

For the gymnastic instruction which occupied the greater part of their time the boys were arranged in squads or "packs" according to age, and these in turn were combined into companies. Each division had its young leader, chosen on the score of ability and longer experience, but all were subject to the direction of special state officers. The course of training included practice in wrestling, running, jumping, throwing the javelin and the discus, marching in time to music, together with other military exercises, swimming in the Eurotas, riding on horseback, hunting and certain rough games. There was also practice in choral dances, for use on religious occasions, and in the war dance, representing the movements of attack and defense. This latter, the so-called Pyrrhic dance, was sometimes executed in armor, and by whole companies moving together in rhythm to the accompaniment of music. Occasional public exhibitions and contests acted as incentives to improvement and furnished opportunity to test it, satisfying at the same time the general fondness for such displays.

With the advent of his eighteenth year the youth left the common training quarters of the boys and entered upon a second stage of discipline. During the next two years his preparation took more and more the form of scouting in outlying districts of the state, and might involve actual warfare. His understanding had been matured meanwhile by constant intercourse with grown men in the affairs of daily public life.

Not much is known of the training imposed upon the Spartan girls; but it included both gymnastics and music, and among the exercises practised were running, jumping, throwing the spear and the discus, dancing, swimming and even wrestling.

In Athens, as at Sparta, weak, deformed or sickly infants were sometimes put out of the way ("exposed"), but in this case the decision rested with the father.   Here, too, the first six years were spent at home, under the charge of the women of the household. The play of childhood took most often the form of active exercise and games, and in the list of amusements, under the thin disguise of strange names, we discover many varieties which have survived to the present day with undiminished popularity: The small box of metal or wood containing stones which rattled when it was shaken; hobby-horses, swinging and seesaw, walking on stilts, trundling hoops, kite-flying; spinning tops, whipping the humming top and a game resembling our peg-top, but played with sharpened sticks; shooting or tossing smooth stones or nuts and the like, as in some of our modern games with marbles; tossing up and catching jackstones, in the shape of pebbles or small bones; making flat stones skip along the surface of the water, various exercises and games with balls, hide-and-seek, blindman's buff, games like our drop-the-handkerchief, and others in which sides were chosen and one side then chased its opponents in the attempt to make them prisoners.   Besides a share in the less violent of these sports, the little girls had, of course, their dolls, made of clay or wax and sometimes painted.   They seldom left the women's quarters, but acquired there whatever training was considered necessary for their later life.

The school age for the boy began with his seventh year.   Custom required that each son of a free citizen should be given instruction in gymnastics and music, but beyond keeping an eye on the morals of teachers and the conduct of their charges the state did not concern itself with education.   It rested with the parent alone to decide how much schooling his boy should receive, and the schools were in all cases private institutions, supported by the fees of pupils. The status of the teacher was not an exalted one—the pay was small, and the position was often the last resort of the unsuccessful. We may be certain, therefore, that the results of education, even at Athens, too often fell far short of the exalted ideal cherished by many of her foremost citizens.   The general features of the system are sufficiently clear, but many details of instruction, including the amount of time devoted to different branches, and the age at which they were begun, remain to be discovered.   The literary training comprised reading and committing to memory selections from the poets, especially Homer and Hesiod, writing and the elements of arithmetic.   For musical training there was practice not only in singing selections from the great lyric poets, but also in the use of stringed instruments—the seven-stringed lyre, or the later cithara—as an accompaniment to the voice.   The flute, as an instrument for ordinary use, was held in less esteem.

Games and gymnastics, however, seem to have occupied the larger part of the boy's time. The private school where these were practised was known as a *palæstra*, a name derived from the Greek word for wrestling. The exercises must have been given out-of-doors originally, and whatever structures were used for them in later times can hardly have contained more than an open court for wrestling, with one or more small rooms adjoining, where clothing might be laid aside or put on and where oil and sand were kept, and some provision for bathing in case there was no stream close at hand. No clothing of any sort was worn during the exercises. These seem to have included most of the forms practised in later life—running, the broad jump with and without weights in the hands, throwing the javelin and the discus for distance, and above all, wrestling, besides the rudiments of boxing, and a form of the

FIG. 1.—Scene in a Palæstra.

pancratium, a struggle which combined certain features of both boxing and wrestling with others of its own.[1] Mention is also made of simple exercises to develop correct carriage and a graceful step in walking, and it is said that the art of swimming was early acquired, and that games, especially those in which the ball was used, were by no means forgotten. Dancing, at least in its more advanced forms, was not a regular subject of instruction at Athens, but was left to choral bands which received special training for their appearance before the public on festal occasions.

Upon reaching the age of eighteen the youth, now known as an *ephebe*, passed under state control for a two-year period of disci-

[1] For details regarding each of these exercises the reader is referred to Part II of E. N. Gardiner's "Greek Athletic Sports and Festivals," and Julius Jüthner's "Uber antike Turngeräthe."

pline comparable to the enforced military service in modern continental Europe. He first took a solemn oath of allegiance, and was
then sent to join the garrisons at the neighboring harbor of the
Piræus, for training in the use of weapons and the performance of
a soldier's duties. At the end of the first year he received from
the state a shield and spear, and might now be employed at other
garrison ports or as a frontier patrol. Hunting afforded additional
preparation for active warfare. Meanwhile the former gymnastic
exercises were continued, but for these, instead of visiting the
palæstra, he now joined the grown men in the city gymnasia. The
ephebes were conspicuous figures in the numerous local festivals
held at Athens, taking part in processions like that represented on
the frieze of the Parthenon, and in various athletic events. Aside
from this later gymnastic and military training there was no higher
education in Greece until the rise of the sophists, or professional
lecturers on rhetoric and philosophy, after the middle of the fifth
century before Christ.

The Greek *gymnasium*, unlike the palæstra, was intended for
ephebes and for grown men who had finished their schooling. It
was a state institution maintained at public expense and administered by public magistrates and other functionaries. Structures of
this sort began to be built, or, more properly, laid out, as early as
the sixth or seventh century before Christ, and by the end of the
fifth century B.C. there was probably no important Greek town, at
home or in the colonies, that did not possess at least one of them.
Almost any open spot would serve the purpose at the start, but, as
population increased and civilization advanced, buildings of special
design became necessary, and these grew in size and splendor with
the addition of new features from time to time. Exact information
with regard to the different parts and their arrangement is almost
wholly lacking for the period under review. Descriptions which
have come down to us, and the remains discovered at Olympia,
Delphi and other places belong to later centuries. The same general
plan seems to have been followed, however, but with considerable
variation in details. Originally, we may suppose, as in the case
of the palæstra, there was only an open space for wrestling, running
and the other exercises, and surrounding or adjoining this covered
colonnades, into which various rooms opened. The essential
features at a later stage seem to have included, besides this spacious
court or course and its colonnades, a room where clothing might be
taken off and left, others for the oil with which visitors rubbed
the body before exercising, and for the dust or fine sand with which
the wrestlers were then sprinkled, and some sort of baths, either
basins set on high supports, or running water issuing from outlets
under which one might stand, as in a modern shower-bath. Before

washing himself the gymnast removed the oil, sand and dirt from his body with a scraper of metal, bone or reed, hollowed out somewhat like a spoon and furnished with a handle, but concave along one edge. Some provision was usually made for playing at ball and for running under cover, in addition to the open spaces intended for wrestling, running and throwing the discus and the javelin. The whole might be enclosed in spacious grounds, as was the case with the three ancient gymnasia outside the walls of Athens, and these were laid out like public parks, shaded with trees and planted with shrubs and flowering plants, watered by streams or fountains, and further adorned with statues of favorite gods, legendary heroes and eminent citizens.

The position of general superintendent of the gymnasium was one of great dignity. Other officials were charged with enforcing good order and decorous behavior, and there was a variety of trainers and servants who gave assistance in one way or another. Like the boys in the palæstra, those who were about to exercise stripped themselves entirely naked before commencing—a practice which must have stimulated each to make himself an object worth beholding, and gave to the sculptor unparalleled opportunities for study of the human body in action and repose. Among the favorite occupations were running, wrestling, the broad jump with stone or metal weights in the hands, throwing the heavy stone or metal discus for distance, and throwing the javelin by means of a leather thong wound about it near the center and ending in a loop for one or two fingers. The javelins commonly used in practice were blunt rods about a man's height in length, and thrown for distance more often than at a mark. A combination of these five exercises, known as the *pentathlon*, or five-fold contest, furnished a popular form of gymnastic competition. Another exceedingly popular sport was boxing, with the knuckles protected by long, thin, leather thongs wrapped about the hand and wrist, and there was also the *pancratium*, a sort of rough-and-tumble fight reduced to orderly form. In this the hands were left bare and the struggle was continued until one of the contestants acknowledged himself defeated.

Besides answering the original purpose for which they were laid out, the gymnasia came to be more and more the centers of Greek social and intellectual life, a gathering place of citizens for conversation and amusement which combined some of the features of a modern clubhouse with those of a city park. Philosophers and rhetoricians found a general audience or met their special pupils there, and thus it happened that each of the three great gymnasia at Athens became associated with a particular school of philosophy —the *Academy*, on the banks of the river Cephissus about a mile to the northwest of the city walls, with Plato, whose followers assembled in a small garden which he owned within the enclosure, and were therefore dubbed the "Academic sect;" the *Lyceum* with Aristotle, whose favorite walk was here, whence he and his disciples were known as "Peripatetics;" and the *Cynosarges* with the school of the Cynics, or followers of Antisthenes, who frequented that spot. It is these later and secondary uses of the gymnasium that alone give significance to such modern words as the German *gymnasium* and the French *lycée* (secondary schools), and to our own "academy" and "lyceum."

The most striking illustration of the important place accorded to physical training among the Greeks is found in their great national festivals. The very beginnings of recorded history show that in every town there were periodic religious festivals, where sacrifices to some hero or divinity were followed by feasting, dancing, choral songs to the accompaniment of the lyre or the flute, and exhibitions of bodily agility, strength and skill in the form of competitive exercises. Gradually, in the case of certain localities, the importance and attractiveness of the festival increased and the circle from which visitors were drawn grew wider, until four of them, all in or near the Peloponnesus, finally developed into national occasions— first and foremost of the number, and as far back as the end of the eighth or very early in the seventh century before Christ, that held at Olympia, and in the first half of the sixth century before Christ three others, the Pythia, the Nemea and the Isthmia. During three centuries in particular, from 600 to 300 B.C., the service they rendered as common centers of interest, binding together the politically distinct members of the Greek race in the parent land and in the far-scattered colonies that dotted the borders of the Mediterranean and the Black Sea, was of the greatest value.

Olympia lies in a plain near the western limits of the Peloponnesus, about ten miles from the Ionian Sea. The sacred enclosure, some ten acres in extent, contained a grove in the center of which stood a great altar to Zeus, and near it his temple, wherein was a wonderful statue of the god in ivory and gold, the most famous work of Phidias and one of the greatest triumphs of Greek sculpture. Besides other temples, there were numerous altars, votive offerings, statues of gods, heroes and victors in the games and treasure houses erected by cities which had sent gifts to the shrine. Just outside the enclosure, to the east, were the stadium and the hippodrome. The stadium, to which most of the contests seem to have been transferred after the middle of the fifth century B.C., was at first merely a stretch of level ground overlooked from the north by spectators who stood or sat on the slope of the Hill of Cronus. Afterward an artificial embankment was raised along the opposite side and straight across the ends of a parallelogram, completely enclosing it, so that 40,000 persons or more might find standing-room, but no permanent seats. Modern excavations have allowed exact measurements of the race course, from the starting to the finish line, and it is found to be just 192.27 m., or a trifle over 210 yards in length. No trace remains of the neighboring hippodrome, intended for chariot races, but it is supposed to have resembled the stadium in general plan, although much longer. A gymnasium, to the northwest of the enclosure, belongs to a much later date.

The festival was held at intervals of four years, at the time of the second or third full moon after the summer solstice, coming therefore in the late summer. During the lunar month in which it occurred a truce of the god was observed throughout Greece. For an armed force to set foot on the soil of the district of Elis within that period, or for anyone to do violence to travellers on their way to or from Olympia, was considered sacrilege. Heralds were sent to announce the coming celebration through all the states of Greece and to carry the news to the Greek colonies which had been established on the islands of the Ægean Sea, in south-western Italy and Sicily, and along the shores of the Black Sea and the coast of Asia Minor, Syria, Egypt, Gaul and Spain. From the whole of this wide area deputations and private citizens made their way to the sacred spot. It was essentially a Greek gathering, though many foreigners were doubtless present in the throng, and except the priestess of Demeter, who occupied a conspicuous seat in the stadium, no women were allowed to view the exercises.

In the games which followed the sacrifices on the altar of Zeus none but free-born Greek citizens, of pure Hellenic descent and untainted by civil or religious crime, were allowed to have a share. Each contestant had passed through a long period of preliminary training, the last thirty days of which were spent in the gymnasia at Elis, thirty miles away to the northwest, or in later years the one at Olympia itself. Originally a single day had sufficed for the festival, but from time to time, as the occasion grew in importance, new features were added until finally the program required five days for its completion. Interest centered chiefly on the competitive exercises, which consumed the greater part of the time. The list of these varied in the course of years, with the addition or dropping out of one item or another, but in general they included the foot race—a single course (210 yards), or down and back, or back and forth a number of times, or a race in armor; the pentathlon; wrestling; boxing and the pancratium; races between men on horseback; and the chariot race, commonly with four horses, less frequently with two. As far back as the seventh century B.C. separate contests for boys in running, the pentathlon, wrestling and boxing were introduced.

So much importance was attached to the games in the popular mind, and the fame of the winner spread so widely over the Hellenic world, that to wear the victor's wreath on such an occasion became one of the highest honors a Greek could covet.   At first the prizes offered possessed intrinsic value; but as victory became more and more a sufficient recompense in itself, they were restricted to the simple crown of sacred wild olive, placed upon the brow of the successful athlete.   There were other rewards than this, however. In recognition of the honor done to them the citizens of the victor's town sometimes received him with extraordinary demonstrations. It might be that, clad in purple, he entered the gates in a chariot drawn by white horses, and made his way through singing and cheering throngs to hang his wreath as an offering in the principal temple.   We even hear of city walls torn down to make a passage, as though where such a citizen dwelt there was no need of other defense.   The choral ode which greeted him might have been composed for the occasion by lyric poets like Pindar and Bacchylides.[1]   His statue would be set up in the home city, or placed within the sacred enclosure at Olympia.   He was perhaps granted a seat of honor in the theater, and provided with board at the public table for the rest of his life.   Solon, at Athens, is said to have offered five hundred drachmæ to an Olympian victor, and one hundred in the case of other national festivals.

At Olympia the gymnastic competitions were the only ones. There were many among the visitors, however, who did not fail to take advantage of the great crowds to advance some private interest.   Historians, philosophers and rhetoricians, poets, painters and sculptors found listeners and patrons.   The occasion was also one of commercial interchange, like the great fairs of the middle ages, or the religious gatherings at Mecca and Medina.   To other proofs of the wide influence exerted by the games are to be added the facts that the length of the race course in the stadium at Olympia was adopted as the standard unit for measuring distances, and that in the third century before Christ Greek historians began generally to employ as a unit of time the Olympiad, or four-year period including one celebration and extending to the next, designating each by the name of the victor in the foot-race at its particular festival.   The first recorded Olympic festival was held in 776 B.C.,

[1] For English translations see Ernest Myers, "The Extent Odes of Pindar" (London, Macmillan & Co.), or Sir John Sandys, "The Odes of Pindar," in the Loeb Classical Library (New York, G. P. Putnam's Sons); and Sir Richard C. Jebb's "Bacchylides" (Cambridge, England, The University Press).   Pindar's forty-four "Odes of Victory" include fourteen in honor of Olympian winners, twelve Pythian, eleven Nemean, and seven Isthmian.   Of the thirteen odes of Bacchylides four are Olympian, two are Pythian, three Isthmian, three Nemean, and one relates to a Thessalian festival.

and they were not finally abolished until 394 A.D.—a period of 293 Olympiads.

Next to the Olympic festival in importance was the *Pythia*, in honor of Apollo, celebrated near the famous shrine of the god at Delphi, a few miles north of the Corinthian Gulf. It was quadrennial, like its greater rival, falling in the third year of each Olympiad. In the case of the two remaining national festivals the contests took place at intervals of only two years. The *Nemea*, in honor of Zeus, was held in Argolis, in a valley near Cleonæ where there was a grove containing a temple of the god. The *Isthmia* was celebrated on the isthmus of Corinth, in a grove of pines sacred to Poseidon. They fell in the second and fourth years of the Olympiad, one occurring in the summer and the other in the following spring. A general truce of the gods was observed during the progress of all three of these festivals. Unlike the Olympia, they added musical and literary competitions to the usual gymnastic contests and chariot races. The victor's reward, at first substantial, was afterward reduced to a wreath of sacred laurel at the Pythia, and to one of wild celery ("parsley") at the Nemea and the Isthmia, replaced at the latter by one of pine in later times.

BIBLIOGRAPHY.

General works in English which will be found of value are J. B. Bury's "History of Greece to the Death of Alexander the Great," E. A. Gardner's "Handbook of Greek Sculpture," T. G. Tucker's "Life in Ancient Athens," and K. J. Freeman's "Schools of Hellas," all four published in London by Macmillan & Co. Freeman's chapter on Physical Education is the least satisfactory in his book, largely because of failure to distinguish between conditions at different periods, and taken alone would prove quite misleading.

The following special works are indispensable, and contain ample references to the older literature: E. N. Gardiner's "Greek Athletic Sports and Festivals" (London, Macmillan & Co., 1910), and Julius Jüthner's "Philostratos über Gymnastik" (Leipzig and Berlin, B. G. Teubner, 1909) and "Über antike Turngeräthe" (Vienna, Alfred Holder, 1896).

E. N. Gardiner's "Olympia," 1926.

CHAPTER II.

THE ROMANS.

THE year 400 B.C. may be taken as marking roughly the close of the two or three centuries which witnessed the gradual development and culmination of physical training in Greece. Meanwhile a people differing widely from the cultured, reflective, beauty-loving Athenian in character and ideals had been establishing itself on the banks of the Tiber, and was already beginning to display a military prowess and a genius for organization that were to make Rome mistress of Italy within the next hundred and fifty years, extend its sway over the Mediterranean states in another century, and finally achieve world empire. The early Roman possessed some traits in common with the Spartan. He was first of all a man of affairs, intensely practical and interested in things whose usefulness was apparent. A stranger to the Greek passion for beauty, he considered vague and worthless the notion of harmonious development as something desirable for its own sake. Education should fit a man for his work in the world. It was to make of him a good citizen and a capable soldier, ready to play his part in public life. Bodily exercise was desirable only as it gave robust health and prepared for military service. Music was an unprofitable art, and anything more than the rudiments of literary training was unnecessary. Until the time of the later emperors the state did not concern itself in any way with education, but left it altogether in the parents' hands.

So long as Roman education was free from foreign influence, *i. e.*, down to the middle of the third century B.C., it was given in the home and by the parents. Schools, if they existed at all, were few and relatively unimportant. In free intercourse with his father and mother the boy received moral and religious instruction and became acquainted with ancestral traditions, mastered the rudiments of reading, writing and counting, and acquired experience in the care of the estate and the management of a household. Among his games, exercises with the ball were especially popular, but even his childish sports must have felt the influence of the military career that awaited him. As he approached the age when he must be enrolled among the citizens and assume a man's obligations, both civil and military, companionship with his father on the streets and in the forum completed the necessary preparation for public life. Now, too, he met with other young men for military exercises on the Field of Mars, which lay between the Tiber and the foot of the city hills. They practised running, jumping, throwing and the use of weapons, and learned to swim in the neighboring stream.

During the larger part of the period of conquest which terminated in universal empire, and until the Roman army was reorganized as a mercenary body of professional troops under Caius Marius, about a hundred years before the beginning of the Christian era, every citizen except those of the lowest class was liable to military service between the ages of seventeen and sixty. The older men (forty-seven to sixty years) acted as home guards or did garrison duty only, except in times of emergency, but the younger legionary might be called out for from sixteen to twenty campaigns in the field, unless earlier disabled by honorable wounds. Army life, therefore, became an educational factor of the first rank. Under the earlier (Servian) plan of enrolment citizens above a certain minimum property rating were grouped in five classes according to wealth, beginning with the richest, and if chosen served without pay and also furnished their own equipment and rations. The first class was protected by helmet, cuirass, greaves and shield, and fought with long lance and sword. The second and third were not so completely armed, but with the first constituted the heavy infantry, arranged in three parallel lines for battle. The fourth and fifth wore no defensive armor, but were supplied with lances and javelins, or other light weapons. Each "legion" contained twenty centuries of the first class, five each of the second, third and fourth, and seven of the fifth—a total of three thousand heavy and twelve hundred light infantry, to which three hundred horsemen were added. The latter, who rode without saddle or stirrups, played only a minor part in the wars of the Republic. Soldiers were called out in the spring, and disbanded at the close of the summer campaign.

Various modifications had been introduced before the conquest of Italy was completed. The state assumed the cost of field expenses, and age rather than wealth became the basis of division into groups. The youngest troops now formed the light-armed centuries, and the older and more experienced men were distributed among the three successive lines which were to withstand the heavy shock of battle. The short, two-edged sword for thrusting had become the favorite weapon. The enemy was first attacked with a shower of light javelins, which might easily transfix a shield and render it useless, and then the sword was used for personal combat at close quarters. The soldier's clothing consisted of nothing but a woolen tunic which did not reach his knees, hob-nailed sandals and a cloak or hooded cape. His ration was usually wheat, served out once a month or oftener at the rate of about a bushel a month per man, ground in hand mills as needed and made into cakes or porridge. Barley might be substituted, and meat was an accessory, if issued at all. The average day's march was fifteen miles, preferably accomplished in the morning hours. Whatever the climate or the condition of the roads, the legionary carried, besides his clothing armor and weapons, a supply of wheat sufficient for two weeks or more, a pot for cooking, several long stakes for the palisade about the nightly camp, and perhaps intrenching tools or other implements—a total estimated by Colonel Dodge at something more than eighty-five pounds, or considerably over half his own weight.

FIG. 2.—Roman soldier, on the march.

The camp site must then be fortified by means of a ditch, mound and palisade extending entirely around it.

For such a strenuous life the recruit was prepared and the veteran kept fit by a training to the severity of which the name of the army (*exercitus*) bears witness. There was steady drill in marching forward and to the rear, or by either flank, in wheeling, changing from line to column and back again, and taking open or close orders. Practice marches of twenty miles or so were executed under full equipment and at the regular rate of four miles an hour, or with forced marching at five miles an hour. They were made to run, jump, climb, swim, hurl the javelin and fight with swords against posts set firmly in the ground, taking care through all the movements of attack and defense to keep the body covered with the shield. The operation of intrenching camp, and of attacking or defending it, was rehearsed. In peace times there might be employment on public works, such as roads, canals, bridges, fortifications, amphitheaters or aqueducts.

It was not until the third century before Christ that the influence of Greek literature, philosophy and art began to be felt in Rome, introduced through contact with Greek colonies in Italy and Sicily, by Greek slaves, and by Romans who had sojourned in Greece. But the new culture awakened such interest and spread with such rapidity that by the time Greece had become a Roman province, soon after the middle of the succeeding century, it had profoundly modified the scheme of Roman education, except on the side of physical training. The boy's earliest instruction, received at home or in a private school, still included reading, writing and reckoning. He was afterward sent to a secondary school, where the chief subject of study was the writings of favorite Greek and Latin poets, and the practical end sought was accuracy and facility in the use of the two languages. To these a little music and applied geometry might be added. Young men who were looking forward to public life received further preparation in schools of rhetoric. These taught the art of effective speaking, as needed in the law courts, before a popular assembly, or in the senate. The home life of the boy had thus lost its earlier place as chief factor in education, and the old training for domestic, political and religious duties had been replaced by one essentially grammatical and oratorical.

Military service, meanwhile, had ceased to perform its part in national discipline, for during the last century of the Republic it was committed to mercenary troops, and these developed into a standing army under the Empire. While the Greek gymnastics was introduced to some extent among the Romans of the upper class, it never acquired a hold upon the popular mind or entered as an important factor into education in the fosterland. Its pedagogical aim had become obscured, and the great national games which once exhibited its most perfect product had fallen into ill repute. The Roman nature lacked that intense love of competition which was so characteristic of the Greek. The exercises of the palæstra and the gymnasium, an inexhaustible mine of subjects for the painters of red-figured Greek vases in the latter half of the fifty century B.C. were nothing more than idle amusements to a people bent upon world conquest. They were disgusted at the nakedness of the performers, which had been the inspiration of sculptors like Myron, Phidias, Polycletus, Praxiteles and Lysippus; and the sight of young athletes contending in generous rivalry in such events as made up the pentathlon could have aroused little interest in a generation accustomed to the thrills of the circus and the amphitheater.

The Greek national festivals, too, were in the last stages of decline. The better class of citizens no longer appeared as contestants, for the religious character of the celebrations had largely disappeared, boxing and the pancratium had become the favorite exercises, prizes more valuable than the wreath had been substituted, trickery and falsehood were less uncommon, and a class of professional athletes had been developed, whose members were usually of low birth and looked upon with little favor. They submitted themselves to an irksome and exacting routine which set them apart from the rest of mankind, left no time for other occupations and made them virtual slaves of their trainers. Numerous attempts by Roman emperors to revive the glory of the ancient games, and to imitate them on Italian soil, met with no enduring success.[1]

A structure quite as typical of its time and habitat as the Greek gymnasium of the Periclean age was the public bath, or *therma*, found in Rome and in every important provincial town in the days of the Empire. Both made provision for exercise, and contained a system of baths; though in the thermæ the baths occupied a greater part of the space, and the rooms and courts for exercise were fewer and smaller. Both added seats and walks and places of meeting and conversation for visitors, were lavishly decorated with objects of art, and were frequented by rhetoricians, poets and philosophers, as well as by the common populace. Although the various forms of Greek gymnastics were introduced and occasionally practised at the baths, that which seems to have been most popular, and which gave the name to one of the halls or courts (the *sphæristerium*) was play with various sorts of ball, filled with air, feathers or hair. Other exercises were movements of the arms with dumbbells in the hands, and fencing with wooden swords against a post, as practised by the soldiers. Besides the large public baths, such as those of Caracalla and Diocletian, almost every private house of any size possessed its own sphæristerium, where light exercises, and especially games with the ball, were engaged in as a preliminary to the bath. All such exercises were taken at the whim of the bather, and only as a means of recreation or to heighten the enjoyment of the bath and meal which followed it. The resemblance to the Greek gymnasium, though at first striking, is therefore much less real than apparent, and the effect of the institution on Roman life was to favor its decay.

[1] For details of this period of decline consult chapter eight (Athletics under the Romans) in E. N. Gardner's "Greek Athletic Sports and Festivals."

Between the pan-Hellenic festivals celebrated in the stadium and hippodrome at Olympia in the time of Pericles, and those public spectacles which crowded the amphitheater and circus of the degenerate Roman world during the first centuries of the Christian era, a greater contrast can be drawn. The chariot races of the Circus Maximus and the gladiatorial combats, the contests of men with beasts, or those of beasts with one another in the Coliseum, reveal the changed type of civilization, and also mark the last stages of athletic professionalism. The charioteer and the gladiator were either prisoners of war, slaves, condemned criminals or freedmen who adopted the calling from choice. They were trained in special schools, and unless the property of private citizens, were commonly let out by their owners to any person who desired their services.

BIBLIOGRAPHY.

General works: Besides the standard dictionaries and handbooks of classical antiquities, the "Companion to Latin Studies" edited by J. E. Sandys (Cambridge, England, at the University Press. See especially the sections on Education and the Roman Army), and T. G. Tucker's "Life in the Roman World of Nero and St. Paul" (New York, The Macmillan Co., 1911).

On Roman education: S. S. Laurie's "Historical Survey of Pre-Christian Education" (second edition. London and New York: Longmans, Green & Co., 1900. Pp. 301–411 are devoted to the Romans), and A. S. Wilkin's "Roman Education" (Cambridge, England, at the University Press, 1905).

On the Roman army: Col. T. A. Dodge's "Hannibal: A History of the Art of War among the Carthaginians and Romans down to the Battle of Pydna, 168 B.C." (Boston and New York: Houghton, Mifflin & Co., 1891), and his "Caesar: A History of the Art of War among the Romans down to the End of the Roman Empire" (Boston and New York, as above, 1892).

CHAPTER III.

THE TEUTONIC INVADERS OF THE ROMAN EMPIRE.

THE Germans as we meet them in the pages of Caesar and Tacitus[1] are a race of sturdy, blue-eyed giants, who dwell in a land of forest and swamp. Their straggling villages consist of low, thatched, dirt-floored huts of rough timber, and in spite of the harsh climate they go about scantily clad in skin mantles or garments of coarse linen. Small fields of barley and perhaps other grains are tilled by the women, but flocks and herds form the chief support of the family, and these, with wild animals taken in the chase, supply the greater portion of their food. For drink there was a crude beer, made without hops. Next to warfare, hunting was the favorite occupation, and for this the surrounding forests yielded the aurochs or bison, the wild boar, elk and bear, besides packs of predatory wolves and numerous lesser animals. Arms were a token of the freeman's position and dignity, and were carried constantly. Only a few could equip themselves with breastplate and helmet, and iron for swords was scarce, but each man had a shield, and short, sharp spears for thrusting or throwing. Their cavalry rode without saddles. A public spectacle much in demand was a dance of naked youths in the midst of drawn swords and upturned spears. Swimming and horsemanship furnished other means of active exercise in time of peace.

With such a people the training of the young could not fail to be a hardy one. Since there was no written language, and the only records were those handed down in ancient songs, formal instruction was unknown. While the girls busied themselves with domestic duties, the boys early learned the arts of the chase and the use of weapons. Hunting and warfare were their chief schoolmasters. At maturity the youth was publicly equipped with shield and spear in the periodical assembly, as a sign of admission to the rights of citizenship. It was the custom of young men to attach themselves to favorite chiefs, who vied with each other in the number and quality of such followers. These promised loyalty in peace and war, and received in turn horses, arms and food.

Among the Northmen of the viking age we find a somewhat more advanced type of civilization, but hunting, fighting and vigorous

---

[1] Caesar, the *Gallic War*, especially book six, chapters 21–28; Tacitus, *Germania*, published in 98 A.D.

sports in the open air are still the chief delight of men. Hawking was a favorite pastime, and the northern falcons were famous throughout Europe. Coats of chain mail, helmets, swords and battle axes are added to the earlier shield and spear, at least in the case of chieftains, and we hear of bows and arrows, clubs and slings. A variety of popular exercises were also practised, which survived throughout the Middle Ages. They included wrestling, foot-races, broad and high jumping, putting the stone, hurling the spear, throwing with knives, racing on snowshoes or skees and several games of ball.

FIG. 3.—Northern warrior of about 300 A.D.

It is difficult, if not impossible, to follow with certainty the particular changes wrought in portions of the Roman Empire which were occupied by the Teutonic invaders. In general, lines of communication were interrupted, the foundations of new and independent nationalities were laid, and city life became less dominant. There was also an admixture of sturdy barbarian stock with native populations, though the latter seem in most cases to have gradually absorbed the conquerors. Roman forces put an end to Vandal dominion in Africa in 533. Neither Vandals nor Suevi were numerous enough in Spain to exert a greater influence than that of bands of roving plunderers, and the Spanish kingdom of the Visigoths fell before the Mohammedan invasion of 711. In Italy, also, Gothic power was broken in 533, and the Lombard kingdom which followed came to an end with Charlemagne's conquest in 774. West Goths and Burgundians in Gaul were overcome by the Franks, who seem themselves to have lost little by little their distinctive national traits and been merged in the earlier Gallo-Roman population. The Normans of the tenth century met a similar fate. In the case of England, where the Teutonic element gained the ascendant, one would like to trace the British fondness for fox hunting, shooting, horse racing, yachting, rowing, games like football and cricket, lawn tennis and golf, and the falconry and archery of an earlier period, to the surviving influence of Anglo-Saxon, Danish and Norman ancestors; but actual demonstration of any such connection could hardly be expected.

BIBLIOGRAPHY.

Edward Gibbon, "The History of the Decline and Fall of the Roman Empire," chapter nine (The State of Germany until the Invasion of the Barbarians, in the Time of the Emperor Decius).

Francis B. Gummere, "Germanic Origins: A Study in Primitive Culture." New York, Charles Scribner's Sons, 1892.

Karl Weinhold, "Altnordisches Leben." Berlin, Weidmannsche Buchhandlung, 1856.

Paul B. Du Chaillu, "The Viking Age: The Early History, Manners, and Customs of the Ancestors of the English-speaking Nations, Illustrated from the Antiquities Discovered in Mounds, Cairns, and Bogs, as well as from the Ancient Sagas and Eddas." New York, Charles Scribner's Sons, 1889.

C. F. Kerry, "The Vikings in Western Christendom, A.D. 789 to A.D. 888." London, T. Fisher Unwin, and New York, G. P. Putnam's Sons, 1891.

CHAPTER IV.

ASCETICISM IN THE EARLY CHRISTIAN CHURCH.

No sooner had the Teutonic tribes overrun Romanized Europe than they began to yield, in turn, to the proselyting activities of the young and lusty Christian Church. And with it came the doctrine óf *asceticism*, which left its mark on education for a thousand years and more, and tended to counteract, in a measure, the invigorating effect of the barbarian strain.

The Hindu fakir, the Christian saint of the desert and the Mohammedan dervish are different expression of a belief which at some time or other has prevailed among a very large proportion of the human race. It has been one of the fundamental ideas of the oriental religions that evil inheres in matter, while mind or spirit is essentially divine and pure. According to this view, the flesh and the spirit wage perpetual warfare on each other; the body is not a useful servant, but an enemy, and to be resisted therefore at every point and struck down whenever its head is raised. The ideal life is one of solitude, contemplation and strict abstinence from sensual indulgence in any form. Asceticism has thus been an important factor in the ancient religions of China, Tibet, Siam, India and Persia, and very early in the Christian Era, or before its dawn, this principle had found its way into Syria and Egypt, and through the Alexandrian schools of philosophy into southern Europe. Brought into contact with Christianity, it helped to prepare the way for the movement now under consideration and in like manner gave its impress to Mohammedanism at a later period.

But in the case of the early Christians, living for the most part in cities and brought into close and daily contact with all the abominations of the decadent pagan society of the Empire, a violent reaction from the prevailing luxury and sensual self-indulgence was inevitable. Men of deep religious feeling desired to escape contamination from such worldliness, and it is not strange if in protest against its excesses they sometimes carried their stern self-restraint so far as to deny themselves the common comforts of life and decline to gratify those cravings of the body which are innocent and natural. The healthy appetites and impulses of the normal man are not to be eradicated without a struggle, however, and the constant discomfort which resulted from unsatisfied desires they

(37)

viewed as insubordination. This in turn led to belief in the innate depravity of human nature. To subdue the rebellious flesh they resorted to renewed and more severe privations, or punished it with self-inflicted tortures. Mortification of the body acquired the dignity of a religious exercise while the idea of pleasure came to be closely associated with that of vice.

A third cause of the outbreak of asceticism is found in the persecution to which many converts of the growing church were subjected. This soon kindled an intense religious enthusiasm which welcomed martyrdom and glorified the sufferings that attended it. The liberated soul, it was taught, entered at once into eternal blessedness. Pain and torment came thus to be considered meritorious of themselves, and the direct road to salvation; and after the persecutions ceased, the self-torture of the ascetic took their place as a means and measure of human excellence. When once the movement to the deserts was started, the desire to escape from the burdens imposed by corrupt government, from social disorders and later from the wretchedness that followed the invasions of barbarian hordes from the North, helped to crowd the ranks of the hermits and swell the numbers gathered into monastic communities.

It was in the latter half of the third century that the first Christian hermits fled to the deserts of Egypt, where natural caverns, or caves easily hewn out of the rock, supplied the only shelter necessary in such a climate, and a grove of date palms with a spring close by it solved the problem of sustenance without labor. But the movement did not gather much headway until the early part of the next century, when Anthony's career had given dignity to the solitary life and made it widely popular. At the time of his death, in 365, the deserts on either side of the Nile from the Cataracts to the Delta were dotted with the retreats of hermits, and it is said that Pachomius, who was the first to gather his disciples into organized communities and formulate a monastic rule, had no fewer than 7000 monks under his authority. By the fifth century the numbers had increased to 100,000 in Egypt alone, and the practice had extended into Syria and Palestine, Armenia, Mesopotamia, parts of Asia Minor and Italy, whence it soon reached the whole of Western Europe.

The greatest extravagances are found among the Eastern "saints of the desert," accounts of whose austerities were collected by wandering pilgrims and excited the admiration of all Christendom. Some dwelt in deserted dens of wild beasts, in tombs and dried-up wells, on the summit of narrow columns, or spent days in the midst of thorn bushes. Others never lay down during months and even years, or they slept naked in swamps, exposed to the stings of insects. Many abstained from food altogether for long periods, or restricted themselves to quantities too small to relieve the pangs of hunger. Bodily cleanliness was frequently abjured, and a long list of strange penances was devised.[1]

Severe self-torture was less common in the Western monasteries, especially after the earlier code had been supplanted by a new one drafted (529) by Benedict of Nursia, founder of the order that bears his name. This is distinguished by the absence of any severe austerities, and substitutes manual labor in place of contemplation and penance. But the conception of supreme excellence was much the same in the West and in the East. Asceticism became a part of the accepted teaching of the Church and the practice of a large proportion of her leaders and adherents. Of Simeon Stylites, the famous Syrian monk of the fifth century, we read that "from every quarter pilgrims of every degree thronged to do him homage. A crowd of prelates followed him to the grave. A brilliant star is said to have shown miraculously over his pillar; the general voice of mankind pronounced him to be the highest model of a Christian saint."

The physical effects of the ascetic life upon the individual must have been disastrous as a rule. Not only did it lead to broken health, such as embittered the lives of some of the greatest among the Church Fathers, but long-continued austerities and over-wrought emotions produced a disordered nervous system and supplied all the conditions for hallucination. Lecky has also called attention to certain moral qualities that suffered from the prevailing conception of excellence. "What may be called a strong animal nature," he says, "a nature, that is, in which the passions are in vigorous, and at the same time healthy action, is that in which we should most naturally expect to find . . . good humor, frankness, generosity, active courage, sanguine energy, buoyancy of temper. (These) are much more rarely found either in natures that are essentially feeble or effeminate, or in natures that have been artificially emasculated by penances, distorted from their original tendency, and habitually held under severe control."

Among the people at large the physical consequences of the prevailing doctrine were hardly less pernicious. It justified the personal and public uncleanliness and the neglect of simple sanitary precautions to which they were already prone enough, and thus became to some extent accountable for the unprecedented succession of plagues which decimated the population of Europe again and again throughout the Middle Ages. None of these widespread epidemics suggested sanitary improvement, but they were regarded as "visitations," and attributed to the wrath of God, or

---

[1] Lecky gives a striking series of examples in his "History of European Morals," vol. 2, pp. 114–119.

to the malice of Satan. It is not unlikely that such phenomena, even, as the dancing mania, the processions of Flagellants, trials of innocence, and the persecutions of Jews and witches depend in part upon the fact that communities and nations, no less than individuals, lacking real physical hardihood, were often crazed by nervous excitement, and impelled by an overstimulated emotional nature fell an easy prey to weird delusions and morbid fancies, of which a series of moral epidemics was the natural result.

BIBLIOGRAPHY.

W. E. H. Lecky, "History of European Morals from Augustine to Charlemagne" (New York, D. Appleton & Co., 1869), **2**, pp. 107 ff.

I. Gregory Smith, "Christian Monasticism from the Fourth to the Ninth Centuries of the Christian Era." London, A. D. Innes & Co., 1892.

Abbot Gasquet, "English Monastic Life." London, Methuen & Co., 1904. Contains illustrations, maps, and plans.

Herbert B. Workman, "The Evolution of the Monastic Ideal from the Earliest Times Down to the Coming of the Friars." London, Charles H. Kelly, 1913.

CHAPTER V.

MONASTERY AND CATHEDRAL SCHOOLS.

In the cities of Northern Italy the dying out of the old Roman schools, as a result of internal decay and the inroads of the Teutonic barbarians, was not followed by the complete extinction of the race of lay teachers, and here, and throughout southern Europe generally, education therefore never became exclusively ecclesiastical; but in transalpine Europe, from the sixth until the twelfth century, the Benedictine monasteries were the chief if not the only seats of learning, and education was almost wholly in the hands of monks of that order. There were schools attached to the cathedrals, also, but they drew their teachers from the monasteries and seldom rose to more than local importance until in the course of the twelfth century intellectual activity was gradually transferred to them and they became the germ out of which the universities of the Middle Ages developed. The reform legislation of Charles the Great fixed this intimate relation between the Church and education by requiring that every monastery and every cathedral throughout his broad empire should have its school. The origin of these institutions is to be found in the need of educated ecclesiastics, and the earliest scholars were candidates for admission to the Benedictine order, or for the priesthood; but about the beginning of the ninth century "exterior schools" began to be added, open to boys who were intended for secular callings.

The course of study, intended to prepare the way for a proper understanding of the Holy Scriptures and the writings of the Church Fathers, was everywhere limited to the so-called seven liberal arts. These included the fundamental *trivium*—grammar, rhetoric and dialectics or logic—and the less important *quadrivium* —music, arithmetic, geometry and astronomy. It was the world to come for which men were trained; theological doctrines and religious interests absorbed human thought, and the present world was deemed unworthy of attention. So long as the spirit of asceticism remained in the ascendant there could be no such thing as physical training in schools conducted by the Church. The soul was the one object of solicitude, and the body was regarded with contempt. Uncleanliness and physical neglect were not incompatible with intellectual eminence. The monastic discipline in all its severity was an essential part of school life. Other forms of pun-

(41)

ishment were common, but the rod was the favorite instrument; it was used on the least occasion, and sometimes periodically, "as a kind of general atonement for sins past and possible." Even the humane Alcuin, Master of Charles the Great's Palace School at Aix (782–796), would have a separate master for every class "that the boys may not run about in idleness or occupy themselves in silly play." Their lessons were to furnish them all the play and diversion needed.

BIBLIOGRAPHY.

S. S. Laurie, "The Rise and Early Constitution of Universities, with a Survey of Mediæval Education." New York, D. Appleton & Co., 1887.

A. F. West, "Alcuin and the Rise of the Christian Schools." New York, Charles Scribner's Sons, 1892.

Any standard history of education, such as F. P. Graves, "A History of Education during the Middle Ages and the Transition to Modern Times" (New York, The Macmillan Co.).

CHAPTER VI.

CHIVALRY.

CHIVALRY, or the body of law and custom relating to knighthood, prevailed almost universally throughout western Europe between the eleventh and sixteenth centuries. Its usages were international, and in its ideal of war, religion and gallantry was summed up the whole duty of the gentleman of that age. The system can be traced in part to various customs of the ancient Germans, developed later under the influence of feudalism; but its final form was not received until the time of the Crusades (1096–1270), when the Church, in order to further her own designs, adopted and modified its practices. It was in large measure the inroads of Mohammedan warriors in Christian territory and their profanation of the Holy City which led to a substitution of military Christianity for the ascetic ideal cherished hitherto, and caused war with the infidels to be pronounced a religious duty and the battlefield a direct road to salvation. This union of chivalry with religion—the consecration of military prowess to the service of the Church—is typified in the three orders of soldier monks, the Hospitallers, the Templars and the Teutonic Knights, which had their origin in the twelfth century. The hermit of early Catholic legends had thus been displaced as a popular hero by the king and the knight who figures in the romances of Arthur and of Charles the Great. The decline of chivalry as a military system began soon after the last crusade (1270), and in the fifteenth century became complete; for the introduction of gunpowder in warfare, with the increased importance attached to infantry and artillery made the arms and armor of the knight of no avail and lessened the opportunities for personal distinction on the field. At the same time the growing centralization of power in the hands of the sovereign was rapidly destroying the independence of the nobility of lesser rank.

The early training of a knight bore no resemblance to the ascetic type seen in the monastery and cathedral schools. Although the boy intended for such a career was sometimes brought up at home, it was the common custom to send him away, at the age of seven or soon after, to the court or castle of some nobleman, in whose household, among other young attendants of gentle birth, he might learn the principles, acquire the breeding and become proficient in the practices of chivalry. As a *page* he was expected to render to his master and mistress personal service of all sorts, even the most humble and domestic, waiting on them at the table, carrying messages, following them to the chase or camp, and in visits to neighboring castles. Meanwhile, under the tuition of the ladies, he was mastering the rudiments of reading and writing, together with the rules of courteous behavior and the first principles of gallantry. He gained some familiarity with Latin and French, the universal languages, tried his hand at playing the harp and in games of chess and backgammon, picked up many facts of history, learned much of heraldry and became acquainted with the songs and poetry of the troubadours. But the principal part of his training was car-

Fig. 4.—Knight Templar (Gasquet).

ried on outdoors, where he was already imitating grown men in his play, learning the business of a *squire*, and seeking to prove himself worthy of advancement to that rank.

Promotion to this second grade did not come until after the age of fourteen, though it is probable that the change from page to squire was not a sudden one. The personal service to his lord became more responsible in its nature, and thus led to a more dig- nified position in the household; but vigorous sports and martial exercises, in which he had already made some progress as a page, now occupied his time increasingly. Instruction in dancing was a part of his discipline in polished manners. He was early taught how to train a falcon and handle him in hawking, and in the pursuit of the stag and wild boar found occasion for the display of greater skill and daring. Running, jumping, wrestling, swimming, climbing ropes and poles and ladders, hurling stones, casting the spear, shooting with the bow and cross-bow, wielding the battle-axe, and fencing, at first with dull wooden swords, helped to harden his body and give mastery of its powers for future need. The most essential exercise, however, was horsemanship, including the adroit use of shield and lance, and the ability to endure the weight and overcome the hindrance of full armor. There was practice in leaping into the saddle without the help of stirrups, dismounting quickly, and reaching down to pick up objects from the ground. Tilting at the ring or quintain, or afterward with a living opponent, developed a firm seat and the skill required to govern the galloping charger with the legs alone while one received and parried a thrust with the shield upon his left arm, and with the right guided the lance so as to lift his antagonist from the saddle, if possible, by striking him squarely in the throat or upon the center of his shield.

The young squire also followed his master to the field, sharing with him all the dangers and privations of a military career. He helped him to adjust and fasten the numerous pieces that composed his armor, after taking care that these were in perfect condition, assisted him to mount, held extra horses, supplied fresh lances as they were needed, raised him if·unseated, attended to his wounds, received and guarded whatever prisoners were taken, sought to release him if he were taken captive, or bore away his dead body to give it proper burial. After this long apprenticeship, in case he had proved his fitness for the dignity and possessed the means to support so costly a profession, the squire who had reached the age of twenty-one might hope to take the final step. By a blow upon the shoulder with the flat of a sword some knight or noble ended his tedious years of waiting and admitted him to the great brotherhood of chivalry.

A public spectacle no less brilliant and fascinating than the pan-Hellenic games or the gladiatorial shows of the Roman world, and equally characteristic of their age, were the tournaments common all over Christendom in the thirteenth and fourteenth centuries. Originally the rough trials of strength and skill that were a natural occurrence whenever knights met at leisure, they were little by little modified and regulated until they became the chief pastime of nobles and gentlemen, a school of war in times of peace, where the young contestant not only displayed but developed his personal bravery, presence of mind and ability to find at once the right means of attack and defense, the field in which he often won his first laurels or attracted the attention and interest of influential men. After the decline of chivalry as a military system tournaments lost their value as an image of war, and became more and more a means of mere amusement and an occasion for display, though they did not pass entirely out of fashion until toward the close of the sixteenth century.

In tournaments proper groups of combatants on each side fought together with lance and sword in a miniature cavalry battle; while in the joust, which was far more frequent, although it also formed a part of many tournaments, two horsemen only met each other, with lance and shield, sometimes continuing the combat on foot with swords after one of them had been unseated. The contestants in both cases appeared in full armor, and commonly, but not always, the swords were blunt and the lances tipped with flat or slightly toothed plates of metal; but injuries, nevertheless, were not infrequent, and heavy falls or suffocation from heat and dust, or serious wounds when the lance struck fair and did not split cost many a life.

BIBLIOGRAPHY.

Paul Lacroix, "Military and Religious Life in the Middle Ages and at the Period of the Renaissance." London, Chapman and Hall, 1874.

Léon Gautier, "La Chevalerie." Paris, 1883.

Alwin Schultz, "Das höfische Leben zur Zeit der Minnesinger." Leipzig, S. Herzel, 1879 and 1880 (second edition, 1889).

Julius Bintz, "Die Leibesübungen des Mittelalters." Gütersloh, C. Bertelsmann, 1880.

F. Warre-Cornish, "Chivalry." London, Swan Sonnenschein, and New York, The Macmillan Co., 1901.

CHAPTER VII.

THE UNIVERSITIES OF THE MIDDLE AGES.

A SUCCESSION of influences operating in the eleventh and twelfth centuries had widened the scope of human interests and produced a vague longing after knowledge which was not to be satisfied by the traditional teaching of the schools. Along with the demand for a different type and more advanced grade of instruction, there arose here and there famous lecturers, such as Abelard (1079–1142) at Paris, who gathered about themselves great numbers of disciples. Centers where thus created to which other teachers and their followers were attracted, and this in turn led to an informal association of masters and pupils, out of which the medieval university developed. The complete university came at length to include four departments—theology, law, medicine and philosophy or the arts. Certain texts were thought to contain explicitly or implicitly the sum of ascertainable secular truth, just as the Bible and the writings of Church Fathers held all religious truth; and this was to be extracted by prescribed methods of reasoning, with no fresh resort to the facts of observation and experience. Instead of seeking new harvests the typical schoolmen of that day were content with the continual threshing over of old straw.

As regards treatment of the body, the influence of asceticism was still supreme. Provision for lawful amusements was rarely made in the university statutes, which appear frequently to regard harmless attempts at pleasure with more hostility than they display toward actual vice and crime. The sports of chivalry—hunting and hawking, jousts and tournaments—were not considered seemly for the student, even if he had the means to indulge in tnem. Dancing was seldom countenanced in any form. "Playing with a ball or bat" is sometimes found included in the list of "insolent" games, and other prohibitions make mention of "profane games, immodest runnings and horrid shoutings." The ideal student would appear to be the one who denied himself all recreation and amusement; but we may be sure that no such suppression of animal spirits was possible for the average full-blooded young man of that age. In the absence of any authorized outlet they found vent in drinking, gambling and grosser forms of vice, in street

(47)

brawls and rough practical joking, and not infrequently in violent outbreaks of organized lawlessness.

BIBLIOGRAPHY.

S. S. Laurie, "The Rise and Early Constitution of Universities, with a Survey of Mediæval Education." New York, D. Appleton & Co., 1887.

Gabriel Compayré, "Abelard and the Origin and Early History of Universities." New York, Charles Scribner's Sons, 1893.

Hastings Rashdall, "The Universities of Europe in the Middle Ages." Oxford, Clarendon Press, 1895.

J. B. Mullinger, article "Universities" in the *Encyclopædia Britannica*, 11th edition.

CHAPTER VIII.

THE PERIOD OF THE RENAISSANCE AND THE REFORMATION.

THE universities of the Middle Ages had made their contribution to the intellectual advancement of Europe, but they could not break the bands of ecclesiastical tyranny that still fettered the human mind. It required the joint action of other and more potent forces to provide escape from a conception of the world and the flesh which associated them with the devil, and to weaken the authority of that theological dogma which centered the thought and imagination of men for centuries upon the rewards and punishments of a future state and meanwhile paralyzed or thwarted every effort to master the resources or investigate the phenomena of the material universe. Man's rightful heritage upon this earth was not yet restored to him. In some way the feeling of personal dignity and independence must be aroused, the spirit of emulation provoked, and his powers of achievement challenged as they had never been before. Among the chief factors in this process of transition from the medieval to the modern world was the Revival of Learning, that appreciative study of the Greek and Latin classics and all the long-neglected records of ancient civilization which supplied the Western nations with a new ideal of life and culture. The recovered masterpieces of literature and art excited the passionate admiration of scholars; they revelled in the free existence of what seemed to them a Golden Age, rich in such treasures as they had begun already to covet for themselves.

To the Italian "humanists" of the fifteenth century we owe what is still known as a classical education. The greatest schoolmaster of them all was Vittorino da Feltra (1378–1446), who undertook the training of the sons of Marquis Gian Francesco Gonzaga at Mantua in 1423. So earnest and successful was this teacher and so widely did his fame extend that other pupils were added from time to time, until most of the princely houses of Italy, together with some in foreign countries, were represented at the school, to which many in humbler station were also admitted. Latin, Greek, and classical archeology formed the basis and main body of instruction. The chief end was to enable pupils to read and understand the best works of the ancients and to express themselves with elegance in these foreign languages. It was, in fact, an attempt to train new citizens of Greece and Rome, and to reproduce for them the life of the past.

The customs of chivalry had not ceased to shape the early training of an Italian gentleman, and it was therefore natural that Vittorino should incorporate in his school some of the characteristic features of knightly education. The staff of assistants included special teachers of dancing, riding, fencing, and swimming, and to these exercises were added wrestling, running and jumping, archery, ball games, hunting and fishing, and mock battles between two parties, or contests in which one side sought to storm the castle or surprise the camp of its opponents. The ample grounds about the villa which has been converted into a school building were well adapted for such sports, and all the pupils were required to share in them. Vittorino himself often joined them, it is said, and occasionally led them on excursions into the surrounding country, extending as far as Lago di Gardo, Venice and the Alps. He insisted on moderation in food and drink, and did not allow weather or season to interfere too much with life in the open air.

Vittorino had thus succeeded in combining physical with mental training and bringing them within the reach of every pupil; but outside of the schools for young noblemen, which continued to exist in various parts of Europe as late as the eighteenth century, he seems to have had few, if any, successors in this respect until Basedow opened the "Philanthropinum" at Dessau in 1774. During the more than three hundred years that intervene, however, much was written by educational reformers and others in commendation of bodily exercises and recognition of its right to a place in the curriculum; and some of these authors, theorists though they were, occupy an important position in the history of physical training, as links between the present and the past. Vittorino, indeed, had only applied in practice the pedagogical principles already outlined by another Italian humanist, *Pietro Paulo Vergerio* (1349–1428), in a brief treatise on education sent to the young Ubertino di Carrara, whose tutor he had been at the court in Padua. This letter, which was afterward printed and passed through many editions, refers repeatedly to ancient Greeks and Romans, as authorities or by way of illustration, and devotes two of its chapters to the subject of physical exercise. *Maffeo Vegio* (1407–1458), who began life as a scholar and poet but later entered the service of the Church at Rome and finally joined the order of Augustinian monks, wrote one of the most notable pedagogical works of the fifteenth century, and in the chapters relating to physical training shows in a similar way the influence of his classical studies. To the same category belong *Enea Silvio Piccolomini* (1405–1464), better known as Pope Pius II, who was at one time a secretary at the court of

Emperor Frederick III, and in 1450 prepared a tractate on the subject of princely education; *Francesco Filelfo* (1398–1481), who wrote to the Duchess Regent of Milan, about 1475, suggesting a method of education suitable for her young son; and *Jacopo Sadoleto* (1477–1547), humanist and churchman, friend of Luther, Melanchthon, Erasmus, and Sturm, and author of a book (1530) on education which indicates a return to the old Athenian ideal and type.

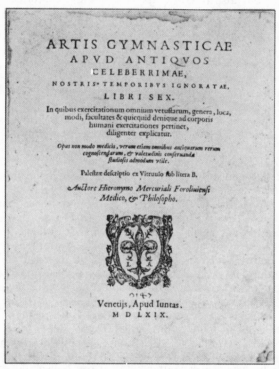

FIG. 5.—Hieronymus Mercurialis: Title-page of first edition of his *De arte gymnastica*.

Two other Italian writers are worthy of more extended notice. *Girolamo Cardano* (1501–1576) had studied at Pavia and Padua, and travelled in France, England, Scotland, the Netherlands and Germany. He obtained his doctorate in medicine and practised that profession, devoting much of his time, however, to researches which bore fruit in a long series of scientific and philosophical works. In his interesting autobiography he tells of his own early practice in running and jumping, riding, fencing and swimming, and elsewhere describes at length a great variety of ancient and

modern feats of strength and skill. His work on the care of health
(*De sanitate tuenda, libri* iv), of which several editions appeared,
contains an independent, systematic, and scientific treatment of
the hygiene of bodily exercise, discussing its value and effects in
general, the physiological classification of exercises into violent or
light, rapid or slow, continuous or interrupted, etc., and the nature
and usefulness of numerous special forms, which belong not only
to past ages but also to contemporary life and customs.

HIERONYMI
MERCVRIALIS
DE ARTE GYMNASTICA
LIBRI SEX,

In quibus exercitationum omnium vetuſtarum
genera,loca,modi,facultates,& quidquid de-
niq. ad corporis humani exercitationes
pertinet,diligenter explicatur.

Secunda editione auɛ̌ti,& multis figuris ornati.

Opus non modo medicis,verum etiam omnibus antiquarum rerum cognoſcendarum , & valetudinis conſer-
uandae ſtudioſis admodum vtile.

AD MAXIMILIANVM II.
IMPERATOREM.

VENETIIS APVD IVNTAS,
M D LXXIII.

Fig. 6.—Hieronymus Mercurialis: Title-page of second edition of his *De arte gymnastica.*

Hieronymus Mercurialis (1530–1606), a famous physician, and
widely known throughout Europe on account of his medical writings, while he was still a young man, in the household of Cardinal
Alexander Farnese at Rome, began his literary career with a treatise
on the gymnastics of the ancients (*De arte gymnastica*)[1]— a book
which seems to have enjoyed a remarkable degree of popularity

[1] The first edition, dedicated to Cardinal Alexander Farnese, has the following
title-page: "Artis Gymnasticæ apud Antiquos celeberrimæ, nostris temporibus
ignoratæ, Libri Sex. In quibus exercitationum omnium vetustarum genera, loca,
modi, facultates & quicquid denique ad corporis humani exercitationes pertinet,
diligenter explicatur. Opus non modo medicis, verum etiam omnibus antiquarum
rerum cognoscendarum & valetudinis conservandæ studiosis admodum utile. Palæs-
træ descriptio ex Vetruvio sub litera B. Auctore Hieronymo Mercuriali Foroliviensi,
Medico & Philosopho. Venetiis, Apud Juntas. MDLXIX." The second edition,
like the third and the fourth, is illustrated, and dedicated to Emperor Maximilian II.

and is often cited by more recent writers. It was first published at
Venice in 1569, but at least three more editions appeared in Venice
and one in Paris during his lifetime, and others after his death,
including one in Amsterdam as late as 1672. Out of his rich store
of classical learning—the first edition contains a list of ninety-six
Greek and Latin authors upon whom he has drawn—Mercurialis
seeks to reproduce for his readers the ancient gymnasia and gymnastic exercises; but in the second half of the volume he leaves the
descriptive and historical and turns to the hygienic and medical
aspects of exercise, as viewed from the critical standpoint of the
physician. Somewhat like Cardano, he first considers the value
of exercise in conditions of health and disease and the general
principles that govern its application, and then takes up the nature
and effects of particular exercises in some detail. According to
the title-page the work was not intended for the use of physicians
only, but for all who were interested in the study of archeology or
in the preservation of health.[1]

In Germany *Martin Luther* (1483–1546) realized the recreative
and moral value of bodily exercise, and recommends especially
such knightly sports as fencing and wrestling. The Swiss reformer
Ulrich Zwingli (1484–1531), writing on the subject of education
in 1524, makes suggestions regarding diet and clothing, and refers
to running, jumping, hurling stones, wrestling, and fencing as a
means of acquiring strength and skill. He also considers wrestling
and fencing a useful preparation for military service. *Joachim
Camerarius* (1500–1574), who taught in Nuremberg, Tübingen, and
the University of Leipsic, and was the friend and biographer of
Melanchthon, published in 1544 a brief dialogue on bodily exercise

---

The title-page is changed to read: "Hieronymi Mercurialis de arte gymnastica Libri
Sex, in quibus exercitationum . . . admodum utile (as in first edition). Secunda
editione aucti, & multis figuris ornati. Ad Maximilianum II. Imperatorem. Venetiis apud Juntas, MDLXXIII." The Paris issue of this second edition substitutes
the words "Parisiis, Apud Jacobum du Puys, via Joannis Lateranensis, sub signo
Samaritanæ, 1577." The third edition ("Tertia editone correctiores, & auctiores
facti") was published "Venetiis, MDLXXXVII. Apud Juntas," and the fourth
edition ("Quarta editione correctiores, & auctiores facti"), Venetiis, apus Juntas.
MDCI."

The title-page of the Amsterdam edition reads: "Hieronymi Mercurialis Foro-
liviensis de Arte Gymnastica Libri Sex: in quibus exercitationum omnium vetustarum
genera, loca, modi, facultates, & quidquid denique ad corporis humani exercitationes
pertinet diligenter explicatur. Editio novissima, aucta, emendata, & figuris authen-
ticis Christophori Coriolani exornata. Amstelodami, Sumptibus Andreæ Frisii,"
(1672).

In this connection may be mentioned also "The Muscles and Their Story, from the
Earliest Times; including the Whole Text of Mercurialis, and the Opinions of Other
Writers Ancient and Modern, on Mental and Bodily Development. By John W. F.
Blundell, M.D., Licentiate of the Royal College of Edinburgh, Author of 'Medicina
Mechanica,' etc." London, Chapman & Hall, 1864.

[1] The table of contents, translated, is given in full at the foot of pp. 477–479 in
the Report of the United States Commissioner of Education for 1891–1892, vol. 1.

(*Dialogus de gymnasiis*).[1] The author believes that boys should be encouraged to run, jump, wrestle, fence, and play ball outdoors, and one of the speakers, after mentioning the gymnastics of the ancients and the performances of the old Germans, describes to his companion a model school for the common people in which the teacher provides for indoor practice in hanging from a bar, climbing a rope, lifting weights, and matching strength with an opponent in various ways, and for a number of active games in the open air, some of them described in the text. Among the most illustrious names in the history of educational reform is that of *Johann Amos Comenius* (1592–1671), a Moravian pastor and teacher who suffered persecution and banishment in the course of the Thirty Years' War. In his writings he allots eight hours of the day to sleep, eight to work, and eight to meals, the care of the health, exercise of the body, etc. He would have about every school building a playground, where the boys might run and jump and enjoy their games, since it is necessary to put the body in motion and allow the mind to rest. A half hour of recreation is to follow each hour of study. He would let pupils play to their hearts' content, but forbids wrestling, boxing and swimming as either useless or dangerous.

Juan Louis Vives (1492–1540), a well-known Spanish scholar, born at Valencia, educated there and in the University of Paris, after 1514 a resident of Bruges and Louvain, but dividing his time between Flanders and England in the years 1522 and 1528 as lecturer at Oxford and tutor in the family of Henry VIII, published several works on education which contain frequent mention of bodily exercise. He regards it as necessary for the health of growing boys, and appreciates the recreative value of games.

The typical figure of the French Renaissance is *François Rabelais* (1490–1553), monk, physician and humorist, whose novels *Gargantua* (1535) and *Pantagruel* (1533) contain his revolutionary views on education. The young gentleman Gargantua is provided with an ideal tutor in the person of Ponocrates. After three hours of lectures in the morning they spend an hour or so in ball games out-of-doors, followed by dinner, an hour of music or quiet games, and three more of study in the afternoon. Now his physical training, the object of which is plainly to prepare for "the gentleman's occupation, war," begins in earnest. With the author's habitual exuberance of detail Esquire Gymnast is made to teach his pupil horsemanship, how to handle the lance while in full armor, vault on horseback and leap from one horse to another, wield the battle-axe, handle pike, sword, dagger and shield, and hunt the bear, deer, wild

[1] Translated by Karl Wassmannsdorff in *Deutsche Turnzeitung*, **17** (1872); 272, 279.

boar and lesser game. He also practises wrestling, running, broad and high jumping, swimming, rowing and sailing a boat, climbing ropes, masts, trees and walls, throwing stones, hurling spears shooting with bow and cross-bow and with firearms, hanging and travelling sideways on a pole fixed in two trees, and putting up leaden dumb-bells.[1]

The eminent French essayist *Michel de Montaigne* (1533–1592), in discussing at some length the education of children, has comparatively little to say of their physical training; but his few words on that subject have been frequently quoted, and will still bear repetition. They are found in Book I, Chapter 25, of the *Essays* (1580). Health and strength are necessary, he says, for "the soul will be oppressed if not assisted by the body. . . I know very well how much mine groans under the disadvantage of a body so tender and delicate that eternally leans and presses upon her. . . Our very exercises and recreations, running, wrestling, music, dancing, hunting, riding and fencing will prove to be a good part of our study. I would have his outward behavior and mien, and the disposition of his limbs, formed at the same time with his mind. It is not a soul, it is not a body, that we are training up; it is a man, and we ought not to divide him into two parts; and as Plato says, we are not to fashion one without the other, but make them draw together like two horses harnessed to a coach. By which saying of his does he not seem to allow more time for and to take more care of, exercises for the body, and to believe that the mind in a good proportion does her business at the same time too? . . Inure him to heat and cold, to wind and sun, and to danger that he ought to despise. Wean him from all effeminacy in clothes and lodging, eating and drinking; accustom him to everything, that he may not be a Sir Paris, a carpet-knight, but a sinewy, hardy, and vigorous young man."

An English contemporary of Rabelais and of Henry VIII, was *Sir Thomas Elyot* (1490?–1546), intimate with Sir Thomas More, deeply stirred by the spirit of the Renaissance, and held in high repute for his scholarship. "The Boke named the Governour," published by him in 1531, relates to the education suitable for a gentleman's son who is preparing to serve the commonwealth. It passed through a half-dozen editions within the next fifty years, and has been recently reprinted in London and New York. Book I, Chapters 16–22, 26 and 27, comprising more than an eighth of the entire work, is concerned with physical training, which is treated under the followed heads: "Of sundry forms of exercise necessary for a gentleman. Exercises whereof cometh both recrea-

---

[1] Chapter 23. The entire passage is given in English at the foot of pp. 472–474 in the report of the United States Commissioner of Education for 1891–1892, vol. 1.

tion and profit" (here he mentions the use of dumbbells of lead or other metal, lifting or throwing the heavy stone or bar, wrestling, running, swimming, handling the sword and the battle-axe, riding and vaulting.) "The ancient hunting of Greeks, Romans and Persians. Dancing. Of other exercises which, moderately used, be to every estate of man expedient. That shooting in a long bow (the 'noble art of archery') is principal of all other exercises."[1] Elyot's fondness for the classics appears in his very numerous references to Greek and Roman examples or authorities.

While Mercurialis was writing his *De Arte Gymnastica* and Montaigne his *Essays, Richard Mulcaster* (1530?–1611) was doing hard work for scant pay as Master of the Merchant Taylors' School in London (1561–1586). Among other striking points of difference, he stands in pleasant contrast with his more successful contemporary Sturm, at Strasburg, in his attitude toward the bodies of the young. His *Positions*, which appeared in 1581 and was dedicated to Queen Elizabeth, deals with the principles to be observed in the training of children, "either for skill in their book or health in their body." A third of the volume is given up to the physical side of education, and the nature of the contents cannot be better revealed in brief space than by a partial list of the chapter headings, slightly altered and condensed: Chapter 4, That exercise must be joined with the book, as the schooling of the body. 6, The importance of exercise and physical training (as an agent of health). 7, The order followed in the present treatment of the subject. 8, Definition and varieties of exercise (athletics, martial exercise, exercises for health, etc.). 9, Choice of exercises. 10–15, Of loud speaking, loud singing, loud and soft reading, much talking and silence, laughing and weeping, holding the breath. 16–27, Dancing, wrestling, fencing, top and scourge, walking, running, leaping, swimming, riding, hunting, shooting (archery), ball games. 28–34, Circumstances to be considered in exercise, nature and quality of exercise, the bodies which are to be exercised; place, time, quantity, and manner of exercise. 35, The training master (the same teacher is to serve for both mind and body). Of all books on gymnastics he says in this last chapter, "I know not any comparable to Hieronymus Mercurialis, a very learned Italian physician now in our time, which hath taken great pains to sift out of all writers whatsoever concerneth the whole gymnastical and exercising argument, whose advice in this question I have myself much used, where he did fit my purpose." Mulcaster seems never to have caught the ear of the age in which he lived, and it is only within the last few

---

[1] Quotations from these chapters will be found in Barnard's *Am. Jour. Educ.*, **16**, 490–496 (1866). In 1545 *Roger Ascham* (1515–1568), author of The Scholemaster, published his "Toxophilus, the schole of shootinge conteyned in two bookes."

decades that he has been rescued from oblivion and rated at his real worth, as a man far in advance of his time. His book was reprinted in London in 1888.

Standing at the very end of this period of the Renaissance and the Reformation is *John Milton* (1608–1674), whose *Tractate on Education* (1644), though not of great value in itself, is yet deserving of mention here because it associates a form of bodily exercise with mental and moral training. In his model school, intended to bring up gentlemen's sons "to perform justly, skilfully, and magnanimously, all the offices both private and public, of peace and war," he would have the young men, between the ages of twelve and twenty-one, live together in barracks, like the Spartan youth. "About an hour and a half ere they eat at noon should be allowed them for exercise, and due rest afterwards; but the time for this may be enlarged at pleasure. . . The exercise which I commend first is exact use of their weapon, to guard and to strike safely with edge or point; this will keep them healthy, nimble, strong, and well in breath; is also the likeliest means to make them grow large and tall, and to inspire them with a gallant and fearless courage. . . They must be also practised in all the locks and gripes of wrestling, wherein Englishmen were wont to excel, as need may often be in fight to tug or grapple, and to close. . ." About two hours before supper they are to be called out for their military motions under sky or covert; "first on foot, then, as their age permits, on horseback, to all the art of cavalry; that, having in sport, but much exactness, and daily muster, served out the rudiments of their soldiership . . . they may as it were out of a long war, come forth renowned and perfect commanders in the service of their country."

BIBLIOGRAPHY.

R. H. Quick, "Essays on Educational Reformers." New York, D. Appleton & Co., 1890.

F. P. Graves, "A History of Education during the Middle Ages and the Transition to Modern Times." New York, the Macmillan Co., 1910.

Foster Watson, "Notices of Some Early English Writers on Education, with Descriptions, Extracts, and Notes." In annual Reports of the United States Commissioner of Education for 1900–01 (I: 861–884), 1902 (I: 481–508), 1903 (I: 319–350), and 1904 (I: 633–701).

W. H. Woodward, "Studies in Education during the Age of the Renaissance (1400–1600)." Cambridge (England), at the University Press, 1906.

W. H. Woodward, "Vittorino da Feltre and Other Humanist Educators: Essays and Versions." Cambridge (England), at the University Press, 1897.

Wilhelm Krampe, "Die italienischen Humanisten und ihre Wirksamkeit für die Wiederbelebung gymnastischer Pädagogik. Ein Beitrag zur allgemeinen Geschichte der Jugenderziehung und der Leibesübungen." Breslau, W. G. Korn, 1895.

O. Richter, "Die Ansichten und Bestrebungen italienischer Humanisten auf dem Gebiete der Leibeserziehung. Ein Beitrag zur Geschichte der Leibesübungen." In *Monatsschrift für das Turnwesen* 14 (1895); 98–107, 139–149, 193–200, and 262–270. Berlin, R. Gaertners Verlagsbuchhandlung.

Carl Rossow, "Italienische und deutsche Humanisten und ihre Stellung zu den Leibesügungen." Leipzig, C. G. Naumann, 1903.

S. S. Laurie, "John Amos Comenius, Bishop of the Moravians: His Life and Educational Works." Cambridge (England), at the University Press, 1895.

M. W. Keatinge, "The Great Didactic of John Amos Comenius now for the first time Englished, with Introductions, Biological and Historical." London, Adam and Charles Black, 1896.

W. S. Monroe, "Comenius and the Beginnings of Educational Reform." New York, Charles Scribner's Sons, 1900.

Foster Watson: On Education. A Translation of the De Tradendis Disciplinis of Juan Luis Vives, together with an Introduction." Cambridge (England), at the University Press, 1913.

Foster Watson, "Vives and the Renascence Education of Women." New York: Longmans, Green & Co.; London, Edward Arnold, 1912.

Arthur Tilley, "François Rabelais." Philadelphia and London, J. B. Lippincott Co., 1907.

Walter Besant, "Readings in Rabelais." Edinburgh and London, William Blackwood and Sons, 1883.

M. E. Lowndes, "Michel de Montaigne: A Biographical Study." Cambridge (England), at the University Press, 1898.

Edward Dowden, "Michel de Montaigne." Philadelphia and London, J. B. Lippincott Co., 1905.

L. E. Rector, "Montaigne: The Education of Children. Selected, Translated, and Annotated." New York, D. Appleton & Co., 1899.

H. H. S. Croft, "The Boke Named The Governour Devised by Sir Thomas Elyot, Knight. Edited from the first edition of 1531." In two volumes. London: Kegan, Paul & Co., 1880.

Sir Thomas Elyot, "The Boke Named the Governour." London, J. M. Dent. & Co.; New York, E. P. Dutton & Co., (Foster Watson's Introduction is dated 1907). Number 227 in Everyman's Library.

R. H. Quick, "Positions: By Richard Mulcaster, First Headmaster of Merchant Taylor's School (A.D. 1561–1586); with an Appendix, Containing Some Account of His Life and Writings." London and New York: Longmans, Green & Co., 1888.

Oscar Browning, "Milton's Tractate on Education. A Facsimile Reprint from the Edition of 1673. Edited with an Introduction and Notes." Cambridge (England), at the University Press, 1890. The Tractate is also published in Barnard's American Journal of Education II (1856): 76–85.

CHAPTER IX.

LOCKE AND ROUSSEAU.

THE best of the Renaissance writers on education had begun to break away from authority and tradition, and with reason as a guide were groping their way toward a training better suited to the nature and present needs of man than any the past could supply. That their ideas gained currency throughout all Europe and the way was thus prepared for practical reforms is very largely

FIG. 7.—John Locke (1632–1704).

due to the powerful influence exerted by two philosophers, *John Locke* (1632–1704) and *Jean Jacques Rousseau* (1712–1778), the former of whom published "Some Thoughts on Education" in 1693, and the latter his "Émile, a Treatise on Education" in 1762.

Locke was an Oxford graduate and lecturer, had studied medicine and been physician in the household of Lord Ashley, afterward Earl of Shaftesbury, and his chief work, the "Essay Concerning Human

Understanding," had already appeared (1690). His views, therefore, commanded attention at once, and whatever relates to the
physical side of education came with the added weight of special
knowledge. The author begins by dwelling at some length upon
the hygiene of childhood. "Keep the body in strength and vigor,"
he says, "so that it may be able to obey and execute the orders of
the mind. . . A sound mind in a sound body, is a short but full
description of a happy state in this world: he that has these two has
little more to wish for; and he that wants either of them will be
but little the better for anything else. . . He whose mind directs
not wisely will never take the right way; and he whose body is
crazy and feeble will never be able to advance in it. . .

"Most children's constitutions are either spoiled, or at least
harmed, by cockering and tenderness." They should not be too
warmly clad or covered, winter or summer, and to prevent colds the
boy's feet are to be washed every day in cold water, and his shoes
made "so thin that they might leak and let in water whenever he
comes near it." For safety and for health's sake he must learn
to swim. He is to be "much in the open air, and very little, as
may be, by the fire, even in winter." Clothing should never be
made tight, especially about the breast, and the diet ought to be
very plain and simple, with only small beer for drink, and that after
eating. Serving his meals at irregular intervals will train him to
endure hunger, if necessary. As regards fruit, "our first parents
ventured paradise for it, and it is no wonder our children cannot
stand the temptation, though it cost them their health." Some
kinds are wholesome and may be taken freely before or between
meals, but others are forbidden. Allow no sweetmeats—"one of
the most inconvenient ways of expense that vanity hath yet found
out; and so I leave them to the ladies." Nothing is more to be
indulged children than sleep, but insist upon early rising, and let
the bed be hard and rather quilts than feathers. All may be
summed up in these rules: "Plenty of open air, exercise and sleep;
plain diet, no wine or strong drink, and very little or no physic;
not too warm and strait clothing; especially the head and feet kept
cold, and the feet often used to cold water and exposed to wet."

Further on, in the body of his work, Locke comes to what we
should now call physical training proper. He recognizes that
"besides what is to be had from study and books, there are other
accomplishments necessary for a gentleman, to be got by exercise,
and to which time is to be allowed, and for which masters must
be had. Dancing being that which gives graceful motions all
the life, and above all things, manliness and a becoming confidence
to young children, I think it cannot be learned too early. . .
As for the jigging part, and the figures of dances, I count that little

or nothing, farther than as it tends to perfect graceful carriage. Music . . . wastes so much of a young man's time to gain but a moderate skill in it . . . that amongst all accomplishments I think I may give it the last place. . . Fencing, and riding the great horse, are looked upon as so necessary parts of breeding that it would be thought a great omission to neglect them: the latter of the two, being for the most part to be learned only in great towns, is one of the best exercises for health which is to be had in those places of ease and luxury . . . and . . . is of use to a gentleman, both in peace and war. . . As for fencing, it seems to me a good exercise for health, but dangerous to the life, the confidence of their skill being apt to engage in quarrels those that think they have learned to use their swords. . . If . . . a man be to prepare his son for duels, I had much rather mine should be a good wrestler than an ordinary fencer; which is the most a gentleman can attain to in it, unless he will be constantly in the fencing school, and every day exercising. . .

"I would (also) have him learn a trade, a manual trade; nay, two or three, but one more particularly. . . Manual arts, which are both got and exercised by labor, do many of them by that exercise not only increase our dexterity and skill, but contribute to our health too; especially such as employ us in the open air. . ." He "is not for painting;" but proposes "one, or rather both these, viz., gardening or husbandry in general, and working in wood, as a carpenter, joiner, or turner; these being fit and healthy recreations for a man of study or business."

The effects produced by Rousseau's educational romance, "Émile," upon the modern pedagogic world it would be difficult to exaggerate. The times were ripe for a revolt, and close upon the radical criticism of existing methods to which this theorist gave such convincing expression followed the actual reforms inaugurated by Basedow, Pestalozzi and other innovators. It will be sufficient here to mention only a single phase of the education which this disciple of Locke would give to his imaginary hero. "The body," says Rousseau[1] in Book I, "must needs be vigorous in order to obey the soul: a good servant ought to be robust. . . The weaker the body, the more it commands; the stronger it is, the better it obeys." Upon the subject of sleep, cold bathing, and the clothing suitable for young children his views are those of Locke.

In Book II we read: "If . . . you would cultivate the intelligence of your pupil, cultivate the power which it is to govern. Give his body continual exercise; make him robust and sound in order to make him wise and reasonable; let him work, and move

[1] These quotations are taken from Rousseau's "Émile," abridged, translated, and annotated by William H. Payne. New York, 1892.

about, and run, and shout, and be continually in motion; let him
be a man in vigor, and soon he will be such by force of reason. . .
It is a very deplorable error to imagine that the exercise of the
body is injurious to the operations of the mind; as if these two
activities were not to proceed in concert, and the second were not
always to direct the first! . . These continual exercises, thus
left wholly to the direction of Nature, not only do not brutalize
the mind while fortifying the body, but on the contrary, they form
within us the only species of reason of which childhood is susceptible,
and the most necessary at any and all periods of life. They teach
us thoroughly to understand the use of our powers, the relations
between our own bodies and surrounding bodies, and the use of the

Fig. 8.—Jean Jacques Rousseau (1712–1778).

natural instruments which are within our reach and which are
adapted to our organs. . . In order to learn to think, we must
. . . exercise our limbs, our senses, and our organs, which are
the instruments of our intelligence; and in order to derive all the
advantage possible from these instruments, it is necessary that the
body which furnishes them should be robust and sound. Thus,
so far is it from being true that the reason of man is formed independently of the body, it is the happy constitution of the body
which renders the operations of the mind facile and sure. . .
". . . Let him learn to make jumps, now long, now high; to
climb a tree, to leap a wall. Let him always find his equilibrium;
and let all his movements and gestures be regulated according to

the laws of gravity, long before the science of statics intervenes to explain them to him. . . When a child plays at shuttlecock he trains his eye and arm in accuracy; when he whips a top he increases his strength by using it, but without learning anything. I have sometimes asked why we do not offer children the same games of skill which men have, such as tennis, fives, billiards, bow and arrow, football, and musical instruments. I have been told, in reply, that some of these sports are beyond the strength of children and that their limbs and organs are not sufficiently developed for the others. I find these reasons bad. . . I do not mean that he shall knock the balls in our tennis courts, nor that his little hands shall be made to hold the racket of an expert; but that he shall play in a hall whose windows are protected; that at first he use only soft balls; that his first rackets shall be of wood, then of parchment, and finally of catgut stretched to accord with his progress. . . To spring from one end of the hall to another, to estimate the bound of a ball still in the air, and to send it back with a strong and steady hand, such sports do not befit a man but they serve to train a youth. . .

". . . I insist absolutely that Émile shall learn a trade," Rousseau continues, in Book III. This is not so much for the trade itself, as for overcoming the prejudices that despise it. "His apprenticeship is already more than half done, through the tasks with which we have occupied our time up to the present moment. . . He already knows how to handle the spade and the hoe; he can use the lathe, the hammer, the plane and the file; the tools of all the trades are already familiar to him. All he has to do in addition is to acquire of some of these tools such a prompt and facile use as to make him equal in speed to good workmen using the same tools, and in this point he has a great advantage over all others; he has an agile body and flexible limbs, which can assume all sort of attitudes without difficulty and prolong all sorts of movement without effort. . . All things considered, the trade which I would rather have be to the taste of my pupil is that of cabinetmaker. It is cleanly, it is useful, and it may be practised at home; it keeps the body sufficiently exercised; it requires of the workman skill and ingenuity, and in the form of the products which utility determines, elegance and taste are not excluded. . ."

As he approaches maturity (Book IV) Émile requires "a new occupation which interests him by its novelty, which keeps him in good humor, gives him pleasure, occupies his attention, and keeps him in training—an occupation of which he is passionately fond and in which he is wholly absorbed. Now the only one which seems to me to fulfil all these conditions is hunting. . . Émile has everything necessary for success in it: he is robust, dexterous, patient, indefatigable. Without fail he will contract a taste for this exercise; he will throw into it all the ardor of his age; for a time, at least, he will lose in it all the dangerous inclinations which spring from idleness. Hunting toughens the heart as well as the body."

Book V is concerned with the education of Sophie, Émile's future wife. ". . . Plato, in his *Republic*, enjoins the same exercises on women as upon men, and in this I think he was right. . . Since the body is born, so to speak, before the soul, the first culture ought to be that of the body; and this order is common to both sexes. But the object of this culture is different; in one this object is the development of strength, while in the other it is the development of personal charms. Not that these qualities ought to be exclusive in each sex, but the order is simply reversed: women need sufficient strength to do with grace whatever they have to do; and men need sufficient cleverness to do with facility whatever they have to do. The extreme lack of vigor in women gives rise to the same quality in men. Women ought not to be robust like them, but for them, in order that the men who shall be born of them may be robust also. In this respect the convents, where the boarders have coarse fare, but many frolics, races, and sports in the open air and in gardens, are to be preferred to the home where a girl, delicately reared, always flattered or scolded, always seated under the eyes of her mother in a very close room, dares neither to rise, to walk, to speak, not to breathe, and has not a moment's liberty for playing, jumping, running, shouting, and indulging in the petulance natural to her age; always dangerous relaxation or badly conceived severity, but never anything according to reason. This is the way the young are ruined both in body and in heart. . . Delicacy is not languor, and one need not be sickly in order to please."

While Locke and Rousseau were urging the necessity of some sort of physical training in the scheme of education, and philologists and students of ancient art kept alive the knowledge of Greek gymnastics, a number of medical writers had been directing attention to the importance of bodily exercise in the restoration and preservation of health. In London, 1705, *Francis Fuller* (1670–1706), a graduate of St. John's College, Cambridge, published "Medicina Gymnastica: or a Treatise Concerning the Power of Exercise with Respect to the Animal Œconomy, and the Great Necessity of it in the Cure of Several Distempers."[1] A German translation appeared

---

[1] London: Printed by John Matthews, for Robert Kanplock, at the Angel and Crown in St. Paul's Church Yard, 1705. A second edition, with additions, followed in the same year, a third ("printed for Robert Knaplock, at the Bishop's Head in St. Paul's Church-Yard") in 1707, a fourth in 1711, a fifth in 1718, a sixth in 1728, another in 1740, and the "ninth and last" in 1777.

in 1750,[1] after the book had already passed through seven or eight editions in England. *Friedrich Hoffmann* (1660–1742), a distinguished German physician referred to several times by GutsMuths in his "Gymnastics for the Young," and the first professor of medicine at Halle University, published in Latin an essay "On Motion, the Best Medicine for the Body"[2] in 1701; and eighteen years later several of his articles on the hygienic influence of exercise appeared at Halle under the title "The Incomparable Advantages of Motion and of Bodily Exercises, and How They are to be Employed for the Preservation of Health."[3] *Joh. Friedrich Zückert* (1737–1778), a Berlin physician quoted by Basedow, in discussing the hygiene of infancy and childhood (1764–1765),[4] mentions various bodily exercises, such as wrestling, dancing, riding, vaulting, bowling, skating and swimming. Upon his appointment to the chair of medicine at Lausanne, in 1766, *Simon André Tissot* (1728–1797) delivered a Latin discourse on the health of the literary class (*De valetudine litteratorum*), in which he recommends games and gymnastics for the youth of both sexes. A French translation of the address was published in 1767,[5] a German one in the following year,[6] besides later editions in both languages, several in English,[7]

[1] Medicina gymnastica, oder von der Leibesübung, in Ansehung der animalischen Oeconomie, oder der zu Erhaltung der Gesundheit des menschlichen Lebens nöthigen Ordnung; und wie solche bey Curirung verschiedener Krankheiten unumgänglich nöthig sey, von Franz Fuller, aus der sechsten Englischen Herausgabe übersetzt. Lengo, Johann Heinrich Meyer, 1750.

[2] "De motu, optima corporis medicina."

[3] "Vorstellung des unvergleichlichen Nutzens der Bewegung und Leibes-Uebungen und wie man sich derselben zur Erhaltung der Gesundheit zu bedienen habe."

[4] "Unterricht für rechtschaffene Eltern, zur diätetischen Pflege ihrer Säuglinge" (Berlin, A. Mylius, 1764. Second edition, 1771); and "Von der diätetischen Erziehung der entwöhnten und erwachsenen Kinder bis in ihr mannbares Alter "(Berlin, A. Mylius, 1765. Second edition 1771).

[5] "Avis aux gens de lettres et aux personnes sédentaires sur leur santé, trad. du latin" (Paris, Herissant Fils, 1767). It was later corrected by the author and published under the title "Del la santé des gens de lettres" (Lausanne, F. Grasset & Cie.; Lyon, Benoit Duplain; and Paris, P. F. Didot le jeune, 1768. Other editions bearing the same title appeared at Lausanne in 1769, 1770, 1772, and 1788; at Lyon in 1769; and a "nouvelle édition, augmentée d'une notice sur l'auteur et de notes, par F.-G. Boisseau, "in Paris (J.-B. Baillière) in 1825 and 1826.

[6] "S. A. D. Tissot, der Arzneygelahrtheit Doctor und öffentlicher Lehrer zu Lausanne, der Königl. Gesellschaft der Wissenschaften zu London, der Medicinisch Physischen Akademie in Basel, und der Oekonomischen Gesellschaft in Bern Mitglied. von der Gesundheit der Gelehrten. Aus dem Französischen übersetzt von Joh. Rud. Füesslin." Zurich, Füesslin und Compagnie, 1768. Later editions are said to have appeared in Zurich in 1769 and 1775. The German translation was also published in Leipzig (J. G. Müller) in 1768 and 1775).

[7] "An Essay on Diseases Incident to Literary and Sedentary Persons. With Proper Rules for Preventing Their Fatal Consequences, and Instructions for Their Cure. By S. A. Tissot, M.D., Professor of Physic at Berne. . The Second Edition, with very large Additions. With a Preface and Notes by J. Kirkpatrick, M.D., London: Printed for J. Nourse . . and E. and C. Dilly. . MDCCLXIX." The English translation was also published in Dublin ("Printed for James Williams, at No. 5, Skinner Row). MDCCLXXII."

and at least one in Swedish,[1] "Italian, and six other languages." A well-known French physician, *Clement Joseph Tissot* (1750–1826), published in Paris in 1780 his "Medical and Surgical Gymnastics: an Essay on the Use of Motion and of Different Exercises of the Body in the Cure of Disease."[2] Translations of the work were printed in Leipsic[3] and Stockholm.[4]

BIBLIOGRAPHY.

R. M. Quick, "Some Thoughts concerning Education by John Locke. With Introduction and Notes." Cambridge (England), at the University Press, 1880. Revised edition, 1884.

J. W. Adamson (Editor), "The Educational Writings of John Locke." New York: Longmans, Green & Co.; London, Edward Arnold, 1912.

W. M. Payne, "Rousseau's Émile; or, Treatise on Education. Abridged, Translated, and Annotated." New York, D. Appleton & Co., 1892.

Thomas Davidson, "Rousseau and Education According to Nature." New York, Charles Scribner's Sons, 1898.

Gabriel Compayré, "Jean Jacques Rousseau and Education from Nature." Translated by R. J. Jago. New York, Thomas Y. Crowell & Co., 1907.

R. L. Archer (Editor), "Rousseau on Education." New York: Longmans, Green & Co.; London, Edward Arnold, 1912.

Karl Wassmannsdorff, "Aerztlicher Einfluss auf die sogenannte Erneuerung der Leibesübungen in Deutschland; ein Beitrag zur Geschichte der Turnkunst," in *Neue Jahrbucher für die Turnkunst*, 15 (1869), 111–133.

[1] "Råd till de Lärde och till dem som föra ett stillasittande lefnadssätt. Af Tissot. Öfversättning i sammandrag. Pendant till Underrättelse om Gymnastik. Upsala, hos Palmblad och C. 1821." The dedication "till studerande corpsen" is signed "Gustav von Heidenstam."

[2] "Gymnastique médicinale et chirurgicale, ou essai sur l'utilité du mouvement, ou des differens exercises du corps, et du repos dans la cure des maladies; par M. Tissot, Docteur en Médecine, & Chirurgien-Major du quatrième Regiment des Chevaux-Légers." Paris: Bastein, Libraire, 1780.

[3] "Medicinische und chirurgische Gymnastik, oder Versuch über den Nutzen der Bewegung oder der verschiedenen Leibesübungen, und der Ruhe bey Heilung der Krankheiten. Aus dem französischen des Herrn Tissot, mit Anmerkungen des Herausgebers bereichert. Mit Churfürstl. Sächs. Privilegio. Leipzig, bey Friedrich Gotthold Jacobäer und Sohn, 1782."

[4] "Medicinsk och Chirurgisk Gymnastik, eller Försök om nyttan af Rörelse och Stillhet vid Sjukdomars botande. Af Herr Tissot, M.D., Öfver Fältskär vid fjerde Regenentet af Franska lätta Cavallerier. Stockholm, Tryckt hos Bokhandlaren Joh. Dahl, 1797."

CHAPTER X.

THE BEGINNINGS OF MODERN PHYSICAL EDUCATION IN GERMANY.

JOHANN BERNHARD BASEDOW (1723–1790), the son of a Hamburg wigmaker, attended school in his native city and was for several years a student of theology in Leipsic, later accepted a position as private tutor, and for eight years, from 1753 till 1761, was professor

FIG. 9.—Johann Bernhard Basedow (1723–1790.)

of moral philosophy and belles-lettres in the school for young noblemen (Ritterakademie) at Soröe, in Denmark. This institution belonged to a type common in Continental countries during the sixteenth and seventeenth centuries.[1] It had been founded in 1623 by Christian IV, who merely followed the custom of the age when along with teachers of the literary branches he appointed professional masters of riding, fencing and dancing, a master of

[1] Dr. Karl Wassmannsdorff has described in the *Deutsche Turnzeitung* (1870, pages 35–40 and 41–42) two of the oldest German *Ritterschulen*, the first founded in 1575 at Slez, in Alsace, and the second the *Collogium Illustre* at Tübingen, Württemberg, opened in 1594. The article is reprinted in Hirth's "Das gesamte Turnwesen," second edition, 1893, 1: 290–303.

gymnastics, and a special teacher of various games of ball. Basedow, therefore, had before his eyes a system of education which
actually made the attempt to combine physical with mental training, in the case of youth of a certain class. After leaving Soröe
he taught for seven years in Altona, near Hamburg. Thoughts
of reform in school life had already begun to fill his mind, and the
appearance of Rousseau's "Émile" (1762) just at this time no doubt
influenced him profoundly. In 1768 he gave up teaching in order
to devote himself wholly to the improvement of educational methods.

For some years Basedow had been pondering plans for a model
school which should embody his ideas and force them upon the attention of educators, and where among other innovations physical
training should be given a place in the daily program. The support
of the Duke of Anhalt, at whose invitation he removed to Dessau
in 1771, enabled him to realize this project, and on December 27,
1774, he opened there his private academy, named by him the
Philanthropinum. A year and a half later the number of pupils
was only fifteen, including Basedow's daughter, and only three of
these were above eight years of age. But in spite of the unwilling-
ness of parents to subject their children to the new methods, and
although the founder himself soon resigned his position at the head
of the institution, the effects produced by the experiment were
far-reaching and it was watched with the greatest interest. Basedow severed all connection with the school in the spring of 1778,
but other men, with greater capacity for organization and administration than he possessed, continued the work in conformity with
his views until 1793, when the Dessau Educational Institute, as
it has been called after the first few years, finally closed its doors.

According to the prospectus issued in December of 1774, five
hours a day were to be allotted to studies, three hours to recreation,
in fencing, riding, dancing, music, etc., and two hours to manual
labor. Basedow promises that if the numbers are sufficient and
the ages suitable there will be drill in military positions and movements, and frequent marches on foot; he also hopes to have the
school dwell under tents in the field for two months of the summer,
and in this way to give opportunities for hunting and fishing, boat-
ing, bathing, climbing and jumping, as well as for the study of
geography and the natural sciences. The physical training of the
pupils was first entrusted, as a part of his duties, to *Johann Friedrich
Simon*, a teacher in the Philanthropinum from January 2, 1776, to
October 20, 1777; and he was succeeded by *Johann Jakob Du
Toit*, whose connection with the school lasted from Easter of 1778
until the end came in 1793. The earliest exercises mentioned are
weekly lessons in dancing, free instruction in fencing for the older
boys, and six lessons a week in the Duke's private riding-school.

The latter's riding-master also gave free instruction in vaulting the (living) horse. Thus the "knightly exercises," as these four were called, had all been introduced, and Basedow himself refers to this fact, evidently recalling the school at Soröe.

But children of such tender age plainly required a different sort of bodily training, and accordingly it was not long before Simon began to give his pupils lessons in what he termed "Greek gymnastics," apparently including under this head nothing more than orderly contests in running, wrestling, throwing, and jumping, such as formed the staple of discipline in the Greek palæstra. For the broad-jumping he used ditches, cut so that they were perhaps eight feet across in the middle, but tapered almost to a point at either end, the pupils starting with a width which they could easily clear and working gradually toward the center as their strength and skill increased. For the high-jump two vertical poles were fixed at a distance of two and a half feet from each other in the ground, reaching about five feet above its surface; into holes bored in these, at intervals of an inch, wooden pegs were set at any desired height, and a stick resting crosswise upon the pegs furnished a barrier which would not injure the person who happened to strike it with his foot. Another of Simon's devices was a long round beam raised about four feet above the ground and fastened firmly between posts at its thicker end and again near the middle, but with the smaller half left unsupported. The pupils were taught to balance themselves upon this beam, first at the fixed end, while the teacher lent a hand from below, and then, as they accustomed themselves little by little to the feat, upon the swaying portion, and without assistance. A simpler exercise of the same character consisted in crossing ditches on a narrow plank. The list of games, all of which were under the oversight of a teacher, included shuttlecock, tennis or fives, skittles, and playing with a large ball filled with air. For the younger children there were also hoops and seesaw.

Under Simon's successor, Du Toit, other varieties of exercise were added from time to time—singing and reading aloud; swimming, skating, shooting with the bow and with firearms; marching in time and playing soldier; making excursions on foot into the surrounding country; walking up the rounds of a ladder set obliquely, without the help of the hands, or swinging from its under side and climbing hand-over-hand; carrying bags full of sand with the arms stretched out horizontally at the sides, while a teacher, walking among them, counted his steps aloud, and the pupils noted the number when their muscles began to pain them, and when they were finally overcome with fatigue, gauging thus the daily increase in strength and endurance. Gardening is mentioned, and in the fall of 1777 working in wood was introduced—the use of the lathe and plane, and cabinetmaking. Thus, at the very beginning of modern physical training, and under these earliest teachers of the art, we find in embryo most of the varied forms which have been advocated at one time or another since that day, i. e., simple games and athletic sports, gymnastics, military drill, manual labor and manual training, and school excursions. It will be observed, further, that these exercises had been incorporated into the plan of education as an essential factor, and that they were entrusted, not to a special master, but to one of the regular teachers in the school.

Other institutions were soon started in imitation of the Dessau Philanthropinum. The first of these was opened in October of 1775 at Marschlins, in Switzerland, but closed its doors in the following year. A second, at the castle Heidesheim, not far from Mannheim, lived only from the first of May, 1777, until some time in 1779. The task of organization in each instance was confided to Karl Friedrich Bahrdt, who had spent four weeks at Dessau and was recommended by Basedow himself. But one philanthropinistic school, the Schnepfenthal Educational Institute, long outlived its parent, and has survived even to the present day. Its founder, *Christian Gotthilf Salzmann* (1744–1811), had been called from a pastorate in Erfurt to become liturgist and teacher of religion in the Philanthropinum at Dessau, remaining there from the spring of 1781 until the end of February, 1784, and he himself attributed much of his later success to what he saw and learned in these three years. A growing desire to carry out independently his ideas of education, upon similar principles but with some important differences in organization and surroundings, finally induced Salzmann to give up his position in order to found a new school in the country, remote from the influences of city life. The site selected for the venture was Schnepfenthal, an estate in the vicinity of Gotha. Toward its purchase Duke Ernst II of Saxe-Gotha contributed four thousand thaler, and the corner stone of the main building was laid June 18, 1784.

Besides the Director's four children, there were during the first year nine pupils, all of them under twelve years of age, and for the instruction of this small number five assistants were employed. On July 18, 1785, *Christian Carl Andre* entered upon his duties as a teacher at the Institute, and to him Salzmann assigned the physical training of the pupils. About eleven o'clock they were called away from other tasks for the gymnastic lesson, commonly given in an open space under the oaks which shaded a neighboring hill. Here a jumping-ditch had been dug, and a balance-beam and pair of upright poles set up, like the ones at Dessau. The new exercises mentioned at this period are throwing at a target, running through the long jumping rope, pole-vaulting, and running up and down hill. When the weather was unfavorable they practised indoors various movements and positions intended to teach the proper carriage of the body—the beginnings of our present "free exercises.' The knightly exercises had not yet been introduced. After the midday meal the children were allowed the time until two o'clock for relaxation and games, and again in the evening these alternated with "musical entertainments." The whole of Sunday afternoons was set apart for amusements, excursions on foot, and games under Andre's direction. Pupils who showed proficiency in the events of the morning were distinguished by a few oak leaves on the hat, and as a further reward they were sometimes permitted by the teacher to choose the exercises for the following day.

In July of 1786 this portion of Andre's work was turned over to *Johann Christoph Friedrich GutsMuths* (1759–1839), who continued to discharge the duties of the position for nearly fifty years. During fifteen years of this time, *i. e.*, from October of 1787 till 1802, Christian Ludwig Lenz assisted him by giving instruction in swimming and vaulting. The preëmince of GutsMuths among pioneers of modern physical education does not rest upon priority in time— as we have seen, he was not the first, but the fourth teacher of gymnastics in a school open to all classes of society—but it is due rather to his long period of service, to the character and results of his teaching and the favorable impression which it made upon visitors, and to the series of volumes from his pen which formed what has been aptly called the first normal school of physical training for other teachers, and not in Germany alone, but elsewhere in Europe and even beyond its borders. For these reasons his career deserves somewhat extended notice.

GutsMuths, son of a tanner in moderate circumstances, was born August 9, 1759, in the ancient Prussian town of Quedlinburg. The boy's first library consisted of a great Bible illustrated with beautiful copper-plate engravings, an old geography with woodcuts of the different races of men, and best beloved of all, the "Acerra philologica," in German. This last book, containing hundreds of selections from the writings of well-known Greek and Latin authors, he read through a score of times, he said, and it may have given him his first introduction to the gymnastics of the ancients. He was also fond of working with tools and skilful with his pencil, and afterward with brush and paints. In the spring of 1773, while he was in his third year at the Gymnasium or classical secondary school of Quedlinburg, his father died. Four years later, upon recommendation of the prorector of the *Gymnasium*, he became private tutor in the family of Dr. Friedrich Wilhelm Ritter, a respected physician in the town and medical adviser to the then

Abbess of Quedlinburg, Princess Anna Amelia, sister of Frederick the Great. GutsMuths now found his time fully occupied. Besides preparing his own school tasks, he must teach the two oldest of Dr. Ritter's four sons and a merchant's boy whom he had also accepted as a pupil, and to fit himself the better to discharge the new duties he studied carefully Basedow's "Elementarwerk" (1774) and especially the "Methodenbuch" (1770).

In 1779 GutsMuths entered the university of Halle, intending to take up the study of theology; but inclination led him to attend as well courses in mathematics, physics, and modern languages (including English and Italian), and pedagogy, too, continued to interest him greatly. After three years in Halle he returned to Quedlinburg to resume his old position in the Ritter household, where there were now six children, five of them boys and the oldest barely nine years old. The next to the youngest, aged three, was Karl, the geographer-to-be. Only two years later, in June, 1784, Dr. Ritter succumbed to a severe attack of typhoid fever. His young widow found herself unable to continue the salary which GutsMuths had been receiving, but he was unwilling to desert the family in its time of need and was easily persuaded to remain for another year in spite of the changed circumstances.

During this same year Salzmann was making preparations to open his new education institution at Schnepfenthal, about seventy miles away to the south and west in a straight line. Already teachers had been selected, but outside of his own large family there were no pupils on the grounds. He decided to receive without charge, as the first of these, some promising lad not yet beyond his sixth year, and having learned of Dr. Ritter's death from a published announcement, sent two friends to Quedlinburg to see whether there might not be among his sons a suitable candidate. As a result, Frau Ritter was asked to part with her favorite Karl. June 7, 1785, taking the boy and his brother Johannes, four years older, she set out for Schnepfenthal, accompanied by GutsMuths, and reached there at noon of the 9th. A stay of several days led to such favorable impressions on both sides that she accepted Salzmann's offer to receive *both* children, and GutsMuths consented to remain as a permanent assistant. He made the return journey to Quedlinburg with the widow, arranged his affairs in the home city, and on the 30th of the same month was again in Schnepfenthal, ready to take up the new tasks.

The life story of GutsMuths during the next century, apart from his work as teacher and author, is soon told. In a letter to a university friend, written in June, 1791, he speaks of his garden, and of cabinetmaking and wood-turning; he has daily gymnastic exercises with the children in good weather, goes shooting in the

Fig. 10.—J. C. F. GutsMuths (1759–1839) and Karl Ritter (Anders monument in Quedlinburg).

Fig. 11.—Portrait of GutsMuths, and Views of Schnepfenthal and Vicinity (Deutsche Turn-Zeitung).

fall, and in winter skates on the meadows and coasts down the neighboring hills; he is an industrious botanist, still takes up his brush occasionally, painting portraits especially, but also landscapes from Nature, and enjoys the use of a very good pianoforte by one of the best German makers; he mentions the many distinguished visitors (Goethe, Wieland, Kotzebue and others), but says that of more importance to him is the Gotha library of seventy thousand volumes from which he has permission to draw whatever books he desires, through a messenger who makes trips back and forth every day or two. The school itself has a good collection of books, and he has been made librarian. Together with an English pupil he has read much in that language.

Twelve years after his arrival in Schnepfenthal, on August 15, 1791, GutsMuths was married to Sophie Echardt, a niece of Salzmann's wife. They occupied a storehouse on the grounds, at first, but after fifteen months moved into a home of their own in the little village of Ibenhain, a half mile distant in the valley. There they gradually improved and beautified the dwelling and its surroundings, laid out a garden which became famous for its flowers and fruit, and by the purchase of adjoining pieces of ground from time to time came at length to be possessors of a considerable estate, the source of much pleasure and not a little profit. The family life seems to have been an ideal one. Eight sons and three daughters were born to the couple, and two of the children who married during his lifetime presented their parents with six grandchildren. "Father" Salzmann died in 1811, but his son Karl succeeded to the directorship and the new administration brought no change in GutsMuths' relations with the school. The completion of fifty years of teaching, celebrated June 1, 1835, found him still in full enjoyment of his powers and busy in his calling. He continued in active service up to the end of March, 1839, and died on the 21st of the following May, after a brief and painless illness.

In the earlier years, while pupils and teachers were few, GutsMuths gave instruction in various elementary subjects, but especially in geography and the French language. Gymnastics was added, as we have seen, in July, 1786. Later, when he had moved to Ibenhain, he confined himself to his favorite subjects—the gymnastic lesson from 11 to 12 daily (until the summer of 1835), and geography and technology between 2 and 4. After 1802 he was swimming teacher as well. Salzmann had expected not more than twelve pupils at the start, but in the fall of 1785 there were already thirteen, including four of his own children, and the numbers steadily increased during the next two decades, to forty-nine in 1790, fifty-two in 1800, and sixty-one in 1803. The war which broke out in 1806 led to a marked falling off, followed by another rise, from twenty-two at the beginning of 1814 to thirty-six three years later, and forty-one in 1823.

For full information regarding the sort of gymnastic exercises which GutsMuths practised with his pupils we turn, of course, to his books. With few exceptions they were taken outdoors, in a spot set apart from the purpose and provided with the necessary apparatus. Already at Dessau, and by his predecessor André at Schnepfenthal, a varied list of suitable forms had been elaborated: Marching in time, walking on the balance beam and crossing ditches on the edge of a plank, jumping over a stick placed on jump stands, pole vaulting, jumping across a ditch, vaulting, carrying weights with outstretched arms, throwing at a target, foot-races, running and jumping through a long rope swung by two persons, simple free exercises indoors, skating and coasting, and long walks. Most or all of these GutsMuths continued to employ, modifying them, however, and making numerous additions as experience suggested. During the summer of 1794, for example, or before it, he has the pupils going up and down a rope ladder, swinging on vertical ropes, climbing a mast, hanging and travelling on the under side of a horizontal beam, balancing rods on the fingers, going through various exercises while standing on one foot, jumping over a rope swung close to the ground, throwing a wooden discus, wrestling, pushing against each other, lifting a weight hung on a rod and moved toward or from the hands according to the strength of the individual, estimating distance with the eye, and reading aloud so as to be heard by a person stationed at varying distances. He kept an accurate record of each pupil's performance in order to note his needs and progress.

Meanwhile gardening and other forms of manual labor and training were not neglected by Salzmann. Terraces were laid out upon the sides of a hill near the school, and here each pupil had his own patch of flowers, vegetables, and fruit to cultivate, earning pocket money by selling produce to the Institute. During the first year a bookbinder in the neighboring village of Waltershausen had given instruction in his trade and in the manufacture of little boxes, pen cases and baskets out of pasteboard; and after the spring of 1796 one of the regular teachers, who had been employed in various mechanical pursuits and was usually skilful with his hands, continued this instruction in pastboard work and also taught the pupils to make wooden models of tools and machines used in the various handicrafts, in milling, etc. Now and then a whole day was passed in the open air by teachers and pupils, who enjoyed their lunch together at some attractive spot in the woods. Longer excursions on foot, when the smaller children were left at home and a wagon was required to carry the baggage of the party are occasionally mentioned. Thus we read of a four day's excursion in October, 1798, undertaken by a company numbering forty-five persons; and in another year the journeys of Salzmann with his pupils amounted altogether to more than a hundred miles.

Joseph Röckl, a professor of pedagogy, passed nine days at the school in 1805, and in a published record of his observations commends the frugal diet there, the light and simple clothing, the unusually airy rooms for sleeping and study, the regard for personal

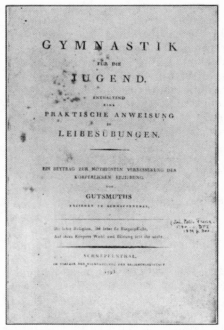

FIG. 12.—Title-page of "Gymnastik für die Jugend" (1793).

cleanliness, the active outdoor life, regular walks, work in the garden, and especially the gymnastic exercises. He visited, with GutsMuths, the newly erected riding school, the grounds for jumping and vaulting, and the swimming pool; watched the pupils handling saw, plane and chisel, or engaged in paste work; and learned of the occasional festivals and the yearly excursions. He doubts whether anywhere in all Germany there is an educational institution which devotes more care to the physical well-being of its scholars.

Other visitors also came to Schnepfenthal, and went away to

spread the news of what was undertaken and accomplished there. The lasting fame of GutsMuths, however, depends less upon the example furnished by his fifty years of teaching than upon his books, two of which, at least, the "Gymnastics for the Young" (1793), and its continuation, the "Games" (1796), not only constitute the first modern manuals on those subjects, but deserve to rank as classics. The former[1] was issued in two volumes, which contain altogether about seven hundred pages, nine copperplate illustrations of various exercises, and a folding sheet with explana-

Fɪɢ. 13.—One of the plates in "Gymnastik für die Jugend" (1793).

tory drawings of apparatus. The first volume is divided into five chapters: 1, We are weak because it does not occur to us that we

---

[1] "Gymnastik für die Jugend. Enthaltend eine praktische Anweisung zu Leibesübungen. Ein Beytrag zur nöthigsten Verbesserung der körperlichen Erziehung Von GutsMuths, Erzieher zu Schnepfenthal." Schnepfenthal: Verlag der Buchhandlung der Erziehungsanstalt, 1793. Bound in two volumes. The centenary of the book's appearance was the occasion of complete and partial reprints as follows:

"Gymnastik für die Jugend von GutsMuth. Unveränderte Ausgabe der ersten, in Jahre 1793 erschienenen Auflage, veranstaltet von Gustav Lukas . . . Mit 11 Tafeln." Wien und Leipzig, A. Pichler's Witwe & Sohn, 1893.

"GutsMuths, 1793, 1893. Die Kupfer und Einiges vom Texte des ersten Turnunterrichtsbuches der Welt, 'Schnepfenthal 1793.' Mit einer turngeschichtlichen Einleitung von Dr. Karl Wassmannsdorff, einem facsimile der Handschrift Jahn's in Schnepfenthal, dem Idealturnplatze Basedow's vom J. 1771 und einem Bilde des Herausgebers." Leipzig, Eduard Strauch, 1893.

could be strong if we only would. 2, Consequences of the common method of education, and especially the neglect of bodily training. 3, All the means hitherto employed against lack of hardihood are insufficient. 4, Gymnastics proposed and objections answered. 5, The effects and object of gymnastics. The second and larger volume is a practical handbook, arranged as follows: Chapter 6, Gymnastics defined, the open-air gymnasium described, the exercises classified. 7–15, Different sorts of jumping, running, throwing, wrestling, climbing, balancing, lifting, carrying, pulling, dancing, walking, military exercises, bathing and swimming. 16, Behavior in case of fire, keeping watch at night, fasting. 17, Loud reading and declaiming. 18, Exercises of the senses. 19, The exercises classified, according to the different parts of the body which each affects. 20, Method, use of time, general rules. 21, Manual labor and training. A second edition of the work, so much altered that it is virtually a new treatise, was published in 1804.[1]

In the volume "Games,"[2] of which two editions appeared in the first year and a third in 1802, an introduction of about fifty pages is followed by detailed descriptions of one hundred and five different games, arranged in natural groups and according to the faculties which they test or tend to develop, *e. g.,* attention, observation, memory, judgment. The other works of GutsMuths include a "Manual of the Art of Swimming" (1798, 2d ed., 1833),[3] "Mechani-

---

[1] "Gymnastik für die Jugend, enthaltend eine praktische Anweisung zu Leibes übungen. Ein Beytrag zur nöthigsten Verbesserung der körperlichen Erziehung. Von J. C. F. GutsMuth, Fürstlich N. W. Hofrath und Mitarbeiter an der Erziehungsanstalt zu Schnepfenthal. Zweite durchaus umgearbeitete und stark vermehrte Ausgabe mit 12 von dem Verf. gezeichneten Tafeln." Schnepfenthal, Buchhandlung der Erziehungsanstalt, 1804.

[2] "Spiele zur Uebung und Erholung des Körpers und Geistes, für die Jugend, ihre Erzieher und alle Freunde unschuldiger Jugendfreuden. Gesammelt und praktisch bearbeitet von GutsMuths, Erzieher zu Schnepfenthal. Mit einem Titelkupfer und sechzehn kleinen Rissen." Schnepfenthal, Verlag der Buchhandlung der Erziehungsanstalt, 1796.

A second edition of the "Spiele" appeared in 1796, and a third in 1802, a fourth, revised and with a new introduction by F. W. Klumpp, in 1845; and a fifth, sixth, and seventh, revised by O. Schettler, with Klumpp's additions and 33 woodcuts, in 1878, 1884, and 1885. An eighth edition, edited by Dr. J. C. Lion, was published at Hof (Rudolf Lion) in 1893, and a ninth at the same place in 1914, "neu bearbeitet von Georg Thiele."

Danish translations of the "Spiele" were published as follows: R. Nyerup, "Beskrivelse over nogle Lege," in *Borgervennen* 1800 nos. 41–44, 1801 nos. 11 and 12, and 1802 no. 4; and Jo. Werfel, "Nyeste Samling af gymnastiske Lege, Selskabslege og Julelege, til Tidsfordriv og Fornöjelse. Efter Gutsmuths," Copenhagen 1801 (The same book was published again in Copenhagen in 1802 under the title: "Walter og hans Elever i deres Fritimer.").

[3] "Kleines Lehrbuch der Schwimmkunst zum Selbstunterrichte; enthaltend eine vollständige praktische Anweisung zu allen Arten des Schwimmens nach den Grundsätzen der neuen Italienischen Schule des Bernardi und der älteren Deutschen, bearbeitet von J. C. F. GutsMuths, Mitarbeiter in der Erziehungsanstalt zu Schnepfenthal. Weimar, im Verlage des Industrie-Comptoirs, 1798." A Danish translation was published under the title:
"J. C. Fr. GutsMuths: Lærebog i Svømmekonsten til Selvundervisning; inde--

cal Avocations for Youths and Men" (1801, 2d ed., 1809),[1] "Book of Gymnastics for the Sons of the Fatherland" (1817),[2] and "Catechism of Gymnastics: a Manual for Teachers and Pupils" (1818).[3] Some idea of the wide influence exerted by these books may be gained from the fact that the "Gymnastics for the Young" was pirated outright in Austria (the 2d ed., Vienna, 1805);[4] appeared in the form of translations more or less altered and condensed in Denmark (Copenhagen, 1799),[5] England (London, 1800),[6] the United States (Philadelphia, 1802. This is a reprint of the London edition, and in both the work is wrongly attributed to *Salzmann* on the title page. See footnote on p. 89),[7] and Holland (The Hague, Amsterdam, and Breda, 1806);[8] was epitomized and issued under a different name in Bavaria (Stadtamhof, 1800),[9] France (Paris,

holdende en fuldstaendig praktisk Anvisning til alle Arter af Svømmen. Overs. og udg. (translated and published) af L. Reistrup." Copenhagen, 1800.

"Kleines Lehrbuch der Schwimmkunst zum Selbstunterrichte; enthaltend eine vollständige practische Anweisung zu allen Arten des Schwimmens nach den Grundsätzen der neuen Italienischen Schule des Bernardi und der alten allgemeinen Schwimmschule bearbeitet von Hofrath J. C. F. GutsMuths, Mitarbeiter in der Erziehungsanstalt zu Schnepfenthal. Zweite genau durchgesehene, verbesserte und vermehrte Auflage. "Weimar: Im Verlage des Landes-Industrie-Comptoirs. 1833.

[1] "Mechanische Nebenbeschäftigungen für Jünglinge und Männer, enthaltend eine praktische, auf Selbstbelehrung berechnete Anweisung zur Kunst des Drehens, Metallarbeitens und des Schleifens optischer Gläser. Als Anhang zu seiner Gymnastik von J. C. F. GutsMuths, Mitarbeiter in der Erziehungsanstalt zu Schnepfenthal." Leipzig und Altenburg, bei J. C. Hinrichs, 1801. Second edition, unchanged, in 1809.

[2] "Turnbuch für die Söhne des Vaterlandes. Von Joh. Chr. Fried. GutsMuths. Mit vier Kupfertafeln." Frankfurt am Mayn: Bei den Gebrüdern Wilmans, 1817.

[3] "Kateschismus der Turnkunst (Kurzer Abriss der deutschen Gymnastik), ein Leitfaden für Lehrer und Schüler von J. C. F. GutsMuths." Frankfurt a. M.: Bei den Gebrüdern Wilmans, 1818.

[4] "Wien: In Kommission bei Anton Doll, 1805. This is the second edition, reprinted with a few unimportant alterations.

[5] "Kort Anviisning til Legemsøvelser. Et Udtog af GutsMuths Gymnastik, Udgivet paa Dansk af V. K. Hjort." Copenhagen: Paa Hofboghandler S. Poulsen's Forlag. 1799.

[6] "Gymnastics for Youth: or a Practical Guide to Healthful and Amusing Exercises for the Use of Schools. An Essay toward the Necessary Improvement of Education, Chiefly as it relates to the Body; freely translated from the German of C. G. Salzmann. Master of the Academy at Schnepfenthal, and author of Elements of Mortality, Illustrated with Copper Plates." London: J. Johnson. 1800.

[7] The title page differs from that of the London edition only in the imprint: "Philadelphia: Printed by William Duane, No. 106 Market Street, 1802."

[8] "Volledig Leerstelsel van kunstmatige Ligschaams-oefeningen. Eeen Bijdrage tot de Opvoeding der Jeugd. Gevolgt vaar het Hoogduitsch van J. C. F. GutsMuths, Hofraad, en Leeraar op de Kweekschool van den Heere Salzmann, te Schnepfenthal, door Jan van Geuns . . . 's Gravenhage, Amsterdam en Breda: Bij de Gebroeders van Cleef en W. van Bergen & Comp. In two volumes, published in 1806 and 1813. A second edition, unchanged, appeared in 1818.

[9] "Entwurf zu einer Gymnastik, oder Anleitung zu Leibesübungen für die Jugend, grössten Theils nach Art der alten Römer und Griechen; aber alle nach den Bedürlnissen und Umständen unsers Zeitalters gesammelt, und in ein regelmässiges Ganze bebracht, von Johann Nepomuck Fischer, Weltpriester. Stadtamhof, bey Joh. Mich. Daisenberger, 1800."

Reprinted under the title. "Des Weltpriesters Joh. Nep. Fischer Auszug aus GutsMuths' Gymnastik für die Jugend v. J. 1793, verfasst i. J. 1799. Neu herausgegeben von Karl Wassmannsdorff. Den Freunden der Geschichte des deutschen Turnwesens gewidmet." Hof, Grau & Co. (Rud. Lion). 1872.

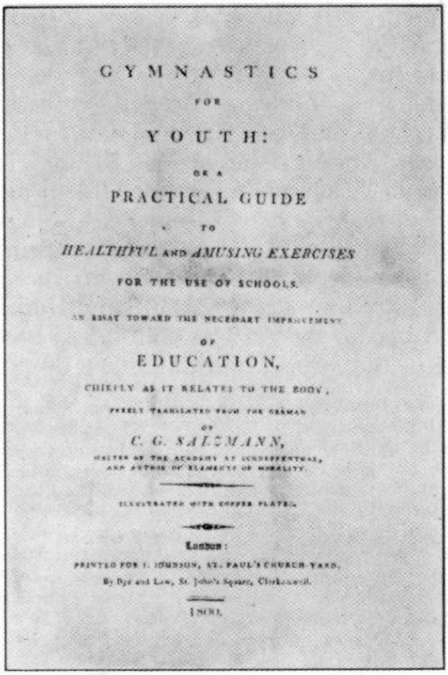

FIG. 14.—Title-page of the English translation of "Gymnastik für die Jugend" (1800).

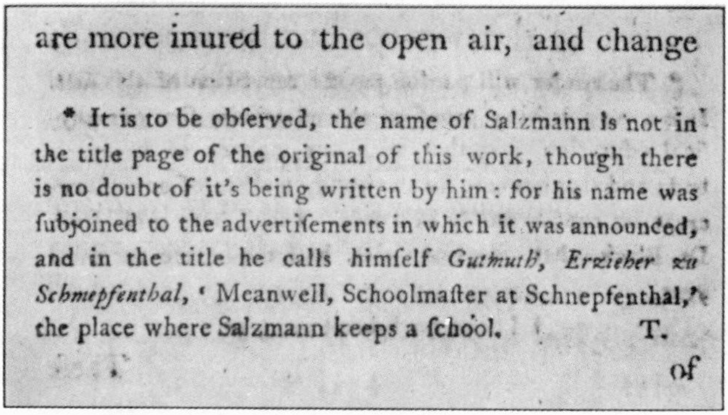

FIG. 15.—Footnote on p. 89 of the English translation of "Gymnastik für die Jugend,"

1803),[1] and Sweden (Lund, 1813);[2] was freely drawn upon by Clias in the "Elements of Gymnastics" which he published in German (1816), French (1819) and English (1823); and with these books of Clias served as the basis of Young's Italian manual (Milan, 1825).[3] Of the "Games," six editions (revised) have been published since the author's death, the last of them in 1914. In addition to his books on physical training GutsMuths wrote numerous ones devoted to *Geography*, and rendered an important service to educational science through the *Bibliothek der paedagogischen Litteratur*, which he edited and published in the years 1800–1820 (53 volumes).[4]

Chronologically the names of *Franz Nachtegall* (1777–1847), *Per Henrik Ling* (1776–1839) and *Friedrich Luduig Jahn* (1778–1853) should follow those of the German pioneers who taught and wrote in Dessau and at Schnepfenthal. These men, however, are best studied in connection with the later results of their life work, *i. e.*, statewise physical education in Denmark, the Swedish system of school gymnastics, and the popular gymnastic societies (Turnvereine) of Germany, to each of which a separate chapter is devoted.

BIBLIOGRAPHY.

General

Encyklopädisches Handbuch des gesamten Turnwesens und der verwandten Gebiete. In Verbindung mit zahlreichen Fachgenossen herausgegeben von Dr. Carl Euler, Schulrat, Professor, Unterrichts-Dirigent der königlichen Turnlehrer-

[1] "La Gymnastique de la jeunesse, ou traité élémentaire des jeux d' exercice, considérés sous le rapport de leur utilité physique et morale; par M. A. Amar Durivier, et L. F. Jauffret. Ouvrage orné de 30 gravures. A Paris chez A. G. Debray, Libraire, près le Louvre, place du Muséum, no 9. An XI (1803)."

[2] "Gymnastik för Swenska Ungdomen, eller Kort Anvisning till Kroppsöfningar. Ofversättning (by H. F. Sjöbeck, docent at the University of Lund). Med ett Kopparstick, Lund, 1813. Tryckt uti Berlingska Boktryckeriet."

[3] "Ginnastica elementare o sia corso analitico e graduato degli esercizi atti a sviluppare ed a fortificare l'organizzazione dell' uomo, estratto dalle opere dei celebri autori di ginnastica Professori Clias e Guts-Muths, compilato da E. Young, colonello . . . ed arricchito di 13 Tavole in rame." Milano: Per Giovanni Silvestri. 1825. "Elementar-Gymnastik oder zergliederte, stufenweise Anleitung zu jenen Leibes-Übungen, welche vorzüglich geeignet sind, den menschlichen Körper zu entwickeln, auszubilden und zu stärken. Nach den Werken der rühmlichst bekannten Gymnastiker und Professoren Clias und GutsMuths bearbeitet von E. Young, Obserst, Kommandant der K. K. Militär Erziehungs-Anstalt in Mailand . . . Mit 22 Kupfertafeln. Aus dem Italienischen übersetzt von K. K. Oberleutnant S. Poschacher. Mailand, aus der kaiserl. königl. Buchdruckerey. 1827."

[4] The "Enclyclopaedia of Bodily Exercises" (*Encyklopädie der Leibesübungen*. Three volumes, 1794, 1795, 1818) published by Gerhard Ulrich Anton Vieth (1763–1836) of the Dessau *Hauptschule* (not the Philanthropinum), and the important pioneer work of Don Francisco Amoros (1770–1848) in Madrid and Paris and of Phokion Heinrich Clias (1782–1854) in Switzerland, England, and France, are omitted here for lack of space, but have been discussed at length in an article which appeared in the *American Physical Education Review* for June, 1904 (IX: 89–110). The sketches of Amoros and Clias, without bibliography, are reprinted as chapters V and VI in the writer's "Pioneers of Modern Physical Training" (New York, Association Press, 1915).

bildungs-Anstalt in Berlin. Wien und Leipzig, A. Pichler's Witwe & Sohn, 1894–1896. Three volumes.

Geschichte des Turnunterrichts. Bearbeitet von Professor Dr. Carl Euler, Unterrichts-Dirigent der Königl. Zentral-Turnanstalt in Berlin. Zweite Auflage. Gotha, E. F. Thienemanns Hofbuchhandlung, 1891. There is also a "dritte Auflage, neu bearbeitet von Carl Rossow, Turnlehrer am Königl. Wilhelms-Gymnasium in Berlin," issued by the same publisher in 1907.

Die Turnübungen in den Philanthropinen zu Dessau, Marschlins, Heidesheim und Schnepfenthal. Ein Beitrag zur Geschichte des neueren Turnwesens. Von Dr. Karl Wassmannsdorff. Sonderabdruck aus der *deutschen Turnzeitung.* Heidelberg, Karl Groos, 1870.

Neue Jahrbücher für die Turnkunst (NJT). Published in Dresden (vols. 1–27) and Leipzig (vols. 28–40) 1855–1894. There were six numbers a year 1855–1881, and twelve numbers 1882–1894. In 1880 the name was changed to "Jahrbücher der deutschen Turnkunst."

Deutsche Turn-Zeitung (DTZ). Leipzig, since 1856. This is the official organ (weekly) of the Deutsche Turnerschaft.

Monatsschrift für das Turnwesen (MT). Berlin, 1882–1920.

Körper und Geist (K.G.) Published under this title, 26 numbers a year, in Leipzig from April 1, 1902 (vol. XI), through December, 1920 (Vol. XXIX). It was started April 1, 1892, as the "Zeitschrift für Turnen und Jugendspiel" (24 numbers a year), and ten volumes were published under that title.

Karl Wassmannsdorff, in NJT 1855; 28, 153, 247, and 323; 1887: 56; MT 1882: 18, 49, and 76; and DTZ 1887: 700 and 715.

Ferd. Brehmer, in DTZ 1911: 806.

G. Meier, in NJT 1890: 257, 311, and 408.

W. Moestue, in KG 13; 213, 327, and 359 (1904 and 1905).

Jaro Pawel, in NJT 1891: 15.

Otto Richter, in DTZ 1890: 470, 603, and 622.

Richard Winter, in DTZ 1910: 189, 358, and 597.

GutsMuths

GutsMuths pädogogisches Verdienst um die Pädagogik, die Georgraphie und das Turnen. Inaugural-Dissertation zur Erlangung der Doctorwürde der Hohen Philosophischen Facultät der Universität Leipzig vorgelegt von Adolf B. Netsch, aus Oberkunnersdorf bei Löbau in Sachsen. Hof. a. S., Rud. Lion, 1901.

Johann Christoph Friedrich GutsMuths. Erweiterter Separatabdruck aus der Festschrift zur Feier des 100 jährigen Bestehens von Schnepfenthal, Von Dr. Karl Wassmannsdorff. Heidelberg, Karl Groos, 1884.

Karl Wassmannsdorff, in DTZ 1865: 400, 409; 1884: 317, 354; NJT 1884: 233, 290, 340, 392, 430, 476; 1888: 3, 49; 1890: 41; 1894; 15, 53, 101, and 145.

H. Brendike, in DTZ 1886: 551.

Carl Euler, in DTZ 1871: 133; NJT 1872: 2, 149; MT 1885: 217; 1886: 201; 1899: 136.

P. M. Kawerau, in DTZ 1859: 61.

M. Kloss, in NJT 1858: 249.

E. Witte, in KG 13: 33 (1904).

Other articles in DTZ 1861: 241; MT 1902: 302; and KG 13: 124, 127, and 142, 1904).

CHAPTER XI.

FRIEDRICH LUDWIG JAHN, AND POPULAR GYMNASTICS IN GERMANY.

FRIEDRICH LUDWIG JAHN, the father of popular gymnastics (*Volks-* or *Vereinsturnen*) in Germany, was born August 11, 1778, at Lanz, a Prussian hamlet lying midway between Hamburg and Berlin and only a few miles distant from the right bank of the Elbe. His father, the village pastor, was a large and vigorous man, faithful to all the varied duties of his office, and at the same time a thrifty manager of the parochial estate, fond of his garden, and with hopfields and sheep of his own. The mother was a strong, brave woman of Puritan type, devoutly religious, severely plain in her manner of living, industrious and economical, and not unlike the peasant women of the parish in outward appearance. Their only other child was a daughter, born two years before.

The first thirteen years of the boy's life were spent at home, mostly outdoors and in the company of older persons. At the age of four he began to read with his mother in Luther's translation of the Bible, a book with which he afterward showed great familiarity. This was followed by Pufendorf's record of the Great Elector's deeds and by the historical writings of Frederick the Great. The latter monarch died when Jahn was eight years old, and was made a very real hero to him by the tales of veterans of the Seven Years' War living in the neighborhood and of troopers attracted by the rich pasturage there. In addition to Latin his father taught him history, geography and the German language, which soon became his favorite studies and continued to interest him deeply throughout his school and university days.

Rich cultivated lands and broad meadows alternate with pine woods and patches of arid, sandy soil on the surface of the alluvial plain which reaches out in all directions from Lanz. Not allowed to mingle much with the peasant children, Jahn roamed these neighboring fields and forests, learned from grown-up acquaintances to ride and swim and shoot, helped his father in the garden, went with him across the Elbe to market the hops at Dannenberg, in the electorate of Hannover, and accompanied other hop-growers as far as Lübeck, Wismar and Rostock, on the Baltic. His mother came from Neustadt, in the adjoining duchy of Mecklenburg-Schwerin, and frequent trips with smugglers across the borders of this state, only ten miles away to the north, made him thoroughly

at home on every road and footpath leading thither.   It was this
frontier life and his early visits to other states that made it easy for
Jahn in later years to disregard sectional barriers and to view as
citizens of a common country all who spoke the German language.
The relation of lord and vassal was unknown in Lanz and most of
the peasants owned the farms they tilled.   Jahn breathed in the
prevailing spirit of self-reliance and independence, and grew up
sturdy and fearless, fond of his native language and customs and
proud of the history of Prussia and of Brandenburg, his own province, in particular.

Fig. 16.—Friedrich Ludwig Jahn (1778–1852).

On October 8, 1791, he entered the higher classical school (*Gymnasium*) at Salzwedel, an old Prussian town about twenty-five miles
to the southwest of Lanz.   Notwithstanding the lack of system
and completeness in his home training the boy's marked natural
ability, his gift of quick perception and his retentive memory must
have led to rapid progress; for three years later (September 27,
1794), at the age of sixteen, he was received into the eighth class
(*Unter-prima*) at the *Gymnasium zum grauen Kloster* in Berlin.   On
the 17th of the following April, after spending only six months at
this second school, he left for home suddenly and without taking
leave, so that for a time the authorities supposed some accident
had befallen him.   In contrast with the outdoor life and the comparative freedom from restraint of his earlier years, he had found
the confinement and orderly discipline of the classroom doubly
irksome; and his country plainness, not to say roughness, of speech
and manners and want of familiarity with city ways, together with
his independent spirit and the absence of intimate companionship

with boys of his own age while he was living at home, had led to repeated misunderstandings with teachers and fellow-pupils alike.

His university career was even more irregular and stormy, but now his native capacity for leadership and a certain rugged eloquence in public speaking began to reveal themselves. For five years, dating from April 27, 1796, he was a student in the University of Halle. In obedience to his father's wish he undertook the study of theology; but it was not in his nature, nor had his imperfect preparation fitted him, to take one of the usual professional courses. Prussian and German history and the German language and literature, subjects generally neglected at that day but dear to his own heart from childhood, absorbed more and more of his time and thought. Thus, after three years we find him selling, for ten thalers, the manuscript of a small treatise on "The Promotion of Patriotism in Prussia,"[1] a glorification of that state and its rulers, and a plea for more attention to the study of Prussian history in the schools and universities as a means of developing love of country. The purchaser published the work a year later, with his own name on the title page. Meanwhile Jahn's habits of study continued to be desultory. Although he attended lectures, and in the philological seminar of F. A. Wolf won that scholar's commendation for his "language instinct," few of the courses begun were completed in orderly fashion, and his work was interrupted by frequent excursions on foot to various parts of Germany.

Another disturbing factor was the war which he soon declared against the student clubs and associations of fellow-countrymen known as *Landsmannschaften*, the predecessors of the present *Corps*. The sectional character of these "circles" is evident from their names—Westphalians, Pomeranians, Silesians, Magdeburgers, Anhalters, etc.; and it seems to have been their spirit of narrow provincialism, coupled with the dissolute life and constant duelling of their members, which roused him to an almost fanatical opposition and was the occasion of incessant brawls. His increasing difficulties with the Landsmannschaften and the effort to unite against them all students outside their ranks brought him at length into conflict with the academic authorities, and he left Halle to continue the same passionate struggle for a time at Jena, where his eloquence gained him a considerable following among the students.

Apparently it was a desire to study the Northern languages that carried him next into what was then Swedish Pomerania, where he was received into the University of Greifswald, May 31, 1802, enrolling himself under a false name. Here, too, in spite of poverty, he soon became a recognized leader. It was rumored that he

---

[1] Über die Beförderung des Patriotismus im Preussischen Reiche. Allen Preussen gewidmet von O. C. C. Höpffner. Halle, 1800.

belonged to the proscribed secret order of Unitists. However this may have been, before many months had passed certain wild student pranks and the violent outcome of a factional feud resulted in his appearance before the academic authorities, by whom he and a fellow student were given, on February 7, 1803, the *consilium abeundi*.

After the turmoil of his school and university life there now succeeded a period of quiet teaching and literary labors, during which the man gathered himself together, formed those settled convictions which were the mainspring of his future career, and gave evidence of his underlying strength and soundness of character. For two years he was a private tutor, in Neubrandenburg until the end of September, 1804, and then at the Torgelow glassworks, twenty-five miles westward. The first of these years witnessed a foreshadowing of the great work begun seven years later in Berlin. Every evening he gave his pupils, the sons of Baron Lefort, instruction in swimming, in a brook near the town, followed by practice in running, climbing, jumping and wrestling on a neighboring height and by a few lively games. Any other boys who happened to be present, although strangers to him and with no claim upon his services, were made welcome, and in this way the number was increased to twenty or thirty. New and equally vigorous outdoor exercises were substituted in the late fall and winter months.

On October 1, 1805, Jahn took public leave of his Mecklenburg friends through the columns of the *Strelitz'scher Anzeiger*. His next move, made in the interest of literary plans and to favor his own advancement, was to Göttingen. Some months were spent in linguistic studies at the University, and in the summer of 1806 he removed to Jena, where he completed a volume of "Contributions to High German Synonymy," embodying material collected in all parts of Germany during the excursions of his university days. The book is the work of an ardent friend of the German language, and not of a scientific philologist; and it reveals the keen observer of the country and its inhabitants, as well as the student of popular dialects.

Jahn had hoped to get a footing in the university at Göttingen, it seems; but in the fall of 1806, while he was sojourning in the Harz Mountains, his plans were suddenly changed and his thoughts turned from the classroom to the camp. Napoleon's incursions and his insolent treatment, which were threatening the very existence of Prussia, had at last compelled Frederick-William III to take up arms against the French. Learning that war was inevitable, Jahn immediately gave up his visit and hastened toward the army which was gathering in Thuringia, intending to volunteer his services. Delayed by swollen streams, he reached Jena on the day of the battle (October 16, 1806), saw the last struggle and the crushing defeat, and joined the fleeing soldiery as a "volunteer fugitive." Frederick-William's ill-prepared and poorly officered troops had proved an easy prey for the French. One by one the great fortresses were surrendered and garrisoned by the enemy's forces, the royal family was forced to flee from Berlin, and by the Treaty of Tilsit (July, 1807) Prussia lost half her territory and became virtually a mere province of France, overrun by the soldiers of the conqueror and entirely at his mercy.

Jahn's flight and later wanderings led him by wide detours to Halle and Magdeburg, down the Elbe, across to the Baltic and westward along the coast to Lübeck (November 5), thence into Silesia, apparently, and back again to Jena, where he remained until the Treaty of Tilsit. Afterward, until the fall of 1809, he spent a portion of his time at home, but lived for the most part with a friend at Dammeretz, on the Elbe, some distance below Lanz. Before the outbreak of the war he had been engaged on two works, a "Handbook for Germans" and "German Nationality" (*Deutsches Volksthum*); but the manuscript of both seems to have been lost in the days following the battle of Jena. The former was not rewritten, but the latter, his chief literary work, was again ready in 1808 (the introduction is dated October 14, at Lanz) and appeared at Lübeck in the spring of 1810. Its central thought is the unity of Germany, and in its pages his controlling passion for the German language, customs and history, his intense love for the fatherland, and his desire to see it bound together into one strong nation, able to throw off the foreign yoke, found full and forcible expression.

Late in December of 1809 Jahn arrived in Berlin, where, as he says, love for the fatherland and his own inclination led him again to teaching. Disappointed in his original idea of finding a position in the new Berlin University, and failing to receive a promised head mastership at Königsberg when the results of his faulty school and university training became apparent, he at first received some private pupils, and the next Easter entered a training school for teachers (the *Königliche Seminar für gelehrte Schulen*). He also began to give instruction in history, German and mathematics at the *Gymnasium zum grauen Kloster*, the school from which he had run away fifteen years before. This position he retained for a year and a half, until Christmas, 1811, and in the meantime he had been given some classes in Dr. Plamann's flourishing Pestalozzian School for Boys.

It was the custom at the Graue Kloster for teachers to spend some of the Wednesday and Saturday half-holiday afternoons outdoors with pupils of the lower classes. In the spring of 1810 Jahn began to make this his practice, meeting the boys from time to time outside the Halle and Kottbus gates for games and simple exercises like running, jumping and wrestling, or going farther south with them to the *Hasenheide*, a hilly and wooded stretch of unused land on the southern slope of the Spree valley, and to the adjoining *Rollberge* and the *Tempelhofer Berg*. Older scholars were welcomed whenever curiosity and inclination tempted them to join the band, and the numbers rapidly increased from week to week. They played at "Black Man," or at "Robber and Traveller" (afterward known as "Knight and Townsman"), using a fowler's hut for the robbers' den and the foot of an oak as the city or castle from which the travellers set forth. The first apparatus, furnished by Jahn, was a pair of light poles tipped with iron points so that they could be thrust into the sand, and a rope with a sandbag at either end, which was placed across the top as a barrier to be jumped over. Long, straight sticks were used like spears for hurling at any mark that might be chosen. The limb of an oak, their first horizontal bar, sufficed for hanging exercises and for attempts to draw themselves up by the arms. Preparatory jumping exercises, borrowed from GutsMuths, were occasionally practised. One afternoon Jahn went on foot with ten or twelve boys as far as the *Britzer Heide*, to the southeast, where they had a game together and then walked back. The report of this first *Turnfahrt* (gymnastic excursion) roused the desire for others of a similar sort.

Jahn knew how to vary the exercises and make each one interesting, and the moments of rest were filled with jokes and banter or with stories drawn from history and from his own experiences. Winning thus the respect and love of all his young companions, he was able to overcome the spirit of dissension which at the start was ready to break out on slight provocation, and made harmony and discipline prevail. During the following winter a part of those who had been regular in attendance still held together, and were allowed a share in the indoor exercises of the pupils at Plamann's school—fencing with light broadswords and shooting at a target with crossbows. This group formed a nucleus for the next year's work.

The spring of 1811 saw Jahn again at the Hasenheide with pupils from the Graue Kloster and Plamann's school. But now he had a more definite plan in mind. Immediately after school hours on Wednesdays and Saturdays work was begun in an opening in the woods, opposite a few public houses. They first fenced in a rectangular area and built in the background a small hut or arbor where clothing could be left, and then set up within the enclosure their simple apparatus. This comprised a horizontal mast or balance-beam, a rope hung from a yard which was fastened crosswise in the limbs of two trees, a group of horizontal bars made by tying three small fir trunks, at a height of seven feet, to three pines which stood at the points of a triangle, a roughly made inclined ladder, two climbing masts, one fifteen and the other twenty feet or more in height, and two sets of fixed standards for use in high jumping and pole-vaulting. They also made a jumping ditch, and laid out a figure-of-eight track, one circle of which served as a wrestling place. Games were to be played outside the enclosure.

Early in June this first *Turnplatz*[1] was opened. Each boy was assessed fourteen groschen (thirty-three cents) to meet the expense of keeping grounds and apparatus in condition; but Jahn evidently advanced much of the original cost himself, and he granted free admission to any boys of good character who were unable to pay the light charge. Meanwhile the attendance had increased to eighty or a hundred, and later in the summer it rose to two hundred. A friend of Jahn came with many of his pupils from the *Friedrich-Wilhelms- und Werder'schen Gymnasium* and two other teachers brought boys from the Schindler'schen Orphan Asylum. Seeing the need of a special suit for the exercises, Jahn appeared one day clad in long trousers and a short jacket of gray unbleached linen, a costume so cheap and durable that its use soon became general on the Turnplatz, and an enemy of the turners was in the habit of referring to them later as "the unbleached rascals." All distinctions of rank and class disappeared with the adoption of this uniform costume. Lunches consisted of bread and salt, or of bread and butter and eggs, and pure spring water was the usual drink. Tobacco and brandy, together with all sweetstuffs, were forbidden.

Tuesday and Friday afternoons were added to the usual half-holidays during the months of July and August. Besides the games, wrestling, in which Jahn was himself uncommonly proficient, retained its popularity in spite of the new apparatus. There was no wooden horse as yet, but one day Friedrich Friesen, a fellow teacher with Jahn at Plamann's school, showed them how to vault from the rear and the side to a seat on the thick end of the balance beam. The exercises were not yet orderly or organized, but every boy was an inventor and shared the result with others, learning from them in turn. It was hardly in Jahn's nature to be systematic, and such a thing as a formal school of gymnastics was foreign to his purpose. The essential thing was the active, wholesome, common life in the open air, and especially the games, training the boys to work together in harmony, and he sought also to

---

[1] In his own opposition to everything foreign Jahn had applied the name *Turnen* to his exercises, believing that it was a term of German origin, and from this root he built up many new compounds—*Turner* (gymnast), *Turnkunst* (the gymnastic art), *Turnplatz* (the grounds where the exercises were practised), *Turntag* (gathering of gymnasts), etc.

kindle in them a public spirit which might some day be of service to the nation.

With the approach of winter all movable apparatus at the Hasenheide was stored away, and now Jahn and his oldest pupils began to read eagerly whatever they could find on the subject of physical training, studying with special care the books of GutsMuths and Vieth.

A year's experience had shown that the first Turnplatz was too small, too near the public houses, too exposed to "weather, wind and wit." With the first spring sun of 1812 work was therefore begun on a new site farther to the east and south, the free use of which was granted by the authorities. It lay on a tableland at the head of the slope, close to the Rollberge, and was protected

FIG. 17.—Jahn's Hasenheide *Turnplatz*, from a contemporary print (1818).

from the wind on three sides by dense thickets of pine, fir and oak. Paths were made leading to this spot, the surface was levelled off, more trees were set out, another hut was erected, in the center of the grounds this time and with a meeting and resting place near it (the *Tie*), and the apparatus was brought away from the old Turnplatz. The equipment received numerous additions. Three vaulting bucks or horses without pommels, three, four and five feet high respectively, were constructed out of tree-trunks. Nearby stood the first crude models of our parallel bars—three pairs of thin beams about twelve feet long, those in each set placed parallel with each other and about two feet apart. They corresponded in height with the bucks, and the original aim in using them was merely to gain the strength of arm and hand necessary for lifting and supporting the body during vaulting exercises. New jumping ditches and running tracks, a larger balance beam, targets with movable iron-mounted heads, and more elaborate devices for hanging and climbing exercises were provided.

Jahn had already begun to note down and arrange the various exercises, but everything was still in process of development. Although the other apparatus was not neglected, the parallel bars and the horizontal bar soon became the favorite pieces, and the boys vied with each other in inventing new performances on them. Three turners who had received private instruction in vaulting during the winter preceding met for further practice at special hours with little groups of skilled companions, and for this purpose Friesen arranged to have a live horse brought to the *Turnplatz* on certain days. Less interest was taken in jumping, and games did not hold such a prominent place as formerly. Once a month Jahn used to stay all night at the grounds, going through the exercises by moonlight with his pupils. It was also the custom for several of them to keep watch there regularly, as a precaution against thieving. The *Turnfahrten* were renewed, and gave a great impetus to excursions of all sorts. More than a hundred turners are said to have gone off on foot during the summer vacation, some of them on very considerable journeys.

Before the season was over the attendance had reached five hundred, new arrivals streaming in from all classes of society. On Sundays adults were allowed to take part. In general, the popular attitude toward the movement was very favorable. Spectators of every rank and by the hundred gathered at the sides of the *Turnplatz*, and the evident physical benefit from the work, the harmony that existed and the strong national feeling cultivated there were at once appreciated. Jahn worked alone, for the most part, assisted, however, by the older and more experienced pupils, whom he was now able to employ as squad leaders (*Vorturner*). If something new was to be practised he selected a few of the most skilful and showed them the exercise himself, and they in turn spread it from group to group. In spite of the numbers, accidents were unknown during this and the preceding summers. Occasionally gentle measures were not sufficient to preserve discipline. It is said that Jahn knew how to use a rope-end, and that when two boys had quarreled he used to furnish each of them with a pliant root, with which they fought it out in the presence of their comrades, clad in their thin linen breeches, and striking with all their might lest they should appear cowardly.

In the winter of 1812–13 some of the best turners, with Friesen at their head, organized a society for the critical study of gymnastics and to work out an artistic arrangement of the material which had accumulated. A hall was also rented, a wooden vaulting horse was purchased with a hundred thalers which some of them had collected, and practice in vaulting and fencing was continued.

The momentous events of the next three years, which drew all Europe into the conflict with Napoleon and culminated in his final overthrow at Waterloo (June 18, 1815), put a temporary check upon the further development of Jahn's work at the Hasenheide, at the same time that they emphasized its value. On March 17, 1813, King Frederick-William III of Prussia declared war upon France and appealed to his people to join in the great War of Liberation. Jahn was among the first to respond. He entered Lützow's famous Free Corps, and his example was quickly followed by most of the turners who were old enough to bear arms. Although he made occasional visits to the Turnplatz in 1813 and 1814, and remained in Berlin during the campaign of 1815 to watch over the work there, he had entrusted it, before joining the Corps, to lottery director Hohann J. W. Bornemann, who had shown great interest in the movement. He had also persuaded one of his earliest and most capable pupils, Ernst Eiselen, the state of whose health incapacitated him for military service, to undertake the direction of the exercises, and this position Eiselen seems to have retained throughout the three seasons. At the suggestion of Minister von Schuckmann and with the approval of Chancellor Hardenberg, Jahn's annual allowance was increased from 500 to 800 thalers, Eiselen was provided with a salary of 400 thalers, and for the support of the Turnplatz a yearly grant of 150 thalers was made, together with free timber for building purposes.

Some important additions were made at the grounds meanwhile, and work went on as usual, though with diminished numbers. In August of 1814 General Blücher paid a visit to the spot, and after watching some of the exercises made a brief address. The Crown Prince, who also appeared there, was especially pleased with the wrestling. The wife of Prince William came with her children, and the sons of Prince Radziwill, the King's brother-in-law, were on intimate terms with the turners. Jahn was married at Neubrandenburg on August 30, 1814, to Helene Kollhof, whom he had met while he was a private tutor in Mecklenburg, nearly ten years before. During the same summer Bornemann published a "Manual of the Gymnastics Revived by Friedrich Ludwig Jahn under the name of *Turnkunst*,"[1] intended to prepare the way for Jahn's

[1] Lehrbuch der von Friedrich Ludwig Jahn unter dem Namen der Turnkunst wiedererweckten Gymnastik. Mit Kupfertafeln, darstellend die Geräthe, Gerüste und Uebungen auf dem Turnplatz in der Hasenheide bei Berlin. Zur allgemeiner Verbreitung jugendlicher Leibesübungen herausgegeben von (Johann Jakob Wilhelm) Bornemann. Berlin, W. Dieterici, 1814. See also his "Der Turnplatz in der Hasenheide," published in 1812.

own book which was not ready until two years later. A society of older turners, consisting originally of nine members, was organized in the fall of 1814, and met every Saturday with Massmann, one of their number, to practise songs, discuss regulations, revise the exercises by series, fix rules for the games and choose leaders for the squads. The first anniversary of the Battle of Leipsic (October 18 and 19) was celebrated at the Turnplatz with huge signal fires, songs by all the turners and a great exhibition. The number of spectators on this occasion was estimated at ten thousand, including many persons of distinction and delegates from six neighboring towns.

In the fall of 1815 and the following winter gymnastics was again made the subject of associated investigation, and now the results of so much study and experience were gradually brought together into book form. Eiselen undertook the technical portions, with the help of Massmann, Dürre and others, while Jahn wrote the remainder, decided in doubtful cases and revised the whole. March 31, 1816, he signed the preface, and on April 29 the finished volume was published under the title *Die Deutsche Turnkunst* ("German Gymnastics").[1]

No analysis of this book can convey any idea of the charm and vigor of its style, or of the lofty patriotism that pervades it. The, preface (pages iii-xlviii) tells the story of the Hasenheide Turnplatz the origin of the word Turnkunst, and how the present volume came to be written. The author believes that, though incomplete, it reveals the spirit of the workers, and will serve as a guide in similar undertakings elsewhere. Only preliminary and fundamental forms of exercises have been described; such others as fencing, swimming, dancing and military exercises must be left for a larger work. The early history of gymnastics, especially in connection with popular festivals. deserves careful investigation, for contests of strength and skill are a necessary feature on these occasions. The German nomenclature of gymnastics is explained and defended. Certain Prussian authorities who have proved themselves promoters and patrons of Jann's efforts are mentioned; and finally a gymnastic annual is promised, the first number to appear the following year at Eastertide. Part I, The gymnastic Exercises (pp. 3–166), is arranged in eighteen sections, devoted respectively to walking, running, jumping, vaulting the horse, balancing, the horizontal bar, the parallel bars, climbing, throwing, pulling, pushing, lifting,

---

[1] Die Deutsche Turnkunst zur Einrichtung der Turnplätze dargestellt von Friedrich Ludwig Jahn und Ernst Eiselen. Mit zwei Kupferplatten. Berlin, auf Kosten der Herausgeber, 1816. The volume, without the plates, has been issued in *Relcams Universal-Bibliothek* (Leipzig, Philipp Reclam jun.), with an introduction by Hugo Rühl dated 1905.

carrying, holding the body outstretched horizontally, wrestling, jumping with the hoop and with the rope, and miscellaneous exercises. In each case the necessary apparatus is described. Part II, Gymnastic Games (pp. 169–183): Gymnastics and games are links in the same chain, and a gymnasium without a playground is inconceivable; games prepare for social life, and in them one comes to know his mates thoroughly; the characteristics of a good game are given, and six elected games are described—black man, prisoner's base, knight and townsman, the hunt, storming, and German ball. Part III (pp. 187–206) tells how to lay out and fit up an outdoor gymnasium, and gives specifications for the complete equipment of one which will accommodate four hundred persons working in squads. Dimensions of each piece of apparatus, and of its parts, are stated in detail, so that the cost in any given locality can be figured out. Part IV (pp. 209–244) discusses the management of the grounds and exercises, with sections on the art of gymnastics, the gymnasium, the teacher, the exercises, the exercise period, costume, meeting place (the *Tie*) and spectators; and gives the general and special rules to be observed by the turners. Part V (p. 247–288) contains a classified bibliography of gymnastics, with about 170 titles; and explains the plan of an outdoor gymnasium shown on the first of two large folding plates. A portion of the first plate and all of the second illustrate various forms of apparatus.

After the appearance of the book work was continued at the Hasenheide throughout the seasons of 1816–18 with little change, from early spring until the exercises of October 18, the anniversary of the Battle of Leipsic. Gymnastics must still hibernate during the winter, from lack of suitable accommodations indoors. On October 22, 1816, Jahn reported that the number of turners in Berlin had passed the thousand mark. The next year it increased to 1074, and life on the *Turnplatz* reached its culmination. Hans Ferdinand Massmann had returned to Berlin at Easter, after a year at Jena, and from July 15 until September 2 he took the place of Eiselen at the grounds, while the latter was absent at Kiel in the interest of his health. More trees were planted, seats were provided around the *Tie*, and other improvements and additions were made. The turners began the afternoon with whatever form of exercise each preferred for himself (*Kurturnen*); then followed a period of rest, after which all took part in the orderly exercises (*Turnschule*), grouped in squads and divisions according to age. Each squad had its leader (*Vorturner*), who also kept a record of the attendance and proficiency of its members. Massmann had prepared a set of instructions for the guidance of these leaders, and there were written lists of exercises in tabular form (*Turntafeln*) to show the steps of progression in each group.

Whole days were often given up to games, which were still popular, and almost every Saturday they were played all night long. Excursions, with older turners especially, and enlivened by Jahn's talk and by many a song, were continued during this and the following summer. The nights were passed in haylofts or on the straw in some shed, and at sunrise they started on, first singing together a selection more or less devotional. For Jahn was an earnest Christian; his knapsack always contained a Bible, and he frequently read aloud from it to his companions, showing a preference for prophetic passages from the Old Testament. At the celebration of October 18 thousands were present. Jahn first gave a review of the year's progress; following this all joined in a song, and then came competitive exercises, a torchlight procession to the Rollberge, more speechmaking and singing, and the lighting of huge bonfires. On the 31st of the same month the universities of Jena and Kiel each conferred on Jahn the honorary degree of Doctor of Philosophy, in recognition of his services to the fatherland in time of need, his stimulating influence on the young, his power as a public speaker and his efforts in behalf of the German language.

The number of turners dropped to 815 in the season of 1818, but there seems to have been no weakening in Jahn's hold upon the love of his followers. We hear again of the close friendships formed among them, the manly qualities encouraged, the earnest effort to be purely German in speech, custom and dress, and the underlying seriousness of their joyous life together. After the day's exercise they used to return to the city in groups, each with some favorite leader as its center. Singing and conversation alternated until the Kottbus gate was reached; there they halted until all had come up, joined in a final song and then scattered to their homes.

The next spring (1819) the *Turnplatz* did not open at the usual time. The Prussian Ministry had in mind a union of gymnastics with the whole scheme of instruction in the schools. Summer and winter exercises alike were to be under its supervision. Additional grounds were to be opened, and one site had already been secured near Berlin. The plan was nearly ready, and Jahn was informed that for the present, until it should be perfected, the authorities desired that the Hasenheide *Turnplatz* should remain closed.

The years 1814–18 had witnessed a rapid and remarkable spread of the Jahn *Turnen* far beyond the narrow bounds of its first home, throughout the length and breadth of the Prussian provinces and

into other German states as well. Outdoor gymnasia had been
opened, for example, at Königsberg, Elbing, Marienwerder, and at
least four other cities in East and West Prussia; at a score of places
in Silesia, beginning with Breslau and Liegnitz, and including
Bunzlau, Frankenstein, Waldenburg, Strehlen, Hirschberg, Neisse,
Leobschütz, Gleiwitz, Brieg and Kreuzburg; at Friedland, Neu-
brandenburg, Neustrelitz and Malchin in Mecklenburg; Potsdam,
Frankfort-on-the-Oder and Prenzlau in Brandenburg; the free
cities of Hamburg and Lübeck; in central Germany at Leipsic,
Helle, Jena, Erfurt, Gotha, Eisenach, Rudolstadt, Mühlhausen,
Nordhausen and Heiligenstadt; at Frankfort, Hanau and Offenbach-
on-the-Main, and along the Rhine at Mainz, Bonn, Cologne and
Düsseldorf; at Darmstadt and Giessen in Hesse, Heidelberg in
Baden, Stuttgart and Tübingen in Württemberg and Erlangen and
Hof in Bavaria.

In general the early history of these Turnplätze resembles that
of the parent organization in Berlin. A majority of them were
started in connection with higher schools for boys, but they often
included in their membership teachers and university students,
clerks and young mechanics—all classes of society. Usually the
prime mover was some teacher, impelled, like Jahn, by a motive
which was patriotic rather than pedagogical; and afterward local,
provincial or state authorities not infrequently added their support.
Sometimes it was the public officials themselves who inaugurated
the movement. The common incentive was the great tidal wave
of love for the fatherland which swept over Germany at the time
of the War of Liberation. Many a teacher who had fought in
Lützow's or some other volunteer corps and joined in the stirring
songs of Karl Theodor Körner about the campfire or on the march
went back to his classroom filled with a desire to see developed in
his young charges a stronger patriotism, a simpler, more vigorous
and more manly type of life, less regard for distinctions of rank
and wealth, a spirit of mutual helpfulness and a willingness to unite
with others for the common welfare. Jahn's *Turnen* had already
shown its fitness for these ends.

In many cases assistance was received directly from Berlin.
Thus in September of 1814 Jahn sent Eduard Dürre,[1] one of his
Vorturners, to Friedland in Mecklenburg, where two teachers were
trying to introduce the exercises in the Gelehrtenschule; and the
same year Massmann started a Turnplatz at Schwerinsburg. At
the request of the *Oberpräsident* of the Rhine Province Jahn recommended in 1816 a teacher of gymnastics for Cologne, and a similar

[1] Dr. Christian Eduard Leopold Dürre. Aufzeichnungen, Tagebücher und Briefe
aus einem deutschen Turner- und Lehrerleben. Herausgegeben von Dr. Ernst
Friedrich Dürre. Leipzig, Eduard Strauch, 1881.

request from two Jena professors was met by persuading Massmann and Dürre to continue their studies in that university for a time. When the *Deutsche Turnkunst* appeared in 1816 it became at once the authority on all *Turnplätze* and the guide in opening new ones. A glance at the contents will show how admirably and completely it meets the requirements of such a manual. Minister von Schuckmann ordered fifty copies sent to the West Prussian authorities in Marienwerder, at their request, and two hundred more for distribution among other provincial officials. In Westphalia, for example, twenty-four higher classical schools for boys were thus supplied. Numerous visitors, too, came to Berlin for a longer or shorter time to be trained as teachers of gymnastics. Some did this at their own motion and expense, and others received state support. In 1816 there were, among others, three normal school students from Weissenfels, and teachers from Neumark, Neustadt a. d. Dosse, Wusterhausen and Neurippen. Jahn made them all welcome, charged no fees, gave his time and personal interest freely in regular hours and out, and saw that each one obtained the best possible preparation.

His own brief trips and longer excursions should also be mentioned in this connection. A short visit which he paid to Frankfort-on-the-Main in 1815 led a band of school boys there to fit up a private Turnplatz. In September of the next year he was very cordially received by a congress of seventy school inspectors, clergymen and teachers at Frankfort-on-the-Oder, and delivered an address on gymnastics which made a deep impression. A month's excursion with eighteen older turners in July and August of 1817 took him through Mecklenburg and Pomerania to the Island of Rügen, in the Baltic. The party was hospitably greeted and entertained by the turners in Neustrelitz, Neubrandenburg and Friedland joining with them in exercises on the *Turnplatz*, or matching strength at tug-of-war and wrestling. They met other turners from Prenzlau, and at Puttbus, before a large audience, gave a sort of gymnastic exhibition with an accompaniment of national songs. Again the next summer he set out with thirteen school boys, intending to be absent four weeks. They journeyed southeast through Hirschberg and Waldenburg to Breslau, spent several days with turners in the Silesian capital, and on the way back visited Liegnitz, Züllichau and Frankfort-on-the-Oder.[1]

Still another agency in the spread of Jahn *Turnen* is found in the *Burschenschcften*, or general student unions, organized in the Ger-

---

[1] Des Berliner Turners Franz Lieber's " Die Fahrt nach Schlesien im Jahre 1818, um vom Tie vorzulesen beschrieben." Eine Turn-Reliquie aus dem Jahre 1818 (with introduction and notes by Dr. Karl Wassmannsdorff). In *Deutsche Turnzeitung* 1895: 637–642, 686–690.

man universities as one result of the War of Liberation. Students who had had served in Lützow's Free Corps, the most national of the volunteer regiments, took the lead in forming the first of these at Jena, where it was publicly announced on the 12th of June, 1815. The new association was intended to correct the abuses of the *Landsmannschaften* or sectional clubs, to promote the physical and moral vigor of its members, and to awaken love for the common German fatherland and a desire to see it free and united. Gymnastics was at once introduced and practised after the Berlin fashion. Jahn watched the inception and spread of the movement with the keenest interest, if he did not himself have a hand in sketching the plan of organization; and he sent to Jena two of his most trusted pupils, Dürre and Massmann, whose activity there was not confined to the Turnplatz. Other *Burschenschaften* were soon formed in the universities at Halle, Leipsic, Giessen, Heidelberg, Bonn, Erlangen and elsewhere, and with them wandering students from Berlin, Breslau and Jena carried the art of the Hasenheide *Turnvater*. Thus Karl Völker, one of the directors of the Jena *Burschenschaft*, after completing his studies there went to Tübingen in 1818 to accept an invitation from students in that university to help them organize a *Burschenschaft* and start a *Turnplatz*. The city offered a site, upon condition that the boys in its *Bürgerschule* and *Gymnasium* should be allowed to share in the exercises.[1]

The key to the history of the Hasenheide *Turnplatz* and the scores of others patterned after it in the years 1814–18 we have found in the spirit of the German War of Liberation. To this also are to be traced the repressive measures which suddenly checked the growth of the seemingly lusty organization before the completion of its first decade, and for more than twenty years banished it as a factor in the popular life. When the common people rose in arms against Naopleon it was with the hope that war would result, not only in freedom from the foreign yoke, but in closer union between the semi-independent German states, and the substitution of constitutional liberty for the absolutism of personal rule. They secured promises of ample concession to these cravings, but found, after peace was declared, that their rulers had no intention of meeting engagements made under duress. The Germanic Confederation of 1815 was a sorry substitute for the vigorous empire anticipated, and under the lead of Prince Metternich, Austrian Minister of Foreign Affairs, the Holy Alliance at once adopted a reactionary policy which was hostile to the free movement of ideas and sought to allay the agitation of the popular mind. The turners represented a political tendency, and therefore incurred suspicion.

[1] See Eduard Dürre's "Rückblicke und Träume eines alten Turners," in *Deutsche Turnzeitung* 1872: 103–107, 127–129, 136 and 137.

Beginning January 17, 1817, Jahn had delivered in Berlin a series of twenty-one semi-weekly public lectures on his favorite subject, German Nationality. Among the great number of persons from all classes who heard him some were offended by his blunt speech, and various extreme, unguarded and misunderstood statements gave a handle to opponents who accused him of revolutionary principles. He was eccentric and independent always, and with his followers on the *Turnplatz* took exception to much that was customary in dress, speech and manners. Disquieting rumors were in circulation regarding his conduct on the Rügen and Breslau excursions, and it was suggested that the large gatherings at the anniversary celebrations of the Battle of Leipsic were dangerous to public order and afforded a chance for demagogues. In the summer of 1817 Jahn was unfavorably criticized by two writers in the Berlin press, who attributed to his work in the Hasenheide injurious physical, mental and moral effects; and the discussion did not cease when reports from the directors of three higher schools and a special investigation made by Medical Councilor Dr. von Könen, at the request of Minister von Schuckmann, had failed to sustain the objections raised, and on the contrary brought complete vindication.

Under the auspices of the *Burschenschaften* hundreds of students from many German universities met in Eisenach, October 18, 1817, to celebrate the anniversary of the Battle of Leipsic and the tercentenary of the Protestant Reformation. There were appropriate exercises in the town and in the Hall of the Minnesingers at the Wartburg Castle, and when evening came all gathered about a huge bonfire for more speeches and singing. Suddenly Massmann appeared with friends carrying bundles of waste-paper done up and labeled to represent books. After recalling Luther's burning of the papal bull he read off from a prepared list the titles of certain reactionary writings hostile to German unity, constitutional government and free institutions; and as each item was reached the corresponding bundle was pitchforked into the fire with suitable comments. Common opinion credited Jahn with being the real originator of this student prank. It naturally aroused the anger of the authors concerned, among whom Kotzebue and Kamptz deserve mention here since their names appear again in the next paragraph. Metternich saw in the performance the indication of a widespread conspiracy.[1]

---

[1] Moritz Zedtler (Zettler), "Das Wartburgfest am 18. October 1817," in *Deutsche Turnzeitung* 1877: 309–313, 331–333, 343–346, 351 and 352. See also his "Ein geckenhafter Gegner des Turnens," in 1880: 9–11, 25–28, 41–45. Other articles published in the *Deutsche Turnzeitung* are Dr. Th. Bach's "Aus Metternich's nachgelassenen Schriften" (1881: 409–411, 422–424, 429 and 430), Karl Wassmannsdorff's "Das burschenschaftliche Schauturnen bei Gelegenheit des Wartburgfestes am 18 Oct. 1817" (1882: 461), and Hans Brendicke's "Die Wartburgfeier der Deutschen Burschenschaft und ihre ältere Literatur" (1887: 624 and 625).

A conference of monarchs at Aix-la-Chapelle in the fall of 1818 did much to confirm Frederick-William III of Prussia in his suspicions of intrigue. Metternich also laid before Prince Wittgenstein, the Prussian Minister of State, a memorial in which he declared that the *Burschenschaften* were nurseries of revolution and the *Turnplätze* preparatory schools for university disorders; both must be suppressed, for no palliative measures would suffice. A more forcible argument was the assassination of the German dramatist Kotzebue by Karl Ludwig Sand at Mannheim, on the 23d of March, 1819. Kotzebue was a paid spy of Russia and a reactionary writer who had attacked with especial bitterness the student unions and the turners. Sand was a turner, and had visited Jahn and others in Berlin the year before; he was a member of the Jena *Burschenschaft* and had been present at the Wartburgfest. Without any proof of the fact, it was assumed that he had carried out the decision of an organization. On the night of July 13–14 Jahn was arrested and taken to the fortress of Spandau, on suspicion of "secret and most treasonable associations." Meanwhile Kamptz had been made Prussian Minister of Police and clothed with extraordinary powers, and a special commission had been charged with the prosecution of demagogues. A little later a conference of German ministers adopted the oppressive Carlsbad Decrees, which were ratified by the Frankfort Diet, September 20. These provided for censorship of the press, police supervision of the universities and a central commission of seven to search out "the origin and ramification of revolutionary conspiracies and demagogic associations." The *Burschenschaft* was dissolved, and January 2, 1820, Frederick-William III decreed that *Turnen* should absolutely cease throughout Prussia.

Jahn was kept at Spandau for a few days, transferred to Küstrin July 17, brought back to Berlin for trial early in October, and by an official report of February 15, 1820, the chief charges against him were declared null and void. A cabinet order of May 31 released him from arrest, but stipulated that he should reside, until further notice, in the fortress of Kolberg, on the Baltic, and placed him under the oversight of the commanding officer there. The 1000 thalers which he had been receiving from the state—800 as teacher of gymnastics and 200 from the Ministry of War—was to be continued. After prolonged investigation the supreme court at Breslau, by its decision of January 13, 1824, absolved him from all suspicion of complicity in the murder of Kotzebue, but sentenced him to two years additional confinement in a fortress on account of "repeated irreverent and insolent utterances regarding existing conditions and regulations in the state." From this decision Jahn appealed, and sent in his "self-defence" (*Selbstvertheidigung*, finished October 9, 1824) to the supreme court at Frankfort-on-the-Oder, by which body he was entirely acquitted March 15, 1825. But a cabinet order of May 3 forbade his living in Berlin or within a radiu of ten miles from the capital, or in any city containing a university or higher school for boys; and wherever he settled he was to remain under police surveillance. The thousand-thaler pension remained unchanged. Jahn selected for his home the Thuringian town of Freyburg-on-the-Unstrut, about thirty miles west and south of Leipsic. The accession of Frederick-William IV to the throne of Prussia in 1840 was followed by the final removal of all police restrictions, and brought him also the long-expected decoration of the Iron Cross. By a cabinet order of June 6, 1842, gymnastics was "formally recognized as a necessary and indispensable part of male education and received into the circle of means for popular education." *Turnen* began to revive with this, but though Jahn followed its development with interest and received hospitably the turners who visited his home, he took no active part in the movement. In 1844 he attended the centennial exercises of his first school, the *Gymnasium* at Salzwedel. Four years later he was present as a delegate in the German national assembly at Frankfort-on-the-Main, but returned to his home bitterly disappointed. He died at Freyburg, after a brief illness, October 15, 1852.[1]

Although Prussia's example in suppressing public *Turnen* was followed by other German states, the procedure was by no means universal. Thus the reaction did not directly affect the Kingdom of Württemberg, the Grand Duchies of Mecklenburg and Oldenburg, the Duchy of Brunswick and the Free Cities of Hamburg and Lübeck; and it was not of long duration in the Kingdom of Bavaria. Between 1820 and 1840 the old organizations continued without interruption, therefore, in scattered cities, and new societies of older boys or young men who met regularly for exercise were formed in Hanover (1831), Frankfort-on-the-Main (1833), Plauen in Saxony (1834) and Pforzheim in Baden (1835). Even in Berlin Ernst Eiselen (1793–1846), Jahn's faithful assistant, was allowed to open a private indoor and outdoor gymnasium in 1828. The venture prospered, and he added a gymnasium for girls in 1832, and four years later opened a branch institution in another

---

[1] Friedrich Ludwig Jahn's Leben. Nebst Mittheilungen aus seinem literarischen Nachlasse. Von Dr. Heinrich Pröhle. Berlin, Franz Duncker, 1855. A second edition, unchanged, was published in 1872.

Friedrich Ludwig Jahn, Sein Leben und Wirken. Von Dr. Carl Euler, Professor, Unterrichts-Dirigent der K. Turnlehrer-Bildungsanstalt in Berlin. Stuttgart, Carl Krabbe, 1881.

Friedrich Ludwig Jahns Werke. Neu herausgegeben, mit einer Einleitung und mit erklärenden Anmerkungen versehen von Dr. Carl Euler, Hof, G. A. Grau & Cie. (Rud. Lion), 1884–1887. Three volumes.

part of the city. The latter was transferred to his helper Wilhelm Lübeck (1809–1879) in 1839. Both men trained many teachers of gymnastics, and wrote valuable manuals,[1] bridging over in this way the gap between the older and the newer *Turnen*.

With the accession of Frederick-William IV to the Prussian throne in 1840 the hopes of his people were kindled afresh, and during the next decade all Germany was stirred by an agitation for reform which steadily gathered force until the outbreak of the French Revolution in 1848 brought it to a climax. One sign of this quickened national and political life was a general revival of the Jahn gymnastics. The incorporation of physical training in school programs led to the formation of separate societies (*Männerturnvereine*) for adults, in which the bond of union was at first merely an agreement to meet for exercise at certain fixed hours; but this was soon followed by the adoption of by-laws, the appointment of boards of directors and the fixing of definite dues. Partly as a result of excursions and exhibitions new societies sprang up everywhere, until at the close of the decade they numbered nearly three hundred. The desire for union which early showed itself was met by holding district conventions (*Turntage*) and gatherings for gymnastic exercises (*Turnfeste*). So we find turners from Frankfort, Hanau and Mainz coming together in Frankfort-on-the-Main September 5, 1841, for the first of several annual *Turnfeste*, and on the Feldberg in 1844 inaugurating the important series of *Feldbergfeste;* and in Saxony, where progress had been especially active and orderly, the first *Turntag* at Dresden, October 31, 1846, attended by delegates from fifty-four societies. Periodicals devoted to the interests of the turners also began to make their appearance—Karl Euler's "Jahrbücher der deutschen Turnkunst" (1843 and 1844)

---

[1] Turntafeln. Das ist: Sämmtliche Turn-Uebungen auf einzelnen Blättern zur Richtschnur bei der Turnschule und zur Erinnerung des Gelernten für alle Turner herausgegeben von Ernst Wilh. Bernh. Eiselen. Berlin, gedruckt und verlegt bei G. Reimer, 1837. The 46 printed pages contain numbered lists of exercises.
    Uber Anlegung von Turnplätzen und Leitung von Turnübungen. Als Vorlaufer einer neuen Auflage der *Deutschen Turnkunst* herausgegeben von E. W. B. Eiselen. Berlin, G. Reimer, 1844.
    Abbildungen von Turn-Uebungen gezeichnet von H. Robolsky und A. Töppe. Durchgesehen, vervollständigt und geordnet herausgegeben von E. W. B. Eiselen. Berlin, G. Reimer, 1845. A fifth edition, prepared by Karl Wassmannsdorff, was published in 1889.
    Friedrich Ludwig Jahns Deutsche Turnkunst. Zum zweiten Male und sehr vermehrt herausgegeben. (Erste Hälfte des Werkes). Berlin, G. Reimer, 1847. The preface is signed "Die vereinten Herausgeber" (Eiselen, Massmann, Feddern, Ballot, Böttcher, and Wassmannsdorf).
    Lehr- und Handbuch der deutschen Turnkunst, von W. Lübeck, Turn- und Fechtlehrer am Königl. Kadetten-Hause zu Berlin und Vorsteher einer Turnanstalt. Frankfurt a. O., Gustav Harnecker und Comp., 1843. A second "ganz umgearbeitete, vermehrte und verbesserte Auflage" was published in 1860.

and "Turn-Zeitung" (1846 and 1847),[i] "Der Turner" (1846–52)[2] the "Mainzer Turnzeitung" (1846),[3] and Ravenstein's "Nachrichtsblatt für Deutschlands Turnanstalten und Turngemeinden" (1846 and 1847).[4] But a second period of reaction set in with the revolutionary movements of 1849, in which many of the turners the Saxon and South German ones especially, took an active part. In carrying out their policy of repression the various governments again disbanded or put under careful supervision the gymnastic societies, and not only those directly concerned in disturbances, but others which had been well-disposed and preferred to keep *Turnen* free from partisan politics. Of the three hundred societies in existence in 1849 hardly a third survived the next ten years. A few, however, continued vigorous and active, and this number included some of the largest and best *Turnvereine* in Saxony and Württemberg. Here Theodor Georgii started his "Turnblatt für und aus Schwaben" (1850–1853),[5] followed by the "Esslinger Turnzeitung" (1854–1856),[6] and this in turn was succeeded by the "Deutsche Turnzeitung" (since 1856),[7] the present organ of the German *Turnerschaft*. In Dresden Moritz Kloss began to publish the "Neue Jahrbücher für die Turnkunst" (1855–1894).[8]

Toward the close of the fifties signs of life began to multiply. The war of France and Sardinia with Austria (1859) and uncertainty as to future relations between France and the German states helped to rouse the slumbering societies and fill abandoned *Turnplätze* once more. A summons printed in the *Deutsche Turnzeitung* in March of 1860 and signed by Theodor Georgii and Karl Kallenberg

---

[1] Jahrbücher der deutschen Turnkunst. Herausgegeben von Karl Euler, Turn- und Fechtlehrer in Königsberg in Preussen, Mitglied der deutschen Gesellschaft zu Berlin. Erstes Heft. Danzig, S. Anhuth, 1843.
Jahrbücher der deutschen Turnkunst. Herausgegeben von Karl Euler, Turn- und Fechtlehrer in Köln a. Rh., Mitglied der deutschen Gesellschaft zu Berlin. Zweites Heft. Solingen, Albert Pfeiffer, 1844.
Turn-Zeitung, von K. Euler und Dr. Lamey, Karlsruhe, 1846.
Turn-Zeitung, von K. Euler und Prof. Schach. Karlsruhe, 1847.

[2] Der Turner. Zeitschrift gegen geistige und leibliche Verkrüppelung. Dresden, H. M. Gottschalk, 1846–1852. Seven volumes.

[3] Mainzer Turn-Zeitung, herausgegeben von Eduard Müller. Mainz, 1846.

[4] Nachrichtsblatt für Deutschlands Turnanstalten und Turngemeinden. Frankfurt a. M., 1846 and 1847. Two volumes.

[5] Turnblatt für und aus Schwaben. Von Theodor Georgii. Esslingen, four volumes, 1850–1853.

[6] Turnzeitung. Zeitschrift für Turn- und Feuerlöschwesen. Von Theodor Georgii. Esslingen, C. Weichardt. Three volumes, 1854–1856.

[7] Deutsche Turn-Zeitung, Leipzig, since 1856. The publishers have been Ernst Keil (1856–1874), Eduard Strauch (1875–1899), and Paul Eberhardt (since 1900).

[8] Neue Jahrbücher für die Turnkunst (volumes 1–25). In 1880 the name was changed to "Jahrbücher der deutschen Turnkunst" (volumes 26–40). Published annually 1855–1881 in Dresden (volumes 1–27) and 1882–1894 in Leipzig (volumes 28–40). There were six numbers a year 1855–1881, and twelve numbers 1882–1894. Beginning with volume 28 Woldemar Bier succeeded Kloss as editor.

resulted in the first general German convention and *Turnfest*, held at Coburg June 16–19 of that year—the anniversary of the Battle of Waterloo. More than a thousand adult turners were present, representing one hundred and thirty-nine cities and villages. Formal organization into a national body was impossible as yet, but notwithstanding this a feeling of union was established and a great impulse was given to further growth. The next year the fiftieth anniversary of the opening of the Hasenheide *Turnplatz* was celebrated by a second convention and *Turnfest* at Berlin, August 10–12. The attendance rose to 2812 adult turners, 1659 of them from outside the capital. Two hundred and sixty-two places were represented. This time a standing "Committee of the German *Turnvereine*," composed of 15 members, was appointed to look after matters of general interest. The committee, at its meeting in Gotha the following December, organized by electing Theodor Georgii chairman and Dr. Ferdinand Goetz business manager; it decided that *Turnvereine* as such must hold themselves unconditionally aloof from all political partisanship, took action which put a damper on those who wished to have military exercises introduced in all societies, and charged Georg Hirth with an investigation which led to the first "Statistical Annual of German Turnvereine" (Leipsic, 1863).[1] According to this there were on July 1, 1862, in 1153 towns and cities, 1284 societies, not less than 1050 of them organized since 1860. In 1863, the semi-centennial of the Battle of Leipsic, more than 20,000 turners gathered in that city for the third convention and *Turnfest*. Another statistical annual issued two years later[2] showed an increase of 650 societies and more than 33,000 members over the numbers recorded in the first volume (July 1, 1862, to November 1, 1864).

Enthusiasm had reached such a pitch that a reaction was inevitable, and the Austro-Prussian War of 1866, by diverting attention and draining the resources of the people, interfered with further expansion and threatened to paralyze the existing *Turnvereine*. In the five years between November 1, 1864, and August 1, 1869, there had been a falling off of nearly 400 societies and 40,000 members, according to the statistical annual of 1871.[3] A *Turnfest* planned for July 22–24, 1866, in Nuremberg, had to be given up; but two years later 168 delegates assembled for the fourth general

[1] Statistisches Jahrbuch der Turnvereine Deutschlands. Im Auftrage des Ausschusses der Deutschen Turnvereine herausgegeben von Georg Hirth. Leipzig, Ernst Keil, 1863.

[2] Zweites statistisches Jahrbuch der Turnvereine Deutschlands. Im Auftrage des Ausschusses der Deutschen Turnvereine herausgegeben von Georg Hirth. Leipzig, Ernst Keil, 1865.

[3] Drittes statistisches Jahrbuch der Deutschen Turnerschaft. Im Auftrage des Ausschusses der Deutschen Turnerschaft herausgegeben von Dr. Ferd. Goetz und A. F. Böhme. Leipzig, Ernst Keil, 1871.

convention in Weimar (July 20 and 21, 1868), and there formally organized the *Deutsche Turnerschaft*, a firm union of all German gymnastic societies, including the Austrian Germans. A constitution was adopted, the old committee was increased to 22 members, and Georgii and Goetz were continued in their positions as chairman and business manager. During the Franco-Prussian War of 1870–71 15,000 turners followed the colors to the field and many gymnasia were converted into hospitals. But in spite of this temporary check the war brought what Jahn and his followers had looked forward to for sixty years and more—the unification of Germany. Experiences of march, battlefield and camp had driven home to the minds of all the need and value of physical efficiency, as nothing else could do it; and after the formation of the new empire popular *Turnen* began, at first slowly and then more rapidly, to flourish as never before, and this time with the full approval of the state.

The following table shows the development that has taken place since the first statistical investigation was made, in 1862. The second column gives the number of German towns and cities in which there were popular gymnastic societies (*Turnvereine*), and the third column the total number of these societies irrespective of membership in the *Turnerschaft*. "Active" turners are those who actually take part in the gymnastic exercises.

Date.	Places.	Turnvereine.	Belonging to Deutsche Turnerschaft (Since 1869).		
			Societies.	Members.	Active Turners.
1862, July 1	1153	1279	....	134,507	96,272
1864, November 1	1769	1934	....	167,942	105,676
1869, August 1	1415	1546	....	128,491	80,327
1876, November 1	1532	1788	1547	156,590	69,872
1880, January 1	1741	2226	1971	170,315	86,159
1885, January 1	2413	3208	2878	267,854	144,134
1890, January 1	3340	4434	3992	388,513	195,375
1895, January 1	4536	6061	5312	529,925	270,528
1900, January 1	5509	7238	6483	647,548	310,374
1905, January 1	6063	....	7264[1]	766,347[1]	357,849[1]
1910, January 1	7621	....	9101	946,115	435,511
1915, January 1	9851	....	11,769	1,072,274	......
1920, January 1	8518	....	10,010	1,008,375	......

[1] District (*Kreis*) XV (German Austria), which on January 1, 1904, contained 525 societies with 61,166 members and 25,316 active turners, withdrew from the Deutsche Turnerschaft on September 25, 1904, and formed an independent association under the name "Turnkreis Deutsch-Oesterreich." It is therefore not included in the figures for 1905 and later.

General German *Turnfest* and conventions (*Turntage*) of the *Deutsche Turnerschaft* (since 1868) have been held as follows:

No.	Turnfeste.		Turntage.	
	Place.	Date.	Place.	Date.
I . .	Coburg	1860, June 17–18	Coburg	1860, June
II . .	Berlin	1861, August 10–12	Berlin	1861, August
III . .	Leipsic	1863, August 2–5	Leipsic	1863, August
IV . .	Bonn	1872, August 3–6	Weimar	1868, July 20–21
V . .	Frankfurt	1880, July 25–28	Bonn	1872, August 3
VI . .	Dresden	1885, July 19–21	Dresden	1875, July 25–26
VII . .	Munich	1889, July 28–31	Berlin	1879, July 27–28
VIII . .	Breslau	1894, July 22–24	Eisenach	1883, July 24–25
IX . .	Hamburg	1898, July 23–27	Coburg	1887, July 19–20
X . .	Nuremberg	1903, July 18–22	Hannover	1891, July 21–22
XI . .	Frankfurt	1908, July 18–22	Esslingen	1895, July 22–23
XII . .	Leipsic	1913, July 12–15	Naumburg a. S.	1899, July 30–31
XIII . .	....	....	Berlin	1904, April 4–5
XIV . .	....	....	Worms	1907, July 28–29
XV . .	....	....	Dresden	1911, July 27–28
XVI . .	....	....	Erfurt	1919, Oct. 15–16

The Bonn *Turnfest* fell in the period of decline, and one planned for Breslau in 1878 was given up because disturbed political conditions threatened its success; but beginning at Frankfort-on-the-Main two years later these great national gatherings have brought together not less than 10,000 turners, and at Hamburg and Nuremberg between 25,000 and 30,000 were present. Successive conventions have left the outward form of the German *Turnerschaft* almost unchanged, although various details have been modified. The Esslingen *Turntag* defined its object to be "the promotion of German gymnastics as a means to physical and moral vigor, and the fostering of patriotic sentiment and a spirit of racial unity among Germans." In 1887 Georgii gave up his position as chairman of the committee and was succeeded by Alfred Maul of Karlsruhe, who resigned in 1894. The next year Dr. Ferdinand Goetz was appointed to that office, and his place as business manager was given to Dr. Hugo Rühl, of Stettin. Dr. Goetz died October 13, 1915. Dr. Theodor Toeplitz then became chairman, but died June 2, 1919, and the position passed to Dr. Oskar Berger, of Aschersleben.

Turnvater Jahn is still held in loyal and grateful remembrance, as the apostle of German unity and the man who gave to the German people a love for gymnastics. The one hundredth anniversary of his birth (1878) and the fiftieth anniversary of his death (1902) were celebrated throughout the entire *Turnerschaft*. That body has erected monuments in his honor at the Berlin *Turnplatz*, and in Lanz, Freyburg and other places; has built a memorial gymnasium (*Turnhalle*) over his grave in Freyburg; and has brought together

FIG. 18.—District Display at the 11th German *Turnfest*, Frankfurt, 1908.

FIG. 19.—A Competitor on the Horizontal Bar at the 11th German *Turnfest*, Frankfurt, 1908.

there, in the "Jahn Museum," numerous relics of the man and his work. In 1903 a separate building was provided for this collection.

FIG. 20.—Mass Exercises (17,000), at the 12th German *Turnfest*, Leipsic, 1913.

BIBLIOGRAPHY.

Dr. Carl Euler's "Encyklopädisches Handbuch des gesamten Turnwesens" and "Geschichte des Turnunterrichts," and files of the *Neue Jahrbücher für die Turnkunst, Deutsche Turnzeitung*, and *Monatsschrift für das Turnwesen* (see page 82).

Das gesammte Turnwesen. Ein Lesebuch für deutsche Turner. 133 abgeschlossene Muster-Darstellungen von den vorzüglichsten älteren und neueren Turnschriftstellern. Herausgegeben von Georg Hirth. Mit den Bildnissen von GutsMuths, Vieth, Jahn, Eiselen, Harnisch, Passow, Spiess, Martens. Leipzig, Ernst Keil, 1865.

Das Gesamte Turnwesen, Ein Lesebuch für deutsche Turner. In erster Auflage herausgegeben von Georg Hirth. Aufsätze turnerischen Inhaltes von älteren und neueren Schriftstellern. Zweite erweiterte Auflage in 4 Abteilungen. Besorgt von Dr. F. Rudolf Gasch. Hof, Rud. Lion, 1893. Three volumes. A "Geschichtliche Einleitung (Ergänzungsband)" was added in 1895.

Moritz Zettler, "Bausteine zur Geschichte des deutschen Turnens." In *Deutsche Turnzeitung* 1885–1900. A long series of articles, based on the study of original documents.

Handbuch der Deutschen Turnerschaft. Im Auftrage des Ausschusses derselben herausgegeben von Dr. med. Ferdinand Goetz, Geschäftsführer des Ausschusses der Deutschen Turnerschaft. Leipzig-Lindenau, Verlag des Ausschusses der Deutschen Turnerschaft, 1879. The second to sixth editions of the Handbuch were published in Hof, by Rud. Lion, in 1884, 1888, 1892, 1896, and 1899; and the seventh, eighth, ninth and tenth in Leipzig, by Paul Eberhardt, in 1904, 1908, 1912 and 1920. The editor, since 1899, has been Dr. Hugo Rühl.

Jahrbuch der Turnkunst: Jarhbuch der Deutschen Turnerschaft. Edited by Dr. Rudolf Gasch, and published in Leipzig-Zwickau by Emil Stock, annually since 1907. The volumes are illustrated and range from eighty or a hundred up to nearly three hundred pages.

CHAPTER XII.

ADOLF SPIESS, THE FATHER OF GERMAN SCHOOL GYMNASTICS.

By the Prussian cabinet order of June 6, 1842, already referred to (page 101), physical training was "formally recognized as a necessary and indispensable part of male education." Minister Eichhorn, who was charged with putting this decree into effect, received that same summer a visitor from Switzerland who for eight years had been teaching gymnastics to boys and girls of all ages, as a regular branch of their school work, and who therefore seemed to have solved successfully, on a small scale, the problem of incorporating the subject into the school plan. He was asked by the Minister to submit in writing a statement of the measures which in his judgment would accomplish the same result in the Prussian state, and the reply to this request, dated at Burgdorf on the 18th of the following October, was contained in some "Thoughts on the method to be followed in making gymnastics an integral element in popular education."[1] The steps therein advocated have since been taken, in part at least, by almost every German state, and the author, Adolf Spiess, now enjoys the undisputed title of "founder of school gymnastics in Germany and of gymnastics for girls in particular."

Spiess was a native of the Grand Duchy of Hesse and born February 3, 1810, in Lauterbach, a small town on the northeastern slope of the Vogelsberg. His father Johann Balthasar Spiess (1782–1841), himself the son of a Thuringian farmer and master smith, had first prepared himself for a position as teacher in the elementary schools, but after some years of professional experience at Frankfort-on-the-Main decided upon further study, and so completed a course in theology at the University of Giessen, and immediatly after passing his examination, in 1807, became teacher and subrector at the Latin school in Lauterbach. Thither he soon brought as bride Luise Werner, of Saarbrücken, first met in Frankfurt, and Adolf was the oldest of their five children. In 1811 the father accepted a pastoral position in the Evangelical Lutheran church at Offenbach, across the Main from Frankfurt, and in addition to his clerical duties opened a private school which prepared for the upper

---

[1] Gedanken über die Einordnung des Turnwesens in das Ganze der Volkserziehung, von Adolf Spiess. Basel, Schweighauser'sche Buchhandlung, 1842. Reprinted on pages 15–41 of "Kleine Schriften über Turnen von Adolf Spiess. Nebst Beiträgen zu seiner Lebensgeschichte, Gesammelt und herausgegeben von J. C. Lion." Hof. G. A. Grau & Cie. (Rud. Lion), 1872. Second edition, 1877.

classes of the *Gymnasium* (higher classical school) or for a mercantile career.   Ten years before this he had observed the methods in use at Schnepfenthal, and made the acquaintance of GutsMuths and other teachers there, renewed by frequent later visits.   It was therefore natural that one feature of the daily program should be gymnastics, as described and practised by GutsMuths—walking the balance beam, jumping. running, climbing, throwing, skating, swimming, etc., and games of all sorts.   Every week throughout the year there were also excursions with teachers, and dancing lessons were given in the winter months.

Adolf entered this school at the age of six or less.   A few years later, in 1819, Fritz Hessemer, just back from the University of

Fig. 21.—Adolf Spiess (1810–1858).

Giessen, made the pupils acquainted with the new Jahn gymnastics, and parallel bars and a horizontal bar were now added to the equipment.   In 1824 some of the boys organized a little society for the purpose of practising gymnastics regularly outside of school hours. They met in the private garden *Turnplatz* of Hofrath A. André, using Jahns' "Deutsche Turnkunst" as a guide and inspiration, and soon afterward entered into friendly relations with other turners in Hanau, a few miles to the east, with whom joint excursions on foot to the Taunus Range were made in 1826 and the following year.

In the spring or summer of 1828 Spiess went to the University of Giessen to pursue the study of theology.   He at once joined the *Burschenschaft*, which had been organized ten years previously and now concealed itself under the name *Waffenverbindung*, and his active habits at once took the form of assiduous practice in fencing, the favorite student exercise.[1] Before the end of the year he had become proficient in the art. There were also many excursions with friends to neighboring peaks and castles, and an acquaintance has borne witness to the skill he displayed in all forms of physical activity—riding, swimming, skating, dancing and gymnastics. Music and drawing, too, for which he possessed both taste and talent, absorbed a portion of his leisure. With other students he left Giessen at Easter of 1829 and journeyed on foot across the Vogelsberg to Schnepfenthal, where as a schoolboy he had met GutsMuths nine years before, and then on to Halle, there to continue his theological studies in the university. An excursion through the Harz Mountains later in the same season was made the occasion of a visit to Jahn. In Halle there were opportunities for renewed practice on the horizontal bar, the parallel bars and the horse, and fencing, too, was not neglected; but the greatest interest was excited by certain outdoor games. For these they used to gather twice a week, and often to the number of a hundred or more, in Passendorf, singing and playing together until nightfall. About Christmas time of the same year Spiess went up to Berlin for some months. This gave an opportunity to frequent Eiselen's private gymnasium, and though that master himself was confined to his home by illness the young student saw and learned many new exercises from Philipp Feddern, his assistant.

For a year or more following the spring of 1830 Spiess was again in Giessen, and active in the life of its *Burschenschaft*.[2] He now began to give regular instruction in gymnastics, first to a dozen boys on a garden *Turnplatz*, and then, as interest grew, to nearly 150 in one of the city parks; and already he was modifying the traditional method by gathering the entire number into one band at the commencement of each period for various simple exercises performed in rhythm as they stood or marched, or for running and jumping under the leadership of a single teacher. But the Hessian authorities were on the lookout for agitation looking toward a united Germany, and had already given notice to the University that no student who was affiliated with forbidden organizations, like the *Burschenschaft*, would be admitted to the regular examinations. The July revolution in France, however, exerted a stimulating influence. Early in 1831 the local association allied itself with the general German

---

[1] See Herman Haupt's "Adolf Spiess, der Begründer des deutschen Schulturnens, als Giessener und Hallischer Burschenschafter 1828–1831," on pp. 306–330 of "Quellen und Darstellungen zur Geschichte der Burschenschaft und der deutschen Einheitsbewegung." Band II, Heft 3–4 (Heidelberg, Carl Winter's Universitätsbuchhandlung, 1911).

[2] To a sword-thrust in the lung received as second in a student duel at this period (November, 1830) his family traced the disease which in middle life brought his career to an untimely end.

Burschenschaft, and members were openly displaying signs of their sympathy with the radical element. Under such circumstances any revival of the old *Turnen* was certain to be viewed with apprehension. In the spring of 1831 the former prohibition was renewed, and there could be no more exercising by groups in public. After some months of private study at Sprendlingen, his father's new parish, Spiess returned to Giessen and successfully passed his examinations in theology, April 2, 1832. He then became private tutor in the family of the Hessian Count Solms-Rödelheim, at Assenheim.

Before taking this position, or on one of his visits home, he received a foretaste of what awaited him if he remained in his native state. A friendly magistrate informed his father one evening that if the young man was found in the house on the following morning he would be subject to arrest. Spiess therefore left at once, and reached Assenheim in safety. The next year (1833) a newspaper notice brought word to Sprendlingen that the city of Burgdorf, in Switzerland, was in search of someone who could take charge of physical training in its elementary school. The clergyman, recognizing that a sojourn in a neutral country was the only safe course for his son, in view of existing political conditions, at once wrote to propose Adolf for the place. Word came in August that he had been appointed teacher of gymnastics, singing, writing and drawing.[1] On October 5 he left home with his youngest brother, Hermann, and travelling by way of Basel reached Burgdorf on the 21st, ready to begin work in the alien state which was to be his fosterland for fifteen busy and fruitful years (1833–1848).

The city authorities had erected a new, attractive and roomy building for the school, and now placed at its head Friedrich Froebel (1782–1852), already widely known for his book "The Education of Man" (1826), and Heinrich Langethal (1792–1879) and Wilhelm Middendorf (1793–1853), who had been associated with Froebel for fourteen years in his school in the Thuringian village of Keilhau and after the few years in Burgdorf were again to be his helpers when the first kindergarten was opened at Blankenburg, another Thuringian town. All three had been members of Lützow's Free Corps during the War of Liberation, and through residence in Berlin had come under the influence of Jahn and his work on the Hasenheide *Turnplatz.* Spiess found these colleagues ready to coöperate with him at every step, and all worked together in perfect harmony to give the broadest possible training to the children under their care. The open-air gymnasium, originally laid out after the Jahn plan in 1824, and beautifully situated in a grove near the left bank of the Emme, overlooked to the east by wooded sandstone

---

[1] Upon his reappointment, for a term of six years, on October 13, 1835, instruction in geography and history was substituted for the writing and drawing.

cliffs beyond the stream and on the west by an ancient castle, was now doubled in size and entirely refitted in accordance with the wishes of the new teacher. In the castle itself, where Pestalozzi had conducted his school for five years (1799–1804) and written "How Gertrude Teaches Her Children" (1801), a hall was equipped for winter use. In the spring of 1834 the boys of the school, including even the youngest, began to receive systematic instruction in gymnastics for two successive hours on three afternoons of each week, and before long the interest of the girls, also, was awakened and special classes were formed and suitable exercises devised to meet their needs. There were frequent excursions on foot into the surrounding country, and once a year, in the autumn, an exhibition or *Turnfest* was held. The new discipline, which reached pupils of

Fig. 22.—The original Spiess *Turnplatz* at Burgdorf, in the grove between the Emme and the Castle.

both sexes and all ages, was regarded as an essential part of their school training.

It was not long before the attention of the cantonal school authorities was attracted to the Burgdorf experiment, and as a result Spiess received in 1835 the added appointment of teacher of gymnastics in the normal school (*Landschullehrer-Seminar*) at Münchenbuchsee, ten miles to the southwest, where in addition to eighty children in the model school he found about a hundred pupils. He also undertook a similar task at various other schools in the neighborhood, among them one for girls in Kirchberg, and for his own pleasure and further training joined a small gymnastic society of adults (*Männerturnverein*) in Burgdorf, visited the turners in Bern and Hofwyl, and attended the annual Swiss *Turnfest* held in Bern (1839), Basel (1841) and Zurich (1842).

Experience with all grades of pupils had proved to Spiess that the material and methods of Jahn's "Deutsche Turnkunst" were not sufficient for his needs. Little by little he began therefore to develop and test new groups of exercises, and first of all what he called "Free Exercises," or those which require either no apparatus at all, or only such as can be carried in the hands. They were intended to secure ready control and graceful carriage of the body under ordinary conditions, while the pupil was standing or walking on the usual supporting surface, and differed in this particular from the forms commonly practised on the old Turnplatz. The attempt to instruct large numbers of pupils at once in these free exercises led to the elaboration of another group, the class exercises in marching (*Ordnungsübungen*), by means of which the entire mass was made to move as one individual, and in this way discipline and order were improved, since each pupil learned to handle himself as part of the whole, and any desired arrangement of the units could be promptly secured. The next step was a review of all the gymnastic material in the effort to devise a more satisfactory classification than the one adopted in the books of GutsMuths, the "Deutsche Turnkunst," and Eiselen's "Turntafeln" (1837). The result of this study was the publication in 1840 of the first part (Free Exercises) of his "System of Gymnastics" (*Lehre der Turnkunst*),[1] followed by a second (Hanging Exercises) in 1842, and a third (*Stemmübungen* or supporting exercises, including balancing and vaulting) in 1843.

In the summer of 1842 Spiess returned to Germany, drawn by the signs of approaching gymnastic revival in Prussia and the desire to discuss his own views with other men of like interests. He found Massmann,[2] at Munich, too firmly wedded to the *Turnen* of student days to receive with any sympathy the propsed innovations; but Jahn, whose guest he was for two days in Freyburg,

---

[1] Die Lehre der Turnkunst von Adolf Spiess. Basel, Schweighauser'sche Buchhandlung. Four volumes, as follows:
I. Theil: Das Turnen in den Freiübungen für beide Geschlechter, 1840. II. Theil: Das Turnen in den Hangübungen für beide Geschlechter, 1842; second edition in 1871. III. Theil: Das Turnen in den Stemmübungen für beide Geschlechter. Mit einem Anhang der Liegeübungen, 1843; second edition in 1874. IV. Theil: Das Turnen in den Gemeinübungen, in einer Lehre von den Ordnungsverhältnissen bei den Gliederungen einer Mehrzahl für beide Geschlechter, 1846; second edition (Basel, Benno Schwabe) in 1885.
[2] Hans Ferdinand Massmann (1797–1874), pupil and friend of Jahn in Berlin, member of the Jena *Burschenschaft* and present at the Wartburg episode in 1817, was summoned to Munich in 1827 to take charge of gymnastics, first in the royal *Kadettenkorps* and then in a public outdoor *Turnanstalt* which was to serve all the schools of the city. In 1841 he was called to Berlin to confer with Minister Eichhorn regarding the revival of physical training in Prussia. Two years later he was entrusted with the carrying out of the plan, but proved unequal to the task, and retired from the position in 1851.

and Eiselen, whom he saw at a watering-place near Berlin, were more cordial in their attitude. The visit of Minister Eichhorn (August 10), and the formal statement of his ideas regarding the essential features of a state system of physical training for the schools which followed it, have been mentioned already in the opening paragraph. Two years before Spiess had married a former pupil, Marie Buri, and the need of finding a larger and more remunerative field of usefulness no doubt had much to do with the journey to Berlin; but the summons of Massmann to the Prussian capital in 1843 put an end to all hopes in that direction.

Fig. 23.—The Basel *Turnplatz*, from a plate in the *Turnbuch* of Spiess (1847).

Attempts to secure a footing in Darmstadt and in Basel met at first with no better success; but afterward he received from the latter city a call to the position of teacher of gymnastics and history in two higher schools for boys—the *Gymnasium* and the *Realschule* —and at the orphan asylum, entering upon these duties in May of 1844. The following March he was relieved of the work in history in order that he might have time for instruction in gymnastics at the public girls' school (*Töchterschule*), and preparations were also made for progressive improvement in physical training at all the city schools. Free at last to devote all his thought to the one subject, he finished in 1846 the fourth and final part (Class Exercises in Marching, *Gemein-* or *Ordnungsübungen*) of his "System of Gymnastics," and the next year was able to publish the first volume of a practical manual for teachers (*Turnbuch für Schulen*),[1] containing graded series of exercises suitable for boys and girls between the ages of six and ten. The second volume, covering the ages from ten to sixteen, was completed in 1851, after he had left Basel and returned to his native land.

In May of 1848 Spiess accepted an offer from Minister von Gagern of Hesse, and moved to Darmstadt, the capital of the Grand Duchy, to undertake the task of introducing gymnastics into the schools of that state, beginning with the higher schools and the common schools of such communities as were prepared to take the step at once. He was also to train the requisite teaching force, and afterward to superintend their work. The salary of the new "*Oberstudien-Assessor*" was fixed at two thousand gulden. Lessons were immediately begun with classes in two secondary schools for boys (the *Gymnasium* and the *Realschule*) and in the higher school for girls (*Mädchen-* or *Töchterschule*), and in a large garden lying near the center of the city the hall of a former public house was converted into a gymnasium by setting up along one side rows of vertical poles and horizontal bars and ladders, and adding to these a giant stride, parallel bars, bucks, jump stands and jumping ropes, stilts and poles for use in valuting. A new gymnasium or *Turnhaus*, surrounded by a double *Turnplatz* and containing a hall 100 by 60 feet which could be changed into two rooms by means of a movable partition, was opened for use June 14, 1852, with classes of boys and girls from various schools. It was the first building of the kind in Germany. Public exhibitions the next year and again in 1855 acquainted parents, teachers, the grand ducal family and the state and city authorities with the nature of his work, and increased their interest in it.

A four weeks' normal course was given in February of 1849 to about thirty teachers in elementary and higher schools, most of them from Darmstadt, but one from Dresden and ten from Mainz, Offenbach, Worms and other Hessian towns. Instruction was chiefly by means of model classes, conducted by Spiess in their presence, and after observing these the teachers themselves were given an opportunity to practice the same exercises. No other formal courses were given in Hesse, but in response to an invitation he took charge of a similar one in Oldenburg, capital of the Grand Duchy of the same name, in the fall of 1851. He also visited many places in Hesse in the interest of physical training, and teachers

---

[1] Turnbuch für Schulen als Anleitung für den Turnunterricht durch die Lehrer der Schulen, von Adolf Spiess. Basel, Schweighauser'sche Buchhandlung. Two volumes, as follows: I. Theil: Die Uebungen für die Altersstufe vom sechsten bis zehnten Jahre bei Knaben und Mädchen, 1847; second, "vermehrte und verbesserte Auflage, besorgt von J. C. Lion," in 1880. II. Theil: Die Uebungen für die Altersstufe vom zehnten bis sechszehnten Jahre bei Knaben und Mädchen 1851; second edition, as above (Basel, Benno Schwabe), in 1889.

from all parts of the state came to Darmstadt from time to time during the next few years to become familiar with his method. To all these he gladly rendered whatever assistance they desired. A list of foreign visitors during the period 1852–1854 has been preserved, and on it are found the names of educators from Sweden,[1] Belgium (1), Switzerland (3), Austria (4), Prussia (6), Saxony (2), Württemberg (2), Baden (5), Oldenburg (4), Frankfort-on-the-Main (8) and others from the smaller German states. More than half of the number remained long enough to receive practical instruction under Spiess, and to this group belong Nyblæus, Kawerau and Kluge from the Central Institute (Royal Normal School of Gymnastics) in Berlin, and Moritz Kloss, Director of the Normal School of Gymnastics in Dresden. Another list covering the same period shows that the Spiess method had been, or was about to be adopted in more than thirty-five schools in ten cities outside of Hesse, including Berlin, Neurippen, Breslau, Frankfort, Dresden, Oldenburg, Vienna and Bern, besides Basel and Burgdorf.

Failing health compelled Spiess to interrupt, in the summer of 1855, his hitherto unceasing activity. Tuberculosis had developed in the lung wounded during his student days, and attempts to stop its progress by residence in the Taunus and for two years at Vevey, on Lake Geneva, proved unavailing. He returned to Darmstadt, vising the *Turnhaus* there for the last time in the fall of 1857, and died the following year, on the 9th of May.

The chief service which he rendered to physical training in Germany, and wherever German influence has been felt, was the attempt to make it a part of the school life. The *Turnplatz* was not to exist side by side with the school, as a counterpoise to the exclusively mental training of the latter, and in charge of some independent individual or society; but the school should concern itself with the whole life of the young, physical as well as mental, and gymnastics, recognized by the state as a means of education, should be thoroughly incorporated and treated on an equality with other branches of instruction and discipline, enjoying the same rights and conforming to the same pedagogic principles. It should therefore be made a required exercise, from which nothing except a physician's certificate of defect or illness would excuse any pupil. In addition to the open-air gymnasium and the playground the community or the state would have to provide and equip closed halls, in or near the school building, so that instruction need not be interrupted by season or weather. Elementary classes require an hour each day for gymnastics and games. Less time might suffice for the older children, but the lesson periods, in either case, should be included

---

[1] Gustav Nyblæus, then teacher of gymnastics at the University of Lund, but afterwards Director of the Central Institute (Royal Normal School of Gymnastics) in Stockholm.

within the school hours, or stand in immediate proximity to them. Periodical examinations in gymnastics coming at the same time with general examinations, and annually recurring exhibitions or *Turnfeste* were to be held. Those who teach the subject must be educators by profession, and closely identified with the life of the school, receiving their training in this branch, as in all others, at the normal schools and the universities, or in part at institutions intended for that purpose exclusively—the normal schools of gymnastics. In elementary schools instruction would be in the hands of the grade- or class-teacher, and in higher schools there should be special teachers of gymnastics, just as in the case of mathematics or languages or science. The exercise-material must be arranged in progressive steps suitable for the different school grades, and a series of manuals prepared to fit the different conditions and needs in country and city schools, in common schools, higher schools for boys and schools for girls.

In preparation for the process of sorting out and distributing to each sex and age appropriate forms of exercise Spiess thought it necessary first of all to collect, analyze and classify the whole mass of possible positions and movements of the body. This he endeavored to do in his "System of Gymnastics" (*Die Lehre der Turnkunst*), but without seeking at the same time to separate the useful from that which is unessential or undesirable. The book is not intended, therefore, as a practical guide for the teacher. That function was reserved for his second work, the *Turnbuch für Schulen*, which has been a mine of instruction and suggestion for authors of later manuals. Here he leads gradually from the simplest exercises to the most difficult combinations, pointing out what material is to be used for each sex and age, and explaining the method to be pursued during the lesson hour. He devised new forms of apparatus on which the whole class, or a considerable fraction of it, could work at once under the teacher's eye and at his command. The "Free Exercises" and the "Class Exercises in Marching" (*Ordnungs-* or *Gemeinübungen*) which he elaborated were a fresh contribution to the stock of German gymnastics, and with his simpler exercises on apparatus supplied material for girls and younger boys. His musical gifts[1] rendered possible that

[1] The father of Spiess had begun to play the organ for church services at the age of nine, and in his school at Offenbach paid particular attention to instruction in singing. Adolf himself learned to play the violin and the pianoforte, and his strong boyish voice developed into a beautiful tenor. He was made an honorary member of the Swiss *Musikverein* in 1838, sang solo parts from the oratorios of Spohr and Neuhaus in the presence of the composers at a musical festival in Lucerne, and the tenor solos in Mendelssohn's "St. Paul" at Zurich, and took the title role in Handel "Samson" at the national musical festival in Basel in the summer of 1840. It was at his suggestion that Max Schneckenburger wrote "Die Wacht am Rhein" that same year, and when it was read to a little company gathered in the Burgdorf "Stadthaus" Spiess was the first to sing it, to an accompaniment which he improvised on the pianoforte.

rhythmical arrangement of the free exercises which has continued to be so conspicuous a feature in the teaching of his followers ever since, and enabled him also to combine artistically certain marching or dancing or other rhythmical movements into a fixed series which could be executed by pupils to the accompaniment of some familiar song, or other musical composition, as in the case of the Miller-*Reigen* and the whole group of *Lieder-* and *Tanz-Reigen*.[1]

BIBLIOGRAPHY.

Euler's "Encyklopädisches Handbuch des gesamten Turnwesens" and "Geschichte des Turnunterrichts" (see p. 82), and the following articles in the *Neue Jahrbücher für die Turnkunst* (NJT), *Deutsche Turn-Zeitung* (DTZ), and *Monatsschrift für das Turnwesen* (MT):

Wassmannsdorff in NJT 1855: 330–334 and 1858: 81–90; and in DTZ 1859: 22–23 and 1863: 137–140.

Lion in DTZ 1858: 91–93, 98–99, and 102–103.

Marx in NJT 1885: 57–66.

Schmeel in DTZ 1910: 82–85, 97–101, 117–120, and 133–136.

Schmuck in DTZ 1911: 453–457.

Neuendorff in MT 1910: 122–128.

The Spiess centenary in 1910 was the occasion of three important publications: (1) Adolf Spiess: Sein Leben und seine Wirksamkeit. Dargestellt nach Vorträgen, gehalten bei Anlass der Spiess-Feier im Basler Turnlehrerverein von J. Bollinger-Auer, Lehrer an der Höhern Töchterschule in Basel (Basel, Helbing & Lichtenhahn, 1910). (2) Adolf Spiess. Ein Gedenkblatt zu seinem hundertjährigen Geburtstage. Von Prof. Dr. Karl Roller, Oberlehrer in Darmstadt (Berlin, Weidmannsche Buchhandlung, 1910) and (3) Adolf Spiess, der Begründer des deutschen Schulturnens. Ein Lebensbild von H. Schmeel, Stadtschulinspektor in Worms (Giessen, Emil Roth, 1910).

---

[1] Spiess committed to Karl Wassmannsdorff, his friend and associate for two years in Basel, the preparation of his material on *Reigen* for publication. See "Reigen und Liederreigen für das Schulturnen aus dem Nachlasse von Adolf Spiess. Mit einer Einleitung, erklärenden Anmerkungen und einer Anzahl von Liedern herausgegeben von Dr. K. Wassmannsdorff." Frankfurt a. M., J. D. Sauerländer's Verlag, 1869. A second "verbesserte und mit einem anhange 'Gang-und Hüpfarten für das Mädchenturnen' vermehrte Auflage" was published in 1885.

CHAPTER XIII.

PHYSICAL TRAINING IN THE PRUSSIAN SCHOOLS.

THE astonishing development of popular interest in gymnastics which has taken place in Germany and other Europena countries can be traced directly to Jahn's work at the Hasenheide, near Berlin, in the years 1810–1818; and between 1833 and 1858, in Switzerland and Hesse, Spiess laid the foundation of German school gymnastics. But although the first defnite step looking toward physical training in the Prussian schools was the cabinet order of 1842 (p. 101), it was not until after the accession of William I to the throne, in 1861, that conditions became at all propitious. During the latter half of the reign of Frederick-William III, from 1819 to 1840, the one man who with his pupils and assistants kept alive the tradition of *Turnen* in Berlin, adding to and further systematizing its content, and won for it gradually increasing recognition, was Ernst Eiselen, among Jahn's earliest followers and his most faithful fellow-worker. Under Frederick-William IV (1840–1861) there were at first encouraging signs of revival, but the unfortunate choice of Massmann to direct the carrying out of the new plans (1843–1850), followed by Rothstein's untactful and somewhat bigoted attempt to substitute the gymnastics of Ling for that of Jahn in the Royal Central Institute of Gymnastics at Berlin (1851–1863), made the whole period a disappointing one of storm and stress, without much evidence of real progress. Each of these early phases deserves a few words of explanation.

Ernst Wilhelm Bernhard Eiselen (1793–1846), after the closing of the Hasenheide *Turnplatz* in the spring 1819, became a teacher in the Plamann school for boys. In April of 1825, using rented quarters, he began to give courses in foil- and saber-fencing and vaulting to students in the University of Berlin, and two years later succeeded in obtaining permission to offer private instruction in gymnastics. May 1, 1828, he opened his own gymnasium, with indoor and outdoor equipment, at Dorotheenstrasse 31d (now 60). Courses for the training of teachers were added in 1831, and the next year corrective exercises for girls, for whose accommodation a special room was provided. By 1836 the number of his pupils had increased to such an extent that a second gymnasium was built in another part of the city (Blumenstrasse 3, now 63a), and placed under the management of Wilhelm Lübeck (1809–1879), who afterward (1839) became its independent director. Arsenical poisoning in his youth had permanently impaired Eiselen's health, and this fact and his retiring disposition may have led the Prussian authorities to prefer Massmann as their agent in 1843. Eiselen was put in charge of a great public *Turnplatz* in the suburb of Moabit in 1846, but died a few months later at Misdroy, a sea-bathing resort on the Island of Wollin. Attention has already been called to his writings (p. 102). Among his pupils and assistants who afterward filled important teaching positions were Wilhelm Ballot, Moritz, Böttcher, Philipp August Feddern and Wilhelm Lübeck.

In 1836 Dr. Karl Ignaz Lorinser (1796–1853), state medical counsellor at Oppeln, in Prussian Silesia, published a striking article on "Safeguarding Health in the Schools,"[1] in which he urged that too exclusive training of the mind in the higher schools was threatening national vigor. His paper and the widespread discussion which followed called the attention of the ministry of education anew to the need of reform, and led to various orders looking toward more or less systematic introduction of bodily exercises under the supervision of teachers. Participation, however, depended upon parental consent and the inclination of pupils. The cabinet order of June 6, 1842, and the summons of Massmann to Berlin in the spring of 1843 to organize a system of statewide physical training aroused expectations which were slow in being realized. Instead of the Spiess plan of separate facilities at each school and a graded scheme of exercises incorporated in the school program, Massmann clung tenaciously to the idea of great central exercising grounds (*Turnplätze*), preferably a single one even for the larger cities, and a gathering here of all ages and classes for free activity, especially on Wednesday and Saturday afternoons—a system of public playgrounds, rather than one of orderly physical training.

But his endeavor to revive the Jahn gymnastics on a new *Turnplatz* laid out in the neighborhood of the old Hasenheide site met with little success, and the numbers in attendance dwindled rapidly. The times had changed, and there was no one to supply Jahn's inspiring leadership. Teachers were needed, but Eiselen's death had cut short a plan to have him give two courses a year, of six weeks each, in his private gymnasium. A "Central Training School for Teachers of Gymnastics" (*Zentral-Bildungsanstalt für Turnlehrer*), under Massmann's direction, was therefore organized instead. It was to give annually two three-month courses, beginning April 1 and August 1, to a maximum of thirty pupils in each. The opening took place May 1, 1848, in the Eiselen gymnasium; but

---

[1] "Zum Schultz der Gesundheit in den Schulen." In *Medizinische Zeitung des Vereins für Heilkunde in Preussen*, 1836, No. 1. Reprinted by T. C. F. Enslin, Berlin, in 1861. Quoted at some length in Euler-Rossow 1907, pp. 115–117.

the courses were discontinued before the end of the following year. The attendance had been disappointingly small, and those who came manifested little interest in their work. Massmann, already a discredited leader with whose projects the school authorities themselves had shown little sympathy, was retired in 1850. The government attitude toward the Jahn *Turnen* was still one of suspicion and antagonism, and meanwhile attention had been drawn to the claims of a new system of gymnastics, built up on foreign soil.

Hugo Rothstein (1810–1865), second lieutenant in the Prussian artillery and teacher in the artillery school at Berlin, paid a visit

Fig. 24.—Hugo Rothstein (1810–1865).

to Sweden in 1843, and upon his return published in *Der Staat* (September, 1844) an article on "Gymnastics in Sweden and Ling's System of Gymnastics." It attracted favorable notice in military circles, and Minister of War von Boyen commissioned him to revisit the country in order to become better acquainted with the subject. Accordingly in June of 1845, now first lieutenant and accompanied by another officer, he went to Stockholm for a full course at the Central Institute of Gymnastics (*Kongl. Gymnastiska Centralinstitutet*), adding three months in Copenhagen to observe the fencing and other instruction at the Danish Royal Institute of Military Gymnastics (*Det Kongelige Militære Gymnastiske Institutet*). During his second sojourn in the Swedish capital he saw much of Director Branting and Head Teacher Georgii, and was also a frequent guest at the palace of King Oskar I.   In the autumn of 1846 both officers were back in Berlin.   The following year Massmann published a translation of Ling's writings on gymnastics,[1] and Rothstein had begun work at once on a series of volumes on the Ling system which appeared at intervals between 1847 and 1859.[2]

A direct result of the reports by Rothstein and Techow (the infantry lieutenant who had been his companion) was the founding in Berlin of a "Central Institute for Gymnastic Instruction in the Army" (*Zentralinstitut für gymnastischen Unterricht in der Armee*), with the two officers as teachers.   Lübeck's gymnasium on Blumen strasse was used for the practical exercises, and the first course there was begun October 1, 1847; but the rioting which broke out in Berlin the next spring, following the February revolution in Paris, brought it to a sudden close.   Two years later, however, the foundations of a new building were laid in Scharnhorststrasse, and now it was decided to train both military and civilian teachers in a single school rechristened "Royal Central Institute of Gymnastics" (*Königliche Zentral-Turnanstalt*) and opened to pupils October 1, 1851.   Rothstein was made director of instruction (*Unterrichtsdirigent*).   In his own teaching he employed the Ling apparatus and exercises, making light of Jahn's *Turnen*, and for anatomical and physiological reasons rejecting the parallel bars unconditionally.   This action gave rise to repeated protests from *Turnvereine* in Berlin and other German cities, who regarded it as a part of the government's reactionary policy, and led to a violent controversy (the *Barrenstreit*) in the years 1861 and 1862.   Dr. Carl Philipp Euler (1828–1901), who became civilian teacher in 1860, had proposed that the banished apparatus be restored.   Petitions, memorials, and opinions for and against its use multiplied, and the discussion was widened to include the whole subject of the comparative merits of the Ling-Rothstein gymnastics and the Jahn *Turnen*.   Emil du Bois-Reymond (1818–1896), professor of physiology in the University

---

[1] P. H. Ling's Schriften über Leibesübungen. Aus dem Schwedischen übersetzt von H. F. Massmann. Dr. Professor &c. Magdeburg, Heinrichshofen'sche Buchhandlung, 1847.

[2] Die Gymnastik, nach dem Systeme des Schwedischen Gymnasiarchen P. H. Ling, dargestellt von Hg. Rothstein. Berlin, E. H. Schroeder. In five parts as follows: I. Allgemeine Einleitung (with life of Ling). Das Wesen der Gymnastik, Grundlegung und Gliederung ihres Systems, u.s.w. 1848 and 1849. II. Die Pädagogische Gymnastik, 1847; second edition in 1857. III. Die Heilgymnastik, 1847. IV. Die Wehrgymnastik, 1851. V. Die Aesthetische Gymnastik, 1854–1859.
With Dr. A. C. Neumann, Rothstein also published four volumes of an "Athenaeum für rationelle Gymnastik." Berlin, E. H. Schroeder, 1854–1857. (Rothstein's name appears alone on the title page of volumes III and IV.)
Other books by Rothstein were "Die gymnastischen Freiübungen nach dem System P. H. Ling's" (Berlin, E. H. Schroeder, 1853; fifth edition in 1861), and "Die gymnastischen Rüstübungen nach P. H. Ling's System" (Berlin, E. H. Schroeder, 1855; second edition in 1861).

of Berlin, entered the lists as a powerful champion on the side of the Turners.[1] On the last day of 1862 appeared an opinion from the highest medical authority in Prussia, the Royal Scientific Deputation for Medical Affairs, to the effect that exercises on the parallel bars "are justifiable and not to be rejected."[2] It was therefore ordered that both parallel bars and horizontal bar should be used with civilian pupils. Rothstein withdrew from the school in 1863, left Berlin for Erfurt, his birthplace and early home, and died there March 23, 1865.

FIG. 25.—Emil du Bois-Reymond (1818–1896).

The later history of the Central Institute may be briefly outlined here. A second civilian teacher, Gebhard Eckler (1832–1907), was added in October of 1864. In 1877 the military and civilian sections, which had existed side by side, were permanently separated, the former retaining the old site on Scharnhorststrasse and hereafter called the Royal Military Institute of Gymnastics (*Königliche Militär-Turnanstalt*),[3] and the latter, under the name "Royal Training School for Teachers of Gymnastics" (*Königliche Turnlehrer-Bildungsanstalt*), opening its doors in temporary quarters on October 8, but after two years occupying its own new home at 229 Friedrichstrasse (October 15, 1879). As early as 1866 Euler had begun to conduct private classes for women who desired to become teachers of gymnastics, and in 1880 regular state courses were added

---

[1] "Ueber das Barrenturnen und über die sogenannte rationelle Gymnastik" (Berlin, Georg Reimer, 1862), and "Herr Rothstein und der Barren" (Berlin, Georg Reimer, 1863).

[2] The report is reprinted in Georg Hirth's "Das Gesamte Turnwesen," second edition, **3**, pp. 492–506 (Hof, Rud. Lion, 1893).

[3] It was moved to Zossen, about twenty-five miles south of Berlin, in 1919.

to meet their special needs. The first of these began April 19 and closed July 6. Euler became "director of instruction" (*Unter-*

Fig. 26.—Carl Philipp Euler (1828–1901).

richtsdirigent) in 1877, and Dr. Ignaz Küppers (1840–   ) was added as second director in 1891. Following Euler's death, September 15, 1901, Eckler was given the same title (1902), but retired

Fig. 27.—*The Prussian Landesturnanstalt* at Spandau.

in 1905, followed by Küppers in October of the next year. A new office, that of director of the school, was now created, and its first incumbent (May, 1905) was Dr. Paul Diebow (1861–1920). In the autumn of 1911, after a further change of name (to *Landes-turnanstalt*, April 1, 1908), the institution was moved to its present home in Spandau, eight miles northwest of Berlin, where it enjoys ample facilities for indoor and outdoor training of all sorts. The full course for men, at the outbreak of the Great War, covered seven months (April-November), and that for women six months (January-June).

To meet the great demand for teachers, examinations for persons trained in city or private courses outside the Central Institute had been given under its auspices after 1866. Beginning in 1889, arrangements for similar state examinations for both men and women have been made in Bonn, Breslau, Halle, and Königsberg, and in the case of women at Bielefeld, Cassel, Danzig, Hanover, Kiel, Magdeburg, Stettin and a few other cities. The next noteworthy step was the introduction of teachers' training courses in the Prussian universities, in each of which (Berlin, Bonn, Breslau, Göttingen, Greifswald, Halle, Kiel, Königsberg, Marburg and Münster) a student could in 1914 take work in the theory and practice of physical education, in preparation for a teacher's certificate in that subject, and could take the examination itself at the university where he was studying.[1] In general such courses are governed by regulations contained in the Prussian ministerial order of July 9, 1892, originally intended for the University of Halle, and a supplemental order of February 20, 1909, which relates to training in outdoor exercises. The former provides for courses under the immediate oversight of the University *Kurator*, to begin in the middle of October and continue until the close of the winter semester—something less than five months. They are open to candidates who have already qualified as teachers in the schools and to university students who have completed four semesters of work. There is no charge for tuition. Each course embraces both theoretical instruction and practical exercises, and occupies about eighteen hours a week. As a rule, one-third of the time is devoted to lectures on the history of physical education, methods, the forms and construction of apparatus (*Gerätkunde*), the structure and functions of the human body, hygiene as related to exercise, and first aid in accidents; and the remaining two-thirds to the attainment of personal dexterity in the field of school gymnastics, and the actual teaching of others, and direction of games, etc. Four hundred and ninety-eight students attended these winter courses in the Prussian universities in the year 1910–1911.

[1] Similar provision was also made in at least three other German universities, Heidelberg, Jena, and Leipzig. Students at the last named took their examination in Dresden, after a final eight weeks at the state *Turnlehrerbildungsanstalt* there.

The later order, directed to the *Kuratoren* of Prussian universities, requires that as soon as possible the above courses be supplemented by summer ones, lasting about four weeks and devoted solely to the subject of games and athletic sports (*Volks- und Jugendspiele und volkstümliche Übungen*). It was recommended that they cover from fifty to sixty hours altogether, including from four to six lectures on the value of games and athletic sports, about eight on theory and method, eight hours devoted to practice in teaching or directing, and the rest to practical exercises. The course may be compressed within four weeks, or made to occupy two or three hours each on two afternoons a week and spread over an entire summer

Fig. 28.—Gymnasium of the *Realschule* at Gross-Lichterfelde, near Berlin.

semester, thus interfering less with the student's other work. In many cases admission has been granted to students in the departments of medicine, theology and law, as well as to those enrolled in the department of philosophy and preparing directly for the examination for a state certificate as teacher of physical education. Hereafter the full certificate is to be granted only to those who have completed both winter and summer courses.

In spite of all this progress, there was at the beginning of 1913 no professorship of physical education in any German university, although the establishment of such a chair had been proposed at the University of Giessen. In 1925, Dr. Herm. Attrack, the first professor of physical education *Pädagogik der Leibesübungen*, was appointed at the University of Leipzig.

The Prussian cabinet order of June 6, 1842, had "formally recognized bodily exercises as a necessary and indispensable part of male education." A ministerial circular of February 4, 1844, sent out to the provincial school authorities, directed that in towns and cities indoor and outdoor space should be provided for gymnastics at all higher schools (*Gymnasien, höhere Stadtschulen*) and training-colleges for teachers (*Schullehrer-Seminaren*), in order that the exercises might be practised uninterruptedly throughout the year. Instruction was to be in the hands of some regular member of the teaching staff who gave only part of his time to this branch, rather than one who taught no other subject. The exercises were to come, as a rule, on the half-holiday afternoons of Wednesday and Saturday, or under certain conditions they might be given daily during the hour following the afternoon session. It was left to his parent or guardian to decide whether or not any pupil should participate. Certificates of graduation from the schools were to note whether and with what success use had been made of the instruction in gymnastics. A later order (November 27, 1866) extended this last provision to cover semester reports as well.

An order of September 10, 1860, reveals the intention of the ministry to introduce gymnastics into *all* schools for boys and young men, from the elementary or folkschool to the university.[1] Special short courses at training-colleges for teachers, to reach those already in service, are recommended as a means of filling the immediate need of competent instruction, which will later be cared for by the regular graduates. The indifference of many members of the teaching body in higher schools is rebuked, together with the excessive number of excuses from attendance, but attention is also called to praiseworthy progress made at other institutions where the new movement receives earnest and sympathetic support. University authorities are advised to furnish their students with facilities for continuing habits of bodily activity, and reminded of the advantage to the state if those who are to be leaders in church

[1] As generally in Europe, there are two distinct kinds of schools in Germany, the elementary or common schools, and the secondary or higher schools. The former (*Volksschule*) does not lead up to the latter, but is designed to furnish that kind and degree of education which the state requires of every citizen irrespective of class or calling. Its course of eight years covers the period of "school age" (six to fourteen). The higher school (*Gymnasium, Realgymnasium, Realschule*) gives a broader training intended to prepare for later study at the university and the professional and higher technical schools, or to meet the conditions for admission to any but the lowest grades of government employ. In order to enter one must be at least nine years old, having obtained his earlier education in special preparatory classes or in the ordinary *Volksschule*, and the average age of those who complete the full nine years' course is between eighteen and twenty.

NOTE. 1926. The Elementary School (*Volksschule*) has now become the basis for all the different types of secondary schools in Germany and is therefore called *Grundschule*.

and school affairs are given an opportunity here to become familiar with a branch of education which they may later be called upon to oversee or inspect.

Early in 1862 an official "Manual for Instruction in Gymnastics in the Prussian Elementary Schools" was published, replaced by a "New Manual" in the summer of 1868. This latter was again revised in 1895.[1] By ministerial order of June 4, 1862, such instruction is declared to be an integral part of the course for males in schools of this grade (*Volksschule*), and attendance at the exercises is made compulsory. Suitable grounds and the equipment called for by the Manual must be provided. Teachers are prepared in training-colleges (*Seminare*), where special attention is given to actual handling of classes in model schools, choosing and arranging suitable material for the different grades from the official manual, and in the senior class to instruction in methods, the installation of apparatus, the recent history of physical education, the hygiene of exercise and first aid.

The apparatus mentioned in the official manual of 1895 includes wooden and iron wands, long jumping rope, jump stands and jumping board, balance beam, climbing ropes and poles, ladders, adjustable horizontal bar and parallel bars. It recommends enough fixed apparatus so that four pupils can exercise at a time. In its one hundred and fifty pages are described a variety of marching and free exercises, and exercises with the different forms of apparatus just mentioned, and in conclusion sixteen selected running games and seven ball games. Beyond outlining the general plan of each lesson, calling attention to the need of orderly progression throughout the year, and indicating which of the exercises are intended for the upper grades, the manual offers no direct assistance to the teacher in laying out his course, *i. e.*, it contains no tables showing sample lessons and no series of exercises arranged in order of increasing difficulty.

A third hour of exercise a week was added to the curriculum in higher schools in 1892, and in elementary schools by order of June 13, 1910, which was intended especially to encourage the use of games and other activities in the open air. This same order made compulsory for all schools the ten-minute periods of exercise for the promotion of good carriage, deep breathing and quickened blood-flow recommended in 1907 for days on which there was no regular

[1] Leitfaden für den Turn-Unterricht in den Preussischen Volksschulen. Mit 29 in den Text gedruckten Figuren in Holzschnitt. Berlin, Wilhelm Hertz, 1862.
    Neuer Leitfaden für den Turn-Unterricht in den Preussischen Volksschulen. Zweite erweiterte Auflage des "Leitfadens für den Turn-Unterricht" 1862. Mit 53 in den Text gedruckten Figuren in Holzschnitt. Berlin, Wilhelm Hertz, 1868.
    Leitfaden für den Turnunterricht in den Preussischen Volksschulen, 1895. Berlin, Wilhelm Hertz, 1895.

lesson in gymnastics. The "Guide for Use with Boys in Elementary Schools without Indoor Gymnasia," published in 1909,[1] lays down principles which are binding for boys' schools of every sort. In it the class exercises in marching introduced by Spiess are omitted. Free exercises and exercises on apparatus are selected with the specific needs of the pupil in mind, and show the influence of Swedish teaching and practice. They are supplemented by running exercises, games, dry-land-swimming and other forms of activity, and attention is called to the value of *Spielstunden* or play-afternoons. A recent development in higher schools is the organization and rapid spread of voluntary gymnastic, running, tramping and athletic clubs of all sorts, conducted under the oversight of teachers.

It was not until the ministerial order of May 31, 1894, that instruction in gymnastics became a required subject in higher schools for *girls*. Two lessons a week were to be given, and by women teachers. An order of March 30, 1905, extended the requirement to elementary (*Volks-*) and intermediate (*Mittel-*) schools in cities and large towns and recommended that teachers encourage also the playing of games after school hours. The manual of 1895 was to form the basis of instruction. A further step was taken on July 11, 1911, when the time allotted to gymnastics was increased to three hours a week for the upper grades, and all elementary schools not covered by former orders were urged to add the subject to their curriculum. An official "Manual for the Physical Training of Girls in Prussian Schools" was published in 1913.[2]

To an American the German universities and technical schools seemed singularly backward in the matter of physical education. At only one of them is there a full professorship devoted to the subject, and at least a third had not even an instructor in gymnastics (*Turnlehrer*) on the teaching staff. It must not be forgotten, however, that some of the instructors are men of university training although they do not hold professorships and since the war physical education has been made compulsory for all students who are physically fit while the student fraternities are devoting more attention to it than formerly. There are two student associations which may be considered the survivors of the *Burschenschaften* of Jahn's day, so far as the practice of gymnastics is concerned. One of them, the *Akademischer Turnbund*, or "A. T. B." (*Verband nichtfarbentragender akademischer Turnvereine und -Verbindungen auf deutschen Hochschulen*), organized June 27, 1883, on the Schweizerhöhe near Jena, included 39 societies and about 1900 student

---

[1] Anleitung für das Knabenturnen in Volksschulen ohne Turnhalle. Berlin, J. G. Cotta'sche Buchhandlung Nachfolger, 1909.

[2] Leitfaden für Mädchenturnen in den preussischen Schulen, 1913. Berlin, J. G. Cotta'sche Buchhandlung Nachfolger, 1913.

members in 1919, and belongs to the German *Turnerschaft*. Its first competitive meet (*Turnbundfest*) was held at Arnstadt, August 5 and 6, 1893, and the sixth at Coblenz, July 28–31, 1912.[1] The other, the *Verband farbentragender Turnerschaften*, or "V. C." (*Vertreter-Convent*), to which 55 societies with about 1800 student members belonged in 1919, was given its present name and form at a convention held in Berlin, June 11 and 12, 1885. Only a small proportion of its societies have affiliated themselves with the German *Turnerschaft*. The first general competitive meet (*Turnfest*) was held at Sangerhausen, May 26–29, 1882, and the sixteenth in Gotha, May 13–16, 1913.[2] In 1911 an *Akademischer Bund für Leibesübungen* was formed, including the two associations mentioned, the *Akademischer Ruderbund*, the *Kartelverband akademischer Rudervereine*, the *Akademischer Sportbund* and other similar organizations. This union held a "German Academic Olympia" in Breslau, August 1–3, 1911, and another at Leipzig, October 17–19, 1913. Another at Hanover, July 1920 and the last one at Merberg, 1924. There had already been gatherings of this sort at Leipzig, July 11, 1909, and Berlin, July 2 and 3, 1910 and sectional championships are held yearly in various sports.

There have been two attempts at a statistical survey of school gymnastics covering all of the German states, the first by J. V. Lion in 1873, and the second by Carl Rossow in 1908.[3] A general convention of German teachers of gymnastics was held in Berlin, August 9–11, 1861, in connection with the second general German *Turnfest*. Others have been held at intervals ever since, and at the twelfth (Hof. a. Saale, July 17 and 18, 1893), a *Deutscher Turnlehrerverein* (German Society of Teachers of Gymnastics) was formally organized. The eighteenth convention met in Breslau, May 29 and 30, 1914.[4]

---

[1] See the Handbuch für den Akademischen Turnbund. Im Auftrage des Bundes herausgegeben von Dr. rer. pol. Kurt Blaum (A. H. Burgund-Strassburg). 1908. Strassburg i. E., Selbstverlag des A. T. B., Universitätsplatz 7.

[2] See Der Turnerschafter. Handbuch des deutschen V.-C.-Studenten. Zehnte Auflage. Bearbeitet von Herbert Meyer. Leipzig-Reudnitz, August Hoffman, 1908.

[3] Statistik des Schulturnens in Deutschland. Im Auftrage des Ausschusses der Deutschen Turnerschaft herausgegeben von J. C. Lion. Leipzig, E. Keil, 1873.

Zweite Statistik des Schulturnens in Deutschland. Mit Unterstützung der Ministerien der deutschen Bundesstaaten, der Deutschen Turnerschaft und des Zentralausschusses zur Förderung der Volks- und Jugendspiele unter Mitarbeit vieler Schulmänner im Auftrage und unter Mitwirkung des Deutschen Turnlehrer-Vereins herausgegeben von Carl Rossow. Gotha, E. F. Thienemann, 1908. The contents of this second survey are summarized in *Jahrbuch der Turnkunst* 1907 (Leipzig, Emil Stock, 1907) pp. 145–157.

[4] See Euler-Rossow, Geschichte des Turnunterrichts (Gotha, E. F. Thienemann, 1907), pp. 415–423.

BIBLIOGRAPHY.

Euler's "Geschichte des Turnunterrichts" and "Encyklopädisches Handbuch des gesamten Turnwesens" (see pp. 81 and 82).

Handbuch des gesamten Turnwesens und der verwandten Leibesübungen. In Verbindung mit zahlreichen Fachmännern herausgegeben von Studienrat Prof. Dr. Rudolf Gasch. Dresden. Mit 44 Tafeln (teils in Farbendruck), mit 394 Einzelabbildungen und 566 Abbildungen im Texte. Wien und Leipzig, A. Pichlers Witwe & Sohn, 1920.

Verordnungen und amtliche Bekanntmachungen das Turnwesen in Preussen betreffend. Gesammelt von Schulrat Prof. Dr. C. Euler und Prof. Gebh. Eckler. (First edition 1869, second edition 1884) Dritte neubearbeitete Auflage herausgegeben von Prof. Gebh. Eckler. Berlin, R. Gaertner, 1902.

Verordnungen und amtliche Bekanntmachungen das Turnwesen in Preussen betreffend. Mit einem Anhang: Die wichtigsten Turnverordnungen anderer Bundesstaaten im Auszuge. Unter Benutzung der Sammlung von Euler und Eckler neu gesammelt und herausgegeben von Dr. E. Neuendorff und H. Schröer. Berlin, Weidmannsche Buchhandlung, 1912.

The *Neue Jahrbücher für die Turnkunst, Deutsche Turn-Zeitung,* and *Monatsschrift für das Turnwesen* (see p. 82).

The *Jahrbuch der Turnkunst* (see p. 108).

CHAPTER XIV.

THE PLAYGROUND MOVEMENT IN GERMANY.

THE beginnings of the playground movement in Germany can be traced back to a time when the Franco-Prussian War was a very recent memory, and its pioneers were men moved by the same spirit and motives which led Jahn to the Hasenheide sixty years before. In the summer of 1872 Konrad Koch[1] (1846–1911), a teacher in the Gymnasium (higher classical school) Martino-Katharineum in Brunswick, with his colleague, Hermann Corvinus, having

FIG. 29.—Konrad Koch (1846–1911).

in mind their own participation as schoolboys in the outdoor exercises of a Jahn club, began to take pupils on free Wednesday afternoons to St. Leonhardplatz, on the outskirts of the city, to practise a variety of running and ball games. Three years of experience with German games, such as *Barlaufen* (prisoners' base), *Kaiserball*, etc., revealed to them the need of something more highly organized, and of a sport which might be practised in the

[1] Born in Brunswick, attended for eight years the Gymnasium Martino-Katharineum, where his father was one of the teachers, studied classical and German philology at the universities of Göttingen, Berlin, and Leipzig, 1864–1867, and for the rest of his life taught Greek, Latin, middle high German, and history at the Gymnasium Martino-Katharineum, becoming *Oberlehrer* in 1874 and Professor in 1886. Consult *Jahrbuch für Volks-und Jungendspiele* 1912, pp. 238–245; *Monatsschrift für das Turnwesen*, **1**, 97–104; **30**, 241–245. For Hermann consult *Monatsschrift für das Turnwesen*, **6**, 321–329; **25**, 130–137; *Körper und Geist*, **14**, 421–427.

winter months. The teacher of gymnastics (*Turnlehrer*) at the *Gymnasium* was August Hermann (1835–1906), whose wife's sister conducted a flourishing private boarding school for girls in Brunswick and in its interest spent several months a year in England. Hermann's own house was a *pension* which usually contained a number of English boys, and Koch's father-in law, Dr. Med. Friedrich Reck, had observed with interest in his travels abroad the widespread popularity of active games in Great Britain.[1]   At Dr. Reck's suggestion Hermann therefore procured from England a football, and one day in October, 1874, threw it among the boys on the playground.   The history of the Rugby game in Germany dates from this moment.   American baseball was introduced in 1875, and English cricket in 1876, as summer games, and the steady increase in the number of players demonstrated the wisdom of the changed program.

Saturday afternoon had now been added to Wednesday's.   In the summer of 1878 the games were made an integral factor of the school life.   Certain classes were freed from other work on two afternoons a week (Thursday and Friday) in order that the pupils might engage regularly, the two teachers whose time had hitherto been given voluntarily to the task were now relieved from a part of their school duties and formally delegated to the duty, Mk. 200 a year was appropriated toward the cost of equipment, and in the spring of 1879 participation in the games was made obligatory for pupils in the lower and middle classes.   The rule was extended to cover the upper classes also in 1882.   The Gymnasium Martino-Katharineum thus became the first school in Germany to give to active games a place in the curriculum. In 1885 the *Realgymnasium* and the new Wilhelm-Gymnasium took the same step.   Other higher schools in the Duchy followed, and the movement reached the intermediate *Bürgerschulen* of the city in 1905, and the lower ones in 1908.

[1] When Thomas Arnold's fourteen years as head master at Rugby Public School were ended by his death in June of 1842, cricket was the recognized summer sport at the English public schools and at Oxford and Cambridge universities; rowing was firmly established as a fall and spring exercise at Eton College, and the Oxford-Cambridge boat race was an annual affair; football was regularly played at Rugby and others of the public schools; and continuous records of the "big-side runs" of the Rugby School Hare and Hounds—forerunners of the later track and field athletics —were already five years old.   By the time Thomas Hughes published his "Tom Brown's School Days," fifteen years later (April, 1857), all of the public schools had adopted football as the chief winter game, and the first steps looking toward organized track and field athletics as a recognized branch of public school and university sports had been taken.   The annual track meets between Oxford and Cambridge date from 1864.   The first of the annual Cambridge-Oxford contests in Rugby football was held in 1872, and two years later a similar series in the Association game began. ("Association football" dates from the publication of rules by the London Football Association, December 1, 1863.   The Rugby Football Union was organized in London, January 26, 1871.)

Skating competed with football for winter popularity, but cricket was still the favorite summer game. Koch, who later became the recognized psychologist and philosopher of the entire games movement in Germany, was impressed from the start with its fundamental educational value. Like Thomas Arnold, he attached great value to the influence of games on the emotions and the will, and was not satisfied with the too exclusively intellectual training of the schools. His "Die Erziehung zum Mute durch Turnen, Spiel und Sport,"[1] a book devoted to the psychical aspects of bodily exercise, deservedly ranks as a classic, and stands almost alone in its field.

Fig. 30.—August Hermann (1835–1906).

The German *Turnlehrer* held their eighth general convention at Brunswick, July 27–30, 1876.[2] August Hermann opened the morning session on the 28th with an address in which he urged the necessity of arousing an interest in competitive exercises and games if bodily exercise was ever to become a truly national custom in Germany, calling attention particularly to English experience and in conclusion referring to what had already been accomplished in Brunswick with English football and cricket. Dr. Reck described at length how he had himself seen all England at play, and not merely those of one class or age or sex. He also spoke of the value of such habits as a means of training the will and developing initiative.

[1] Berlin, R. Gaertner, 1900.
[2] Consult the *Deutsche Turn-Zeitung*, 1876, pp. 305–310 and 313–319; and *Neue Jahrbücher für die Turnkunst*, 1876, pp. 94–95, 145–150, 163–186, 241–247.

Others who took part in the debate (Kloss of Dresden and Jäger of Stuttgart) had been witnesses of the athletic sports of English residents in German cities. On Saturday, the 29th, pupils from the intermediate classes of the Gymnasium gave the visitors an impressive exhibition of their skill and interest in football and cricket on St. Leonhardplatz, under the direction of Hermann and Koch.

Five years later (November, 1881) the movement in favor of games and other outdoor sports, which had been slowly gaining headway among German teachers of gymnastics and educators in general, received a sudden impetus and gained a powerful champion, when Emil Hartwich (1843–1886), judge in the Prussian district court at Düsseldorf, issued his pamphlet "Woran wir leiden. Freie Betrachtungen und practische Vorschläge über unsere moderne Geistes-und Körperpflege in Volk und Schule."[1] Hartwich was the son of a leading pioneer in German railroad construction, and educated at the Friedrich-Wilhelmstädtische Gymnasium at Cologne (1856–1862) and the universities of Heidelberg and Berlin (1862–1865). After completing the required year of military service in a regiment of dragoons at Berlin he began to practise his profession of public magistrate, and became judge in the Düsseldorf court in 1873. By enthusiastic application in his leisure moments he had acquired skill in gymnastics, music and painting. Deeply impressed with the importance of the problems which modern education is called upon to solve, and convinced that the physical point of view, though fundamental, was too much neglected, he determined to undertake the task of agitation for reform.[2]

The pamphlet of 1881 was the first result of the decision. A second edition, enlarged, was published the following year, and later a third made its appearance. "Next to untarnished honor, health is the greatest good on earth." This is the motto with which he begins. While in England, the home of open-air sports, many an old man has a youthful look, the German schoolboy too often shows a pale, precocious face. What has become of the games which freshen body and soul alike, and the school excursions and long walks? Our modern pedagogy, he complains, has forgotten the great outdoors. With thirty hours or more a week given to mental training in stuffy classrooms, and only a pitiful two hours to gymnastics as the sole counterpoise, the harmonious balance between body and mind cannot fail to be disturbed. A sound body and good spirits must be recognized as of equal value with a well-trained mind. Give the morning to the mind, he says, and the afternoon to body and spirit, to what brings enjoyment and

---

[1] Düsseldorf, L. Voss & Co. Second edition, enlarged, 1882.

[2] Consult *Monatsschrift für das Turnwesen*, 1887, pp. 29 and 30, and *Neue Jahrbücher für die Turnkunst*, 1887, pp. 14–24.

strengthens the will to withstand the trials of everyday life. This quality of courage and good spirits is vastly more important than the training of the intellect now so excessively emphasized.

To coördinate and direct all efforts for improvement and reform Hartwich proposed the organization of a *Zentralverein für Körperpflege in Volk und Schule*—a permanent national body which should hold itself aloof from all political, sectarian and other factional discussions, should unite all classes of society for the common end, and should allow complete independence in the sections which it was to comprise and entire freedom in town and country were to be bound together by the common purpose to promote care of the body and its active exercise. The following divisions were suggested: (1) For gymnastics; (2) for skating; (3) for school interests; (4) for bathing, swimming and rowing; (5) for games and festivals suited to both old and young; (6) a section to serve as a propaganda working through the public press; and (7) a medical section.

The appearance of "Woran wir leiden," which was widely read and quoted throughout Germany, led at once to a lively discussion of the claims of the body and the value of open-air exercise, and to a great accession of popular interest in these subjects. Men of letters, government officials and others in high position rallied to the support of Hartwich, and Gustav von Gossler, Prussian minister of public worship and instruction, invited him to an interview (November 4, 1882). Meanwhile the *Zentralverein* became a reality —it was formed in Düsseldorf, March 6, 1882—and in this and the following year local societies (*Vereine für Körperpflege*) were organized in Witten, Bonn, Barmen and Hagen, in each case with an address from Hartwich as part of the program at the initial gathering.[1] Playgrounds were secured and equipped in Düsseldorf,[2] Bonn, Witten, Berlin (Park bei Treptow) and other cities; much continued to be written on school conditions in general and on brain forcing in particularly; and a number of handbooks of games made their appearance. Bremen and Chemnitz opened playgrounds in 1884, and public games were introduced in Dresden, Salzburg, Darmstadt and Frankfort-on-the-Main. At the sixth national *Turnfest* of the German *Turnerschaft*, in Dresden, July 19–21, 1885, there was an exhibition of games by schoolboys and -girls.

To keep members of the *Zentralverein* in touch with the movement and furnish newspapers with reports and items of information Hartwich had started a periodical, *Körper und Geist*, to be issued

---

[1] Hartwich's addresses were collected and published by M. Eichelsheim, city *Turnlehrer* in Düsseldorf, in 1883 under the title "Reden über die vernachlässigte leibliche Ausbildung unserer Jugend von Emil Hartwich" (Düsseldorf, L. Schwann). A second edition, enlarged, was published in 1884.

[2] Opened June 21, 1882. See *Neue Jahrbücher für die Turnkunst*, 1882, pp. 248 249, and *Monatsschrift für das Turnwesen*, 1882, p. 206.

at irregular intervals. Only five numbers were actually published, the first in the spring of 1883 and the last in April of 1886. In his address at the organization of the society he had referred to the educational value which the English attribute to their games, and to the obligatory school games in Brunswick. He wrote to Koch at Brunswick, requesting a few lines from him on the subject of English games for German playgrounds, having in mind already as part of the program for his *Volks-* and *Kinderfeste* competitions in running, swimming, throwing the spear and the discus, wrestling, football, cricket, etc. Koch replied under date of November 1, 1883, with a recital of his own experience.[1]

The *Vereine für Körperpflege* were largely confined to Rhenish Prussia and Westphalia, a fact explained by the support which newspapers in these provinces, and notably the *Kölnische Zeitung,* gave to the movement. The membership, in both size and character, and the sums contributed fell short of what had been expected, and proved that a considerable portion of the public remained to be won over. Some teachers of gymnastics were hearty and loyal in their coöperation, but not a few *Turnvereine* and leaders in the national *Turnerschaft* adopted an attitude of apathy, or of positive opposition. "Into the open" was the cry of Hartwich, and he seemed to them to ignore, or not to appreciate, the solid achievements of the followers of Jahn and Spiess. There were many, too, who protested against the importation of English games and athletic sports in seeming disparagement of German *Turnen* and native games. The early and tragic death of Hartwich—he was shot in a duel and died December 1, 1886—brought with it the collapse of the *Zentralverein,* for no other leader possessed of equal skill and courage came forward to take his place.

Elsewhere, in Germany, however, new adherents were at work, and the movement which had begun in Brunswick and been greatly extended by the Düsseldorf judge was soon to become national in its scope. One state, and that the leading one, had already given its official sanction. Gustav von Gossler (1838–1902), Prussian minister of public worship and instruction in the years 1881–1891, himself trained in gymnastics as a schoolboy in Potsdam and Königsberg, an expert fencer in his university days, a good oarsman and a strong swimmer and skater, had been an interested listener at the sessions of the ninth national convention of German teachers of gymnastics, held in Berlin, June 7–9, 1881, while he was still under-secretary. There the first morning was taken up by two papers which urged the necessity of systematic use of games and school excursions on foot as a supplement to formal gymnastics,

[1] The letter is published in *Neue Jahrbücher für die Turnkunst,* 1888, pp. 242–252.

and by a discussion which led to the adoption of recommendations to that effect.[1] In the following November Hartwich's pamphlet appeared, and a year later von Gossler, as we have seen, invited him to an interview; but before this took place the minister had already issued (October 27, 1882) his momentous "Order relating to the provision of playgrounds for the promotion of gymnastics in the open air and to stimulate participation in active games."[2]

He begins by saying that when gymnastics was first made an integral part of the instruction in higher and lower schools, effort was naturally directed toward securing room indoors where the exercises might be carried on without regard to season and weather. But the playground is not less valuable, and he sums up impressively the beneficial influence it may exert on the entire life of the pupil, concluding with these words: "The school must foster play as an expression of youthful life, salutary for body and mind, for heart and soul alike, along with the increase in physical strength and skill and the ethical effects which attend it, and this must be done not merely now and then, but as a matter of course and in a systematic way." Attempts in this direction have been few and scattered hitherto. He then refers to the books of GutsMuths and Jahn and to some recent works, mentions a number of suitable games, calls attention to certain articles which contain useful hints, and among them one of Koch's on the history and organization of the Brunswick school games, and suggests at some length practical ways of carrying out the purpose of the order. School excursions, swimming and skating are also recommended. Other ministerial orders and announcements which followed within the next few years touch upon every phase of gymnastics and games, and for girls as well as for boys and young men.

While the von Gossler *Spielerlass* of 1882 met with general approval and exerted a stimulating influence felt beyond the bounds of his own state, the immediate and visible results were disappointing. One experiment which it inspired was, however, momentous in its consequences. The scene was Görlitz, in Prussian Silesia, and the prime mover, soon to become a national figure, was Emil von Schenckendorff (1837–1915), formerly member of the city council and later member of the Prussian chamber of deputies. He had spent ten years in the army (1855–1865) and nine in the telegraph service (1867–1876), resigning from each on account of

---

[1] For reports of the convention consult *Neue Jahrbücher für die Turnkunst*, 1881, pp. 97–105, 208–212, 273–276; and *Deutsche Turn-Zeitung*, 1881, pp. 190, 257–260, 281–284, 301–304, 325–330.

[2] Printed in full in *Neue Jahrbücher für die Turnkunst*, 1882, pp. 409–412; *Monatsschrift für das Turnwesen*, 1882, pp. 321–325; Neuendorff and Schröer, "Verordnungen und amtliche Bekanntmachungen das Turnwesen in Preussen betreffend" (Berlin, Weidmannsche Buchhandlung, 1912), pp. 56–61.

impaired health, and having made his home in Görlitz occupied himself altogether, for the balance of his life, with public affairs in city, state and nation.[1]

In Sweden, in 1872, August Abrahamson (1817–1898) had opened a sloyd school for boys on his estate at Nääs, about eighteen miles from Gothenburg, under the direction of his nephew, Otto Salomon (1849–1907), and in the autumn of 1874 a training-school for teachers of that branch of education was added. Adolph Clauson-Kaas (1826–1906) had made societies for home industry

FIG. 31.—Emil Theodor Gustav von Schenckendorff (1837–1915).

popular in Denmark. Von Schenckendorff was familiar with both movements, and in his desire to provide some counteragent to the one-sided mental exertion of the schools organized in 1881 the Görlitz Manual Training Society (*Verein für Handfertigkeit*) and opened a workshop for boys. He was also, that same year, one of the founders of the German Central Committee for Manual Training and Home Industry (in 1886 the name was changed to *Deutscher Verein für Knabenhandarbeit*). As early as 1882 he was in communication with Hartwich at Düsseldorf, approving his efforts and asking advice with regard to the introduction of games among the young people of Görlitz. In 1883 he persuaded the Görlitz Manual Training Society to add this new form of activity to its program.

[1] Consult *Jahrbuch für Volks- und Jugendspiele*, 1915, pp. 1–26; *Körper und Geist* **16**, 33–41, and **24**, 4–16; and *Monatsschrift für das Turnwesen*, 1912, pp. 201–208, and 1915, pp. 129–137, 193–200.

With the hearty coöperation of his friend Gustav Ernst Eitner (1835–1905), director of the city *Gymnasium*, a beginning was made with boys from the lower classes of that school, who met for the purpose on Wednesday afternoons. Soon the pupils of the intermediate classes became interested, and in the spring of the following year the older boys, who viewed the innovation with indifference at the start, were gradually drawn into the ranks of players. *Oberturnlehrer* Friedrich Wilhelm Jordan (1842–1896) and several younger teachers in the *Gymnasium* assumed the direct oversight of the games. The next step was to make provision for the elementary schools, and thus the movement spread from year to year, and methods of organization and administration were perfected until not only the school children, but older boys and young men and even adults had been reached by the efforts of the society. Annual *Spielfeste* helped to make the playing of games more and more a matter of habit among the entire populace.[1]

An opportunity to bring the results of all this experience to the attention of German teachers generally was afforded by the fortieth national convention of philologists, held in Görlitz, October 1–5, 1889. Eitner realized that in spite of widespread desire for a revival of games in the schools few teachers were familiar with them, or knew how to set about introducing them among the children, and these in turn had forgotten how to play. He thought it would be of service to show the Görlitz plan in actual operation, and so arranged for an exhibition of games as a part of the program for the second afternoon. The applause which greeted the spectacle was gratifying. One of the visitors deplored the fact that in his home there was no one capable of introducing and directing a similar plan, and he therefore proposed that there should be started in Görlitz a teachers' course in games for such persons as were interested in the subject, in order to diffuse a knowledge of it more widely. Von Schenckendorff took up the idea with enthusiasm, readily secured the approval and support of Minister von Gossler, and it was arranged that Eitner should undertake the direction of such a course with the assistance of *Oberturnlehrer* Jordan.

After careful preparation on the part of these two men the first course was given during the week of June 9–14, 1890, and a second September 1–6. In the following year there were two more, June 22–27 and August 31–September 5. The total attendance for the four weeks, not counting about 30 who remained for a few days only, was 120 teachers, of whom 82 were from various parts of Prussia (Silesia 48, Posen 11, Pomerania 2, East Prussia 4, Brandenburg 3, Hanover 4, the province of Saxony 2, Westphalia 1,

---

[1] Consult Eitner's own account in *Jahrbuch für Volks- und Jugendspiele*, 1892, pp. 59–61 and 79–82.

Hesse-Nassau 3, and the Rhine province 4), 2 from Baden, 1 each from Saxony, Oldenburg, Lauenburg, Thuringia and Anhalt, 30 from Austria (13 of these from Vienna), and 1 from Russia. There was no tuition fee. Each morning of the week Eitner lectured for an hour on the theory of games in general and discussed individual ones in some detail, with demonstrations of the apparatus used, until about 60 had been covered, including 34 ball games. Then followed two hours of practice under Jordan, and in the afternoons between four and six o'clock there was a demonstration of the methods employed in the different city schools. A much wider audience was reached by Eitner's manual of games,[1] six editions of which were called for in the year of publication (1890), a seventh in 1891 and an eighth in 1893.

Meanwhile other measures looking toward nationwide agitation and instruction were being taken. As a preliminary step it was desirable to ascertain the exact present status of the games movement in Germany, and for the collection and tabulation of such statistical information von Schenckendorff was able to secure the services of a man who had already made an important contribution in the realm of physical education. Hermann Raydt (1851–1914), born in the Prussian province of Hanover, educated in the Lingen *Gymnasium* of which his father was rector and in the Universities of Berlin, Heidelberg and Göttingen, was from 1878 until 1892 teacher (*Oberlehrer*) in the *Gelehrtenschule* at Ratzeburg, a town twelve miles southeast of Lübeck. In 1886, as the first appointee under the terms of the Bismarck-Schönhausen foundation for the advancement of teaching, he travelled in England and Scotland, studying especially the methods of education and manner of life in the English public schools. The results of his observations were embodied in an interesting and stimulating volume[2] published three years later, in which he proposes an adaptation of the English playground to German school conditions. The book appeared at an opportune moment and met with a favorable reception everywhere. The Prussian ministry of instruction warmly recommended it to the attention of all higher schools and teachers' colleges. It also brought Raydt into communication with von Schenckendorff, who persuaded him to undertake the task already mentioned. The Görlitz Society for the Promotion of Manual Training and School Games bore the expense of the investigation, and in April of 1890 circulars were sent out to all German cities with a population of

---

[1] "Die Jugendspiele. Ein Leitfaden bei der Einführung und Übung von Turn- und Jugendspielen, verfasst von Dr. Eitner, Gymnasialdirektor in Görlitz." Kreuz- nach und Leipzig, R. Voigtländer, 1890.

[2] "Ein gesunder Geist in einem gesundent Körper. Englische Schulbilder in deutschem Rahmen nach einer Studienreise aus der Bismarck-Schönhausen Stiftung geschildert von H. Raydt, Subrektor in Ratzeburg." Hannover, Carl Meyer, 1889.

8000 or more, asking what had already been done in the way of games and playgrounds, and whether the authorities were inclined to welcome their introduction. Two hundred and seventy-three replies were received. Raydt studied these carefully and made them the basis of another volume[1] which appeared early in the following year.

The time for organized endeavor on a large scale 'had evidently arrived. Von Schenckendorff therefore invited a number of prominent men—leaders in the German *Turnerschaft*, pioneers in the games movement, and persons of influence—to meet in Berlin on May 21, 1891, and then and there the "Central Committee for the Promotion of Games in Germany" (*Der Zentral-Ausschuss zur Förderung der Volks- und Jugendspiele in Deutschland*) was formed. The thirteen in actual attendance included Director Bier of the Dresden *Turnlehrer-Bildungsanstalt*, *Unterrichtsdirigent* Euler of the Berlin *Turnlehrer-Bildungsnastalt*, Goetz and F. A. Schmidt of the Committee of the *Deutsche Turnerschaft*, Koch and Hermann from Brunswick, Raydt from Ratzeburg, von Schenckendorff and teachers or public officials from Hamburg, Hannover, Magdeburg, Rendsburg and Stralsund. After an opening address by von Schenckendorff, and a general exchange of views it was agreed that the committee type of organization, with great freedom of action, was peferable to an association bound by a constitution and a fixed program. Three subcommittees of seven members each were decided upon, and the chairmen of these together with the officers of the Central Committee were to constitute a board of directors. Von Schenckendorff was the unanimous choice for chairman of the Central Committee, Schmidt of Bonn was elected vice-chairman, Raydt corresponding secretary or business manager, Koch treasurer, Eitner of Görlitz chairman of the sub-committee on games for boys, Hermann of Brunswick chairman of the sub-committee on games for girls, and Schmidt of Bonn chairman of the sub-committee on games for older persons (*Volksspiele*). The Central Committee itself, in its original form, was composed of thirty-five men, whose names are attached to the formal summons to the German people (*"Aufruf zur Förderung der Jugend- und Volksspiele in Deutschland"*) prepared at the Berlin meeting.[2]

A good idea of the methods adopted by the Central Committee, and the results of its work during the twenty years 1891–1911,

---

[1] "Die deutschen Städte und das Jugendspiel. Nach den amtlichen Berichten der Städte bearbeitet von Konrektor H. Raydt in Ratzeburg." Hannover-Linden, Karl Manz, 1891.

[2] This summons, and von Schenckendorff's account of the formation and plan of organization of the Central Committee, are contained in the first year-book of the Committee ("Über Jugend- und Volksspiele," Hannover-Linden, 1892), pp. 103–111. The miuntes of the Berlin meeting were printed in *Körper und Geist*, **16**, 41–47 (May 21, 1907).

can be gained from a review of that period which von Schenckendorff, still chairman, prepared and published in 1912.[1] The Committee endeavored from the start to supplement and support the
work of individuals or local organizations and to prepare the way
for the actual introductions of games into any community. Its
membership was limited to one hundred, selected from men and
women in all parts of the empire who have had experience and met
with success in the field of physical education. Besides games in
the narrower sense, it aimed to foster all forms of active exercise in
the open air, such as excursions on foot, swimming, rowing, skating, skeeing, bob-sledding, etc. There were the following sub-com-
mittees in 1912: (1) Technical, (2) on public exhibitions of games
(*Jugend- und Volksfeste*), (3) on the German universities, (4) on
continuation and professional schools, (5) on promotion of national
defense (*Wehrkraft*) through education, (6) on country children and
youth, (7) on excursions (*Wandern*) and winter exercises in the open
air, and (8) on measures for increasing the physical fitness of girls
and women. The activities of the Central Committee may be classified in three main groups, as follows: Information, constructive
work proper, and indirect measures.

Information. To bring its work to the attention of the public
at large the Committee made use of the organs which moulded
and gave expression to public opinion, *i. e.*, about three hundred
newspapers and other periodicals—political, social, pedagogical and
medical, as well as those published in the interest of physical education and athletic sports. It possessed also two organs of its
own, the semi-monthly *Körper und Geist*, started in 1892 (April 1)
under the title *Zeitschrift für Turnen und Jugendspiel*,[2] and a year-
book[3] averaging more than three hundred pages. In addition to
these a long list of pamphlets and small volumes were issued. The
first of a series of national congresses in the interest of games was
held in Berlin, February 3 and 4, 1894, and others have followed
in different parts of the empire, at intervals of one or two years.[4]
Persons whose official position gave them an influence which might
be of great value in furthering the objects of the Committee were

---

[1] *Jahrbuch für Volks- und Jugendspiele*, 1912, pp. 1–11. Printed also in *Monatsschrift für das Turnwesen*, 1912, pp. 201–208.

[2] Ten volumes appeared under the latter title, and volume 11, beginning April 1,
1902, bears the new name.

[3] *Jahrbuch für Volks- und Jugendspiele*. The first number is that for 1892. Both
organs are published by B. G. Teubner, Leipzig and Berlin.

[4] (2) Munich, July 10–13, 1896; (3) Bonn, July 2 and 3, 1898; (4) Königsberg,
June 25 and 26, 1899; (5) Nuremberg, July 7 and 8, 1901; (6) Dresden, July 5–7,
1903; (7) Frankfurt, September 15–18, 1905; (8) Strasburg, July 6 and 7, 1907;
(9) Kiel, July 19–21, 1908; (10) Gleiwitz, July 2–5, 1909; (11) Barmen, July 1–4, 1910;
(12) Dresden, July 1 and 2, 1911; (13) Heidelberg, June 28–July 1, 1912; (14) Stettin,
June 28–30, 1913; (15) Altona, June 19–22, 1914.

approached directly. In this way permanent relations were established with about five thousand town and city authorities, district magistrates and school inspectors, provincial school commissioners, heads of institutions for the training of teachers and members of state ministries of instruction.

Constructive Work Proper. Here belongs first of all the arranging of courses for men and women teachers who wish to prepare themselves as playground leaders. By the end of 1904, *i. e.*, in fifteen years if we include the Görlitz courses of 1890 and 1891, a total of 175 courses for men had been held in 54 different places, with 580 participants, and 74 for women in 20 places, with 2814 participants. For the entire period 1890–1911 the totals were 409 courses to 14,269 men, and 206 courses to 6287 women.[1] In general the Görlitz pattern, as already described, was followed. There were no fees for instruction, and the persons in charge of the work gave their services in every case. Since 1905 the Prussian school authorities have also offered playground courses (about 60,000 teachers had been trained in them up to the time when von Schenckendorff wrote his review), and others have been given at the various state normal schools of gymnastics. Next in importance to the demand for competent leaders was that for authoritative descriptions of the most important games, with the rules which govern them. The technical committee met this need by issuing and frequently revising a series of pocket-size booklets, in board covers, which sell for about five cents each and have become the standard guides on nearly all the German playgrounds. By 1912 there were twelve of these little volumes, covering sixteen games. The Central Committee also published ten booklets ("Kleine Schriften") containing information and suggestions on such subjects as how to set about introducing games into a community, the management of competitive and other exercises for public exhibitions, active games for girls, games at the German universities, winter sports, excursions on foot, *Geländespiele*, games for use in the army, etc.

The World War then came on and following it the Deutsches Reichsausschuss für Leibesübungen was formed to replace the committee and to take charge of all popular physical training outside of the schools, including the Olympic Games, and the new high school was formed under their auspices. They supervise courses also at the Spandau School, as well as in other states of Germany besides Prussia. Their Committee has charge of the stadium at Berlin, in the use of which all parties have equal rights. The new sports forum, now under construction, is to replace the stadium for

[1] These are the official figures. Dr. F. A. Schmidt, in a review of "Zwanzig Jahre Spielkurse" on pp. 143–152 of the 1911 *Jahrbuch für Volks- und Jugendspiele*, gives the totals as 14,301 men and 6233 women.

the students of the Hochschule, and to provide laboratories and lecture rooms as well, for students who are to be teachers.   These courses attract, as well, physicians, sculptors and scholars.   In this they approach the ideal that was characteristic of the Greek gymnasium.[1]

The free exercises given are much influenced by the work of Neils Bukh of Denmark, referred to elsewhere.

In the University of Berlin, and all other German Universities, a movement was started in 1920, to make Physical training compulsory for at least two years and this is now almost universal. Athletic games and gymnastics are both on the program, although

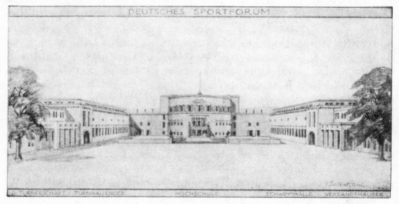

FIG. 32.—The new sports forum, showing the lecture room, swimming pool (right), gymnasium (left) and turnplatz (foreground).

a wide option is allowed, following the American custom, and the instructors are educated men and are given academic rank.

Indirect Measures.   For a number of years the Committee worked energetically to bring about the inaguration of periodical German *Nationalfeste*, which should serve as an inspiration and pattern for smaller public exhibitions (*Jugend- und Volksfeste*) all over the country, and at the same time stimulate national spirit.   Growing opposition on the part of the German *Turnerschaft*, which saw in such occasions a menace to the success of its own quadrennial *Turnfeste*, together with other difficulties, finally led to the abandonment of the plan.   The Committee then sought to work from the bottom

---

[1] Athletic competition began to attract attention as early as 1896, and became more and more popular, attracting members from the Turners Society.   In 1913 Carl Deim visited the United States and took back with him, Alva Krantzlein, as coach for the German athletes who were expected to take part in the Olympic Games of 1916, for which a new stadium had been built.

up, by encouraging regular exhibitions with competitive sports in separate localities. The conviction that national efficiency (*Volks-kraft*) and national defense (*Wehrkraft*) are merely different expressions of the same thing, and that whatever promotes or disturbs the one affects the other similarly, led to careful study of the latter question. A volume of some size ("Wehrkraft durch Erziehung"), published in 1904, in place of the usual year-book, sets forth educational measures which foster *Wehrkraft* by increasing *Volkskraft*, and a special "Committee of Defense" (Ausschuss zur Förderung der Wehrkraft durch Erziehung) has met repeatedly to discuss the subject, with representatives of the Prussian war ministry and the head of the general staff present on one occasion (March 12, 1911). Games were incorporated in the course of military gymnastics by imperial order of May, 1910, and the Committee's manual ("Militärisches Spielbuch") is now in use everywhere.

Looking back over twenty years of effort along these varied lines of activity, von Schenckendorff was forced to admit that much remained to be accomplished. In the schools, while play-afternoons with voluntary attendance had spread widely, the obligatory play-afternoon on a par with required instruction in gymnastic had been introduced only here and there. Brunswick, Würtemberg, Baden and Saxony are farthest advanced in this respect. The continuation schools have taken only the first step looking toward physical development. At the universities there is increased interest in gymnastics and atheltic sports, but facilities for their practice are still inadequate. The state has not met its responsibility in the matter of building gymnasia, fitting up playgrounds and providing the means for swimming, rowing and the like.

Von Schenckendorff, the foremost figure in the German playground movement, died March 1, 1915, and was succeeded as chairman of the Central Committee by Dr. F. A. Schmidt of Bonn, the former vice-chairman. Of the other members of the original board of directors, Raydt died December 6, 1914, Koch April 13, 1911, Eitner September 4, 1905, and Hermann February 20, 1906. The board in 1915 was constituted as follows: Chairman, Schmidt; corresponding secretary, Kohlrausch of Hanover (since Raydt's death); treasurer, Dominicus of Berlin-Schöneberg (following Koch); and Hagen of Schmalkalden, Sickinger of Mannheim and Neuendorff of Mühlheim-on-the-Ruhr.

CHAPTER XV.

PER HENRIK LING, FATHER OF PHYSICAL EDUCATION IN SWEDEN.

FOR more than a century gymnastics in Sweden has been undergoing development along three more or less distinct lines, educational, military and medical, *i. e.*, as an integral factor in school life, as an agent in the training of men for the army and navy, and as a therapeutic measure. The Royal Central Institute of Gymnastics at Stockholm, where teachers of these various branches receive their preparation, was opened in 1814, and its originator and first director (1814–1839) was Per Henrik Ling. He was born November 15, 1776, in Småland, one of the southern provinces

FIG. 33.—Per Henrik Ling (1776–1839).

where his ancestors had lived for seven generations or more. Up to the time of his grandfather, Mathias Månsson (1687–1748), they had belonged to the peasant class; but this man, taking the name Ling, prepared himself for the ministry and married a clergyman's daughter. His son, Lars Peter Ling (1723–1780), who followed the same calling, was settled in the country parish of Ljunga, in Kronoberg county and died there when Per Henrik, the youngest of six children, was only four years of age. A year and a half later the mother, a great granddaughter of the famous Swedish author Olof Rudbeck and herself a woman of superior intelligence, married the new pastor, but died in 1789.[1]

These early bereavements, acting on the serious, sensitive, and

[1] E. Wrangel in *Lunds Universitets Årsskrift*, **9** (1913), Nr. 6; and Richard J. Cyriax in *Svenska Gymnastiken i In- och Utlandet*, **9**, 92–94 (1913).

affectionate nature of the boy, and in spite of his stepfather's watchful care, gave a touch of sadness to the whole period of his childhood, to which he rarely referred in later years, and then only in the fewest possible words. The romantic scenery about his home must have heightened this effect, besides producing others of its own. The church and parsonage stood near the border of a lake encircled by forests, and all around stretched desolate heath, a strange jumble of hills and broken rocks, swamps and reedy lakes, and forests of pine and deciduous trees with here and there a cleared space in their midst. In 1784 he left these scenes to attend the *läroverk* (higher classical school) in Vexiö, capital of the same district, where the botanist Linnæus had studied sixty years before. Here he gave evidence of rich mental gifts, a strong will, and a fondness for independent and original thinking and acting; but in November of 1792, taking part in certain boyish pranks, he broke a pane of glass in the rector's house one Sunday morning, and left the school rather than accept the harsh terms imposed as the condition of his reinstatement. In February of the next year, however, upon furnishing proof of repentance, continued progress in his studies, and good conduct meanwhile, he received from the rector a certificate admitting to the university in Lund.[1]

The young Ling was registered as a student in the Småland *nation* at Lund—the "nations" are provincial clubs at the Swedish universities, and each student is expected to enroll himself in one of them, according to his birthplace—on April 19,1793, and remained there during the spring and fall semesters. In September of 1796 he wrote to Lund from Stockholm requesting a university certificate, and on the 22nd of the following November applied for a clerkship in one of the city offices at the capital, where an older brother, Carl, was already installed in a similar position. Two days later he received the appointment. April 9, 1797, in a letter to his stepfather, he refers to "these years" in Stockholm, and tells of private lessons in French and German which he is giving to bookkeepers outside of office hours. Although he registered with the Småland nation at Upsala, December 21, 1797, and took out his certificate there on June 5, 1799, he seems never to have attended that university through an entire semester, and there is no record of the theological examination which he is reported to have passed on the former date.[2]

It will be seen that not much is definitely known, then, regarding his life in the years 1794–1799. It was plainly a time of poverty and struggle, and it is not strange that even the members of his own family and his nearest friends learned little or nothing of its secrets from his lips. By the time he left Stockholm for Copen-

[1] Westerblad 1904, p. 6.   [2] Ibid., p. 7.

hagen, in the summer of 1799, he was able to speak French, German, and English—the first of the three with especial ease—and this fact alone may explain the legend of extensive wanderings on the Continent and in England. He possessed, however, a quick mind and undoubted talent for language, and was a diligent and enthusiastic student of any subject that aroused his interst. Moreover, it was not necessary to leave Sweden in order to find natives of those countries with whom he might converse, and it now seems probable that he resided at first near Stockholm as private tutor and later in that city itself as clerk during most or all of the period in question. Although there is nothing impossible in the frequently repeated story of travel and military service in foreign parts, but very little direct evidence has been urged in its support.[1]

In July of 1799 Ling arrived at Copenhagen, and remained in the Danish capital for more than five years, until September or October of 1804. According to his own statement he entered the university there March 27, 1801. Although he was voluntarily enrolled on the side of the Danes when Nelson and his English fleet, by the battle fought in Copenhagen harbor April 2, 1801, broke up the Northern Alliance, the company to which he belonged was not brought into action on that occasion. Linguistic studies continued to engross his mind at first. He worked diligently in the Royal Library, took every opportunity to extend his knowledge by conversation with foreigners, and acquired complete mastery of the Danish language, both written and spoken. Afterward his attention became transferred from language to literature. Schelling, the distinguished Jena professor and the favorite philosopher of the Romantic school of writers in Germany, was then at the height of his fame. Among his enthusiastic auditors had been a young Norwegian, Henrik Steffens, who appeared in Copenhagen in 1802, full of the new doctrines, and began to lecture there on philosophy and on Goethe. Through him Oehlenschläger, soon to be hailed as Denmark's foremost poet, caught the spirit of the Romantic movement and began to breathe new life into the old Norse mythology, rousing in the breasts of his countrymen a feeling of Scandinavian nationality. These men introduced Ling to the treasure-house of the Eddas and the Northern sagas, whose gods and heroes were thenceforth never absent from his thought. After composing short poems in French, German, and Danish, and translating into Swedish the "Balders Död" (Balder's Death) of Johannes Evald, the chief lyric poet of

---

[1] The story appears, along with other statements unsupported or flatly contradicted by later investigations, in Atterbom's address before the Swedish Academy May 29, 1840 (Proceedings **20**, 82–202), von Beskow's memoir of 1859 (pp. vi and vii), and Georgii's "Biographical Sketch" of 1854 (p. 2). On the contrary see Törngren in *Tidskrift i Gymnastik*, **4**, 415 (1896), Westerblad 1904 pp. 7–12, and Norlander in *Lunds Universitets Årsskrift*, **9** (1913).

Denmark, he wrote himself, in Danish, a three-act comedy, *Den Misundelige* (The Envious Man), which was published in Copenhagen in 1804. Here also he conceived the plan of his later dramatic works, designed to set forth momentous epochs in Swedish history. "Eylif the Goth," printed in Stockholm in 1814, was written at this period, and reveals his desire to revive in the rising generation the old Norse vigor.

Perhaps it was the opportunity afforded for practice in a foreign language that first attracted Ling to the fencing school in Copenhagen conducted by two French *émigrés*, Beuerneir and the Chevalier de Montrichard. For three years he continued to frequent the place, and made such progress that Montrichard gave him a paper which certified to his great skill with the foil and his ability to give instruction in the art. There is a story that Ling had suffered from gout in the arm, as one result of the privations to which he was constantly subjected, and finding the case much relieved by his fencing, was thus led to study the effects of exercise in general. At any rate, he visited the private gymnasium which Nachtegall had started in Copenhagen in the fall of 1799 (see page 181). GutsMuths's "Gymnastics for the Young" appeared in 1793 and Hjort's translation into Danish six years later, and two volumes of Vieth's "Encyclopedia of Bodily Exercises" were published at this time; but how much Ling was indebted to these German sources for inspiration and suggestion is purely a matter of conjecture.[1]

In the fall of 1804 he returned to Sweden, to act as substitute for the aged fencing-master at the University of Lund. The latter died shortly after his arrival, and Ling, who had applied for the position December 8, was appointed his successor, at a small salary. Writing to a Copenhagen friend December 28th he says that the fencing-master at a Swedish university must be able to give instruction in vaulting the horse, and he wishes therefore to have a good vaulting buck sent him. A riding-school, also, is about to be opened, and his assistance is wanted there. Though he has almost entirely lost his skill in that art he is confident that practice will to some extent restore it. At that time gymnastics proper was unknown in Sweden, but Ling soon arranged apparatus for general exercise, and some years later, when a new university building had been completed, he was allowed to use an older one for this purpose and as a fencing hall.[2] In 1806 he began to apply himself to the

---

[1] The chief authority for this Copenhagen period is E. C. Werlauff's "Bidrag til P. H. Lings Biographie," in *Frey: Tidskrift för Vetenskap och Kunst* (Upsala), 1848, pp. 92–105. Werlauff (1781–1871), later well known as historian and teacher in the University, was employed in the Royal Liberty at the time of Ling's sojourn in Denmark and became his close friend. See also Westerblad 1904, pp. 13–21.

[2] See Carl Norlander, "Per Henrik Lings första Gymnastik- och Fäktsal med dithörande redskap" (Lund. Ph. Lindstedts Univ. Bokhandel, 1908).

study of anatomy and physiology. A year later he had worked out a system of bayonet fencing and was practising it with his pupils. He seems to have won the respect and esteem of teachers and students alike. The new exercises became very popular, and it was not long before interest in his fencing method, a simplification of the French, and in his gymnastics as well, spread beyond the bounds of Lund. Invitations to introduce the double art were received from Gothenburg, Malmö, and Christianstad, and in the first and second of these cities, at least, he gave instructions repeatedly during the course of the long summer vacations. Thus Gothenburg papers of July 9 and 10, 1807, announce his presence there for six weeks to give instruction "in all parts of the art of fencing and in gymnastics;" another of July 25, 1809, informs the public that he will remain three months to teach fencing, gymnastics, and swimming; and again July 5, 1811, he gives notice that until the middle of August he will receive pupils in sabre and foil fencing and gymnastics. On the occasion of this last visit arangements were also made to have him give instruction in "the art of swimming and other gymnastic exercises" to certain poor children of the city.

Ling remained eight years in Lund. In 1809 he married Sofia Maria Rosenqvist, and a daughter, Jetta, was born April 8th of the following year. "Agne," a tragedy in five acts, his most successful dramatic work, was printed there in 1812, and a year after his death was presented on the stage in Stockholm at the opening of the new theater. The condition of Sweden just at this time was a desperate one. Gustavus IV had allowed intense hatred of Napoleon to draw him into the great coalition of 1805 (the third, formed by England, Russia, Austria and Sweden), and as a consequence French troops had occupied Swedish Pomerania and in 1807 had taken Stralsund and Rügen, the last of the Swedish possessions south of the Baltic. By opening his ports to English vessels the King next incurred the enmity of Russia, whose troops invaded and conquered the whole of Finland in 1808, and so deprived the Swedes of territory which had been theirs for centuries. Gustavus was meanwhile deserted by his English allies, his armies were driven back from Norway, and the Danes invaded the southern provinces. In 1809 he was dethroned, and succeeded by his uncle, Charles XIII. One of Ling's poems, "Gylfe" (1810, 1812, 1816), deals with this loss of Finland, which the Swedes bitterly deplored, and shows how intense was his patriotism and his hatred of Russia. We have here the reason for his desire to see his countrymen strong in body and soul, and hence prepared to meet the enemy. This was the inspiring motive of his poems and his gymnastics alike, though in the latter he saw a means of restoring health, as well as developing the race and defending the fatherland. One who visited him in Lund in

1812 refers to his enthusiasm and to the system introduced into his methods of instruction. During these eight years he had been thinking out the principles upon which his later work was based, seeking first of all to understand the human body and discover its needs, and then to select and apply his exercises intelligently, with these needs in view. Nachtegall, in Copenhagen, had already begun to train teachers of gymnastics for the army and the schools of Denmark, and now Ling conceived the idea of opening in Stockholm a central training school from which all Sweden should be supplied with teachers of the new art.

With this plan in mind he went up to the capital early in 1813, applying first for the position of fencing-master in the Royal Military Academy at Karlberg, just outside the city to the northwest, and then, on January 29th, handing in to the recently appointed Committee on Education a written proposal of the new institution. He refers to what he has already accomplished in Lund, Malmö, and Gothenburg, explains his purpose in seeking to make Stockholm a center of influence for the physical training of the young, and asks government approval and support for the project. To the secretary of the Committee, Jakob Alderbeth, he brought a letter of introduction (dated January 15, 1813) from Esaias Tegnér, at that time a teacher in the University at Lund, who had roused the Swedes in 1808 by his "War Song for the Militia of Scania," three years later won for himself national fame and the great prize of the Swedish Academy by his patriotic poem "Svea," and was soon to receive worldwide recognition as the author of "Frithiofs Saga" (1825) Ling was already favorably known for his own literary labors, and appears to have been fortunate in his Stockholm quest from the start. He was given the Karlberg position, at a salary of 250 rix-dollars and lodging; the Committee received his proposal February 1st, and the same day reported the matter to the King with its strong recommendation; and a royal letter of May 5th formally approved the plan. Ling was to receive a salary of 500 rix-dollars as director of the school, an annual allowance of 100 more to cover the rent of a room for his exercises, and a single grant of 400 rix-dollars for the purchase of equipment. The salary was doubled in 1830, and before his death was raised again to 2000 rix-dollars. The school was opened in 1814, and at the Committee's suggestion the King gave it some time later the name it still bears—The Royal Central Institute of Gymnastics (*Kongl. Gymnastiska Central-Institutet*).[1]

In the northern suburb Norrmalm, at what is now the corner of

---

[1] Kungl. Gymnastiska Centralinstitutets Historia 1813–1913. Med Anledning av Institutets Hundraårsdag utgiven af dess Lärarekollegium. Stockholm, P. A. Norstedt & Söner, 1913.

Hamn-Gatan and Beridarebans-Gatan and on the site ever since occupied, Ling equipped the necessary rooms—a gymnasium, a fencing hall, and others—in some old buildings which had once belonged to a cannon-foundry. Soon considerable improvements were possible, for in a letter dated December 13, 1815, the King informed the Committee that a further grant of 9800 rix-dollars had been made, in order to provide for the better housing of the Institute and its director. The next fall means were furnished for an assistant, and others were added from time to time until in 1830 the personnel included, besides the director, a head teacher and two ordinary teachers. Lars Gabriel Branting, who had already been his assistant for a year at Karlberg, became second teacher at the Institute in 1818, and head teacher in 1830; Carl August Georgii was made extra teacher in 1829 and regular teacher six years later; and Gustav Nyblæus joined the staff as assistant teacher in 1838.

Ling believed that gymnastics had a rightful place in education, medicine, and national defence, and almost from the start instruction was accordingly given in the three corresponding branches, educational, medical and military gymnastics. He continued to teach fencing to the cadets at Karlberg until 1825, and on the 4th of December, 1821, was also appointed instructor in gymnastics and fencing at the Artillery School in Marieberg, about equally distant to the southwest, in the latter capacity receiving a salary of 300 rix-dollars. In 1810 the Swedish Diet had elected Bernadotte, one of Napoleon's marshals, to succeed the childless King Charles XIII. He assumed the title Crown Prince at once, and from 1818 to 1844 reigned as Charles XIV. Quick to see the importance of Ling's work for the army, he had officers detailed to complete the course at the Institute and afterward employed to teach gymnastics and bayonet fencing to the rank and file. Soldiers from cavalry and artillery regiments in the city were also sent to the school to receive practical instruction in the same arts, and Branting and Ling were allowed to introduce them among the troops assembled in the various training camps. The later order giving these exercises a place in all Swedish regiments did not meet with a cordial reception at the start; but afterward, when it was learned that French and Prussian soldiers were being drilled in bayonet fencing, investigation and comparison led to the choice of Ling's method in preference to either of the others, and thus won for it a somewhat tardy recognition. In 1836 he published a manual of gymnastics (*Reglemente för Gymnastik*) and another of bayonet fencing (*Reglemente för Bajonettfäktning*) for use in the army, and in 1838 a small handbook covering both subjects (*Soldat-Undervisning i Gymnastik och Bajonettfäktning*). In view of the general absence of well-equipped gymnasia and teachers thoroughly trained in the system he found it necessary to limit the exercises to simple forms, and to such as require little or no apparatus.

Medical gymnastics he had begun to develop after the first year in Stockholm. The new ideas not unnaturally aroused much bitter opposition on the part of conservative physicians, but he went his way nevertheless, and was content to let the future determine the value of his method of treatment. His school gymnastics comprised only a few strong movements, in which the pupil himself and his fellows constituted the most important apparatus. Swedish educational gymnastics in its present form is a comparatively recent growth, and its introduction in the elementary schools of the state and in schools for girls was not brought about until long after Ling's death. The first law requiring physical training in the secondary schools for boys was published in 1820.

In spite of his regular duties as director and teacher, Ling's literary activity was unceasing. For some years he belonged to the Gothic Society, organized by Tegnér in 1811, and the moral support of its distinguished members was of no slight assistance in the long struggle to win recognition for his work at the Institute and to see it firmly established in spite of small beginnings and scant resources. In 1816 he delivered public lectures on the Northern Myths. Three years later appeared his "Symbolism of the Eddas, for the Unlearned," a prose work; and his "Asarne" (the Aesir, or Northern gods), including the entire mythology and ancient legendary history of the Scandinavian race, first published in 1816, was reissued in revised and more complete form in 1833, winning for him the great prize of the Swedish Academy. This august body of eighteen scholars, created by Gustavus III in 1786 after the pattern of the French Academy, paid him the further tribute of election to a seat in its midst, and he was accordingly made a member by the King in 1835. He was also given the title Professor, and decorated with the Order of the North Star. A long series of dramatic and other poetical works was added to those already mentioned, so that his collected writings[1] fill three large volumes, of whose more than 2500 pages only about 350 have to do with gymnastics.

Ling's first wife died in 1817, and he had previously lost two sons, leaving him only the daughter Jetta. About two years later he married Charlotta Catharina Nettelbladt (1798–1889). Of their seven children only five survived him, and three of these became teachers of gymnastics—Hjalmar (1820–1886) and Hildur (1825–

---

[1] Samlade Arbeten af P. H. Ling. Utgifne under ledning af Bernhard von Beskow. Stockholm, Adolf Bonnier, 1859–1866. Pp. 433–786 of vol 3 were also published separately, under the title "P. H. Lings Gymnastiska Skrifter. Aftryck ur Lings Samlade Arbeten" (Stockholm, Adolf Bonnier, 1866).

1884) at the Institute, and Wendla (1834–1911) both there and at two normal schools for women. After some years of impaired health, his own death occurred in 1839, on the 3d of May. He was buried at Annelund, a few miles north of the city, where he owned some property, and the grave, on a high bank overlooking Brunns-viken, a bay of Lake Mälaren, is now marked by a memorial stone erected by friends in 1848. Branting and Georgii were the men he considered best fitted to carry on his work. The task of arranging his literary remains he laid upon the latter of the two in company with Dr. P. J. Liedbeck (1802–1876), who had been one of his pupils and afterward taught anatomy at the Institute and had married his daughter Jetta in 1833. The year after his death they

Fig. 34.—Ling's grave at Annelund, near Stockholm.

accordingly published, in the incomplete and often fragmentary form in which he had left it, his "General Principles of Gymnastics,"[1] a treatise begun as far back as 1831. After an opening section devoted to the laws of the human organism, the book takes up, in order, the principles of educational, military, medical, and esthetic gymnastics, and closes with a few pages of miscellaneous suggestions and comment. It is a small volume of less than 250 pages, and like the rest of Ling's writings possesses little of present interest to any but the student of history. As one of his successors at the Institute

[1] Gymnastikens allmänna Grunder af Ling, dels af Författaren, dels enligt dess yttersta vilja, efter dess död, redigerade och på trycket utgifna. Upsala, Leffler & Sebell, 1840. On Ling's writings see Kåre Teilnann. "Lings Gymnastik og dens udvikling," in *Gymnastisk Selskabs Aarsskrift* 1912 (Copenhagen, H. Hagerup, 1913), pp. 65–134; C. A. Westerblad, "Den Lingska Gymnastiken i dess upphofsmans dagar" (Stockholm, P. A. Norstedt & Söner, 1913); and also Dr. E. M. Hartwell in the *American Physical Education Review* 1 (1896). 1–13 (Reprinted in Report of the United States Commissioner of Education for the year 1898–99, 1, pp. 539–546).

has said, his greatest service to gymnastics was the attempt to give it a scientific basis, and it must therefore change and develop with every advance in the sciences upon which it rests.

BIBLIOGRAPHY.

All the earlier sketches of Ling's life must now be viewed in the light of recent critical studies by Carl August Westerblad, of Upsala, and particularly his "Pehr Henrik Ling: en lefnadsteckning och några synpunkter" (Stockholm, P. A. Norstedt & Söner, 1904). His later discussion of "The Ling Gymnastics in the Days of Its Founder" (1913) has just been mentioned in a footnote. To other articles referred to in footnotes should be added one by Jetta Ling Liedbeck in *Tidskrift i Gymnastik* **3**, 870–891 (1893), originally published in *Aftonbladet* (Stockholm) in 1852.

Massmann's translation of Ling's writings, and Rothstein's version of the Ling gymnastics, were spoken of on p. 123.

CHAPTER XVI.

LING'S SUCCESSORS AT THE CENTRAL INSTITUTE IN STOCKHOLM.

IMMEDIATELY after Ling's death, and in accordance with his wishes, *Branting* was appointed Director in his stead, and retained the position for twenty-three years (1839–1862). Born July 16, 1799, he had grown up a weak and sickly boy, and in the very first year of the Institute had been sent to Ling for treatment by means of medical gymnastics. Improvement was rapid, and the master

FIG. 35.—Lars Gabriel Branting (1799–1881).

was so impressed with the evident talent of his young patient that he offered to train him as a teacher of the art. Thenceforth the relation between the two resembled that of father and son. For several years Branting was a student at the Karolinska Mediko-Kirurgiska Institut (the largest medical college in Sweden) and attended clinics in the Serafimer-Lazarett (hospital), receiving instruction in chemistry under Berzelius, and showing such a fondness for anatomy and physiology that A. A. Retzius bore witness to his skill in the former subject. He learned to speak German, French and English fluently and travelled repeatedly in Germany and Austria. For more than twenty years he had been a member of the teaching staff at the Institute, under Ling, assisting the latter with his fencing at Karlberg and Marieberg, successfully introducing gymnastics among the girls at the large Hillska School, just outside the city, where he became teacher of gymnastics and music in 1831, and applying himself with marked enthusiasm to medical gymnastics. Ling gave him the first place among all his pupils, and turned over to him gradually a large share of the responsibility for both theoretical and practical instruction.

As director, Branting devoted himself chiefly to the development of medical gymnastics in accordance with the theories of his predecessor, and brought that branch to a high degree of perfection. He insisted that the beneficial effects are due not alone to changes produced in the muscular system, but mainly to the influence exerted upon the nerves and bloodvessels—a novel view at that time. He also elaborated a rich store of gymnastic material and worked out a terminology which with a few changes is still generally employed in Sweden. It was at this period, too, that the work of the Institute began to awaken interest in other countries. As we have seen (pp. 122 and 123), two Prussian army officers, Lieutenants Rothstein and Techow, were sent to Stockholm to take the regular course of instruction in 1845–1846, and Rothstein afterward wrote extensively on the Ling gymnastics and in 1851 became the first director of the Berlin "Central-Institute," founded on the pattern of the Swedish school but without its department of medical gymnastics. Many other foreigners came for visits of varying duration, and physicians, especially, were attracted by the new system, among them Drs. Eulenburg and Neumann of Prussia, Melichor of Vienna, and Mathias Roth of London. Branting was made a knight of the orders of the North Star and the Red Eagle (Prussian) in 1847 and of St. Olaf and Dannebrog (Danish) in 1855, and in 1873 Commander of the Order of Vasa. After retiring from the position of Director in 1862 he was still actively engaged in the practice of his profession until his death, March 27, 1881.[1] During his term of office the staff of instruction was enlarged, provision having been made for one additional teacher in 1841, and for two more, a man and a woman, in 1848. Some of these teachers deserve particular mention. *Carl August Georgii* (1808–1881), trained at the Karlberg Military Academy and made lieutenant in the army in 1836, had entered upon his service at the Institute ten years before Ling's death, was chosen by the latter to edit and publish, with Dr. Liedbeck, his "General Principles of Gymnastics," and in 1859 married the oldest daughter of Liedbeck, and Jetta Ling. He became head teacher in 1839, giving instruction in anatomy and in the three branches of practical gymnastics. In 1846 he went to Paris to introduce the

---

[1] *Tidskrift i Gymnastik* **1**, 931–941 (1881).

Swedish system, and the next year published in French a treatise on the Ling method of kinesitherapy and physical education. Two years later, in 1849, he with drew from his Stockholm position and removed to London, where for twenty-eight years he presided over a private institution, giving lessons in fencing and conducting school gymnastics in addition to his medical work. His published writings in England include "Kinesipathy" (1850), a biographical sketch of Ling (1854), a lecture on "Rational Gymnastics" (1873), and "Kinetic Jottings" (1881). The last four years of his life were spent in Stockholm.[1] The first woman to be regularly appointed as teacher at the Institute was *Gustafva Lindskog* (1790–1851), in 1848, and at her death she was succeeded by Ling's daughter Hildur

Fig. 36.—Gustaf Nyblæus (1816–1902).

(1825–1884). Besides assisting in medical gymnastics they both devoted a portion of their time to the physical training of school girls. Two other teachers, Hjalmar Ling and T. J. Hartelius, who began their activity during this period, will be referred to again at some length farther on.

Branting's successor was Col. *Gustav Nyblæus* (1816–1902), who filled the position of director for twenty-five years, from 1862 until 1887. He was trained as an officer in the army, and had been added to the staff of instruction at the Institute during the last year of Ling's life. The school, which had hitherto been under the control of the Stockholm educational authorities, was now given its own board of directors appointed by the King; the length of the course was increased from one year to two years of six months each (October

[1] *Tidskrift i Gymnastik*, **1**, 989–999 (1881).

1 to April 1), and a regular course for women was opened; and the royal statutes of January 8, 1864, reorganized it into three sections, the pedagogical or educational, the military, and the medical, each with a head teacher and a second teacher. Provision was also made for extra teachers, both men and women, and a sum of over 167,000 rix-dollars was granted in 1863 for remodelling and adding to the buildings. Nyblæus himself became the head teacher in the section of military gymnastics, and the corresponding positions in the other sections were given to Ling's son Hjalmar, in school gymnastics, and to Hartelius in medical gymnastics. Nyblæus visited at various times other European countries to study the systems of physical training employed in their schools[1] and armies, and published several manuals of fencing for use at the Institute and in the Swedish army, and others of gymnastics and military exercises to meet the needs of teachers in elementary schools.[2]

Truls Johan Hartelius (1818–1896) had taken the course at the Institute in the year 1851–1852, and began to give instruction there immediately after his graduation. He afterward completed a course in medicine, became a regularly qualified physician, and held the position of head teacher in medical gymnastics from 1864 until 1887. Finding no text-books suitable for his classes, he prepared small manuals of anatomy, physiology and histology, and hygiene, and wrote a larger work on medical gymnastics which was translated into German, French and English. When the corps of teachers decided to start a semi-annual periodical devoted to gymnastics in all its phases and therefore began the publication of the *Tidskirft i Gymnastik*[3] in 1874, Hartelius undertook the editorship, and for fifteen years served in this capacity, contributing many articles on his own and related subjects and important biographical sketches of fellow workers along similar lines.[4]

To *Hjalmar Fredrik Ling* (1820–1886) Swedish educational gymnastics is largely indebted for its present form, and the school gymnasium for the nature and arrangement of the equipment now in common use. He also made it possible to introduce physical training generally in the elementary schools and in schools for girls. The only surviving son of Per Henrik Ling, he was born in Stockholm, April 14, 1820, received an education equivalent to that given in the Swedish secondary schools, completed the course at the Institute (1842), and was installed at teacher there in 1843, devoting himself to educational and medical gymnastics under Branting's

---

[1] See page 117 for his visit to Adolf Spiess at the Darmstadt *Turnanstalt.*
[2] *Tidskrift i Gymnastik,* **5,** 680–687 (1904).
[3] Tidskrift i Gymnastik. Utgiven af Svenska Gymnastikläraresällskapet. Stockholm, P. A. Norstedt & Söner. Two numbers a year through 1904, and four numbers a year since 1905. Organ of the Swedish Association of Teachers of Gymnastics.
[4] *Tidskrift i Gymnastik,* **4,** 449–455 (1896).

direction, and studying anatomy with Dr. Liedbeck. In 1854 at Georgii's suggestion he went to Paris to spend the better part of a year in study there, paying particular attention to anatomy, both human and comparative, but attending also Claude Bernard's lectures on experimental physiology and the clinics at the Hôtel Dieu, and meanwhile acquiring a thorough knowledge of the French language and literature. During this same period he also paid two long visits to Berlin, to assist in introducing the Swedish method of medical gymnastics at the institutions of Drs. Eulenburg and Neumann, and took advantage of the opportunity to familiarize himself with the German language. From Paris he returned to

Fig. 37.—Hjalmar Fredrik Ling (1820–1886).

Stockholm, became head teacher under Branting in 1858, and upon the reorganization of the course in 1864 was placed at the head of the section of school gymnastics. This position he continued to fill for eighteen years, until his retirement on a pension in September of 1882. For some years he was also in charge of the physical training in one of the city's higher schools for boys (the Nya Elementarskola).

Following closely the ideas of his father, and with the sole thought of completing the latter's work, he devised new forms of apparatus adapted to the needs of the school and so arranged them that large numbers could exercise at the same time, in this way greatly increasing the number of useful exercises and bringing them all within the reach of every pupil. Then collecting a mass of gymnastic material he selected the most suitable exercises and arranged them in groups according to the effects produced upon the individual, providing further an orderly progression in each group, and combining these into a complete lesson-scheme—the original "day's order." It was now possible to assign to different ages and degrees of ability, and to the two sexes, the appropriate material from the graded series of exercises, so that the benefits of gymnastics could be extended to girls and younger boys.

Hjalmar Ling published two pamphlets[1] intended primarily as guides for his students at the Central Institute, and in 1866 a work on kinesiology (*Rörelselära*) or the science of bodily movements. He also assisted Hartelius with the *Tidskrift i Gymnastik* and for ten years (1874–1883) was one of its associate editors and a frequent contributor. Although not a clear writer, he was a deep thinker and an industrious compiler, familar with the whole range of gymnastic literature—German, French and English—as a glance at the pamphlets just mentioned will show. He left behind a carefully arranged collection of nearly two thousand pen-drawings of positions and movements used in gymnastics, made by himself. These are preserved in the library of the school, and about a quarter of the entire number appear in a book[2] since published with the help of a gift from Mrs. Mary Hemenway, the founder of the Boston Normal School of Gymnastics. The younger Ling died March 9, 1886, and was buried near his father at Annelund.[3] He sought first of all to analyze the conditions of school life and the needs of the growing child, and then to devise forms of exercise, to select, invent, and arrange apparatus, and to elaborate a lesson plan which should meet these conditions and needs efficiently and with the greatest economy of time and effort. Opinions my differ as to the merits of particular details in the system he helped to perfect, but his method of approach to the problem deserves ungrudging commendation.

The head teachership in school gymnastics left vacant in 1882 was filled by the promotion of Captain *Lars Mauritz Törngren* (1839–1912), at that time second teacher in the same section and an officer in the navy; and he was further advanced to the position of director upon the retirement of Nyblæus in 1887. A third year

[1] Tabeller för Gymnastiska Central-Institutets Lärokurs (och för "friskrotar" af vuxne). The first (1866), second (———), third (1869), and fourth (1876) editions are by Hjalmar Ling. A fifth (1888) and sixth (1897) were edited by L. M. Törngren.
Tillägg vid användningen af de Tabeller hvilka varit begagnade för Gymnastiska Centralinstitutets pedagogiska lärokurs. The first (1869), second (1871), and third (1880) editions are by Hjalmar Ling. The fourth (1894) was edited by L. M. Törngren.
[2] En Samling Gymnastiska Ställningar och Rörelseformer, utgifven af Kungl. Gymnastiska Centralinstitutet i Stockholm. Stockholm, P. A. Norstedt & Söner, 1893. An English edition bears the title-page: "A Collection of Gymnastic Positions. Issued by the Royal Gymnastic Central Institute, Stockholm. Stockholm: Royal Print, P. A. Norstedt & Sons, 1893."
[3] *Tidskrift i Gymnastik*, **3**, 365–367; **6**, 891–903, 950–952. *Gymnastik Selskabs Aarsskrift* (Copenhagen) 1912, pp. 93–134.

(medical gymnastics only) was now added to the course, the school year was lengthened, and other minor changes were made. In 1894 a grant of 80,000 kronor made possible improved facilities for instruction and practice. Among Professor Törngren's earlier writings had been a book on school games (*Fria Lekar*, Stockholm, 1879; 2d ed., 1880), the fruit of a visit to England in 1877, and an official manual of gymnastics for the Swedish navy (1878; 2d ed., 1879). *Tidskrift i Gymnastik* for 1890 (3:145–195) contains further observations on physical education in English public schools, based on a second visit in 1889. In the spring of 1893 he came to the United States, and was present at the department Congress of

Fig. 38.—Lars Mauritz Törngren (1839–1912).

Physical Education and the eighth annual meeting of the American Association for the Advancement of Physical Education held in Chicago in July of that year. He was on the editorial staff of the *Tidskrift i Gymnastik* from its beginning in 1874, assuming more direct responsibility after Hartelius withdrew in 1888, and revised and reissued the pamphlets (*Tabeller* and *Tillägg*) prepared by Hjalmar Ling. His last and most important book was a manual of gymnastics[1] for use in institutions which train teachers for the elementary schools. Major *Carl Silow* (1846–1932), second teacher in the section of school gymnastics 1883–1906, was very active and successful in the work of his department and made further improvements in the construction and arrangement of apparatus. The official handbook of gymnastics for the Swedish army and navy

[1] Lärobok i Gymnastik för Folksskollärare- och Folksskollärarainneseminarier. Stockholm, P. A. Norstedt & Söner, 1905. A German translation ("Lehrbuch der schwedischen Gymnastik") by G. A. Schairer was published in 1908 (Esslingen a. N., Wilh. Langguth).

published in 1902[1] is largely his work. For careful arrangement of material, detailed treatment of the different exercises, and clearness and beauty of the illustrations it is probably the most satisfactory manual of gymnastics yet issued anywhere.

Törngren was succeeded as director by Col. *Viktor Gustav Balck* (1844–1928) in 1907, and two years later retired from his position as head teacher in the section of school gymnastics. Balck, who in turn gave place to Major *Nils Fredrik Sellén* in 1909, had been head teacher of military gymnastics since 1887, following Nyblæus. He has been an ardent advocate of outdoor and other sports for young and old, organizing societies for their promotion, editing a series of a dozen volumes devoted to the various forms,[2] and founding in 1881 the *Tidning för Idrott* (Sporting Times). He also has done much to promote the formation and spread of popular gymnastic societies, and to make Swedish gymnastics known in other countries. With this object in view he accompanied squads of fellow countrymen to *Turnfeste* at Brussels in 1877 and 1880, and in Paris in 1889 and 1900. Exhibitions were also given in London, Copenhagen, and Berlin, in connection with these trips. Together with Major Silow and other teachers he was a member of the committee which prepared the new handbook of gymnastics for the Swedish army and navy.

THE CENTRAL INSTITUTE IN 1900.

The influence of the system of school gymnastics perfected by Hjalmar Ling and his associates and successors in the Central Institute at Stockholm began to be felt abroad, in Europe and America, in the years just preceding and following the appointment of Törngren as director. For this reason, as well as its age and intrinsic merits, a description of the institution as it was in the fall of 1900, based on first-hand studies[3] deserves a place here.

Leaving behind him the cluster of rocky islands which once held all there was of Stockholm, and passing north on the mainland through one of the linden-bordered promenades of the "King's Garden," the visitor soon reaches Hamn-Gatan, its farther limit. If he turn to the left along this busy thoroughfare his eye will be caught by a steep hill just ahead, and at its summit a slight bend of the street to the right reveals on the south side a low and very plain two-storey building constructed, like most of its neighbors, of

---

[1] Handbok i Gymnastik för Arméen och Flottan, utgifven på nådigste befallning. Stockholm, P. A. Norstedt & Söner, 1902. Two volumes.

[2] Illustreradt Bibliotek för Idrott. Stockholm, C. E. Fritze.

[3] During three months, from September 17 to December 15, 1900, the writer was a student at the Central Institute, in almost daily attendance at some of its classes and a frequent visitor at others. A more detailed description was published in the *American Physical Education Review* (**5**, 301–311) for December, 1900.

large bricks coated with plaster over the entire free surface, and painted a weather-worn buff. From the crest of this hill the ground is seen to fall away rapidly on the other side, so that the building gains an additional storey at its corner on Beridarebans-Gatan. The north front stretches for about two hundred feet along Hamn-Gatan. Beridarebans-Gatan crosses this street obliquely, the two forming an acute angle in which the property of the Institute lies. This explains its unsymmetrical arrangement; for half way down the Beridarebans-Gatan side, which measures about two hundred and forty feet, a building forty feet wide has been carried in at right angles to that street. Near the center of the Hamn-Gatan front is a large archway, and over this in raised gilt letters are the words "*Kongl. Gymnastika Central-Institutet.*" It leads into a triangular

Fig. 39.—The Stockholm Central Institute of Gymnastics.

paved court (A) surrounded by plain structures of plastered brick, and a second archway, bisecting the opposite side of this court, communicates with a gravelled yard (B) at the rear. The director and some of the other teachers make their homes in the three-storey sections C and D, which also contain servants' quarters and on the ground floor a few dressing-rooms. The lower storey of E is devoted to medical gymnastics for free patients, and overhead are the library (remarkably rich in the older literature of physical training) and a reading room, two lecture rooms, and others for student use and for the storage of anatomical collections and the like. A hall-way starting from the east angle of the court opens into the men's dressing room (F), with shower baths adjoining. G and H, two storeys in height, contain on the ground floor large halls equipped for school gymnastics and fencing, and above these two other halls intended for patients who pay for treatment by medical gymnastics, and employed also for school gymnastics and as classrooms. There is a small one-storey building (I) for practical exercises in anatomy, and opposite this in the yard is a low shed (J) about 80 by 30 feet, with corrugated iron roof and smooth concrete floor, supplied with a variety of gymnastic apparatus. It is open except on the street side. In the narrow rooms marked KK the schoolboys who receive their physical training at the Institute store their slippers and hang up coats and caps.

The general control is vested in a Board appointed by the King and composed of a president and three other members, of whom

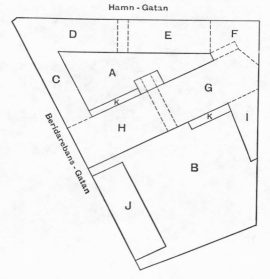

FIG. 40.—The Stockholm Central Institute of Gymnastics (Diagram showing arrangement of rooms.)

one must belong to the army or navy, one must be a teacher (*skol-man*), and one a physician. The corps of instruction includes a head teacher and a second teacher in each of the three departments, the hygienic or educational, the military, and the medical; two women teachers, one of them in hygienic and the other in medical gymnastics; and extra teachers, both men and women, as these are required—a total of fifteen persons in 1900–1901. The royal statutes provide that all who give instruction at the school must be graduates from its courses. From among the head teachers the King selects one to act as director of the Institute, in immediate charge of the buildings and their contents and of the work that goes on in the halls and classrooms. This appointment is for five years, and is renewable.

The school year, divided into a fall and a spring semester, begins on the 15th of September and closes on the 25th of May, with an intermission of two weeks at Christmas time. For male pupils three courses are offered. The "Instructor's Course," extending through a single school year, gives the one who completes it the right to teach gymnastics in the elementary schools (*folkskolor*) or in one of the lower (five-year) secondary schools (*lägre allmänna lärverk*). In the "Gymnastic Teacher's Course" a second year is added, and the graduate is eligible to a position as teacher of gymnastics in any public educational institution, civil or military, in the country.

Fig. 41.—Students (men) at the Stockholm Central Institute in 1900–1901.

The course in medical gymnastics, leading to the title "Gymnastic Director," requires still another year of study and practice, although for students of medicine the prescribed work may be shortened. No person, unless he is himself a physician, is allowed to give treatment by means of medical gymnastics in Sweden except in cases where a duly authorized physician has prescribed it in writing. Young women can complete both the gymnastic teacher's course and that in medical gymnastics in two years, on account of the smaller range of practical exercises to be covered.

The men in attendance are for the most part young army and navy officers who have received orders to take the course. The balance consists of non-commissioned officers in the army and of young men in civil life. All must have passed such an examination as would entitle them to admission into one of the national universities;

they must also possess a sound constitution and some aptitude for gymnastic exercises, and for all but physicians the age limit is thirty years. Young women must present certificates which would allow them to enter the national Higher Normal School for Women. There are no charges for tuition in any of the courses, and foreigners are admitted to them within certain limits. The total number of men present at any one time is commonly about sixty, and the women, formerly not half so numerous, are now rapidly approaching the same figure. During the autumn of 1900 there were in the student body two men from Greece and one each from Norway, Denmark, Finland and the United States, while Russia, Holland and England were represented among the women.

Fig. 42.—Class of women students at the Stockholm Central Institute.

Work begins on Monday morning and continues through Saturday afternoon, as in other Swedish schools, for Sunday is the only holiday. The theoretical courses come at nine and at one o'clock, and the practical courses at seven, eleven and two. At ten o'clock three hundred boys from the New Elementary School (it is a higher school, in spite of the name) visit the Institute to receive their gymnastic lesson in three of the large halls, affording material for practice in teaching, and further opportunity is given at three. When two hundred more arrive from the Jakobs Secondary School. The hours from eight to nine and twelve to one are free, and there are no exercises after four o'clock. The theoretical courses of the first-year men include: (1) Lectures and recitations on the anatomy of the bones, ligaments, and muscles (three times a week through the year); (2) the physiology of the circulation and of the organs of nutrition, including respiration (twice a week during the second semester); (3) the theory of school gymnastics, covering the discussion of the various positions and movements, the commands employed and the common faults observed, the arrangement of exercises in a lesson, and progression in each lesson and from day to day (twice a week through the year); (4) military gymnastics (twice a week during the first semester), and (5) the theory of fencing (twice a week through the year). There is one hour of practical instruction each day in school gymnastics, another in fencing with foils, and a

Fig. 43.—Class of schoolboys at the Stockholm Central Institute.

third in fencing with sabre and bayonet, together with daily practice in teaching under the supervision of the director and members of his staff. The five hundred boys who come to the Institute meet in the various halls according to school grade, and the hundred or so in each room are subdivided into a half-dozen squads, which exercise separately under the direction of first-year students during part of the lesson and are watched and corrected by them when the whole roomful is receiving commands from a single leader.

The theoretical courses of the second year include (1) the study of anatomy three hours a week in the lecture room, and in addition two exercises a week in the dissecting room during a large part of the year; (2) two lectures a week on the physiology of the blood, the circulation, respiration, digestion, and excretion; (3) lectures on kinesiology or the theory of bodily movements (twice a week); (4) the theory of school gymnastics (twice a week); and (5) instruction and practice in the forms of treatment employed in medical gymnastics, followed by special study of the class of cases likely to be met with in the schools. The practical work, besides that just mentioned, again covers the branches of school gymnastics, fencing with foils, fencing with sabre and bayonet, and actual teaching, the students in the two years meeting in each case at the same hour and in the same rooms. In the hour devoted to school or hygienic gymnastics, however, the division of the class into two sections for exercises in hanging and climbing and in jumping and vaulting allows some difference to be made in the work of the two years; and in the fencing, where the men are grouped in squads, the work of each corresponds with the stage of progress reached by its members, and the second-year students also meet twice a week by themselves, in the presence of their instructors, for practice, in free fencing. Each man is now required to take his turn at directing one of the classes of a hundred or more schoolboys for a week at a time, making out his own "day's order" for the opening exercises, in which the entire class work as a unit, then supervising the exercises of the different squads, and handling the whole number again during the marching and running. One of the instructors at the Institute is always present, but the student assumes all the responsibility of leadership for the time being. The second-year man is also called upon to give individual instruction in foil fencing twice a week to men of the lower class, as assistant to the regular instructor, and a somewhat similar plan is followed in the courses in sabre and bayonet fencing. Though swimming is not included in the curriculum, no one can receive a certificate as graduate from the "Gymnastic Teacher's Course" without furnishing evidence that he possesses a satisfactory degree of skill in that art.

Third-year pupils attend lectures six times a week in anatomy, the physiology of the muscles and the nervous system, and pathology, are further instructed in the theory and practice of medical gymnastics, and assist in giving treatment to patients who visit the Institute. Women in both courses receive separate instruction throughout, for there is no such thing as coëducation at the school. Their theoretical work includes anatomy, physiology, the theory of bodily movements and of pedagogical gymnastics, medical gymnastics, and pathology; and there is practice in pedagogical and medical gymnastics, and opportunity to teach gymnastics daily, under supervision, at one or the other of two private schools.

PROPOSED REORGANIZATION OF THE CENTRAL INSTITUTE (1912).

On April 8, 1910, the King of Sweden appointed a special committee to consider plans for the reorganization of the Royal Central Institute of Gymnastics, and the provision of a new site and buildings. Their report,[1] dated March 7, 1912, recommends numerous radical and far-reaching changes in the venerable institution, and would substitute civilian for military teachers of gymnastics in the great majority of Swedish secondary schools. As was to be expected it has called out much discussion on either side. Whatever the outcome may be, the document remains a memorable study of every public aspect of physical education, and the committee has rendered a service of the very highest value, not only to the Swedes, but to all who are confronted by the problem of training teachers for the physical education of the people.[2]

---

[1] Underdånigt Utlåtande och Förslag angående Omorganisation af Gymnastiska Centralinstitutet äfvensom rörande anskaffande af nya lokaler för detsamma. Stockholm, Ivar Hæggström, 1912.

[2] A brief summary of the report is contained in the *American Physical Education Review* (**19**, 192–199) for March, 1914.

CHAPTER XVII.

PHYSICAL EDUCATION IN THE SCHOOLS OF SWEDEN.

In Sweden, as in Germany,[1] there are two types of public schools, the elementary, common, or *folkskola* (people's school), and the secondary, or *allmänna läroverk*, corresponding in general to the German *Gymnasium* and *Realschule* and the French *lycée*. An American college student at the end of his sophomore year has received an education roughly equivalent to that of the graduate from a Swedish *allmänna läroverk*. In the matter of equipment, organization, and method there is such uniformity throughout Sweden that if allowance is made for less favorable conditions in smaller cities and in country regions a fairly accurate, and more definite conception of physical training in the schools will be obtained by confining attention to Stockholm, the capital and largest city.[2] It will be convenient to consider, in order, the *folkskola*, the *allmänna läroverk*, the higher schools for girls, and private schools.

Of the more than 35,000 children of school age in Stockholm over three-fourths attend the thirty *folkskolor*. These are grouped in eight school systems, corresponding to the parishes or districts into which the city is divided, and at the head of every such system is placed a "first teacher." The different grades in a single building are cut up into parallel sections, so that the average number of children under one teacher does not exceed 35. The great Kungsholms *folkskola*, intended to accommodate 3500–4000 children, and one of the largest school buildings in the world, is in many ways typical of them all, in spite of its greater size. It consists of two L-shaped portions, each four storeys high with a basement, their long arms forming the opposite ends of a rectangular gravelled yard and separating this from the street, and their short arms turned toward each other on one side of the yard. At the center of this third side is an archway, flanked by one-storey structures which

---

[1] See footnote page 128.

[2] A description based primarily on extensive personal observation, supplemented by interviews and the study of official documents, has so many advantages over a compilation made at a distance that this chapter has been left substantially in the form given to it soon after the period of residence in Stockholm referred to on page 163. It therefore applies to conditions as they existed in 1900. A second, briefer visit in the spring of 1913 revealed minor changes, but the general impression given by the article as it first appeared in the *American Physical Education Review*, (6, 1–13) for March, 1901, and in condensed form in *Mind and Body* (11, 105–111) for July, 1904, remains essentially correct.

contain offices and the janitor's quarters. Next to these the loftier gymnastic halls complete the front by joining on to the ells. The area of the yard is not far from one and a half acres. The classrooms, ninety-four in number, occupy the entire street side of the building, and open into long corridors which look out upon the central yard and lead down into it. On every floor drinking fountains and stationary washbowls supplied with hot and cold water are distributed at frequent intervals along these passage-ways. Besides the recitation rooms there are eight larger halls for pasteboard, wood and metal sloyd and the sewing classes; three rooms for the use of cooking schools, two gymnasia; two bathing outfits, which include dressing-rooms, a hot-air chamber, shower baths, and a pool 7 by 14 feet; steam disinfection apparatus, laundry and drying rooms; dining rooms, and counters where milk and bread are sold to the children; the living apartments of the First Teacher, and a room for the use of other teachers; offices, and janitor's quarters. The old wing is heated by steam and the newer one by hot air. The total cost, exclusive of the site, was over $200,000.

In the classrooms of this building the single desks are arranged one behind the other so as to leave aisles between adjacent rows and next to the wall at the sides and rear. Space is thus afforded for simple marching exercises and for others with either require no apparatus or may be practised with the help of desks and seats. The two halls set apart for gymnastics measure about 55 by 25 feet, and have a height considerably greater than that of the other rooms. Their side walls are lined with stallbars, and the floor space is divided crosswise into three nearly equal parts by two pairs of Swedish horizontal bars, when these are set up; but the bars and central post of each pair can be dropped below the floor and concealed from view by trap-doors when not in use, and then the entire area from wall to wall is left free. The remaining equipment includes Swedish ladders, climbing poles, ropes and rope ladders hanging from the ceiling, long benches for use at the stallbars, and bucks for vaulting exercises. Each of the other school districts has also its special room or rooms for gymnastic instruction.

The three lower classes of the various *folkskolor* have marching and other exercises without apparatus daily, in the schoolroom, the work alternating with other instruction and directed by the same teacher. In the case of higher classes special periods, three a week as a rule, are set apart for the gymnastic lesson, and this is given sometimes in the schoolroom, utilizing the desks and seats as apparatus, but at least once a week in the gymnasium, where its duration is commonly about half an hour. Little or no change of costume is attempted, beyond the laying off of coats by the boys. The school report for 1898 relates that "since many of the children wear wooden shoes, unsuitable for the gymnastic lesson, four hundred pairs of special shoes were brought and distributed among the districts for use in the gymnasia."

As regards teachers in the *folkskolor*, the women outnumber the men five to one. All must have completed a four-years' course at one of the twelve Swedish training colleges for this grade of instructors, and of that course gymnastics everywhere forms a part, directed by a graduate of the Central Institute at Stockholm and occupying three hours a week throughout the entire four years. There is always a model school attached, which affords the future teacher an opportunity to test his skill and to acquire experience in this as well as other branches of instruction. In Stockholm teachers receive additional counsel and direction from a special instructor in gymnastics, who divides his time among all the *folkskolor* in the different districts; but the general guide followed is C. H. Liedbeck's "Manual of Gymnastics."[1] Besides the formal exercises this book contains a large number of games. These are introduced occasionally as part of the gymnastic lesson, and are also encouraged in the schoolyards during recess. Of the twenty-eight tables of exercises contained in the manual only six call for no apparatus of any sort, six can be given with nothing more than desks and seats, and the balance require a hall supplied with stallbars, Swedish horizontal bars, poles, ropes, ladders, benches, mats, etc.

Instruction in military tactics and target shooting is given to the older boys in the spring and early fall, under the general direction of an army officer who is assigned to this service in all the elementary schools of the city. There is drill by squads in exercises for the recruit, together with occasional company drill, a few longer marches in battalion, and training as subalterns for the most advanced. During the summer months pupils may also receive instruction in swimming, at a large swimming school in Lake Mälaren, near one of the city bridges. Over 3000 boys and 2500 girls availed themselves of this privilege in 1899, and a total of 6000 in 1900. The number of these who could swim increased in the former year from 602 at the beginning of the season to 1510 at its close.

There are seven *higher schools* for boys at Stockholm. At two of these the gymnasium is a separate building of brick, located at one side of a gravelled yard at least an acre and a half in extent. Each

---

[1] Gymnastiska Dagöfningar för Folkskolan. Stockholm, P. A. Norstedt & Söner, 1881. Second edition in 1891. A German translation by J. A. Selter and J. H. Jarisch, under the title "Das schwedische Schulturnen," was published in 1907 (Marburg, N. G. Elwert).

This book has now been superseded by Törngren's manual of 1905 (see footnote on p. 162). Special attention should also be called to Elin Falk's three-volume "Dagövningar i Gymnastik för Stockholms Folkskolor" (Stockholm, P. Palmquist, 1915 and 1916).

cost about $17,000 and consists of a lofty main hall, 80 by 40 or 45 feet, with a wing containing dressing-rooms, the teacher's office and a few shower baths.   At a third school the gymnasium occupies a spacious two-storey wing which projects from the rear of the main building; in two other cases a hall in the main building is fitted up for gymnastics, and pupils in the remaining two schools go for their exercises to the halls of the Central Institute.   The following list of apparatus noticed in the gymnasium of the Real-läroverk (a non-classical higher school for boys) is fairly represent-ative.   Sixty sections of stallbars, seven Swedish horizontal bars, two vertical Swedish ladders and two horizontal ones, eight rope ladders, twenty-four climbing ropes and eight poles, two double inclined ropes, a few sections of stallbars continued to the ceiling

Fig. 44.—Rear view of a higher school for boys (*Norra Latinläroverket*) in Stock-holm.   (The gymnasium occupies the lower half of the projection in the foreground.)

as ladders, storming boards and short benches for use with stallbars, bar saddles, two Swedish horses, two vaulting boxes, two bucks, jump stands with cord and pins, some thin mats about 4 feet by 3, and a number of cheap fencing foils.   The horizontal bars are arranged to drop beneath the floor.   The inclined ropes are attached to the ceiling at either end, and to a hook beneath the floor, when in use, by means of a tackle block at the center.   Near the ends they are crossed by vertical ropes, used by the pupils in reaching or leaving the inclined ropes.   All of these ropes can be hoisted out of the way readily, and a small trap-door conceals the hook.

The royal statutes require that in every public secondary school in Sweden there shall be at least three hours a week of pedagogical gymnastics, arranged in daily half-hour periods when possible.   In Stockholm the division into half-hour lessons is the most common one.   Less frequently there are three periods of an hour each, and in a few cases a class meets twice for a half-hour and twice for an hour, or fifty minutes four times a week, or forty minutes six times, or in four one-hour periods. In a majority of cases the time chosen for exercise lies between ten and one o'clock, though the hours from two to four in the afternoon are used not infrequently. Military exercises take the place of gymnastics for boys of the sixth to ninth years in the early part of every fall semester, occupying three hours daily for twenty days as a rule, and during this period their usual school duties are cut down by a corresponding amount. Each of the seven schools has its special teacher of gymnastics, and no one is eligible to such a position until he has completed a two-years' professional course at the Central Institute of Gymnastics. In the fall of 1900 these teachers and their assistants were all officers in the army, and five of the nine were on the staff of instruction at the Institute. One had the rank of major, and the rest were captains and lieutenants.

Occasionally a "weak section" is formed of boys selected from the whole or part of the school, but in general the division into classes is based upon school grade, the boys of the sixth to ninth years exercising together as a rule, and the rest variously subdivided according to their numbers. The size of some of these classes is noteworthy. They rarely contain fewer than 60 or 70, while 100–125 is not an unusual number, and 150–200 are sometimes seen together under a single teacher. To facilitate the handling of so many it is usual to separate them into squads of from 12 to 20, on the basis of physical fitness, and to place at the head of each squad one of the best pupils, who sees that his portion of the lines is correctly formed at the beginning of the hour, reports upon attendance, and directs the work of his division when the teacher is not giving commands for the whole class. Before exercising it is the practice to remove coats, collars, cuffs, and suspenders, and the dickey, or detachable shirt-front, if a boy has arrived at the dignity of wearing that common article of clothing. Shoes are exchanged for rubber-soled canvas slippers, of the sort so often seen in American gymnasia.

The ease and quickness with which apparatus is made ready or put out of the way by pupils must strike every observer. It is this which allows such frequent changes during a single lesson, and the great variety of forms given to the "day's order." As a rule the teaching which one sees is remarkably well done. Perfect discipline and prompt and accurate execution of commands are secured, and yet there is no oppressive military strictness, nor anything but the pleasantest relation between teacher and pupils. Opportunities for relaxed attention and brief outbreaks of high spirits are frequent, the boys take hold with vigor which proves their interest, and many squad leaders, even the youngest, show uncommon earnest-

ness and ability to direct.   In a few cases it will be found that when
the control over a class is less perfect and listless, slovenly work is
tolerated.   Where pupils are sent to the Central Institute for their
instruction, and receive it largely from students at that school,
the frequent change of leaders and the great variety of personality
among them produce a natural mingling of good and bad teaching.

So far as the fencing instruction given to boys of the four higher
grades was observed it formed a portion of the gymnastic lesson,
and included brief practice in the fundamental positions and movements by the whole class, and an exchange of thrusts and parries
between two opposing lines.   The military exercises of the same
boys in the fall semester cover target practice with the rifle, besides

Fig. 45.—The gymnasium of a mixed school in Trelleborg, Sweden.

squad and company drill and the manual of arms.   The school
yard serves not only for these evolutions and for games, but part
or all of the gymnastic lesson is often given outdoors when the
weather is favorable.

In all Sweden there are only two *higher schools for girls* under
state control.   These are the Royal Higher Normal School for
Women (*Kungl. högre lärarinneseminarium*), in Stockholm, and the
model school associated with it.   One of the halls in the school
building used by the two in common is fitted up as a gymnasium,
and except in the lowest classes at the model school a half-hour of
gymnastic instruction is given daily throughout the entire course
of study at both institutions.   In the case of *private schools*, the
great majority of which are for girls only, or admit boys to none

but the lowest classes, there is no law prescribing the amount of physical training to be given, and the practice varies accordingly. Thus in 1899 there were 46 such schools, with a total of 5157 pupils, and out of this number 2909, in 33 schools, were reported as receiving instructions in gymnastics. The oldest institution of them all, with 240 pupils, has (1900) nothing but a small room some 40 by 25 feet and 9 feet high, supplied with a Swedish horizontal bar six climbing ropes, three long benches with balance beams on the under side, a vaulting box, jump stands, and a rubber ball. Most of the lower classes exercise here for half an hour every other day, and the higher ones twice a week, under a special teacher. Another school for girls provides for nearly the same number of pupils a room 60 by 20 feet and of good height, situated on the ground floor, and for its size as well equipped with apparatus as any of the *allmänna läroverk*. Its gymnastic instruction is in the hands of Major Silow, of the Central Institute, assisted by students in the course for women at that school. His capacity as an organizer and his rare talent as a teacher render the quality of work done by these girls quite as good as the best to be seen in the boy's schools of the city.

BIBLIOGRAPHY.

Dr. F. A. Schmidt of Bonn and Captain C. J. J. Lefebure of Brussels, who visited Stockholm in 1899, have recorded their observations and impressions in the following:

Dr. Schmidt—"Die Gymnastik an den schwedischen Volksschulen nebst einem Anhang: Die Militärischen Übungen an den höheren Schulen in Stockholm." Berlin, R. Gaertner, 1900 (Reprinted from the *Monatsschrift für das Turnwesen* for 1900). Second edition 1909. Third edition, revised and enlarged under the title "Die schwedische Schulgymnastik," in 1912 (Berlin, Weidmannsche Buchhandlung).

Captain Lefebure—"L'Éducation Physique en Suède." Brussels, H. Lamertin; Paris, A. Maloine, 1903. Second edition 1908 (Paris, Felix Alcan).

The Swedish Department of Church Affairs and Education (*Kungl. Ecklesiastik-Department*) publishes statistical reports covering the work of the common schools (*Berättelse om folkskolorna*) and the higher schools for boys (*Berättelse om Statens Allmanna läroverk för gossar*). The board of directors of the common schools and the rectors of the various higher schools for boys in Stockholm also prepare elaborate annual reports which contain information regarding the physical training of pupils.

CHAPTER XVIII.

PHYSICAL EDUCATION IN DENMARK.[1]

DENMARK was the first European state to introduce physical training into its schools as an essential part of the course, and to prepare teachers of that subject by offering systematic instruction in theory and method of gymnastics. The leader in this movement, and its director for more than forty years, was Franz Nachtegall (1777–1847), the son of a Copenhagen tailor. His early education

FIG. 46.—Franz Nachtegall (1777–1847).

was received in a private school, and he had begun the study of theology in the university; but the death of his father prevented him from taking the final examination for his degree and threw upon him the support of an invalid mother. For a time he gave private lessons in Latin, history, and geography, but the small pay necessitated such long hours that his health began to suffer. From boyhood he had been interested in forms of physical activity, and

[1] This chapter is condensed from one of two "Studies in the History of Physical Education" published for the author by the Society of Directors of Physical Education in Colleges in 1918.

(180)

as a university student gained considerable proficiency in fencing and vaulting. Inclination, therefore, and the reading of GutsMuths's *Gymnastik für die Jugend*[1] started him upon what was to become a life-work. He began to teach gymnastics, first to some students at his own home, and then, early in 1798, to a club of university students and tradesmen which he organized and directed. This brought him, a year later, an invitation to give lessons in the private school which Court Chaplain Christiani had opened in May of 1795, in accordance with the philanthropinistic ideals of Basedow and his followers. A rival institution, the Schouboe school which Nachtegall had himself attended as a boy, soon secured a share of his time for the same purpose. Other schools in the city, public as well as private, followed the example of these two, so that by 1805 at least nine were furnishing instruction in gymnastics to their pupils.

On November 5, 1799, having definitely decided to give himself wholly to the new calling, Nachtegall opened a private outdoor gymnasium in the yard of number 45 Østergade, the first institution in modern times devoted exclusively to physical training. The 5 pupils with whom he began had increased to 25 by the end of the year, and in the winter of 1803–04 the number reached 150, both children and adults, under six teachers whom he had himself trained. When in 1804 the King appointed him professor of gymnastics in the university he had already given, for two years, lectures on the history and method of physical training, with the help of a former pupil, to an audience made up of students there and in a college for teachers, with an admixture of military men. Meanwhile the training of military and naval cadets and the instruction in gymnastics given in schools for non-commissioned officers had also been entrusted to him, and when the King established a Training School for Teachers of Gymnastics in the Army (*det militære gymnastiske Institut*), by decree of August 25, 1804, Nachtegall became its first director. From this as a center the new teaching was to be spread throughout the entire army and navy, including the Norwegian regiments. Four years later civilians were also admitted to the courses, the institution now attempting to do for the schools and the people at large what it had already accomplished for the army, and to prepare instructors for teachers' colleges and the elementary schools especially. The usual length of the course was fifteen to eighteen months, though the first pupil was graduated in August of 1809. By 1814 the civilian training school, caught in the stress of hard times, had ceased to exist. Mean-

---

[1] See page 77. An abridged translation of this book, by V. K. Hjort, curate at Holmens Kirke, was published in Copenhagen in 1799 (see page 79).

while a total of only 31 students had completed its course, but 10 of these went out to occupy positions at *Seminarier* (teachers' colleges), and so became in turn the instructors of other teachers-to-be.

The disastrous results of collisions between Denmark and Great Britain during the Napoleonic wars (1801–1814) and the economic distress which followed the loss of Norway (1814) made the period 1809–1825 an unfavorable one for educational reforms, and yet the efforts of the Danish government to introduce gymnastics into the curriculum of the schools did not stop altogether with provision for the training of teachers. An ordinance of November 7, 1809, stated in general that grammar or secondary schools (*"de lærde Skoler"*) should furnish instruction in gymnastics "when and where it was possible" to do so. In the school code of 1814 gymnastics was made an integral part of the course for boys in all elementary schools (*Folkeskoler*)—nearly three decades before any other European country took such action. Whenever the teacher possessed the requisite ability he was to give his pupils a daily lesson in gymnastics, outside of school hours proper, and for this purpose every school must have the necessary apparatus and an outdoor space of 800–1200 *Alen* (3200–4800 square feet). At the *Seminarier* gymnastics became a required subject under the regulations of 1818, and in 1821 Nachtegall was appointed *Gymnastik-direktør* (Director of Gymnastics), with oversight of both civil and military gymnastics throughout the state. But with here and there a notable exception, the result of so much favorable legislation left much to be desired. Teachers were most of them without training, hard times interfered with the purchase of grounds and apparatus, and appreciation of the importance of school gymnastics as a pedagogical measure was by no means general.

Beginning with the middle twenties and lasting till the death of King Frederick VI (December 3, 1839) there was some improvement. In Copenhagen itself gymnastics was now introduced in many public and private schools, and some of the village schools in Copenhagen county took similar action, assisted by the government (1826), which desired to see all the schools in a single county reached before further statewide measures were attempted. Within a few years this had been accomplished. November 25, 1826, a circular was sent out to the school authorities all over Denmark urging them to do what they could to favor instruction in gymnastics. In the summer of the next year a considerable number of teachers from Copenhagen county came to the city for a course in gymnastics. They felt the need of some opportunity for practice with children along with the instruction they themselves received.

At Nachtegall's suggestion the King therefore ordered (August 21, 1827) that 40 to 50 children from one of the public schools should be received at *det militære gymnastiske Institut,* for instruction in gymnastics, and that this public school should establish such relations with the Institute that both together would constitute a teachers' college which might serve as a normal school of gymnastics (*Normalskole for Gymnastikken*), where not only the military and civil pupils at the Institute but also teachers in public and private schools could have an opportunity to conduct classes under supervision. The Normal School, under this new arrangement, was opened on January 28, 1828 (at the same time a new building, at Solvgaden barracks, was ready for use), and during that year more than 200 teachers were in attendance, 160 boys from the garrison school coming to the Institute to serve as a model school. In summer their place was taken by pupils from charity schools.

June 25, 1828, the King approved the *manual of gymnastics*[1] for use in the middle and common schools (*Folkeskolerne*) on which Nachtegall and four other members of a commission appointed for the purpose had been at work for a year. This was the first book of the sort to be authorized by any European government. Copies were sent (4000 of them) at the King's expense to all Danish schools and school authorities. On the same day, June 25, was issued an order which required the immediate introduction of instruction in gymnastics in all schools throughout the state. A city inspector of gymnastics was appointed in Copenhagen, where every child received three lessons a week and the teachers were most of them non-commissioned officers. It was estimated that by the end of 1830, 2000 elementary schools (*Almueskoler*) were already complying with the order, and that by the time of the King's death 2500 out of the (approximately) 2600 public schools in Denmark were making at least some provision for systematic bodily exercise.

The secondary schools were at first slow to take adequate measures, but a special order of September 20, 1831, directed that this be done just as soon as circumstances permitted. An administrative order of February 14, 1832, made the introduction of instruction in gymnastics a necessary condition of permission to open any private school for boys. September 14, 1833, Nachtegall's manual

---

[1] Lærebog i Gymnastik for Almue- og Borger-Skolerne i Danmark. Kjøbenhavn 1828. "Trykt hos Andreas Seidelin, Hof- og Universitets-Bogtrykker." A German translation was published: "Lehrbuch der Gymnastik für Volks- und Bürgerschulen. Aus den Dänischen übersetzt von C. Kopp, Gymnastiklehrer am Königl. Schullehrer-Seminar in Tondern, Dannebrogsmann. Mit vier Steindrücken. Tondern 1831. Gedruckt in der Königl, privilegirten Buchdruckerey der Wittwe Forchhammer." Tondern was then a Danish town, but the German language was used in the *Seminarium.* State aid was given toward the publication of the book.

and regulations for secondary schools[1] received the King's approval, and it was published the following year. In 1836 he was sent on a tour of inspection among the *Seminarier*, to see what was being done in them and to give any needful counsel and suggestions. He found the interest in gymnastics general, but lack of sufficient apparatus in some places and in others faulty methods, and therefore arranged to have the teachers of gymnastics at three of the *Seminarier* take a summer course of the Normal School in 1837. In obedience to an order of March 7, 1838, he made a second tour, primarily to inspect the Latin schools, but took advantage of the opportunity to visit the *Seminarier* again.

Hitherto it had been boys and young men alone who were reached by gymnastics in the schools, but an order of March 28, 1838, given in response to Nachtegall's proposal, established an experimental school for girls. Thirty pupils, ranging in age from six to fifteen years, were selected from among the girls at the garrison school, and beginning in the spring of the same year these received three lessons a week from five teachers (three sergeants and two women) at the Military Gymnastic Institute, under the general direction of Nachtegall and a physician. The success of this experiment suggested a normal school of gymnastics for women (*Normalskole for Kvindegymnastik*). An order of February 20, 1839, approved the plan, and prescribed that women teachers, and others who wished it, should receive an opportunity at the Institute to become acquainted with methods of teaching and that the exercises practised there and the mode of progression adopted should serve as a model for the schools for girls which introduced gymnastics. These latter were also put under Nachtegall's supervision. The number of pupils at the Normal School now increased. In the summer of 1839 lessons in the new subject were begun with girls in the royal navy schools (*Søetatens Skoler*), and many other Copenhagen schools took a similar step.

After the death of Frederick VI, December 3, 1839, Nachtegall's own efforts (he was now sixty-two years old) began to slacken. In 1840 and 1843 he made new tours of inspection among the

---

[1] "Lærebog i Gymnastik til Brug for de lærde Skoler i Danmark. Ved F. Nachtegall, Direkteur for og Professor i Gymnastikken; Ridder af Dbr. og Dbm. Kjøbenhavn. Trykt i det Poppske Bogtrykkeri. 1834." Bound with the above: "Regulativ for den gymnastiske Underviisning ved de lærde Skoler i Danmark." Of this book also a German translation appeared: "Lehrbuch der Gymnastik zum Gebrauch für die gelehrte Schulen in Dänemark. Von F. Nachtegall, Directeur und Professor der Gymnastik, Ritter von Dannebrog und Dannebrogsmann. Aus den Dänischen übersetzt von C. Kopp, Gymnastiklehrer am Königl. Schullehrer-Seminar in Tondern, Dannebrogsmann. Tondern, 1837. Gedruckt in der Königl. privilegirten Buchdruckerei der Wittwe Forchhammer." Bound with the above: "Regulativ für den gymnastischen Unterricht bei den gelehrten Schulen in Dänemark."

Seminarier. In 1842 he turned over to la Cour the headship of *det militære gymnastiske Institut,* but continued to discharge the duties of *Gymnastikdirektør* until his death, which occurred May 12, 1847. He was not the inventor of a system of his own, but borrowed his types of exercise from Dessau and Schnepfenthal, and used the manuals of GutsMuths as a guide. He was a good teacher and organizer, tactfully winning the good will and support of leading men, skilful in accommodating himself to actual conditions, and indefatigable in his efforts to advance the work to which he had committed himself with so much devotion. Denmark owes it to him that during the first third of the nineteenth century she held the leading place among European nations in the realm of physical education.[1]

Captain Niels Georg la Cour (1797–1876), who succeeded Nachtegall as Director of Gymnastics in Denmark (1847–1870) met with little success in his endeavor to improve conditions. As head of the Military Institute he published a new manual for the army, upon which was based his later manual for the elementary schools.[2] But interest was now at low ebb. Beginning in 1859 it came to be the practice to supply the need of teachers of gymnastics in the *Seminarier* by "loaning" them non-commissioned officers for a term of three years. (This continued to be the rule until 1901!) In the schools of Copenhagen, also, and in garrison towns, such instruction was in the hands of military men. But in the army the broad educational aims of gymnastics had been subordinated to mere attainment of skill, so that the soldier too often regarded it with dread as a means of discipline and punishment. These officers, too, held themselves aloof from the general school life and from the other teachers. When la Cour, who possessed more energy than

---

[1] Sources for Nachtegall and his time:

1. Joakim Larsen, "Gymnastikundervisningen i Danmark paa Nachtegalls Tid (Foredrag ved Gymnastiklærermødet i Stockholm 1895; her meddelt i en noget udvidet Skikkelse)." In *Vor Ungdom* (periodical, Copenhagen), 1895, pp. 465–512.

2. Joakin Larsen, article "Nachtegall" in C. F. Bricka's "Dansk Biografisk Lexikon," 12 (Copenhagen, 1898).

3. Joakin Larsen, "Gymnastikundervisningens Indførelse i vore Folkeskoler for 100 Aar siden." In Gymnastisk Selskabs Aarsskrift 1913–1914 (Copenhagen, 1914), pp. 5–28.

4. K. A. Knudsen, article "Gymnastik" in "Salmonsens store illustrerede Konversationsloksikon," 8 (Copenhagen, 1898).

5. K. A. Knudsen, "Gymnastikken i Danmark i hundrede Aar 1814–1914." Foredrag ved de baltiske Lege i Malmö 1914. Copenhagen, 1914.

6. Jens Bergmann, "Hærens Gymnastikskole og Skolegymnastikken." In Gymnastisk Selskabs Aarsskrift, 1904.

7. Illeris og Trap, "Grundtræk af Gymnastikkens Historie" (Copenhagen, 1909), pp. 72–79.

[2] "Lærebog i Gymnastik for Borger- og Almueskoler." Copenhagen, 1856 (1855?). Second edition 1860. There was also a "Tillæg til Lærebog i Gymnastik for Borger- og Almueskolerne." Copenhagen, 1869.

tact and lacked Nachtegall's conciliatory manner, called attention to neglect or defective equipment revealed by his tours of inspection, and when official circulars directed the school authorities to exercise a keener and more vigorous oversight, the result in many cases was to arouse a feeling of irritation and indignation.

Upon la Cour's retirement from the position of *Gymnastikdirektør* in 1870 this office was abolished, and a new one was created—that of inspector of gymnastics (*Gymnastikinspektør*) for civil schools only. But there was no actual separation from military control, for until 1904 it was the army which supplied candidates for the place. The first man to fill it (1870–1886) was Col. Johann Theodor Wegener (1810–1886). He chose for his assistant Captain (later Lieut.-Col.) Julius Amsinck (1833–1902), Director of the Military Institute[1] 1867–1885, who later became his successor (1886–1899). Amsinck published in 1883 a manual for school use, based on that of la Cour.

After the war of 1864 with Prussia and Austria, in which the Danes lost Schleswig-Holstein and Lauenburg, there was a period of great depression, soon followed, however, by a variety of measures looking toward national regeneration. In two institutions which date from this time, the rifle clubs (*Skytteforeninger*) and the people's or folk high schools (*Folkehøjskolerne*), gymnastics was among the means employed, as it had been in Germany by Jahn and his followers a half-century before. For some years before the outbreak of the war the attitude of Germany in the Schleswig-Holstein dispute had been growing more and more threatening, and in January, 1861, an artillery captain, Valdemar Mønster, proposed in the columns of the Danish paper *Fædrelandet* the organization of voluntary clubs on the plan of the English National Rifle Association, in order that young men subject to military service might have opportunity to become familiary with the use of weapons and fit themselves to defend the country's right by force of arms. The suggestion met with general approval, and a few months later a Central Committee, with Captain Mønster as its secretary, was formed to guide and assist the rifle clubs which were being started all over Denmark.[2] By the close of 1863 there were over a hundred of them in existence.

At first the *Skytteforeninger* confined their attention to rifle shooting and military drill, but after the war had given great headway to the whole movement gymnastics began to be intro-

---

[1] Now known as the "Army School of Gymnastics" (*Hærens Gymnastikskole*).

[2] For the history of the Rifle Clubs consult Lieut.-Col. Peter Ramsing's "Gymnastiken i de danske Skytteforeninger," published in the "Beretning om det skandinaviske Gymnastiklærerselskabs femte almindelige Møde i København den 12–14. August 1899" (Copenhagen, 1902), pp. 48–73; and Kristen A. Lange's "Den Lingske Gymnastik i Danmark 1884–1909" (Copenhagen, 1909), pp. 60–87.

duced as a related activity, and gradually won for itself a more and more prominent place. A firmer organization had now been effected, for the smaller clubs, whose number had increased to several hundred, united into county rifle clubs (*Amts-Skytteforeninger*. Denmark is divided for administrative purposes into eighteen counties or *Amter*), and in 1871 the original Central Committee was succeeded by a Board of Directors (*Overbestyrelse*) chosen by representatives of the various units. According to information gathered by the new *Overbestyrelse*, eleven clubs practised gymnastics in 1872, and nine of these had 2100 members actively engaged, of whom 763 belonged in Svendborg county alone, where the efficient leadership and persevering efforts of Captain Edward Nielsen had contributed largely toward such a favorable showing and had made that club a model for others.

The exercises were necessarily limited at the start to what could be done in the open air and with little or no apparatus, or use was made of barns or rooms for public gatherings. In 1871, at Ryslinge (island of Fünen), the first special *Øvelseshus* (house for exercise, gymnasium) was erected. Other places were quick to follow the example, so that by 1897 there were nearly 300 such buildings, provided by the club members themselves, and in them 10,000 young countrymen were practising gymnastics. Trained instructors could be borrowed from the army in garrison towns and the regions adjacent to them, or school teachers were employed or men who had returned from military service. Many clubs, in order to secure better qualified squad leaders, organized brief teachers' courses (*Instruktionsmøder*) in charge of army instructors. When various people's high schools, notably those at Askov and Vallekilde, opened their doors for such leaders' courses (*Delingsførerkursus* in gymnastics they became an important source of supply. The first course of this kind at Vallekilde was given in 1878. A handbook of gymnastics ("Vejledning i Gymnastik") prepared for the rifle clubs by *Hærens Gymnsatikskole* in 1882, at the instance of the *Overbestyrelse*, does not appear to have been widely used, but Captain Amsinck's manual of 1883 was made the basis of instruction.

At the general *Skyttefest* (gathering of rifle clubs for competitive shooting) in 1869 at Horsens the Svendborg county club, the university club from Copenhagen, and others gave exhibitions of gymnastics which must have contributed toward its spread, and this was still more true of the general *Gymnastikfest* at Svendborg in 1878 and the general *Skytte- og Gymnastikfest* at Nyborg in 1881, both of them arranged by the Svendborg county rifle club. At the former there were nearly 1100 participants, who came from 16 towns and 110 country parishes. Six hundred were from Svendborg county alone. County and lesser *Skyttefester* exerted a similar influence. Advantage was taken of the interest thus aroused to seek state aid for the purchase of apparatus. Captain Edward Neilsen proposed such a measure at the meeting of delegates in 1879, and a motion requesting the *Overbestyrelse* to take suitable steps led to an initial annual grant of 2000 Kr. from the government, increased to 5000 Kr. in 1882 and to 6000 Kr. the following year. Attempts to obtain similar grants to assist in the erection of *Øvelseshuse* and the giving of courses of instruction for squad leaders (*Delingsførere*) met with no success at this time.

The people's or folk high schools (*Folkehøjskoler*),[1] like the rifle clubs, date from before the Schleswig-Holstein war of 1864; but their great popularity and rapid spread began with the period of reform which succeeded it. They are not public institutions, though nearly all now receive a certain amount of government aid, but are privately owned in most cases, or belong to a self-perpetuating corporation, and depend for their success upon the personality of the director and his associates. The total number opened in the years 1844–1911 was 143, and 80 of these were in existence at the close of the period. The great majority of the students are young countrymen eighteen to twenty-five years of age, who after completing the required course at free rural elementary schools have been engaged in practical agriculture and household duties, either at home or on some model farm. The attendance in the years 1864–1884 averaged about 3000 annually, but doubled in the following decade, and in the school year 1898–1899 reached a total of 3491 young men and 2646 young women. In 1906 the numbers at the different high schools ranged from 10 to 400; 53 per cent of the pupils were males, and it was estimated that a third of the young people among the rural population passed through these schools, although attendance is altogether voluntary. A few are coëducational, but the usual plan is to offer a winter course of five to six months (November–May) to young men, and a summer one of three months or more to young women. An hour a day is allotted to gymnastics as a rule.

The people's high schools and the rifle clubs have stood in close relation with each other, some of the former organizing clubs of their own, or supplying leaders for neighboring clubs, and others, like the ones at Askov and Vallekilde, arranging for teachers'

[1] Sources: "Le Danemark. État actuel de sa civilisation et de son organisation sociale. Ouvrage publié a l'occasion de l'exposition universelle de Paris 1900 par J. Carlsen, H. Olrik, C.-N. Starcke" (Copenhagen, 1900), pp. 180–190; Harold W. Foght, "The Educational System of Rural Denmark" (U. S. Bureau of Education Bulletin 1913, No. 53. Washington, 1914); L. L. Friend, "The Folk High School of Denmark" (U. S. Bureau of Education Bulletin 1914, No. 5. Washington, 1914); and Kristen A. Lange's "Den Lingske Gymnastik i Danmark 1884–1909" (Copenhagen, 1909) pp. 14 and following.

courses in gymnastics and rifle-shooting under professional instructors from the army. The aims of the two institutions are similar in many ways. Although the people's high schools all give instruction in handwork and household economics for women and many offer courses in agriculture, horticulture, masonry, carpentry, etc., their chief purpose is cultural—to mold character and ideals, inspire patriotism, train the students to think for themselves, reveal the dignity and possibilities of country life, and lay the foundation for later work in local agricultural schools and schools of household economics. The lecture method prevails in the classroom. Courses in history and literature may be considered the backbone of the curriculum, with frequent discussion periods and much singing of folk and patriotic songs and hymns. Students room in the school dormitories, and are thus brought into close and sympathetic association with each other and with their teachers—the foundation of that spirit of coöperation which is so characteristic of rural life in Denmark today.

The revival of general interest in physical education in Denmark had its origin thus among young adults, and not in the schools. At first it was the GutsMuths gymnastics as developed by Nachtegall which they practised in the rifle clubs and the people's high schools, with the gradual addition of exercises borrowed from the Jahn *Turnen;* but beginning in 1884 the Ling or Swedish system was introduced, and made rapid headway until by the close of the century it had been generally adopted in the people's high schools, had outstripped its Danish-German rival in the rifle clubs, and formed the basis of a new official manual for the schools.[1]

It was not to be expected that the friends of the GutsMuths-Nachtegall gymnastics would watch the encroachments of the foreign system without a vigorous protest. The struggle began as early as 1885, with army officers almost without exception opposed to the innovation, and a few years later was at its height. The attention of school authorities was drawn to the subject by conflicting claims put forward in the press and by what the followers of Ling were already accomplishing in Denmark, and some of them

---

[1] For the history of the Ling gymnastics in Denmark consult: Ramsing 1899 (as above, under rifle clubs); Knudsen 1914 (as above, under Nachtegall), pp. 12–30; Kristen A. Lange's "Den Lingske Gymnastik i Danmark 1884–1909" (Copenhagen, 1909); Kåre Teilmann's "Den Lingske Gymnastik i Danmark," in *Gymnastisk Selskabs Aarsskrift* 1913–1914 (Copenhagen, 1914), pp. 94–152; "Haandbog i Gymnastik" (Copenhagen, 1899); Prof. K. Kroman, "Den nye danske Skolegymnastik," in "Beretning om det skandinaviske Gymnastiklærerselskabs femte almindelige Møde i København den 12.–14. August 1899" (Copenhagen, 1902), pp 20–30 (see also pp. 31–40); "Die Leibespflege in Dänemark: Bericht über eine einjährige Studienreise von Turnlehrer Otto Plaumann (Beilage zu dem Jahresbericht des Reform-Realgymnasium zu Kiel." Kiel, 1910. 48 pages); "Leibesübungen in Dänemark: Bericht über eine einjährige Studien-Reise von J. B. Masüger, Turnlehrer an der Kantonsschule in Chur" (Chur, 1912. 104 pages).

recognized that with the help of the new exercises school gymnastics might perhaps be resuscitated, especially in the country, where conditions were quite unsatisfactory.

The most important result of all this agitation was the appointment (April 5, 1887) of a commission of three by the ministry of church and school affairs (*Ministeriet for Kirke- og Undervisningsvæsenet*), to recommend improvements in gymnastics as taught in the schools and to present plans for the founding and organizing of an institution in which men and women should be trained as teachers of gymnastics. Its members were Lieutenant-Colonel Amsinck, the new state inspector of gymnastics, chairman, communal physician (*Kommunelæge*) Axel Hertel, and Professor K. Kroman. They spent several weeks in Stockholm, at the *Central-institut* and in the schools, and then went to Berlin for a similar purpose. Upon their return they submitted a report (April, 1888) containing a number of definite suggestions for the better organization of physical education, the training of teachers, and the grouping of exercises in a lesson plan. They also proposed the appointment of a second and larger commission which should prepare a new manual of school gymnastics along the lines indicated. This body was accordingly named November 30, 1889. It included the former members, with the addition of *Kommunelæge* Chr. Fenger, regimental surgeon (*Korpslæge*) Johan Kier, Cand. polyt. N. H. Rasmussen, and the head of *Hærens Gymnastikekole*, Captain L. V. Schleppegrell. The result of their labors was the "Handbook of Gymnastics" (*Haandbog i Gymnastik*) published in 1899[1] and at once authorized by the government for use in all schools under its control. The new manual follows the general principles of the Ling gymnastics and adopts practically all of the Swedish exercises, but uses also many of the forms already current in Denmark, and introduces exercises on the horizontal and parallel bars, flying rings, and trapeze along with others which require the apparatus commonly found in gymnasia in Sweden.

The commission of 1887 had proposed that the government should start an institution for the training of men and women as teachers of gymnastics (*Gymnastik Læreranstalt*), with a two-years' course of study and practice. But in view of the unsettled condition of the whole question the authorities were unwilling to take such action. Professor Hans Olrik, director of the State Teachers' Course (*Statens etaarige Lærerkursus*, later known as the *Lærer-højskole*) then suggested, in 1897, that instruction in gymnastics be included as a separate division in that course. The government gave its approval to the plan, the *Rigsdag* voted the necessary

---

[1] Copenhagen, J. Frimodt.

funds, 13,500 Kr., and on March 30, 1898, an official announcement of the organization and character of the new course (*det etaarige Gymnastikkursus*) was published. It was opened September 1 of that year in N. H. Rasmussen's *Gymnastikhus* on Vodroffs Vej, under the direction of Cand. theol. K. A. Knudsen.[1] The next year (1899) Amsinck retired from his position as state inspector of gymnastics. His successor, Lieutenant-Colonel Ramsing (1837–1904), already over sixty years old when he was appointed to the office, died August 18, 1904, and now, for the first time in the history of the inspectorship, it was given (September 2) to a non-military man, K. A. Knudsen, the director of the one-year teachers' course.[2]

The training school for civilian teachers of gymnastics (*det civile gymnastiske Lærerinstitut*) founded in 1808, and the normal school of gymnastics (*Normalskole for Gymnastikken*) opened twenty years later were both short-lived and both had been appendages of *det militære gymnastiske Institut;* since 1859 the teachers of gymnastics in the *Seminarier* had been non-commissioned officers in the army, assigned to this duty for three-year periods only; and though the non-military schools were given a state inspector of their own in 1870, this position had always been held by an army officer. But with *det etaarige Gymnastikkursus* of 1898–1899, the *Haandbog* of 1899, and the appointment of Knudsen to the state inspectorship in 1904 gymnastics in the Danish schools entered upon an independent career. This fact was made plain by a new school law (1899) which prescribed, among other things, that no one should be regularly employed as teacher in the public schools unless he had received professional training in a *Seminarium*. The *nur-Turn-*

---

[1] Born at Orte, Island of Fünen, August 21, 1864, and graduated from the Latin school in Odense in 1883. He had completed his theological studies in Copenhagen in 1889, and the two-years' course at the Stockholm *Centralinstitut* in 1891, taught in the Ryslinge (Fünen) people's high school 1891–1895 (and during this time was active in spreading the Ling gymnastics in the Svendborg and Odense county rifle clubs), and besides practising medical gymnastics had been connected with Frøken Natalie Zahle's school and the Rasmussen gymnasium in Copenhagen 1895–1898.

[2] Inspector Knudsen has written the following, all of them published in Copenhagen, "i Hovedkommission hos J. Frimodt."
1. "Grundsætninger for Gymnastikundervisning." 1897. Fourth edition, 1908.
2. "Øvelselære. Forklaring af typiske gymnastiske Øvelser." 1900. Fourth revised edition 1911. A German translation (*Turnerische Ubungslehre*) by Ana Iversen, was published by B. G. Teubner, Leipzig and Berlin, in 1915.
3. "Timesedler til Brug ved Gymnastikundervisning for mandlige Elever." 1900. Fourth edition, 1912.
4. "Timesedler til Brug ved Gymnastikundervisning for kvindelige Elever." 1900. Fifth edition, 1912.
5. With Sigrid Nutzhorn, "Legemsøvelser for Pigeskolen, ordnede efter Skoleaar." Udgivet med Understøttelse fra Ministeriet for Kirke- og Undervisningsvæsenet. 1913.
6. "Lærebog i Gymnastik for Seminarierne." 1916. An English translation ("A Text-book of Gymnastics") by Ruth Herbert and H. G. Junker was published in 1920 (London, William Heinemann; Philadelphia, J. B. Lippincott Co.).

lehrer was thus to give place to the *auch-Turnlehrer*, and integral part of the teaching staff, and payment for instruction in gymnastics was to be at the same rate as for any other subject in the curriculum. It was therefore chiefly *Seminarium* -trained teachers, both men and women, who attended the one-year course, and from 1901 onward examinations based on the *Haandbog* of 1899 were given to all candidates for graduation at the sixteen *Seminarier*.[1]

In the higher (secondary) schools also gymnastics was to be taken out of the hands of special or professional teachers and entrusted to instructors who give a part of their time to other subjects. University graduates already occupying positions in such schools and university students who looked forward to teach-

Fig. 47.—Knud Anton Knudsen (1864–   ).

ing as a profession were therefore found among the pupils in the one-year course, and in 1905 the government decided to permit the work of that course to be spread over three or four years in the case of students who wished to complete it at the same time they were carrying on their studies in the university. April 1, 1911, the one-year course ceased to be a part of *Statens Lærerhøjskole*, and September 1, 1911, under a new name and as an independent institution (*Statens Gymnastik Institut*), it moved into a building

[1] For the later history of physical education in the Danish schools consult Knudsen in "Salmonsens store illustrerede Konversationsleksikon," **19** (Copenhagen, 1911), pp. 631–634; his "Gymnastikken i Danmark i hundrede Aar 1814–1914" (Copenhagen, 1914), and "Beretning om Statens Kursus i Gymnastik og om Gymnastikkens Tilstand i de danske Skoler i 1911" (Copenhagen, 1912); Docent J. Lindhard, "Akademiske Gymnastiklærere," in *Gymnastisk Selskabs Aarsskrift* 1912, pp. 169–177; and Kristen A. Lange, "Den Lingske Gymnastik i Danmark 1884–1909" (Copenhagen, 1909).

of its own.[1] Two years before this (November 1, 1909) the authorities of the University at Copenhagen had added to the faculty of that institution, on a six-year appointment, a *Docent* in anatomy, physiology, and theory of gymnastics (Johannes Lindhard, a physician), under whose direction students who desired to add instruction in gymnastics to other teaching after graduation were allowed to take one of their minor courses in preparation for the final examination (*Skoleembedseksamen*) leading to a degree, and so qualifying them to become candidates for positions in higher schools. The instruction in practical gymnastics and games was to be given

Fig. 48.—Interior of the Danish Central Institute of Gymnastics, at Copenhagen.

at *Statens Gymnastik-Institut*, or under the oversight of its director, and was to be at least equal to that given in the one-year course.

The demand for teachers trained in the *Haandbog* of 1899 could not be met by graduates from these more extended and thorough courses of preparation, however. For men and women already employed in the schools who could not afford to leave their regular duties the state therefore arranged short vacation courses of four weeks each. Thirty-four attended the first one of these, given in Copenhagen in 1899. The next year it was decided to move them out into the country, to *Seminarier* and *Folkehøjskoler*, and the numbers rose at once to 200. Between 1900 and 1911 the work thus offered was completed by 1027 men and 1680 women—an average

[1] Temporary quarters, on rented land in a corner of the University Ball Club's grounds (*Akademisk Boldklubs Bane*), out Tagensvej near the corner of Jagtvej. On April 1, 1921, the *Rigsdag* voted the sum of 500,000 Kr. for new buildings.

attendance of 225. In 1913 it reached 349. Still briefer courses, of a single week's duration (*Instruktionskursus*), brought a measure of preparation to older teachers who were unable to leave their homes, and these were often attended by the same persons for several years in succession. Two thousand five hundred and twenty-six men and 519 women were enrolled in them in the years 1901–1911. The total number of teachers trained in the newer gymnastics, in the state one-year course, the university, the sixteen *Seminarier*, and the longer and shorter vacation courses reaches therefore well into the thousands, and to these should be added the other thousands who have attended the month-long leaders' courses (*Delingsførerkursus*) arranged by the rifle clubs or their *Overbestyrelse* since 1889.

The Danes have not been the only ones to profit by the agencies just enumerated. Up to 1911 the one-year course had been taken by 15 foreigners (4 men and 11 women), from Norway, Finland, Poland, Germany, Switzerland, Holland, England and America; and 49 foreigners (25 men and 24 women) had completed vacation courses. At the invitation of Yorkshire school authorities *Gymnastikinspektør* Knudsen conducted a special vacation course for English teachers at Scarborough in 1905, and two graduates of the one-year course, H. G. Junker and H. P. Langkilde, were afterward employed to train teachers in the schools of West Riding, Yorkshire. Langkilde was engaged by the British ministry of war in 1906 to introduce the Ling gymnastics in the army gymnasium at Aldershot. Two other graduates of the one-year course, Braae-Hansen (in 1908, as director) and Frøken P. Brandt (in 1909), were installed as instructors in state-supported training schools for men and women teachers of gymnastics, organized at the Southwestern Polytechnic Institute in London. In 1908 Junker began to give one-month courses for English teachers at Silkeborg, in Denmark, which have been largely attended by both men and women (more than 80 in each of the years 1910 and 1911), and in 1910 he opened in the same place a one-year course for Englishmen. Danish women have also served as teachers of gymnastics at various English teachers' colleges and in the schools of that country.

The school code of 1814 had made practice in gymnastics obligatory, in the case of boys, at all elementary schools (*Folkeskoler*), whether town or country. A law of 1904 extended its provisions to include girls, as well; and within six years of that date more than 95 per cent of the girls in town and city elementary schools and nearly 50 per cent of those in the country were receiving such instruction. Lack of suitable rooms was the greatest difficulty which confronted the country schools. To meet this condition the *Rigsdag* voted that beginning with April 1, 1907, the state should bear one-half of the expense (up to 15,000 Kr.) incurred by any community in building a gymnasium (*Gymnastikhus*) for its schools. Two years later the grant was increased, so as to include town schools, and made to cover the cost of providing playgrounds also. It became necessary to withhold state aid after April 1, 1911, on account of financial stringency, but up to that time nearly 300 gymnasia had been erected in the country regions, at an average cost of about 5000 Kr. By the following year (1912) 488 country schools had gymnasia of their own, and 559 others were using rented gymnasia, usually those which belonged to rifle clubs. The other two-thirds of the 3500 or more country schools were obliged to content themselves with exercise out of doors on the playgrounds, which are gradually being equipped with such gymnastic apparatus as stallbars, Swedish horizontal bars, bucks, vaulting boxes, etc.

Not content with merely providing facilities for physical education, the *Rigsdag* also appropriated funds sufficient for the appointment of 17 *Gymnastikkonsulenter* (14 men and 3 women, most of them trained in the one-year course) or assistants to the state inspector of gymnastics, who are able to visit nearly 900 schools a year, arousing interest in teachers, pupils, and parents, demonstrating the proper handling of a class, meeting the teachers for conference and suggestions, and in general working for a better understanding of the object and means of physical education and greater uniformity in methods. A step which has done much to improve the standing of gymnastics in higher schools was the decision to grade pupils on their work in this subject, in connection with two of their public examinations (the *Mellemskoleeksamen*, since 1907, and *Realeksamen*, since 1908, but not yet in the final or *Studentereksamen*), and to give to such a grade (*Aarskarakter*) equal value with those secured in any other branch of study or practice.

Starting thus among young adults in the people's high schools and rifle clubs, the newer gymnastics has made its way into the elementary schools and the *Seminarier* and thence into the higher schools and the university. In contrast with what one sees in Sweden, the instruction is almost wholly in the hands of civilians, regular members of the teaching staff who give only a portion of their time to this branch; the average number of pupils in a class is only about 30, instead of the 150 or even 200 sometimes led by a single teacher across the Sound; and the rooms provided for exercise are smaller and more numerous—so frequently two for a single school that this may be considered the rule. On the other hand the Danish teacher receives at most a ten-months' course of special training, in contrast with the two years usually spent at the Stockholm *Centralinstitut*.

It is now more than a hundred years since Denmark made gymnastics an essential part of the curriculum of its public schools, antedating Prussia in the step by over a quarter of a century; but her German neighbor, on the other hand, takes precedence in the matter of systematic efforts to foster games among school children. Minister von Gossler's playground order was issued in 1882, fourteen years before its Danish counterpart, and the German "Central Committee for the Promotion of Games," formed in Berlin in 1891, was six years old before a corresponding body was organized in Copenhagen. The beginnings of the movement, in each country, reveal the influence of English customs, and the ball games of the English schoolboy were among the first forms introduced. In certain of the higher schools of Denmark, particularly in boarding schools located in the country, open-air games were already firmly established when in 1891 the Copenhagen Playground Association (*Legepladsforening*) first undertook to bring them within the reach of children in public elementary schools (*Folkeskoler*), by opening playgrounds in various sections of the city and organizing the playlife there. This attempt suddenly took on national proportions when Wilhelm Bardenfleth, Minister of Church and School Affairs, on August 31, 1896, sent out his "Circular to all school authorities regarding the introduction and regular use of games for children in the public schools."[1]

Games which require agility and strength, the Minister said, deserve a place side by side with formal gymnastics, not only as healthful forms of recreation, but because they train the players to make decisions promptly and carry them out energetically, rouse a feeling of responsibility, require subordination and coöperation, and play a large part in the development of personality. Hitherto this valuable educational agency, which supplements, but should not replace, gymnastics, has been left too much to the initiative of the young themselves and the results have been largely a matter of chance. School authorities should make it their business to provide playgrounds of sufficient size and conveniently located. Teachers must interest themselves in the matter, joining the pupils in their sports, preserving order, and supplying the necessary supervision and direction, and a place ought to be found in the curriculum for such activities, in addition to voluntary practice outside of school hours. The Minister announces his readiness to render assistance in furthering the movement, by including the subject of organized play in the annual vacation courses for teachers. Attention is called to a list of books containing directions for a variety of games. The Commission of 1889, appointed to work out a new manual of gymnastics, was also preparing a brief guide to the use of appropriate games,[2] and this, it was hoped, could be sent out to all public and private schools.

[1] "Circulære til samtilge Skoledirektioner om Indførelse af ordnede Lege for Folkeskolens Børn." The circular is given in full in the appendix to the first report (Første Beretning, 1897–1899) of *Udvalget for danske Skolebørns Fælleslege* (Copenhagen, 1899).

[2] "Lege, Boldspil og anden Idræt. Kort Vejledning til Brug for Skoler undarbejdet af Gymnastikkommission." Copenhagen, 1897. The same material, somewhat modified, is contained on pp. 275–404 of the "Handbog i Gymnastik" of 1899.

On December 1, 1896, three months after the appearance of the Bardenfleth circular, the Copenhagen Playground Association proposed to the ministry an annual grant from state funds to be used in making it effective, and offered to form a committee which should undertake to manage the practical details of the project. The suggestion was approved, the *Rigsdag* voted an appropriation of 5000 Kr. a year for three years, and the expenditure of the fund was entrusted to a group of men and women from all parts of the country who met in Copenhagen April 11, 1897, at the invitation of the Playground Association, and constituted themselves a National Committee for Promoting Group Games among School Children.[1] The original membership included Fru Rigmor Bendix, Copenhagen, chairman; school principal Emil Slomann, Frederiksberg, vice-chairman; wholesale merchant Carl H. Melchior, Copenhagen, treasurer; Dr. med. H. Forchhammer, Copenhagen, secretary; district physician Axel Hertel, Copenhagen, and school director Joakim Larsen, Frederiksberg, additional members of the executive committee; and fifteen other persons residing in various parts of Denmark, among them Professor Poul la Cour of the Askov people's high school, and Cand. theol. K. A. Kundsen, then living in Frederiksberg.

The regulations adopted at the time of organization have governed the operations of the Committee ever since. They define its object as the furtherance of group games in the open air. Among the means employed are lectures and the distribution of pamphlets explaining its work, guidance in the use of games, the training of teachers, grants of money to help in procuring apparatus and hiring teachers, and assistance in securing and equipping playgrounds. As a rule it is expected that in each case the community concerned, or private individuals, will provide an amount equal to that furnished by the Committee from the funds placed at its disposal. The Committee also reserves the right to supervise activities toward which it contributes, and to require annual reports regarding them; but local organizations are independent in matters of detail. It does not solicit contributions outside of the state grant, although it has a small income from other sources. Effort has been largely centered, from the start, on two lines of work, the preparation of teachers to act as play leaders in the schools, and the furnishing of expert advice and direct assistance in particular cases where these are requested.

Minister Bardenfleth, in his circular of 1896, had offered to include instruction and practice in group games in the annual vacation courses for teachers conducted by the state. Special

[1] *Udvalget for danske Skolebørns Fælleslege.* The Committee, whose headquarters are in Copenhagen, at Holsteinsgade 11², has issued six reports, covering respectively the years 1897–1899, 1899–1902, 1902–1905, 1905–1908, 1908–1911, and 1911–1914.

courses of this sort, under the direction of the secretary of the National Committee, were therefore provided for men in the summers of 1897–1900, and for women in 1898 and 1899, and the subject of games was added to the vacation course in gymnastics for women in 1897 and 1898. Since the fall of 1898 group games have been taken up as a regular part of the state's one-year course in gymnastics. In the spring of 1897 and again in 1898 the Committee offered short courses of its own for women teachers, especially those in the Copenhagen schools. With its help group games were made a part of various teachers' courses organized primarily for other purposes, and later it arranged a long series of special courses, beginning and repetition, term-time and vacation, for men, for women, and for both sexes.

The usual length of these special courses has been three weeks. Men have devoted four or five hours daily to the work, or a total of eighty to ninety hours, and most of it has been practical, with chief emphasis on the more complicated games, such as *Langbold* (a Danish-Norwegian ball game), cricket, football and hockey. The aim has been to give a complete understanding of the theory of each game, and enough practice in it to make the teacher a capable guide for his pupils. Not much time has been allotted to the simpler games. In the early courses for women instruction was more elementary, and limited at first to a total of eighteen to twenty-four hours, since most of the participants were quite unused to strenuous bodily exercise. *Langbold* was the favorite game, but later football was found to be excellent for young girls up to the age of puberty, and hockey after that period. The amount of time given to daily practice was also increased, until it reached three or four hours, and the total advanced from between thirty and thirty-five hours to between fifty and sixty. Hockey steadily gained in popularity, but children's games received relatively more attention than was the case in courses for men. Fr. Knudsen, secretary of the National Committee, has published a handbook of games, a guide to hockey, and with Ahrent Otterstrøm a football manual.

The demands upon the National Committee in its other field of effort, the giving of expert advice and direct assistance in particular cases, have been numerous and constant from the start. In 1897 help was given to 43 schools or communities; 64 others were added to the list the following year, and 120 in the period 1890–1901, and since that time the additions have averaged about 25 a year, so that by the end of 1913 a total of 532 had received aid. The needs of public elementary schools (*Folkeskoler*) have naturally been the first to receive attention, but a few *Realskoler* and *Højskoler* in the provinces are included in the number. Experience demonstrated the importance of competent oversight, and since April 1,

1901 assistance has been granted in new cases only when a professionally trained teacher of gymnastics is employed, or a graduate of one of the state or Committee courses in group games. Tours of inspection are made by the secretary of the National Committee, who visited 387 schools or communities in the years 1900–1913. Other trips were made to give advice or help in the laying out of playgrounds. Commonly the Committee first suggests the games which seem most appropriate in the locality concerned, and then sends on the necessary apparatus (for *ball* games, exclusively), except such as can be bought on the spot without much expense. A sum of money to be used in procuring or improving playgrounds is sometimes added; but the original idea of providing compensation for teachers has not been carried out.

The Folk High Schools, already alluded to, are residential, state-aided schools for adult continued education. Men attend usually from November to April. Women from May to August. There are now 83 schools, attended by 8000 students, mostly sons and daughters of small farmers. The school at Ollerup specializes in Physiology and the History, Theory and Practice of gymnastics, games and athletics, and the graduates, on their return to their native villages lead the village clubs in gymnastic games and dancing. The principal of this work is Niels Bukh, whose primary or fundamental gymnastics have been the greatest recent contribution in the field of Physical Education.

Following the principles laid down by Ling, it differs radically from the present day Swedish gymnastics in its application in increasing mobility, strength and agility with emphasis on mobility for which various stretching exercises are designed. He takes the useful movement of free athletics rather than the artificial movements of Swedish gymnastics.

His "day's order" has eight divisions. Exercises for legs, arms, neck, lateral, abdomen, dorsal, marching, vaulting; omitting the Swedish divisions, span bending, heaving, balance and breathing. In his mobility exercises he not only uses free but also duplicate or assisted movements to increase the mobility of contracted stiff joints and he moves the joints throughout their entire range, first free then forced, and finally with assistance.

In 1925 he made a tour of United States with his class of both men and women and his classes in Denmark draw students from America, England and elsewhere as well as from his own country.

BIBLIOGRAPHY.

The chief sources of information have already been given in the footnotes. Others will be found in the chapter as originally published in 1918 (see page 178).

CHAPTER XIX.

GREAT BRITAIN.

WHILE the *Turnverein*, or popular gymnastic society, was spreading over Germany, and systems of school gymnastics were being developed in that country and in Sweden, a variety of sports and organized games had become an established feature of life in the English public schools and universities.[1] As might be expected, these different types or phases of physical training have later begun to react upon each other, and each has been copied in more or less modified form in other countries. Most European states now have societies modelled after the German *Turnverein*, and the gymnastics of Spiess won friends among educational authorities far beyond the bounds of Switzerland and Hesse. We have found the playground movement making headway in Germany and Denmark, but shall also see the Swedish system of school gymnastics gain a foothold in England, as it had already done in Denmark.

In the first chapter of his "Athletics and Football" (The Badminton Library of Sports and Pastimes) Montague Shearman has reviewed the history of athletic sports in England. He attempts to show "that competitions in running, jumping and hurling of heavy weights are not only indigenous to the land, but have been one of the chief characteristics of both town and country life in England as far back as chronicles will reach; and that athletic sports, though they have had their days of waxing and waning, have always been a feature of life in 'Merrie England.' " Young Londoners in the reign of Henry II (1154–1189) practised "leaping, wrestling, casting of the stone, and playing with the ball," together with other exercises, in open spaces set apart for their use near the city. We have seen (p. 55) that Sir Thomas Elyot, in *The Boke* published in 1531, refers to lifting or throwing the heavy stone or bar, wrestling, running, swimming, handling the sword and the battle-axe, riding, vaulting and shooting in a long bow. Some idea of the universal prevalence of vigorous forms of recreation in the early part of the seventeenth century we gain from a passage in Robert Burton's *Anatomy of Melancholy*. Writing of exercise as a cure (Partition 2, section 2, member 4), he first considers hunting and fishing, and then goes on to say that "many other sports and recreations there be, much in use, as ringing, bowling, shooting (archery), which Ascham

---

[1] See footnote, page 134.

recommends in a just volume (*Toxophilus*, 1545) . . .; keelpins, tronks, quoits, pitching bars, hurling, wrestling, leaping, running, fencing, mustering, swimming, wasters (fencing with wooden swords), foils, football, balloon, quintain, etc., and many such, which are the common recreations of the country folks; riding of great horses, running at rings, tilts and tournaments, horse-races, wild-goose chases, which are the disports of greater men. . . ." The ordinary occasions for the pastimes of the common people were Sundays and church festivals, and the numerous country fairs. Joseph Strutt's volume on "The Sports and Pastimes of the People of England," published in 1801, gives an entertaining description of town and country recreations practised "from the earliest period to the present time," and it also reflects the general interest in such matters at the opening of the nineteenth century.

Fig. 49.—Eton College: The Wall Game (from "Football, the American Intercollegiate Game," by Parke H. Davis).

When we come to the particular forms of active sport or pastime which have been popular in Great Britain at one time or another we are amazed at their number and variety. Activities once practised as a necessary part of daily life survive in the sports of hunting, shooting, falconry or hawking, fishing with rod and line, and archery, and the same is true of walking, mountaineering, rowing and sailing, swimming, skating and the like. The primeval joy of combat has been furnished by wrestling, boxing, fencing with foil and sabre, single-stick and quarter-staff. Man has matched himself against man in footraces, broad and high jumping, weight-throwing and putting the stone or shot, the hammer-throwing and caber-tossing of the Scottish highlands, and the pole-vaulting which probably had its origin in contests between messengers whose calling required them to cross ditches and hedges with the help of jumping-poles. The game of bowls has been traced back to the thirteenth century or farther, and curling has been popular in Scotland for three centuries or more. Skittles, quoits, and hockey or shinny (shinty) have been played time out of mind. Golf was a formidable rival of archery in Scotland as far back as the middle of the fifteenth century; but English interest in the sport is comparatively recent. Polo was not introduced from the East until about fifty years ago. Tennis and fives, racquets and squash racquets have long had their

FIG. 50.—Football at Rugby School. (From H. H. Hardy's "Rugby.")

devotees, and lawn tennis is now added to the list. Cricket, while it existed in England as long ago as 1600, did not become widely popular until toward the middle of the next century; but football "is undoubtedly the oldest of all English national sports. For at least six centuries the people have loved the rush and struggle of the rude and manly game" (Shearman).

Certain ones of these sports are common to several or many countries, and no nation has a monopoly of games; but Great Britain has been preëminently the home of such pastimes, and nowhere else have they won such an enthusiastic following among all classes of society or affected so large a part of the population. In variety of sports cultivated, elaborate attention to details, and the perfection of play attained in games like cricket and football she was long without a rival. Price Collier, in the chapter on sports in his "England and the English from an American Point of View" (New

York, 1909), quotes some figures which "an accepted authority upon all matters of sport in England has compiled as to the investment and expenditures upon sport by the forty odd millions of inhabitants of Great Britain. His estimates, when they have been criticized, have been criticized mainly because they were too low." From these figures Collier concludes "that some $233,066,250 are invested permanently, and $223,887,725 spent annually for sport." He goes on to say: "Travel by train or motor anywhere in England and you see games being played—particularly if it be a Saturday— from one end of the country to the other. The open spaces of

FIG. 51.—Oxford University: The "Eights" on the Thames.

England seem to be given over to men and some women batting, kicking, or hitting a ball. The attendance at games on a Saturday is very large. . . Even at the beginning of the football season the gate receipts show an attendance of more than 200,000 people. When the big and final games take place, I have calculated that out of the male adult population of England and Wales on a great football Saturday one in every twenty-seven is in attendance at a game of some sort, and this leans to the error of being too few rather than too many."

Foreigners visiting England, and particularly men interested in education and brought into contact with the athletic life of the great public schools and Oxford and Cambridge Universities, could not fail to be impressed by such facts as we have mentioned, and to report them in the books which were the outcome of their travels. The influence of English practices on Koch, Hermann and Hartwich, pioneers of the playground movement in Germany, and Raydt's journey of 1886 and the volume embodying the result of his observations (1889) have been already cited (Chapter XIV). Professor Törngren, from the Central Institute of Gymnastics in Stockholm, visited England in 1877 and published a volume on school games shortly after (p. 162). The results of a later visit (1889) are reported in the *Tidskrift i Gymnastik* for 1890 (3 :145–195). English customs, also, seem to have been partly responsible for starting the playground movement in Denmark (p. 194). Paschal Grousset, the French journalist, recorded his impressions in "La vie de collège en Angleterre" (Paris, J. Hetzel, 1880), writ-

FIG. 52.—Oxford University: The "Eights" Passing the College Barges.

ing under the *nom de plume* "André Laurie." Pierre de Coubertin, who began his visits to England in 1884, has done the same in his "L'éducation en Angleterre: collèges et universités" (Paris, Hachette, 1888). Chapters II–IV in the volume on Physical Education of the Young by Professor Angelo Mosso, the Turin physiologist (German translation, 1894; French translation, 1895) reveal his indebtedness to English experiences. In the United States we have had Caspar Whitney's "A Sporting Pilgrimage" (New York Harper & Brothers, 1894), and John Corbin's "School Boy Life in England" (New York, Harper & Brothers, 1898) and "An American at Oxford" (Boston: Houghton, Mifflin & Co., 1902).

To an outsider, attempting to review the earlier history of physical education in England, it seems that apart from her outdoor sports, in the form they have assumed at the public schools and universities, her greatest contribution has been made through the teaching and writings of Archibald Maclaren, for many years proprietor of a gymnasium at Oxford. He was born in 1819 or 1820[1] at Alloa, a seaport on the north bank of the Forth, in Scotland. His daughter writes that she believes his father was the minister of a neighboring kirk, and the boy was brought up a Presbyterian. At the age of sixteen or a little older he went to Paris, and for some years was a student of fencing and gymnastics there. He also studied medicine; but was most interested in physical training, and determined to reform gymnastics, make a real science of it, and put it on a plane where it belonged as a part of education. He therefore settled in

FIG. 53.—Archibald Maclaren (C. 1820–1884). Copied from a portrait made about six years before his death.

Oxford, and opened a fencing school in Oriel Lane, afterward converting it into a gymnasium. In 1858 he erected a building of his own, the University Gymnasium, on Alfred Street at the corner of Bear Lane.[2]

An interesting sidelight on Maclaren's qualities of mind and heart is afforded by certain events which belong to this period. William Morris and Edward Burne-Jones, poet- and painter-to-be, entered Exeter College, at Oxford, in January of 1853, and both young men soon began to frequent the fencing rooms on Oriel Lane. J. W. Mackail[3] recalls how "between them and Maclaren himself, a man

[1] He died February 20, 1884, at the age of sixty-four.
[2] Described in the *Deutsche Turn-Zeitung* for January, 1860 (V: 8).
[3] In "The Life of William Morris" (London and New York: Longmans, Green & Co., 1899).

in the prime of life, cultivated and full of enthusiasm, a mutual intimacy and liking sprang up, and grew into a warm friendship. Three or four times in the term they would go and dine with him in Summertown. . ." And Lady Burne-Jones[1] speaks of Maclaren as a "man of the highest character and with warmth and tenderness underlying reserve of manner. His home at Summertown, then a small village separated by a stretch of country road from Oxford, was a sanctuary seldom opened to the outer world."[2] She calls him one of the truest friends her husband ever had, and one whose eyes discerned his pupil's genius from the first.[3]

About 1860 Maclaren was asked to work out a system of physical education for the British army. The result was "A Military System of Gymnastic Exercises for the Use of Instructors" (London, H. M. Stationery Office, 1862), "approved by the General Commanding in Chief and to be adopted at all stations where the means of carrying it out may be provided," according to a general order issued in February, 1862. Already, in 1861, a gymnasium built on the plan of the Oxford one had been erected at Aldershot, and Maclaren himself has described[4] the next step in carrying out the plan of the military authorities. "Two detachments of non-commissioned officers, under the command of the officer (Major Hammersley) selected by the authorities to direct its introduction (i. e the Maclaren system) and conduct its future extension—an officer specially selected for his high qualifications for the difficult work of introducing into the Army a new and hitherto entirely untried institution—were sent to Oxford to be qualified as instructors, and thence removed to Aldershot to form a normal school for the preparation of other teachers, and form the center of the military gymnastic system.

"The first detachment of non-commissioned officers, twelve in

---

[1] In "Memorials of Edward Burne-Jones" (New York, The Macmillan Co., 1904).

[2] "Mrs. Maclaren was the daughter of D. A. Talboys, the Oxford printer, and under her father had been trained as a first-rate classical scholar" (Charles L. Graves, in "Life and Letters of Alexander Macmillan," London, Macmillan & Co., 1910).

[3] The first step in the artistic life of Burne-Jones, she says, "was a series of pen-and-ink designs made at the suggestion of his friend Mr. Maclaren. These drawings were intended for illustrations to a volume of Ballads upon the Fairy Mythology of Europe, which Maclaren had written with the intention of publishing immediately. . . . The scheme included a frontispiece, title-page, illustrations and ornamental letters. They were begun early in 1854 and carried on for about two years and a half, and in the series may be traced his development from the time that he first went into the Wytham woods to draw leaves and branches until the day when he discovered that the human form was the alphabet'of the language which he was henceforth to use." The frontispiece, title-page, and a tail-piece on page 279 are all that appear in "The Fairy Family: a Series of Ballads and Metrical Tales Illustrating the Fairy Mythology of Europe," which Maclaren published anonymously in 1857 (London: Longman, Brown, Green, Longmans, and Roberts). A second edition, published in 1873, bears Maclaren's name on the title-page and is dedicated "To my daughter Mabel (London, Macmillan & Co.).

[4] In his "System of Physical Education," 1869, pp. 72, 73 and 93.

number, sent to me to qualify as Instructors for the Army were selected from all branches of the service. They ranged between nineteen and twenty-nine years of age, between five feet five inches and six feet in height, between nine stone two pounds and twelve stone six pounds in weight, and had seen from two to twelve years' service. I confess I felt greatly discomfited at the appearance of this detachment, so different in every physical attribute; I perceived the difficulty, the very great difficulty, of working them in the same squad at the same exercises; and the unfitness of some of them for a duty so special as the instruction of beginners in a new system of bodily exercise. . . But I also saw that the detach-

FIG. 54.—Maclaren's Oxford Gymnasium (From frontispiece to his "A System of Physical Education," 1869).

ment presented perhaps as fair a sample of the army as it was possible to obtain in the same number of men, and that if I closely observed the results of the system upon these men, the weak and the strong, the short and the tall, the robust and the delicate, I should be furnished with a fair idea of what would be the results of the system upon the Army at large. I therefore received the detachment just as it stood, and following my method of periodic measurements, I carefully ascertained and registered the developments of each at the commencement of his course of instruction, and at certain intervals throughout its progress."[1]

[1] Maclaren's "system of measurements to determine the rate of growth and development" is given in Appendix H of the volume just quoted. Appendix E contains a "table of measurements of first detachment of non-commissioned officers selected to be qualified as military gymnastic instructors," showing increases for the seven and a half months between September 11 and April 30; and a similar table of measurements of the second detachment, with increases for the period extending from October 27, 1862, to July 12, 1863.

To this period belong Maclaren's article on "National Systems of Bodily Exercise," published in *Macmillan's Magazine* for February, 1863 (VII :277–286), and another on "Military Gymnasia" which appeared in Volume VIII of the *Journal of the Royal United Service Institution* (Oxford, 1864). He also compiled "A System of Fencing, for the Use of Instructors in the Army" (London, H. M. Stationery Office, 1864). A general order of July 31, 1864, states that this system, "having been approved by the Field Marshal Commanding in Chief, is to be adopted in the Military Gymnasia, and at other stations where the means of carrying it out may be provided."[1] The next volume, "Training in Theory and Practice,"[2] reveals Maclaren at his best. He centers his remarks about a single exercise, rowing, and "in a great measure the mode in which that exercise is practised at our Universities and Public Schools." This selection is made because he believes rowing to be "the exercise most susceptible of being influenced by a judicious system of bodily preparation, being at once an art of considerable intricacy, demanding long and assiduous practice, and an exercise of considerable difficulty, involving the possession—although not in an equal degree —of both muscular and respiratory power, to promote which is the object of all training." Exercise (pp. 2–59), diet (60–119), and sleep, air, bathing, clothing (120–158) are discussed in turn in a clear, sane and masterly fashion, with frequent sharp and skilful thrusts at time-honored customs and beliefs. Fourteen appendices contain diagrams and tables relating to boats, diet, training systems, etc. It remains today one of the most valuable books of its class. A second edition, in 1874,[3] is enlarged by the addition of a practical course of training for the several kinds of boat-races practised at the university (pp. 119–160), a review of J. E. Morgan's "University Oars" (161–192), reprinted from *Nature*,[4] and an appendix on the subject of the sliding seat.

Outside of England, at least, Maclaren is best known through his latest volume, "A System of Physical Education, Theoretical and Practical," published in 1869.[5] The book is arranged in three

[1] In September of 1864 Mrs. Maclaren opened at Summertown a private school intended to prepare boys for the (endowed) public schools. The venture proved a very successful one from the start, and was continued by her son-in-law. Alexander Macmillan, one of the founders of the publishing house which bears that name, had made the acquaintance of the Maclarens in the summer of 1864, and by his efforts did much to enlist the interest of influential patrons, in addition to sending his own son George and two nephews. See pp. 225–227 in the "Life and Letters of Alexander Macmillan," by Charles L. Graves (London, Macmillan & Co., 1910).

[2] London, Macmillan & Co., 1866.

[3] London, Macmillan & Co.

[4] Vol. 7, 397–399, 418–421, and 458–460 (March 27, April 3 and 17, 1873).

[5] Oxford, Clarendon Press. A second edition, unchanged, was issued the year after the author's death (Oxford, 1885), and a third, reëdited and enlarged by his son, Wallace Maclaren, appeared ten years later (Oxford, 1895).

parts: (1) Growth and Development (pp. 3–101), (2) Practical System of Gymnastic Exercises (105–472), and (3) Appendices A-K (475–518). While the second part, which makes up nearly three-quarters of the volume, is not without interest as a manual of gymnastics embodying the author's ideas and the results of his long and varied experience,[1] it is the first hundred pages and certain of the appendices which have raised it to the rank of a classic in its field. After pointing out that "exercise alone of all the agents of growth and development can be regarded in an *educational* light— alone is capable of being permanently systematized and administered as a means of progressive bodily culture," he proceeds to discuss its nature and effects in terms of the physiological science of his day, much of it now outgrown. Health, rather than strength, should be the aim, he says. "Scholarships Junior and Senior, Examinations, open Fellowships, speculations, promotions, excitements, stimulations, long hours of work, late hours of rest, jaded frames, weary brains, jarring nerves—all intensified and intensifying— seek in modern times for the antidote to be found alone in physical action." School-games, sports and pastimes he finds, "from their very nature, are inadequate to produce the uniform and harmonious development of the entire frame, because the employment which they give is essentially partial. . . Recreative exercise in sufficient amount is usually in itself sufficient to maintain health and strength after growth and development are completed, but it does not meet the many wants of the rapidly-changing and plastic frames of youths spending a large portion of their time in the constrained positions of study."

He dwells at length upon conditions in the army, the attempt which he had made to meet them with his military system, and the results secured (pp. 64–94). "Now if all this arrangement and method were considered necessary in the organization of the bodily exercise of full-grown men—men of mature frame and hardy habit, and at the period of life when all the physical energies are at their highest point of power, at least as much precaution and forethought and method, it would be expected, would be adopted on its administration with boys and lads at school, whose frames are all incomplete and impressionable in the highest degree; capable of being affected for good or evil by every surrounding agency. But what are the

---

[1] "The system which I advocate is the result of my professional life—developed and matured by every means which I could bring to bear upon it by physiological theory or practical test. The period of its preparation extends over nearly a quarter of a century, for during that period I have been, as it were, standing in the midst of a living stream of men and boys flowing in from every school, public and private, in the kingdom; youths possessing every degree of physical power—presenting every phase of physical weakness. On these, *by* these, every exercise in the system has been tested; its nature, its character defined and its results ascertained, its place in the progressive courses slowly and carefully determined" (pp. 89 and 90).

facts? Except the two Military Colleges of Woolwich and Sand-hurst, and Radley College, not one of our large educational establishments is provided with a regularly organized Gymnasium with properly qualified teachers. . . In our day if gymnastics mean anything—that is, anything worth the serious thought of parent, teacher, or pupil—they mean a gradual, progressive system of physical exercise, so conceived, so arranged, and so administered, that it will naturally and uniformly call forth and cultivate the latent powers and capacities of the body, even as the mental faculties are developed and strengthened by mental culture and mental exercise."

In the appendix Maclaren illustrates certain forms of growth and development, regular and irregular, at different ages (A. Figs. 1–14); gives tables showing the state of growth and development between the ages of ten and eighteen years (B), and of men on arriving at the University (C); one which shows the influence of systematized exercise, extending over periods of several years, on boys of different conditions of growth and development, and on men of different degrees of physical power (D); and others containing measurements of non-commissioned officers before and after their course of training under him (E), and corresponding figures for youths at the Royal Military Academy, Woolwich (F), and for two pupils of his own (G); explains his system of measurements (H), goes into some detail regarding the construction and requirements of gymnasia (I), and closes with tables of best performances at certain athletic meetings (K). It is this practical demonstration of what regular exercise will accomplish, as well as his impessive setting forth of the need for it, that has caused his book to be so often quoted and makes it one of permanent value.

The first trace of the Ling system of medical gymnastics in England we find in 1838, when Lieutenant Govert Indebetou (the name is also written *In de Betou*), after completing the course at the Central Institute of Gymnastics in Stockholm, moved over to England and began the practice of that art in London. His work was continued for a time by an English physician, John W. F. Blundell. Another Swede, Lieutenant C. Ehrenhoff, settled in London for the same purpose in the early forties. Much more significant was the arrival of Carl August Georgii from Stockholm, where he has been a teacher at the Central Institute since 1829 and head teacher after 1840. He opened a private institute in London in 1850, and continued in active practice and teaching there until 1877. One of his pupils was the English physician M. J. Chapman, and another was Dr. Mathias Roth.[1] All of these men published

---

[1] Born in Kassa (Kaschau), Hungary, in 1818; studied in Vienna and Pavia, and won his medical degree at the latter university in 1839; took part in the Hungarian War of Independence (1849), and afterward made his way to England as a political refugee. See *Tidskrift i Gymnastik* **2**, 225–235 and **9**, 293–297.

pamphlets or more elaborate treatises on the subject. Of the Swedish system of school gymnastics, originated by P. H. Ling, but given its present form by his son Hjalmar in the years 1864–1882, we hear first in 1878. Dr. Roth had interested Mrs. Alice Westlake, a member of the London School Board, in this form of physical education, and in that year she persuaded the Board to engage Miss Concordia Löfving, a graduate of the Central Institute in Stockholm in 1870, to give a course in the theory and practice of Swedish gymnastics to women teachers under the Board, leading to a special certificate.

In 1881, at the end of the summer term, Miss Löfving withdrew from the service of the Board, and Miss Martina Bergman (later Mme. Bergman Österberg)[1] was appointed superintendent of

Fig. 55.—Martina Bergman Österberg (1849–1915).

physical exercise in girls' and infants' schools. Within the next six years, under her direction, the system was introduced into 300 schools, and 1000 teachers were trained. September 23, 1885, Miss Bergman opened a Training College for (women) Teachers of Physical Education at Reremonde, Broadhurst Gardens, Hampstead, N. W. (a borough of London), removing it ten years later to Kingsfield, Dartford Heath, Kent, and in her thirty years at the head of this school she built it up into an institution of more than national influence and importance. In 1893 she was present at the eighth annual convention of the American Association for the Advancement of Physical Education and the Congress of physical Education in Chicago, and in 1900 she attended the International Congress of Physical Education in Paris and gave a demonstration there with her pupils.[2] Captain J. D. Haasum, graduated at the

---

[1] Born in Skåne, south Sweden, October 7, 1849; graduated from the Central Institute of Gymnastics in Stockholm in 1881; died July 29, 1915.

[2] See *Tidskrift i Gymnastik*, **6**, 687–694 (1908).

Stockholm Central Institute in 1872 and teacher there since 1873, spent six months in London in 1884 and gave the first training course in Swedish gymnastics to a number of men teachers under the School Board, with the help of a gymnasium fitted up at the Crampton Street schools, Walworth. This work was continued by Allan Broman (Stockholm Central Institute of Gymnastics 1883), who at a later period (October, 1911) opened in London a "Central Institute for Swedish Gymnastics, for Men Students of Physical Training." This college together with the one at Bedford and Chelsea are the main sources from which teachers are obtained for the schools.

How the Swedish system was introduced into the British Navy and substituted, in large part, for the Maclaren gymnastics in the Army, may be told in a few words. Commander N. C. Palmer of the Navy spent some weeks in Stockholm in the autumn of 1902, in order to study the organization and management of instruction in gymnastics there, and upon his return set in motion plans for the training of instructors from among officers and non-commissioned officers. In the summer of 1903 Allan Broman was put in charge of the first course at Portsmouth, given to sixty officers in the British Navy. That same year a *Handbook of Physical Training,* published by authority of the Lords Commissioners of the Admiralty was issued.[1] Part I (pp. 4–73) is evidently based upon the Swedish Army and Navy Manual of 1902 (see p. 163), in both text and illustrations. A new Handbook, much enlarged and altogether Swedish, was published in 1910, the work of Lieutenant Lockhart Leith, who during a winter in Stockholm had taken part in the exercises at the Central Institute of Gymnastics. In 1906 the Army authorities decided to introduce the same system, but instead of going to Sweden they applied to the Danish government for a man capable of teaching it at the Aldershot training school for instructors. H. P. Langkilde (p. 192) was selected for the task. He began a course with the sixteen teachers at the school in August, and the next month a regular four-month course with non-commissioned officers. By the first of the next year (1907) the transition to the new system was complete. A *Manual of Physical Training,* worked out by Major Moore in collaboration with Langkilde on the basis of the Danish *Haandbog* of 1899, the Army and Navy Manual (Danish) of 1905, and the books of Knudsen was published in 1908.[2]

It was in 1867 that Archibald Maclaren, at Major Hammersley's suggestion, took to his gymnasium at Oxford Sergeants Rafferty, Kearney, Flanagan, Riley, Bartlett, Smith, Jackson, Tarbottom, Beer, Cox, Steele, and Sheppard, and gave them the course so graphically described in his classic work on physical education.

[1] London, H. M. Stationery Office.
[2] London, H. M. Stationery Office.

The group-picture, a little faded, still hangs on the wall of the Aldershot Gymnasium and their neatly tabulated measurements, copied by hand and signed by him on the parchment, can still be seen in the book of their photographs.

It is a far cry from this small beginning; and the way was through bypaths of Sandowism and other fads to the system that required a four months' course in Swedish gymnastics, gymnastic games, and clearing of obstacles, designed for the training of sergeant instructors and embodied in the official manual (1908).

When the World War broke out in August, 1914, the staff of instructors melted overnight. Every man rejoined his regiment up to the Inspector of Gymnasia, Colonel Walter Wright, who was, however, speedily recalled to his important post. This crisis he met by rapidly enlisting old graduates of the course who had left the service and taken positions in public and board schools, and private institutions. These formed the nucleus of the new staff with the half dozen he was able to retain in their positions. Soon he was to increase their numbers in another way. From the front, men kept coming back; one with a bullet through his shoulder blade; another with a piece of shrapnel in his face; and a third with a ragged scar on his leg or part of his foot gone—all wounds that made them useless in the fighting line, but did not prevent them from using their knowledge of teaching. Among them Colonel Ronald Campbell who afterwards succeeded Colonel Wright as Inspector of Gymnasia.

The war started with the machinery for training 100,000 and the numbers to be attended to within a year mounted to nearly 3,000,000 The number of instructors that could adequately manage the ordinary army of peace times scarcely touched the enormous masses of raw men in the training camps—recruits who had to be turned into trained soldiers in months instead of years—so he sent out a call to all commanding officers to select candidates, both officers and men, from their regiments. These men were to be sent to Aldershot for a special course to fit them as teachers in their own regiments. Among other things the qualifications required were: (1) Sufficient force of character to inspire respect; (2) intelligence and enough education to grasp the system of physical training; (3) sufficient activity to perform and illustrate the various exercises correctly; (4) age not under twenty or over thirty years, as those under twenty years have not, as a rule, developed the force of character necessary for discipline and those over thirty do not easily acquire certain positions which are important.

The response was such that even after quadrupling the numbers taken, there were always three or four waiting for every place vacant in the gymnasium course.

To make the course as simple as possible, the work that usually spread over four months was cut down to twenty-one working days, and the exercises were arranged into eight tables of movements, Swedish in character but arranged somewhat differently from the accepted Swedish day's order.   Each table consisted of two parts, the first part being subdivided into three, as follows:

PART I.—(a) Introductory exercises, five in number, for the leg, neck, arm, trunk and leg, in that order.

(b) General exercises consisting of span bending, balance, lateral, abdominal, dorsal; marching and jumping.

(c) Final exercises—leg and arm, to slow down the circulation, the arm exercise consisting of side upward raise and lower, with deep breathing, the rhythm being governed by the rate of respiration and not *vice versa*.

The progression was logical and carefully designed, the exercises becoming more difficult and complicated from table to table.   Having mastered these, it was a simple matter to teach the special tables designed to give the trained soldier a stiff thirty minutes of work or the light morning table of five or ten minutes taken usually after a cup of cocoa or tea, or the remedial table with its emphasis on the abdominal muscles.

Part II consisted of class formations, marching in quick, slow and double time, jumping, hopping, the surmounting of obstacles, and gymnastic games like leapfrog and fox and geese.   The object was to provide exercises for large numbers that could be taught by comparatively untrained instructors and also to round out the day's work by these additions to the pure Swedish gymnastics.

The staff instructors laid stress on accuracy, alertness, speed and discipline; most of the movements were in themselves far from violent, but the attention was kept at the highest pitch of intensity and any wandering of the mind received a quick and efficient check.

The day's work began at 9 A.M., when the table for the day was gone through again and again, with criticism and explanation, until 10.30 A.M.   After a brief rest the class divided into couples, each putting the other through the table of exercises done the day before.   The staff instructors criticized and instructed in the important art of teaching, the proper emphasis in the word of command, the adequate pause, the intonation, and the attitude of domination necessary for discipline.   This part of the day justly received quite as much attention as the actual performance of the movements, for each officer and man was trained as a teacher rather than as a gymnast.

The colossal armies that poured from the training camps into France, Egypt, Gallipoli, and Servia, were composed of men from every walk of life—lawyers, doctors, clerks, bookkeepers, brokers and students—unaccustomed to the fatigues of marching, and the heavy manual labor of digging. Miners, masons, bricklayers, carpenters, ploughmen, and iron workers, often bent and stiffened by long hours of hard slow labor, all had to be strengthened, quickened and made supple and agile, to fill the rôle of the modern soldier.

The physical training and bayonet fighting as taught at Aldershot, were designed to cultivate the qualities necessary for success in the field, and they did so admirably. It made easier the work of the drill sergeant. If the object would be put in two words only they would be "executive action," the training that would apply equally well in marching, digging, throwing bombs, jumping trenches, using the rifle and bayonet, or handling a gun. The very artificiality of most of the movements gives a special training to the will power and attention by isolating muscle groups against natural inclination.

It was planned to give every soldier, after passing his recruit stage, one hour a day, equally divided between physical training and bayonet fighting.

The visit of men from the trenches impressed more than ever the importance of the use of the bayonet, and the old and picturesque bayonet exercise that was always an attractive display, was replaced by a less beautiful, but much more practical method.

The drill movements and positions were abolished except those of "on guard" and "point." The men were paired off to teach each other by signs rather than words. The application of this teaching was demonstrated on sacks or faggots, hanging from gallows, set up on tripods, or set in trenches, and the bayonet course over which the recruit passed gave him experience in every combination of conditions with which he was likely to meet. He leaped trenches, climbed parapets, thrust down into trenches or at hanging sacks, and the four simple parries he learned were considered not so much as a means of defense, as the clearing of an obstruction for his attack. There was no sparring for an opening.

This bayonet fighting formed the basis for that of all the allied armies and the American Expeditionary Force, and was widely taught.

Since the war the course of four months has been resumed at Aldershot and the bayonet fighting has been greatly curtailed. Special emphasis now is being placed on the teaching of games along with the more formal work of the Swedish Gymnastics.

March 31, 1902, King Edward VII appointed a commission of nine "to enquire into the opportunities for physical training now available in the State-aided schools and other educational institutions of Scotland; and to suggest means by which such training may be made to conduce to the welfare of the pupils; and further, how such opportunities may be increased by continuation classes and otherwise, so as to develop, in their practical application to the requirements of life, the faculties of those who have left the day schools, and thus to contribute towards the sources of national strength." This commission reported under date of March 14, 1903,[1] and perusal of the second volume shows the Swedish system still in use in elementary schools for girls under the London School Board, and in two Merchant Company's higher schools for girls in Edinburgh, the Edinburgh Ladies' College and George Watson's Ladies' College. Having regard to the findings of this Royal Com-

Fig. 56.—Eton College: The Gymnasium (1913).

mission an "Interdepartmental (*i. e.*, English and Scotch) Committee on the Model Course of Physical Exercises," under date of March 10, 1904, presented to both Houses of Parliament a report directed to "the Right Honorable the Lord President of the (English) Board of Education and the Right Honorable the Vice-President of the Committee of the Privy Council on Education in Scotland."[2]

On pp. 10–49 is the proposed Syllabus of Physical Exercises, based in general on the Swedish system. In consequence of this report the English Board of Education published its first official "Syllabus of Physical Exercises for Use in Public Elementary Schools" in 1904.[3] The next year it was reprinted, with slight alterations;

[1] Report of the Royal Commission on Physical Training (Scotland), presented to both Houses of Parliament by Command of His Majesty. Edinburgh, H. M. Stationery.
[2] London, H. M. Stationery Office.	[3] Ibid.

but the third edition,[1] four years later, contains "further amendments and extensive revisions, which are based upon experience. . . . Speaking generally the new Syllabus, like its predecessor, is based on the Swedish system of educational gymnastics which has been adopted in several European countries, and is now the basis of physical training in the Army and Navy in this country" (p. vi).

The part played by Denmark in this transplantation of an alien system to British soil has been already indicated (p. 194). Even in the endowed Public Schools, the very strongholds of athletic sports,

Fig. 57.—Rugby School: The Gymnasium (From H. H. Hardy's "Rugby").

we find it introduced as a general requirement, to supplement the effects of outdoor recreation. Lieutenant F. H. Grenfell, who had taken work at the Stockholm Central Institute of Gymnastics, brought it to Eton College in 1907, and Captain E. C. Brierly, of the Army, undertook a similar task at Rugby in September of 1911. Harrow and Winchester, at least, among the other public schools, also possess gymnasia in addition to their extensive playgrounds.

To this fragmentary review of certain phases of physical education in Great Britain a paragraph on the Dunfermline College of Hygiene and Physical Training should be added. The Carnegie Dunfermline Trust was formed in August of 1903, and in the hands of its

[1] The Syllabus of Physical Exercises for Schools. 1909. London, as above.

Trustees Andrew Carnegie placed a princely fund to be used for the benefit of the town of his birth. A gymnasium was opened October 21, 1904, and the New Baths March 31, 1905. Physical training was introduced into the schools soon after the Trustees came into office, and medical inspection of school children was begun in 1906. October 4, 1905, a College of Hygiene and Physical Training (for women) was opened, offering a two-year course and housed at first in the Gymnasium and Swimming Pool, on Pilmur Street. Three years later a men's department was added, and the two departments were united in 1911. By the next fall 75 students had received diplomas for the full course. Meanwhile, in July of 1909,

FIG. 58.—Dunfermline College of Hygiene and Physical Education: The New College and Clinics Building.

the Trustees learned that the College had been recognized by the Scotch Education Department as a Central Institution for the purpose of the Education (Scotland) Act of 1908, *i. e.*, for the training of teachers for the schools of that country; and by an arrangement approved in 1912 the services of certain teachers on the college staff are available for the work of inspecting the teaching of physical exercises in schools throughout Scotland. Venturefair Park, seven acres in extent, was leased for the games of the College students and opened July 27, 1909, and in September of 1914 a new building, the foundation stone of which had been laid by Mr. Carnegie two years before, was occupied by the College and the School Clinics. Early in 1911 the original gift to the Trust had been increased by one half, raising the fund to $3,750,000.

Additional material on Great Britain, especially on Government cooperation in the Physical Fitness program, may be found in Chapter XXXII.

BIBLIOGRAPHY.

The Badminton Library of Sports and Pastimes (London: Longmans, Green & Co.; Boston: Little, Brown & Co., 28 volumes, 1885–1896) is unique in its field. Robert Scott Fittis, in "Sports and Pastimes of Scotland" (Paisley and London, Alexander Gardner, 1891), offers some material of historical interest. Other sources have been mentioned or suggested in the text.

A Visit to the Home of Archibald Maclaren, R. Tait McKenzie.

Physical Training of the New British Armies, American Physical Education Review, December, 1915. R. Tait McKenzie.

The Making and Remaking of a Fighting Man, American Physical Education Review, March, 1917. R. Tait McKenzie.

Relation of Physical Education to the Business of War, American Physical Education Review, December, 1917. R. Tait McKenzie.

Treatment of Convalescent Soldiers by Physical Means, R. Tait McKenzie, R.A.M.C. Proceedings Royal Society of Medicine, 1916.

A National Scheme of Physical Education, Journal of Royal Sanitary Institute, No. 4, 1916. R. Tait McKenzie.

CHAPTER XX.

INTERNATIONAL GATHERINGS.

THE types or systems of physical training found in Europe can all be reduced to three elemental forms, illustrated by the *Turnverein* or popular gymnastic society of Germany, the athletic sports and active games of the English public schools and universities and the school gymnastics of Germany and Sweden. Corresponding to each of these, in a way, there have been international gatherings of three sorts in recent years, *i. e.*, conventions and competitive meets of the European gymnastic federations, "games" and congresses held under the auspices of the International Olympic Committee, and a series of congresses organized with a view to better understanding of the principles and methods of physical education.

In 1881 Nicolas Jan Cupérus of Antwerp, president of the *Fédération belge de Gymnastique* (*Belgische Turnbund*), proposed an association of the various national organizations of popular gymnastic societies in Europe. Preliminary conventions were held at Liège on July 23d of that year and again on August 14–16, 1896, and arrangements were completed in Brussels, July 3–5, 1897. A permanent committee (*Bureau*) was appointed, with Cupérus as president. The articles of agreement provided for an exchange of publications and official documents, established rules governing invitations to national meets and conditions of participation in them, recognized only such national organizations as held themselves aloof from political and religious controversies, and stated the attitude of the union towards professionalism and in regard to the sort of prizes which should be awarded in competitions. The following federations subscribed to these articles: the Belgian, Czech, French, British (the National Physical Recreation Society, Amateur Gymnastic and Fencing Association, Irish Amateur Gymnastic Association, Scottish Amateur Gymnastic Association, and later the Welsh Amateur Gymnastic Association), Italian, Luxemburg (Grand Duchy), Hungarian, Netherlandish, Norwegian, and Swedish. The Danish federation was added later, but the German *Turnerschaft* and the Swiss *Eidgenössischer Turnverein*, together with smaller organizations in Austria, the Balkan States, Russia, Finland, and Portugal have never become affiliated. Seven statistical "Annuals"[1] have been published under the editorship of Cupérus. Since 1897 conventions have been held at Antwerp (August 14, 1903), Berne (July 14, 1906), Prague (July 1, 1907), Paris (November 21, 1908), and Luxemburg (July 21, 1909); and there have been international meets for competition at Antwerp (1903), Bordeaux (1905), Prague (1907), Luxemburg (1909), Turin (1911), and Paris (1913).

The story of the modern Olympic Games, and the events which led up to them may best be told in the words of Dr. Albert Shaw[2] and Professor William Milligan Sloane.[3] Its central figure in the early years is Baron Pierre de Coubertin, scion of an old French

Fig. 59.—Pierre de Coubertin (1863-1937).

family, born January 1, 1863, and educated in the schools of Paris. "It was in 1884, when only twenty-one years of age," says Dr. Shaw, "that M. de Coubertin began his visits to England, with the prime object of acquainting himself intimately with the life of the great public schools—Rugby, Eton, Harrow, and the others of that type. He had become strongly convinced that there was an element in

---

[1] Annuaires des Fédérations Européenes de Gymnastique, 1898 (14 pages), 1899 (16), 1900 (21), 1901 (47), 1902 (32 pages of text and 17 plates containing portraits), 1906 (49), and 1913 (? Not seen, but reviewed in *Deutsche Turn-Zeitung* 1913, pages 138 and 141).

[2] In "The Evolution of France under the Third Republic," by Baron Pierre de Coubertin. Translated from the French by Isabel F. Hapgood. Authorized edition with special Preface and Additions and Introduction by Dr. Albert Shaw, Editor of *The Review of Reviews*. New York and Boston, Thomas Y. Crowell & Co., 1897. See Introduction, pages iii-xxiii.

[3] First American member of the International Olympic Committee. Quoted from his chapter (pages 71-83) in "Report of the American Olympic Committee, Seventh Olympic Games Antwerp, Belgium, 1920."

English education that was sadly lacking in the French schools. Obviously and conspicuously, the English training in athletics and the English devotion to outdoor sports and exercises, were almost totally unknown in the French lyceums and collegiate institutes. But Coubertin clearly perceived that something even more serious was concerned than the mere question of physical culture. He understood that in the rowing, football and cricket of the English schools, and all their other games, contests, and field-day exercises, there was involved an element of moral discipline and strength that supplied in some sense a key to the secret of England's power. Not merely a manliness expressed in muscular force and physical bearing was developed in the English arena of school sports or neighborhood contests and pastimes, but also a fine spirit of fair play, a hatred of meanness, lying, and all forms of deceit, and that fundamental kind of honor and integrity of character that causes Englishmen to be trusted and respected, even if not greatly beloved, by all races, in all lands. Furthermore, this love of hardy games and contests seemed to Coubertin the best sort of protection to the young men of our times from the temptation to unworthy indulgences that tend to undermine personal vigor and thereby to diminish the vitality of the nation.

"The drift in France among young men of education was toward softness and overrefinement, and the vices that are somewhat dangerously akin to certain phases of aesthetic development. The ideals of youth in England seemed, as compared with those of France, to make for the clear eye, the steady hand, the firm will—in short, for self-control and the conservation of energy. It was, therefore, with no mere boyish fondness for the excitement of athletic contest, considered as a thing desirable in itself, that M. de Coubertin devoted himself to the development or the revival of a high type of manhood among French students. . . He was ready at length in 1888, at the age of twenty-five, to publish his book *L'Éducation en Angleterre* (see p. 202), an account of school life in England, which, while valuable on any account, was of particular use in the advancement of the cause to which all his efforts were really devoted. The book attracted very favorable attention in France, and its success gave the young author and reformer prestige enough for the public launching of his practical movement, this taking the form of a 'committee for the propagation of sports and physical exercises in education,' with that eminent statesman, scholar, and educational authority, Jules Simon, as president of the committee."

In 1889, in connection with the Paris Exposition, he organized a congress on physical education, and that autumn visited the United States, under commission from the National Department of Public Instruction, to study the organization, work, and life of American colleges. "Meanwhile," continues Shaw, "all this work for the encouragement of the athletic spirit in the French institutions had begun to tell strongly; and in the season of 1891–1892 it was possible under M. de Coubertin's leadership to organize what is now the well-known *Union des Sociétés des Sports Athlétiques*. This central body is a confederation of abut two hundred French athletic clubs and societies, half of which are in the universities and colleges. With a view to keeping the French student's interest from flagging, M. de Coubertin endeavored to make some plans for English and American competitions. Thus, in 1892, international football matches were begun between French and English teams, Lord Dufferin himself presiding over the first one held at Paris. M. de Coubertin also succeeded in securing the recognition of the French Union by the Henley Regatta Committee, and the admission of French rowing crews to the university contests on the Thames. Again, in that same season, he secured the visit to Paris of a team of American university athletes, as the result of the efforts of an American committee which he had organized and in which his friend Professor Sloane, then of Princeton University, was especially active. . .

"To crown the work of the year, M. de Coubertin, at the end of November (1892), gave a lecture in the amphitheatre of the Sorbonne, in which he disclosed his plan for the reëstablishment of the Olympic games. The enlistment of American interest in this ambitious project for a modern quadrennial tournament of games and sports that should be open to amateurs—particularly those of the student class—from all nations, was much facilitated by M. de Coubertin's second visit to the United States, which occurred in 1893. . . Before leaving this country in the autumn of 1893 he has aroused a very general interest, especially in the college world, in his plan for the Olympic games. A little later, in the early weeks of 1894, he was actively at work in England holding conferences and forming his committee for the promotion of the idea of the quadrennial athletic tournament. In June of that year the subject was taken up by a great conference or congress, held at the Sorbonne in Paris (June 16–24), a dozen or more nations being represented. King George of the Hellenes sent his best wishes; and the eight-day conference, with its accompanying fêtes and sports in the Bois du Boulogne, was fairly successful, resulting in the formation of an international committee to carry the Olympic plan into effect."

So far Dr. Shaw. Professor Sloane quotes from a preliminary circular of January 15, 1894, the final sentence of which reads as follows: "The reëstablishment of the Olympic Games on a basis and under conditions conformable to the needs of modern life would bring together every four years representatives of all nations, and it is permissible to suppose that these peaceful and courteous contests would supply the best of internationalism." "To this circular," he says, "came a very irregular and scattering response. The German federations took no notice whatever, the gymnastic element in France was hostile, the British were lukewarm, the Belgians frankly and actively embattled. They had always held and still were of the opinion that gymnastics and sports were two inimical things, and would always combat the latter as opposed to the former. Italy, Spain, Greece and above all Sweden sent regular delegates. Somehow or another seventy-nine persons representing something or another appeared at the congress. The many sessions

FIG. 60.—The Stadium at Athens (1906).

were well attended, the accompanying festivities were dignified and inspiring. No one present can ever forget the great assemblage at the Sorbonne, the inspiring address of Courvel, the superb poem of Sicard, the wonderful execution of the hymn to Apollo, recently discovered at Delphi, nor the enthusiasm of the closing banquet. These were but a few of the notable events of the week. The climax of the proceedings was a unanimous vote for the reëstablishment of the Olympiads with the opening of the new century; but second thoughts were even more enthusiastic than first and it was finally determined to hold the first one at Athens in 1896.

"Greek royalty was already enrolled among the patrons of the scheme, Greek patriotism might be relied upon for material and effective support. Such at least was the opinion of M. Bikelas, the Greek member, the greatest modern Greek man of letters, exerting by the charm of his manner, the weight of his character and the gifts of his liberal hand, such an influence on the evolution of modern Greece as no other single man has been able to deploy. The event showed the correctness of his judgment and the weight of his personal influence. The president of the International Committee was received in Athens with enthusiasm, a wealthy Greek merchant of Alexandria, M. Averoff, caused the ancient Stadium to be restored and newly lined with Pentelic marble at his personal cost. A princely gift of a million drachmæ, other lavish personal contributions, and what amounted to a subsidy from the Greek Government completed the necessary fund. A very considerable legacy to the state from the brothers Zappas, designated for the furtherance of physical culture, was through the untiring persistency of M. de Coubertin, aided by two devoted Greek friends, M. Antonopoulo and Alexander Mercati, appropriated by government consent for Olympic purposes. The enterprise was therefore brilliantly launched.

"The succession of Olympic Games is well known: after Athens in 1896, Paris in 1900, St. Louis in 1904, London in 1908, Stockholm in 1912, Berlin (designated for 1916 and actually prepared but lapsed owing to war), Antwerp in 1920 and Paris in 1924. Baron de Coubertin resigned the presidency in 1925, and was succeeded by Count Balliet-Latour of Belgium. Each has been more amazing than its predecessor: in the number of nations represented, in the number and quality of competitors, in the greater perfection of preparation for each sport, in the number of sports clustered around the Olympic week of field and track events, in the social arrangements for better acquaintance among competitors and the ever-growing throng of visitors, and above all in the passionate interest of all peoples in all lands. . . While track and field sports are the nucleus of the sport-plexus, they are not the whole of it. Nor is sport in the narrow sense the whole of it. All kinds of outdoor exercises and games have attached themselves to the Olympic week of track and field athletics—central and focal in modern as in ancient Olympiads—to such an extent that no national Olympic council can provide for all in the arrangements for the Olympiad to be held. Instead of an Olympic week we already have Olympic months and a very powerful movement was started some years ago to include winter sports of every kind, and expand into an Olympic year. It has become absolutely necessary, if there are to be Olympiads, that contraction should be substituted for expansion in the number of admitted sports or games represented by federations, national or international.

"Furthermore, the Olympic idea comprehends something, yes much, quite aside from contests of foremost experts in sport and play. For the Antwerp Olympiad arrangements included lectures,

FIG. 61.—The Stockholm Stadium (1912)

preliminary in the not too distant future to contests in belles lettres and the fine arts. Such competition is already in evidence as actually existent though still inchoate. In particular, however,

FIG. 62.—Stockholm, 1912: The Swedish Gymnasts Marching into the Stadium.

and poignantly the Olympic idea as represented by its carriers proposes 'all sports for all' in the literal sense of the words. The Committee hopes that the day is not far distant when through its moral influence, orient as well as occident may be nationally organized for competition and that the benefits of 'play for country' as

Fig. 63.—Stockholm, 1912: Swedish Women on the Long Horizontal Bar (*Bom*).

Fig. 64.—Stockholm, 1912: The Danish Gymnasts.

well as for self may by such organizations be alluringly offered to youths and adults of both sexes in every walk of life. To this end its plans are already laid, and already great portions of the globe hitherto inert athletically are girding themselves for Olympic organization. The field therefore of the Olympic idea is not merely sportive

Fig. 65.—Stockholm, 1912: The Finish Gymnasts.

Fig. 66.—Stockholm, 1912: Finnish Women on the Ladders.

and social, it is educational and sociological as well. The intercourse of athletes and their friends makes for reciprocal good will and international peace; but in its largest aspect the idea makes for the general uplift and personal purity of untold millions. . ."

The first international congress for the promotion of physical education was held at Paris, June 8–15, 1889, in connection with the Universal Exposition. Its organizer and general secretary was Pierre de Coubertin, and the presiding officer was Jules Simon. At the same time came the fifteenth annual *fête* (*Turnfest*) of the *Union des Sociétés de gymnastique de France*, attended also by representatives from gymnastic societies in Belgium, Holland, the Grand Duchy of Luxemburg, the three Scandinavian countries,

Fɪɢ. 67.—Georges Demeny (1850–1917).

Bohemia and Switzerland. The Scandinavians did not take part in competition, but the delegations from each of the three countries went through their exercises separately in front of the tribune. In addition the group of Stockholm gymnasts, under the direction of Captain Viktor Balck of the Central Institute, appeared before the international congress on the 14th, at the Nouveau Cirque, rue St. Honore, in another exhibition of the Swedish system. A second *Congrès international de l'Éducation physique* met in Paris August 30–September 6, 1900, during the progress of the *Exposition universelle* of that year, with M. Georges Demeny (1850–1917) as general secretary.[1]

Demeny, at first won over to the Swedish system by what he saw

[1] See his "Procès verbaux sommaires," Paris, Imprimerie Nationale, 1900.

and heard at Paris in 1889 and during a mission to Sweden with Dr. Fernand Lagrange (1845–1909) in the autumn of 1890, afterward withdrew from association with men like Dr. Philippe Tissié who advocated the Ling gymnastics for French schools, and sought to build up an eclectic (French) system of his own. Both parties were represented at the *Congrès Olympique international de Sport et d'Éducation physique* in Brussels June 9–14, 1905, and the *Deuxième Congrès international de l'Éducation physique de la jeunesse* at Liège, August 28–September 1 of that year,[1] and there were preliminary skirmishes at the latter; but the first real battle was fought a few weeks later, at the *Congrès international d'Expansion économique mondiale*, in Mons (September 24–27). Five years later each group organized its own congress, the friends of the Swedish system a *Congrès international de Gymnastique pédagogique, militaire, médicale et esthétique*, which met in Brussels, August 4–6, 1910,[2] and Demeny and his followers a (third) *Congrès international d'Éducation physique* in the same city a week later (August 10–13).[3] A Danish committee representing friends of the Ling system organized another international congress, which held its sessions in Odense, Denmark, July 7–10, 1911.[4] The last congress to be called together before the outbreak of the Great War met in Paris under the auspices of the *Faculté de Médecine*, March 17–20, 1923.[5]

---

[1] See the *Règlement et rapports préliminaires* and the *Compte rendu* of the second congress (Nivelles, Lanneau & Despret).

[2] See the *Rapport général*, Brussels, 1910.

[3] There is a report by the delegates from the United States in the Bureau of Education Report for 1910 (I: 598–601).

[4] See "procès verbal du Congrès international de l'Éducation physique à Odense (Danmark)" (Copenhagen, J. H. Schultz, 1911).

[5] "Congrès international de l'Éducation physique (programme and announce, ment), Paris, Faculté de Médecine, 17–20 Mars 1913."

CHAPTER XXI.

THE FIRST INTRODUCTION OF THE JAHN GYMNASTICS INTO AMERICA.

THE different systems or sorts of physical training which were brought forward for trial and the agencies which promoted its spread in the United States during the nineteenth century fall into three groups, centered about 1830, 1860 and the decade from 1880 to 1890. The first group includes Captain Alden Partridge and his military academies;[1] the introduction of the Jahn gymnastics and the opening of school, college, and city or public outdoor gymnasia under the direction of the German refugees Beck, Follen, and Lieber; the attempt to provide manual labor as a system of exercise in educational institutions;[2] and the use of "calisthenics" for girls and women, by Catharine Beecher in her schools in Hartford and Cincinnati.[3] Space limits have prevented the discussion of any but the second member of this group in the present volume.

The first school, college, and public gymnasia in the United States—all of them outdoor ones of the early Jahn type—were opened in the years 1825 and 1826 in Massachusetts, at Northampton, Cambridge and Boston. All three were laid out and directed by university trained Germans, who had been active participants in the Jahn gymnastics in their student days and had left their native land for the United States in order to escape arrest or constant persecution under the reactionary policy adopted by the Holy Alliance.

One of these men was Charles Theodore Christian Follen (German *Karl Follenius* or *Follen*), born September 4, 1796, in Romrod, a market-town north of the Vogelsbert. His father was counsellor at law and judge at Giessen, in the Grand Duchy of Hesse, and he

---

[1] See *Mind and Body* for November, 1906, (**13**, 257).
[2] See *Mind and Body* for May-July, 1906, (**13**, 65, 97, 129).
[3] See *Mind and Body* for December, 1906 (**13**, 289).

received his own early training at the classical secondary school and
the university in that city.   When the German War of Liberation
broke out, in 1813, like most of the Giessen students he joined the
army, with his brothers August (later called Adolf Ludwig) and
Paul, but was taken sick with typhus fever within a few weeks, and
though he returned to his regiment afterward he was never under
fire.   When peace was concluded (1814) he resumed the study of
jurisprudence at Giessen, and in March of 1818 received his diploma
from the university as doctor of the civil and ecclesiastical law.

Like many another German student, Follen had come back from
the war filled with ideas of moral and social reform.   In place of the
provincial clubs (*Landsmannschaften*), with their carousing and the

Fig. 68.—Charles Follen (1796–1840).

duel as their only arbiter of quarrels, he desired to see the entire
student body united in one Christian brotherhood, with no distinctions of class or rank, ruled by the will of the majority determined in open assembly after free discussion, and settling all dis-
putes according to the principles of right and justice.   The purity
of his own life and the moral greatness of his character, the eloquence
with which he urged his views, and his confident enthusiasm soon
won a following of like-minded friends, in whose eyes he took on
the dignity of a very prophet.   The first motion toward union was
taken in the late summer of 1816.   A few days after the following
Christmas, at a general gathering of students, a formal "code of
honor" (*Ehrenspiegel*), Follen's work in great part, was proposed.
A majority of those present evinced their hostility to the project
by withdrawing at once; but about sixty who remained organized

themselves into an association, under Follen's leadership. Looked upon with suspicion by the authorities on account of their liberal tendencies, hated and proscribed by a majority of the students, who nicknamed them "Blacks" (*Schwarzen*) from the dark clothing they affected and their somber demeanor, the reformers became only more extreme and uncompromising in their attitude. Reaching far beyond the bounds of the university, their plans already contemplated a great Christian republic formed of freed and united Germany. Tyranny was to be met with resistance, and Follen now taught that armed insurrection, and even perjury and assassination, were justified when other measures failed in the struggle for popular freedom. Some of the Blacks drew back at this, but others, known as "Unconditionals" in contrast with the "Moderates," were undismayed at the radical doctrines of their revered leader.

Development of the physical powers formed an essential part of the program of the Giessen "Blacks," just as in the case of the *Burschenschaften* at other universities. In the summer of 1816 a gymnastic society was formed, enrolling boys in the secondary school, young merchants and others, as well as university students. Here again the leadership fell to Follen, who is described as an excellent gymnast, a skilful hand with the broadsword, and a powerful swimmer. The "Deutsche Turnkunst" of 1816 was the guide in Giessen, as elsewhere, and Jahn's rules formed the basis of order during the exercises. National anniversaries were celebrated, a *Turnfest* was held at the end of July, 1818, excursions were organized, and trips were taken with companions from Darmstadt, Heidelberg, and other places. Upon leaving Giessen students transferred their membership to *Turnvereine* in the new home, or sought to form such societies where they did not already exist. The efforts of Karl Völker at Tübingen have already been mentioned (p. 98) in describing Jahn's life and work.

Upon completing his courses in jurisprudence Follen remained at the University as *Privat-docent*, studying at the same time the practice of law in his father's court. Early in the fall of 1818 he undertook the cause of several hundred communities in the province of Upper Hesse which desired to remonstrate against a government measure directed against the last remnant of their political independence, and drew up a petition to the Grand Duke in their behalf. It was printed and widely circulated, and aroused public opinion to such a pitch that the obnoxious measure was repealed; but it also brought upon its author such unrelenting hatred on the part of the influential men whose selfish plans were thereby thwarted that any thought of a further career in his home city became impossible. He therefore accepted an invitation from Professor Fries to lecture on the Pandects as *Privat-docent* in the University of Jena, and left Giessen in October of 1818.[1]

An attempt to force upon the Jena *Burschenschaft* his radical views regarding moral and political reform excited the opposition of all but a small minority.   Friends, even, were alienated by his stern, intolerant attitude, and by the charge of weakness or cowardice with which he met dissent from the extremities to which he pushed his principles; so that the number of "Unconditionals" at Jena was never more than a small handful.   One of these, however, was Karl Sand, whose murder of Kotzebue on March 23, 1819, was the logical outcome of Follen's teaching, acting upon a mind unbalanced by fanatical zeal in the cause of popular liberty.   To the authorities all student associations became objects of suspicion, and under the reactionary measures that followed the Giessen "Blacks" and the *Burschenschaften* at Jena and other universities suffered alike. Follen was forbidden to lecture any longer at Jena, and he therefore returned to his home in Giessen.[2]   Here, however, he found himself a proscribed man.   Learning that the government intended to send him to prison, he left Giessen for Strasburg in the winter of 1819–20, visited for a time in Paris, where he made the acquaintance of Lafayette and, through him, of other distinguished men, and in the summer of 1821 settled in Basel, as public lecturer on jurisprudence and metaphysics in the recently organized University.

Among the German refugees whose friendship Follen enjoyed during his three years at Basel were the distinguished theologian De Wette, and his stepson Charles (German, *Karl*) Beck.   Beck was born in Heidelberg August 19, 1798.   His father, a merchant, died when the boy was still young, and his mother afterward became

---

[1] For the Giessen period consult:

Robert Wesselhöft, "Deutsche Jugend in weiland Burschenschaften und Turngemeinden." Magdeburg, W. Heinrichshofen, 1828.

Friedrich Münch. "Erinnerungen aus Deutschlands trübster Zeit." St. Louis, Conrad Witter, 1873.

Ferdinand Marx. "Die Giessener sogenannten *Schwarzen* als Verbreiter des Turnwesens," in *Neue Jahrbücher der Turnkunst* **27** (1881): 23–30, 66–73, and 106–113.

Moritz Zettler, in *Deutsche Turnzeitung*, 1882, pp. 9, 25, 45.

Karl Wassmannsdorff, in *Deutsche Turnzeitung*, 1882, pp. 269, 295, 319, 333, 345, and 355.

Kuno Francke, "Karl Follen and the German Liberal Movement," in Papers of the American Historical Association, **5**, parts 1–2 (January and April 1891).

Herman Haupt, "Karl Follen und die Giessener Schwarzen." Giessen, Alfred Töpelmann, 1907.

Herman Haupt, "Zur Geschichte des Giessener Ehrenspiegels." Pp. 202–214 in "Quellen und Darstellungen zur Geschichte der Burschenschaft und der deutschen Einheitsbewegung," Band II, Heft 1–2. Heidelberg, Carl Winter's Universitätsbuchhandlung, 1911.

[2] For the Sand episode, and Follen's relation to it, consult J. Sauerbrey in *Neue Jahrbücher der Turnkunst* **35** (1889): 98, 149, 196, 253, 301, 341, and 405; and Hermann and Münch in *Deutsche Turnzeitung* 1880, pp. 185 and 403.

the wife of Wilhelm De Wette, professor in the university of Heidelberg. In 1810 the family removed to Berlin, whither De Wette had been called to fill the chair of theology in the new Prussian university. There, as a student in the Werder'sche *Gymnasium*, Beck soon came under Jahn's influence, began to frequent the Hasenheide *Turnplatz*, and owing to his natural robustness of body, and the enthusiasm with which he applied himself to the exercises, developed more than usual proficiency in all the arts of the *Turner*. After the assassination of Kotzebue in 1819, De Wette, who had long been a friend of the Sand family, wrote a letter to the mother, in which he endeavored to console her with the thought that her son's act,

Fig. 69.—Charles Beck (1798–1866). (From a portrait in the Library of Harvard University.)

though wicked, arose from a mistaken notion of duty. The Prussian authorities, upon learning of this letter, accused the eminent teacher of seeking to excuse the crime, and in token of their displeasure deprived him of his chair and even banished him from the kingdom. After several years in retirement he accepted, in 1822, the professorship of theology in the University of Basel, and passed the remainder of his life in that city. Beck, meanwhile, had become an accomplished classical scholar at the University of Berlin. He afterward studied theology, was ordained to the Lutheran ministry at Heidelberg, July 7, 1822, and the next year obtained his doctor's degree in theology from the University of Tübingen. He has been active in the movement for a true Christian *Burschenschaft*, and finding that his republican sentiments stood in the way of a successful career in Germany, he, too, removed to Switzerland and joined the rest of the family at Basel, where he found an opportunity to teach the Latin language and literature.

Meanwhile the allied sovereigns of Austria, Russia and Prussia had requested repeatedly that Follen be surrendered to them for trial on the ground of complicity in revolutionary movements, and acting on the advice of friends he left the city for a few months, seeking concealment in Baden at first, and in the spring of 1824 revisiting Paris. Here he again saw much of Lafayette, who introduced him to the American Minister (James Brown) and sought his company on an approaching visit to the United States. Although longer residence in Basel appeared unsafe, he returned to his duties in the university; but in October 27, 1824 he again left the city, and three days later, travelling by mail-coach and provided with a false passport, he reached Paris. Here he found Beck, who had already left Switzerland a few days in advance, convinced that even this asylum was no longer free from danger for Germans known to cherish liberal opinions. The two men went at once to Havre, engaged passage on the vessel "Cadmus," and sailed for the United States on the 5th of November.

They reached New York December 19. Three days later Follen wrote to General Lafayette, who was then revisiting this country at the invitation of Congress and receiving everywhere a welcome which gave to his movements the character of a triumphal procession. Acting at once on his suggestion that they go first of all to Philadelphia, they reached that city on January 12, and were soon busily engaged in the study of English. Letters from Lafayette secured them a kind reception and introduction to agreeable and influential men, among others to Duponceau, a prominent lawyer of French descent, who had been his friend for more than half a century. George Ticknor, professor of the French and Spanish languages and literature and of belles-lettres at Harvard University 1819–1835, was then visiting in Washington. Lafayette sought to interest him in the two German refugees, and on his return through Philadelphia, early in February, Ticknor accordingly hunted them up, and found in Follen's possession a letter from Friedrich Gottlieb Welcker, a friend of the Follen family and one of the son's favorite teachers in Giessen, and afterward professor in the University of Göttingen, where Ticknor, a student there in the years 1815–1817, had made his acquaintance.[1]

Ticknor's letter to George Bancroft, to whom De Wette had already directed a letter recommending his stepson, secured for Beck an immediate appointment at instructor in Latin and gym-

[1] See "Life, Letters, and Journals of George Ticknor" (Boston, 1876), vol. 1, p. 351.

nastics at the Round Hill School, Northampton, Massachusetts, and by the middle of the month (February, 1825) he had left Philadelphia to take up his new duties.   Except for a visit to Beck at Northampton the next summer, Follen continued to reside in or near Philadelphia, applying himself with diligence and success to his English studies, and preparing a course of lectures on the civil law, which he hoped to deliver in the following fall and winter.   He had also enrolled himself with Duponceau as a law student and was reading Blackstone.   But in November, owing to the efforts of Professor Ticknor, Duponceau and others, Harvard University offered him the position of Instructor in German, at a salary of $500—the first time that subject had been included in its curriculum.   Expecting to add to his income by lectures on the Roman law, to be delivered in Boston, he at once accepted the offer, visiting Beck once more on the way, and before Christmas was settled in Cambridge.

One of the most important and successful educational innovations of its time was the Round Hill School, opened on the first of October, 1823, by Joseph Green Cogswell (1786–1871) and George Bancroft (1800–1891).   A descriptive circular issued a year after Beck's appointment—it is dated March 25, 1826[1]—reveals the serious purpose with which they undertook the introduction of gymnastics and other forms of physical training.   "It may be impossible," they say, "to engraft on any modern nation a system of education corresponding to that which prevailed in ancient Greece. But something must be done.   Food, sleep, and exercise must be regulated, purity protected, life guaranteed against casualties, and temperance and exercise be set, even in the dawn of existence, to keep watch over health.   Games and healthful sports, promoting hilarity and securing a just degree of exercise, are to be encouraged. Various means of motion are to be devised and applied; and where there are regularly used everything is done to assist nature in strengthening the youthful constitution.   If in addition to regularity in the use of exercise, the kinds of it are so arranged that the several powers of the body may successively be brought into action and gradually led to greater exertions, it will not be long before the physical being assumes a new appearance, and in addition to the acquisition of a control of the body, beneficial results will be visible in general industry, deportment and morals.   The attempt, therefore, to provide the various means for gymnastic exercises merits to be encouraged; and whether the methods are by turns strange or common, complicated or simple, the best that are known should

---

[1] Same Account of the School for the Liberal Education of Boys, established on Round Hill, Northampton, Massachusetts, by Joseph G. Cogswell and George Bancroft.   19 pages.

be employed. We are deeply impressed with the necessity of uniting physical with moral education; and are particularly favored
in executing our plans of connecting them by the assistance of a
pupil and friend of Jahn, the greatest modern advocate of gymnastics. We have proceeded slowly in our attempts, for the undertaking was a new one; but now we see ourselves near the accomplishment of our views. The whole subject of the union of moral
and physical education is a great deal simpler than it may at
first appear. And here, too, we may say, that we were the first in
the new continent to connect gymnastics with a purely literary
establishment."

Of the nature of this "first gymnasium on this side of the Atlantic,"
and the work done in it, not much direct evidence has come down
to us. One former pupil (Thomas G. Appleton)[1] writes: " 'Pitching
the bar' was generally done near the schoolhouse; but the regular
exercise of gymnastics was upon a plateau just below the hill, where
gymnastic appliances, then freshly introduced from Germany,
were in abundance."   Dr. George C. Shattuck, another "Round
Hiller," is quoted by Dr. E. M. Hartwell[2] as follows: "Dr. Beck,
the teacher of Latin, afterward the professor of Latin in Harvard
University, was the teacher of gymnastics. A large piece of
ground was devoted to the purpose and furnished with all the apparatus used in the German gymnasia. The whole school was divided
into classes, and each class had an hour three times a week for
instruction by Dr. Beck."   A newspaper article copied in the
American Journal of Education for July, 1826, states that classes
begin at 5.30, others at 6.15, and breakfast comes at 7; from 7.30
until 9 the only exercises are in declamation and dancing, 9 until
12 other classes, 12 until 1 rest, dinner at 1, 2 until 5 more classes,
5 until 7 "exercise and amusement. At this time the classes in
gymnastics have their instruction, when the weather permits."
The evening meal follows, and devotional exercises are held at 8,
after which the smaller boys go to bed, and the rest study for a
hour longer.

Indirect proof that the Round Hill "gymnasium" was only a
miniature Hasenheide · *Turnplatz* is abundantly furnished by the
"Treatise on Gymnasticks, taken chiefly from the German of F. L.
Jahn," a translation of the "*Deutsche Turnkunst*" of 1816, which
Beck completed and turned over to the publisher in January, 1828.[3]

---

[1] "Some Souvenirs of Round Hill School." In *Old and New* (Boston) **6**, 27–41
(July, 1872).

[2] In his "Physical Training in American Colleges and Universities." Circulars
of Information of the Bureau of Education, No. 5, 1885. Washington, 1886. See
page 22.

[3] A Treatise on Gymnasticks, taken chiefly from the German of F. L. Jahn. Northampton, Mass., Simeon Butler, 1828.

In the preface he tells us that "The same causes which occasioned the publication of the original, in Germany, about twelve years ago, render a translation desirable in this country. . . The school of Messrs. Cogswell and Bancroft, in Northampton, Mass., was the first institution in this country that introduced gymnastick exercises as a part of the regular instruction, in the spring of 1825. Since that time, the interest for this branch of education has been rapidly increasing, and frequent inquiries have been made respecting a subject much esteemed for its expected salutary effects, but little known as to its particulars. . . Wishes were expressed to me, by several of the most zealous and able friends and advocates of physical education, to translate a work which would be suitable. . . or compile one. . . I did not doubt to which of the two ways proposed to give the preference. I fixed upon the treatise of Jahn, for reasons contained in the preceding lines." Jahn's preface and Part V (containing the bibliography) are omitted altogether by the translator; Parts III and IV have been transposed, a chapter on dumbbell exercises is introduced in Part I, and there are a few other omissions and additions suggested by recent experience. Plates VII and VIII are reproductions of the two in the original, but the sixty-three figures in the remaining six plates are new.

Leaving Beck at work in the first school gymnasium established in the United States, we have now to return to Charles Follen, waiting in Cambridge, in late December of 1825, to begin his duties as first teacher of the German language in Harvard University. Within a year he also was introducing the Jahn gymnastics in his new field, and had opened the first college gymnasium this country had seen, at Harvard University, and the first public gymnasium, in Boston. He had visited Beck at Northampton in July of 1825 and again early in December, and on March 5 of the next year, only a little more than two months after his arrival in Cambridge, used these words in a letter to his friend: "I expect our University will particularly apply to you on the subject of gymnastics. I have commenced gymnastic exercises with the students. The College furnishes the implements, and will give us a place. At present I use one of the dining-halls. All show much zeal. In Boston a gymnasium is soon to be established."[1]

The third instalment of "Reminiscences of Harvard, 1822–26," by Rev. Cazneau Palfrey, printed in *The Harvard Register* of October, 1880, contains this passage: "The first movement in the direction of gymnastics made in college was made in my senior year. . .

---

[1] Pages 104 and 105 in "The Life of Charles Follen," by (his wife) E. L. Follen. Boston, Thomas H. Webb & Co., 1844. This "Life" also forms Vol. I of "The Works of Charles Follen, with a Memoir of His Life." In five volumes, Boston: Hiliard, Gray & Co., 1842.

The medical professors of the College published an appeal to the students, strongly recommending to them the practice of gymnastic exercises; and a meeting of all the classes was held in the College chapel (such a meeting as I do not remember hearing of on any other occasion), at which a response was made to this appeal, and resolutions passed expressing our readiness to follow the suggestions made in it. One of the unoccupied commons halls (on the first floor of University Hall) was fitted up with various gymnastic appliances; and other fixtures were erected on the Delta, the enclosure now occupied by Memorial Hall. But Dr. Follen did not confine his operations to these two localities. One day he was to be seen issuing from the College yard at a dogtrot, with all college (the total number of undergraduates at that period was not more than two hundred) at his heels in single file, and arms akimbo, making a train a mile long, bound for the top of Prospect Hill. Great was the amazement and amusement of all passersby. I was one of the bobs of that living kite; but, as I dropped prematurely, I cannot speak confidently of the end. . ."

Anyone familar with the appearance of a German *Turnplatz* of the Jahn type will readily understand the allusions made by Thomas Wentworth Higginson in his chapter on "The Gymnasium, and Gymnastics in Harvard College," in the second volume of "The Harvard Book" (Cambridge, 1875). "One of my most impressive early reminiscences," he says, "is of a certain moment when I looked out timidly from my father's gateway, on what is now Kirkland Street, in Cambridge, and saw the forms of young men climbing, swinging, and twirling aloft in the open playground opposite. It was the triangular field then called the 'Delta,' where the great Memorial Hall now stands. The apparatus on which these youths were exercising was, to my childish eyes, as inexplicable as if it had been a pillory or a gallows, which indeed it somewhat resembled. It consisted of high uprights and crossbars, with ladders and swinging ropes, and complications of wood and cordage, whose details are vanished from my memory. Beneath some parts of the apparatus there were pits sunk in the earth, and so well constructed that they remained long after the woodwork had been removed. This early recollection must date as far back as 1830."

In the "Catalogue of the Officers and Students of the University in Cambridge," October, 1825, appears the name "Charles Follen, J.U.D., Instructor in German, and Lecturer on the Civil Law." The next catalogue (September, 1826) retains the name and title unchanged, but in that "for the Academical year 1827–1828" (published in 1827) he is called "Instructor in German, and Superintendent of the Gymnasium;" and in both these catalogues the following paragraph occurs: "The regular Gymnastick exercises, when the Superintendent of the Gymnasium is present, are on Wednesday and Friday, from 12 to 1 o'clock; or when the length of the day admits, after evening Commons. On Monday, the Monitors and Vice Monitors meet separately with the Superintendent, to prepare for the general exercises." The catalogues for 1828–1829 (published in 1828) and 1829–1830 (published in 1829) make no mention of "Gymnastick exercises," and give Follen the title "Instructor in the German Language, in Ethics and in Civil and Ecclesiastical History." From 1826 through 1829 this further paragraph is included: "Military exercises are allowed on Tuesday and Thursday, from 12 to 1 o'clock, or after evening Commons; with music not oftener than every other time, and liberty of a parade on the afternoons of Exhibition days."

In a letter to Beck dated March 5, 1826, Follen had written: "In Boston a gymnasium is soon to be established." The gentlemen interested in the project offered him a liberal salary if he would "superintend the erection of the proper apparatus and become the principal instructor," and authorized him to engage a suitable assistant. September 26 he again wrote to Beck: "The day after tomorrow my rope-dancing begins in Boston. The gallows stand, in significant majesty, on the spot. There is no lack of gallows-birds, large and small, genteel and vulgar. . ." A petition had been presented to the Board of Aldermen of Boston on March 13 asking for the use of a certain piece of ground "for the purpose of establishing a school of gymnastic instruction and exercise." April 17 the city authorities granted this request. Following a call which appeared in the Boston *Daily Advertiser* of June 12, a meeting of citizens was held June 15, at the Exchange Coffee House, to take steps to carry out the plan for a public gymnasium. The official report is published in the *American Journal of Education* for July, 1826 (Vol. I, p. 243). The meeting unanimously resolved "that it is expedient to attempt the establishment of a Gymnastic School in the city of Boston," and appointed William Sullivan, Dr. John C. Warren, Prof. George Ticknor, Dr. John G. Coffin and John S. Foster, with others to be selected by them, a committee to carry the resolution into effect, by securing and applying contributions from the citizens of Boston. Others mentioned as especially interested in the project are Judge Prescott, Josiah Quincy, Daniel Webster, Peter O. Thacher, John A. Lowell, Thomas Motley and John B. Davis. Two hundred and fifty shares, at twenty dollars each, were offered by the committee, and according to Dr. Warren the contributions were "very liberal," permitting the opening of the establishment "on a large scale."

The open-air gymnasium or *Turnplatz* was ready for the public on September 28, not on the site originally selected, but in Washington Gardens, at the corner of West and Tremont Streets, opposite the Common. A notice in the *American Journal of Education* for October mentions "the large number of pupils of various ages and the high gratification it seems to afford;" and the November number of the same Journal uses these words, in the course of a more extended reference: "A month's opportunity of observing its progress and participating in its exercises enables us now to say that thus far it gives the utmost satisfaction to those who have made the experiment of taking a course of lessons. The physical effects of the gymnastic exercise, on pupils of very different ages—from ten to fifty—are surprising. Many have doubled their vigor. . . Pupils belong to great diversity of situations in life—physicians, lawyers and clergymen are inter mixed with young men from the counter and the counting house, and with boys from the public schools." Follen was assisted by George F. Turner, a Harvard student. Mrs. Follen, then Miss Eliza Lee Cabot, first met her future husband in the autumn of 1826. She says: "He accompanied us and some other ladies to his gymnasium, to see his class of boys go through their exercises. He took us, when we first entered the place, to look at a very amusing caricature of his school, particularly of his elder pupils and himself, in the act of performing some of their most difficult exercises."[1]

In June of the following year (1827) Follen resigned his position at the Boston Gymnasium. To a committee of pupils there, who sent him a letter[2] expressing their appreciation of his services and their regret at losing him, he replied under date of July 3, referring to "the patriotic views to which the Boston Gymnasium owes its existence and the efficient zeal with which these exercises have been carried on." Meanwhile an attempt had been made to secure the services of no less a person than Friedrich Ludwig Jahn himself. Dr. Warren tells us[3] that he "addressed a letter to the distinguished philosopher and gymnasiarch, Professor Jahn, through my friend, William Amory, Esq., who was at that time residing in Germany. Mr. Jahn was so situated that we could not without obtaining more means than were at our disposition, lead him to abandon his own country and establish himself for life in ours. The idea of obtaining his aid was therefore relinquished; and I afterward addressed Dr. Lieber. . ."

This latter gentleman who succeeded Follen at the Boston gymnasium late in June or early in July of 1827 was Francis (German, *Franz*) Lieber, born in Berlin on March 18, 1800. In 1811 he

---

[1] Page 107 in her "Life of Charles Follen."

[2] July 2. Quoted in part in the *Boston Medical Intelligencer*, **5**, p. 133, (July 10, 1827).

[3] The Life of John Collins Warren, M.D. (Boston, Ticknor & Fields, 1860).

became acquainted with Jahn, at the Hasenheide *Turnplatz*. Although too young to join his older brothers in the first campaign of the War of Liberation, upon Napoleon's return from Elba he entered (May 26, 1815) a volunteer regiment, the Pomeranian Rifles or Kolberg Regiment, took part in the battle of Ligny, was severely wounded at Namur and later suffered from a prolonged siege of typhus fever in the hospitals at Aix-la-Chapelle and Cologne. After his return home he attended for a time the *Gymnasium zum grauen Kloster* and now became one of the most ardent and tireless of Jahn's turners accompanying him on the month-long excursions to the Island of Rügen in 1817 and to Breslau the following year.[1] In July of 1819, a few days after Jahn's arrest, Lieber was also seized as an enemy of the state. After four months in prison he was

Fig. 70.—Francis Lieber (1800–1872). (From Harley's "Francis Lieber.")

allowed to go free, but forbidden to study in any Prussian university. The universities of Heidelberg and Tübingen also refused him admission, but he met with better success at Jena, where he received his doctor's degree (Ph.D.) in 1820, studying afterward for brief periods in Halle and Dresden (1821). In December of that year Lieber joined at Marseilles a band of Philhellenes, who sailed from that port to give their services in the cause of freedom to a foreign race, since the reaction at home left no opportunity there for patriotic endeavor; but disgusted with the cowardice, incapacity and lying met at every step in Greece, he returned in a small vessel to Ancona, on the eastern coast of Italy, reached Rome about the first of June, and spent the next year as private tutor

[1] A manuscript account of the latter trip, written by Lieber, was found among Massmann's papers, and published in the *Deutsche Turnzeitung* for 1895 (pp. 637–642 and 686–690), with introduction and notes by Dr. Karl Wassmannsdorff.

in the family of Barthold Georg Niebuhr, the celebrated German historian, at that time Prussian ambassador to the Papal Court.

The Prussian King, and later Kamptz, the Minister of Police, had assured Lieber that no further persecution need be feared in his own country, and for some months after his return to Berlin, which he reached August 10, 1823, it seemed as though all was well. But in time it appeared that every movement was watched by the police. Foreseeing the fate that awaited him if he remained longer in Germany, he now took steps looking toward a career in some foreign land. Lessons in English were begun in February of 1826, and among other things he secured from Major-general von Pfuel, in charge of a swimming school in Berlin, a testimonial as to his skill in that art and his ability to conduct a similar institution with success. When all was ready he left Berlin, May 17, 1826, and ten days later reached London, travelling by way of Hamburg and Gravesend.

Although he passed a year in the English metropolis, supporting himself by private instruction in German and Italian at six shillings a lesson, Lieber's thoughts were soon turned from this uncertain means of livelihood to the possibility of a career in the United States. As early as August his diary contains this entry: "Mrs. Austin, the authoress, introduced me to Mr. Bentham and to Mr. Neal" (p. 252). The *American Journal of Education* for November of that year (Vol. I, pp. 699–701) quotes as follows from "a recent letter of our literary countryman Mr. Neal, who has taken a very active part in aiding the interests of Prof. Voelker's establishment in London, and to whose attention we have been repeatedly indebted for intelligence on gymnastics:" "You know my zeal about gymnastics. I have been heartily engaged for above a year in the study and practice of them in every variety; and under a hope that I may be of use to my countrymen. I have found three men who I am told are qualified, almost beyond example, for teachers. I enclose you the proposals and the certificate of one, who was a chief personage with Professor Jahn himself."

The certificate of Professor Jahn: "Francis Lieber, Doctor in Philosophy, has during several successive years, both in summer and winter, gone through the whole course of gymnastic exercises in the gymnasium over which I, the undersigned, presided; he has also accompanied me in several pedestrian excursions, among other in 1817 to the Island of Rügen, and in 1818 to the Riesen mountains, on which travels we visited many Prussian gymnasiums. Having found him of good moral behavior, ingenious and clever, and being a good leader and teacher of gymnastics, I thought it right as early as the year 1817 to propose him to the government of the Rhenish Provinces at Aix-la-Chapelle for the situation of a teacher of gymnastic exercises. Beloved by the young scholars, esteemed and respected by those of the same or a more advanced age than himself, he was elected a member of the committee which was intended to represent the society of 'Turners' and to promote the art generally, with a view as well to the art itself as to morals and science. At the time when Dr. Lieber was daily with me he zealously adhered to those external maxims of truth, duty and liberty which form the only basis of the progress of human kind. The journeys which he has performed through Germany, Switzerland, to France, Italy and Greece have no doubt still further formed his understanding and enlarged his mind; but on this point I cannot judge from my own knowledge, having since lost sight of him although he lives in my recollection. At the request of Dr. Lieber I have given this testimonial, stamped according to law, written with my own hand, with my seal affixed and certified by the municipality of my present abode. Freiburg on the Unstrut, in the Prussian Duchy of Saxony. August, 1, 1826. (Signed) Frederick Lewis Jahn, Doctor in Philosophy."

"In addition to the above," the editor of the *Journal* concludes, "Dr. Lieber has a very satisfactory certificate from Major-general Pfuel, who invented the new method of teaching to swim and established the Prussian Military Swimming Schools. It may be proper to, add that Dr. Lieber is known and approved by Dr. Follen, Professor (!) of civil law in Harvard University and Superintendent of the gymnasium in Boston."

April 13, 1827, in response to an invitation just received, Lieber wrote accepting a position as Follen's successor at the Boston Gymnasium, and agreeing to establish a swimming school in that city. June 20 of the same year he landed in New York City, and proceeded at once to the scene of his new duties. The *Boston Medical Intelligencer* of July 3 (Vol. V, p. 118) announces his arrival "to take charge of the gymnasium in Washington Garden and to open a swimming school;" and an advertisement in the same journal, dated July 14, gives notice that "Dr. Lieber's Swimming School, situated on the north side of the Mill Dam, will be opened for the reception of pupils on Wednesday next, 18th inst. . ." The swimming school seems to have proved a successful venture from the start, and was still in existence at least as late as the season of 1832. The popularity of the gymnasium, on the other hand, soon waned. From a sketch of the life of William Bentley Fowle contained in Barnard's *American Journal of Education* for 1861 (Vol. X, p. 607) we learn that "about four hundred gentlemen attended at the opening term. Mr. Fowle was chosen treasurer, and was in fact the chief executive officer. When Dr. Follen resigned Dr. Lieber was invited over from London; but no talent could keep the gymnasium alive after the novelty had ceased, and some of the gymnasts had been caricatured in the print shops. The institution lingered about two years, when, only about four gymnasts remaining, Mr. Fowle closed its accounts."[1]

Beck left the Round Hill School in 1830 to take part in establishing another boys' school in Phillipstown, on the Hudson River opposite West Point. Two years later he was elected "University Professor of Latin and Permanent Tutor" in Harvard University, and for eighteen years discharged the duties of that position in a manner which won the respect and affectionate regard of pupils and colleagues. Upon resigning his chair, and until his death, which occurred suddenly on March 19, 1866, he was occupied with literary pursuits and classical studies, and also held various offices of public trust, representing Cambridge for two years in the State Legislature.[2] Bancroft, too, had withdrawn from the school at Northampton in 1830.[3] For some years longer, in the face of financial losses and in spite of failing health, Cogswell struggled to maintain its efficiency. In the spring of 1834 he finally gave up the attempt, and after two years at the head of a boys' school near Raleigh, North Carolina, turned his back forever on a profession in which he had been in many ways singularly successful.

Follen, as we have seen, resigned his position at the Boston gymnasium early in the summer of 1827; the title "Superintendent of the Gymnasium" at Harvard is given him only in the catalogue for 1827–1828, which also contains the last reference to "gymnastick exercises." August 21, 1828, the Corporation of Harvard College appointed him "Instructor in Ethics and in Civil and Ecclesiastical History" in the Theological School, in addition to his work in the College. Two years later he received a five-year appointment as Professor of the German Language and Literature, three friends having guaranteed a portion of his salary for that period. The professorship was not renewed in 1835, and his connection with the University came to an end. In the summer of 1833 he became interested in the Anti-slavery Society which had been formed the year previous in Boston, and soon joined it, assisting later in the formation of a similar society in Cambridge, and at one time serving

---

[1] Leiber's own ideas regarding the nature and means of physical training are preserved for us in two articles contributed by him to the *American Journal of Education* of August, 1827 (**2**, pp. 487–491), and the *American Quarterly Review* of March, 1828 (**3**, pp. 126–150).

[2] The main facts regarding Beck's life are given in "The Christian Citizen. A Discourse Occasioned by the Death of Charles Beck." Delivered March 25, 1866, before the First Parish in Cambridge, by William Newell. Cambridge, Sever and Francis, 1866. See also pp. 124–126 in Andrew P. Peabody's "Harvard Reminiscences" (Boston, Ticknor & Co., 1888).

[3] The first volume of his "History of the United States" was published four years later.

as a manager of the Massachusetts Society. As early as the winter 1826–1827 he formed the acquaintance of Dr. William Ellery Channing, and decided to prepare himself for the ministry with the assistance of that distinguished Unitarian clergyman. On January 13, 1840, three days after completing a well-attended course of six lectures on German literature under the auspices of the Merchants' Library Association of New York, he left that city for Boston on the steamboat "Lexington." About fifty miles out, on the Sound, the vessel caught fire, and Follen, together with all but four of the crew and passengers, met his death. Charles Sumner, who had been his pupil, wrote to a friend "Dr. Follen is gone; able, virtuous, learned, good, with a heart throbbing to all that is honest and humane;" and Dr. Channing said of him that he was, on the whole, the best man he had ever known.[1]

The career or Francis Lieber in the United States was more notable than those of either of his compatriots. A testimonial from Niebuhr, and his own force of intellect and character, secured him at once a very cordial reception on this side of the Atlantic, and upon the recommendation of the same distinguished patron a half-dozen leading periodicals in Germany appointed him American correspondent. At the close of his first season at the swimming school he turned with great energy to literary labors, and soon made up him mind to edit an encyclopedia, modelled after the seventh edition of the Brockhaus *Conversations-Lexicon* and in part a translation of that famous German work, but adapted to English readers and supplied with numerous additional articles by distinguished American contributors. The first volume of the new "Encyclopædia Americana" appeared in 1829, and the thirteenth and last in 1833. It proved a successful venture financially and brought him also the acquaintance of prominent men in all parts of the country. In September of 1833 he moved his family from Boston to Philadelphia and by Ocober 19 had finished the draft of a constitution for Girard College. June 5, 1835, he was unanimously elected Professor of History and Political Economy in South Carolina College, at Columbia. May 18, 1857, he was elected Professor of History and Political Science in Columbia College, New York City, but later, in July of 1865, was transferred by the trustees to the chair of Constitutional History and Public Law in the Law School. Here he continued in active service until his sudden death, October 2, 1872.[2]

[1] See also pp. 116–123 in Andrew P. Peabody's "Harvard Reminiscences" (Boston, Ticknor & Co., 1888).
[2] Sources: Thomas S. Perry, "The Life and Letters of Francis Lieber" (Boston, James R. Osgood & Co., 1882); and Lewis R. Harley, "Francis Lieber: His Life and Political Philosophy" (New York, The Columbia University Press, 1899). See also Eduard Dürre's "Erinnerungen" in *Deutsche Turn-Zeitung* 1872, pp. 286 and 293; and Karl Ulrich in *Deutsche Turn-Zeitung* 1874, pp. 227 and 228.

The outdoor gymnasia at Northampton, Cambridge and Boston, although for the historian they possess the greatest interest, were not the only ones established during the period (1825–1830) under consideration. Each had its imitators, and there were other attempts of a similar nature which seem to have been more or less independent, or inspired by direct contact with European models. The following information deserves a place as a contribution to this study of beginnings, and it is offered in the hope of arousing a curiosity which will result in additions to our present knowledge of the subject.

No school of the period attracted more attention or enjoyed greater prosperity than did the New York High School, a private institution for boys, which the son of its founder[1] calls, at the time of its organization, "the first and the only pay school in this country established on the professed principle of cheap and efficient instruction based on . . . the adoption and employment of the monitorial system, by which one teacher can communicate his knowledge to a large number of pupils." It was located in New York City, on Crosby Street, above Grand, and opened March 1, 1825, with about 250 boys; but the numbers rapidly increased to more than 600, and there were still about 400 at the time of its discontinuance, near the close of 1831. The founder was John Griscom (1774–1852), who during a year of foreign travel had examined many famous European schools, and refers in the published account of his observations[2] to the gymnastic exercises which he saw in Paris, at the school of Amoros[3] (August 27, 1818), and in Switzerland at the schools of Fellenberg, in Hofwyl (October 2 and 3, 1818), and Pestalozzi, in Yverdon (October 8 and 9, 1818). In writing of the visit to Amoros he remarks: "A systematic course of instruction, with proper exercises, on the right use of their limbs, I have long thought would be very advantageous to boys;" and his opening address at the New York High School[4] contains the following: "I shall refrain from dwelling longer on the literary pursuits of this seminary; but I cannot dismiss my subject without adverting to one branch of instruction which it is equally the wish, I believe, of the trustees and principals to establish as a constituent part of our general plan, from a conviction of its advantages to the bodily vigor and, of course, to the intellectual strength and

---

[1] "Memoir of John Griscom, LL.D., "by his son, John H. Griscom, M.D. (New York, Robert Carter & Bros., 1859). An article based on this volume was published in Barnard's *American Journal of Education* for June, 1860 (**8**, pp. 325–347).

[2] "A Year in Europe, Comprising a Journal of Observations in England, Scotland, Ireland, France, Switzerland, the North of Italy, and Holland, in 1818 and 1819." Two volumes. New York, Philadelphia, and Boston, 1823.

[3] The word is spelled *Amonton* in Griscom's book!

[4] See the *American Journal of Education* for January, 1826 (**1**, pp. 50–52).

activity of our pupils. I allude to *gymnastics*." The second annual report of the Trustees[1] informs the public that "Gymnastic exercises have been introduced, under the superintendence of an experienced and careful teacher, and they have been attended with evident advantage to the spirits and health of the pupils."

Other schools which introduced gymnastic exercises, or planned to do so, during the period under review, were the New Haven Gymnasium, conducted by two sons of President Timothy Dwight of Yale; the Berkshire High School, at Pittsfield, Mass.; the Mount Pleasant Classical Institution, at Amherst, Mass.; the Livingston County High School, near Geneseo, New York; the Buffalo High School; Gideon F. Thayer's private school for boys, in Harvard Place, Boston; the Noyes School, at Andover, New Hampshire; Walnut Grove School, at Troy, New York; a High School in Utica, New York; the Brookline (Mass.) Gymnasium; Mount Hope Literary and Scientific Institution, near Baltimore, Maryland; and the Classical and Scientific Seminary at Ballston, New York.[2]

After Harvard, Yale College seems to have been the first to introduce gymnastics among its students. A letter received from the University Library states "that the idea was taken from the gymnasium recently established at Harvard; that Tutor William M. Holland was sent to Cambridge in the summer of 1826 to procure the apparatus, and that he superintended the exercises, which was begun with the opening of the fall term of 1826." At a meeting of the Corporation held September 12, 1826, it was "Voted that a sum not exceeding three hundred dollars, to be expended under the direction of the faculty, be appropriated to the clearing and preparation of grounds for a Gymnasium and to the erection of apparatus for Gymnastic exercises, with a view to the promotion of the health and improvement of the Students."

A book entitled "Student Life at Amherst College." compiled by George R. Cutting and published at Amherst in 1871, contains the following account of a similar movement at that institution: "In the summer of 1826 the students of the college petitioned the Faculty for a holiday in which to clear up the college grove. The petition was granted, and a second day was given for further completion of the work. Thus logs, stumps and rubbish were removed, and the students had a fine grove at their command for outdoor exercise. Several months afterward a Gymnastic Society was formed, whose chief object was the erection and support of gymnastic apparatus in this grove. The first president of the society was Joseph Howard, M.D., of '27. The Faculty concurred

---

[1] See the *American Journal of Education* for January, 1827 (**2**, pp. 58–60).

[2] See an article in *Mind and Body*, **12**, 313–319, based on an examination of volumes **1**-**3** of the *American Journal of Education* (1826–1828).

in the plans of the society, and as a result of their efforts a variety of useful apparatus was placed here, which was eminently service-able to the students and contributed not a little to their health and happiness. By the enthusiasm and public spirit of the society a bathing house (10 x 12 feet) was also erected in the southwest corner of the grove. Here shower-baths were provided for the members. This was afterward burned down. In 1827–1828 the society contemplated the erection of bowling alleys, but the Faculty would not suffer the innovation. . . Addresses were occasion-ally pronounced before the society, in the chapel, upon 'physical culture.' The society did not really cease to exist until 1859–1860, when the present (Barrett) gymnasium was erected. Its appara-tus, ever and anon increased and repaired by the liberality of the students, was not removed from the grove until after that time. Dr. E. M. Hartwell, in his "Physical Training in American Colleges and Universities" (Washington, 1886), tells us that "One who entered Amherst as a student in 1829 describes a gymnasium which consisted of 'a few horses and parallel bars, with one or two swings in the grove, but even these belonged to a society of students who guarded their property with jealous care.' "

May 9, 1827, the Trustees of Williams College voted "That a sum not exceeding one hundred dollars be appropriated to the procuring and erection of apparatus necessary to the practice of the gymnastic exercises, if the Faculty should think proper to introduce the same at this College." At a meeting of the Faculty held June 15 "The President and Tutor (Mark) Hopkins,[1] a com-mittee who had been appointed for this purpose at a former meet-ing, reported a plan of a gymnasium, and recommended a site for its location. The same committee were authorized to prepare the ground according to the plan reported." The Trustees, again, on September 5, of the same year, voted "to appropriate a sum not exceeding $50, in addition to the $100 granted at the last meeting, to be expended on the Gymnasium." The *Boston Medical Intelli-gencer* for September 25, 1827 (vol. v, p. 311) contains this note: "A traveller observes, 'On a portion of the College grounds in Williamstown, I perceived one day a large number of students at work, headed by their venerable President, and on examination found that they were preparing a Gymnasium. Here is a fine spot for exercise, and we may hope that our students will no longer, as in former years, leave college with emaciated frames and pallid countenances, through want of proper exercise.' "

[1] Dr. Hartwell (Report to the Boston School Committee, December, 1891, page 20) says that Tutor Hopkins "had been sent on a mission to Round Hill to investigate the construction and working of its gymnasium."

The following extracts are taken from a long letter[1] to the editor of the *Boston Medical Intelligencer* by a correspondent who signs himself "G. F.," and writes under date of September, 1827: "Having lately been in Providence, Rhode Island, I have had the best opportunity of informing myself with respect to the success of the Gymnastic Exercises in Brown University, and knowing the interest you take in this subject I submit to your disposal some remarks on it. On the 11th of June last, near the commencement of the present term, the exercises opened under the most auspicious and flattering circumstances. Nearly all the students, with the exception of the senior class, to the number of about seventy, presented themselves on the exercise ground. The exercises were countenanced, and consequently enlivened, by the presence of the president, professor and tutors of the university. . . The officers, as I stated, appeared with the students, and under the direction of the teacher of gymnastics, performed the exercises. . . The students have taken a great interest in the exercises throughout the term, though not so much at the latter part of it as at first. . ." Late in July of 1827 Charles Follen spent a day in Providence on his way to Newport, and refers to the visit as follows in a letter to Beck: "I was, for the most part, with Dr. Wayland,[2] and my ex-assistant Haskins, and held in the evening a strict Gymnastic review. I spoke much with Dr. Wayland on education. He stated many fine views and seemed to be respected and beloved by the teachers. He exercises with all." The University catalogue of 1827–1828 announces that "a very complete Gymnasium, with every variety of apparatus for exercise, has lately been erected on the college grounds;" and the Treasurer's Reports contain these items:

1827—June	28, Cash paid for digging, etc. for gymnasium . .	$ 26.06
July	27, Materials and labor for gymnasium	231.81
"	31, Lumber for gymnasium	24.14
Aug.	17, Dynamometer for gymnasium	27.00
"	27, Lumber, etc.	3.00
"	27, George F. Haskins, on account of services as teacher in gymnasium	15.00
Sept.	4, George F. Haskins services in full	135.00
1828—Jan.	5, Spar for gymnasium	10.00
Feb.	4, Work on gymnasium	10.22

President Jasper Adams, D.D., of Charleston College, Charleston, S. C., is thus quoted in the *Quarterly Review and Journal of the American Education Society* for May, 1830 (Vol. II, p. 244): "A system of bodily exercise was adopted three or four years ago, and

[1] It was published in the *Intelligencer* for September 18, 1827 (**5**, pp. 291–294).
[2] Francis Wayland, appointed President of Brown University in February, 1827.

suitable apparatus was constructed; but it was not found useful
and the apparatus has been destroyed."

In speaking of Lieber's year in England reference has already been
made (p. 244) to an American, John Neal,[1] who was at that time
residing in London. Neal had spent his early life in New England,
in 1815 established himself in business in Baltimore, studied law in
that city and was admitted to the bar in 1819, and meanwhile in
order to support himself, had been writing articles for the *Portico*
and had followed these with a two-volume novel and a book of
poems. A whole series of novels was produced within the next
few years, and some of these were reprinted in London. Late in
1823 he left America to try his fortune as a pioneer of American
letters in the British metropolis, and during his residence in London,
from January of 1824 until April of 1827, became a frequent contributor to the most important magazines and reviews, residing
much of the time at the house of Jeremy Bentham, by invitation
of that distinguished jurist and philosopher. While still in Baltimore he had been moved by signs of mental overwork to take
lessons in boxing, fencing and riding; in London these were continued, and when Carl Voelker[2] (German, *Karl Völker*), like Beck,

---

[1] Born in Portland, Maine, in 1793; died there in 1876. The chief source of
information concerning Neal is his "Wandering Recollections of a Somewhat Busy
Life. An Autobiography" (Boston, Roberts Brothers, 1869). His letters from
England are quoted in the *American Journal of Education*, 1 (1826), pp. 375 and 699–
700; and 2 (1827), pp. 55 and 56. Consult also *The* (New York) *Continental Monthly*
for September, 1862 (2, pp. 275–281), and *The New American Cyclopædia*, 12, pp. 150
and 151 (New York, 1861).

[2] Voelker, born in about 1796, was according to his own story a pupil of Jahn and
had served among the volunteers in the War of Liberation. As a student at the
University of Jena he assisted in organizing the first *Burschenschaft*, became one of its
directors, and exercised on the Jena *Turnplatz*. In September of 1818 he went to
Tübingen, at the request of a delegation of students from its university, to help
them start a *Burschenschaft* and open a *Turnplatz* (see p. 98). In the course of the
investigation that followed the murder of Kotzebue by Sand the government of
Württemberg was asked to surrender Voelker for arrest as a suspected accomplice.
This was refused, but so much pressure was at length brought to bear that in order
to save the ministry further embarrassment he crossed into Switzerland. Some
years later he arrived in London, bearing letters of recommendation to Jeremy
Bentham and Henry Brougham (later Lord Chancellor). Apparently in the spring
or early summer of 1825, after three months study of the English language, he opened
with Bentham's help a garden *Turnplatz* at No. 1 Union Place, New Road, near
Regent's Park, at the same time receiving pupils in German. Later in the same
season he rented Mr. Fontaine's riding-school on Worship Street, Finsbury Square,
using this also as a gymnasium. He afterwards returned to Switzerland, and lived
there until his death at Kappel, in St. Gall, October 2, 1884. The fullest account of
Voelker's life is that by Eduard Dürre ("Rückblicke und Träume eines alten
Turners") in the *Deutsche Turn-Zeitung* for 1872 (17, pp. 103–107, 127–129, 136 and
137). See also *Neue Jahrbücher für die Turnkunst* for 1881, p. 72, and 1885, p. 43. On
the London gymnasium consult the *American Journal of Education*, 1 (1826), pp. 375,
430–432, 502–506, 625 and 626; and 2 (1827), pp. 55 and 56. Volume 1 of "The
Every-Day Book" by William Hone (London, 1826) contains under date of September
25 (1825) some additional particulars, and a drawing made for this article "by Mr.
George Cruikshank, after his personal observation of Mr. Voelker's gymnasium in
the New-road."

Follen and Lieber, a German refugee, opened there his gymnasia patterned after the Jahn *Turnplatz*, Neal became one of his most enthusiastic pupils and supporters. Returning to America in the summer of 1827, he opened a law office in Portland, Maine, where the remainder of his life was passed. The following words from his autobiography (pp. 333–335) evidently refer to the first year (1827–1828) of this residence:

"The late Governor Enoch Lincoln was my mother's nextdoor neighbor. Having understood that I was familiar with gymnastics, which he wanted to have introduced here, he proposed a lecture. A lecture! I had never been guilty of such a thing, in all my life; but as soon as my mind was made up about staying here I determined to establish a gymnasium, take charge of it myself, and, refusing all compensation, see what could be done for the people in that way. Our first gathering was in the upper story of the old town-hall, which I asked of the authorities; and succeeded in obtaining for certain purposes, though vehemently opposed by such young men as the late Colonel John D. Kinsman, then exceedingly popular with the militia power. . . From the old town-hall we went to Silver Street, where we succeeded in obtaining a large hay magazine. There we set up our ladders and ropes and masts parallel bars, wooden horses, etc., with such success that before a month had gone over I had under my charge at least fifteen or twenty full classes. Among these were many capital gymnasts. After this, when the spring opened, we took the old fort on the top of Munjoy Hill, and established another gymnasium there, with ditches and leaping-poles; and then, having got into other and better business, with my law and literature, and fencing and sparring classes, at my office, I threw up these gymnasia; being, to say the truth, heartily sick of them after I found how little the members were inclined to do for themselves; not one of the whole being disposed to let me off, although I had trained forty or fifty for class-leaders, and they understood that I had my own living to get in other ways. Meanwhile I had established a gymnasium at Brunswick,[1] which has continued to this day (he is writing late in December, 1868), with two or three long interruptions, and another

---

[1] In the pines back of the present site of Sargent Gymnasium. A report of the Visiting Committee to the Board of Trustees and Overseers of Bowdoin College, dated September 2, 1828, contains the following: "The committee would introduce to the favorable notice of the Trustees and Overseers the Gymnasium which has been recently established. We have had some opportunity of witnessing its exercises and are convinced that its effects are highly salutary. . . . These exercises are voluntary, few however decline them. Those who have associated as Gymnics have presented a request that a shed may be erected for their accommodation. But highly as we approve of the association we think that this request cannot now be acceded to. Other and more pressing wants of the college demand all its funds." This outdoor gymnasium was in existence until the early sixties, when the college fitted up for similar uses a building formerly occupied as a college common.

at Saco; and all this without asking or receiving a penny for my time and trouble; nay, more, at considerable expense to myself. . ."[1]

Dr. John Collins Warren, who had helped to start the gymnasium at Harvard University and in Boston, bore reluctant testimony to the brevity of the period now under review in a lecture "On the Importance of Physical Education," delivered at Boston in August of 1830 before the convention which organized the American Institute of Instruction.   After urging the importance of suitable bodily exercise, for young women as well as young men, he adds: "The establishment of gymnasia through the country promised at one time the opening of a new era in physical education.   The exercises were pursued with ardor, so long as their novelty lasted; but owing to not understanding their importance, or some defect in the institutions which adopted them, they have gradually been neglected and forgotten, at least in our vicinity.   The benefits which resulted from these institutions, within my personal knowledge and experience, far transcended the most sanguine expectations."   And he still believes that "the diversions of the gymnasium should constitute a regular part of the duties of all our colleges and seminaries of learning."

BIBLIOGRAPHY.

In addition to the references given in the text and footnotes consult Dr. E. M. Hartwell, Report of the Director of Physical Training, December, 1891 (Boston, School Document No. 22—1891), pp. 12–23; and B. A. Hinsdale, "Notes on the History of Foreign Influence upon Education in the United States," Chapter XIII in the Report of the Commissioner of Education for the year 1897–1898 (Vol. I, pp. 591–629).

[1] For references to private gymnasia opened in New York and Philadelphia at this period see *Mind and Body*, **12**, 350 and 351 (February, 1906).

CHAPTER XXII.

THE "NEW GYMNASTICS" OF DIO LEWIS.

In the third and fourth decades of the nineteenth century four different systems of physical training had been brought forward for trial in the United States—the drill and discipline of the military academy, the Jahn gymnastics, manual labor on the farm or in the shop, and "calisthenics" for girls and women. The claims of each were pressed by enthusiastic advocates, and there was no lack of imitators of the educational institutions in which each had first become incorporated; but for various reasons not one of the four was generally adopted or won for itself more than temporary foothold. From 1835 until 1860, though educators were increasingly alive to the importance of physical training,[1] no one appeared with

[1] Horace Mann (1796–1859), secretary of the Massachusetts Board of Education 1837–1848, in the annual reports of the Board and in the ten volumes of the *Common School Journal* which he edited (1839–1848) had much to say of school sanitation and the importance of instruction in personal hygiene. In pp. 56–160 of the sixth report (1843) he attempted to vindicate the title of a study of physiology and hygiene to "the first rank in our schools, after the elementary branches." Perusal of successive reports of the annual meetings of the American Institute of Instruction from the first (1830) to the thirtieth (1859), and of the *Massachusetts Teacher* from 1850 to 1860 (Vol. **3–12**) and Barnard's *American Journal of Education* 1855–60 (Vol. **1–8**) reveals a cumulative interest in the problem of physical education as the end of that period approached. A. A. Livermore's article in the *North American Review* for 1855 (**81**: 51–69), Dr. D. W. Cheever's in the *Atlantic Monthly* for 1859 (**3**, 529–543), and Thomas Wentworth Higginson's series which began in the latter magazine in March of 1858 (afterward collected and published under the title "Outdoor Papers") point in the same direction, as do also the twenty-first and twenty-second reports of the Massachusetts Board of Education (1858 and 1859), that of the Boston School Committee for 1859 (pp. 52 ff.), and a report to the New York State Teacher's Association in the same year. "Tom Brown's School Days," first published in April of 1857, presented an attractive picture of vigorous boy-life; and the fourth chapter (Physical Education) of Herbert Spencer's "Education" (New York, 1860), which had already appeared in the *British Quarterly Review* of April 1, 1859, was certain to attract attention. The following were the recent manuals available:

Paul Preston's Book of Gymnastics (Boston, Munroe & Francis, 1842). A new edition, revised, was published in 1861 (New York, Charles S. Francis).

Walker's Manly Exercises, revised by "Craven" (Philadelphia, John W. Moore, 1856).

P. A. Fitzgerald, "The Exhibition Speaker" (New York: Sheldon, Lamport & Blakeman, 1856). Pp. 223–268 are devoted to "Gymnastics and Calisthenics."

N. W. Taylor Root's "School Amusements" (New York, A. S. Barnes & Co., 1857). Pp. 95–143 have to do with gymnastics.

R. T. Trall, "The Illustrated Family Gymnasium" (New York, Fowler & Wells, 1857).

George Forrest (John George Wood), "A Handbook of Gymnastics" (London and New York, G. Routledge & Co., 1858).

Perhaps we should add that literary and pictorial curiosity, Henry de Laspée's "Calisthenics, or the Elements of Bodily Culture on Pestalozzian Principles" (London, Darton & Co., 1856). A second edition was published in 1865 (London, Charles Griffin & Co.).

anything that seemed more likely to meet the conditions and needs of the time. Then came Dio Lewis, with his "new gymnastics for men, women and children," something definite and practical. His contagious enthusiasm created a wave of popular interest that spread to all parts of the country, and the "Normal Institute of Physical Education" which he opened in Boston in the summer of 1861 was the first attempt in America to prepare teachers of a subject whose right to a place in the school curriculum had long been conceded.

FIG. 71.—Dio Lewis (1823–1886).

Dioclesian, or as he called himself in after life Dio Lewis came of vigorous Welsh stock and was born March 3, 1823, on a farm in Cayuga County, New York within a few miles of Auburn. Loran L. Lewis, born two years later, who served two terms in the Senate of his native state, and from 1882 until 1896 was Justice of the New York, Supreme Court, has written as follows regarding the early life of his elder brother:

"At the age of twelve Dio was as large and mature as ordinary boys of fifteen. His mind was remarkably active; so were his movements. He could do anything he desired to do with more rapidity than any person I ever knew. When accustomed to committing to memory he could read a page in a book once, close the book and repeat it all. He had an investigating inquisitive mind. He liked miscellaneous reading, but did not relish digging into study. He learned a great many facts, but did not read many books thoroughly. He was enthusiastic in everything in which he engaged. He developed as a child a talent for declaiming even before he could read much, and as a youth he engaged in debates and talked on temperance. . . He was cheerful and full of fun. . . . At the age of twelve Dio left school and went into a cotton factory in Clarksville, near Auburn, where he remained perhaps six months, working some sixteen hours a day and receiving from $1.25 to $2.50 a week in orders on stores in Auburn. After this he worked in Wadsworth's hoe, axe and scythe factory for about two years, attending school at intervals. . .

"At about the age of fifteen he began teaching school in our district. He surprised the patrons with novel ways of teaching and managing the school. Heretofore the masters had moved around the room with ferule in hand, always ready to deal a blow as occasion might offer. The young teacher discarded the whip and went to singing, and for a change he would march with the children into a piece of woods near the schoolhouse, and sometimes, after the children got tired, he would allow them to play hide-and-seek. Dio continued teaching near home for a year or two, and when eighteen years of age he went to what was then Lower Sandusky, now Fremont, Ohio, and organized a select school. Here he began the study of Latin and Greek, and the classes which he soon formed in them, as well as in algebra and geometry, kept him hard at work with his own studies in order to keep well ahead of his pupils. The school was patronized by most of the leading citizens, and gave so great satisfaction that in a few months some of them volunteered to erect a handsome school building. They obtained an act of incorporation, naming it, in compliment to Mr. Lewis, 'The Dioclesian Institute,' and the new quarters were occupied just before the close of the school year."

A severe and prolonged attack of ague compelled the young teacher to give up his work in Fremont at the end of a year, and he did not return to it. Having made up his mind to study medicine, he now entered the office of the physician at the Auburn State Prison, Dr. Lansing Briggs, with whom he remained for three years, with the exception of one winter devoted to teaching. In 1845 he went to Boston and spent some time in the Medical Department of Harvard University, but seems to have been prevented from completing the course by lack of means, and therefore came back to Port Byron, not far from his home, to enter at once upon the practice of his profession. By his partner, Dr. Lewis McCarthy, he was won over to the new system of homeopathy, and a little later, after establishing himself in Buffalo in 1848, began to edit a monthly publication called *The Homœopathist*. The honorary degree of Doctor of Medicine was conferred upon him in 1851 by the Homœopathic Hospital College of Cleveland, Ohio, then only two years old.

A year after his removal to Buffalo Dr. Lewis married Miss Helen Cecelia Clarke, daughter of a physician whose country residence was in the neighborhood of Port Byron. Three of her sisters had died of consumption, and in the fall of 1851 she herself began to exhibit unmistakable symptoms of the same disease. Her husband, who was already urging in his medical journal the importance of *preventive* measures, at once undertook the treatment of her case by hygienic means. These appeared to be successful for a time; but in the fall of 1852 her cough reappeared, and Dr. Lewis thereupon determined to give up his practice and go South with her for the winter. Early in January they reached Fredericksburg, Virginia. It was not in the man's nature to remain idle, and he was soon talking on health subjects to pupils in the schools. To identify himself with a cause which had excited his interest ever since boyhood he now joined "The Sons of Temperance," but with a protest, his biographer[1] tells us, "against the exclusion of women from membership. He urged upon the leaders that in failing to enlist woman in the work they were leaving out the element most essential and indispensable to success. . . Meeting only indifference to his appeal for the admission of women to the organized temperance work, he wrote a paper on 'The Influence of Christian Woman in the Cause of Temperance,' and read it in a hall in the old town of Fredericksburg, Virginia, the same year (1853). This was his first appearance on the public platform. Directly afterward he gave lectures on this subject and on health topics in Fredericksburg, Richmond, Petersburg, Norfolk and Portsmouth, Virginia." The two succeeding winters were also spent with his wife in the South, where among other places he lectured in Paris, Lexington and Georgetown, Kentucky. The same occupation was continued in New York State in the intervening summers. At the end of this time, after renewed and more careful attention to the matter of dress and exercise, Mrs. Lewis found herself fully restored to health.

The next five years, until the summer of 1860, were devoted almost entirely to platform work in "the Middle and Northern United States and Canada. . . It was his custom to speak on six evenings in the week on the laws of health, laying special stress on his favorite axiom, adapted to suit himself, 'An ounce of prevention is worth a ton of cure.' On Sunday evenings he presented in the churches, or, by preference, in a large hall, where such could

---

[1] "The Biography of Dio Lewis," prepared at the desire and with the coöperation of Mrs. Lewis by Mary F. Eastman. New York, Fowler & Wells Co., 1891.

be obtained, his favorite subject, 'The Duty of Christian Women in the Temperance Work.' " In 1856 he made a short visit to Paris, chiefly to secure material suitable for demonstration in his popular lectures on physiology, although he also improved the opportunity to attend clinics at some of the city hospitals. Referring to this period he speaks of himself as "burdened with what I felt to be my life-work, that of urging upon the people their right to 'a sound mind in a sound body,' and the introduction of a new system of physical training into the schools of the country. . ;" and how his thoughts were turned to gymnastics is told in these words: "During the eight years of lecturing the spare hours were devoted to the invention of a new system of gymnastics. The old, or German gymnastics, the one so common throughout our country,[1] was obviously not adapted to the classes most needing artificial training. Athletic young men, who alone succeeded in the feats of that gymnasium, were already provided for. Boat clubs, ball clubs and other sports[2] furnished them in considerable part with the means of muscular training. But old men, fat men, feeble men, young boys and females of all ages—the classes most needing physical training—were not drawn to the old-fashioned gymnasium. The few attempts that had been made to introduce these classes to that institution had uniformly and signally failed. The system itself was wrong."

After experimenting for some years with the new exercises he had devised Dr. Lewis determined to concentrate his efforts on the attempt to introduce them to the public, and in June of 1860 established his home in the vicinity of Boston for this purpose. "I thought," he says, "that Boston would prove more hospitable to an educational innovation than any other city in the country;" and he was not disappointed. Evening classes in gymnastics were soon organized in West Newton, Newtonville, Newton, Newton Upper Falls and Watertown. The English and classical school of Mr. N. T. Allen, in West Newton, was the first to introduce the new system, according to Dr. Lewis, and it was soon followed by the

---

[1] The oldest gymnastic society (*Turnverein*) of the German type in the United States was the Cincinnati *Turngemeinde*, organized November 21, 1848. By October of 1853 there were at least seventy in existence, and by September of 1856 ninety-six societies, with a membership of about five thousand, had united into a national body and at least twenty more were known to have been formed. At the outbreak of the Civil War there were a total of one hundred and fifty-seven societies, in twenty-even states of the Union. See pp. 294 and 295.

[2] The beginning of rowing clubs in the United States goes back to 1833 and the few years following, and in the decade 1850–1860 interest in the sport spread all over the country. Baseball, starting in the forties and fifties, did not become a truly national pastime until the period immediately succeeding the Civil War. The "Caledonian games" of Scotch immigrants, forerunners of our track and field athletics, had been shown in Boston in 1853 and Hoboken in 1857, but did not become widely popular till the later sixties and seventies. Football existed only in its primitive form.

Normal School at Framingham, and in Boston by the institutions of Mr. Gannett in Pemberton Square and Madam de Maltchyce in Pinckney Street, the Concord Hall school, and many others in and near the city. A public gymnasium, also, for men, women and children was opened at 20 Essex Street, in Boston. Among others, a class of clergymen and their wives met there regularly for an hour on Mondays—"blue Monday"—to exercise with the proprietor and, as one of them expressed it, to "inhale hygiene in his presence, and in the atmosphere of his room."

In August of 1860 the "new system" was all at once brought to the notice of leading educators gathered from the length and breadth of the United States. Dr. Lewis himself related the circumstances to a Boston audience, several years afterward,[1] as follows: "I may remark that the hour of my coming was most fortunate for my cause. Just then the American Institute of Instruction held its great Convention—the largest ever held in this country—in this city. I was so fortunate as to be invited to appear before that most august of all educational bodies, to explain and illustrate the new system of gymnastics. They told me 'You may have half an hour on the second morning; we have the business so arranged that we cannot give you more.' But when the half-hour had expired they said, 'Go on;' and I went on until two hours had passed, and then they voted that the next morning they would meet at half past eight (having announced important business for nine o'clock), to hear more about the new gymnastics. The next morning was foggy and dark, but the hall (Tremont Temple) was full, and they passed over their important business and gave me nearly two hours more, and at noon another hour. With such an opening as this, it is not remarkable that the interest spread over the entire country."[2]

One of Dr. Lewis's objects in coming to Boston had been the establishment of a training school for teachers of the "New System," and in the spring of 1861 the *Normal Institute for Physical Education* was incorporated. President Cornelius C. Felton, of Harvard College, readily consented to serve as its president, and continued to take an active interest in the enterprise until his death, a year later. Upon the list of twenty-eight Directors appear the names of Governor John A. Andrew, Hon. George S. Boutwell, Dr. H. I. Bowditch, Rev. James Freeman Clarke, Rev. E. E. Hale,

---

[1] At the fourth commencement exercises of his Normal Institute for Physical Education, March 18, 1863.

[2] See also the "Lectures Delivered before the American Institute of Instruction, at Boston, Mass., August 21, 1860, including the Journal of Proceedings, and a List of Officers" (published under the direction of the Board of Censors. Boston, Ticknor & Fields, 1861). The references to Dio Lewis occur on pp. 19–21, 23–25, 45 and 46, and 77 of the Journal of Proceedings. Another report of these sessions is printed in the *Massachusetts Teacher*, **13**, 378–393 (October, 1860).

N. T. Allen, Professor A. Crosby and others of recognized standing. The members of the first faculty were Thomas H. Hoskins, M.D., Professor of Anatomy; Josiah Curtis, M.D., Professor of Physiology (the instruction in this subject, as well as in anatomy, was later given by Dr. Hoskins); Walter Channing, M.D., Professor of Hygiene; and Dio Lewis, M.D., Professor of Gymnastics. The next year a department of Elocution was created, and Professor T. F. Leonard was called to the new chair. The first course opened July 5, 1861, and continued ten weeks. Other similar courses were to be given twice each year thereafter, beginning regularly on the second of January and the fifth of July.

This Institute was not, as Dr. Lewis supposed, "the first ever established to educate guides in Physical Culture," since normal schools of gymnastics had already been opened in Europe, *e. g.*, at Stockholm (1814), Dresden (1850) and Berlin (1851); but it was the first attempt of the sort to be made in the United States, and as such merits more than passing notice. A report of the first course and announcement of the second, published in pamphlet form at Boston in 1861, yields the following: "Readers of our educational journals are, to some extent, familiar with Dr. Lewis' system of Gymnastics, since in connection with his appearance before the American Institute of Instruction last year these journals, as also large numbers of the daily press, gave somewhat full accounts of the principal features of that system.[1] It is a novel system, novel alike in its philosophy and in its practical details. Dispensing with the whole cumbrous apparatus of the ordinary gymnasium, its implements are all light, easily managed and designed less to impart mere strength of muscle than to give flexibleness, agility and grace of movement. The exercises are accompanied by music and all of them so arranged that both sexes participate in each. . .

"The second course of the Institute will open on the second day of January, 1862, and continue ten weeks. Many peculiar and marked advantages will be enjoyed by the pupils of the winter term. D. B. Hagar, Esq., Ex-President of the American Institute of Instruction, Hon. Geo. Bradburn, Rev. Warren Burton, Rev. T. W. Higginson and several other well-known gentlemen, will deliver lectures before the class of the Institute. . ." In addition to the regular instruction in anatomy, physiology, hygiene and gymnastics, the class will

---

[1] Lewis had himself published articles on "Physical Culture" in the *Massachusetts Teacher* for October and November of 1860 (**13**, 375–377 and 401–406), and in the latter month issued the first number of a monthly periodical, *Lewis' New Gymnastics for Ladies, Gentlemen and Children, and Boston Journal of Physical Culture*. Vol. **2** (1862, January–November, with one extra number) bore the title *Lewis's Gymnastic Monthly and Journal of Physical Culture*.

be taught "the principles of the 'Swedish Movement-Cure,'[1] a department of the institution devoted to the treatment of curvature of the spine, paralysis and other chronic maladies, affording rare opportunities to study in detail the application of Ling's methods in treating such forms of chronic disease. . . Each pupil, on being received into the Institute, will be critically examined with reference to strength, form and health; and any deficiency thus disclosed will be at once placed under the most thorough treatment. . . Each will be drilled by Dr. Lewis in person, which such care that he or she cannot fail to become a competent teacher of gymnastics. And each will have two drills a day. . . All will be made familiar with at least two hundred different exercises . . .; and will be allowed, every one in turn, to lead a small class. . ."

At this point a bit of contemporary testimony from a well-informed, but more impartial, source may be introduced. During the years 1858–1862 Mr. Thomas Wentworth Higginson contributed to the *Atlantic Monthly* a series of vigorous and stimulating articles, full of good sense and literary charm, which were afterward collected and published in book form under the title "Outdoor Papers" (Boston, 1863; New York, 1894). One of them, on "Gymnastics," which appeared in March of 1861, contains this reference to the "New System:" "It would be unpardonable, in this connection, not to speak a good word for the favorite hobby of the day—Dr. Lewis and his system of gymnastics, or, more properly, of calisthenics. Dr. Winship[2] had done all that was needed in

---

[1] It has already been noted (p. 159) that under Branting's directorship of the Central Institute in Stockholm (1839–1862) foreign physicians began to be attracted by the new system of treatment, and among them Mathias Roth of London. Roth afterward published "The Prevention and Cure of Many Chronic Diseases by Movements" (London, 1851), a translation of "The Gymnastic Free Exercises of P. H. Ling, arranged by H. Rothstein" (London, New York, and Boston, 1853), and "Handbook of the Movement Cure" (London, 1856). The first American physicians to write at length on the subject were the Taylor brothers of New York, George H. Taylor "An Exposition of the Swedish Movement Cure" (New York, Fowler & Wells) in 1860, and Charles F. Taylor his "Theory and Practice of the Movement Cure" (Philadelphia, Lindsay & Blakiston) a year later. Bayard Taylor spent the late winter and spring of 1857 in Stockholm, visiting the Central Institute regularly as a "patient," and described his experiences in letters to the *New York Tribune* and in his volume "Northern Travel" (London and New York, 1857. Consult pp. 202–206).

[2] George Barker Winship, born at Roxbury, Mass., January 3, 1834, and died at the same place (of heart disease) September 12, 1876. He was educated at Harvard University (A.B. 1854, M.D. 1857), and in June of 1859 gave his first lecture on physician training, with an exhibition of heavy lifting, in Music Hall, Boston, repeating these afterward in many places throughout the northern states and Canada. In the sixties and early seventies he conducted a private gymnasium on Washington Street, Boston, next door to the Boston Theater. See his "Autobiographical Sketches of a Strength-Seeker," in the *Atlantic Monthly* for January, 1862 (**9**, 102–115), an article on "Physical Culture" in the *Massachusetts Teacher* for April, 1860 (**13**, 126–132), and an item in the latter magazine for April, 1861 (**14**, 159). Among the literary announcements of Ticknor & Fields in the *Atlantic Monthly* for August, 1862, a book on "Health and Strength" by Dr. Winship is mentioned as "in press," but it seems never to have been published.

apostleship of severe exercises, and there was wanting some man with a milder hobby, perfectly safe for a lady to drive. The Fates provided that man, also, in Dr. Lewis—so hale and hearty, so profoundly confident in the omnipotence of his own methods and the uselessness of all others, with such a ready invention, and such an inundation of animal spirits that he could flood any company, no matter how starched or listless, with an unbounded appetite for ball-games and bean-games. How long it will last in the hands of others than the projector remains to be seen, especially as some of his feats are more exhausting than average gymnastics; but, in the meantime, it is just what is wanted for multitudes of persons who find or fancy the real gymnasium to be unsuited to them. It will especially render service to female pupils, so far as they practise it; for the accustomed gymnastic exercises seem never yet to have been rendered attractive to them, on any large scale, and with any permanency."

In a volume published in 1868 Dr. Lewis says that more than two hundred and fifty persons had taken the diploma of the Normal Institute in the nine sessions which had been held. His biographer, on the other hand, makes this statement: "During the next seven years (after its establishment) four hundred and twenty-one ,ladies and gentlemen in about equal numbers, were graduated from it. These were able to answer the demand for instructors in the 'new gymnastics' which soon came from the schools and from private classes in the larger cities of New England, and later from the remoter parts of the country, until at length the system was taught in every State in the Union."

Dio Lewis was a voluminous writer, but only two of his books require particular mention here—"The New Gymnastics for Men, Women and Children," first issued in 1862; and the tenth edition, practically a new work although it bears the same title, which appeared in 1868. Both were published in Boston, by Ticknor & Fields. The leading article, "The New Gymnastics," in the *Atlantic Monthly* for August of 1862 (Vol. X, pp. 129–148) is from his pen, and another of sixty-five pages was published in two instalments in Barnard's *American Journal of Education* for June and December of the same year (Vol. XI, pp. 531–562; Vol. XII, pp. 665–700). Of the 275 profusely illustrated pages in the book of 1862 only a little more than a third are filled with material of the author's own devising. Pp. 102–115 ("Free Gymnastics") contain exercises selected from Schreber's "Aerztliche Zimmer-Gymnastik;"[1]

---

[1] *Aerztliche Zimmer-Gymnastik*, oder Darstellung und Beschreibung der unmittelbaren, keiner Geräthschaft und Unterstützung bedürfenden, daher stets und überall ausführbaren heilgymnastischen Bewegungen für jedes Alter und Geschlecht und für die verschiedenen speciellen Gebrauchszwecke, entworfen von Dr. med. Daniel

on pp. 117–164 "The Dumb Bell Instructor for Parlor Gymnasts," by Maurice Kloss,[1] is given in condensed form and free translation; and pp. 165–255 are occupied with a similar translation of Schreber's "The Pangymnastikon; or All Gymnastic Exercises brought within the Compass of a Single Piece of Apparatus."[2] The first portion of the book begins with ten pages of introductory discussion relating to the need of special gymnastic training for children, the inadequacy of military drills and other forms of exercise commonly employed, the use of music with gymnastics, the gymnasium and the gymnastic dress. Then follows (pp. 18–101) Lewis's own exercises, grouped as follows: Bag exercises (30), exercises with rings (54), exercises with wands (68), dumbbell exercises (34), club exercises (22), pin running (a game with clubs), games with birds nests (played with bean-bags), the arm pull, the gymnastic crown and the shoulder pusher.

In the tenth edition of "The New Gymnastics" (1868) the translations from German authors are omitted. In the words of the preface, "their places have been supplied by original exercises, now for the first time published. At the same time changes have been made in that portion of the book which was devoted to an illustration of the author's system of Gymnastics. In the constant practice of the system for the past five years, among thousands of pupils, a multitude of new exercises have been added, and the entire method has been improved in many respects. This edition is an attempt to reflect upon the pages of a book the changes which have taken place in actual practice." A few of the introductory pages are worth quoting here, since they contain Dr. Lewis's own statement of the advantages of his system, his claims to originality, and the order in which the exercises were developed.

"The advantages of the New System of physical culture are in part, the following: (1) The varied movements of the New System

---

Gottlob Moritz Schreber, pract. Artze und Vorsteher der orthopädischen und heilgymnastischen Anstalt zu Leipzig; 45 Xylographische Abbildungen enthaltend, Leipzig, Friedrich Fleischer, 1855. The third German edition of this work was translated by Henry Skelton and published by Williams & Norgate, London and Edinburgh, in 1856, with the title "Illustrated Medical Indoor Gymnastics, or a system of medico-hygienic exercises requiring no mechanical or other aid, and adapted to both sexes and all ages, and for special cases."

[1] *Das Hantel-Büchlein für Zimmerturner*, von Dr. Moritz Kloss, mit 20 in den Text gedruckten Abbildungen. Leipzig, J. J. Weber, 1858. Lewis's translation is made from the second edition.

[2] *Das Pangymnastikon*, oder Das ganze Turnsystem an einem einzigen Geräthe ohne Raumerforderniss als einfachstes Mittel zur Entwickelung höchster und allseitiger Muskelkraft, Körperdurchbildung und Lebenstüchtigkeit. Für Schulanstalten, Haus-Turner und Turnvereine, von Dr. med. D. G. M. Schreber, Director der orthopäd und heilgymnast. Anstalt zu Leipzig. Mit 108 Holzschnitten im Texte und 107 auf Tafeln. II. Theil der "Aerztlichen Zimmer-Gymnastik." Leipzig, Friedrich Fleischer, 1862.

give opportunity for the full play of every muscle in the body, resulting in an all-sided development. (2) The exercises are constantly changed from one set of muscles to another, thus obviating weariness and undue disturbance of the circulation. (3) The centrifugal impulse of the predominating series secures a completeness and *grace* attained by no other means, while the centripetal character of the old or German method has long been the opprobrium of physical culture, with the philosophical. (4) In the New System the exercises are subordinated to personal or individual wants, while in the old the person is entirely subordinated to the performance of difficult feats. (5) The physiological purpose of all muscle training is to perfect the intermarriage between nerve and muscle. The skill exacted by the accurate lines, changing attitudes, and difficult combinations of the new methods compels the most complete interaction between soul and body. (6) The New School employs apparatus which cannot strain and stiffen the muscles, not even in the extremely old and young or feeble, while the old school sanctions weights which must produce the slow, inelastic muscles of the cart-horse. (7) The New Gymnasium invites to its free and social life persons of both sexes and all ages, while every attempt that has been made to introduce the old, or the very young, or women, to the Old Gymnasium has failed. (8) In the New Gymnasium persons of both sexes unite in all the exercises with great social enjoyment, thus adding indefinitely to the attractions of the place, while the attractions of the Old Gymnasium are about equal to those of a ballroom from which ladies are excluded. (9) In the New Gymnasium everything is set to music. Marches, free movements, dumb-bells, wands, rings, mutual-help exercises. No apathy can resist the delightful stimulus. The one hundred persons on the floor join in the evolutions inspired by one common impulse. Under the old system each individual works by himself, deprived of the sympathy and energy evoked by music and the associated movement."

For three years, 1864–1867, Dr. Lewis conducted at Lexington, Massachusetts, a school for girls, in which Theodore Dwight Weld, once the confident advocate of manual labor as a system of exercise, was a leading teacher, and Catharine Beecher was for a time one of the lecturers.[1] In September of 1867 the school building was burned, and although temporary quarters were at once secured in a summer hotel at Spy Pond the project was abandoned at the close of another year. The number of pupils rose to 140 in the third year, drawn from all over the country, and nearly 300 were enrolled during the whole period. In the words of Dr. Lewis, "The

[1] See the "Catalogue and Circular of Dr. Dio Lewis's Family School for Young Ladies, Lexington, Mass., 1867" (Cambridge: Welch, Bigelow & Co., 1867).

character of the announcement, with what the public knew of my interest in physical education, drew together a company of bright girls, with delicate constitutions, such girls as could not bear the exclusively mental pressure of the ordinary school. . . The girls went to bed at half-past eight every evening. They rose early in the morning and went out to walk, which walk was repeated during the day. They ate only twice a day, and of very plain, nourishing food. They took off their corsets. They exercised twice a day, half an hour, in gymnastics, and danced an hour about three times a week. This was the general course, and upon this regimen they rapidly improved. The gymnastic exercises proved invaluable, but the nine hours in bed, I believe, played a still more important part." The Eastman biography states that "On entering the school pupils were measured about the chest, under the arms, about the waist and around the arm and forearm. The average gain for eight months was in chest measure, two and a half inches; waist measure, five inches; size of arm, one and a half inches; of forearm, about one inch. The work was so hard that with all this remarkable development the weight of the pupils was often lessened."

The closing of his school for girls, in 1868, may be said to mark the end of Dio Lewis's greatest activity in the interest of physical training. He had never relinquished altogether the lecture field, and now found more leisure for the work, speaking in Massachusetts and New Hampshire on his favorite topics, physical education and temperance. The winter of 1873–1874 was given up to an extensive course of lyceum lectures in the West, under the suspices of a lecture bureau, and again, as in the fifties, he devoted Sundays to the cause of Temperance, "always keeping in mind what he had for twenty years desired to see inaugurated, a practical movement on the part of women to close the saloons." The balance of the year 1874 was filled with temperance work exclusively, and out of the "Women's Crusades" which he inspired and helped to organize at this time was developed the Women's Christian Temperance Union, formed at Cleveland in November. In 1875 he was obliged to heed the signs of approaching physical collapse, and went to California for three years of outdoor life.[1] The year 1884 saw him located on a farm at Smithtown, Long Island, in search of rest and trying meanwhile to "concentrate his attention on chickens," but in July able to deliver a course of lectures and teach gymnastics at the Martha's Vineyard Summer Institute. His death occurred at Yonkers, May 21, 1886.[2]

[1] Described in his "Gypsies" (Boston, Eastern Book Company, 1881).

[2] Lewis's published works include, in addition to those already mentioned, "Weak Lungs, and How to Make Them Strong" (1863), "Talks about People's Stomachs" (1870), "Our Girls" (1871), and "Five-Minute Chats with Young Women" (1874), "Talks about Health" (1871), "Chastity" (1872), and "In a Nutshell" (1883). In 1864 Amherst College conferred on him the honorary degree of Master of Arts.

Mr. James C. Boykin pays the following just tribute to Dio Lewis: "It may be true that 'he was unconventional, sympathetic, plausible, oracular and self-sufficient,' and 'not a scientist in any proper sense,' as one writer has said.[1] But, notwithstanding all this, he rendered a real service. Even if he had nothing in his favor but the undoubted fact that he gave gymnastics in America a greater impulse that any man before him had done, that would be sufficient to earn for him the gratitude of all interested in physical training. But he did more. He first awakened the American public to the appreciation of the fact that the mere development of huge muscles is not the true idea of physical training. His contribution to the list of exercises and to gymnastic material was by no means insignificant, though, to be sure, his claims were out of all proportion to their value; but, more than all else, he lifted the gymnasium above the low plane it had occupied in the public mind as the resort of prizefighters and bullies, and carried gymnastics into the schoolroom to an extent never before approached in this country and into the home to an extent that no one else had ever attempted."[2] His so-called "system" was not of a sort to survive for many years the loss of the founder's energetic leadership, and yet he prepared the soil for the broader and more substantial type of work of a later day.

BIBLIOGRAPHY.

This chapter was first published in the *American Physical Education Review* for June and September, 1906 (**11**, 83–95 and 187–198). It is given here in condensed form, with a few footnotes added. The chief sources of information have been already mentioned.

[1] Dr. E. M. Hartwell, in his first report as Director of Physical Training in the Boston Schools (School Document No. 22, 1891), pp. 35 and 36.
[2] Report of the Commissioner of Education—1891–1892 (Washington, 1894), **1**, pp. 517 and 518.

CHAPTER XXIII.

PHYSICAL EDUCATION IN AMERICAN COLLEGES AND UNIVERSITIES.

Each of the four systems or sorts of physical training brought forward for trial during the decade whose middle point was 1830 had been adopted by one or more institutions of college rank. Under Follen's guidance Harvard students were introduced to the Jahn gymnastics in the spring of 1826 (pp. 239–241) and other outdoor gymnasia of the Hasenheide type were prepared soon afterward at Yale, Amherst, Williams, Brown (pp. 249–251), and Bowdoin (p. 253). In "A Memorial of the Class of 1827, Dartmouth College," written by Jonathan Fox Worcester (second edition, Hanover, N. H., 1867), there is also mention of "the interest awakened, during the latter part of our career, in the subject of physical education; the gymnastic apparatus set up behind the 'College' in 1826, by the students themselves . . .; the cricket clubs which covered the green the next spring, adding this excellent game to our previous list of modes of exercise. . ." Manual labor, combined with study, played a large part in many sections of the country, and particularly in new colleges founded while that movement was at its height. Norwich University made military exercises and long marches on foot a regular part of the course, under Captain Partridge, its first president (1835–1843); and Mount Holyoke College, chartered as Mount Holyoke Female Seminary, opened in 1837 with both domestic work and "calisthenics" included in its plan. The latter was more properly dancing steps, accompanied by singing.[1]

In the fifties there were many signs of a reviving interest in gymnastics as a means of exercise, culminating at the end of the decade in the erection of brick or stone gymnasia at Harvard, Yale and Amherst colleges, at a cost of approximately $10,000 each. In the "Catalogue of the University of Virginia—Session of 1851–1852" (Richmond, 1852), following the list of "Faculty, Instructors and Officers" and the name of the "University Hotel-keeper," is the note: "Gymnastics are taught under the authority

---

[1] Mrs. J. H. McCurdy, "The History of Physical Training of Mount Holyoke College," in the *American Physical Education Review* for March, 1909.

of the Faculty, by Mr. J. E. D'Alfonce."[1] The Board of Visitors reported in 1852 that they "have read with pleasure that J. E. D'Alfonce proposes to give instruction in that subject (gymnastics), and hereby renew the permission formally given for a site on the University grounds for a gymnasium, and are disposed to offer proper facilities. . ." John S. Patton, in Chapter XXII of his "Jefferson, Cabell and the University of Virginia" (New York and Washington, The Neale Publishing Co., 1906), says that "the gymnasium authorized by the Visitors was erected on the site of the present Academic Building and on the banks of the little stream nearby was built a house for Russian baths. Both enterprises were directed by D'Alfonce, but fell into disuse during the Civil War, when the buildings were destroyed. As a teacher the Frenchman is said to have been unusually successful. . ."

The note regarding D'Alfonce appears again in the same place in the catalogues issued by the University in 1853 and 1854, and in those from 1855 to 1860 inclusive his name is listed under "Faculty, Instructors and Officers." Professor William M. Thornton contributes the following picture: "A pretty sight might have been seen from the foot of the Lawn. As the visitor reached the apex of the triangle his eye would have rested on a great, circular framed building in the midst of the field below. Near it would have been seen a company of two or three hundred students, all in an easy uniform of blue blouse and grey trousers, drawn up in rank and file. At their head stood a lively Frenchman, an ex-soldier, issuing the word of command. And under his orders this regiment of college boys would go through a series of complex exercises, marching and countermarching, . . . all out in the open air. . . Or, entering the building at an earlier hour, he would have found these same boys turning upon bars, swinging upon ropes, brandishing broadswords or foils, dumb-bells and clubs. And then, as the sun descended and before the great bell of the Rotunda rang out its evening summons, he would have heard the Frenchman, in his splendid baritone, raise the chant of the Marseillaise, or some other martial strain, and all the boys would join in, and the great chorus of many voices would rise . . . upon the . . . air. The soldierly Frenchman was D'Alfonce. . ."[2]

[1] See "Instructions in Gymnastics, containing a full description of more than eight hundred exercises, and illustrated by five hundred engravings. By J. E. D'Alfonce late Professor in the Military School in St. Petersburgh, and in Paris." New York George F. Nesbitt & Co., 1851. The author speaks in the preface of "seven years' practice with pupils of all ages," and of "the debt which I owe to America for the freedom I enjoy, and for the hospitality and friendship I have received from her citizens. . ."

[2] Page 60 of "The University of Virginia: Glimpses of Its Past and Present," by John S. Patton and Sallie J. Doswell (Lynchburg, Va., 1900). See also a letter ("Due Tribute") published in The Outlook for May 18, 1907 (**85,** p. 122).

Frederick Chase, writing on "the beginnings of athletics at Dartmouth,"[1] says that "gymnastics were introduced in a small way by the erection in 1852, by the enthusiasts, in the ravine east of the observatory, of a frame popularly called the gallows, by some the 'Freshman's Gallows. . .' The apparatus consisted of nothing but two suspended ropes with rings, and a horizontal bar (it is referred to elsewhere as 'two posts and a rude horizontal rail'). . . . It was a feature of that spot until superseded by Mr. Bissell's Gymnasium building, with its wealth of apparatus, in 1867."

Allan Marquand, in "The Princeton Book,"[2] recites that "in the year 1856–1857 Robert Tarleton and Hugh L. Cole, of the class of 1859, resolved that Princeton should have a gymnasium. When a sufficient sum of money had been raised a single-boarded structure was erected, and painted with the inevitable *red*, that it might resist the storms of heaven as its founders had resisted the objections of an unpropitious Faculty. All winter long, in this stoveless shanty, with the winds sweeping through from one end to the other, might have been seen a few enthusiastic gymnasts, at work on parallel bars, springboard, trapeze and ladder, or swinging upon the rings and shaking the rafters in their efforts to touch the beam. . . . In the year 1864 the building was sadly in need of repair. Through an effort made by the class of 1866 sufficient money was raised to supply it with a stove and a new set of apparatus. Thus renovated, it answered the purpose of a gymnasium, until one night during the summer vacation of 1865, a report was circulated that a tramp sick with the yellow fever was sleeping there. The next day the building was reduced to ashes by the frightened people of the town."

The Board of Trustees of Miami University, Oxford, Ohio at a meeting held July 2, 1857, adopted the following resolution, presented by William M. Corry, one of their number: "Resolved that the Committee on Finance be instructed to report an appropriation of two hundred dollars for the construction of a plain and substantial gymnastic apparatus for the use of the students of the University." J. C. Christin, M. D., a Cincinnati German, who was Professor of the German and French Languages and Literatures at Miami University from 1856 to 1860, was made manager of the project, and thus outlined its history in a report to the Board of Trustees under date of July 4, 1859: "When in the fall of 1857 the gymnastic apparatus purchased by your committee was offered to the use of the students, a number of them organized themselves

---

[1] In Bartlett and Gifford's "Dartmouth Athletics" (Concord, N. H., 1893).

[2] The Priceton Book. A Series of Sketches Pertaining to the History, Organization and Present Condition of the College of New Jersey. By Officers and Graduates of the College. Boston: Houghton, Osgood & Co., 1879. See p. 268.

at once into a society called the Miami Gymnastic Association, engaged Mr. F. H. Roemler (a German) of Cincinnati as teacher at a salary of $40 a month, and rented a building (a little west of the campus) for their gymnasium at a cost of $60 a year.[1] During that entire first year the classes practised regularly three times a week, and with what success you have seen at our festival, where the young gymnasts of M. U. carried off the first honors of the day over their competitors, delegates from several of the old Turners' societies. But to bring about this happy result we were obliged to complete our gymnasium by purchasing about $300 worth more of apparatus. This the Association did, encouraged as they were by a generous donation of $150 from the citizens of Oxford and other friends, and believing that they could pay their debt soon by the aid of friends and the proceeds of some exhibitions. At the beginning of the fall session of 1858 the society was reorganized, and Mr. Roemler again engaged as teacher at a salary of $480; but as the number of members during these two sessions was on an average only about 75 (out of 220 students) they were, for want of funds, obliged to rescind the contract with their teacher at the end of March last, whereupon Mr. Roemler went to Dayton. . . After his departure the number of students at the exercises of the gymnasium, which under their faithful teacher's direction had always been from 60 to 80, dwindled down in a few weeks to about a dozen, and today the gymnasium is closed altogether, for want of interest in the students and citizens to continue their exercises without a teacher."

The annual catalogue of Miami University issued in May of 1859, apparently oblivious of the sudden collapse of the plan, announces that "An extensive Gymnastic Apparatus has been erected in the College Campus, and an expert Teacher instructs the students in all the branches of Gymnastics under the direction of Professor Christin, M.D." The "festival" to which the latter refers took place June 29, 1858,[2] on the day before Commencement. Apparatus had been set up on the campus between the Main Building and the South Dormitory, and "thousands of spectators of both sexes came." A report published in the *Cincinnati Daily Gazette* of July 2, 1858, states that about twenty-five representatives of the Hamilton *Turnverein* and other delegates from the Cincinnati *Turngemeinde* and Young Men's Gymnastic Association were present. The program opened at 2 P.M. with a song by the Hamilton Turners. William M. Corry then addressed the audience on the subject of

---

[1] It was opened for use December 8, 1857, according to an item in the *Deutsche Turn-Zeitung* for 1858, p. 44.

[2] This is the date given in *Jahrbücher der Deutsch-Amerikanischen Turnerei* (New York), **3**, 55 (December, 1893). See also a reference in, **2**, 267 (July, 1893).

physical education, and the gymnastic exercises followed, continuing until late in the afternoon. The eight young men to whom the judges awarded prizes, four of them members of the Miami Gymnastic Association, "were each crowned with a wreath of evergreen in the presence of the multitude."[1]

In the Williams College catalogue for 1851–1852, published in the former year, it is stated that "A well-furnished Gymnasium, with which are connected facilities for bathing, is now provided." The same sentence is repeated in catalogues for 1852–1853 and 1853–1854, but modified in those for 1854–1855 and the three years following to read: "For their physical training a well-furnished Gymnasium, with which are connected facilities for bathing, is owned and controlled by the students." The catalogue for 1858–1859, issued in 1858, announces that "a new stone Gymnasium, to be owned and controlled by the students, is about to be erected, with which will be connected facilities for bathing;" and in the next year we are told that "a convenient Gymnasium, owned and controlled by the students, has just been erected."

President James Walker, of Harvard University, in his annual report dated December 31, 1858, after remarking that "the need of great facilities for exercise suited to our climate, and for the physical education of students, has long been felt, and is felt more and more," announced that "a friend of the College, whose name is not divulged, has given $8000 to be expended in the erection and equipment of a Gymnasium, for the use of 'all undergraduates and officers of the College, and such other persons as the College Faculty may permit.' . ." The next December he reported that "a suitable building has been erected during the past year, with all the necessary apparatus, accommodations and means of instruction. Almost all the students, both undergraduates and members of the professional schools (there were then 431 undergraduates, and the total enrollment was 839), have begun to avail themselves of the advantages thus supplied, each one paying a small fee (two dollars a term) in order to defray the current expenses of the establishment." The Treasurer's Statement dated December 1, 1859, noted that "the want of a Gymnasium has been supplied by the presentation of $8000, through Rev. Dr. Huntington, by a gentleman who declines to be known except as a 'Graduate' of the College.[2] The building has been erected and furnished, at a cost of $9488.05." Further details are supplied by *The Harvard*

---

[1] For references in the University catalogue and the records of the Board of Trustees, and for a copy of the report in the *Cincinnati Daily Gazette* I am indebted to the kindness of Professor J. E. Bradford, of the department of history at Miami. The first hint of any such episode as the above was gained from the *Jahrbücher* mentioned in the footnote preceding this one.

[2] The donor was Henry Bromfield Rogers, Harvard 1822.

Magazine for October, 1859 (VI, 38): "The spot selected for the building was the little Delta at the junction of Cambridge Street and Broadway. The ground was broken March 23, 1859. The building is in the Italian style, and was erected under the direction of Mr. E. C. Cabot, architect, Boston. . . The Gymnasium was opened for use on Wednesday, September 14. Meanwhile, most fortunately, the services of Professor (!) A. Molineaux Hewlett had been secured. He came with an experience in gymnastic training of fourteen years, the last five of which had been devoted most acceptably to the citizens of Worcester. . ."

In "The Harvard Book" (Cambridge, 1875) Thomas Wentworth Higginson describes the gymnasium as "of brick, octagonal in form, 74 feet in diameter and 40 feet high. It includes as great a variety of apparatus as is compatible with the size of the building; there are

Germanic Museum, Harvard College, Cambridge Mass.

Fig. 72.—The Harvard Gymnasium of 1859.

also two bowling alleys, and there are dressing-rooms, but no bath-rooms. . . The first teacher of gymnastics in Harvard College was Abram Molineaux Hewlett. He was a professional teacher of boxing, and had established a gymnasium of his own in Worcester, Mass., where he was highly esteemed. He was a mulatto, of very fine physique, and of reputable and estimable character. He was, moreover, a fair gymnast and a remarkably good teacher of boxing. In the first years of his term of service there was a good deal of activity in the Gymnasium, and regular class-exercises went on. After a few years the interest fell off in some degree, or concentrated itself chiefly on the rowing-weights. Mr. Hewlett died December 6, 1871, and . . . Mr. Frederic William Lister was appointed in 1872." Hewlett's name does not appear in the list of "Officers of Instruction and Government" in the Harvard catalogues, but from 1867 to 1871 he is mentioned with the title "Instructor and Curator" in a brief statement regarding the "College Gymnasium."

Fig. 73.—The Yale Gymnasium of 1860.

Fig. 74.—The Yale Gymnasium of 1860.

At Yale College a gymnasium was erected in 1859, on Library Street, near the corner of High, behind the college grounds proper, and "dedicated on Monday evening, January 30th" of the following year.[1] It was a plain brick structure 100 by 50 feet, with a

[1] The *Yale Literary Magazine* of March, 1860 (**25**, 230).

main hall 25 feet high to the crossbeams and large gable windows. Across the front (south) end of the hall stretched a gallery 25 feet deep in which were dressing-closets and a room or rooms for an instructor or janitor. A basement story, about 10 feet high, contained bath-rooms and bowling alleys. The total cost was something over $11,000, of which $10,000 was appropriated by the Corporation and George Merriam of Springfield, Mass., contributed $500 of the balance. Yale catalogues from 1860 on through the decade state that for the privileges of the gymnasium, "including instruction, the sum of $4 a year will be charged to each academical student." Catalogues of 1867 and later years add that "those who use the bathing-rooms connected with the Gymnasium pay a small fee for ticl ets." Lyman B. Bunnell, B.A., is listed as Instructor in Gymnastics in 1860 and 1861, and Follansbee G. Welch[1] during the years 1867–72.[2]

The fourth president of Amherst College, Rev. William Augustus Stearns,[3] in his inaugural address (November 22, 1854) and his annual reports to the trustees urged impressively, again and again, the adoption of measures desigr ed to protect the health of students. "Physical education is not the leading business of college life," he said in 1854, "though were I able . . . to plan an educational system anew, I would seriously consider the expediency of introducing regular drills in gymnastic and calisthenic exercises." And in 1859 he states his belief that "if a moderate amount of physical exercise could be secured to every student daily, I have a deep conviction . . . that not only would lives and health be preserved, but animation and cheerfulness, and a higher order of efficient study and intellectual life would be secured." At their meeting in August of 1859 the trustees took steps to carry out at once the president's wishes. Work on the new building was

---

[1] Follansbee Goodrich Welch was born at Concord, N. H., June 8, 1843, and graduated from Dio Lewis's Normal Institute for Physical Education. In addition to his duties at Yale he served as "Instructor in Physical Culture" at Dartmouth College from the spring of 1867 through the year 1867–68, and instructor in gymnastics, at Wesleyan University 1868–69, besides conducting for a number of years an eight weeks summer "Normal Institute for the Training of Teachers in Dio Lewis's New Gymnastics," at the Glenwood Ladies' Seminary, West Brattleboro, Vermont. In 1869 he published "Moral, Intellectual, and Physical Culture; or the Philosophy of True Living" (New York, Wood & Holbrook), Part I of which deals with "The Gymnasium," and Part II with "the Dio Lewis System of Gymnastics." The New York Homeopathic Medical College conferred on him the degree of M.D. in 1870, and he afterward practised medicine in New York City.

[2] See "Four Years at Yale," by a Graduate of '69 (Lyman H. Bagg) (New Haven, Charles C. Chatfield & Co., 1871), pp. 31 and 402–405; and Dudley A. Sargent in "Yale College: A Sketch of Its History. . . ." (New York, Henry Holt & Co., 1879), **2**, pp. 458 and 459.

[3] He had been a student in Harvard College at the time when Follen introduced the Jahn gymnastics there, and was in Andover Theological Seminary while the "Mechanical Association" was still flourishing.

begun in the fall of that year, and the next summer "Barrett Gymnasium" was completed.[1] The name commemorates a liberal donor, Dr. Benjamin Barrett, of Northampton, who had been a near neighbor of the Round Hill School throughout its entire life history. August 6, 1860, following still the lead of the president, the trustees voted to establish a department of hygiene and physical education, the head of which should be a thoroughly educated physician, and the equal of any other member of the college faculty. "It is distinctly understood that *the health of the students* shall at all times be an object of his special watch, care and counsel." John Worthington Hooker (1833–1863), a graduate of Yale College and Medical School (1854 and 1857), was appointed to the position at once; but failing health led to his resignation within a year, and by

Fig. 75.—The Amherst (Barrett) Gymnasium of 1860.

the action of the trustees on August 8, 1861, Dr. Edward Hitchcock[2] was called from Williston Seminary to take the place thus left vacant. His connection with the department continued without interruption for only a few months less than fifty years, until his death on February 16, 1911.

[1] It was 72 by 50 feet and two stories high, with walls of Pelham gneiss or granite. The first floor contained an office, dressing-rooms, and bowling-alleys, and above this was the main hall for gymnastic exercises. The architect was Charles E. Parkes of Boston, and the total cost of the building and fixtures amounted to $15,000.

[2] He was born May 23, 1828, at Amherst, Massachusetts, where his father had been appointed professor of chemistry and natural history in the college three years before and was afterward to become its third president (1845–1854). Upon completing his preparatory studies at Amherst Academy, and at Williston Seminary, in Easthampton, eleven miles to the southwest, he entered Amherst College and graduated with the class of 1849. Then from 1850 to 1861, with the exception of a single year (1852–53), he was teacher of elocution and natural science at Williston Seminary, and early in this period obtained the degree of doctor of medicine from the Harvard Medical School (1853).

His own attitude toward physical training, and a foreshadowing of what he was soon to undertake, will be found in the course of nine pages of "Remarks upon Muscular Development" in an "Elementary Anatomy and Physiology, for Colleges, Academies and other Schools," which Dr. Hitchcock had just published (New York, 1860) in conjunction with his father. An article which he prepared in 1878 for the Tenth Annual Report of the Massachusetts Board of Health sums up as follows the essential features of the "Amherst plan" as it had been worked out under his direction: "This department was not created, nor has it been developed, for the purpose of extraordinary attention to the muscular system. Its sole object has been to keep the bodily health up to the normal standard, so that the mind many accomplish the most work, and to preserve the bodily powers in full activity for both the daily duties of college

FIG. 76.—Edward Hitchcock (1828–1911). (From a photograph taken in 1867.)

and the promised labor of a long life. . . At the same time it has been equally desired that the so-called exercises of this department should be mentally as well as physically enjoyed by the students, and not be made a tedious, mechanical, or heavy drill. . . . An essential feature of it is, that each student with his class by itself, at a stated hour on four days of the week, appears at the gymnasium, and performs his part in systematic and methodical exercises timed to music. Each class has its own organization of officers and men. . . The exercises are commonly known as those of light gymnastics, which consist of various bodily movements accompanied and guided by music; the larger part of them with a wooden dumb-bell in each hand. . .[1] Especially during

[1] See the "Manual of Gymnastic Exercises, Arranged on Hygienic Principles and Adapted to Music. Compiled by E. H. Barlow, Captain of the Class of '66, Barrett Gymnasium, Amherst College" (Amherst, 1863). A second edition was published in 1866, and a third in 1875. It will be recalled that in 1864 Amherst College conferred on Dio Lewis the honorary degree of Master of Arts.

the colder season of the year, running is practised by the class on the floor of the gymnasium. A few marching movements are also undertaken by the classes. This amount of exercise is required of every student who is sound of limb." In the fall of 1861 Dr. Hitchcock began to note in the case of each freshman the age, weight, height, girths of chest, arm and forearm, and strength of upper arms (pull-up), repeating the examination afterward at the end of each year of the course. Other measurements were added from time to time, and about twenty years later the list was considerably extended. The tabulated results appear in the Anthropometric Manual published in 1887, and in the revised editions of 1889, 1893 and 1900.[1]

As a matter of record the following data regarding other college gymnasia erected or equipped during the sixties and seventies deserve a place here. At *Bowdoin College* in 1860 or soon afterward a gymnasium was fitted up in what had been a dining hall. Before the middle of the next decade it was removed to unfinished Memorial Hall, and in 1882 to the lower floor of Winthrop Hall. William Colyer Dole was "Director of the Gymnasium," 1863–1869, and Dudley Allen Sargent, 1869–1875. Men students in *Oberlin College* organized a Gymnasium Association in 1860, and erected a one-story wooden structure about 75 by 25 feet, opened March 30, 1861. Samuel Putnam, member of the Worcester, Mass., Gymnastic Club and highly recommended by Rev. Thomas Wentworth Higginson, was secured as instructor of the classes, which were at once organized, but left within a month to join the Massachusetts troops at Washington. Another wooden building of similar size, and again the result of student effort, was opened in October of 1873, the earlier one having been removed in 1867. At *Wesleyan University* a one-story wooden structure with one room 70 by 40 feet was built and equipped in 1863–1864 at a cost of $5000. A large room in Goodrich Hall, erected at *Williams College* in 1864, was fitted up with gymnastic apparatus, and there was a bowling-alley on the lowest floor. A wooden gymnasium built in 1881 was blown down in 1883. Charles Russell Treat served as Professor of Physiology, Vocal and Physical Culture 1866–1869, Henry Wilson Smith (A.B., '69) as Instructor in Physical Training 1870–1874, and Luther Dana Woodbridge (A.B., '72) in the same position 1874–1876.

[1] The gift of a new gymnasium to Amherst College in 1884, by C. M. Pratt of the class of '79, brought new and much-needed facilities, to which important additions have been made during more recent years; but the unique contribution of the College, and of Dr. Hitchcock, himself, to the advancement of physical training in America was made in the two decades which succeeded the trustee meeting of August, 1859. Dr. Hitchcock was chairman of the meeting in Brooklyn at which the American Association for the Advancement of Physical Education was organized (November 27, 1885). He was also its first president, a member of the committee on statistics and measurements, and a frequent contributor to the early programs.

A gymnasium hall 80 by 30 feet and 19 feet high was ready for use at *Mt. Holyoke Seminary* in the summer of 1865. After 1862 the Dio Lewis gymnastics had replaced the earlier "calisthenics" there. *Vassar's* gymnasium (80 by 30 feet) and riding school was occupied at the opening of the second college year, in the fall of 1866. Here, too, the Dio Lewis exercises were employed. In March of 1867 a two-story gymnasium of brick with stone trimmings was opened at *Dartmouth College*, to which George H. Bissell gave nearly $24,000 for the purpose. The architect was Joseph R. Richards of Boston. F. G. Welch was Instructor in Gymnastics 1867–1868, Charles Franklin Emerson (A.B.,'68) 1868–1871, Devinel French Thompson (B.S., '69) 1871–1872, Solon Rodney Towne

Fig. 77.—Vassar College: "The Calisthenic Hall" of 1866.

(A.B., '72) 1872–1875, and Thomas Wilson Dorr Worthen (A.B., '72) 1875–1893. "In the spring of 1869 and during the greater part of the year 1869–1870 the students (of *Brown University*) had the use of a private gymnasium on Canal Street, the college bearing half the expense" (Bronson 1914, p. 377). *Princeton's* gymnasium, the gift of Robert Bonner and Henry G. Marquand, was a two-story structure of gray stone, planned by George B. Post of New York, and with the ground on which it stood cost $38,000. The main hall was 80 by 50 feet. George Goldie[1] was Superintendent of the

[1] Born in Edinburgh, Scotland, 1841, March 16; removed to New York City at the age of thirteen, and in 1861 became a professional gymnastic; as a member of the New York Caledonian Club was a leading figure in its annual games, and at national Caledonian meets he twice won the championship medal. He died at Princeton, February 23, 1920.

Gymnasium 1869– (it was opened January 13, 1870) 1885. The annual report of the Board of Regents for the year ending September 30, 1870, records that at the *University of Wisconsin* "a building for drill and gymnastic exercises has just been completed at a cost of about $4000. . . The main building is 100 by 30 feet," with a wing containing an armory. Before 1870 *Washington University* (St. Louis) had provided for its students a one-story gymnasium with a main hall 70 by 50 feet, at a cost of $7000. Other institutions known to have made similar provision were Pennsylvania College, at Gettysburg (1870, wood, $3000), Beloit (1874, wood, $5000), University of California (1878 wood, $12,000) and Vanderbilt University (1879, brick, $22,000).[1]

The three decades which witnessed the gradual revival of interest in gymnastics in the colleges were not without other signs of a growing desire for some sort of physical activity suited to the conditions and needs of the undergraduate world. The Civil War brought inevitably to the front the idea of a trained citizen soldiery which had animated Captain Patridge's endeavors forty years before, and the beginnings of athletic sports in the colleges go back to the period immediately preceding and following the death-grapple between North and South.

The momentous Land-Grant Act of 1862, introduced by Justin S. Morrill of Vermont, passed by both houses of Congress in June and signed by President Lincoln July 2, allotted to each state a quantity of public land equal to 30,000 acres for each senator or representative in Congress, the proceeds from the sale of these lands to be used for "the endowment, support and maintenance of at least one college, where the leading object shall be, without excluding other scientific and classical studies and *including military tactics*, to teach such branches of learning as are related to agriculture and the mechanic arts in such manner as the legislatures of the states may respectively prescribe in order to promote the liberal and practical education of the industrial classes in the several pursuits and professions in life." The clause relating to military instruction "was not in the original bill, but was introduced . . . because the advantage of the South over the North at the beginning of the war was attributed to the numerous military schools there, and it was thought that at least one college in each state should teach military subjects."[2]   In accordance with this Act nineteen states, among them Connecticut, Iowa, Kansas, Michigan and New

---

[1] See Dr. E. M. Hartwell, "Physical Training in American Colleges and Universities" (Bureau of Education, Circular of Information No. 5, 1885. Washington, 1886), pp. 39, 60–67. It is possible that Cornell University and Hamilton, Union, and Wabash College should be added to the list.

[2] See "The Life of Daniel Coit Gilman," by Fabian Franklin (New York: Dodd, Mead & Co., 1910) pp. 70–73

Hampshire, have organized independent colleges of agriculture and the mechanic arts; in twenty-one others the college of agriculture is a part of the state university, as in California, Illinois, Maine, Minnesota, Missouri, Nebraska, Ohio and Wisconsin; and in a few cases all or a part of the income goes to a privately endowed institution, like Cornell University, Massachusetts Institute of Technology, Purdue University and Rutgers College. Army officers are detailed to serve as instructors in military science and tactics, and in 1915–1916 the number of young men who received such instruction under the Act of 1862 was 33,445.[1]

Rowing was the first sport to gain a foothold in American colleges. The earliest organizations were the boat clubs formed at Yale in 1843 and at Harvard in 1844. Crews from the two colleges met for a race on Lake Winnipiseogee, August 3, 1852. The next year the Yale Navy was organized, University of Pennsylvania students formed a university barge club in 1854, 1856 marks the beginnings of rowing at Dartmouth, Brown's first crew was the one of 1857, and on May 26, 1858, Harvard, Yale, Brown and Trinity organized the College Union Regatta, the first races occurring July 26, 1859, and the second July 24, 1860, both at Worcester, Massachusetts. The outbreak of the Civil War interrupted the series of regattas, and after its close the crews of Harvard and Yale were the only ones to renew the annual contest. But the Harvard-Oxford race over the Putney-Mortlake course August 27, 1869, attracted the attention of other colleges to the sport, and interest in rowing culminated in the years 1870–1876. Amherst, Princeton, Cornell and the Massachusetts Agricultural College formed boat clubs in 1870, and Trinity became active again. In the spring of 1871 representatives of Amherst, Bowdoin, Brown and Harvard organized the Rowing Association of American Colleges, and in July of this and the five succeeding years this body held regattas, on the Connecticut River at Springfield for three years, and afterward at Saratoga Lake. Thirteen colleges sent crews to the great regatta of 1875. The list of those who competed at one or more of the races during this period includes Amherst, Bowdoin, Brown, Columbia, Cornell, Dartmouth, Hamilton Harvard, Massachusetts Agricultural College, Princeton Trinity, Union, Wesleyan, Williams and Yale. Rutgers and the College of the City of New York had also sought admission to the Association, and at the University of Pennsylvania a boat club was organized in 1872.

College baseball had its beginning in the years 1858–1860, with the appearance of teams at Amherst, Princeton, Williams and Yale.

[1] See Bulletin 1918, No. 13 of the United States Bureau of Education (Benjamin F. Andrews, "The Land-Grant of 1862 and the Land-Grant Colleges"), and an article by Herman Balson in *The Outlook* for May 4, 1901 (pp. 81–85).

The first intercollegiate game seems to have been that between Amherst and Williams representatives at Pittsfield, Massachusetts, July 1, 1859. During the course of the Civil War the game was introduced at Harvard and Brown, and Bowdoin had a nine as early as 1864. In the years immediately following the war interest in the game became general and intense over the entire United States, and clubs were formed everywhere, in the colleges and outside of them.

Intramural football, in a primitive form, was all that existed in American colleges up to 1869. Traces of it are found at Yale, Princeton, Harvard, Dartmouth, Rutgers, Brown and Amherst. The first intercollegiate football game in this country was played by Princeton and Rutgers teams at New Brunswick, New Jersey, November 6, 1869, and by 1876 the present form of game was definitely established.

The general practice of track and field athletics can be traced back to three influences—the example of students at Oxford and Cambridge Universities, the "Caledonian Games" of Scotch immigrants organized into clubs for the purpose of keeping up interest in their native language and customs, and the contests arranged as appendages of the rowing events at Saratoga in 1874, 1875 and 1876. A letter from George Rives, a graduate of Columbia University, who was present at the annual meets of the two English universities in 1868, led to the formation of an athletic association at Columbia, and to its first meet, in June of 1869. The first of the Caledonian Clubs was organized in Boston March 19, 1853, and its earliest games were held later in the same year. The New York Caledonian Club dates from 1856, and its first meet was on St. George's Cricket Grounds, Hoboken, in October of 1857. Similar clubs were formed in Philadelphia, Baltimore, Washington, Montreal and other cities. The annual games of these organizations were especially popular in the ten or fifteen years following the Civil War, and they may be considered the precursors of our modern amateur athletic clubs. George Goldie, long a member of the New York Caledonian Club, at one time director of its gymnasium, and twice a winner of the championship medal at national Caledonian meets, was director of the Princeton gymnasium from 1869 to 1885, and under the inspiration of his presence the Princeton Athletic Club was organized in the spring of 1873. The club had its first field day on June 21 of that year. Yale students held a field meet May 4, 1872. In the fall of 1873 the University of Pennsylvania Athletic Association was formed, and the Harvard Athletic Association a year later. Among the colleges which competed in five events at Saratoga in 1874 were Columbia, Cornell, Harvard, Princeton, Wesleyan, Williams and Yale. Amherst,

University of Pennsylvania and Union were added in 1875, and Dartmouth in 1876. Although an intercollegiate athletic association was organized in this last year (1876), the present widespread interest in track and field athletics was not reached until the following decade. Nineteen colleges were represented at the Mott Haven (New York) games in 1886. The New York State Intercollegiate Athletic Association, made up of seven colleges, was already in existence (1885), and delegates from seven other colleges formed the New England Intercollegiate Athletic Association on November 23, 1886.[1]

FIG. 78.—Dudley Allen Sargent (1849–1924).

Twenty years after the octagonal gymnasium on Cambridge Street and Broadway was opened to students in Harvard University a structure ten times as costly, the gift of Augustus Hemenway, Harvard 1875, to his *alma mater*, was nearing completion at the corner of Cambridge Street and Holmes Place, facing the College Yard. The selection and arrangement of apparatus and the details of system and method were left to the newly appointed director, Dr. Dudley Allen Sargent, a man whose stimulating and molding influence upon physical training in American colleges in the next few decades was to be more potent and more widely felt than any other than can be named. His interest in gymnastics reached back to boyhood days, and during ten years of experience as a teacher in that field he had evolved certain unique plans of equipment and

[1] See "Rowing and Track Athletics: Rowing by Samuel Crowther, Track Athletics by Arthur Ruhl" (New York, The Macmillan Co., 1905); and "Football, the American Intercollegiate Game," by Parke H. Davis (New York, Charles Scribner's Sons, 1911).

administration which were now to be carried out under most favorable conditions.

He was descended from New England ancestry, the son of a ship carpenter and sparmaker in Belfast, Maine, on the west side of Penobscot Bay, and was born there on September 28, 1849. The harbor and the bay furnished abundant opportunity for youthful activity and enterprise, and the early death of his father made it necessary to give much of the time outside of school hours and in the long vacations to varied forms of manual labor on land and sea, under the direction of an uncle. Meanwhile he had joined with other high-school boys in putting up a horizontal bar and some other apparatus on the school grounds and starting a gymnastic club. Reports of exhibitions given at Bowdoin College, in Brunswick, sixty miles away to the southwest, added to their zeal, and constant practice brought such a degree of skill that they ventured to give similar public exhibitions of their own, first in the town-hall at home, and later in some of the neighboring towns.

An invitation to become director of the gymnasium at Bowdoin College, in the fall of 1869, opened the way to further study for the young expert and started him on a career which was followed thenceforth without interruption. Two years later he was ready to enter the college as a freshman, retaining still the position to which he had been originally appointed, and now the authorities required all students to attend regular class exercises in the gymnasium for a half-hour daily during most of the fall and winter terms, *i. e.*, when they were not occupied with military drill. During his sophomore year Sargent spent three months at Yale College, introducing there the same plan of work, and he continued to divide his time between the two institutions until his graduation from Bowdoin (A.B.) in 1875. The fall of that year found him instructor in gymnastics in Yale College and a student in the Yale Medical School, and from the latter he obtained the degree of M.D. in January of 1878.

The next move was to New York City, where for a year he conducted a private gymnasium on the site afterward occupied by the Madison Square Theatre Company. "I elaborated my old system of measurements," he says, referring to this period, "and had the first patterns of my long-contemplated developing appliances constructed. These consist of what are familiarly known as chest-weights, chest-expanders and developers, quarter-circles, leg-machines, finger-machines, etc., to the number of forty different pieces. . ."[1] The attempt was made to ascertain the strength

[1] The idea of the pulley weight is an old one. See an illustrated article in the *Deutsche Turnzeitung*, 1902, pp. 289–292, and Captain Chiosso's "The Gymnastic Polymachinon" (London, Walton & Maberly; Paris and New York, H. Ballière, 1855).

and physical condition of the individual by dynamometers and other testing and measuring appliances, and then to adapt the apparatus by means of pulleys, levers, adjustable weights, etc., to the strength or weakness of the person as determined by the physical examination."

Meanwhile the Hemenway Gymnasium was nearing completion, and the attention of the Harvard authorities, in search of a man able to insure the best use of such splendid facilities for physical training, was turned to Dr. Sargent by alumni living in New York, and especially by William Blaikie (1843–1904), whose "How to

Fig. 79.—Frontispiece to Captain Chiosso's "The Gymnastic Polymachinon" (1855).

Get Strong and How to Stay So" had just been published (New York, Harper & Brothers, 1879). In the chapter on "What a Gymnasium Might Be and Do" he sets forth Harvard's opportunity in language that now sounds prophetic, and here and elsewhere in the book makes repeated mention of Dr. Sargent's work at Bowdoin and Yale and of the new apparatus which he was then introducing. On September 22, 1879, the Corporation appointed him assistant professor of physical training and director of the Hemenway Gymnasium.[1] His first task was to determine

[1] The appointment as assistant professor was for the usual term of five years. After that period, and until his retirement in September of 1919, his title was simply "Director of the Hemenway Gymnasium."

the equipment and to superintend its construction and installation, and the building, therefore, was not ready for use until the following January. In the *Harvard Register* a month later he explains that the older gymnasia were "filled with crude appliances that have been handed down in sterotyped forms for several centuries (!). To use this apparatus with benefit, it is necessary for one to have more strength at the outset than the average man possesses. . . When it is considered that only one man out of five can raise his own weight with ease, the need of introductory apparatus to prepare one for the beneficial use of the heavy appliances becomes quite apparent. It was the realization of this need that led to the invention of the numerous contrivances that have been introduced into the Hemenway Gymnasium; the desire to strengthen certain

Fig. 80.—Harvard University: Hemenway Gymnasium (1885).

muscles, in order to accomplish particular feats on the higher apparatus, was the original motive. . . The results which followed were so satisfactory that the same appliances were afterwards used as a means of attaining a harmonious development. For this last-named purpose each machine has its own use. Each is designed to bring into action one or more sets of muscles, and all can be adjusted to the capacity of a child or of an athlete. . ."

According to the university catalogue published in 1880, "The attendance is voluntary, and the system adopted in one designed to meet the special wants of each individual. Realizing the great diversity in age, size and strength, as well as in health, of the students who attend the University, the Director makes no attempt to group them into classes which pursue the same course of exercises. Upon entering the University, each student is entitled to an examination by the Director, in which his physical proportions are measured, his strength tested, his heart and lungs examined and information is solicited concerning his general health and inherited tendencies. From the data thus procured, a special order of appropriate exercises is made out for each student, with specifications of the movements and apparatus which he may best use. After working on this prescription for three to six months, the student is entitled to another examination, by which the results of his work are ascertained, and the Director (is) enabled to make a further prescription for his individual case."[1]

Fig. 81.—Harvard University: Hemenway Gymnasium (1885).

A "Handbook of Developing Exercises" was printed in 1882, and a revised and enlarged edition, with illustrations, in 1889. The skeleton Anthropometric Chart (percentile) described in *Scribner's Magazine* for July, 1887 (II: 3–17), had been issued the year before, and in 1893 table charts were ready, "designed to show the distribution of any American community as to physical power and proportions," and ranging "from ten to twenty-six years of age for either sex, there being one for each age, except that the ages from twenty-two to twenty-six for men, and from eighteen to twenty-six for women are combined." In this same year the life-size statues of typical American students, man and woman, were exhibited at the World's Fair in Chicago.

As early as 1881 Dr. Sargent had begun to train teachers, in the "sanatory Gymnasium" opened in Cambridge that year, primarily

[1] See Dr. Hartwell's Report on "Physical Training in American Colleges and Universities" (Washington, 1886), pp. 41–59.

to meet the needs of young women studying in the "Harvard Annex," now known as Radcliffe College. In 1883 accommodations were secured at 20 Church Street, and here during the next two decades more than two hundred and fifty women completed the prescribed two years' normal course of theory and practice. The commodious new building on Everett Street was ready for use in the school year 1904–1905, and the course, now extended to cover three years, was thrown open to men also. Summer courses in physical training, lasting five weeks and given in Hemenway Gymnasium under the auspices of Harvard University, have been offered since 1887. The annual attendance in the first twenty-five years averaged over one hundred students, of whom nearly one-third were men.[1]

The continuous and rapid development of physical education in American colleges and universities which has taken place in recent years may be dated from the opening of the new Hemenway Gymnasium at Harvard University, with Dr. Sargent's novel equipment and methods, in January of 1880, and the publication of Dr. Hartwell's report by the Bureau of Education in 1886. First came an era of gymnasium building. In the brief interval between the two events just named the list of institutions includes Smith College (1880, $4000), Lehigh University (1882, $40,000), Cornell University (1882–83, $40,000), Tufts College (1882–83, $10,000), University of Wooster (1882–83, $4200), Johns Hopkins University (1883, $10,000), Amherst College (1883–84, $65,000), Bryn Mawr College (1884, $18,000), Dickinson College (1884, $8000), Lafayette College (1884, $15,000) and University of Minnesota (1884, $34,000). Twenty-five years later 114 institutions reported gymnasia, and in 1920 the number had increased to 209.[2]

---

[1] At the meeting in Brooklyn which resulted in the organization of the American Association for the Advancement of Physical Education, in 1885, Dr. Sargent was elected one of three vice-presidents. In 1890 he was chosen president, and held the same office again in the years 1892–94 and 1899–1901. He was also an active member of the Society of Directors of Physical Education in Colleges from the time of its organization in 1897, serving as president in 1899. Outside of these professional associations he has been busy with voice and pen in the interest of wholesome and nationwide physical training, and against excesses in athletics, the abuse of military drill in the public schools, and other unwise measures. A list of his more important papers and addresses would include no less than forty titles (see pp. 9–22 in the "Fiftieth Anniversary" volume prepared in 1919 and presented to Dr. Sargent at a dinner given in his honor at Hotel Vendome, Boston, on the evening of December 27th of that year). Twelve papers and essays were collected into a volume under the title "Physical Education" and published in 1906 (Boston, etc., Ginn & Co.), and two years earlier another volume, "Health Strength and Power," had appeared (New York and Boston, H. M. Caldwell Co. Reissued in 1914 by the Dodge Publishing Co., New York).

[2] See the reports of a standing committee of the Society of Directors of Physical Education in Colleges, based on questionnaires sent out in 1909, 1915, and 1920, and published in the *American Physical Education Review* for February, 1912, March, 1916 and November, 1921. These reports supply the other figures quoted in succeeding paragraphs.

Next came the organization of departments of physical education. By 1909 at least 111 institutions were giving regular instruction in gymnastics, and in 1920 such departments existed in 199 colleges and universities. In 187 of them the head of the department had a seat in the faculty, and in 157 the rank of a full professor. It must be recalled in this connection that postgraduate courses like those offered in theology, medicine, law and general education have not hitherto been available for men and women looking forward to a career in physical education, so that not many candidates have been able to measure up to the standards of general and special preparation which have determined appointment to other college professorships. A course in medicine, which has seemed to many the natural portal of entry to the new profession, cannot be viewed as anything but a makeshift solution of the problem, and until this need is met in some more adequate way it must be difficult for the department of physical education to win and hold a status equal to that of others long established. A national Society of (men) Directors of Physical Education in Colleges was organized in New York City December 31, 1897, and has held annual meetings during the Christmas holidays ever since. A corresponding Association of Directors of Physical Education for Women has been in existence since 1910, but until 1915 it included only the New England colleges.

It early became the practice to prescribe courses in physical education for students as a part of their required work. This was the case at 95 institutions in 1909, and at 180 in 1920. Freshmen were included in the requirement at 157 colleges in the latter year, sophomores at 137, juniors at 44 and seniors at 29. The next step was the giving of positive credit toward graduation for courses in physical education. By 1909, 60 colleges were doing this, and in 1920 there were 139. More recently the department has begun to take over the control and administration of intercollegiate athletics,[1] to develop recreational activities for the entire undergraduate body of students on a large scale, and to offer both theoretical and practical courses of instruction and training open to students who intend themselves to teach the subject later on. These courses are sometimes grouped into a major, like those offered in other departments of the college or university, and may be considered the first step toward regularly organized professional courses for graduate students. The relation of a department of physical education to instruction in hygiene, the care of student health and the sanitation

[1] An important step looking toward effective faculty control of intercollegiate athletics was taken when the Intercollegiate Athletic Association of the United States was formed in 1906. Four years later the name was changed to "National Collegiate Athletic Association." Annual conventions have been held during the Christmas holidays since 1906.

of the college community varies in different institutions. In some a part or all of the latter functions are entrusted to a separate "students' health service."[1]

Perhaps present-day tendencies can be best indicated by printing here in full the report of a special committee appointed in 1919 by the Society of Directors of Physical Education in Colleges to formulate the aims and scope of physical education. It was published in the *American Physical Education Review* for June, 1920, and adopted by the Society without change at the annual meeting in Chicago, December 30, 1920, as expressing its attitude in general on the various questions involved. After an introductory paragraph the report proceeds as follows:

"DEFINITION. The term physical education is sometimes regarded as identical with the hygiene of childhood and youth. Others would limit it to more or less systematic exercise of the neuromuscular apparatus in order to promote and conserve the perfect functioning of the entire human mechanism, to make it what Huxley called 'the ready servant of the will,' and to develop correct motor habits. A usage more in conformity with the present conception of man's nature as a unit is that which sees in measures insuring bodily health and the right kind and amount of motor activity an avenue of approach through which the whole individual may be influenced for good, in mind and character as well as in body; it employs the word physical to denote the means, and not the end. Probably no one would contend that education in general is identical with hygiene in its broader meaning, which takes account of mental and moral soundness, and there seems no better warrant for making physical education synonymous with hygiene in the narrower sense. Obviously something more than health is in the mind of one who adopts the newer definition proposed above, and improved coördination is not the only goal in sight.

"AIMS. 1. If we conceive the perfecting of the individual in his social relations to be of greater importance than more purely personal values we may well begin our list of aims with certain qualities developed by appropriate group activities, particularly games and athletic sports, practised under favorable conditions. It is through these agencies that the child and youth most readily and naturally acquired habits of obedience, subordination, self-sacrifice, coöperation and friendliness, loyalty, capacity for leadership, ability to lose without sulking and win without boasting, a spirit of fair play, and all that is implied in the word sportsmanship.

"2. Other qualities of marked, though indirect, significance to the community are self-confidence and self-control, mental and

[1] An "American Students Health Association" was organized in Chicago, March 4, 1920, and held its first annual meeting in that city on December 31 of the same year.

moral poise, good spirits, alertness, resourcefulness, decision and perseverance, courage, aggressiveness, initiative. These traits, developed by the farm life and varied home activities of an earlier age, must now be insured through other means than those which the average family can itself supply.

"3. Underlying such aims must be the purpose to promote the normal growth and organic development of the individual, conserve his health and provide a fair degree of strength and endurance, and to secure an erect and self-respecting carriage of the body and the neuromuscular control required for prompt and accurate response and graceful and effective movements. Emergencies should be anticipated by training in exercises of which swimming may be taken as a type, and by others which accustom one to bear physical punishment coolly and to defend himself successfully.

"4. But the teacher's vision should not be bounded by the limits of the school or college or university period. To engender in youth an intelligent and healthful interest that shall lead to lifelong practice of forms of active exercise which favor not only a continued high level of physical efficiency, but also mental sanity and stimulating social contact is certainly not the least service he may seek to render.

"SCOPE. 1. The scope or range of physical education is suggested by what has already been said. Physical examinations intended to reveal the condition and needs of the individual and to allow the application of various tests constitute a necessary introduction and accompaniment. The educational procedure itself involves *two related lines* of work: (1) An orderly and progressive program of *activities* designed specifically to develop the qualities listed above, including regular and frequent exercise of the fundamental muscle groups, and suitable employment of corrective exercises in cases of faulty posture and other remediable defects reached through such agencies; and (2) *instruction* in personal hygiene and public sanitation, and inculcation of health habits, together with advice and suggestions to students confronted by individual health problems. Special courses in school hygiene and in the theory of physical education should be added in normal schools, colleges and universities, in order that students preparing for the teaching profession may be adequately trained under the most favorable conditions.

"2. *Vocational training* and industrial occupations supply a certain amount of motor activity for a large part of the population, it is true, but in forms which are in general too one-sided and too much limited to the accessory mechanisms of the hand and fingers to be of serious hygienic value, and too often they are practised under insanitary conditions. The isolated exercises of *formal gymnastics*, if wisely chosen, are serviceable for corrective purposes, and may be utilized for bringing into play the fundamental muscle groups, and securing erect posture and a good degree of neuromuscular control. They permit a maximum economy of time and space and offer the advantages of skilled supervision, and they may be made to yield a foundation of strength and skill without which interest and success in games are likely to be lacking. Carefully selected and arranged exercises in *hanging and climbing* and in *jumping and vaulting* are especially valuable as supplying elementary training in self-confidence, alertness, decision and courage, in addition to their hygienic and corrective uses and the advanced training in coördination which they furnish. *Combat exercises* make their unique contribution in the form of capacity for self-defense and ability to take punishment coolly. Folk, esthetic and athletic *dancing* have an obvious place with relation to fundamental muscle groups and graceful control of the body as a whole. *Group games*, which are lacking in corrective value and compare unfavorably with formal exercises as a school of good posture and general coördination, may give excellent results in the way of improved health, and their special field is the development of sturdy character and right ethical standards.

"3. The *relative importance* to be assigned to the different aims and means of physical education mentioned varies, of course, with the age, sex, environment and other conditions of life and work. The teaching of hygiene and the health habits emphasized must be related to the grade of intelligence and the special needs and interests of the individual at each stage, from early childhood to full maturity. The activities of the *kindergarten* and the *lower school grades* should be directed chiefly toward promotion of normal growth and organic development, by exercise of the fundamental muscle groups, and particularly through the agency of simple games, which also furnish a valuable social training at this period. In the *upper grades* and the *high school* training in coördination, with suitable attention to posture, should become a prominent feature. Too often, nowadays, the *college or university* department of physical education is called upon to adopt measures which would be quite unnecessary with an adequate system in the elementary and secondary schools, and to remedy conditions of malgrowth and maldevelopment which ought never to have been allowed to develop. After the high school period conservation of health and the higher social values would normally become the dominant objectives. Outside the limits of school life, *i. e.*, in dealing with *industrial or professional groups*, conditions of occupation and environment must determine the aim and content of whatever plan is adopted.

"RELATIONS. 1. Closely associated with the purposes of physical education are *other procedures* which any complete health program in a school, college, university or system of schools will include. These are measures intended to secure (1) prompt *detection of illness* and physical defects, through preliminary and periodic medical inspection and physical examinations, and (2) *adequate treatment*, by means of hospital, dispensary or private service, and (3) to provide *sanitary safeguards*, such as attention to food and water supplies, sewage disposal, light and ventilation, rooming conditions and the early recognition and isolation of cases of communicable disease. Such measures call for the employment of a practising physician and health officer, whose services might also be utilized in the examinations given by the department of physical education and in the instruction in personal hygiene and public sanitation. For all other purposes mentioned in this report the oversight of a specially trained educator is required.

"2. The influence of a well-organized department of physical education ought to be felt in every phase of school work, through *coöperation* in attempts to promote mental hygiene and to follow hygienic principles in the choice of methods of instruction and management. Teachers in other departments may be stimulated and helped to maintain themselves in a condition which renders their own work more effective."

BIBLIOGRAPHY.

The portions of this chapter which have to do with the life and work of Dr. Edward Hitchcock and Dr. Dudley Allen Sargent have already appeared in print, as Chapters XIII and XIV in the writer's "Pioneers of Modern Physical Training" (New York, The Association Press, 1915). Other references are given in the text and footnotes.

CHAPTER XXIV.

GERMAN–AMERICAN GYMNASTIC SOCIETIES AND THE NORTH AMERICAN TURNERBUND.

THE first introduction of the Jahn gymnastics into the United States, in the years 1825–1828, we owe to Follen, Beck, Lieber, and Völker, men who had been associated with the German *Turnvater* or had come under his influence during their university days in Europe and who fled from their native land to America·or England in consequence of the reactionary measures adopted by the Holy Alliance after the murder of Kotzebue by Karl Sand in 1819. Although Prussia's example in suppressing public *Turnen* was followed by other German states, the procedure was by no means universal, so that between 1820 and 1840 not only did the old organizations continue without interruption in certain cities, but a number of new societies of older boys or young men, who met regularly for exercise, were formed here and there. One sign of the quickened political life which followed the accession of Frederick-William IV to the Prussian throne in 1840 was a general revival of the Jahn gymnastics, we have seen (p. 102). New societies sprang up everywhere, until at the close of the decade they numbered nearly three hundred. The desire for union which early showed itself was met by holding district conventions (*Turntage*) and gatherings for gymnastic exercises (*Turnfeste*). Agitation for reform in state and nation found many bold and able adherents among these later disciples of Jahn, and Saxon and South German turners, especially, took an active part in the revolutionary movements of 1848 and 1849. The prompt suppression of all such popular outbreaks and the new reactionary policy pursued by the various governments led to an exodus of thousands of disappointed patriots to the United States, and these brought with them, together with other institutions and customs of the fatherland, the German *Turnen*.

The Cincinnati *Turngemeinde*, the oldest German-American gymnastic society in this country, was organized November 21, 1848, at the temporary home and with the coöperation of Friedrich Hecker, now an exile, but the popular hero of a republican uprising in South Germany earlier in the same year. He had been one of the foremost leaders of the advanced revolutionary party. A week later another group of men, most of them turners before their migration and former followers of Hecker and Struve, met in Hoboken and organized the New York *Turngemeinde*. Other societies

followed in rapid succession, so that within three years there were
25 or more in existence, with an aggregate membership of nearly
2000. These were scattered all the way from *New England* (Boston)
New York (New York, Brooklyn, Poughkeepsie, Utica, and Rochester), *New Jersey* (Newark), *Pennsylvania* (Philadelphia, Reading,
Pittsburgh, and Allegheny), and *Maryland* (Baltimore), to *Ohio*
(Cincinnati, Columbus, and Cleveland), *Kentucky* (Louisville), *Indiana* (Indianapolis), *Illinois* (Peoria), and *Missouri* (St. Louis) in
the west, and as far as New Orleans in the southwest. Four
societies, in New York, Philadelphia, Baltimore, and Cincinnati,
contained about half of the total membership.

The first steps looking toward union through the formation of a
national *Turnerbund* were taken in New York as early as July of
1850, and at Philadelphia on the 5th of the following October
delegates from Boston, New York, Brooklyn, Philadelphia and
Baltimore effected a provisional organization, under the name of
the "United *Turnvereine* of North America." The next August
(1851) the Philadelphia *Turngemeinde* invited all the societies
in the country to join in a general *Turnfest* (the first) in that city
on September 29 and 30. Between six and seven hundred turners
responded, and at a second convention held on October 1 and 2
delegates from nine societies completed the details of permanent
organization. The name was now changed to the *"Socialistic
Turnerbund."* New York was made the headquarters of the
Executive Committee (*Vorort*), the members of which were to be
chosen by the New York *Socialistischer Turnverein*. The first
number of the monthly *Turnzeitung*, the official organ of the *Bund*,
was issued November 15, 1851, and reported that 11 societies, with
1072 members, had already joined.

By October of 1853, when Philadelphia became the seat of the
Executive Committee, the number of societies had increased to
about 60, and 10 others, recently organized, were expected to
announce their accession shortly. Seven years later there were
altogether above 150 societies, and the total membership had
risen to between 9000 and 10,000. A list of all those in existence
at the outbreak of the Civil War in 1861 reveals the following
distribution: Massachusetts (4 societies), Connecticut (5), Rhode
Island (1), New York (12), New Jersey (13), Pennsylvania (7),
Delaware (1), Maryland (1), District of Columbia (2), Virginia (1),
West Virginia (1), Ohio (11), Indiana (8), Michigan (3), Illinois (29),
Wisconsin (13), Minnesota (7), Iowa (11), Missouri (6), Kansas
(5), Kentucky (4), Tennessee (2), South Carolina (1), Alabama (2),
Louisiana (2), Texas (1) and California (4)—a total of 157 societies
in 27 states of the Union.

These early societies, most of whose members had been pro-

foundly stirred by the popular uprising in Germany, did not confine
their activity to the practise of gymnastic exercises. On the other
hand, leavened by men of education, character, and superior ability,
they were centers of agitation for a great variety of reforms. American socialism, for example, found here its first home. The
"Statutes" adopted by the Convention in Philadelphia October 5,
1850, announce that the organization aims to secure the most
complete independence of the individual, along with his physical
development, and declare the promotion of socialism and the
efforts of the Social-democratic Party a matter of supreme importance. The *Turnerbund* sought to assist each member to a clear
understanding of purposed political, social, and religious reforms,
to the end that in a spirit of radical progress he might lend them
effective aid, either individually or through the agency of the *Bund*.
The shadow of approaching Civil War helped to give to love of freedom immediate objects of thought and endeavor. The Buffalo Convention of 1855 (September 24–27) put itself on record as opposed to
slavery, and especially to its extension into free territories; to the so-
called American Party or Know-nothings, and to any other body of
similar spirit; and to all temperance legislation, which was deemed
undemocratic in principle and unjust and unpractical in operation.

In view of this multiplicity of interests it is not strange that the
history of physical training in the early societies was a checkered
one. For a time the official *Turnzeitung* contained excellent articles
on gymnastics by Magnus Gross and Eduard Müller. The first
Executive Committee of the *Turnerbund* distributed drawings of
pyramids, and employed Louis Winter, an expert turner from
Leipzig, to visit the smaller societies as itinerant teacher and to
assist them in fitting up outdoor gymnasia. Among the members
of the larger societies were usually to be found men able to direct
the exercises of adults and older boys. At the Cincinnati Convention of 1852 the Committee was asked to arrange for the preparation of a suitable manual of gymnastics. The task was committed
to Eduard Müller (1803–1886), who completed it before the end of
the year.[1] Müller was born in Mainz, and becoming acquainted
with the Jahn *Turnen* while a student of drawing and painting at
the Munich Academy organized a *Turnverein* in his native city, and
later became its leader, city teacher of gymnastics, and editor and
publisher of the *Mainzer Turnzeitung* (p. 103). When the disturbances of 1848 drove him to America he continued his activity
in the New York *Turnverein*, and until 1858 was teacher of gym-

---

[1] "*Das Turnen. Ein Leitfaden für die Mitglieder des Sozialistischen Turnerbundes
und alle Freunde der Leibesübung. Im Auftrage des Vororts dargestellt von Eduard
Müller, Turnlehrer. Mit erlaüternden Zeichnungen.*" New York, Buchdruckerei
von John Weber, 58 Chatham St., 1853.

nastics in its school.   His manual of nearly 350 pages was illustrated
with numerous lithographed plates.   It did not prove as satisfactory
a guide as had been hoped, partly on account of the clumsy terminology adopted, and not half of the thousand copies printed were sold
at the published price (seventy-five cents).

A few years later a period of decline set in.   Membership fell off,
for the older turners began to discontinue their gymnastic practice
and the young German-Americans, trained in this country, did not
always sympathize with the ideals of their parents.   *Turnen* in
Germany was suffering from reactionary measures which followed the events of 1848–1849, so that good gymnasts were less
numerous among recent immigrants, and this continued to be the
case until the marked revival of interest in the sixties.   The Executive Committee was absorbed in politics and aside from offering
prizes to the victors in *Turnfest* competitions did little or nothing
to make physical training other than a subordinate phase of society
life.   The same retrogression was manifest in the pages of the
Turnzeitung and the proceedings of the national Conventions.
Only the larger societies employed professional teachers of gymnastics, and nothing was done to recruit their ranks or to provide
well trained assistants.   An attempt was made to remedy the latter
condition in 1858 by establishing *Vorturner* schools in various cities,
but it met with slight success.   By this time, as a result of dis-
sensions, the *Bund* was divided into two mutually suspicious and
unfriendly groups of societies, and Eastern and a Western, each with
its own Executive Committee.   One noteworthy feature of the
report of the Western Committee, presented at a Convention in
Indianapolis (September 4–8, 1858), was the statement that fifteen
gymnastic societies had been organized by native Americans (in
Cincinnati, Indianapolis, Louisville and New Orleans, for example)
after the German model and were in flourishing condition, and that
these had held their first *Turnfest*, with competition for prizes, in
Oxford, Ohio (June 29, 1858.   See p. 271).

A list of national *Turnfeste* held by the societies of the *Turnerbund*
between 1851 and 1860 is added here, as a matter of record:

I.	1851, September 29 and 30 . . .	Philadelphia.
II.	1852, September 11–14	Baltimore (Eastern societies).
III.	1852, September 26–28 . .	Cincinnati (Western societies).
IV.	1853, May 30 and 31	Lousville (Western societies).
V.	1853, September 3–7	New York (Eastern societies).
VI.	1854. September 2–7	Philadelphia.
VII.	1855, September 15–18 . . .	Cincinnati.
VIII.	1856, August 26–29	Pittsburgh.
IX.	1857, August 29—September 2 .	New York (Eastern societies).
X.	1857, August 29—September 2 .	Milwaukee (Western societies).
XI.	1858, August 30—September 2 .	Belleville, Illinois.
XII.	1859, August 20–23	Williamsburgh, N. Y. (Eastern societies).
XIII.	1859, August 27–30	Baltimore (Western societies).
XIV.	1860, June 30—July 5 . . .	St. Louis.

As early as 1851, at the Philadelphia Convention, the *Turnerbund* had announced itself in favor of the Free-soil party platform. The delegates to the Pittsburgh Convention in September of 1856 announced their adhesion to the platform of the new Republican party and to its candidates, Fremont and Dayton. In October of 1860 the Executive Committee, now located in Baltimore, sent out letters calling upon societies everywhere to support the Republican platform and vote for Lincoln in the coming election. This advice was generally followed, even in the slave states. The next spring, during the riot of April 19 and 20, a mob sacked the hall of the Baltimore society when their demand that the national flag floating above it be replaced by the state one was refused, and on the 22d the office of the *Turnzeitung* met a like fate. The editor and most of the members of the *Turnverein* were forced to flee from the city. The *Turnerbund* was therefore left without headquarters or official organ, and since no attempt at recovery could prove effective in the face of the approaching struggle, which engrossed all attention, each society was left to shift for itself throughout the years of the Civil War as best it could.

President Lincoln's call for volunteers, issued just before these events in Baltimore, met with an immediate response among the German-Americans, whose actions at this time demonstrate beyond question the sincerity of their enthusiasm for freedom and human rights. Exact figures are not available, but it seems tolerably certain that out of the total membership of nine or ten thousand at the outbreak of the war between five and six thousand turners joined the Union army, and to this number should be added about two thousand more who had formerly belonged to societies and now fought side by side with their old comrades. In the St. Louis *Turnverein* three full companies, well drilled and completely equipped were ready to take the field at once. The Seventeenth Missouri Regiment was made up chiefly of members of societies in the Southwest and was therefore known as the Western *Turn-regiment*. The Twentieth New York State Volunteer Regiment, twelve hundred strong, contained three companies of New York turners, two from Williamsburg, one from Newark, and others from societies along the Hudson and in the interior of the state, with some men from Boston and Philadelphia. More than half the membership of the Cincinnati *Turngemeinde* enlisted at the first call, and these and other turners from neighboring cities composed a large part of the Ninth Ohio Volunteer Infantry. On the evening that the Philadelphia *Turngemeinde* decided to raise a battalion of volunteers 86 men out of a membership of about 260 signed their names to the roll, and within eight days four companies were formed.

These were attached to the Twenty-ninth New York or Astor Regiment. The Chicago *Turngemeinde* met in extra session the day following Lincoln's summons, to hear the excuses of such members as were unable to enlist, and had a company of 105 men ready to march by the night of April 17. A second company was organized immediately afterward. Turners from the Milwaukee and other Wisconsin societies were incorporated in the Fifth Wisconsin Regiment as Company C, known as the "Turner Rifles." Many societies were so reduced in numbers by enlistment that they found it necessary to disband and effort was everywhere centered on the support of those who were hastening to the field, or had already gone. The roll of turner dead is a long and honorable one.

During the years of the Civil War the *Turnerbund* retained only a nominal existence. The old Executive Committee remained in office, but few societies kept up their connection with this central body and it received no financial support. Immigration from Germany, where *Turnen* was now making rapid strides forward, had given an impetus to gymnastics in the larger societies meanwhile, and *Turnvereine* in and near New York City had effected a district organization, with monthly conventions and *Turnfeste*. At their suggestion the New York *Turnverein* undertook to manage a general *Turnfest*, in which societies all over the country were invited to share, and after which the matter of reorganizing the *Bund* was to be discussed. On September 14, 1864, accordingly, delegates from twenty-two societies outside the New York District met with their hosts in a sort of improvised national convention, which reaffirmed the former platform and appointed a provisional central committee. In less than five months six other district organizations, after the New York plan, had reported their existence. The next spring at Washington (1865, April 3–5) fifty-eight societies were represented by delegates in regular convention, and on the first day the details of reorganization were completed under the name *Nordamerikanischer Turnerbund* (North American Gymnastic Union).[1] The headquarters of the Executive Committee were established in New York, and its members were to be chosen by the New York district (*Turnbezirk*). Physical training was declared to be the first object of the societies. All active members were to take part in the gymnastic exercises up to their thirtieth year, after a uniform system based on the Jahn-Eiselen model and the "free exercises" of Spiess, and suitable classes for boys and girls were also to be provided.

---

[1] The name was changed to *American Gymnastic Union* June 24, 1919.

The following table reveals the progress made in the next two decades:

Year.	Societies.	Membership.	Active members.	In classes for Boys.	In classes for Girls.	Teachers employed.
1866	96	6,320	3,240	3,317	120	..
1868	148	10,200	....	....	....	..
1872	187	9,920	4,500	4,770	394	..
1877	167	11,653	3,906	6,318	1,069	..
1878	162	11,313	3,799	7,307	1,795	..
1879	178	12,376	3,044	6,972	2,083	..
1880	186	13,387	4,199	8,337	2,388	..
1881	188	14,885	5,586	9,286	2,701	..
1882	183	16,349	7,357	10,141	3,040	97
1883	187	17,537	7,372	10,312	3,186	111
1884	199	19,713	8,439	11,392	3,572	106
1885	213	21,809	5,117	12,228	4,005	98
1886	231	23,823	5,562	13,161	3,888	95

During the same period national *Turnfeste* were held as follows:

XV.	1865, September 2–6	Cincinnati.
XVI.	1867, June 10–13	Baltimore.
XVII.	1869, August 7–11	Chicago.
XVIII.	1871, August 5–10	Williamsburg (now Brookly, E. D.).
XIX.	1873, June 26–29	Cincinnati.
XX.	1875	New York.
XXI.	1877, July 18–23	Milwaukee.
XXII.	1879, August 2–6	Philadelphia.
XXIII.	1881, June 4–7	St. Louis.
XXIV.	1885, June 20–24	Newark, N. J.

A paragraph added to the by-laws of the *Turnerbund* at the Convention held in Pittsburgh September 1–5, 1856, provided that a school for the complete preparation of teachers in the theory and practice of physical training should be established in the city where the Executive Committee was located. This was almost five years before Dio Lewis opened his Normal Institute for Physical Education in Boston. The next September the Executive Committee, whose headquarters at that time were in Cincinnati, reported to the Detroit Convention that lack of means had prevented the carrying out of the provision. At the Rochester Convention in 1860 (July 30 to August 2) the Committee reaffirmed the necessity of establishing a central normal school, at the same time that it acknowledged the want of success which had hitherto attended its efforts. Soon after the reorganization of the *Turnerbund* in 1865 the new Executive Committee, in New York City, took up the matter again, and worked out a plan to be laid before the next national convention. Resolutions adopted by a conference of teachers of gymnastics which followed the Cincinnati *Turnfest* of 1865 also recommended that the step be taken. Both actions were reported to the St. Louis Convention of 1866 (April 1–4), and it was decided to open such an institution at once, with a one-year course which should include lectures on the history and aims of German *Turnen*, anatomy and aesthetics in their relation to gymnastics, and first aid, together with gymnastic nomenclature, the theory of the different systems, and practical instruction with special regard to the training of boys and girls. Only persons whose qualifications as teachers were attested by some *Turnverein* were to be admitted, and certificates of attendance and proficiency were to be awarded to pupils who were successful in examinations given at the close of the course. The direction of instruction was entrusted to three persons to be appointed by the Executive Committee.

In accordance with this decision the normal school was opened in *New York City*, November 22, 1866, ten years after the original proposal, with an attendance of nineteen men from different parts of the country. The practical instruction was given by Wilhelm Heeseler, formerly a pupil at Hermann Otto Kluge's gymnasium in Berlin, and the lecturers were Dr. H. Balser, Dr. Julius Hofmann, Eduard Müller, and Heinrich Metzner. Nine men remained for the final examinations, on February 13, 1867, and five of these received diplomas. The second course was opened in New York January 3, 1869, and at its close on July 2 of the same year diplomas of the first grade were granted to five pupils and those of the second grade to three. At the Pittsburgh Convention of 1870 (May 29 to June 1) it was voted to move the normal school from New York to *Chicago*. The third course (six months, beginning in January, 1871), conducted in that city under the direction of August Lang, John Gloy, and George Brosius, fell short of expectations, although there were ten participants, of whom four obtained diplomas as teachers and two as *Vorturner*. The great fire of October 8–10, 1871, made another change necessary, and the fourth course was therefore held in *New York City* again, from October 27, 1872, to the end of May, 1873. Seven diplomas of the first grade and four of the second were granted, and three pupils received certificates as *Vorturner*. The Rochester Convention of 1874 (May 24–27) transferred the school to *Milwaukee*, and there in the years 1875–1888 ten courses were completed.

The technical director of the Normal School during all these years in Milwaukee was George Brosius, who becomes therefore the most important single figure in the earlier history of *Turnvereine* of the German type in America. His father was born in Hesse-Darmstadt in 1815 and his mother near Leipsic in 1818, but both came to this country with their parents in the early thirties, and settled in

Lancaster, Pennsylvania. Here they met and married and here the boy was born, September 9, 1839. In 1842 the family moved to Milwaukee, which was thenceforward to be his home except for a few brief intervals. He was educated first in the public schools and afterward in the Engelmann School, now known as the German-English Academy. Eduard Schulz, a political fugitive from Berlin, was conducting a private gymnasium in the city, and this the boy attended. When the *Turnverein* "Milwaukee" opened its classes for children in 1854 he joined one of them, becoming a junior member (*Zögling*) of the society soon after and entering into full membership in 1858. Already he had developed such great ability as a gymnast that he was able to win the first prize for juniors at the *Turnfest* of the Western societies held in Milwaukee in 1857. In

Fig. 82.—George Brosius (1839–1920).

that year he was also admitted to the militia company commanded by his father. After the latter's death (1859) he moved to St. Louis, and was following there the trade of painter and decorator at the outbreak of the Civil War. Although married only a few months before, he immediately returned to Milwaukee, enlisted as a volunteer for the three-year term, and was made sergeant in Company E of the Ninth Wisconsin Regiment, later receiving a commission as second lieutenant in the Thirty-fifth Regiment of Wisconsin Volunteers.

The career of Brosius as a teacher of gymnastics, which was to continue without interruption for fifty fruitful years, began in the autumn of 1864, when he undertook the direction of the various classes of *Turnverein* "Milwaukee." The regular exercise soon restored his former degree of strength and skill, and a long list of successful appearances in local, district, and national *Turnfeste* gave evidence of his own merit as a practical gymnast and of his gift for developing a corresponding proficiency in his pupils. In 1866 the Engelmann School, one of the first to introduce physical training into its curriculum, secured a part of his time as teacher, and during the same period he was also conducting the exercises at the Milwaukee Gymnasium, frequented chiefly by native Americans. Then followed a year in Chicago (1870–1871), in the service of the "Aurora" and Scandinavian societies. When the third course of the *Turnerbund's* Normal School was opened there, in January of 1871, he became one of the three teachers who directed it. But the great fire of October sent him back to Milwaukee, to open a private gymnasium and take up again his work at the Engelmann School, and in 1873 to resume his former position at *Turnverein* "Milwaukee."

The next period of his life, and the most fruitful one, opens in 1875, with the transfer of the Normal School of the *Turnerbund* to *Turnverein* "Milwaukee." Brosius became its technical director, as we have seen, and in the ten courses held between 1875 and 1888 more than a hundred teachers of gymnastics were graduated from the institution, to become leaders in *Turnvereine* all over the country, and many of them to undertake the direction of physical training in important city school systems or in other positions of large influence. From 1875 to 1883 Brosius himself served as superintendent of physical training in the public schools of Milwaukee, and after 1878 as instructor in the National German-American Teachers College (*Lehrerseminar*), which had been established there.[1] The rules in

---

[1] The "Central *Turnverein*" of New York City drew him away for two years (1889–1891) with its $800,000 building and its membership of 3000, to take charge of classes which soon enrolled 160 actives, 100 older men, 150 women, and from 1400 to 1500 children. Meanwhile the Normal School of the *Turnerbund* had been moved to Indianapolis, but a building of its own was now ready in Milwaukee, connected with the new home of the Teachers College and the German-American Academy (the model school of the College), and in these commodious quarters Brosius took up again the task of training teachers. Seven courses were held and 59 more men were graduated under him between 1891 and 1899. In the latter year he retired permanently from the Normal School, but took up his earlier position in *Turnverein* "Milwaukee," to continue there his active teaching until in June of 1914 he had rounded out a full half-century of professional achievement. He died in Milwaukee March 17, 1920

No account of his career would be complete without mention of the famous "Frankfort Squad" of 1880. The fifth general German *Turnfest* was to be held at Frankfort-on-the-Main on July 25–28 of that year, and *Turnverein* "Milwaukee" decided to send a team of seven members, under their teacher Brosius, to take part in the exercises and compete for prizes. To the amazement of everyone, at home and abroad, they succeeded in winning second, third, fifth, sixth, thirteenth and twenty-first place in the competitions. Herman Koehler, whose mother was the oldest sister of Brosius, carried off the second prize. He afterward completed the course at the Normal School (1882) under his uncle, and since 1885 has been Master of the Sword and director of physical training at the West Point Military Academy, with the present rank of Colonel.

force at the time the ninth course was given in Milwaukee (1885–1886) required that it should last not less than ten months, and should include systematic instruction in the following subjects: Practical gymnastics, gymnastic nomenclature, the value and uses of the different pieces of apparatus, the preparation of series of graded lessons in gymnastics; the history and literature of physical training, including systems and methods, with special attention to modern times; the history of civilization, in connection with the preceding course, the essentials of anatomy and physiology; hygiene, medical gymnastics, and first aid; the principles of education, and practical

Fig. 83.—Gymnasium of the Milwaukee *Bundesturnhalle*.

hints derived from them; the German and English languages and literature; simple popular and *Turner* songs; foil, sabre, and bayonet fencing; swimming. There was also to be frequent observation of classes in gymnastics, for adults and for school children, and practice in conducting them. It was deemed desirable that every graduate should be able to use the English language in his teaching.

Some idea of the organization and activities of the *Turnerbund* as it was in January of 1886 may be gathered from the annual statistical summary published by the Executive Committee in that year. This shows 231 societies, grouped in 30 districts (*Turnbezirke*). The total membership reported was 23,823, of which number 18,164 were citizens of the United States, 5562 were on the list of active turners, and 3201 actually took part in the gymnastic exercises. Ninety-five professional teachers of gymnastics were employed. There were 1028 members in the junior societies (*Zöglingsvereine*), and 587 had passed from these into the regular *Turnvereine* during the preceding year; 13,161 boys and 3888 girls were enrolled in the classes for children; 436 members took part in fencing, and 399 in rifle-shooting; 1722 belonged to singing sections. The society libraries contained 44,139 volumes; 224 lectures had been delivered and 283 debates conducted, and during a single month 109 meetings for intellectual improvement were held. The attendance at day schools supported by the societies was 1921, at night schools 428, and at Sunday schools 1482. One hundred and forty-four societies occupied buildings of their own, and the total value of society property was $2,556,018, of which amount $1,662,583 was free from debt.

The year 1886 may be regarded as a turning point in the history of the German-American gymnastic societies, and there is some reason for calling the period which precedes this date the German one, and that which follows the American. The immigrants not unnaturally gravitated toward cities or sections where communities of fellow-countrymen were already established. They continued to use the mother-tongue among themselves, and the consequent imperfect command of English, together with certain continental customs which they retained, serve to explain the fact that few Americans outside of their own ranks appreciated the aims of the *Turnvereine* or knew how much they were doing to provide physical training for children and adults. For example, Dr. E. M. Hartwell, for two years a resident of Cincinnati, and director of the gymnasium at Johns Hopkins University at the time he was asked to prepare for the Bureau of Education a report on physical training in American colleges and universities, had travelled widely in states east of the Mississippi before completing his manuscript in the spring of 1885, and yet did not learn of the existence of *Turnvereine* in the United States until his visit to Germany that summer. Two pages of the appendix to the report, added after his return, are devoted to the North American *Turnerbund*.

At its national convention in Boston in the summer of 1886 the *Turnerbund* authorized its executive committee to appoint delegates to the second annual meeting of the American Association for the Advancement of Physical Education, and before this body, in Brooklyn on the 26th of November following, three papers were accordingly read by representatives thus named, and an exhibition of German gymnastics was given by classes from New York and Brooklyn societies. This was the beginning of a systematic campaign undertaken to acquaint American educators and the public in general with the claims and merits of the German system. Representation by delegates at the annual meetings of the American Association for the Advancement of Physical Education was continued, and at Philadelphia in 1892 a paper by William A. Stecher made an especially favorable impression; a special committee of well-known men (Doctors Hitchcock, Sargent, and Hartwell) was invited to attend the national *Turnfest* in Milwaukee in 1893 as guests of the *Turnerbund*, and other similar committees were appointed at several succeeding *Turnfeste;* there were demonstrations and exhibits at the World's Fair in Chicago (1893), together with the distribution of great quantities of printed matter; a monthly periodical, *Mind and Body*, started in March, 1894, has been issued regularly ever since;[1] a summer school was held at Milwaukee under the auspices of the *Turnerbund* in 1895 and the three years following; and a "Text-book of German-American Gymnastics" was published in 1896.[2]

For years the *Turnvereine* had provided classes for children of school age, directed by their own teachers of gymnastics and held in their own gymnasia. These enrolled 13,161 boys and 3888 girls in January of 1886, and ten years later the numbers had risen to 18,582 boys and 10,274 girls. But within the same decade of expansion (1886–1896) falls the introduction of physical training into the public school systems of many cities under the supervision of graduates from the Normal School of the *Turnerbund*. Among the very first to take such a step was Kansas City, Missouri, in 1885, and the career of Carl Betz, the man who proposed the action and himself directed the work during the next thirteen years, may be taken as typical of this phase of the second period in the history of German-American gymnastics.

His father and mother, both natives of Bavaria, came to America in 1843 and 1844, and were married at Baltimore in the latter year. Their second home was Belleville, Illinois, where the boy was born June 1, 1854. Two years afterward they moved again, to St. Paul, and in this young capital the father's social and political activity made him member of the common council and of the school-board, United States assessor, one of Minnesota's Presidential electors, and a speaker (in German) in the Greeley campaign of 1872. Carl was educated in the public schools, and took one year of the high school course, but then discontinued his studies to enter a bank as office boy. Four years later he had advanced to the position of general bookkeeper and assistant teller. In April of

[1] The editors have been Hans Ballin (March, 1894—June, 1896), Franz Pfister (August, 1896—December, 1906), and William A. Stecher (since January, 1907).

[2] A Text-book of the German-American System of Gymnastics, Specially Adapted to the Use of Teachers and Pupils in Public and Private Schools and Gymnasiums. Edited by W. A. Stecher, Secretary of the Committee on Physical Training of the North American Gymnastic Union. Boston, Lee and Shepard.

1875 he was employed as teacher of gymnastics by the St. Paul *Turnverein*, and the next autumn decided to fit himself further for the work by attending the Normal School of the *Turnerbund*, which had just been transferred to Milwaukee. The four-month course there was completed early in 1876, and for most of the decade following he was actively engaged in the practice of his new profession in various western societies—at South Bend, Indiana (1876–1877), Louisville, Kentucky (1877–1882), Terre Haute, Indiana (1882–1883), St. Paul again (1883–1884), and finally in the *Socialer Turnverein* of Kansas City, Missouri, beginning in January of 1885.

At a meeting of the Kansas City Teachers' Institute on May 2, 1885, Mr. Betz was present with a class of a dozen girls and led them in a series of exercises with wands and Indian clubs which excited

Fig. 84.—Carl Betz (1854–1898).

much interest. In the discussion that followed, the need of some sort of physical education in the schools was generally recognized. He assured the teachers that he could work out a plan which might be successfully introduced, and a motion was carried requesting him to do so. The result was a little pamphlet of eighteen pages, published by the *Socialer Turnverein*. The next October the School Board accepted his proposal to conduct gymnastic exercises in the public schools for three months without pay. Before the end of that period, however, on December 5, 1885, they appointed him director of physical training, and thus he was launched upon the career which ended only with his death, on April 28, 1898. During the last two years of his life he was also supervisor of music in the city schools. The executive committee of the *Turnerbund* made him a member of the committee which represented the German-American gymnastic societies at the second meeting of the American

Association for the Advancement of Physical Education (November 26, 1886, in Brooklyn), but the paper which he presented there,

Fig. 85.—Gymnasium of the Washburn School, Cincinnati. (From a photograph loaned by Dr. Robert Nohr.)

Fig. 86.—Gymnasium of the Westwood School, Cincinnati. (From a photograph loaned by Dr. Robert Nohr.)

on the introduction of gymnastics into the public schools, does not appear in the published *Proceedings* of that year. Another, read at the sixth annual meeting (April 4, 1891, in Boston) describes the system and methods employed in Kansas City, and will be found, much abridged, in the corresponding volume of *Proceedings*. Mr. Betz was also director of the first summer school conducted under the auspices of the national *Turnerbund*, at its Normal School in Milwaukee (July 1 to August 10, 1895).

A letter written in 1887 explains his plan of instruction as follows: "On every Saturday the director of physical training drills the principals of the different ward schools. These in turn drill their assistants, the regular teachers, on every Monday. The assistants take up the new drill for the week on every Tuesday. The drill is obligatory, and is taken as any of the other studies. At ten o'clock all principals strike a gong, and at this signal all teachers take up the drill at once (daily). Thus at the same time all school children throughout the city have the same exercise. Each teacher is furnished with a manual of instruction, which clearly marks the work to be accomplished. The scholars, of course, do not leave the schoolroom. . . As yet we have only free gymnastics, but as soon as possible dumb-bells, wands, poles, rings and clubs will follow. Then gymnastic games and popular gymnastics will be taken up, and lastly heavy gymnastics on apparatus." The little manual of instruction to which he refers was afterward expanded into a *System of Physical Culture in a Series of Four Books*, *i. e.*, *Free Gymnastics* (Kansas City, 1887), *Gymnastic Tactics* (1887), *Light Gymnastics* (1887) and *Popular Gymnastics: Athletics and Sports of the Playground* (1893). Later editions of these books, all more or less revised, were published in Chicago (A. Flanagan Co.). Additional volumes were planned, and even announced as "in preparation," but never completed. The ones named were adopted as guides in the schools of numerous other cities, and also served as models for similar works prepared by fellow-graduates of the Normal School who occupied corresponding positions elsewhere.

Among the considerable number of cities which soon followed the example of Kansas City in introducing systematic instruction in gymnastics into the public schools under the direction of graduates from the Normal School of the *Turnerbund* were Chicago, in 1886, under Henry Suder (class of '75); Davenport, Iowa, 1887, under William Reuter ('78); Cleveland, Ohio, 1887, under Karl Zapp ('75); St. Louis, 1890, under George Wittich ('82); Sandusky, Ohio, 1890, under Hans Ballin ('90); Columbus, Ohio, 1892, under Anton Leibold ('77); Cincinnati, Ohio, 1892, under Carl Ziegler ('86); Milwaukee, 1892, under Hans Rasmussen ('88); and Dayton, Ohio, 1892, under Robert Nohr ('90). Schoolroom manuals like those of Betz were published by Ballin, Leibold, and Ramussen.[1] Karl Kroh ('79) was head of the department of physical training in the Cook County, Illinois, Normal School 1891–1899, and in the University of Chicago School of Education 1901–1907. William A. Stecher ('81), after three years as supervisor of physical training in the public schools of Indianapolis (1904–1906), was appointed director of physical education in the Philadelphia schools in January of 1907; and in the same year George Wittich ('82), who had been successor to Brosius at the Normal School of the *Turnerbund*, became supervisor of physical training in the Milwaukee schools. Reports from societies to the National Executive Committee under date of January 1, 1920, show that in 51 cities 171 men and 91 women graduated from the Normal School of the *Turnerbund* (now known as the Normal College 'of the American Gymnastic Union) were employed as teachers in the public schools.

The varying fortunes of the *Turnerbund* since 1886 are suggested by the following table, compiled from statistical reports which reveal conditions in the constituent societies on January 1 of the year mentioned.

| Year. | Societies. | Membership. | Active members. | In classes for | | Teachers employed. |
				Boys.	Girls.	
1887	237	26,722	5704	14,123	4,765	104
1890	277	35,912	7337	17,145	7,735	148
1893	316	41,877	7604	17,389	8,702	172
1895	314	39,870	7647	18,879	9,992	180
1900	258	33,964	5675	17,252	9,756	166
1905	244	37,090	5843	18,033	10,823	167
1910	234	39,207	5134	12,870	7,897	146
1915	218	37,941	4989	9,264	7,958	165
1920	186	33,853	4135	6,782	6,958	125

On January 1, 1920, there were also 2760 juniors (boys fourteen to eighteen years of age), 1904 older men, and 6565 women enrolled in classes; 123 in fencing, 971 in singing, and 283 in dramatic sections; and 6404 in the Women's Auxiliary, organized at the time of the Twenty-seventh National Convention of the *Turnerbund*, held in Louisville, Kentucky, June 22–24, 1919, and intended to "unify as much as possible the efforts of the women's societies connected

[1] Gymnastics in the School Room: A Manual for the Use of Teachers. By Hans Ballin. Erie, Pa., Herald Printing and Publishing Co., 1891.

Manual of Physical Culture for Public Schools, by Anton Leibold. Columbus, Ohio, Journal-Gazette Press, 1892.

Physical Culture for Public Schools: A Manual for the Use of Teachers. By Hans Rasmussen. Chicago, Geo. Sherwood & Co., 1893.

with the gymnastic societies, and to increase their efficiency." One hundred and forty-two societies owned their gymnasia, and the total value of the property of all societies was $6,842,224, of which amount $4,995,718 was free from debt.

Fig. 87.—Kansas City Turners at the Thirty-first *Bundesturnfest*, Denver, 1913.
(From a photograph loaned by Dr. Robert Nohr.)

To the list of national *Turnfeste* given on p. 300 the following have been added:

XXV. 1889, June 22–25 . . . . Cincinnati.
XXVI. 1893, July 21–25 . . . . Milwaukee.
XXVII. 1897, May 6–10 . . . . St. Louis.
XXVIII. 1900, June 18–23 . . . . Philadelphia.
XXIX. 1905, June 21–25 . . . . Indianapolis.
XXX. 1909, June 23–27 . . . . Cincinnati.
XXXI. 1913, June 25–29 . . . . Denver
XXXII. 1921, June 29—July 3 . . . . Chicago.

We have seen (p. 303) that in the years 1889–1891, while Brosius was in New York City and the new gymnasium of the *Turnerbund* was being built in Milwaukee, its Normal School occupied temporary quarters in Indianapolis, with the *Socialer Turnverein* and under the direction of William Fleck (class of '81). Two courses were given here, and 32 men and 1 woman were graduated. The last three courses under Brosius (1895–1899) covered two years each. Upon his retirement George Wittich (class of '82) was called from St. Louis to serve as technical director, the scope of the school was broadened, and in the years 1902–1907 five more courses, each of one year's duration, were held in the Milwaukee *Bundesturnhalle*, graduating a total of 36 men and 23 women. At the close of that period the building was sold, and on September 23, 1907, the newly christened "Normal College of the North American Gymnastic Union," incorporated under the laws of Indiana and authorized to confer academic titles and degrees, was opened in the German House of the Indianapolis *Socialer Turnverein*. The name was changed to "Normal College of the American Gymnastic Union" in June of 1919. Karl Kroh (class of '79) was the technical head for two years (1907–1909), and was succeeded by Emil Rath ('98), who resigned in 1934. Then followed Dr. Carl B. Sputh, who continued in this capacity until the merger with Indiana University, September 1, 1941.

Shortly after the organization of local societies, as noted above, they established a national organization known as the *North American Turnerbund*, which in 1853 adopted the policy of local schools to help inculcate the thousands of German immigrants into American ideals. As early as 1853 the *Bund* went on record as being "opposed to slavery, regarding this institution as unworthy of a republic and not in accord with the principles of freedom." The services of the *Turnerbund* in defense of freedom and democracy during the civil war is one of the brightest chapters in its history. It is estimated that 75 per cent of their membership enlisted in the Union army.

With freedom and national democracy assured, the *Bund* adopted the policy of emphasizing individual and group health through physical, mental and social activities. So in 1865 delegates from 58 local societies completed a national reorganization under the name of *North American Gymnastic Union*, which name was shortened in 1919 to *American Gymnastic Union*, and in 1939, by referendum vote, to *The American Turners*.

By 1870, there were insinuations that the *Turnerbund*, being a German membership, was alien minded. So to define its position the national executive committee issued a clarifying statement from which the following is quoted:

"The *Turners* of America have nothing in common with the *Turners* of the old fatherland (Germany), except the system of health and physical education. Of our endeavors for reform in political, religious and social fields, of the struggle against corruption and slavery in all forms, the *Turners* of Germany know nothing, although this has been the object and inspiration of our *Turner-bund*."

Interest and activity in promoting social and political reforms continued to be characteristic of the more progressive *Turners*. Because of criticism on this account, the key note of a new emphasis was struck by the chairman of the executive committee in 1880 with a proposal:

"We in America have gained that personal liberty the *German Turners* (in Germany) once dreamed of . . . . . . and it now remains to find a new field for our energies. How would it be for us to work with all our might to introduce physical training into the public schools of this country? We could not conceive a more beautiful gift to bestow upon the American people."

This policy was adopted and followed diligently with the result that many cities were induced to include physical training in their schools. Among these may be mentioned Philadelphia, Buffalo,

Cleveland, Indianapolis, Chicago, Milwaukee, Kansas City, St. Louis and Los Angeles. In these, as well as in many other cities, strong local societies were formed.

Practical results of the *Turner* system may be indicated by the fact that in World War I, 93 per cent of the *American Turners* examined for service with the American forces were found to be physically fit, whereas the national average was not more than 67 per cent.

Normal College of the American Gymnastic Union.

At the 1940 Convention of the *American Turners*, held at Camp Brosius, Elkahart Lake, Wisconsin, the Normal College Committee recommended "That it is deemed to be to the best interests of the *American Turners* and of the *Normal College of the American Gymnastic Union*, that the school and property operated by the latter, be absorbed by some well established University, or other institution of learning in the United States capable and willing to conduct the school in the future." This was unanimously adopted together with the authorization of the Board of Trustees to conduct such transfer.

In his annual message of the National Executive Committee for 1940–1941, President, Judge Carl Weideman, reported the completion of a merger with the University of Indiana, effective September 1, 1941, whereby the Normal College became a school of the University, with Dr. W. W. Patty, Dean of the Physical Welfare Training Department of the University, as Director of the school. This was but an extension of a working affiliation, operative between these institutions, for several years.

The *American Turners* agreed to offer, to selected members, seven two-year scholarships, and ten partial scholarships. The College arranged to offer six scholarships, one half regular tuition, to high school graduates of high rank.

BIBLIOGRAPHY.

Jahrbücher der Deutsch-Amerikanischen Turnerei. Dem gesammten Turnwesen mit besonderer Berüchsichtigung der Geschichte des Nordamerikanischen Turnerbundes gewidmet. Herausgegeben und redigirt von Heinrich Metzner. Three volumes of six numbers each, published in New York from November, 1890, through October, 1894.

Jahresberichte des Vororts des Nordamerikanischen Turnerbundes. In 1920 the English language was substituted for the German in these and the title now reads "Annual Report of the National Executive Committee, American Gymnastic Union." Each report covers a period extending from April 1 to April 1.

The *Amerikanische Turnzeitung* (weekly), the official organ of the *Turnerbund* since January 1, 1885.

Proceedings of national conventions, reports of national *Turnfeste*, catalogues of the Normal College, and numerous other occasional publications issued by the National Executive Committee.

The "Brosius 1864–1914" illustrated souvenir.

I am indebted to Mrs. Carl Betz for material relating to her husband's life and work. Most of what is said of Brosius and Betz has already appeared in print, as Chapters XV and XVI in the author's "Pioneers of Modern Physical Training" (New York, 1915).

CHAPTER XXV.

PHYSICAL TRAINING IN THE YOUNG MEN'S CHRISTIAN ASSOCIATIONS.

In 1869, eighteen years after the introduction of the Young Men's Christian Association into America, the first Association buildings to contain gymnasia were dedicated, in San Francisco and New York, and in the latter city William Wood took up his duties as the first director of an Association gymnasium. By the close of another eighteen years, when the number of gymnasia reported had increased to 168, and the paid directors to 50, it had become apparent that steps must be taken to provide adequately trained leaders for this phase of work in individual Associations and some sort of general oversight for the whole country. Accordingly in 1887 a department of physical training was added to the Young Men's Christian Association Training school in Springfield, Massachusetts, a summer school for gymnasium directors was opened at that institution, and the International Committee established a department for supervision of the physical work with a special secretary at its head. Luther H. Gulick, a young student who had just finished his first year in the medical department of New York University, was chosen to fill the office thus created, and was also made one of two instructors in the new department at the Springfield Training School. The other, Robert Jeffries Roberts, was a veteran of twelve years' experience as director of the gymnasium at the Boston Young Men's Christian Association, and at that period the most influential and widely known teacher of gymnastics engaged in Association work.

His colleagues in the earlier days had been drawn in many cases from the ranks of professional gymnasts, trained in difficult and showy feats of strength and skill. William Wood, an Englishman born in December, 1819, had conducted a private gymnasium in New York for thirty years before he was called upon to superintend the equipment and exercises in the new Twenty-third Street building (1869–1889).[1] At the Brooklyn Association in the eighties was James Douglas Andrews, born in Kilmarnock, Scotland, July 25, 1839, who became proficient in gymnastics and athletics under the tuition of the Huguenins in London, and for nearly a score of years

[1] See his "Manual of Physical Exercises: Comprising Gymnastics, Calisthenics, Rowing, Sailing, Skating, Swimming, Fencing, Sparring, Cricket, Baseball. Together with Rules for Training and Sanitary Suggestions." New York, Harper & Brothers, 1867. Second edition, enlarged, in 1870.

had been in charge of private and other gymnasia in Glasgow, Belfast, Ottawa, Toronto, and at various points on the Pacific coast. John C. Doldt, of the Providence Association, was the first manager and instructor at the Tremont Gymnasium, on the corner of Eliot and Tremont Streets in Boston (opened in 1859), and afterward travelled about the country as a professional athlete. Roberts himself had come under the influence of Doldt and of Dr. George Barker Winship, a graduate of Harvard College and Medical School, who went about lecturing on physical culture and giving exhibitions of heavy lifting in the sixties, and whose interesting "Autobiographical Sketches of a Strength-Seeker," published in the *Atlantic Monthly* in 1862, have already been mentioned (p. 262).

Fig. 88.—Robert Jeffries Roberts (1849–1920).

It was such models as these that Roberts sought to copy during his own years of apprenticeship. Born in England June 29, 1849, he was brought to America in early infancy, and thereafter resided in Boston with the exception of three years in Springfield and Utica (1887–1890). He nearly completed the course of study at the Phillips Street Grammar School, at fifteen entered the service of the Western Union Telegraph Company, first as messenger boy and afterward as delivery clerk, and finally gave up this position to earn his living by the wood-turner's trade. Primarily to escape from the evil influences of the streets, he joined the Tremont Gymnasium in 1864, and a few years later was both exercising and giving instruction at the Union Gymnasium, 300 Washington Street, and also visiting Dr. Winship's gymnasium across the way, next door to the Boston Theater. When the Young Men's Christian Association bought out the Tremont Gymnasium, in 1872, he continued his membership there, and now made it his practice to go two nights a week each, in regular rotation, to the Union, Association, and Winship gymnasia. In 1875, having determined to devote himself to the new calling, he asked to be made superintendent of the Association gymnasium, and on the first of July began to discharge the duties of that position.

A list of his best performances at about this time will serve to show the aims and results of the strenuous course of discipline to which Roberts had subjected himself hitherto. Although only five feet five inches high, he weighed 145 pounds and had a 43-inch chest, 32-inch waist, 23-inch thigh, 14½-inch calf, and 15-inch upper arm. With a yoke on his shoulders he lifted 2200 pounds, could rise from a lying to a sitting posture while holding a 100-pound weight back of his neck, push up a 120-pound dumbbell with each hand, pull himself up to the chin 3 times with either hand and 35 times with both, had covered more than 12 feet in one broad jump and 35 feet in three, cleared 4 feet 6 inches in a standing high jump from either side, 5 feet 4 inches in a leap with running start, and 9 feet with the pole, put the 16-pound shot 35 feet right and left, threw the 16-pound hammer 70 feet, walked a mile in less than eight minutes and 6 miles an hour, ran 100 yards in eleven seconds and 5 miles in thirty minutes, had learned to box and wrestle, and was a good swimmer and oarsman.

But this is not the type of work which Roberts advocated in 1887, when he was called from Boston to Springfield, or for which he is remembered in Association circles today. After a few years of experience, he says, it began to dawn upon him that health did not necessarily improve as strength increased, and that the Winship plan of heavy lifting was not calculated to yield "the greatest good to the greatest number, physically speaking," any more than the Dio Lewis exercises, which he considered too light and easy. "I noticed when I taught slow, heavy, fancy, and more advanced work in acrobatics, gymnastics, athletics etc.," he writes,[1] "that I would have a very large membership at the first of the year, but that they would soon drop out because they could not do the work, and . . the weak members would not renew the next season. . . I give most of my attention to those who need it most, the beginners and those who cannot for various reasons do the more advanced work. By . . . pushing simple work I can get more men to go into it, and find it easier to find leaders to teach it, and also can run more classes in a day. . . In competitive work and the harder kind of safe exercises . . . the men leave the classes and become

---

[1] Quoted by Dr. Gulick in the *Association Seminar* for May, 1908, in the course of an authoritative and exhaustive paper on Roberts and his work.

spectators, but when I teach easier work the crowd do the work and the few look on." He was also led to emphasize trunk exercises rather than those of the legs and arms, in order to influence respiration and circulation favorably and keep the abdominal organs in a condition of healthy activity; and special attention was given to those muscles which expand the chest, draw back the head and shoulder, and hold the body erect.

According to the Roberts "platform," as it came to be known, all exercises should be "safe, short, easy, beneficial and pleasing." They must be safe for the man who does them, *i. e.*, well within the limits of his capacity at the time. When apparatus is employed such work must be selected that the members of the squad or class follow each other rapidly, without tedious waits. No exercise must represent more than a slight advance over others which have preceded it. Each "must serve some definite and useful end," instead of being chosen at random and with nothing in mind beyond the mere desire to keep the class busy. It must give pleasure if it is to exert its full effect and not degenerate into a sort of monotonous and mechanical "grind." These principles found illustration in the *Roberts Dumbbell Drill*, the *Home Dumbbell Drill*, and the little volume of *Classified Gymnasium Exercises, with Notes*,[1] which were very generally used in Association gymnasia thirty years ago.

While he was still in Boston, Roberts had been conducting a sort of training school, and during the years 1885–1887, 25 or 30 men went out from his gymnasium to become instructors. At Springfield the summer session of 1887 (six weeks) was attended by 24 men, or 48 per cent of the whole number then engaged in Association work; that of 1888 (July 17 to August 21) by 50 men; and the third, in 1889 (June 30 to July 31), by 57 men. At the regular sessions of the Training School there were 5 juniors and 1 senior in the Gymnasium Department in the year 1887–1888, and 6 juniors and 2 seniors in 1888–1889. After two years in Springfield Roberts resigned to take charge of a new Association gymnasium in Utica, New York, but the next year (1890) accepted an invitation to return to his old position in Boston, where he continued his activities as teacher almost to the day of his death, December 22, 1920. Together with several assistants he conducted four-week summer courses there in July of 1893 and 1894, himself giving instruction in the system of floor work which he had made so widely popular.[2]

Luther Halsey Gulick, associated with Roberts at the Springfield Training School in 1887–1889, was superintendent of its physical department for twelve years (1889–1900), and for sixteen years

[1] Compiled by A. K. Jones. Cedar Rapids, Iowa, 1889. Other editions later.
[2] See "The Body Builder, Robert J. Roberts," by B. Deane Brink. New York and London, Association Press, 1916.

special secretary charged with supervision of his physical work in the Young Men's Christian Association of North America, under the International Committee—the first man to be appointed to such a position. He was the third son and fifth child of Dr. Luther Halsey Gulick, a missionary located for a time in the Hawaiian Islands, and was born in Honolulu December 4, 1865.[1] The first

FIG. 89.—Luther Halsey Gulick (1865–1918).

[1] Some knowledge of Dr. Gulick's ancestry is required if one seeks to explain the work he accomplished with such limited preparation of a formal sort. Peter Johnson Gulick (1797–1877), the third of seven sons of a New Jersey farmer, and a descendant of Hendrick Gulick, who came to this country from the Netherlands in 1653, was graduated from Princeton College in 1825, studied afterward in Princeton Theological Seminary, married Fanny Hinckley Thomas, of English ancestry, and in November of 1827 sailed with her from Boston under appointment as a missionary of the American Board. The following March, only eight years after the opening of the mission to the Hawaiian Islands, they reached Honolulu by way of Cape Horn, and in this field he remained in active service for forty-six years. Of his eight children one died during student days in America, and all the rest became missionaries. Luther Halsey, the oldest son (1828–1891), came to the United States and entered an academy in Auburn, New York, in the fall of 1841, and after further study with a physician in Amboy, New Jersey, went to New York City for three years in medicine, first in the College of Physicians and Surgeons and then in the medical department of the University of New York, from which he was graduated in the spring of 1850. The next year he was ordained as a missionary, married Louisa Lewis, daughter of a New York merchant, and started back on the long journey around Cape Horn. For eight years (1852–1860) he was stationed at Ponape and Ebon Islands, in Micronesia. At the end of that time, broken in health, he returned to Honolulu. Several years of public speaking on missionary topics in the United States followed, and then from January of 1864 till February of 1870 he was secretary of the Board of the Hawaiian Evangelical Association, the agent of the American Board on the Hawaiian Islands and in Micronesia. See "Luther Halsey Gulick, Missionary in Hawaii, Micronesia, Japan, and China," by Frances Gulick Jewett (Boston and Chicago, Congregational Sunday School and Publishing Society, 1895).

fifteen years of the boy's life were far from monotonous.   In 1870 the father was called to New England, to act as a temporary district secretary of the American Board, and here his family soon joined him.   Late in 1871, upon the Board's decision to undertake missionary work in Roman Catholic countries, they sailed for Spain, to make their home in Barcelona for two years and a half.   August of 1873 found them settled in Florence, but the closing of the mission in Italy the next year was followed by Dr. Gulick's return to the United States, and in 1875 he accepted a call to become the agent of the American Bible Society in China and Japan, with headquarters in Yokohama.   Meanwhile the family had remained in Europe for six months after his own departure for America, and now Mrs. Gulick and four of the children were left behind in California, and did not follow him to Japan until 1877.   Three years later Luther Halsey, Jr., again crossed the Pacific, to make his home for a time with an older sister whose husband had just been appointed to a professorship in Oberlin College.

Two uncles had graduated from Williams College, and his two older brothers, Sidney Lewis and Edward Leeds, completed the course at Dartmouth in 1883, but his own desire for a college education was not to be gratified.   Although he was enrolled in the preparatory department of Oberlin College during a part, at least, of the school years 1880–1882 and 1883–1884, severe headaches which now made their appearance rendered continuous application to study impossible and finally compelled a change of plan.   He had entered the middle preparatory class in the fall of 1885, but was taking some work in the college department and rooming with a sophomore, Thomas D. Wood, later Dr. Wood of Teachers College, Columbia University.   What happened just at this time may be told in his own words.[1]   "The advent of one of Dr. Sargent's graduates, Miss Delphine Hanna, later Dr. Hanna, had brought to our minds in a more vivid way than ever before, that there was really such a thing as scientific teaching of gymnastics, genuine body building.   We had both of us been very much interested in the gymnastics and athletics of the college, had identified ourselves thoroughly with all the work that was going on in these lines, and had read as far as we were able what had been written on the subject at that time. Blaikie's *How to Get Strong*, particularly the chapter entitled 'What a Gymnasiúm Might Be and Do,' filled us with enthusiasm.   One Sunday afternoon we took a long walk out into the woods, and sitting beside a rail fence (I can picture the situation even now), we looked forward to the future of physical training.   We spoke of the relation of good bodies to good morals, we thought of the

[1] *Physical Education*, 1, 25 (April, 1892).

relation of bodily training to mental training. . . The glimpse which we secured that day of the future has remained . . . a prophecy of the work which each of us was to do. . ."

His own course thus determined upon, Gulick at once left Oberlin for Cambridge, Mass., to spend the winter in Dr. Sargent's Normal School of Physical Training. On April first following (1886) he began his professional career, as superintendent of the gymnasium with the Young Men's Christian Association of Jackson, Michigan; but withdrew from this position the next fall in order to take up the study of medicine at the University of New York, from which his father had graduated thirty-six years before. For six weeks in July and August of 1887, together with Robert J. Roberts, he conducted the first summer school for directors of Association gymnasia, at the Springfield, Massachusetts, Training School, and these two men constituted the special teaching staff of the department of physical training which was added to the school at this time and opened its first regular session on Armory Hill early in September of the same year. The next month the International Committee secured a part of his time for the task of supervising the physical side of Association work in the country at large. Meanwhile his medical studies in New York were continued, and completed in 1889. He also served in 1887–1888 as medical examiner at the Twenty-third Street Association, where William Wood was still superintendent of the gymnasium, and during a part of the New York period was in charge of the physical training at a girls' school in Harlem.

For thirteen years, until the close of the school year 1899–1900, Dr. Gulick retained his position at the International Young Men's Christian Association Training School in Springfield, after 1888 as superintendent of the physical department and during most of the time as instructor in the history and philosophy of physical training. The service under the International Committee was continuous from October of 1887 until his appointment as director of physical training in the public schools of Greater New York, in 1903. The problem that confronted him was two fold—first to find and train new men for the physical directorship and to unite and guide and stimulate those already in the field; and second to develop a type and methods of work suited to Association conditions. In 1887 there were only 50 "superintendents" and 3 assistants employed in the 168 gymnasia reported by American Associations. By 1900 the number had increased to 244 physical directors and 22 assistants, in 491 gymnasia, and nearly 80,000 men and 20,000 boys were being reached by physical agencies. The regular course at the Springfield Training School covered two years until 1895, when it was extended to three, and meanwhile, in 1890, a second and independent institution of similar sort had been incorporated in Chicago. For five years, from 1887 through 1891, summer courses, lasting from four to six weeks, were given at the Training School, and attended, respectively, by 25, 50, 57, 33, and 23 men. A western section, at Lake Geneva, Wisconsin, in July of 1890, had an attendance of 16. These were succeeded by summer "conferences," more informal and intended for directors already in the work, which met for a week or ten days each year from 1892 through 1895. In 1896 and thereafter the conferences were held under the auspices of the International Committee. Additional educative means were the correspondence courses for physical directors, first offered by the Training School in the fall of 1891 and continued for four years, and the monthly Athletic League Letter, beginning in November of 1898. The Physical Directors' Society of the Young Men's Christian Associations of North America was organized during a conference held at Lakewood, on Chautauqua Lake, New York, June 16–18, 1903.

The relation of physical training to Association work as a whole, and the type and methods suited to Association conditions, Dr. Gulick considered in a paper on "Our New Gymnastics," read at the Twenty-eighth International Convention (Philadelphia, May 11, 1889), and one on "The Distinctive Features of the Physical Work in the Association" at the Twenty-ninth Convention (Kansas City, May 9, 1891). He urged that man is a unit, that the Associations "are working for *young men*, not simply for their bodies, minds and souls, but for the salvation, development and training of the whole man complete as God made him," and that physical education therefore forms a vital part of the Association program. The objects of exercise and the sorts needed in Association gymnasia were discussed at the first and second summer conferences of physical directors (1892 and 1893) and in the columns of *Physical Education* for May, 1892, and January and October, 1893. He furnished the chapter on the Physical Department for a "Hand-Book of the History, Organization and Methods of Work of Young Men's Christian Associations," issued by the International Committee in 1892 (pp. 297–339), and presented the claims of "The Physical Directorship of the Young Men's Christian Association as a Life Work" in a pamphlet published by that body in 1890.

A desire to render anthropometric methods uniform and useful resulted in a "Manual for Physical Measurements in connection with Association Gymnasium Records," which was ready in 1892. An anthropometric chart was also compiled and published. He read a paper on "The Value of Percentile Grades" before the American Statistical Association February 10, 1893, and for Volumes II and III of *Physical Education* (November, 1893, to January 1895), prepared a series of articles on "Physical Measurements and How They Are Studied." In connection with the summer conferences various "hygienic drills" and lists of exercises on apparatus suitable for Association use were elaborated. James Naismith, an instructor at the Training School, invented basket ball in the autumn of 1891 to meet the need of a good indoor game, and it was described in the *Triangle*, the school paper, for January 15, 1892. To promote all-around development a *Pentathlon*, comprising the hundred-yard dash, throwing the twelve-pound hammer, the running high jump, the pole vault, and the mile run, was recommended, with a scheme for uniform scoring. Some years of agitation and discussion led in 1895 to the formation of the Athletic League of Young Men's Christian Associations of North America, designed primarily "to band together those who feel that athletics are often large elements in the formation of character, and to arrange for them lines of co-operation;" and "to foster a better spirit of manliness in connection with these activities that will banish from them the discourtesy and dishonesty by which they have been too often disgraced." The first official handbook of the League was issued in 1897.

Gymnastic therapeutics formed the subject of a course of lectures given at the Thousand Islands Conference in 1900, and a series of articles published in Volumes I and II of *Physical Training* (November, 1901, to April, 1903); and material prepared originally for classes at the Training School and for the Athletic League Letter appeared later under the title "Physical Education by Muscular Exercise" as Part II of the seventh volume ("Mechanotherapy") in *A System of Physiologic Therapeutics*, edited by Dr. S. S. Cohen (Philadelphia, 1904). The duty and opportunity of the Association in its relation to boys was emphasized at the Mobile, Alabama, Convention in 1897, in Volumes VII and VIII of the *Association Outlook* (1897–1899), and before the Physical Directors' Conference at Dayton, Ohio, in June of 1899. Other studies led to papers on "Some Psychical Aspects of Muscular Exercise" (Appleton's *Popular Science Monthly*, October, 1898) and "Psychological, Pedagogical, and Religious Aspects of Group Games" (*Pedagogical Seminary*, March, 1899). How indefatigable was Dr. Gulick's pen may be gathered from the bare enumeration of the periodicals which he employed successively as a regular means of expression: The Physical Department of the *Young Men's Era* (1890, to September 1) the *Triangle* (February, 1891, to January 15, 1892), *Physical Education* (March, 1892, to July, 1896), *International Training School Notes and Association Outlook* (January to July, 1897), the *Association Outlook and Training School Notes* (October, 1898, to July, 1900, two volumes), and *Physical Training* (November, 1901, to June,

1903, two volumes). He was also editor of the *American Physical Education Review* from June of 1901 through 1903.[1]

In the summer of 1890 the Springfield Training School, hitherto a department of Rev. David Allen Reed's "School for Christian Workers," was separately incorporated under the name "Young Men's Christian Association Training School," changed early the next year to "International Young Men's Christian Association Training School," and in the spring of 1891 thirty acres of land bordering on Massasoit Lake, on the outskirts of Springfield, were secured as a site for future buildings. A gymnasium, the first structure erected on the new grounds, was completed in the summer of 1894 and formally opened October 26, a dormitory and recitation hall was added in 1896, Woods Hall, a social center, in 1904, Pratt Field in 1910, the west gymnasium in 1911, and a library and a natatorium in 1913. Dr. James Huff McCurdy, who was to become Gulick's successor as director of the physical course, joined the staff in the fall of 1895, and at that time the course of study and practice was extended to cover three years. In 1905 the Massachusetts Legislature authorized the school to confer the degrees bachelor and master of physical education (B.P.E. and M.P.E.), and in April, 1912, its name was changed to "International Young Men's Christian Association College." Three years later the trustees voted to make the course for physical directors a four-year one, beginning in September of 1916.

At a secretaries' conference held in Montreal in June of 1884 the plan of a permanent summer camp and "institute" was proposed, and in August, while a number of Association men were together at Camp Collie, Lake Geneva, Wisconsin, a committee settled upon that lake as the site of such a camp, adopting the name "Western Secretarial Institute." Land was purchased in the spring of 1886 and on the 6th of October the institute was incorporated under the

---

[1] In 1900, not yet thirty-five years old, Dr. Gulick resigned his position at the Springfield Training School in order to become principal of the Pratt Institute High School, in Brooklyn. Three years later he was appointed director of physical training in the public schools of greater New York, but retained his office only until 1908, and then accepted the directorship of the department of child hygiene under the Russell Sage Foundation. In 1913 he became president of the "Camp Fire Girls." A study of his labors since 1900, in these new fields, in organizations like the American Physical Education Association and the Playground Association of America, and as an advocate of the Efficient Life by spoken and written words which reached an evergrowing audience would carry us beyond the immediate object of this sketch, which is to suggest the place he has filled in the evolution of ideals, means, and methods of physical training in the Young Men's Christian Associations of North America. He died at Camp Gulick, on Sebago Lake, Maine, August 13, 1918. The following books suggest his later interests: "The Efficient Life" (1907); "Mind and Work" (1908); "Medical Inspection of Schools" (with Leonard P. Ayres, 1909); "The Healthful Art of Dancing" (1910); "The Dynamics of Manhood" (1917), and "A Philosophy of Play" (1920).

laws of Wisconsin. July 1–29, 1890, a summer school for physical directors was held on the camp grounds, under the auspices of the Springfield, Massachusetts, Training School and the direction of Dr. Luther H. Gulick. Meanwhile, on June 28 of the same year, the "Young Men's Christian Association Training School" (Chicago) had been incorporated, with the object of training young men for the duties of general secretary, physical director, and other Association officers. It opened its first two-year course September 10th, in rooms of the Central Young Men's Christian Association, 148 Madison Street, with Dr. E. L. Hayford "principal of the physical department," and in 1891 and following summers conducted at Lake Geneva courses similar to those given there in July of 1890. In May of 1896 the Chicago school and the Lake Geneva Institute were consolidated under the title "Secretarial Institute and Training School of Young Men's Christian Associations," changed to "Institute and Training School of Young Men's Christian Associations" in 1903, and ten years later to "Young Men's Christian Association College." The summer school at Lake Geneva was made an integral part of the Training School, *i. e.*, a required summer term, in 1901, and the course for physical directors became a three-year one in the fall of 1908. The purchase of a block of land lying between Fifty-third and Fifty-fourth Streets and Drexel and Ingleside Avenues, as a site for an independent College home, was announced early in 1912, and the new building erected there (5315 Drexel Avenue) was formally dedicated November 30, 1915. George W. Ehler was principal of the physical department 1892–1897, John W. Shaw 1897–1900, and Dr. Winfield S. Hall 1900–1903. Dr. Henry F. Kallenberg, who had been assistant principal since 1896, then became director of the department of physical training, and retained the position until the fall of 1917, when he was succeeded by Martin I. Foss.

January 1, 1898, the International Committee added to the part-time services of Dr. Gulick as secretary for the Physical Department the whole time of George T. Hepbron, whose chief task was to promote the Athletic League. Hepbron resigned in 1905, and the next year Dr. George J. Fisher was called to the position from the physical directorship of the Brooklyn, New York, Association. He was already serving as president of the Physical Directors' Society of the Young Men's Christian Associations of North America and editor of its official organ, *Physical Training*, which had resumed publication under the new auspices in November of 1905 (Volume III. Volumes I and II had been published by Dr. Gulick at Springfield between November, 1901, and June, 1903). A second secretary, Dr. John Brown, Jr., was added to the department in June of 1910, and a third, William H. Ball, in November of the same year. Dr.

Fisher resigned November 1, 1919, to become Deputy Scout Executive of the Boy Scouts of America, and Dr. Brown then became senior secretary. The years since 1900 have seen the influence of the Associations reaching beyond the bounds of their own membership into the community at large. Work for boys, as well as young men, has been organized, and leadership has been furnished to a great variety of social agencies providing physical training and working for health betterment—to playgrounds, Sunday-school athletic leagues, swimming campaigns, summer camps, etc., etc. A handbook of "Physical Work: Management and Methods" was compiled by a special committee of the Physical Directors' Society and published in 1913 (New York, Association Press). This served as the basis of discussion at an eight-day conference held early in the following year, out of which grew a new volume, "Physical Education in the Young Men's Christian Associations of North America," issued in 1914 (New York, Association Press), and revised and republished under the same title in 1920 (New York, Association Press). Chapter ten in the above revision describes briefly the very great service rendered by the physical department of the Young Men's Christian Associations in organizing recreative work during the Great War, in army camps and naval stations at home and among the allied troops in Europe.[1] The Physical Directors' Society has held annual converences since 1903 (except in 1917 and 1920), and has continued the publication of *Physical Training* (monthly, except July and August) since November of 1905.

The number of Associations reporting attention to physical training, through gymnasia or other means, the number of members participating, and the number of physical directors and assistants employed, as reported in the *Year-Books*, have been as follows:

	Associations.	Gymnasia.	Other means.	Participating.	Directors.
1885	131	101	54	. . . . . .	35
1890	466	407	262	. . . . . .	151
1895	559	495	355	. . . . . .	227
1900	556	507	357	80,433	294
1905	673	571	. .	133,627	342
1910	724	658	. .	271,506	495
1915	1112	728	. .	447,351	650
1920	899	838	. .	488,478	663
1925	. .	808	246	409,557	820

The number of swimming pools increased from 151 in 1905 to 293 in 1910 and 610 in 1920; and the number of athletic fields from 143

[1] See the "Army and Navy Athletic Handbook," New York, Association Press, 1919.

in 1905 to 205 in 1920. The *Year-Book* covering the period from May 1, 1919, to April 30, 1920, reports 151,209 men and 157,772 boys enrolled in regular classes at the Association gymnasia, 2927 men and 6469 boys in leaders' clubs, 916 leaders in community service, and 107,580 persons aided by this community service. Nine summer schools for physical directors were held in 1920, attended as follows: Springfield, Mass. (86 men); Silver Bay, N. Y. (101); Blue Ridge, N. C. (45); Lake Geneva, Wis. (100); Hollister, Mo. (14); Estes Park, Colo. (20); Asilomar, Calif. (34); Seabeck, Wash. (16); and Lake Couchiching, Ontario (43).

Recent History of the Young Men's Christian Association.[1]

Standards for admission to the Secretaryship of Physical Education in the *Young Men's Christian Association* have increased markedly since 1920. A college education and two years of successful experience are now prerequisites for full Secretarial status. Since men without technical background are seldom recruited, large summer schools for basic training are unnecessary. In response to these changes, the Association's summer schools since 1920 have modified their curricula and have become: (1) centers for informal conferences at which solutions to current problems are sought by means of group thinking; or (2) accredited schools offering formal courses for credit on the graduate level.

During the summer of 1941, twelve institutes or schools were held as follows:

Secretaries' Study Institute, New Jersey.

School of Arts, Geneva Park.

Canadian Conference on Public Affairs, Geneva Park.

YWCA–YMCA Secretarial Conference, Geneva Park.

Eastern Association of Secretaries Conference, Silver Bay.

Estes Park Association of Secretaries Conference, Colorado.

Mid-West Conference of the Association of Secretaries, Lake Geneva.

Pacific-Northwest Summer School, Washington.

Summer Institute, California.

Southern Conference, North Carolina.

George Williams College Summer School, Chicago.

Springfield College Summer School, Massachusetts.

In common with schools and colleges, there has been during the past two decades, a renewed emphasis on the contribution of Physical Education to the development of the broader personality. Significant evidence of this trend is presented in "The New Physical Education

[1] Acknowledgement is made for the contribution of Dr. Royal H. Burpee who supplied this material.

in the Young Men's Christian Association," prepared by a special committee under the chairmanship of John R. McCurdy by the *Association Press*, 1938.

In this study the essential objectives of Physical Education are classified as follows:

Health and Physical Fitness.

Education for Leisure.

Personality and Social Adjustment.

Social Participation.

A Philosophy of Life.

This renewed emphasis on the contribution of Physical Education to the development of personality has given group experience as much importance as the form and content of activities. To many workers, Physical Education and Health Education become part of a program of diversified activities pointed toward all-round character development.

The recent period has seen also the development of a National Aquatic Program with methods, tests, and a manual on beginner, intermediate, advance and lifesaving levels.

With the entrance of the United States into the world conflict in 1941, there has been an increasing emphasis on the contribution of Physical Education to physical fitness and bodily vigor. Special short term conditioning classes, in which objective tests of physical fitness are used to measure condition and progress, have been developed for selectees.

Because of the timeliness of the topic, Springfield College published in 1941, a 192 page supplement to the *Research Quarterly* entitled *"Physical Fitness."* This contains fourteen chapters, contributed by members of the college staff, and is illustrated by numerous tables, charts, diagrams and photographs.

Since its inception in 1869, physical education in the *Young Men's Christian Association* has developed from the phenomenal growth of its early days to a steady increase in participation, variety of program and enlarged facilities.

BIBLIOGRAPHY.

Catalogues of the Springfield and Chicago colleges and the Springfield periodicals mentioned on page 323, official Handbooks of the Athletic League of the Young Men's Christian Associations of North America, *Physical Training*, and the Yearbooks and other publications of the International Committee. The biographical sketches of Roberts and Gulick have already appeared in print, as Chapters XVII and XVIII in the author's "Pioneers of Modern Physical Training" (New York, 1915).

CHAPTER XXVI.

SWEDISH SCHOOL GYMNASTICS IN THE UNITED STATES.

THE system of medical gymnastics which we owe to the labors of Per Henrik Ling and his successors at the Royal Normal School of Gymnastics (the "Central Institute of Gymnastics") in Stockholm was brought to the attention of Americans as long ago as the early fifties (see p. 258). By the end of that decade writers on physical education had begun to refer to it under the name of "the Swedish movement cure," and authors of manuals intended for school use were borrowing some of their exercises from this source. But to meet the needs of growing boys and girls Ling had also devised a system of school gymnastics. This had been further elaborated by his son Hjalmar (1820–1886), and teachers trained in the Central Institute, or by its graduates, were everywhere using it in Sweden, in common schools and high schools alike. Of the aims, content, and methods of this branch of the "Ling gymnastics" little or nothing was known in this country until near the close of the eighties in the last century. Hartvig Nissen, a native of Norway and the head of a "Swedish Health Institute" in Washington, D. C., began to use it with teachers and pupils in the Franklin school in that city in 1883, and with students at Johns Hopkins University, in Baltimore, early in 1887. A Swedish gymnasium with its equipment was also shown at the World's Industrial and Cotton Centennial Esposition held in New Orleans 1884–1885, in connection with the exhibit of the Bureau of Education, and Commissioner Eaton had placed Mr. Nissen in charge of this and other gymnastic apparatus. Other isolated instances might be cited, but it was not until 1889, however, that the claims of Swedish educational gymnastics were brought forward in the United States so prominently and stated with such clearness and cogency as to attract general attention. Boston was the center from which the movement radiated, and its initiation was due to the public spirit and liberality of Mrs. Mary Hemenway (1820–1894) and the executive ability of her assistant, Miss Amy Morris Homans, coupled with the thorough professional training and forceful personality of Baron Nils Posse (1862–1895), the agent who first made their plans effective and afterward conducted an independent and vigorous campaign of enlightenment until his untimely death.

Baron Posse was born in Stockholm, Sweden, where his father, Baron Knut Henrik Posse, a major in the army, was at one time head of the Royal Army Staff College (*Kungl. Krigshögskolan,* at Marieberg). Both parents ranked among the Swedish nobility. The boy, as only son, was graduated from a private high school at the age of eighteen, and afterward completed the fifteen-month course at the Royal Military School (*Kungl. Krigsskolan,* at Karlberg), and the two years of study and practice then offered at the Central Institute of Gymnastics, including medical as well as educational and military gymnastics. Meanwhile for five years

Fig. 90.—Nils Posse (1862–1895).

he had been enrolled in the Swedish army, half of that time as a private and later as second lieutenant, first in the Life Grenadier Regiment and then in the Royal Svea Artillery. Outside of this formal training his fondness for physical activity led him to join the Stockholm Gymnastic and Fencing Club, the Gymnastic Association, the Rowing Club, and two skating clubs, and in fancy skating he won his title as amateur champion over some of the most accomplished masters of that art in all Sweden.

It was on his twenty-third birthday (May 15, 1885), that Baron Posse graduated from the Central Institute of Gymnastics. Three months later he was on his way to America, and in October, after a visit to Nissen, then vice-consul of Norway and Sweden in Washington, he took up his residence in Boston with the hope of interesting physicians there in medical gymnastics and building up for himself, with their coöperation, a practice in that method of treatment. The first attempts were not encouraging, and progress was slow, yet after three years of such efforts opportunity at length knocked at his door—an opportunity not of his own choosing, but it found him ready. In the interval he had been married to Miss Rose Moore Smith of Newburyport. Besides writing a sixteen-page pamphlet on Medical Gymnastics (Boston, 1887), he had also completed an abridged translation into Swedish of an article on Massage by Dr. Douglas Graham (Lund, 1889), and was at work on an English translation of the Swedish physician Björnström's work on "Hypnotism: Its History and Present Development" (in the *Humboldt Library* of Science, New York, 1889). These labors help to explain that rare command of the language of his adopted country for which he was afterward conspicuous.

Mrs. Mary Hemenway, whose only son had given the new gymnasium to Harvard College in 1879, was herself widely known as one of the wealthiest women in Boston and as a wise and generous dispenser of her riches for the promotion of worthy objects, at home and elsewhere. The introduction of systematic training in sewing and of the kitchen garden and school kitchen into the city schools were among the results of her efforts. Together with Miss Homans, who has been called "one of her right hands" in the execution of such projects, she had been impressed with the need of some efficient system of physical training for school children. A friend suggested Swedish gymnastics, and spoke of the graduate of the Stockholm Central Institute of Gymnastics who was at that time living in Boston. Baron Posse was accordingly consulted, and in October of 1888 Mrs. Hemenway employed him to demonstrate the system in a course of lessons given to twenty-five or more women teachers gathered from the public schools. A small room on Boylston Place was leased for the purpose, and larger quarters, in Park Street, were afterward secured.

On the twenty-fifth of the following June the Boston School Committee accepted her offer to furnish free training for one year, beginning in September, to "one hundred public-school teachers, who may be permitted to use the system in their school work, thus enabling your Honorable Board, and educators in general, to decide upon its merits by actual results produced upon the school children within the environment of the school-room." At the same meeting the Board of Supervisors was authorized "to report in print upon the subject of physical training in the schools." September 24 the committee accepted Mrs. Hemenway's further offer to provide "a teacher of the Ling system of gymnastics for service in the Normal

School for one year, free of expense to the city." October 8 the Board of Supervisors reported, recommending "that the Ling system of gymnastics be the authorized system of physical training in the public schools," and at the same meeting a letter was read in which Mrs. Hemenway expressed her willingness "to provide instruction, free of expense to the City of Boston, for those masters and sub-masters who may desire to make a thorough study of the Ling system for the benefit of the Boston public schools." The report was laid on the table, but the offer was accepted two weeks later. Baron Posse continued to give instruction to all these various classes up to January of 1890. Several small normal classes were also organized in 1889, which mark the beginning of the Boston Normal School of Gymnastics, established and afterward endowed by Mrs. Hemenway, and with Baron Posse as its first director. In his annual report dated March 31, 1890, Superintendent Seaver writes that these demonstrations of Swedish educational gymnastics had already been attended by "30 masters, 24 submasters, and 166 other teachers. These have imparted their knowledge to yet other teachers, so that there are now 360 teachers prepared to use the 'Ling system' in their classes. In addition to these may be counted 97 recent graduates of the Normal School, who have all received instruction in this system."

Mrs. Hemenway and Miss Homans were also responsible for the calling together and successful conduct of that notable "Conference in the interest of Physical Training" which was held in Boston on November 29 and 30, 1889.[1] From one to two thousand persons attended each of the four sessions, which were presided over by William T. Harris, United States Commissioner of Education, and addressed by many well-known educators and by representatives of a variety of systems. At the beginning of the second session Baron Posse set forth "The Chief Characteristics of the Swedish System of Gymnastics" in a masterly paper, followed by a demonstration of that system by a class of women under his leadership. One result of this wisely planned and persevering agitation of the subject was the action of the Boston School Committee taken June 24, 1890, in line with the report and recommendation of its committee on physical training presented two weeks before, which ordered "that the Ling or Swedish system of educational gymnastics be introduced into all the public schools of this city." In November of that year Dr. Edward Mussey Hartwell of Baltimore was elected Director of Physical Training, to hold office from January 1, 1891.

Meanwhile Baron Posse had been succeeded at the Boston Normal

[1] See "A Full Report of the Papers and Discussions of the (Physical Training) Conference held in Boston in November, 1889. Reported and edited by Isabel C. Barrows" (Boston, 1890).

School of Gymnastics by Claës J. Enebuske in the middle of January, 1890; but on the first of the following month he opened a gymnasium and training school of his own in the Harcourt building, on Irvington Street. The six years of life that remained were crowded with incessant teaching and writing. During this period, it is said, "gymnastics according to his methods were officially introduced into the public schools of fifty-two cities and towns, and into as many more private institutions and academies. Clinics for medical gymnastic treatment were established by him in most of the larger Boston hospitals, and instruction was given to the nurses of many hospitals in adjacent towns." Summer courses for teachers and others were conducted at the Martha's Vineyard Summer Institute (1890, 1891, 1892), in his Boston gymnasium (1892, 1894, 1895), and at Harvey, Illinois, while he was in charge of the elaborate exhibit sent to the Chicago World's Fair by various Swedish gymnastic societies and athletic clubs.

A book more complete than anything published in the Swedish language, at the time it appeared, was his volume on "The Swedish System of Educational Gymnastics" (Boston, Lee and Shepard; New York, Charles T. Dillingham, 1890), republished the next year with additions. In a third edition (1894), considerably enlarged, the title was changed to "The Special Kinesiology of Educational Gymnastics" (Boston, Lee and Shepard). His small "Handbook of School Gymnastics of the Swedish System" (Boston, Lee and Shepard) was ready in 1892. Among his more important papers were "How Gymnastics Are Taught in Sweden" (The *Academy*, Boston, V: 485–493, December, 1890), a series on "The Scientific Aspects of Swedish Gymnastics" (*The Doctor*, New York, October, 1890, to August, 1892, Volumes IV–VI), "The Necessity of Physical Education and the Means of Introducing it into American Schools" (*Popular Educator*, Boston, IX: 122 and 123, December 1891), "Modifications of the Swedish System of Gymnastics to Meet American Conditions" (*Physical Education*, Springfield, Mass., I: 169–174, November, 1892), and "Swedish Gymnastics *vs.* German" (*Posse Gymnasium Journal*, Boston, July, 1893). Four of these are included in his "Columbian Collection of Essays on Swedish Gymnastics" (Boston, 1893). The first number of the *Posse Gymnasium Journal* (monthly) was issued in December of 1892, and for four years thereafter nearly every number contained at least one contribution from his pen. Baron Posse's death occurred on December 18, 1895, but as late as 1905 the *Journal* was still publishing material selected or prepared from his literary work.

The Boston "Conference in the Interest of Physical Training," held in November of 1889, is a landmark that grows in significance as the years give perspective. Leading educators attended its sessions, and the published report of papers and discussions reached a larger audience. German and Swedish gymnastics, the systems employed at Amherst College and Harvard University, the claims of military drill, physical training for purposes of emotional expression, and for mental and moral quickening—these were all set forth by able champions. But the first place on the program, after the opening remarks by Commissioner Harris, was assigned to a judge and not an advocate, to a trained biologist and thorough scholar, able to speak with authority regarding the effects of exercise upon body and mind, familiar with the history of this phase of education at home and abroad, and made acquainted with the various systems by travel and personal observation. It was peculiarly fitting that Dr. Edward Mussey Hartwell should be chosen to discuss "The Nature of Physical Training, and the Best Means of Securing Its Ends," on that occasion, and his appointment as director of physical training in the Boston schools a year later came as a further testimonial to proved ability. There was need in those years of just such a keen and fearless critic, impatient of assumption and half-knowledge, conscious of adequate mastery of his theme, and gifted with a pungent vigor of expression that compelled attention.

Dr. Hartwell came from a long line of New England ancestry. Shattuck Hartwell, his father, a graduate of Harvard College and Law School, was just closing the fourth year of service as tutor in Latin at Harvard when the boy was born (May 29, 1850, at Exeter, New Hampshire). The mother was a daughter of Dr. Reuben Dimond Mussey, who after holding for almost a quarter-century a professorship in the medical department of Dartmouth College, his *alma mater*, had moved to Cincinnati twelve years before to become professor of surgery in the Medical College of Ohio. In the fall of 1850 Shattuck Hartwell took up his residence in the same city, but after less than seven years in the practice of law returned to Littleton, Mass., his birthplace, thirty miles northwest of Boston. This was henceforward the family home. With the exception of a few years, he was employed in the Boston Custom House from the fall of 1865 until his death in 1899.

Edward, the oldest of eight children, graduated from the Public Latin School in Boston at the age of nineteen. It is worth noting that as one of Captain Hobart Moore's orderly sergeants in the school battalion he gained experimental knowledge of military drill at this period. Then followed four years at Amherst College (A. B. 1873, A.M. 1876, LL.D. 1898), and the fact that he was chosen captain of his class in the gymnasium in the junior year, rowed on class and other crews, and was at one time commodore of the navy, suggests not only physical fitness and gifts of leadership, but also the influence of Dr. Edward Hitchcock and the department of hygiene and physical education. In 1871 he won the gold medal for excellence in human physiology. College days were succeeded by four years of teaching, first as vice-principal of the high school in Orange, New Jersey (1873–1874), and then as "usher" in the Public Latin School in Boston (1874–1877), where he had once been a student. At the latter Hobart Moore was still instructor in military drill, and in obedience to the wish of the head master Hartwell introduced the Amherst plan of class exercises in light gymnastics among the smaller boys.

Greatly interested in natural science, he had already attended the summer school at Penikese Island, and this inclination now led him to abandon teaching for a time. An uncle, Dr. William Heberden Mussey, was professor of surgery in the Miami Medical College in Cincinnati, and prominent in scientific and educational circles in the city. Thither he came, therefore, to take up the study of medicine (1877–1878), but interrupted the course for three years in biology at Johns Hopkins University (1878–1881), leading to the degree of Ph.D., and did not receive his M.D. in Cincinnati until 1882. In Baltimore, where he was fellow in biology for two years in succession (1879-1881), he made animal physiology, under Professor H. Newell Martin, his principal study, and the subordinate ones, animal histology and morphology, under Dr. William K. Brooks. Membership in and papers before the Scientific Association, the History and Political Science Association, and the Metaphysical Club attest the breadth of his view at this time, and reveal a fondness for historical as well as biological research.

After a summer's work in Baltimore in 1881, and before entering upon the second and final year in Cincinnati, Dr. Hartwell went home to Littleton for a brief vacation, and in Cambridge looked over the new Hemenway gymnasium and made the acquaintance of Dr. Sargent. Interested in what he saw and heard, he spoke of the visit to Herbert B. Adams, another Amherst man, then associate in history at Johns Hopkins University. The students at the university were agitating the subject of a gymnasium. It was therefore natural that his advice should be sought, and the next fall (1882) he was offered the position of instructor in physical culture. The death of Dr. Mussey in Cincinnati, on the first of August, had left him without definite plans for the future, and a leaning toward hygiene moved him to accept the call to Baltimore. In June of 1883 the trustees authorized the construction of a $10,000 gymnasium, which was ready for use before the Christmas holidays. It was supplied with the Sargent developing appliances, and he at once introduced the Sargent plan of physical examinations and prescribed individual work, in place of class exercises, and also gave lectures to undergraduates on health topics. After two years of service he became Associate in Physical Training and Director of the Gymnasium, and remained at Johns Hopkins in that capacity until the end of 1890.

An address which Dr. Hartwell delivered to the students of the university and others on the occasion of the formal opening of the new gymnasium, December 7, 1883, contained a review of the history of physical training in ancient and modern Europe and in America. Soon afterward Commissioner John Eaton, of the United States Bureau of Education, asked him to prepare a special report for that department. The result was a visit to college and other gymnasia from Maine to Tennessee, in the summer of 1884, and the manuscript for a volume of 150 pages on "Physical Training in American Colleges and Universities," with illustrations and plans which was handed in on the fourth of March following. Immediately upon completing it he sailed for Europe, to look up matters relating to hygiene as well as gymnastics. After a brief visit to England he spent most of the time in Frankfort and Berlin, with a side trip to Dresden for the Sixth General Gymnastic Festival of the German *Turnerschaft*, and some attendance upon clinics in Vienna. A 25-page appendix on "Physical Training in Germany" was now added to the former report, and 2 pages on the North American *Turnerbund*, whose existence he had discovered while abroad, and the whole was issued as No. 5—1885 of Circulars of Information of the Bureau of Education (Washington, 1886).

It seems to have been this visit of Dr. Hartwell to Germany which led, directly or indirectly, to the presence of representative German-Americans at the second annual meeting of the American Association for the Advancement of Physical Education, in Brooklyn November 26, 1886, where for the first time the work of the North American *Turnerbund* was brought prominently before native American teachers, by descriptive and historical papers and by illustrative classes of men and children. Dr. Hartwell himself was elected treasurer of the Association at this meeting, and read a paper on "The Physiology of Exercise," not printed in the *Proceedings* but later amplified and rewritten and published in the Boston *Medical and Surgical Journal* for March 31 and April 7, 1887 (Vol. 116, pp. 297–302 and 321–324). As far back as September of 1884 Commissioner Eaton had introduced him to Hartvig Nissen, at the latter's Health Institute in Washington. Early in 1887 Mr. Nissen was invited to give a course of lessons in "Swedish free movements" and German apparatus exercises to Johns Hopkins students, and this instruction was continued in 1887–1888, from November to the middle of April. From the following May until the end of August, 1889, Dr. Hartwell was in Europe on leave of absence, interested especially in the hygienic and medical application of exercise and with the thought of developing a practice in this specialty upon his return. The winter was spent in Stockholm, with almost daily visits to the Zander Institute and the Royal Central Institute of Gymnastics. He went also to St. Petersburg, revisited Vienna, and received six weeks of instruction in Bonn. December 20, 1889, he read a paper on "Mechano-Therapy in Sweden and Germany" before the Clinical Society of Maryland, and repeated it in March before the Johns Hopkins Hospital Medical Society. In this connection attention may be called to the 45 pages on General Exercise which he prepared for Vol. I of Dr. H. A. Hare's "System of Practical Therapeutics" (Philadelphia, 1891), and to his translation, from the Swedish, of Dr. Emil Kleen's Handbook of Massage" (Philadelphia, 1892).

Meanwhile he had been consulted in the preparation of plans for the Boston Conference of 1889, and an examination of the printed proceedings will show how conspicuous a part he played at the various sessions. The summer of 1890 was devoted to a third visit to Europe, this time to gather material relating to school gymnastics and playgrounds. The trip took him to England, France, Switzerland, parts of Austria and Germany, and again to Stockholm. June 24 the Boston School Committee had voted to introduce the Ling or Swedish system of educational gymnastics into all the public schools, and on November 25 they elected him director of physical training. Still hoping to become eventually the head of an institution for mechano-therapy, he consented to inaugurate the work of the new department, and his resignation was therefore presented to the Johns Hopkins trustees, to take effect December 31.

A part of the story of the next seven years is contained in his series of five "Reports of the Director of Physical Training" to the School Committee of Boston, dated December 31, 1891 (75 pages. School Document No. 22—1891), June, 1894 (151 pages. School Document No. 8—1894), 1895 (82 pages. In School Document No. 4—1895), March 15, 1896 (pages 159–192 in School Document No. 4—1896), and March 15, 1897 (pages 135–143 of School Document No. 5—1897). On September 1, 1897, he resigned his position in the Boston Schools to become secretary of the newly created Department of Municipal Statistics in that city. One must also examine the contents of the published *Proceedings* of the American Association for the Advancement of Physical Education, from the sixth meeting (1891) onward, and of their successor, the *American Physical Education Review*, to appreciate fully the yeoman's service he rendered to physical training in the country at large, during these years and also after his direct connection with the work had ceased. In 1891–1892 he was president of the Association, and again from

1895 to 1899, and he was author of the plan of reorganization on the basis of local and district societies which was adopted in 1895. Chapter XII (Physical Training) in the Report of the Commissioner of Education for 1897–1898 (Washington, 1899), and Chapter XVII (On Physical Training) in that for 1903 (Washington, 1905), give final expression to the results of his years of study and observation. His long series of reports and papers which began in 1885 constitute the most scholarly contribution hitherto made to the literature of physical training in English, and no other man in America has done so much to win for physical training a position of dignity and recognized worth.   Dr. Hartwell died in Boston, February 19, 1922.

Fig. 91.—Hartvig Nissen (1855–1924).

Other pioneers of Swedish school gymnastics who deserve further mention, or should be included here, are Hartvig Nissen, Claës J. Enebuske, Jakob Bolin, Louis Collin, and William Skarstrom. Nissen, born in Kongshavn, near Christiania, July 13, 1855, was educated in the large private higher school (*Latin- og Realskole*) opened in the Norwegian capital by his father, Ole Hartvig Nissen, studied gymnastics and massage with private teachers here and later in Dresden (1878–1879, in the *Allgemeiner Turnverein*) and Stockholm (summer of 1890), for three years taught gymnastics in towns near Christiania, and in March of 1883 established a "Health Institute" in Washington, D. C., as we have seen.   1891–1897 he worked with Dr. Hartwell in the Boston public schools as assistant director of physical training, and 1897–1900 himself served as director.   In 1891 he became instructor in Swedish gymnastics and massage in the Harvard University Summer School, and five years later in the Sargent Normal School of Physical Education. 1900–1912 he was director of physical training in the Brookline public schools, and then resigned to remove to Portland, Oregon. But he soon returned to Boston, and in May of 1915 acquired a controlling interest in the Posse Normal School of Gymnastics, of which he became president.[1]

Enebuske was born in Ystad, southern Sweden, May 6, 1855, graduated as a student of pharmacy in Stockholm (1877), and took his doctor's degree (PH.D.) at the University of Lund in 1886. After a year of special work in school and medical gymnastics, under

FIG. 92.—Claës Julius Enebuske (1855–   ).

Colonel Norlander, fencing-master and teacher of gymnastics at the university, he came to New York City in 1887. Dr. William G. Anderson, then in charge of physical training in Adelphi Academy Brooklyn, had begun to train teachers there (February 1, 1886), and at Chautauqua, New York (summer school, in 1886), and he secured Enebuske's services at the latter in the summers of 1889 and 1890, and in his normal school in Brooklyn during the intervening year. We have said that Enebuske succeeded Posse at the Boston Normal School of Gymnastics early in 1890. Here his chief work was done in the eight years that followed, and meanwhile (1896) he graduated from the medical department of Harvard University. In 1898 he

<hr />

[1] The numbers of the *Posse Gymnasium Journal* for February and May, 1920, contain portions of an autobiography by Nissen, covering his early years in Norway. He also published in 1891 an "ABC of the Swedish System of Educational Gymnastics" (Philadelphia, F. A. Davis).

left the Normal School, and in 1902 removed to Paris, receiving the degree *Docteur en Médecine* from the *Faculté de Médecine de Paris* four years later. He was a scholarly gentleman and a thorough teacher.[1]

Bolin, born in Stockholm November 5, 1863, and educated in the higher schools of Visby and Stockholm and at the Stockholm University, spent two years in the United States (1885–1887) and then returned to Sweden for a year to study medical gymnastics in Liedbeck's Institute (Stockholm). From 1888 until he accepted the professorship of physical education in the University of Utah (Salt Lake City) in 1910 he practised medical gymnastics and massage in New York City, but in the meantime followed Enebuske as teacher

Fig. 93.—Jakob Bolin (1863–1914).

of Swedish gymnastics at the Anderson Normal School of Physical Education (transferred from Brooklyn to New Haven, Conn., in

[1] His chief literary work was the "Progressive Gymnastic Day's Orders, according to the Principles of the Ling System," first published in Boston in 1890 and reissued in 1892 (New York, etc., Silver, Burdett & Co.). Other publications include: "The Place of Physical Training in a Rational Education" (in *Boston Conference Report*, 1889, pp. 35–41), "The Gymnastic Progression of the Ling System" (*Proceedings* of the American Association for the Advancement of Physical Education, **5** (1890), pp. 21–35), "The Pedagogical Aspect of Swedish Gymnastics," read before the American Institute of Instruction at its annual meeting in Bethlehem, N. H., July 8, 1891, (*Popular Educator*, Boston **9**, 52 and 53, October, 1891), "Some Measurable Results of Swedish Pedagogical Gymnastics" (*Proceedings* of the American Association for the Advancement of Physical Education, **7** (1892), pp. 207–235), "An Anthropometric Study of the Effects of Gymnastic Training on American Women" (Quarterly Publications of the American Statistical Association, December, 1893, **3**, pp. 600–610), "A Diagram of Working Capacity and Resistance as Manifest in Gymnastic Exercises" (*Proceedings* of the American Association for the Advancement of Physical Education, **9** (1895), pp. 11–17), and "Pedagogical Gymnastics" (*American Physical Education Review*, **2**, 81–88, June, 1897).

1892 and since 1901 known as the New Haven Normal School of Gymnastics), until 1907, and at Chautauqua Summer School of Physical Education 1891–1909. He died in Salt Lake City May 15, 1914.[1]

Carl Oscar Louis Collin, born February 1, 1866, at Sölvesborg, a seaport near Kristianstad in southern Sweden, graduated from the higher classical school in Kristianstad in 1884 and as a student there was for four years class leader under Major Carl Silow, who afterward became second teacher in the section of school gymnastics at the Stockholm Central Institute of Gymnastics. From September of 1884 until October of 1888 Collin was a student in the University of Lund, taking courses in gymnastics under Colonel Carl Norlander at that time, and in November of 1888 joined Enebuske in New York City. He taught gymnastics at Chautauqua with the latter in the summers of 1889 and 1890, and went with him to Boston in the fall of 1890 to become instructor in practical gymnastics and afterward in anatomy also at the Boston Normal School of Gymnastics. From April until August of 1892 he studied under Major Silow in Stockholm, in 1898 graduated from the medical department of Harvard University, spent six weeks of the summer in the medical gymnastic clinic of Dr. Anders Wide in Lysekil, Sweden, succeeded Enebuske that fall as chief instructor in the theory and practice of gymnastics at the Normal School, and continued in that position for three years after it became the department of hygiene and physical education of Wellesley College, in September of 1909. He taught in the Battle Creek Normal School in 1912–1913, and in the latter year became an instructor in the Chicago Normal School of Physical Education.

William Skarstrom was born in Stockholm June 15, 1869, and educated in the Nya Elementarskola (higher school for boys), whose pupils received their physical education in the halls of the Central Institute of Gymnastics. For two years following the fall of 1891 he was in New York City, a member of the Twenty-third Street Young Men's Christian Association and volunteer instructor of

---

[1] His publications were: Three articles on "Den svenska gymnastiken och dess representanter i Amerika" (*Valkyrian*, New York, January, February and March, 1891, **2**, pp. 28–30, 91–94, 138–143), "Mental Growth through Physical Education" (18-page pamphlet, 1893), "The Physical Processes Involved in the Nutrition of Muscle" (*Proceedings* of the American Association for the Advancement of Physical Education, **10**, 1895, pp. 83–89), President's address at the annual meeting of the Physical Education Society of New York and Vicinity, December 4, 1896 (*American Physical Education Review*, **2**, 1–11, March, 1897), another President's address (*American Physical Education Review*, **3**, 25–29, March, 1898), "On Group Contests" (*American Physical Education Review*, **3**, 288–294 and **4**, 66–72, December, 1898, and March, 1899), "What is Gymnastics" and "Why Do We Teach Gymnastics" (28- and 57-page pamphlets, New York, by the author, 1902 and 1903), and a posthumous volume, "Gymnastic Problems" (New York, Frederick A. Stokes Co., 1917).

classes in its gymnasium, and during one winter taking a correspondence course with the Springfield Training School. He entered the
Boston Normal School of Gymnastics as a student in the fall of
1893 and completed the course there in 1895, acting as Bolin's
substitute at Chautauqua in the summer of 1894, and in 1901
received the degree of doctor of medicine from Harvard University.
From the fall of 1899 through the spring of 1903 he gave instruction
in gymnastics at the Massachusetts Institute of Technology, and
also at the Boston Normal School of Gymnastics. 1903–1912 he was
instructor in the Columbia University gymnasium, giving courses
in Teachers College also and in the Summer School. In 1912 he
was appointed associate professor and later (1918) professor in the
department of hygiene and physical education at Wellesley College.
He has written "Gymnastic Kinesiology: A Manual of the Mechanism of Gymnastic Movements" (Springfield, Mass., The F. A.
Bassette Co., 1909), and "Gymnastic Teaching" (Springfield,
Mass., the American Physical Education Association, 1914).

Alice Tripp Hall, a graduate of Wellesley College (1881) and the
Woman's Medical College in Philadelphia (1886) visited the
Central Institute of Gymnastics in Stockholm in the spring of 1889,
and that fall when she took up her duties as professor of physiology,
hygiene, and physical training in the Woman's College of Baltimore
(now Goucher College) classes in the new gymnasium, Bennett
Hall, were put in charge of a graduate of the Central Institute,
Mathilda Kristina Wallin (class of '85). Miss Wallin was followed
two years later by Gulli Öberg ('85) and Maria Palmquist ('91),
under whom a demonstration of Swedish gymnastics was given
April 7, 1892, before visitors on their way to the seventh annual
convention of the American Association for the Advancement of
Physical Education, in Philadelphia. Thereafter the instructors
employed in the gymnasium were regularly graduates of the Stockholm Central Institute, or of the Physical Training College at
Dartford Heath, England, which was directed by Madame Bergman
Österberg, herself a graduate of the Central Institute in 1881.

In a similar manner Dr. Kate Campbell Hurd, also a graduate of
the Woman's Medical College in Philadelphia, and under appointment as the first medical director at the Bryn Mawr School for Girls,
in Baltimore, spent the winter of 1889–1890 at the Central Institute
in Stockholm and the spring with Madame Bergman Österberg in
London (her Physical Training College was removed to Dartford
Heath, Kent, in 1895), and engaged as her first assistant in the
gymnasium Fanny Schnelle (Stockholm Central Institute, class of
1891), whom she had met in Sweden. After Miss Schnelle came one
of Madame Bergman Österberg's graduates, to be succeeded in
turn by young women trained at the Boston Normal School of

Gymnastics. Miss Senda Berenson, a graduate of the latter school, introduced the Swedish system at Smith College, in Northampton, Mass., where she was director of physical training in the years 1892–1911.

In this connection attention may be called again to Mrs. Hemenway's gift which made possible the publication of a portion of Hjalmar Ling's collection of pen-drawings illustrating positions and movements used in gymnastics (see p. 163). One half of the edition was presented to the Boston Normal School of Gymnastics. Director Törngren of the Stockholm Central Institute also accepted her invitation to come to Boston as her guest, reached that city May 14, 1893, and spent some time at the Normal School, in June watched the classes in gymnastics at many of the Boston schools, and the next month read a paper on "The Royal Central Institute of Gymnastics in Stockholm" at the eighth annual meeting of the American Association for the Advancement of Physical Education, in Chicago (see *Proceedings* VIII: 50–52). The clearest and most intelligent exposition of the system under discussion which has yet been written by an American is "A Review of Swedish Gymnastics," by Theodore Hough, first prepared as a lecture in 1899 while its author was assistant professor of biology in the Massachusetts Institute of Technology and instructor in physiology and personal hygiene at the Boston Normal School of Gymnastics. It was published in pamphlet form (Boston, George H. Ellis, 1891, forty pages), and later reprinted in the Report of the United States Commissioner of Education for 1898–1899 (Vol. I, pp. 1209–1226, Washington, 1900).

BIBLIOGRAPHY.

The first part of this chapter, including the biographical sketches of Posse and Hartwell, has already appeared in print as Chapters XIX and XX in the author's "Pioneers of Modern Physical Training" (New York, 1915). It is based on personal correspondence and conversations with the persons concerned, supplemented by information gleaned from catalogues, reports, and other authentic sources.

CHAPTER XXVII.

THE PLAYGROUND MOVEMENT IN AMERICA. STATEWIDE PHYSICAL EDUCATION.

THE playground movement, which we have already traced in Germany (pp. 132–145) and Denmark (pp. 194–197), was slow in gathering headway in the United States. Minister von Gossler's playground order was issued in Prussia October 27, 1882, and the German "Central Committee for the Promotion of Games" was organized in Berlin May 21, 1891. The Danish minister Barden-fleth sent out his games circular August 31, 1896, and a group of men and women met in Copenhagen April 11, 1897, to form a "National Committee for Promoting Group Games among School Children." In this country certain Boston children had access to a sand pile, under supervision, as far back as the summer of 1885, and a public outdoor gymnasium was opened in that city August 27, 1889; but not more than 10 cities are known to have established playgrounds before 1900, and 26 others in the years 1900–1905, *i. e.*, up to the founding of the Playground Association of America, at Washington, D. C., in April of 1906. In the four years following (1906–1909) 83 cities were added to the list, and by the end of 1916 a total of 480 had been reached, according to a report in *The Playground* for March, 1917.

The first step in the Boston experiment is recorded as follows by Mrs. Kate Gannett Wells, chairman of the executive committee of the Massachusetts Emergency and Hygiene Association, in the second annual report of that body (May, 1886. The Association was organized in 1884): "Last summer (1885), at the suggestion of Dr. Marie Zakrzewska, and in accordance with the plan in Berlin, which has proved so useful to children, a large heap of sand was placed in the yard attached to the Parmenter Street Chapel. . . An average of fifteen children connected with the chapel came there three days in the week, through July and August, and under the guidance of Mrs. Gamble, dug in the sand with their little wooden shovels and made countless sand-pies, which were remade the next day with undismayed alacrity. They sang their songs and marched in their small processions, and when weary, were gathered in the motherly arms of the matron. . . The same plan was tried at the West End Nursery, but as the children there were hardly two years old they cared little for it. Your committee hope, however, that the success of the experiment in Parmenter Street may have sufficiently demonstrated the usefulness of the sand-garden to secure its adoption elsewhere. . ."

The third annual report (May, 1887) announces that three sand-gardens "are now permanently established during the summer seasons in the playyards of Parmenter Street Chapel, of Warrenton Street Chapel, and of the Children's Mission. They are maintained in the interest of hygiene and amusement. . . An awning has been placed over the sand at the Children's Mission; and there, with wooden shovel, broken bricks, and much sand, the long days are passed out of doors. . ." In 1887 "the number of these gardens increased from three to ten. No rent was paid for them. The sand was given . . ., and the school Committee granted the use of the Wait Schoolyard. . . The matrons in charge of each garden were generally women who lived in the neighborhood, and who watched, in their play, the children, to whom shovels and pails were given, with which they made castles and pies. At the end of the season the sand was stored in barrels for future use. . . This spring (1888) the Association petitioned the School Committee for the use of schoolyards which would be suitable as playgrounds for little children kept in town through the summer. . ." As a result, during this fourth season (1888) "seven schoolyards situated in the neighborhoods where children swarm, were open for three hours on four fair days of each week. A kindly matron was ready to welcome the children, and offered them sandheaps and shovels, balls, tops, skipping-ropes, reins, beanbags, building-blocks, flags to march under, and transparent slates to draw upon. Besides these seven yards which were dignified by the name of 'Playgrounds,' there were three 'Sand-Gardens,' where only sand and shovels were furnished. . ." A year later "there were eleven playgrounds instead of seven; there were 1000 instead of 400 children; there was double the number of tops, twice the amount of sand. . ."

In the seventeenth annual report of the Boston Board of Park Commissioners, for the thirteen months ending January 31, 1892, the open-air gymnasia at Charlesbank are described in detail. The site is a strip of land containing about ten acres, and lies along the Boston shore of the Charles River between the Craigie and West Boston bridges. It measures about 2200 feet in length by 200 in width. A sea-wall and the filling behind it were completed in 1886, and the plan of the grounds was drawn up by Frederick Law Olmsted, the landscape architect. It included a level promenade, 25 feet wide, overlooking the salt waters of the Back Bay, and behind this, on the side toward the city, stretches of lawn planted with trees to resemble a natural grove, but with a space 500 by 150 feet at the north end fitted up as a gymnasium for men and boys, and another at the south end, 370 by 150 feet in extent, enclosed with a screen of shrubbery and prepared especially as an exercise-

Fig. 94.—View of Charlesbank, Boston, looking north.

ground for women and girls. At either end there was to be a landing for boats, offered for hire, and near this and the entrance a house with waterclosets, toolrooms, and offices of administration.

Fig. 95.—Charlesbank:　Men's Gymnasium.

The men's gymnasium, surrounded by an iron fence, was reached only from the upper story of one of the houses just mentioned, connected with the grounds inside by a bridge on which turnstiles were placed, for registering attendance. The equipment, designed by Dr. Sargent of Harvard University, consisted of two sheds with twelve sets of chest-weights in each, including six high and six low pulleys, "two giant-strides, eight sets of horizontal bars, eight sets of parallel bars, six jumping-boxes, seven boxes for quoit-pitching and shot-throwing, two sets of jumping standards and ropes, two sets of sandbags and attachments, four vaulting poles, three shots, two heavy weights, twenty-four quoits, twenty pairs of dumb-bells, ten sets of hurdles, and two large frames, each 160 feet long, to which are attached the following apparatus: four balance-swings, eight breast-bars, four single swings, two double swings, five swinging-ropes, one rope ladder, one iron Jacob's ladder, one perpendicular ladder, one inclined ladder, four pairs of flying rings, four single trapezes, one climbing-pole, two inclined poles, two perpendicular poles. Around the outside of the ground there is a running and bicycle track 15 feet wide and $\frac{1}{5}$ mile long." The men's grounds were opened to the public on August 27, 1889, in charge of Superintendent John Graham, and the next season extended from April 1 to about the middle of December, an average of 447 men and boys a day entering for use of the apparatus during this period. In May of 1891 thirteen electric arc-lamps were added, and thereafter the gymnasium was kept open until 9.30 P.M. The total number of visitors this year was 169,219, and on the three days showing the largest attendance the turnstiles registered 1649 (May 3), 1480 (July 30), and 1572 (July 31) admissions.

Entrance to the women's gymnasium and the children's playground was likewise through the upper story of the women's lavatory building. The apparatus included "two balance-swings and frames, two seesaws (with side-rails and guards), two seesaws (plain), two single swings, two pole ladders, two perpendicular ladders, four hanging ropes (fastened at the bottom), one long inclined rope and attachments, four long and four short inclined poles, four perpendicular ladders combined, five serpentine ladders united (with guard-rails), two perpendicular climbing-poles, twelve swinging-ropes, one horizontal rope-ladder, two sets horizontal bars and stanchions (with heights adjustable), one set of movable parallel bars, one set of high parallel bars, one set of vaulting-bars, eleven travelling rings and attachments, two single trapezes (with height made adjustable by pulley and chain attachments), two sets of flying-rings (with height made adjustable as above), twelve pairs of chest-weights to run in wooden boxes, one set of jumping standards and ropes, two giant-strides (ropes, handles, and fixtures), twenty-four ring quoits and pins, twelve jumping-ropes, twelve hoops, twenty-five long and ninety-eight short wands, ninety-eight pairs dumb-bells, ninety-eight pairs Indian clubs." In the rear of the building were sand courts for the younger children. "The problem of the proper supervision, management, and care of this gymnasium was satisfactorily settled by our acceptance of the proposition of the Massachusetts Emergency and Hygiene Association, which is under the management of well-known ladies, to take the entire charge and oversight of it without expense to the city, beyond the furnishing of supplies, cleaning the rooms, and taking care of the grounds and apparatus." Miss Elizabeth C. McMartin, a pupil in Dr. Sargent's Normal School, was appointed superintendent, and the matron had had six years of experience as assistant in a kindergarten. The informal opening occurred at noon on June 1,

Fig. 96.—Charlesbank: Women's Gymnasium.

1891.   From this time until November 1 the average daily attendance was 945, and the largest was 2477 (July 6), 2368 (July 9), and 2389 (July 11).[1]

At Wood Island Park, in East Boston, another outdoor gymnasium and playground, nine acres in extent, was opened September 6, 1895.   Men were admitted on four days of the week, and women on two.   Beginning in 1896, and with the effective coöperation of Mayor Josiah Quincy (1895–1899), there was a rapid expansion of public facilities for recreation of all sorts in and about Boston, including playgrounds, indoor gymnasia, beach baths, floating bath-houses, swimming pools and all-the-year baths, and provision for

[1] For a full account of this first year see the eighth annual report (May, 1892) of the Mass. Emergency and Hygiene Association, pp. 13–17.   See also *Reports of Proceedings*, American Association for the Advancement of Physical Education, **9** (1894), pp. 125–130, and *The Bostonian* for June, 1896 (pp. 258–266, illustrated).

skating and coasting in winter. This whole series of progressive steps is outlined in Joseph Lee's "Constructive and Preventive Philanthropy" (New York, The Macmillan Co., 1902), along with corresponding steps in other cities, and details will be found in reports of the Boston Park Commissioners, the Boston Department of Baths, and for the North End Playground the instructive annual reports of the Massachusetts Civic League (after 1900). The first municipal indoor gymnasium was the East Boston (Paris Street) building, a one-story, truss-roofed structure 137 by 98 feet, with a main hall 100 by 80 feet. Originally a skating rink, it was purchased by Esther P. (Mrs. Daniel) Ahl and turned over to the East Boston Athletic Association for use as a combined gymnasium and bath, and in 1897 given to the city and opened to the general public. The South Boston (D-Street) gymnasium, the first to be built by the city, was opened in the winter of 1899–1900.

Next to Boston, Chicago occupies a prominent place in the early history of the playground movement. As Mrs. Charles Zueblin points out in *The Playground* for July of 1907 (pp. 3–5 and 11–13), it has passed through three distinct phases of growth in that city, represented by the independent, schoolyard, and municipal playgrounds. The independent experiments, now almost forgotten, deserve mention, to quote Mrs. Zueblin, "because their experiences and lessons and accomplishment were of proved value later on. In 1893 Hull House opened a large playground in an empty lot, the land belonging to Mr. William Kent; it was equipped with swings, seesaws, giant stride and sandbins, and was maintained under their management for five years. . . Play was totally disorganized both on the part of the children and of the supervisors, and everything from games to management had to be learned. . . This playground later passed under the number of municipal playgrounds. In 1896, under the auspices of the University Settlement of the Northwestern University, and through the great generosity of Mr. Livingston Fargo, a large and splendidly equipped playground was opened accommodating from three thousand to four thousand children. Besides a fine equipment for play, there was a large shelter with plenty of benches and retiring rooms. A police officer and matron had charge of the grounds, which were maintained for two years, until the playground had to be abandoned, owing to the extension of the tracks of the Northwestern Railway Company. For six years, beginning in 1896, the University of Chicago Settlement, under the leadership of Miss Mary McDowell, maintained a very successful playground, where there was provision also for mothers with little babies."

"The first school playground in Chicago," according to Mrs. Zueblin, "was maintained in the Washington School's yard in 1897 by the West End District of the Associated Charities. In the spring of 1898 an appropriation of $1000 was obtained from the City Council ($750 additional being later subscribed by individuals) for 'temporary small parks,' the administration of which was turned over to the Vacation School Committee of Women's Clubs." Miss Sadie American, chairman of that committee, writing of "The Movement for Small Playgrounds" in the *American Journal of Sociology* for September of 1898 (pp. 159–170) says that "the use of six schoolyards, basements, and one room to be used on hot and rainy days was asked of the board of education, and, being granted, the yards were equipped with swings, seesaws, sandbins, and cedar buildingblocks. The *Turnverein* was greatly interested, and loaned portable apparatus for each school, such as parallel bars, horizontal bars, horse, ladders, etc., which were taken into the building at night. The playgrounds chosen were all in densely populated districts and among various nationalities. . . For each there were engaged a kindergartner and a man who should be a 'big brother to the boys,' for the older boys were considered equally or more than the younger ones. . . The men were inexperienced, but entered into the spirit of the work with enthusiasm, and from week to week rose in efficiency on the mistakes of the foregoing days."

But it is the municipal aspect of the movement that demands more than passing mention. The *City Club Bulletin* of March 4, 1908, presents the significant features of the story as follows: "During the last half-dozen years Chicago has achieved a development of small parks and playgrounds more remarkable than has taken place in any other city of the world. It is remarkable, first, because of its extent, and second, because of its unique character. Eight years ago there were, besides the six main parks of the city fifteen or sixteen small public parks and squares, some maintained by the three divisional park commissions and some by the city Department of Public Works. There was not a public playground, however, in all Chicago nor a public bathing beach. Today there are in the city over 30 such small parks and squares, 13 public playgrounds, 17 combination small park-playgrounds and 3 bathing beaches—in all, 63 public neighborhood centers of rest, beauty, recreation and culture. This number is also being added to and does not include school playgrounds.

"This expansion has been carried out by four separate authorities, *i. e.*, the Lincoln Park Commission, the regular park authority for the north side of the city; the South Park Commission, the regular park authority for the south side; the West Park Commission, the regular park authority for the west side; and the Special Park Commission, whose field is the entire city. The first three commissions were created by the legislature about 1870. The Special

Park Commission was created by the City Council in 1899, to investigate and report upon the need both for small parks and playground and for an outer belt park system. While investigating and reporting upon these two subjects it also became, by the very pressure of the subject with which it was dealing, both a promoting and an administrative body. In 1900 it secured from the City Council an appropriation of $10,000 and opened four 'municipal playgrounds' in thickly populated neighborhoods of the city. The next year it secured legislation authorizing the three regular park commissions to raise and expend $2,500,000—that is, $1,000,000 each on the south and west sides, and $500,000 on the north side—for small parks and playgrounds.

"The Park Commissions of the north and west sides were slow in securing the necessary amendment, and approval on referendum, of their laws in this matter, but in 1903 the South Park Commission secured the amendment of the law applying to its district, together with legislative authority for a still larger expenditure for like purposes, and the proposed bond issues having been approved at the polls, the Commission entered upon an unparalleled career of small park and playground development.[1] In 1904 and 1905 it acquired fourteen sites, ranging in size from 7 to 300 acres, and equipped ten of them on an entirely novel plan. Two more of these are being thus equipped, and three more sites are being acquired. The proposed bond issue for the west side was approved on referendum in 1905, and the West Park Commission has within the last year and a half secured and nearly finished the equipment, after the south side plan, of two sites in crowded neighborhoods. It is now acquiring a third site. It has also made 'Holstein Park' a very attractive playground. The Lincoln Park Commission, having secured approval on referendum for its proposed $500,000 bond issue, has now acquired three sites, and they are nearly equipped in somewhat like fashion. Two of the three lack park features proper, on account of limited space, but they provide equipment similar to the park-playgrounds, among which they are here counted. The sites for these various park-playgrounds range in size from 4 to 60 acres, have cost from $40,000 to $290,000 each, and the buildings cost from $60,000 to $100,000 for each site. Each of these centers calls for an annual maintenance budget of from $20,000 to $30,000. . .

"Small park and playground development in Chicago is even more remarkable because of its unique character than because of its extent. The assemblage of functions represented in the small park-playgrounds which we have been considering is a new thing in the

[1] See Reports of South Park Commissioners for 1904, 1905 and 1906 (illustrated).

world, and its creation three or four years ago by the South Park Commission was an event of civic imagination and adventure of which Chicago is worthily proud. A typical center includes both outdoor and indoor activities. The outdoor activities comprise as the central feature a liberally planned bathing pool, with sandbank, dressing-rooms, cleansing showers, life-guards and bathing suits.

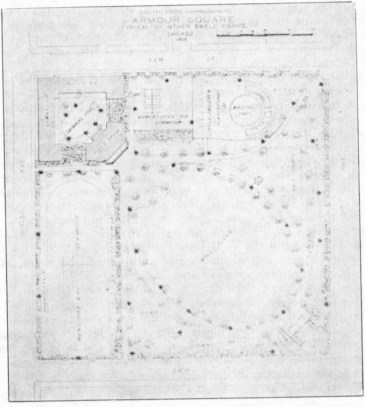

Fig. 97.—South Parks, Chicago: Plan of Armour Square.

Collateral to this are an outdoor gymnasium for men, another for women, another for boys, another for girls, running tracks, wading pools, and sand courts for the youngsters; also tennis courts and ball fields—turned into skating rinks in the winter time. The interior features include a thoroughly equipped gymnasium for men, another for women, each having a trained director and being furnished with baths and lockers, a lunch room, reading and library room, one or two small club rooms for small gatherings, and a large and beautiful assembly hall for neighborhood meetings, lectures or pleasure

FIG. 98.—South Parks, Chicago: Typical Outdoor Gymnasium for Girls.

FIG. 99.—South Parks, Chicago: Typical Swimming Pool Scene.

parties. The entire construction is on a liberal plan and is carried out in accordance with high standards. So is the maintenance. . .''

It is not necessary to repeat here in detail the experiences of other cities in connection with the playground movement. A special report ("General Statistics of Cities, 1916") of the United States Bureau of the Census relating to the recreation service of cities having a population of over 30,000 contains this statement of progress prepared by Joseph Lee, president of the Playground and Recreation Association of America:

"Thirty years have passed since the birth of the movement to protect children's play—an era which has seen the spread of the movement from Boston, Baltimore, Philadelphia, and New York to Chicago and the Pacific coast; which has witnessed at least the theoretical establishment of the children's right to play in safety under good influences and of a man's right to spend his leisure hours, through the provision of the proper facilities by the city in which he lives, in a way which will fit him to make the best use of his working hours, and will keep alive in him those ideal interests for which his work too often furnishes no scope.

"In these thirty years playgrounds have been established in large and small cities and in rural communities throughout the country. A national organization, the Playground and Recreation Association of America, has been called into existence to act as a clearing house for information and, through the publishing of literature and educational work, to further the recreation movement. Buildings used wholly for recreational purposes have been erected. Reports made to the Playground and Recreation Association of America in December, 1916, show that 38 communities have recreation buildings, valued at $4,093,525. In rural communities has come a great awakening to the need of wholesome recreation to counteract immoral influences and to conserve for the community its young men and women who would otherwise go to large cities to find their opportunities. Both large and small cities have established systems, at the head of which have been placed workers employed throughout the year, corresponding to school superintendents in our educational system. Schools have introduced organized play in connection with their school playgrounds and specially trained play directors are employed, who spend their entire time directing the play of the pupils. Cities have come to see the economic waste of great buildings used a few hours each day for educational purposes and have thrown their schoolhouses open at night for the use of all the people for evening recreation-center activities, for dramatic clubs, orchestras, social dancing, gymnasium work, mothers' clubs, civic forums, lectures and motion pictures. In December, 1916, 127 cities reported that their school buildings were being used as neighborhood recreation centers. Legislation making possible such a use of school buildings has been passed in a number of states. The creation of special recreation departments and playground and recreation commissions to administer playground work has been authorized by law in many states and cities. Increasingly has the emphasis been laid on the importance of considering recreation work as a governmental function and of administering it as one of the duties of a municipality to its citizens.

"These facts are borne out by the information gathered by the Bureau of the Census in its study of playgrounds and athletic fields, the results of which are to be found in Table II. It is a very significant fact that during the fiscal year 1916, the 213 cities of more than 30,000 population conducted 2190 playgrounds with a total area of 4662.1 acres. There were, in addition, 19 athletic fields, exclusive of those located in parks, with an area of 148.7 acres. For this work there were payments from public funds for expenses amounting to $2,502,902; and for outlays, $1,017,539. Three thousand seven hundred and ninety-four workers were in charge of the activities of these playgrounds. Graphic as these figures are, they by no means represent the total municipal provision for play and recreation even in the 213 cities themselves. In many of these cities the schools have playgrounds equipped with apparatus and with play leaders in charge, and organized play periods are conducted in connection with their school program. Nor do these figures attempt to include the evening recreation-center work conducted at many schools at a considerable expense to the school board, nor the municipal golf courses, tennis courts, skating facilities, and community music provided for the public from city funds. The public provision of recreational facilities is by no means limited to cities of over 30,000. Reports sent to the Playground and Recreation Association of America show that many cities of less than 30,000 inhabitants are maintaining playgrounds and neighborhood recreation centers, while approximately 50 communities of less than 5000 carried on recreational work privately or publicly during the year ending December 1, 1916."

The founding of the Playground and Recreation Association of America has already been mentioned on p. 344. One must turn to the *Proceedings* of the first, second, and third "Annual Playground Congresses," the volumes of *The Playground*, and other publications of the Association for the full story of its achievements.

Although there had been legislation favoring statewide physical education prior to the outbreak of the Great War (*e. g.*, North Dakota, 1899; Ohio, 1904; Idaho, 1913), it was without doubt the same military motive which has operated in the case of European countries, or that realization of the fundamental values of physical fitness which always comes with the approach of war, that led twenty-five of our states, in the years 1915–1921, to enact laws requiring or permitting the introduction of physical education into their schools. The list is as follows: In 1915—Illinois; 1916— New York; 1917—California, Nevada, New Jersey, Rhode Island; 1918—Delaware, Maryland; 1919—Alabama, Indiana, Maine, Michigan, Oregon, Pennsylvania, Utah, Washington; 1920— Georgia, Kentucky, Mississippi, Virginia; 1921—Connecticut, Massachusetts, Missouri, North Carolina, West Virginia. These laws differ considerably in their statement of the educational aims in view and the means to be employed in attaining them, in the ages or school grades affected, and the time requirements, and in the provision made for a central authority, supervision, the training of teachers, and financial support to make the legislation effective.[1] Some of the state authorities have already published manuals of physical training.[2]

Three examples, quoted from Bulletin 40, 1918, of the United States Bureau of Education, will serve to illustrate the general character and range of the State laws already adopted. The Illinois law (approved June 26, 1915) "provides for physical training in all of the public schools and in all of the normal schools of the State. Apparently, no special provision has been made in that State for the operation of the law; no appropriation for the development of a program or the publication of a syllabus; and no resources for the employment of State supervisors, inspectors, or other administrators of physical education. . .

"The New York law, approved May 15, 1916, and amended at the legislative session of 1918, provides that: 'All male and female pupils, above the age of eight years, in all elementary and secondary schools of the State, shall receive, as a part of the prescribed courses of instruction therein, such physical training under the direction of the commissioner of education as the regents, after conference with the military training commission, may determine, during periods

[1] See United States Bureau of Education *Bulletin*, 1918, No. 40 (Recent State Legislation for Physical Education). Part IV contains copies of the State laws of Illinois, New York, Rhode Island, New Jersey, Nevada, California, Delaware, and Maryland. Bulletin 1922, No. 1, brings the story up to July, 1921.

[2] For example, the following: General Plan and Syllabus for Physical Training in the Elementary and Secondary Schools of the State of New York, as adopted by the Board of Regents of the University of the State of New York upon the report and recommendation of the Military Training Commission of the State of New York. Albany, 1917. A second edition (Book 4, Complete Syllabus) was published in 1921.—By the Department of Public Instruction, Trenton, New Jersey, September, 1917, Courses in Physical Training as follows: For Grades I to VI (Manual 1), Grades VII and VIII (Manual 2), and Grades IX and XII (High School Manual).—Manual in Physical Education for the Public Schools of the State of California—Part IV: Syllabus on Physical Training Activities with Methods of Management and Leadership. Sacramento, 1918.—A Course in Physical Training for the Graded Schools of Michigan. Bulletin No. 2 (Third Edition). Lansing, published by the Superintendent of Public Instructions, 1919.—Manual of Physical Education. Department of Education, State of Alabama, Montgomery, 1920.

which shall average at least twenty minutes each day. . .' The administration of this law in the State of New York is a function of the regents of the University of the State of New York, that is, of the State department of education. A bureau of physical training has been established as a subdivision of the State military training commission. The State inspector of physical training, the chief officer of this bureau, is required, in accordance with the law, to observe and inspect the work and methods described under the provisions of the education law relating to instruction in physical training. The State law in New York also provides that all public schools in the State employing special teachers of physical training, qualified and duly licensed under the regulations of the regents, may receive ,financial support from the State to the extent of half the salary of each teacher so employed, provided that half the salary does not exceed $600. . ." In the *State Plan and Syllabus for Physical Training* that subject "is interpreted as covering: '(1) Individual health examination and personal health instruction (medical inspection); (2) instruction concerning the care of the body and concerning the important facts of hygiene (recitations in hygiene); and (3) physical exercise as a health habit, including gymnastics, elementary marching and organized supervised play, recreation, and athletics.' For the direction and supervision of the State program there is a force of inspectors, consisting of a State inspector of physical training and nine assistant inspectors. . .

"On May 26, 1917, an act providing for physical education became a law in the State of California. This law provides that the school authorities in the public schools of the State, elementary and secondary, shall prescribe suitable courses of physical education for all pupils, except such as may be excused from such training on account of physical disability. The California law makes it a duty of the superintendent of schools in every county and city, and of every board of education, board of school trustees, and high-school board, to enforce the courses of physical education prescribed by the proper authority, and to require that such physical education be given in the schools under their jurisdiction or control. In the elementary schools the time requirement in California shall 'average twenty minutes in each school day,' and in the secondary schools 'at least two hours each week while that school is in session.' This law requires that, if the number of pupils in a given school system is sufficient, there shall be employed a competent supervisor or such special teachers of physical education as may be necessary. The enactment further specifies that the State board of education shall require a course in physical training in all the normal schools of the State and provides that the State board of education shall prescribe a course in physical education for such schools and shall make the completion of such course a requirement for graduation. Under this law, it is the duty of the State board of education: '(1) To adopt such rules and regulations as it may deem necessary and proper to secure the establishment of courses in physical education in the elementary and secondary schools in accordance with the provisions of this act; (2) to appoint a State supervisor of physical education; (3) to compile, or cause to be compiled or printed, a manual in physical education for distribution to teachers in the public schools of the State.' The sum of $10,000 was appropriated for the purpose of carrying out the provisions of the California law. . ."

Attempts are now being made to secure federal aid to physical education in the various states, through laws passed by the Congress of the United States. A commission on the reorganization of secondary education, appointed by the National Education Association, has also recently approved a report on Physical Education in Secondary Schools, which is published by the Bureau of Education as 1917 *Bulletin* No. 50.

National Recreation Association.[1]

Closely related as it has been to physical education throughout much of its history, it is to be noted that the play and recreation movement in the United States was actually initiated by individuals and organizations unconnected with the already active gymnasium and physical training movement in this country. Sand gardens, accepted by authorities as one of the first expressions of the American play movement, were instituted by philanthropic organizations and social service agencies. Various currents of influence contributed to the establishment of these modest beginnings of organized play, but their nature suggests that they were inspired more by the teachings of Froebel, who first stressed the educational side of play, than by any other individual.[2]

The first sand gardens bore a close resemblance to kindergartens. They were quite unlike outdoor gymnasiums, or even the outdoor playgrounds of Germany which were founded long before as an earlier chapter in this volume indicates. They were intended distinctly for the use of small children. This resemblance to kindergartens is perhaps not surprising, since by 1885 many American cities had established kindergartens for which training schools had been set up in this country as early as 1880; and in 1884 the National Education Association had a kindergarten department.

[1] Appreciation is expressed for this contribution by Weaver W. Pangburn of the National Recreation Association.

[2] Mitchell, Elmer D., and Mason, Bernard S., *The Theory of Play*, p. 24. New York: A. S. Barnes and Company, 1934.

Having established the precedent of supporting the sand garden playgrounds, the city of Boston was early followed by Philadelphia, New York, Providence and Chicago. As in Boston, the playgrounds in these cities up to 1895, and in others until a still later period, v ere of the sand garden type. They were founded by philanthropic r gencies; the *City Club* and *City Park Association in Philadelphia*, the *Parks and Playgrounds Association* in New York, the *Union for Practical Progress and Kindergarten Association* in Providence, and *Hull House Settlement* in Chicago. Intended for children of pre-adolescent years, the playgrounds were operated in July and August; were equipped for outdoor uses only; were located in densely populated parts of the cities; and their activities included both free and directed play, the latter of the kindergarten type.[1]

Gymnasiums and Sand Gardens Combine.—While the sand garden playgrounds were spreading to other cities, enlargements and adaptations of them appeared early in Boston and Chicago, anticipating in some respects features of present playgrounds. In 1889, the Boston Board of Park Commissioners opened the Charlesbank outdoor gymnasium for men at the north end of a ten-acre tract designed by Frederick Law Olmstead. This was the forerunner of park playgrounds. Two years later a women's gymnasium and a children's sand garden playground were opened at the south end of the property. Judged by modern practices, these gymnasiums were equipped with a staggering quantity of apparatus.

The equipment was designed by Dudley Allen Sargent, director of the new Hemenway gymnasium at Harvard University and already one of the leading physical education authorities of the country. The Charlesbank gymnasium was constructed during a period of widespread indoor gymnasium building in the United States, particularly at colleges and universities. The two gymnasiums comprised only about three acres of the total Charlesbank property, the remainder of which included a park area with a boat landing and facilities for bathing in the Charles River. The gymnasium and playground adjoining it were significant as an example of unified planning for outdoor recreation. Also noteworthy were the installation of thirteen electric arc lamps at the men's gymnasium in 1891 permitting night use until 9:30 o'clock, and the fact that service to all age groups was concentrated in one place. There was nothing new in having a gymnasium outdoors; that it was public was significant.

In recognition of its success with the sand gardens, the Massachusetts Emergency and Hygiene Association was placed in charge of

[1] Rainwater, Clarence E., *The Play Movement in the United States*. Chicago: The University of Chicago Press, 1922.

the women's gymnasium and sand garden at Charlesbank, the city assuming no expense except supplies, cleaning and maintenance. The Association turned to a pupil of Dr. Sargent, Elizabeth C. McMartin, as first superintendent. The matron who assisted her

Fig. 100.—Boys and girls fishing in a swimming pool.

was also trained, having had six year's experience as a kindergarten assistant.

The Charlesbank equipment reflected interest in body building, rather than games as there were no game courts or sport fields except the running and bicycle track. However, this development was an important contribution to the outdoor play area idea and exerted a widespread influence.

For many years the sand garden playgrounds of Boston continued to be operated for little children and featured principally kindergarten activities. In 1899, however, three of the twenty-one play areas "were provided with a limited outfit of gymnastic apparatus and under the care of young men trained in the art of physical culture were designed especially for boys from twelve to fifteen years of age."[1] This experiment succeeded and was repeated the next year, reflecting the growing influence of physical education on the playground movement.

Model Playgrounds.—An early "model playground" was established in 1892 at Hull House, Chicago. Its area comprised three-quarters of an acre; it served children and youth; its apparatus and equipment were of the sand garden type for little children with a giant stride and handball and indoor baseball for adolescent boys. It was staffed by an experienced kindergartner and a policeman. Two other playgrounds were established in Chicago by settlements in 1896 and in 1898.

Philadelphia, establishing a new type playground in 1898, utilized a three-acre site on which were constructed a central circular area for games and for skating in the winter, a fenced bicycle track, tennis courts, swings, parallel bars and swinging rings, sand piles, a music stand, a promenade for the wheeling of baby carriages and strolling, rows of seats, and two small steam heated buildings on either side of the playfield for winter use. Reflecting the advancing conception of play leadership was a discerning comment on the Philadelphia playground by Stoyan Vasil Tsanoff.

"What really counts is the use made of the playground. . . . The teachers are to study the nature of the child and so to conduct the play as to guide the children and not unnecessarily to restrain them. New games are to be invented, old ones revived, foreign ones introduced, and all necessary modifications made to answer the natural and growing taste of youth. A thorough coöperation with the home, the school, and the church is to be had for achieving the highest ends. The parents and the teachers in the neighborhood are to direct the children to the playground after school hours and not let them drift into the streets as they do now. . . . Thus the playground

---

[1] Tower, Ellen M., "Playgrounds and Sand Gardens." *World Wide*, April 2, 1902. Cited by Rainwater.

will become the center of delight and of moral and social culture in the neighborhood."[1]

In New York City the Outdoor Recreation League induced the city to construct the Seward Park Playground opened in 1899. It had a gymnasium, baths, apparatus, kindergarten platform, and instructors. Although New York City had numerous other public play areas at the time, including 31 schoolyard sand gardens, none of these was as completely equipped as Seward Park Playground.

In 1900 the Massachusetts Civic League opened a playground in North End Park, Boston, which incorporated features from the Charlesbank gymnasium and the sand gardens and added still others. The area had three distinct divisions: (a) A children's corner in which were installed a wooden shelter with a bench for mothers, two sand boxes, four swings, two teeter ladders, carts, and kindergarten and sewing materials; (b) a section for older girls which, among other facilities, provided for baseball and other lively games and for sewing; and (c) a section for older boys where there were installed gymnasium apparatus, space for team games, and facilities for quoits and handball for men. The separate sections for little children and for older boys and girls are still standard in good playground design.

Of even greater significance was the program which sought to create a spirit of loyalty among youth through team games, classified games according to the ages of the participating children, and organized interscholastic competition among grammar school teams of the neighborhood. All competitors from the schools were required to furnish certificates of good standing in deportment and scholarship. Prizes were awarded not to individuals but to schools. Class work on the gymnasium apparatus was encouraged. The program included the use of quiet games, construction activities, and gardening.

In this Boston model playground careful educational approach to organized play was manifested, and among other advances, the importance of competitive games was recognized. Although school intramural games and sports on a widespread democratic basis had not developed in the 1880's and 1890's, the colleges were excited over varsity intercollegiate contests, and professional sports were popular.[2] The standards of the North End Park playground marked the thoughtful planning of persons of much insight into the nature of children and of play. One of these persons was Joseph Lee, who was later to write " Play in Education" and to serve as president of the National Recreation Association for twenty-seven years.

[1] Tsanoff, Stoyan Vasil, "Children's Playgrounds." *Municipal Affairs*, 1898, p. 578, as cited by Rainwater.

[2] Steiner, Jesse Frederick, *Americans at Play*, p. 9. New York and London: McGraw-Hill Book Company, 1933.

The common characteristics of the "model" playgrounds were provision of facilities of interest to youth and adults as well as to small children; the use of trained leaders or instructors; a growing understanding of the proper role of the leaders; better adaptation of equipment to age and interest groups; greater familiarity with the educational values of play; and a tendency to shift responsibility from the private agency to the public. Furthermore, the neighborhood nature of the playground function was recognized. Many of these characteristics reflected the influence of physical education.

Recreation Areas in Parks.—The playground movement in the United States began at a time when most park officials were not favorable to much active recreation in parks. However, during the period when the playgrounds were being developed on or transferred to public school grounds, the city park systems also began to feel the new influence. Besides its precedent-making developments at the Charlesbank gymnasium and in North End Park, Boston, in 1894, purchased Franklin Field, one of the first great playfields in the country with 40 acres given to team games, although without supervision and with no provision for small children.

Soon after the turn of the century, Chicago created recreation areas which marked the most comprehensive and, from the viewpoint of property, the most elaborate conception of public recreation centers yet achieved in the United States. These new centers profoundly influenced American recreational planning for a quarter of a century, and were a direct outgrowth of official efforts in Chicago to extend playgrounds. In 1903 the citizens voted a five million dollar issue of bonds which resulted in the building of small recreation parks for the crowded neighborhoods of South Chicago. President Theodore Roosevelt hailed the creation of ten of these parks in 1905 as "the most notable civic achievement of any American city." These Chicago centers were epoch making in that they were planned to serve both outdoor and indoor needs on a varied scale throughout the year and for all age groups. They sustained the idea of neighborhood planning, one of the principal contributions of social workers to recreation. They also incorporated previous experience as to the necessity of leadership. Above all, they reflected a new and powerful *municipal initiative* in playground and recreation work.

The assemblage of so many facilities and areas in one unified design reflected the inclusive field of play and recreation. The parks, varying from 300 to 7 acres in size, were planned with large sections for active recreational use, but with provision for extensive landscape beauty. Facilities for a wide variety of activities both indoor and outdoor were provided, and trained personnel responsible to a general director of field houses and playgrounds were placed in charge of these facilities. Among other contributions to the movement for play and recreation, the Chicago centers emphasized the importance of beautifying playgrounds.

Special Governing Board for Play.—Far-reaching as was the Chicago achievement in the design and construction of areas and equipment for recreation, an equally important event took place which was to influence the administration of public recreation. In 1904 a Board of Playground Commissioners was appointed in Los Angeles which indicated that play was to be held of such importance that a special municipal department was required for its development. The first Los Angeles playground under the new board was opened in 1905 and a supervisor of recreation was employed in that year. As in the Chicago plan, the playgrounds and buildings in Los Angeles provided varied year-round activities for all ages, and facilities for these were among the very first located outside park or school property. Although recreation was a new function compared with parks and schools, the separate department for it was destined to outstrip all other forms of administration in American communities.

School Sponsored Recreation.—The development of physical training in American public schools was widely extended during the decade 1886–1896 when the sand gardens were being established in a number of cities. However, Milwaukee had in Brosius a superintendent of physical training from 1875 to 1883. The development of such training and the construction of gymnasiums and other facilities in schools were helping to lay the foundations for the later development of physical education and games in public schools. In 1903 Luther Gulick organized in New York City the first public school athletic league, one of the first steps in promoting amateur sport. As school plants acquired auditoriums, swimming pools, libraries, and other special rooms as well as gymnasiums, the economy of using them for recreation when idle became apparent. Prior to 1900 many states passed laws permitting school buildings to be used as civic or social centers. As early as 1898 schools were open for supervised evening recreation in New York City as a continuation of the summer playground program. The use of schools for recreation received a great impulse in 1907 when a demonstration of school centers was organized in Rochester, N. Y., under an appropriation of $5000. This experiment induced the wider use of the school plant in other communities. Wisconsin, in 1911, passed a state law authorizing school authorities to levy an 0.2 mill tax for recreation purposes. It was under the encouragement of this law that Milwaukee developed its well known "lighted schoolhouse" program.

National Agency Founded.—The scattered and poorly related systems of playgrounds and recreation centers in the United States obtained a unifying national headquarters in 1906 when physical education teachers and social workers founded the Playground Association of America in Washington, D. C. The first president was Luther H. Gulick and the first secretary, Henry S. Curtis. President Theodore Roosevelt gave his hearty endorsement. Jacob Riis, colorful anti-slum crusader of New York, became an honorary vice-president. Joseph Lee and Felix Warburg were among the many individuals active in the young organization during its first year. The Russell Sage Foundation helped very substantially with

Fig. 101.—Joseph Lee.

moral backing and funds. The purpose of the Association as stated in its constitution was "To collect and distribute knowledge of and promote interest in playgrounds throughout the country, to seek to further the establishment of playgrounds and athletic fields in all communities and directed play in connection with the schools." This document also contained provisions for the holding of an annual Play Congress and the publication of a magazine to be known as "The Playground."

These constitutional provisions were carried out together with the appointment of promotional field secretaries, the issuance of publications, and the establishment of an information clearing house. An early activity was the publication of "The Normal Course in Play," a book which came to be widely used by schools and colleges in the training of play leaders. Joseph Lee became president of the organization in 1910 and Howard S. Braucher was made executive secretary in 1909. Prominent among the men highly influential in shaping the Association's basic philosophy and methods were George E. Johnson and Clark W. Hetherington. The name of the association was changed to Playground and Recreation Association of America in 1911, and later to the National Recreation Association. In 1931, at a 25th Anniversary meeting in the White House in the nation's capitol, President Herbert Hoover was to say, "The Association has taken a most significant and magnificent part in the whole recreational development of the country."

Growth of the Association's Services.—The establishment of some of the principal services of the Association reflected the broadening scope of the play and recreation movement. These services and the years when they were initiated include the following:

Advisory service on training to normal schools, colleges, and universities, by Clark W. Hetherington, 1910.

Physical fitness tests for boys and girls, 1912 and 1915, respectively.

War recreation service for the government, 1917.

Short-term intensive training institutes, 1917.

Community Dram Service, 1917.

Music Service, 1918.

Social recreation and games institutes, 1918.

National Physical Education Service, 1918.

Comprehensive study of parks and field service to park departments, 1925.

National Recreation School, 1926.

Rural Recreation training institutes, 1927.

Field service on athletics and recreation for women and girls, 1928.

Field service in the interest of recreation areas in real estate subdivisions, 1928.

Field service for play in institutions, 1930.

Study of public school training for leisure and recreation, 1931.

Lecture tour of United States by Dr. L. P. Jacks of England in the interest of recreation, 1931–32.

First International Recreation Congress in Los Angeles, 1932.

Since the year 1932 and in spite of the economic depression, the Association added field services in arts and crafts, gardening, and the design of areas and facilities. It expanded its community studies and research and issued many manuals, texts, and other publications. "The Playground" magazine became "Recreation."

The Play Congress early became a Recreation Congress and grew into a largely attended and influential exchange of information on the varied aspects of community recreation. The 1941 Congress in Baltimore was attended by 1500 delegates from 42 states, Canada and Hawaii.

Fig. 102.—C. W. Hetherington.

In response to the vigorous work of the Association there was a rapid increase in cities establishing playgrounds after 1906. During the six-year period prior to that year, 26 cities had established playgrounds, an average of four a year. In the six-year period following 1906, 158 cities, or an average of 26 a year, started playgrounds. The time from 1906 up to American participation in the

World War in 1917 was not only a period of great extension of neighborhood recreation areas and buildings, but also one of rising interest in play and recreation enterprises for the community as a whole. Only 41 cities reported playgrounds in 1906, while in 1917, 481 cities reported 3944 playgrounds and neighborhood recreation centers and 8748 employed workers. Of the workers, 1474 were employed year round in 141 communities. Enrichment of programs was shown in the large number of cities reporting folk dancing, gardening, lectures, libraries, orchestras, festivals, pageants, singing, social dancing, storytelling and hiking. High School athletics gathered momentum during this period. Many cities reported the establishment of units of the Boy Scouts, Camp Fire Girls, and Girl Scouts, the Boy Scout movement having started in this country in 1910 and the other two organizations in 1912. There was a wide extension of camping and outdoor life. About 100 camps were reported between 1900 and 1910, after which there was a marked increase, due largely to the use of the automobile which encouraged outdoor recreation.

World War I Period.—On request of the government, the National Recreation Association organized the War Camp Community Service when this country entered the World War. This service mobilized the recreational resources of communities near military camps and provided wholesome recreation for soldiers and sailors. A sense of community responsibility for recreation, the importance of leadership, the value in voluntary service, the significance of community singing, the opportunity of the church in relation to recreation, and an interest in community buildings gained great appreciation as a result of the wartime program. An awareness of the importance of physical fitness and physical training was another important outcome.

Leisure and the Recreation Movement.—Working time for millions of factory workers and others had been growing shorter for decades but the full implications of growing leisure did not become apparent in the United States until the 1920's. In 1876 to be sure, Horace Greeley had asked, "Who will teach us incessant workers how to achieve leisure and enjoy it?" and James A. Garfield, speaking at Chautauqua, N. Y., five years later had gone so far as to say, "We may divide the whole struggle of the human race into two chapters; first the fight to get leisure and then the second fight of civilization, what shall we do with our leisure when we get it?"[1] The National Education Association focused the attention of educators on the subject in 1918 by including the worthy use of leisure as one of its seven cardinal objectives of education.

[1] Dulles, Foster Rhea, *America Learns to Play*, p. 209. New York: D. Appleton-Century Company, 1940.

Yet it was not until the American industrial machine had got into high gear in peacetime production and organized labor had with fresh power urged reduced working hours, that the short work period heralded the advent of leisure for the general public. In 1840 the average work week was seventy hours, but by 1930 it was less than fifty. Interest in play and recreation was enormously increased. The shift of large population to the cities, the mechanical and monotonous nature of factory work, the inadequacy of rural play in the urban setting, the decline of religious opposition, and surplus spending power, all combined to introduce a golden decade of recreation. Leisure had become democratized; it was time to democratize recreation. Between the World War and the onset of the depression in the 1930's books and magazines were flooded with articles on leisure.

Recreation for the first time, says Jesse F. Steiner, took its place beside work and was recognized as one of the major interests of life.[1] The expansion of public recreation service was marked, and it became difficult to secure qualified leaders. The National Recreation Association established a professional school in New York for the training of recreation executives, since leadership was being emphasized. President Coolidge called a Conference on Outdoor Recreation in 1924, focusing national attention on the subject under governmental and other auspices. In the relatively neglected rural communities the National Recreation Association undertook short training institutes sponsored by the Extension Service of the United States Department of Agriculture. Beginning with May 1927, 54,000 individual teachers, farm bureau agents, clergymen, 4-H Club leaders, and other rural leaders had been trained in these courses. Not only playgrounds but golf courses, swimming pools, bathing beaches, picnic areas, winter sport facilities, and game fields were constructed in unprecedented numbers. Park acreage grew faster than in any other period. Many cities began to acquire and develop parks outside their limits. The National Recreation Association established a Bureau of Colored Work in 1919, after which far more attention was given to the recreational needs of Negroes. Industrial recreation, recreation for girls and women, church recreation and the work of the youth-serving agencies expanded. The Jewish Welfare Board, an outcome of war work, stimulated the growth of community centers. Play and recreation had a big part in the YMCA and YWCA movements. The data on municipal recreation show the expansion of the decade 1920–1929: employed leaders, 10,218 to 22,920; and expenditures, $7,199,000 to $33,539,000.

[1] Steiner, Jesse F., *Research Memorandum on Recreation in the Depression,* p. 38. New York: Social Science Research Council, 1937.

By the time the Association had completed twenty-five years of service it was true, as Steiner asserted, that recreation was securely entrenched in the folkways of America. It was, he said, "a dominating force wielding strong influence in many directions."[1] One such influence was exerted on education and particularly physical education which itself had contributed much to recreation. Games from the playgrounds were introduced into the formal curriculum of physical training and the social, mental, and moral objectives of the recreation movement were adopted in physical education. Also, "it is not too much to say that the recreation movement created public sentiment for physical education and equipment. . . With its emphasis on all activities that are creative and its inclusion of adults in its scope, it revolutionized the plans and use of school buildings."[2] The emphasis on carry-over activities in the physical education curriculum, the adoption of training for leadership, much of the content of school intramural programs, and the spread of state-wide legislation for physical education have been credited in considerable measure to the recreation movement.[3]

State Legislation for Recreation. —The establishment of children's playgrounds in large cities did not require general state legislation. Most of the larger metropolitan communities had home rule charters permitting them to establish playgrounds through local legislation, or they secured special acts relating only to themselves. However, when small cities undertook to develop playgrounds and recreation, the importance of state enabling acts became apparent. An early example was the Massachusetts playground referendum bill for cities and towns of over 10,000 population which was passed in 1908. Commencing in 1917 and during the 1920's the National Recreation Association influenced legislation in 21 states permitting the localities broad powers in planning recreation programs. A distinctive feature of these acts was to give each locality the freedom to set up recreation under park boards, school boards, or separate recreation commissions in accordance with the local conditions. The Association also assisted in securing the passage of referendum tax legislation providing for establishment of playground and recreation work upon the favorable vote by the people of the locality on a tax levy. Prior to 1931 such tax referendum laws were passed in Florida, Georgia, Illinois, Indiana, Iowa, New Jersey, New York, North Carolina, Ohio, Vermont, Virginia and West Virginia.

[1] Steiner, Jesse F., *Americans at Play*, p. 12. New York and London: McGraw-Hill Book Company, 1933.
[2] Mitchell, Elmer D., "Contribution of the Recreation Movement to Physical Education," *Recreation* Magazine, Vol. XXV, p. 92. New York: National Recreation Association, 1931.
[3] Ibid.

During the period from 1930 through 1941, laws were passed in Minnesota, Arkansas and other states defining more strictly the conditions under which local school authorities could conduct or share in the administration of recreation.

The Depression Decade.—A severe test of the full integration of recreation in American life in the depression years of the 1930–1940 decade was successfully met. Play emerged with a positive philosophy, matured under changing social and industrial conditions. In contrast with the idea current in 1900 that play was the mere release of surplus energy, it was now defined as effort at self-expression. In contrast with totalitarian ideas, American thinking continued to dignify the human personality and to conceive of recreation as a means of growth and lasting satisfactions for the individual as well as first-rate group training for citizenship.

The decade saw an enormous expansion of governmental enterprise in recreation and steady expansion of it among quasi-public and private agencies.[1] By 1937, 35 units in twelve departments of the Federal government were engaged in promoting leisure-time programs. The national park acreage rose to 17,000,000, the national forests to 173,000,000. In these areas there was a great extension of camping, picnicking, fishing, hiking, also of winter and water sports. The Works Progress Administration, created as an employment agency, constructed thousands of playgrounds, athletic fields, swimming pools, picnic areas, and other projects; and in 1939 it reported 41,780 individuals in recreation leadership positions.

Municipal recreation expanded both in numbers and variety. Cities reporting employed workers increased from 828 in 1930 to 1204 in 1939. The number of year-round employees grew from 2660 to 3450. Outdoor playgrounds were 2000 more than the 7677 recorded in 1930. Indoor recreation centers more than doubled. The tendency toward diversification of areas and facilities, already apparent in the previous decade, was accentuated. Archery ranges, handball courts, horseshoe courts, shuffleboard courts, and softball diamonds, among other facilities, were built for park and recreation departments. New York City alone constructed 300 new playgrounds and the WPA built 2078 of them throughout the United States, between 1935 and 1939. However, neighborhood playgrounds, especially in the older sections of cities, lagged behind other expansion. Better functional design for playgrounds and playfields, the widespread use of hard surfaces for game courts, an increase of night lighting, and the expansion of multiple-use areas

[1] See Pangburn, Weaver W., "Play and Recreation," *Annals of the American Academy of Political and Social Science*, November, 1940, pp. 121–129. Philadelphia: American Academy of Political and Social Science.

were noteworthy developments of the decade. Programs gave more attention to youth, ages 16–24 whose needs were revealed by the American Youth Commission.

In spite of the vogue of the movie, the radio, and spectator sports, the recreation of "action" gained in all directions. Swimming became the country's most popular sport. Winter sports too entered a popular phase. Hiking was emphasized by the Youth Hostel movement transplanted from Europe. Camping, now mustering 5000 private organizations and camps, moved toward greater informality and decentralization. An informal recreational approach to nature study brought many naturalists and nature guides to the service of the national, state, and municipal recreational agencies. School training for leisure expanded in several subjects. School intramural sports thrived, while 30,000 orchestras of symphonic proportions and other thousands of choruses and bands in high schools played an important part in changing the whole American attitude toward good music. Activities involving recreational skills and the teaching of such skills greatly increased among the youth-serving organizations.

Far from being the concern of government agencies only, play and recreation had now been taken up widely by Catholic and Protestant churches, by institutions for the mentally ill, by prisons, and other agencies. The government housing projects incorporated provisions for both indoor and outdoor play, and recreation rooms became a standard feature in better class residential construction.

Training.—The extended field of play and recreation brought about increased activity in leadership training. The National Recreation Association conducted institutes for in-service training in 40 cities with a total enrollment of 10,000. Municipal recreation agencies developed numerous courses for their own staffs and for representatives of churches, private agencies, and other groups. Ten colleges and universities organized major courses in recreation for the training of leaders. Several universities appointed inter-departmental faculty committees charged with the responsibility of setting up the best possible recreation training courses. A professional organization, the Society of Recreation Workers of America, came into being.

Impact of World War II.—During the year 1941, with the United States girding its strength for war on a huge scale, the recreation movement was still expanding in the face of a sharp decline in assistance from the Works Progress Administration and the loss of some of its best workers for government service, together with a decline in the construction of facilities. For the first time in ten years the reserve supply of able public recreation personnel became depleted, although volunteer workers increased to 35,000, the largest total yet recorded. While trying to maintain service for the civilian population, public and private agencies gave first attention to the

Fig. 103.—Model playground in 1908.

needs of men in uniform and of employees in defense industries. Recreation in the camps and ports was supplied by Army and Navy authorities. The Federal government appropriated $16,500,000 for community recreation buildings which were to be government property though operated by the United Service Organizations. In large cities public recreation departments and local committees began to operate recreation centers and develop extensive entertainment programs for service men on leave. Special physical fitness programs, the introduction of more utilitarian projects in crafts, and other adaptations of the recreation program to war needs were noted.

Conclusion.

The mission yard sand garden in Boston has become ten thousand neighborhood playgrounds and numerous other recreation areas, and its fifteen little patrons have grown into at least fifteen and a half million individual participants in the recreation program. Community recreation is recognized as a governmental responsibility but the movement has spread also into numerous other institutions. City parks today are providing generously for active as well as passive recreation. Physicial education is play motivated Adults by the millions, as well as children, are served. The immense variety of human recreational interests is met by a corresponding diversification of facilities and activities. In recent years there has been an upswing in individual sports and hobbies. City planning has not yet solved the problem of slums where playgrounds are still relatively far too few. There is need in many large cities for a closer coöperation between the schools and the city governments in recreational planning. The community idea in recreation has gained less headway than hoped for because of the strength the movement has attained among a wide variety of organizations. Property development has outstripped advances in personnel for leadership and management. Yet the progress of so young a movement has been marked and the faith of its founders has been proved sound. The dignity and importance of play for the child and recreation for the adult have become firmly lodged in the American way of life.

BIBLIOGRAPHY.

Butler, G. D.: Introduction to Community Recreation. New York, McGraw-Hill, 1940.
Gloss, G. M.: Bibliography of Masters Theses and Doctoral Studies in the Field of Recreation. Res. Quar. 11 (March, 1940): 150–63.
Hjelte, G.: Administration of Public Recreation. New York, Macmillan, 1940.
Jacks, L. P.: Education through Recreation. New York, Harper & Bros., 1932.
Lipovitz, F. J.: Recreation Handbook of Playground, School and Public Recreation. Minneapolis, Birgess, 1940.
Lundberg, G. A., Mirra Komarovsky and Mary Alice McInerny. New York, Columbia Press, 1934.
Mitchell, E. D., and Mason, B. S.: Theory of Play. New York, Barnes, 1934.
Neumeyer, M. H., and E. S.: Leisure and Recreation. New York, Barnes, 1936.
Kurtz, R. H. (Editor): Social Work Year Book. Russell Sage Foundation, New York, 1941.
U. S. Department of Interior, National Park Service, Municipal and County Parks in the United States, 1935. Washington, Government Printing Office, 1937.
U. S. Department of Labor, Bureau of Labor Statistics: Park Recreation Areas in the United States, May, 1928. Washington, Government Printing Office, 1932.
Workman, E. C.: Trends in Public Recreation. Recreation, August, 1938, p. 267.

The student of the playground movement in America will need to be familiar with the following, in addition to the publications already mentioned: G. E. Johnson, "Education by Play and Games" (Ginn & Co., 1907); Joseph Lee, "Play in Education" (The Macmillan Co., 1915); Henry S. Curtis, "Education through Play" (The Macmillan Co., 1915), "The Practical Conduct of Play" (1915), "The Play Movement and its Significance" (1917), and other volumes; E. B. Mero, "American Playgrounds" (Baker & Taylor Co., 1908); A. and L. H. Leland, "Playground Technique and Playcraft" (Baker & Taylor Co., 1910). See also "The Play Movement in the United States," by Clarence E. Rainwater (The University of Chicago Press, 1922).

CHAPTER XXVIII.

THE TRAINING OF TEACHERS.

THE earliest attempt in America to prepare teachers of physical education was made by Dio Lewis in the years 1861–1868, at his Normal Institute for Physical Education in Boston (see pp. 260–263). Its first course opened at 20 Essex Street July 5, 1861, and at the commencement exercises held nine weeks later, on September 5, 7 men and 7 women were graduated. The second course, which extended from January 2 to March 13, 1862 (ten weeks), was completed by a class of 18, the third (July 5 to September 15, 1862) by one of 12, and the fourth class, graduated March 13, 1863, numbered 22. Details of later courses are lacking. In a volume published in 1868 Lewis says that more than 250 persons had taken the diploma of the Normal Institute in the nine sessions which had been held, but his biographer states that "421 ladies and gentlemen, in almost equal numbers," were graduated in the seven years following its establishment.

The second normal school, that of the North American *Turnerbund*, was projected as far back as 1856, but not actually opened until November 22, 1866. After two courses in New York City (1866–1867, 1869), one in Chicago (1871), and a third in New York (1872–1873), it became firmly established in Milwaukee under Brosius (1875–1888). Then followed two years in Indianapolis (1889–1891), a return to more ample quarters in Milwaukee, under Brosius and Wittich (1891–1907), and finally a permanent transfer to Indianapolis (in 1907). Its present name, Normal College of the American Gymnastic Union, was received in 1919. Four summer courses were given at Milwaukee, 1895–1898 inclusive. The history of the school is given at some length on pp. 301–304 and 311.

We have already mentioned Dr. Sargent's contribution to the training of teachers (p. 287). During his forty years at Hemenway Gymnasium (1879–1919) his influence in this direction was more widely felt than that of any other man in America. The beginning was modest enough, at Witneys Block, corner of Palmer and Brattle Streets in Cambridge (1881–1883), where a single pupil, Mrs. Mary E. W. Jones, completed the one-year course in 1882. A second year was now added, and 4 women were graduated in 1884. Meanwhile quarters had been secured and equipped at 20 Church Street, and here in the years 1883–1904 a total of 261 women finished the prescribed work in theory and practice. About 70 others remained for a single year only. In 1902 the course became a three-year one, with attendance at a summer camp in New Hampshire added in 1912. When the new "Sargent Gymnasium," on Everett Street, was occupied, in the school year 1904–1905, men as well as women were received as students, and in the next five years 130 more women and 6 men were graduated. In the year 1918–1919 the total enrollment had reached 406, with 22 names on the list of "officers of instruction," not counting student assistants and special camp instructors and assistants.

In connection with the Harvard University Summer School five-week courses in physical education, under the direction of Dr. Sargent were first given in 1887, attended that year by 18 men and 37 women. The total registration in the years 1887–1898 was 982 (329 men and 653 women), or an average attendance of 82. For the next three years the course was lengthened to two summers, and the enrollment was 98 men and 204 women, or a total of 302 and an average of 101. Thereafter the graded course covered four successive summers of theory and practice. The figures reached in the period 1902–1919 were 971 men and 2211 women, or a total of 3182 and an average per season of 177. For the entire period of thirty-three years, from 1887 through 1919, the enrollment was 4466 (1398 men and 3068 women), with an average attendance of 135.

The Brooklyn-Anderson-New Haven Normal School of Gymnastics and the Chautauqua (summer) School of Physical Education stood in much the same relation, in the years 1886–1904, as the Sargent Normal School and the Harvard University summer courses. William Gilbert Anderson, the prime mover in each, was the son of Edward Anderson, a Congregational clergyman, and grandson of Rufus Anderson, assistant secretary of the American Board of Commissioners for Foreign Missions 1824–1832 and secretary 1832–1866. He was born at St. Joseph, Michigan, September 9, 1860. From 1874 to 1880 his father was pastor in Quincy, Illinois, and early in this period the boy became "an ardent champion of advanced work in gymnastics, possessed of considerable skill as a performer on the horizontal bars, a tumbler and a batule-board and springboard leaper. . . Attainment as an acrobat had come, in part, from association with the circus men who wintered" in Quincy, and his enthusiasm was further stimulated by William Blaikie's "How to Get Strong" (New York, 1879) and Archibald Maclaren's "Physical Education" (Oxford, 1869). In the year 1877–1878, while a student in the Roxbury Latin School, Boston, Anderson was a pupil of Robert J. Roberts in the Young Men's Christian Association at 68 Eliot Street. Then came two years (1878–1880) as freshman and sophomore in the classical course the University of Wisconsin, where military drill was the only required form of exercise, though there was a crude outdoor gymnasium which the catalogue described as "well-furnished," and "open to students at fixed hours." After teaching school for a year in Clayton Illinois, he became superintendent of the Cleveland, Ohio, Young Men's Christian Association gymnasium (1881–1882), and received the degree of doctor of medicine from the Cleveland Medical College in 1883. The next two years were spent in Columbus and Toledo, Ohio. He had now decided to follow physical training as a profession, and in the fall of 1885 accepted an appointment as director of the gymnasium at Adelphi Academy (now Adelphi College), Brooklyn, New York.

Here, early the next year, he organized the "Brooklyn Normal School for Physical Education." Its first announcement, which lists a faculty of ten, calls attention to the fact that "no school in the country pays more attention to the physical education of its scholars than the Adelphi Academy. The number of scholars enrolled is within a few of one thousand the majority of whom take daily exercise (obligatory). Members of the Normal Class will have opportunity to observe and assist in the instruction of these classes. . . . The gymnasium of Adelphi Academy, corner of St. James Place and Lafayette Avenue, has been secured for the use of Normal classes. . . The first course in reading and study will extend from February 1 to October 1, 1886. The course in practical training in the gymnasium will begin February 1 and end June 1, 1886. The second term will begin October 4, 1886, and end June, 1887." A class of 10 students was graduated in 1887, and 87 altogether in the period of 1886–1892. At the end of that time Dr. Anderson removed to New Haven, Connecticut, to become associate director of the Yale University gymnasium, and the school, rechristened the "Anderson Normal School of Gymnastics," was opened in the new location in September of 1892. In the next eleven years its graduates numbered 140. Meanwhile, Dr. Ernst Hermann Arnold[1] had been associated with Dr. Anderson in the management of the school, and in 1903 the latter's active connection with it ceased altogether.[2]

---

[1] Born in Erfurt, Germany, February 11, 1865, of German and Polish ancestry educated in the *Realgymnasium* at Halle until 1883; completed the ten-month course at the normal school of the North American *Turnerbund*, in Milwaukee, in April of 1888, and was teacher of gymnastics in *Turnvereine* in Trenton, New Jersey (1888–1891), and New Haven, Connecticut (1891–1894); M.D., Yale University Medical School, 1894, and the next year took courses in surgery and orthopedics in the universities at Halle and Leipsic; became associate director of the Anderson Normal School of Gymnastics in 1895, and its director in 1896.

[2] Dr. Anderson published a volume on "Light Gymnastics" in 1890 (New York, Effingham Maynard & Co.), and another on "Methods of Teaching Gymnastics" in 1896 (Meadville, Pa., Flood & Vincent).

The name had again been changed in January of 1901, this time to "New Haven Normal School of Gymnastics."

In 1886 Dr. Anderson went to Chautauqua, New York, to take charge of physical education in the summer school established there by the Chautauqua Institution seven years before, and gave some free instruction to a normal class of three pupils. The next season there was a charge for such tuition, and certificates were given to the few who finished the work; but the normal course was not formally established until the following summer (1888). An old skating rink at the corner of Palestine and Scott Avenues served as headquarters until a new gymnasium, started in 1890 and completed in the winter of 1890–1891, was ready for use. Meanwhile a company had been organized to erect the building and conduct the normal course, and the summer school of physical education was managed by this company in the years 1890–1912. Dr. Anderson held the position of principal from 1890 to 1894, and dean 1895–1904. By the addition of an advanced year in 1891 the course was extended to cover two summers, and in 1903 a third term was offered for the first time. In 1902 a second gymnasium, for classes in Swedish and corrective gymnastics, was available. Upon Dr. Anderson's retirement Jacob Bolin, a member of the faculty since 1891, succeeded him as dean (1905–1909). In 1913 the school passed into the hands of the Chautauqua Institution. Dr. Jay W. Seaver[1] had been an instructor at the summer school since 1889 and president of the company 1895–1912, and now became director of the courses in physical education. After his death Dr. Joseph E. Raycroft was acting director for two years (1916 and 1917), and in 1918 the position was given to Professor Charles Winfred Savage of Oberlin College, who had already served for two seasons as a member of the faculty.

The history of the physical training departments of the International Young Men's Christian Association College at Springfield, Massachusetts (since 1887) and the Young Men's Christian Association College in Chicago (since 1890) had been given in a previous chapter (pp. 315–325). In the absence of other opportunities for the professional training of men, these schools have enrolled among their students some who were not looking forward to Association service, and on the other hand many of their graduates have withdrawn from Association positions to accept others in public schools,

[1] Born at Craftbury, Vermont, March 9, 1855; prepared for college at Craftsbury Academy and Williston Seminary; A.B., Yale, 1880, and M.D., Yale Medical School 1885; instructor in physical training at Yale University 1883–1892, and medical examiner in the department after 1885; died at Berkeley, California, May 5, 1915. Published "Anthropometry and Physical Examination" (New Haven, 1890. New edition in 1909).

in secondary and state normal schools, in colleges and universities, in church or settlement or playground work, or with athletic clubs or Boy Scouts.

We have already noted (p. 332) the beginning of the Boston Normal School of Gymnastics, in 1889, the teaching done there by Posse, Enebuske, and Collin, and that in September of 1909 this school became the department of hygiene and physical education of Wellesley College. Mrs. Hemenway, at her death in 1894, had endowed it for a period of fifteen years, and Miss Amy Morris Homans was its director from the start until her retirement from the Wellesley faculty in the summer of 1918. After occupying temporary quarters at Boyleston Place and on Park Street, in Boston, the school was housed in Paine Memorial Building, 9 Appleton Street, between Tremont and Berkeley, and then from September of 1897 until the transfer in 1909 in the building of the Massachusetts Charitable Mechanic Association at 97 Huntington Avenue, near Exeter Street. At Wellesley the new Mary Hemenway Hall, constructed with a view to the needs of the Normal School and also to provide for the physical training of all Wellesley College students, was ready for its use. Twelve women had graduated from the first class, in 1891, and 433 women and 9 men in the years 1891–1909 inclusive.

Upon severing his connection with the Boston Normal School of Gymnastics Baron Posse at once opened a small gymnasium of his own in the Harcourt Building, 23 Irvington Street, on February 1, 1890. Afterward more spacious quarters in the same building were occupied. From the normal classes, during the next six years (1890–1895), a total of 96 women and 6 men were graduated, 3 of them receiving the diploma from the medico-gymnastic course only. A still larger number had come under his instruction in the brief summer courses conducted in the Boston gymnasium, at the Martha's Vineyard Summer Institute, and at Harvey, Illinois (see p. 330). Following Baron Posse's death, on December 18, 1895, Baroness Rose Posse became director of the school. In the fall of 1900 it was transferred to the Fensmere Building, 206 Massachusetts Avenue, and in June of 1911 incorporated under the name "Posse Normal School of Gymnastics," with Baroness Posse as president. That same summer (1911) the building at the corner of Garrison and St. Botolph Streets, originally constructed (1886) for the (Mary E.) Allen Gymnasium and later used by the Women's Athletic Club of Boston, was secured. This was completely destroyed by fire in the spring of 1913. A plot of land at 773–781 Beacon Street, near its intersection with Commonwealth Avenue, was now purchased, and the formal opening of the new building erected here took place on November 17 of that year. Baroness

Posse retired from active connection with the school in May, 1915, and was succeeded as president by Mr. Hartvig Nissen (see p. 338).

No attempt is made here to trace the growth of the numerous other privately owned gymnasia, most of them of later origin, which have offered training courses for teachers. Nor have the data been collected which would make possible a history of physical training at the various state normal schools. One recalls, however, in the case of the latter, the long service of Dr. and Mrs. C. E. Ehinger at West Chester, Pa., Dr. H. B. Boice at Trenton, N. J., and Professor Wilbur P. Bowen at Michigan Normal College, Ypsilanti (since 1894). Much more significant, as pointing the way to the final solution of the problem of adequate professional preparation for leadership in physical education, are the beginning of teachers' courses at our colleges and universities. Such courses, counting toward a bachelor's degree, have been offered at the University of California since 1898, the University of Nebraska since 1899, Oberlin College since 1900, University of Missouri at about the same time, Teachers College of Columbia University since 1903, Wellesley College since 1909, and University of Wisconsin since the fall of 1911. University of Pennsylvania 1923. These courses cover four years of work of which about 20 per cent is actual exercise and practical teaching of exercises and games, the rest consisting of courses, in anatomy, physiology, hygiene and the more purely cultural courses that lead to the degree of B.A. or B.S., which is given to those students who "major" in physical education. Summer courses, with university credit allowed, have been conducted at Columbia University since 1899. Carefully coördinated courses leading to advanced degrees have been organized in many colleges, universities and normal schools.

The Training of Teachers.[1]

Before 1910 the training of leaders in physical education was left largely to private normal schools. But the need for a broader and higher professional education in physical education was accentuated by several adult organized social movements illustrated by the Young Men's Christian Association, the playground movement, the Boy Scouts of America, and the child health movements under many auspices. With the rapid expansion of physical education in many social institutions there developed a constant demand for better qualified teachers. The question of personnel became in-

[1] Acknowledgement is made for the coöperation of Dr. N. P. Neilson, Silver Spring, Maryland, who contributed this article.

separable from that of the consistent enlargement and enrichment of the physical education program.

Previous to World War I, which came to an Armistice in 1918, the majority of the colleges and universities gave scant recognition to the professional education of experts in physical education. The professional training opportunities for men students were especially limited. Most of the abler men in the field came into physical education teaching through their interest in athletics. They went from an athletic career to a teaching career. Some men substituted a medical training for training in physical education even though a medical education gives no special competence to solve the educational problmes of physical educaton.

Following World War I, the passage of state laws making physical education compulsory in the elementary and secondary schools created such a demand for leaders that many positions had to be filled by candidates with very little training. To meet the emergency, colleges and universities were induced to initiate new courses, to modify others, and to organize curricula leading to a bachelor's degree. Special and emergency efforts, including summer sessions and extension courses coupled with low teacher certification requirements, were employed to meet the demand. Yet so rapid was the development of teacher training that by 1930, in most states, the supply of physical education teachers had caught up with the demand and the need had changed from one of quantity to one of quality.

At present a large number of institutions require some physical education as a part of the undergraduate course leading to a bachelor's degree. The general tendency is to require physical education for two years and to allow four semester hours of credit for it. The fact that physical education is now included as a part of the required work of practically every undergraduate course indicates that it is no longer considered something apart from general education. In 1916 Congress passed the national defense act which among other things created a definite system of civilian military training in preparatory schools and colleges. This act and the amendment of 1920 provided for the senior and junior dvisions of the Reserve Officers' Training Corps whose primary object is to provide systematic military training to qualify selected students for appointment as reserve officers in the military forces of the United States. Of 182 institutions studied 83 provide instruction in military training and of these 49 are land-grant colleges.[1] A large number of the institutions require one hour of theory and two hours of practice

---

[1] United States Department of the Interior. "Physical Education in American Colleges and Universities," Bureau of Education Bulletin (1927), No. 14.

each week in the basic course. The number of semester hours of credit allowed for the required work in military training varies from two to twelve.

Professional Education Curricula in Physical Education are affected by certification requirements adopted by State Departments of Education. These requirements vary in the different states from two to five years of college work with a variable number of units specified in a major or minor in physical education. The general tendency is to require four years of college work with a major in physical education for teaching in a secondary school. However, there is a tendency in some states and in some colleges or universities to increase the requirement by an additional year thus allowing the course in "Observation and Practice Teaching" to be located in the fifth year rather than the fourth year. In fact, the professional education curriculum in physical education is rapidly coming to be a seven year curriculum because of the great amount of content that is necessary for trained competence in the field. School administrators tend to insist that athletic coaches meet the same certification requirements as those met by general physical education teachers.

Recently the movement in colleges and universities to establish a higher professional education has gained momentum but there is no professional education course which is recognized by leading physical educators as standard. A study of the courses listed in 28 college catalogs, given and recommended for the preparation of physical education teachers, revealed the astonishing fact that there were 671 differently named courses.[1] It is also claimed that there are approximately 400 institutions in the United States now giving professional education courses in physical education. Few of them have sufficient weight in the foundation sciences to give their students the ability to understand the real problems of physical education. Hence, there is need for a study of the problem from the standpoint of classes of workers serving in the schools, the functions of these workers, the preparation needed by the workers if they are to perform their functions, and the evaluation of professional courses given in teacher education institutions.

Several attempts at evaluation have been made. In 1913 at the Second Annual Conference of the Middle West Society of Physical Education and Hygiene, Dr. Charles H. Judd of the University of Chicago presented a report which advocated that a permanent committee be appointed to be known as the "Committee on Standards for the Training of Physical Educators." This Committee

[1] California State Department of Education. "A Curriculum for the Professional Preparation of Physical Education Teachers for Secondary Schools," Bulletin E-1, 1930, p. 7.

was to prepare classified lists of institutions and to devise a system of classification of individuals for approval by the society. The report recommended that a minimum of two years of professional study be required and that this include floor work in games and other exercises; at least 120 hours of practice teaching; the fundamental physiological, biological, and social sciences to give a scientific background; and some work in the liberal arts. Technical courses in medicine were omitted deliberately from this recommended professional course.

A Conference on Professional Training in Physical Education, arranged by the U. S. Bureau of Education, was held in Washington, D. C., March 30, 1927. The Conference presented and discussed reports on the aims of physical education, entrance requirements, a three-year curriculum, a four-year curriculum, and to what department of a university does the physical education training belong?

In 1929, Dr. J. H. McCurdy, Chairman of a committee, reported on the Curriculum of 139 institutions in the United States preparing teachers of physical education. The purpose of the study was to make accessible the detailed analysis of the courses required in institutions giving four-year courses leading to a degree, also three-year courses and two-year courses; to give a standard terminology for the various courses; and to recommend the median requirements for each course. The study gives detailed information about the hours required for all courses in each of the 139 institutions.

The Department of School Health and Physical Education of the National Education Association at its meeting in Los Angeles on July 1, 1931, passed a resolution, authorizing the President of the Department, Dr. Jay B. Nash, to appoint a National Committee whose duty it should be to formulate a suggested set of standards to be used in the evaluation of institutions professing to train physical education teachers. Dr. Nash appointed N. P. Neilson, then State Director of Health and Physical Education for California, as chairman of the Committee, and agreed to the plan of having all of the other State Directors of health and physical education serve as members of the general Committee. Some preliminary suggestions were prepared and were discussed by the State Directors at their annual meeting in New York City, December, 1931. Discussion of a report presented at the Convention of the American Physical Education Association held in Philadelphia, April, 1932, resulted in the suggestion that six national organizations sponsor the study and that at least two years of time be taken to complete it. In conformity with this suggestion, a national committee of six members was chosen with G. B. Affleck representing the American Physical

Education Association; W. G. Moorhead representing the Society of State Directors of Health and Physical Education; E. M. Sanders representing the City Administrators of Health and Physical Education; Gertrude Moulton representing the Women Directors of Physical Education in Colleges and Universities; Harry A. Scott representing the College Physical Education Association; and N. P. Neilson, Chairman, representing the Department of School Health and Physical Education of the National Education Association.

The general problem was analyzed in great detail and the study became known as "The National Study of Professional Education in Health and Physical Education." A state committee was organized in each of the 48 states thus involving approximately 250 different persons in the study. A report was made each year at the National Convention held in April.

In 1935 a report on Standards was published in the December issue of the Research Quarterly outlining the problem under the generalized headings: (1) Basic Characteristics of the Secondary School Program, (2) General Standards, (3) Standards for the Selection of Students to be Trained, (4) Course Standards, (5) Standards for Staff, and (6) Standards for Facilities. It was suggested that a National Rating Committee of twenty-five members be organized as a sub-committee of the National Study Committee. During the school year 1936–37, the committee developed a rating chart containing the standards, and a report form to be used for the experimental rating of institutions. The programs for men and for women were rated on an experimental basis in a number of institutions and the results were sent to the institutions concerned.

In 1938 this committee was discharged and a new committee was appointed later under the chairmanship of Dr. E. C. Davis of the University of Pittsburgh. The new standing committee of the American Association for Health, Physical Education, and Recreation became known as the "Committee on the Coöperative Study of Professional Education in Health, Physical Education, and Recreation."[1]

The aim of the Committee is to improve professional education in these fields by sponsoring and aiding research studies, by discovering existing conditions, by determining better practices, and

[1] Serious attempts were made in 1928, 1932, and 1936, to combine the American Physical Education Association with the Department of School Health and Physical Education of the National Education Association. Conferences held at Chicago, Portland, New Orleans, and New York City during 1936 and 1937, ironed out most of the difficulties which had existed. At the Detroit meeting (N. E. A.) in the summer of 1937, the merger was completed and the new organization became known as "The American Association for Health, Physical Education, and Recreation—A Department of the National Education Association."

by rendering advisory services. The organizations represented on the Committee are the American Association for Health, Physical Education, and Recreation; the National Association of Directors of Physical Education for College Women; the College Physical Education Association; the City Administrative Directors Society; and the National Society of State Directors of Physical and Health Education. As a first step the Committee has arranged to have statements written of the working philosophies of professional education in health education, physical education, and recreation, feeling that such statements will serve as common frames of reference as the study progresses.

Because of the close relationship that exists between physical education and the health program the present tendency is for students to complete a combined major in health (or hygiene) and physical education. Positions in both large and small secondary schools are available to candidates with such a major. A combination major with recreation is also being developed. Three national conferences on the College training of recreation leaders have been held, the first at the University of Minnesota, December, 1937; the second at the University of North Carolina, in April, 1939; the third at New York University, January, 1941. These conferences studied the recreation curriculum on the undergraduate and graduate levels and the associated problems of training methods, organization, administration and research.

The University of Minnesota has announced a curriculum for the training of recreation leaders. This curriculum leads to the degree of bachelor of science with a major in recreation. It begins with the Junior year but is based on fundamental courses taken in the first two college years in the fields of biological science, physical science, social science, English Composition and Speech, skills and their appreciation, and a survey of recreation activities. The major includes courses listed under psychology and education, sociology and group work, recreation administration, advanced skills and their application, practice and field work, and campus activities.

In a recent survey Jack E. Hewitt[1] found that there are 56 institutions in the United States offering a graduate major in physical education for an advanced degree. The schools of education offer 85 per cent of all doctor's degrees and 51 per cent of all master's degrees available for the graduate major in physical education. To show the tendency for physical educators to take the Ph.D. rather than the M.D. degree one needs only to refer to the list of Contributing Editors to the Research Quarterly published by the American Association for Health, Physical Education and Recre-

[1] Jack E. Hewitt. "The Graduate Major in Physical Education." Research Quarterly, May 1942, p. 252.

ation in May 1942. Of the 32 persons listed with degrees, 25 hold the Ph.D., 4 the M.D., and 3 the Ed.D. degrees.

The method of work is also undergoing change. Recently summer school "Workshops," first sponsored by the Progressive Education Association have been organized in a considerable number of institutions. They represent an effort to utilize a variety of methods and the total resources of the institution to provide experiences which will most effectively meet the needs of the individuals who participate. These workshops mean a chance to work on a problem without the necessity of attending routine classes and lectures. Some workshops have been devoted exclusively to problems in health, physical education, or recreation while in others these problems are attacked under the program of a general educational workshop.

BIBLIOGRAPHY.

Catalogues, announcements, and lists of graduates published by the institutions or in connection with the summer courses of which mention has been made.

CHAPTER XXIX.

PREWAR CONDITIONS IN EUROPE.

FRANCE.

THE budget for physical education in France (1924) is under that of the Minister of War, and is administered by the High Commissioner of Physical Education. Bonuses are given by him for various sports on application, and the recipient must give reports to him of all money spent. This applies to the sports clubs, "les amis des sports," as well as to the schools.

1. The law requires one hour a week of physical training of all children in the schools up to thirteen years of age. This is enforced to a certain extent in Paris, and it amounts to about three units of gymnastics. In provincial schools it is practically a dead letter.

2. In children over thirteen years the same requirement obtain except in the (a) Ecoles Professionelles, (b) Ecoles Superieures, (c) Lycées and Colleges, but is well enforced only in exceptional cases; perhaps 15 per cent of this time is devoted to football without special instruction.

3. For students from eighteen to twenty-five years of age, there is no provision for physical education. There are a few voluntary clubs for football (soccer), but there is no alumni interest or support by the state.

4. The training for the army is conducted at the school at Joinville, of which a description follows later.

5. There are a number of private clubs in France, about ten important ones, and many small ones in the provincial towns, where sports are practised voluntarily, depending on bonuses from the Government in part, and on football, for their income; whenever the income from gate receipts becomes considerable, recruiting is rife, and players are stolen and bought. The budget is increased by membership fees, as well as by the receipts of the football games. Track and field athletics do not draw crowds or pay in France, and the football receipts are never used to support track and field sports, which are not much practised except in a few big and wealthy clubs, and then the athletes, as in the old New York Athletic Club or Mahattan Club, are active members or competing athletes.

There are three governing bodies in France for sport.

(a) Committée Olimpique Français.—Largely honorary, and not closely in touch with the details and management of sport.

(*b*) Committée National des Sports, which is practically the same.

(*c*) Union des Federations Française Athletism (Secretary Vidal), which is a true federation having under its control football, athletics, and Rugby football, with sections for schools, colleges corporations, and the army, like the National Amateur Athletic Federation of America. This is the law-making and governing body for competition and sport in France.

Athletic clubs in Paris: (*a*) The Paris University Club, a private club of university men, the president and moving spirit of which is Dr. Petitjean, a college man and electrical engineer, who wished to found a club for college men, and to buy or hire grounds for the practice of sports, especially track and field athletics. This club is not official, but aims to represent the University of Paris. The headquarters are at 55 Quai La Tournelles, and consist of a secretary's office, meeting rooms for track and field, football, Rubgy committees, records, trophies, etc.

Their stadium is just outside the gate leading to the Bois de Vincennes; it replaces a section of the old fortifications. It has a good 500-meter track with 200-meter straight-away, jumping pits, circles for shot-putting, and a tribune or grandstand with roof and concrete seats for 10,000 people, beneath which are dressing rooms. Further south are about a dozen dirt tennis courts with dressing rooms and showers. The lockers are of wood, badly designed and poorly ventilated. A court for "jeu de paume" is to be situated close by.

(*b*) The Stade Francais, founded in 1883 and approved by the Minister of War is for the encouragement of physical education by practice of sports in the open air (1) by exhibitions and athletic meets, (2) by lessons to members, (3) by the publication of a bulletin. The ministers of the Interior and Public Instruction reserve the right to visit and report on its activities. Women may become members under certain restrictions, and every member must be an amateur. They have about 3000 members.

It has its headquarters at 3 Rue Volney, Paris, where are offices for secretaries, committee rooms, trophy room, and examining rooms for members. Subscription for active members is 150 francs, for members over twenty years, and 80 francs for members under twenty years of age. They choose their sport on joining, and those under twenty years must, and those over twenty years may, have a medical examination, under the Consulting Medical Commission of the club. This examination is done, where possible, upon having the attached blank filled by the private medical attendant of the member. Reports of the members physical condition are made to him when desired from time to time by the club doctor.

Their club-house and stadium are beautifully situated at the Parde de St. Cloud, at the junction of the Marne and Porte Jaune Avenues. There are fields for football, turf track with jumping pits, circles for shot-putting, and seventeen tennis courts, with one very beautiful court for exhibitions, surrounded by a stand embowered in green. The club-house has lockers and showers and dining rooms and outdoor cafés. Close to the club-house is a beautiful monument to members who fell in the war. The whole atmosphere is that of an American country club, and the membership is of the same class. The Olympic tennis tournament should have been held here just as the P. U. C. stadium should have been chosen for the Olympic games proper.

(c) L'École Dubigneau de Lannau, situated at L'Ancien Parc des Eaux Mineredux de Passy, 21 Rue Raymond, is more strictly educational in its aim than either of the other two bodies. Originally a private school on the Boulevard Periera, the proprietor has taken this park to demonstrate his theories on physical education for schools. The park consists of an upper terrace where the springs were found, which had great vogue from 1657 till 1806, with varying fortunes. On a lower level is the field with 250-meter track, jumping pits, circles for shot-putting, and some gymnastic apparatus, all under fine old trees. There, where in the seventeenth and eighteenth centuries lords and ladies came for the mineral water that would cure them of anemia and dyspepsia, today boys and young men from the Central School of Mines run, leap over hurdles, put the shot, discus, and javelin, clothed only in short running breeches. A row of good but plain dressing rooms, with clothing hung on hooks, a dozen showers, and a massage-room with two low tables complete the equipment, except for the office of Dr. Pierre Minelle, member of the consulting board of the Société Médicale de L'Education Physique et des Sports. Here he measures and examines the pupils from time to time and keeps records of progress. This stadium, by arrangement, is open for certain hours to the 3000 members of the Stade Français, and so tends to bring these two bodies together, but they have no dealings with the P. U. C.

Dr. Bellin de Couteau has compared the three bodies to classes of society, the aristocracy being the Stade Français, the bourgeoisie the Ecole Dubigneau de Lannau, and the bolsheviki the Paris University Club. The attendance is voluntary and irregular.

There are many other private clubs founded by great companies and schools, but in organization they are but repetitions of one of these three.

The school l'École Militaire de Joinville is at the far end of the Bois de Vincennes, in a flat plain, with barracks and exercising ground. Just inside the entrance is an open-air shed with horizontal and parallel bars and climbing ropes with pits of loose earth instead of mattresses. At one end of the shed is a full size boxing ring on wheels, to be moved out into the open in good weather. A tribune or grand-stand overlooks the field on which are the standard jumping pits and circles, and a rather poor cinder path with about sixty yards straight.

The Laboratory of Physiology has two glass spirometers, Dufestel thoracrometer, and ergograph for the quadriceps extensors of the leg, and a modified Goldie rowing machine for giving a regulated muscular load as a preparation for tests of the heart, before and after exercise.

Other rooms have anatomical models and charts and apparatus for urinalysis.

Two special investigations were in course in 1914. (1) Chemical analysis of urine, before, during, and after exercise; (2) changes in the electric conductivity of the blood during exercise—evidence showing that it is enormously increased.

(1) The drills and exercises at Joinville are continuous, varying in speed, but never stopping till the end of the lesson and with no standing about. (2) The rhythm is left to the individual in breathing and most other movements; no attempt is made to enforce a uniform rate. (3) The movements themselves are modifications of normal actions; walking—erect, crawling, and on all fours, fast and slow—swinging, striking, bending, etc. Sharp, static, angular movements are absent. In this it resembles Bukh's primitive and fundamental gymnastics, and differs from the Swedish movements.

For example, a group of Senegalese students will play gymnastic games, in which one or more dances in a circle of handclapping, gesticulating men, evidently an adaptation of one of their own games or dances.

CZECHO-SLOVAKIA.

The new state, Czecho-Slovákia, is composed of Bohemia, to which has been added Moravia, lower Silesia, Slovakia, Ruthenia, and parts of German and Austrian territory.

It has about 14 million inhabitants of mixed Slavic, Teutonic and Magyar origin. The name of the capital has been changed from Pressburg to Bratislava (Slavic brotherhood). This combination has never been united before, and it is of doubtful stability. The organized physical training centers about the three institutions at Bratislava, Brno, and Prague, but one must not forget that in the Sokols, or Falcons, these people have an old patriotic gymnastic organization that is deeply rooted, and gives exhibitions of gymnastics with 12,000 men and 6,000 women at once, as was done recently

at Prague, and this is likely to remain the national expression of
physical education and sport.

There are three colleges in which sports are practised:

1. The University of Comeniuş in Bratislava.
2. University Schools in Brno, Technical School University, Agricultural College, Veterinary School.
3. The University of Prague.

At Comenius University in Bratislava (formerly Pressburg)
physical education is not officially recognized. In 1922 a Y. M. C. A.
was formed and, with the traditions of sport brought by the organization, a playground was developed in the grounds of the university,
and volley ball, basket ball, and playground ball began to be played.
The Association also furnished equipment for track, football, boxing,
and handball, and large numbers of students entered into these
games. In 1923 a Sports Club was formed, still not connected with
the university, and the original playground has become too small
for the demands upon it.

This university sent out an invitation for the first interuniversity
track meet in Czecho-Slovakia, in which three universities took
part. The contest was in volley ball, but next year track and field
sports were introduced. They need a new field. The secretary of
the students' Y. M. C. A. is Vladimir Stefanovic, of the faculty of
Brno.

The first intercollegiate meet between Brno and Bratislava took
place October 26, 1924, on the playground in Bratislava. It was
a good contest, Dr. Kostlivy, Dean of the University of Bratislava,
was referee, and professors and Y. M. C. A. members acted as
officials. There was an audience of 150, mostly students. The
meet was followed by a dinner of 100 to competitors and friends
at the Y. M. C. A. At the dinner, plans were made to have a return
meet at Brno, in May, 1925.

They owe much to Mr. L. W. Reiss for his untiring efforts to
further this work among them.

Before the war there was only one technical school which had a
university sports club, playing soccer, football, and fencing, which
still continues.

After the war, three new schools were founded in Arts, Agriculture,
Veterinary, but as yet they have no recognition from the original
club, and have formed their own Sports Club at University Brno.
They lack space and equipment, have no swimming pool or fencing
hall, or even a place to store apparatus. In spite of this they practise
track and field athletics, soccer, football, swimming, rowing, fencing,
tennis, volley ball, skating, skeeing, and hockey, and hold an annual
intramural tournament, in which almost all students take part.

The backing of the Y. M. C. A. under Mr. L. W. Reiss, has been most valuable, and the movement has extended down to the high schools, which have already organized and will act as feeders to the University Sports Club. The man most interested is Professor F. Majda, University of Prague.

In the University of Prague the growth of sports has been phenomenal. From a meager beginning ten years ago there are today about 5000 taking part in some sport.

The popularity of the sports is about as follows: tennis, volley ball, track and field. The chief man in this movement is Dr. Smotlocks, who has supplied tennis courts, and a track for the students.

FINLAND.

There are three universities:

1. The State University of Helsingfors, founded in 1640, with a three-year course of training of physical education for school teachers in preparatory schools. About 15 women and 5 men are now taking this course. In the schools they rank as regular teachers, giving three lessons a week, and leading the voluntary evening classes for students, who form gymnastic clubs and hold classes with an attendance up to 70 at most. They have no athletic fields, and the work is largely gymnastic.

2. The Finnish University at Abo, with 300 students. No course in Physical Education.

3. The Swedish University at Abo, with 300 students, and nothing done in physical education. In both universities however, private clubs are formed for gymnastics. No clubs have been formed for the practice of athletics. Popular athletic and gymnastic clubs are common in the country districts of Finland, and many students belong. Lewis Pikala, the Olympic trainer, has given courses of lectures at the universities on athletics, and is physical education officer to the National Guard, or militia, being attached for that purpose; but there is little official action of supervision. It is at their private clubs that the Finnish champions are developed, and not at the universities where athletics have not made any great headway. Their champion runner works in a factory, and their best javelin thrower is the keeper of an inn.

GREECE.

The modern movement for university sports in Greece dates from 1898, when the university gymnasium was established, and it lasted till 1912. In this time athletic contests were held with both military and civilian teams in which the University held its own. On the outbreak of the Balkan War in 1912, the students were mobilized and the teams dispersed.

The history of Greece since then has been a depressing one to read, and athletics have shared in this depression. Since the advent of peace they have been revived, and the faculty itself has prepared an elaborate plan for universal athletics.

All the professors are interested because they look on athletics as a national legacy from the glorious past, and they desire technical information and guidance. The interest of the students is great, but they require to develop interdepartmental athletics, there being only one University of Greece, until the day comes when Greece may head a Balkan league for sport. The only organized body that can give this leadership is the Y. M. C. A.

BIBLIOGRAPHY.

R. Tait McKenzie: Report to National Collegiate Athletic Association on Physical Education and International Relations in Europe, 1924.

CHAPTER XXX

AUSTRALIA.

For years, the Commonwealth of Australia has advocated systematic physical education for its citizens, having in mind the production of a race of strong, virile, stalwart individuals, trained to serve the nation in peace and to be a bulwark of defense in case of crisis or emergency. It was recognized that while physical fitness was primarily an individual responsibility, yet as an essential qualification for socially efficient leadership it was obviously a matter of direct concern to the State.

A National Fitness Council was appointed and an appropriation of £20,000 yearly for five years was passed. Great care was exercised to see that all related organizations were included. The State Department of Health is represented by E. Sydney Morris, M.D., Director-General of Public Health, and the educational interests are cared for by Sir Robert Wallace, Chancellor of Sydney University, and by members of the Teaching College staff. This Council has increased its membership to 35.

Chancellor Wallace visited Canada and the United States to interview candidates for the position of Executive Secretary of the Council and National Physical Director. Selection was made of Mr. Gordon Young, B. S., Springfield 1927, and later Mr. E. Harold LeMaistre, M.P.E., Springfield 1940, was added to the staff.

In January, 1938, the state of New South Wales took the initiative in local organization by appointing a Physical Education Advisory Committee which in 1939 held its inaugural meeting under the auspices of the Hon. D. H. Drummond, President of the National Fitness Council, who explained that it was the policy of the Government to place in the State Council the power to initiate and carry into effect a State-wide program for New South Wales. President Drummond said in part:

"Your body will virtually have executive powers and you will coördinate your efforts with the National Fitness Campaign through your representation on the National Council. In this way a coördinated effort will be effected throughout the entire Commonwealth. Through the Director of Physical Education you will plan a campaign to care for the pre-school, the adolescent emerging

(394)

from school and the adult population, to foster interest in extended facilities and to secure public interest and financial assistance."

Because of the urgent need for trained teachers and volunteer leaders, the Government established a Board of Studies in Physical Education. This Board, under the supervision of the Hon. Minister for Education, published in 1941, a circular descriptive of the Physical Education Certificate Course, the aims of which are stated thus:

"*a*, General Culture; *b*, a general training in the Principles of Education, and especially in the problems of health and physical fitness; *c*, the skill which enables holders of the Certificate to give instruction in physical education in all its varied forms in schools, playgrounds, community centers, camps, and in association with delinquency institutions and churches, etc."

Admission to this 3-year course is open to those who: (1) have passed the Leaving Certificate, or its equivalent; (2) pass a medical examination and (3) satisfy the Board in a personal interview. The curriculum is divided into Theoretical and Practical courses, the latter of about eight hours per week. An analysis of the requirements reveals a striking similarity to undergraduate teacher training courses in United States, but certain different emphases are included, *viz.*: (1) Speech training; (2) applied physiology; (3) artistic anatomy, and (4) squad drill.

In the third year, specializing or "majoring" is offered in activities for the following groups: (1) Pre-school children; (2) pre-adolescents; (3) adolescents and post-adolescents, and (4) adults. Facility in teaching and skill in leadership is sought through experience: (1) Teach first- and second-year students in practical work; (2) undergo a course of practice teaching in schools; (3) undertake work in community centers, and (4) undertake work in vacation swimming schools. All practice work is under close supervision.

For the training of instructors of less than university standard, schools and short courses have been established, a board of examiners has been appointed for these volunteer leaders, and many are in training for service in the Volunteer Defense Corps, Women's Australian National Services and similar organizations.

Other facilities provided under National approval include community centers, vacation playgrounds and vacation camps. The Lands Department has established a National Fitness Camp Trust to provide and control these camp properties, and a special Committee is exploring the possibility of developing Youth Hostels.

To forestall any misapprehension as to the responsibility of the Council, it may be noted that it is not in any sense a Government agency. It has been called into being by the Minister for Education as a voluntary body to assist in the promotion of a nation-wide community effort, and the Council may soon register as a separate corporate body. The Government is behind the work of the Council to the extent of providing accommodation and facilities for the administrative work, and making available to the Council much information and expert assistance by the coöperation of the various Departments. The purpose is the promotion of the welfare of the citizens, which can be achieved only by the coöperation of individuals and organizations throughout each local community. The set up has every appearance of being decidedly democratic.

BIBLIOGRAPHY.

Hembrow, C. H.: Physical Education. Med. Jour., Australia, May 8, 1937.
Horder, (Lord): Health with Happiness. Brit. Med. Jour., October 30, 1937.
Morris, E. S. (M.D.): Report on Physical Education—An Outline of Its Aims, Scope, Methods and Organization. Camberra, Government Printer, 1939, 16p.
National Fitness: Report Submitted to Local Government Executive. Sydney, 1939, 5p. (Mimeo.).
National Fitness and State Education: Sydney, 1939, 5p. (Mimeo.).
Physical Education, Certificate Course. Sydney, Teachers' College, 1941, 12p.

CHAPTER XXXI

CANADA.*

GYMNASTICS.

THE people of Canada are still largely agricultural. Their traditions were derived from the native Indians and the immigrants from Great Britain and France. Thousands have never seen a gymnasium, while the vast majority have been accustomed to a wide variety of athletics and sports. Leadership in gymnastics came largely from Europeans who migrated to Canada.

Such a leader was Mr. F. S. Barnjum who came from England about 1858 and settled in Montreal where he with a group of 40 gentlemen formed the Montreal Gymnastic Club, which influenced McGill University to build a gymnasium for use by the high school and university students. This building cost $4000 and the Montreal Gymnastic Club signed a 5-year lease at £80 per year for the use of certain parts during specified hours per week. In 1862 the Board of Governors of McGill employed Mr. Barnjum as Drilling and Gymnastic Master at a salary of $600 per year.

His forceful leadership soon brought popularity and success, especially in the high school, where parent, public and press, invited to exhibitions, concerts and demonstrations, spread most favorable reports. He was by nature a showman and used his art to make public recitals fascinating by introducing mass classes in dumb bells, Indian clubs and calisthentics to which were added novelty events such as inclined ladder, ladder bridge and "peghole," tumbling and pyramids. He added his Pedestrian Club in 1867, and introduced a promotion-for-merit plan, by which at the end of each day he selected the best 10 of the group and placed them at the head of the class on the following day.

At McGill, interest in gymnastics was stimulated when the Board of Governors, in 1882, accepted the proposal of Dr. R. J. Wicksteed who offered $100 in medals and prizes for "general efficiency in the exercises followed in the gymnasium by Mr. Barnjum and to the leading gymnast of the graduating class from the various faculties." Up to the present (1946), the Wicksteed com-

* Appreciation is expressed hereby to Dr. A. S. Lamb, Director, Department of Physical Education, McGill University, and to his associates on the staff, F. W. Wagner, E. M. Orlick and D. E. MacLachlin for their exceptional coöperation in collecting the data on which this article is based.

petitions are still carried on. In 1883 McGill adopted in part the system of gymnastic used by Harvard several of Dr. Sargent's machines were purchased and medical examinations were begun.

Upon the death of Mr. Barnjum (1888), James Naismith, later Dr. Naismith, the inventor of basketball, a graduate in Arts from McGill, and winner of the Wicksteed trophy, was appointed Physical Director. He resigned in 1890 to join the staff at Springfield College, recommending as his successor R. Tait McKenzie, winner of the Wicksteed medal in 1889. (Details of Dr. McKenzie's administration may be found under his name in the biographical sketch in this volume.)

Mr. Jacomb followed Dr. McKenzie and was succeeded in 1912 by A. S. Lamb. Taking his medical degree at McGill, Dr. Lamb has continued as Director of the Department of Physical Education up to the present.

The University of Toronto about 1865 erected a building where the men of residence, and other students who so desired, might exercise during inclement weather. In 1893 Toronto erected a gymnasium at a cost of $25,000 with the arrangement that the students would equip and manage it. The Student Directorate appointed as their representative Sgt. Williams, known to later undergraduates as "Prof." Until his death in 1922 he did excellent work in organizing classes in physical training, gymnastics, boxing, fencing, wrestling and bayonet fighting. He also served as trainer for the rugby and ice hockey teams. The Hart House, containing facilities for the Physical Education and Athletic Departments, is one of the finest structures in Canada.

The great majority of colleges and universities are equipped with gymnasia, a few large athletic clubs contain them and some of the "Societies" among immigrant Europeans retain their gymnastic traditions. Public schools are fairly well equipped and have required attendance.

FOOTBALL.

Both the association (soccer) and rugby games were imports from England. The earliest authentic mention of football available for Canada is that the Montreal Football Club was formed in 1866 and competed mostly with Her Majesty's Regiments quartered in Montreal. In 1872 McGill University permitted baseball and football teams to use its fields for a rental of $1 per player, students of previous session exempt. No public matches were allowed. The *McGill University Gazette*, a student paper, of May 2, 1873 explains that baseball and lacrosse had never been popular in the University and that football was the game most favored and was the sport in which the University was most successful, because it could be played later in the fall than any other game and also because a novice required less experience to render the game enjoyable than in any of the other sports. Evidently reference was made to soccer.

The Dominion Football Association (soccer) was formed in the spring of 1873 and the Montreal club donated a Challenge Cup which for many years was the emblem of soccer supremacy. McGill played intramural matches, "Arts *vs.* Medicine," also outside contests such as "Town *vs.* Gown."

McGill is credited with introducing English rugby in 1874 and meeting Harvard, using Harvard rules and losing the game to the Americans, then on the following day playing a tie using McGill rules. McGill had been accustomed to play with a "melon-shaped" ball which had been left at home, so they had to use an ordinary round ball which handicapped McGill in carrying and passing.

The Britannia Club, organized in 1875, was victorious over McGill for several years, but McGill continued to meet Harvard up to 1881, when the marked difference in rules necessitated the breaking off of relationships.

In 1884, delegates from the Rugby Clubs in Ontario and Quebec formed the Canadian Rugby Football Union which did not hesitate to modify the rules of the English game. The Montreal Club defended the Challenge Cup through 1886 when it won the Dominion Championship in Toronto. The University of Toronto-Ottawa College match, 1887, lined up the teams with one back, two halves, two quarters, two wings and eight forwards. The Ontario and the Dominion Championship was won by University of Toronto in 1895. The snap back from center was first used in Canada when the University of Michigan met the University of Toronto on the latter's grounds (1897). In this same year the Canadian Rugby Union adopted a uniform code of rules including the 10-yard requirement, the elimination of the throw in from touch, and separation of opposing players during scrimmage, all must stand clear of the ball.

Over the country in general, soccer is more widely played, rugby (Canadian) is confined almost entirely to colleges and universities, larger cities and clubs, also military posts.

CRICKET.

The time and place where cricket originated cannot at present be established but it has existed in England as the national game for centuries, and is one of the sports introduced into Canada by enthusiastic devotees. "Wherever Englishmen plant the Union Jack, they are sure to set up the wickets as well."

The earliest record of the game in Canada is that it was played in Upper Canada College ever since the opening of that institution in 1829. Three officials of the college, F. W. Barron, G. A. Barber and John Kent have been called the Fathers of Cricket in Canada. The college organized its Cricket Club in 1836 and played matches with such city teams as Toronto. Montreal and Sherbrooke had their teams in the 1830's.

The first international match between United States and Montreal was scheduled in 1845 and in the following year Toronto traveled, mostly by coach, the 665 miles to meet Montreal, and won the match. Within three years Montreal was able to return the match. Montreal in 1859 invited a team from England, guaranteeing this first team to cross the Atlantic $3750 for expenses and losing $500 on the venture. Other English teams visited Canada in 1868 and 1872, and in 1878 an Australian team visited Canada as guests of the Montreal Club. It was not until 1887 that England was visited by a Canadian eleven composed mainly of Upper Canada College graduates.

But this imported game never "took" particularly with Canadians. The fact that a match might last into a second day and that one player might remain at bat for hours failed to appeal because of its comparative lack of action. In the match against Ottawa, 1880, Mr. Browning, captain of the Montreal team, scored 204 runs, believed to be a record individual score for America. There was a certain spurt in cricket during World War II due to the large number of Old Country boys coming to Canada for aircrew training, but it is mainly where groups of Britishers are found that the game retains popularity.

LACROSSE.

Lacrosse is certainly indigenous to Canada. Menke (p. 431) claims that "The Canadian Indians are responsible for the game of lacrosse, which is Canada's national outdoor game by legislation." Since the game was played in so many parts of the country and there were no rules, many different types of games existed, so reports of travelers differ concerning its details and range all the way from practically unlimited number of players (200 in some cases) with no defined limits of grounds to 5 players per team on fields restricted by some natural landmarks or by the position of medicine men who are reported as shifting even to a distance of miles.

Various reasons are assigned for participation in the game. Some writers claim that it was a preparation for war, training in close combat and crippling opponents; others that it was of a religious nature preceded by elaborate ceremonies, pow wow, feasting and dancing. Another group asserts that the impelling motive was simply the joy of contest.

Of the various names given the game by the Indians, baggataway was the most common. But when the French-Canadians first saw it played they were impressed with the resemblance of the "stick" to a bishop's crosier so called it "LaCrosse" which has become permanent.

The prevailing type of play was that of the Iroquois Indians. Catlin (p. 179) reminds his readers that towards the close of the Revolutionary War a large proportion of the Six Nations migrated to Canada, where the British Government gave them reservations because of their military aid to the Crown.

W. G. Beers, the Father of LaCrosse, recalls the significant historical event of July 4, 1763, when two Ojibway teams played a game of lacrosse near Fort Michilimackinac. In the course of the game the Indians, ostensibly after the ball, crowded close to the open gates of the fort, gave their war whoop, seized weapons from spectator squaws who had concealed tomahawks, etc., under their blankets captured the fort (Beers, p. 70).

There is a record of a lacrosse game between Iroquois and Algonquins in September, 1834, but it appears that the whites did not participate in the sport until some time in the 1840's. The Olympic Athletic Club was organized in Montreal, 1842, for racing and outdoor athletics. In their annual events they, to add interest and variety, scheduled a lacrosse match between a team of 7 whites and 5 Indians; and in 1844 a contest was held on August 28th between 2 Indian teams of 6 men each, then on the day following the Indians defeated a team of whites. Contests between Indians and whites are also reported in 1848. In its annual games the Caledonian Society staged an exhibition game of lacrosse between 2 Indian teams, 1848, and in 1856 also under their auspices, the Iroquois defeated the Algonquins for a purse of $40.

The Olympic Club disbanded and in 1856 a group of players formed the LaCrosse Club of Montreal. A meeting of interested sportsmen to discuss the future of the game was held in Montreal and in 1858 the Hochelaga Club merged with the Lacrosse Club of Montreal, retaining the name of the latter. Many other clubs sprang into existence about this time, especially in the provinces of Quebec and Ontario. The first attempt to systematize the game and formulate rules for its conduct was in 1860 when W. G. Beers published a brochure of preliminary suggestions. He also advocated that lacrosse be made the national sport of Canada.

The visit of H. R. H. the Prince of Wales to Canada in 1861 was the occasion of a grand exhibition match between teams selected from the Montreal and the Beaver clubs and the Caughnawaga and St. Regis Indians, with 25 men on each team.

The year 1867 was marked by both the Confederation of the provinces and the nationalization of lacrosse. Beers (pp. 57-58) outlined his share in promotion:

"I believe I was the first to propose the game of Lacrosse as the National game of Canada in 1859. A few months preceding the proclamation of Her Majesty, uniting the Provinces, a letter head, 'Lacrosse, Our National Field Game,' published by me in the Montreal Daily Paper, in April, 1867, was distributed throughout the Whole of the Dominion, and was copied into many of the public papers, resulting in the organization of many clubs across Canada. On the day which created the greater part of British America a Dominion, the game of lacrosse was adopted as the National Game."

In September of the same year the Montreal Club, following discussion of the previous year, framed the first laws of the game and called a Convention of the Canadian clubs, meeting in Kingston, to organize an Association for the guidance of the clubs and government of the game. Celebration of the nationalization of the game took the form of a match in Montreal, between the Caughnawaga Indians and the Montreal Club, July 1st (Dominion Day). Two senior clubs, the celebrated "Shamrocks" of Montreal and the "Toronto Club," organized this year. In July, Mr. Johnson of Montreal took 18 Caughnawaga Indians to England for several exhibition games, and Mr. L. Weir of the Montreal Lacrosse Club organized a club in Glasgow, Scotland.

In July, 1868, the Mohawks of Troy, N. Y., entertained the Montreal Club, the first International Match, and in August a team from the Dominion and Crescent Clubs visited United States, playing in Troy and New York. The National Lacrosse Association of Canada made important amendments in its Constitution and the laws of the game. The Montreal Club again entertained royalty by a tournament of several days in honor of H.R.H. Duke of Connaught, then Prince Arthur (1869), and in 1876, took a team of Caughnawaga Indians across the Atlantic to further demonstrate the game to the British public. By Royal Command they visited Windsor Castle and had the honor of playing before and being presented to the Queen.

The Montreal Club, in 1882, visited the Prairie Provinces as guests of the hospitable "Gary Lacrosse Club" of Winnipeg, and this same club, in conjunction with the Toronto Club, took another Caughnawaga team to England (1883), playing 60 games, several of which were attended by H.R.H. The Prince of Wales, an honorary member of the Montreal Club. A lacrosse team from the North of Ireland visited Canada in 1885, as guests of the Montreal Club, and played such prominent teams as the "Shamrocks," "Montreal Clubs" and the "All Canada Club." Further evidence of the leadership of the Montreal Club is indicated by the fact that in conjunction with the Montreal Snowshoe Club and the Montreal Bicycle Club, it formed the Montreal Amateur Athletic Association (1881).

A few changes in rules were made in 1889 and the plan of playing for championship honors modified from the old challenge system to a series of home and home games, with gratifying results (1885). Outstanding recent rule changes include the distribution of the players on each team to certain positions on the field with limitations as to when they may participate in active play, thereby discouraging the "bunching" of players in pursuit of the ball. Skillful running, dodging, stick handling, passing and receiving also encourage open play. Penalties, minor and major, in the form of different length of "time out" are intended to handicap the team guilty of fouling. The "sticks" themselves show an interesting evolution as to size and form.

In addition to educational institutions and larger cities, lacrosse continues its popularity in smaller towns and country districts. The young men practice during the long evenings of certain days, and have their matches on Saturdays, public holidays or special local occasions.

BASKETBALL.

Of the original basketball team organized by James Naismith at the YMCA Training School (now Springfield College) in 1891–2, 4 players were Canadians, *viz.*, McDonald from Nova Scotia, Archibald and Thompson from New Brunswick, Patton from Ontario.

When Lyman Archibald graduated from Springfield in 1892 he went to the St. Stephen, New Brunswick, YMCA and introduced the game there, playing 9 men on a side. He arranged games among different sections of the Association membership, but later in the season extended the sport to the nearby centers of Milltown, N. B., and Calais, Maine, arranging matches among these 3 towns. Leaving St. Stephens in 1893, Archibald, through the YMCA, introduced Hamilton to this new sport, and soon Hamilton became the first "real hotbed" of basketball in Canada. An international flavor was added in 1896 when a team from the Buffalo Central "Y" visited Hamilton. The local team won, 16–13, but Buffalo captured the return match at home, 16–6, and Hamilton won the decisive game on its own floor 20–6.

T. D. Patton, Springfield '92, returned to his home in Toronto and imparted his enthusiasm to the local YMCA members and soon basketball was played widely in Toronto and vicinity. Under the capable leadership and coaching of J. H. Crocker, Toronto Central became one of the most prominent teams in Canada. Mr. Crocker had in 1894 introduced the game into Nova Scotia at the "Y" in Amherst.

Montreal was introduced to basketball by W. H. Ball, Springfield '91, who came to the YMCA as physical director in 1891 and by 1892 had the game well organized. McGill University interfaculty trophy games began in 1894 under R. T. McKenzie. By 1900 the game had advanced in importance so that the trophy was transferred to interclass competition and in 1901 the McGill Athletic Association authorized an official representative team for competition. The first intercollegiate match was in 1904 with Queens University and during the 1904–5 season other games were played with Rochester University and the University of Vermont as well as with local teams. The Canadian Intercollegiate Basketball Union was formed during the 1908–09 season.

The provincial organizations met in 1922 and organized the Canadian Amateur Basketball Association, appointing C. E. Race, Registrar of the University of Alberts, as its first president.

Girls' basketball at McGill dates from 1902 when men's rules were used, but women's rules were substituted in 1906 and in 1908 2 girls' teams played outside games, using 7 players on a side. Basketball for women was given its greatest impulse by the success of the team coached by Percy Page, Principal of the Commercial High School of Edmonton, Alberta. He organized the "Edmonton Grads," hailed as the greatest women's team of all time. They took the Alberta title in 1915, the Dominion championship in 1922, and, in the following year, the International. In 1924 they attended the Olympic Games, played exhibition matches and while in Europe defeated 15 teams to win the World's Championship, a title they never lost. They disbanded shortly after the outbreak of World War II.

CURLING.

Curling may not have originated in Scotland but has been played there for hundreds of years, and during the last century has been the outstanding winter sport, and is regarded by many as the National Sport of that country. It is, on ice, the counterpart of Bowling on the Green.

The first successful club in Canada was in Montreal where the Grand Caledonian Curling Club, later known as the Royal Caledonian Curling Club was formed (1807). It is still regarded as the parent club, and is credited with being the oldest organization for outdoor sport in America. Kingston and Quebec followed in 1820 and 1821. Details of the game at the Drumcragie Curling Club of Fergus, Ont., 1834, state that ". . . wooden blocks of maple, fitted with iron handles, were used as late as 1850; and it is reported that wooden blocks into which bent railroad spikes were driven, were sometimes used in the bush by engineers and others who have a taste for Curling. . . ."

The Glamborough Club at Glamborough, Ont., and the Thistle Club of Toronto were soon added and interclub matches began in 1838 between Montreal and Quebec. Several of these clubs affiliated with the Royal Caledonian Curling Club of Scotland, but later the Canadian Branch of the Royal Caledonian Clubs, authorized (1852), had by 1874 enrolled 33 clubs. The Montreal Amateur Athletic Association in 1893 donated a trophy to be competed for annually among the various city clubs. This stimulated interest, so in 1897 women were admitted to membership and competed. The first real "bonspiels" began in 1902 when 6 teams representing the Royal Caledonian Curling Club of Scotland toured Canada and the United States. It was not until 1929 that artificial ice equipment was installed at the Montreal Club.

Curling has a technical language all its own. Each player on the 4-man team uses 2 stones, team representatives alternating and endeavoring to make the play called for by the "skip." Good plays are greeted with cheers, hence the "Roarin' Game." In the last twenty-five years the game has grown increasingly popular.

SNOWSHOEING.

It seems to be generally believed that the Canadian Indians used snowshoes prior to the discovery of America by Europeans. They were thus aided in overcoming the obstacles to travel in the deep, dry, powdery snow of the long winters.

Catlin (pp. 291-292) found that, buoyed up by the aid of webs, the Indians easily overtook the short-legged and heavy buffalo which often sank to the middle of their sides. Thus the Indians secured meat and robes at their prime. What was originally an indigenous, utilitarian activity has become also a popular sport.

The Esquimaux had a triangular shaped type while the Indians used their oval (bear paw) shapes for the woods and longer, narrower models for the open country. As was true of mocassins, each Indian tribe had its peculiar sizes and shapes of snowshoes.

The sport-loving French of Quebec province early discovered in the snowshoe a source of pleasure and sport. A group of a dozen enthusiasts meeting in "L. Tetu Restaurant" so enjoyed their evening of eats, drinks, song and fellowship that they decided to organize the Montreal Snowshoe Club (1840). This Club fostered competition, chiefly with the Indians and was the chief factor in popularizing the sport. By 1944 there were in Quebec alone 75 clubs with a total membership of 25,000.

This parent club influenced the formation of many others, *e. g.*, St. George (1857), Aurora (1858), and introduced this sport into the Victoria Rifles Club. It adopted the now famous blue toque headgear and since then the club has been known as the "Old Toque Bleue." It assisted in the first torchlight tramp over the mountain (1873) in honor of His Excellency, the Earl of Dufferin, Governor-General of Canada. In 1879, 50 members of the "Old Toque Bleue" in their gaily-colored blanket uniforms erected an arch of ice in honor of Their Highnesses, the Princess Louise and the Marquis of Lorne.

Many women are enthusiastic members in the various clubs and share even in competition, but especially in the "tramps" which frequently cover 5 miles or more in an evening and bring the members back with a healthy glow and an appetite calculated to do justice to the refreshments awaiting them.

Initiation into a Snowshoe Club usually includes "The Toss," in which the novice lies in a gay blanket, held on the sides and ends by a dozen fellow members who toss the victim high in the air, catch him (her) and repeat, continuing with shouts and laughter until all are satisfied.

SKIING.

Skiing was probably introduced into Canada from Northern Europe, but the exact date is not known although there is mention of skiis at an ice carnival in Canada in 1759 (Menke, p. 551). The *Canadian Illustrated News*, February 8, 1879, under the caption "From Montreal to Quebec on Norwegian Snow Shoes" reports: "Mr. Birch, a Norwegian gentleman of Montreal, has a pair of patent Norwegian snowshoes on which he has taken a trip to Quebec city, starting on Friday last. The snowshoes are composed entirely of wood, are about 9 feet long, 6 inches broad and have a foot board and toe strap. He walks with the aid of a pole, and crossed ice not strong enough to bear the weight of a good sized dog, so buoyant are these shoes in their action."

The first significant organization was that of the Montreal Ski Club in 1904, from which time this club exercised a strong influence over skiing over the entire country. Its ski jump constructed immediately established the record jump of 49 feet. Techniques at this period were quite elementary. In 1907 one writer states: "When we wanted to stop we just sat down. When we finally learned to

Telemark to the left and a sort of a Christie to the right we were pretty well pleased with ourselves. No ski poles were used at this stage."

Ottawa, stimulated by an exhibition by some Swedes, organized its club in 1910, and British Columbia's Phoenix Club was the first to enroll women in Western Canada. Revelstoke introduced the cross country run for women in 1914. Dartmouth University met McGill in 1914, with McGill winning the jump—62 feet, and Dartmouth taking the relay.

World War I caused a slump in Canadian skiing, but Mr. H. P. Douglas took over the presidency of the Montreal Ski Club with its 30 discouraged members and by the end of 1919 built the membership up to 300, including 50 ladies. The Canadian Amateur Ski Association emerged in 1920 and by 1944 had more than 400 clubs enrolled. In 1932, the year of the Olympic winter games at Lake Placid, a combined Oxford-Cambridge team visited Canada, and in the following season a McGill-Redbird team returned the compliment. This friendly exchange resulted not only in fine fellowship and renewed enthusiasm but also in new ideas in ski techniques.

Skiing, as a winter sport, continues to increase in popularity as competition reaches higher planes and events or rules are modified on the basis of experience. The most spectacular event is the jump which has improved from 62 feet in 1910 to more than 200 feet. The jump is scored on a point system which includes not only *distance* but also *courage, control* (while racing down, in flight, landing and slowing to the finish), and *form*. The jump therefore includes some of the fundamental principles of gymnastics—probably more than does any other so-called athletic event.

The important annual intercollegiate meet is that usually held at Dartmouth where the Host Club and McGill are always in close competition.

THE MONTREAL ICE PALACES.

During the winters of 1883, '84, '85, '87, and '89 Montreal erected on Dominion Square its famous Ice Palaces which grew in size and splendor each year. Somewhat typical was that of 1885, constructed of ice blocks 40 inches by 20 inches, was 190 feet long, 120 feet wide and 100 feet high. They were all lighted by electricity, the reflections from the walls giving the interior a veritable fairyland impression. In 1887 and 1889 tubular chimes were installed as an additional attraction to the thousands of visitors who flocked to this wonderland.

At night the members of the snowshoe clubs would divide into two groups, one to defend the "Fort" or ice palace and the other to attack it. The offensive group would meet on Mount Royal.

tramp through the city on snowshoes, carrying torches and attack the "Fort." A mock battle would ensue, giving a most impressive and colorful spectacle.

Reasons for the discontinuance of these palaces are given as the excessive expense and the occupation of their site by permanent structures. But there is a suspicion that this form of advertising was not wholly beneficial since Montreal began to be known as the "Ice-Bound City." The present Curator of the Chateau de Ramsay admits this and adds that after the rush of immigration began about 1885, those arriving "would often come in summer, wearing winter clothing and carrying snowshoes."

ICE HOCKEY.

The name "hockey" seems to be derived from the old French term "hoquet" (a shepherd's crook) referring to the hooked staff with which the game is played. This suggests that in France the game was played before modern times. Greek plaques show players using a curved stick very similar to that used in field hockey.

But, according to Menke (p. 367 ff): "The game of hockey on ice is of most modern invention. It originated in the enlightened and neighboring country of Canada."

Yet no one knows positively in what city, or what province, the game first was played, although all the evidence now seems to point to Halifax; no one knows the year, or the approximate year, none knows who pioneered it, what inspired it, or who were the first players.

Many think that hockey on ice, as known today, is a development from an old game somewhat common in parts of Europe and known in Ireland as "Hurley," in Scotland as "Shinty" or "Shinney," in Wales as "Bandy" and in England as "Field Hockey."

The earliest mention found of the game in Canada is in the *Montreal Gazette* (December 22, 1836), which states that hockey was being played in Halifax.

There is evidence that, in 1875, Mr. J. G. A. Creighton, a student at McGill University, but a native of Halifax, suggested that hockey sticks be purchased from his home city of Halifax. Report has it that this was done but there is little mention of the game during the next few years.

R. Tait McKenzie in his article, "Hockey in Eastern Canada" (*Dominion Illustrated Monthly*) claims that "Hockey as at present played has been evolved from an old Scottish game 'Shinty.' It was first played in Canada at Montreal by a club of McGill College students, one of whose number had played it in Glasgow. It was played then on an open-air rink on the St. Lawrence River, but for some years little progress was made."

Evidently there was sufficient interest at Montreal where according to *Americana* (Vol. **14**, p. 306) "Development of the game in North America is due mainly to the efforts of McGill University" to widen the sphere of the sport. The Winter Carnivals at Montreal, beginning in 1884, in the old Victoria Skating Rink (built in 1862) gave hockey its first great impetus. In this year the Amateur Hockey Association of Canada was organized. The many good features of the game attracted favorable attention and Clubs flourished in most of the larger cities or towns, *e. g.*, Kingston, Toronto, Hamilton, London, Sherbrooke, Ottawa, Quebec and Montreal. In the latter city there soon were five first-class Clubs with numerous junior teams to serve as feeders for the seniors.

The A.H.A.C. adopted rules of play, organized each team into "positions" of offense and defense and reduced the number of players to 7. This limited number of players was necessitated by reduced area of play on indoor rinks. Formerly, in the days of shinney as many as 200 players per team had been used, *e. g.*, at Kingston.

With increase of popularity of hockey, promoters saw in it a source of financial profit, and even cities began to use it as a means of advertising. Expert players were "induced" to group themselves in locations profitable to themselves. Thus arose the problems of professionalism. The Canadian Hockey Union, organized in 1886, sought to prohibit this as well as to protect itself against unsportsmanlike players, adopted stringent regulations.

Its Article XIII reads: "No clubs shall admit, or retain a person, a member thereof who has been censured or punished by this Association for foul play, or other reprehensible conduct, or who shall henceforth be convicted under the laws of the country of a criminal charge, shall be entitled to continue as a member of Association, or be admitted to membership thereof, and no new Club shall be admitted to membership therein which has among its members anyone who has been convicted of such action. No Club in this Association shall play a match with any such Club, under penalty of forfeiture of membership of such Association."

While there may be indefiniteness regarding the origin of hockey in Canada, there is certainty as to its remarkable growth. For this there are several reasons. Inherent in the game itself is the speedy, spectacular action which involves not only unusual endurance but also a degree of skill probably not surpassed in any sport. In addition to the control of a moving object by a stick held in the hand is the complication of a rapidly-moving player on the smooth, slippery ice. To be efficient in "combination" or "team play," the individual must first be a good skater and stick handler.

To supplement the approximately four months possible **for play** on outdoor ice, covered skating rinks sprang up in many sites and towns all over the Dominion. These had the great advantage of protection from inclement weather, afforded spectators a better view of the game from seats in galleries or elevated tiers of seats, and stabilized playing schedules. The introduction of artificial ice extended the playing season by months. Electric lighting made possible rink playing at night, thereby encouraging greater attendance. In fact, most of the important matches became night games. Ice hockey has, without doubt become Canada's national winter sport. When in the 1890's, professional ice hockey began to flourish in United States, many players were imported from Canada.

Lord Kilcoursie visited Canada and witnessed several hockey games, and when he learned that the dashing, daring lads played this game for nothing other than glory and honor, he communicated with his friend, Lord Stanley, who donated 10 pounds sterling for the purchase of a trophy cup. This Stanley cup, now tarnished and battered, remains as the most-prized professional hockey treasure in North America. The Allan Cup, donated by Sir Montagu Allan of Montreal in 1908, became the emblem of championship for amateur teams.

The National Hockey League, organized in 1917, composed of the Montreal Wanderers, Montreal Canadiens, Toronto Arenas and Ottawa Senators, became international in 1924–25 when Boston took a franchise followed by the New York Americans, later by the New York Rangers. These franchises in the United States did much to bring the professional game into prominence.

Credit for the origin of ice hockey in Canada has been a matter of perennial interest. So many claims and counter claims were made that research along this line were undertaken by the Department of Physical Education staff of McGill University. The Amateur Hockey Association of Canada finally accepted a request that an effort be made to settle the much disputed question. A committee was appointed in 1941 to investigate and report. This committee reported in 1942 favoring Kingston and its findings were accepted. While there is far from unanimous concurrence in this decision, the fact remains that Kingston has been selected as the site of the proposed Hockey Hall of Fame.

BIBLIOGRAPHY.

Farrell, A.: How to Play Ice Hockey. New York, Am. Sports Pub. Co., 1907, 71p. Spalding Ath. Lib., Group VI, No. 304.
Hodge, M. H.: The Technique of Ice Hockey. Grad. Thesis, Springfield College, 1918, 80p. (Typewritten).
McKenzie, R. Tait: Hockey in Eastern Canada. Dominion Illustrated Monthly.
Orlick, E. M.: McGill Contributions to the Origin of Ice Hockey. McGill News, Winter, 1943, pp. 14–7.
Whalen. M.; Winter Sports in Canadian Colleges. Outing 64: 407-15, Jan. 1915.

CANADIAN INTERCOLLEGIATE ATHLETIC UNION.

On May 27, 1906, the Canadian Intercollegiate Athletic Union was organized at Montreal by representatives of Queens University, University of Toronto and McGill University as active members. A constitution was accepted and the object of the Union agreed upon as: "The encouragement of systematic physical exercise and the supervision and control of all Canadian Intercollegiate Athletics."

The controlling body of the Union consisted of three Governors, elected annually, from each of the active members, at least one of the Governors from each of the active members must hold a seat on the faculty of his institution and be qualified to represent the teaching body of that University.

One of the most difficult problems of all such governing bodies is that of defining an amateur. The first attempt by this Union was one of those Old Testament type, legalistic delineations of what an amateur must NOT do. After some years of experience, and various amendments, this Union had the courage, November 15, 1945, to adopt the following:

> "An amateur is one who engages in sport solely for the pleasure and the physical, mental and social benefits he derives therefrom, who receives no material remuneration, either directly or indirectly, and to whom sport is nothing more than an avocation."

In elaboration of the above SPIRIT of amateurism is the emphasis that it stands for a high sense of honor, fair play and courtesy on the part of participants, hosts, guests, officials and spectators. It stoops to no petty technicalities to twist or avoid the rules or to take an unfair advantage of opponents.

The Board expressed itself as strongly opposed to the granting of "athletic scholarships," proselytising, scouting and subsidization in any form, and urges all colleges and universities to continue directing their activities toward the spirit and ideals of amateurism and sportsmanship with a sincerity of purpose in promoting interest and participation by as many students as possible in the joy of effort and love of the game for the game's sake.

Eligibility for intercollegiate competition, either as an individual or as a member of a team, is issued to students having: (*a*) amateur rating; (*b*) registration as a "bona fide" student, regularly in attendance on the regular lectures of the institution he represents; and (*c*) written on his final sessional examinations in his preceding year of attendance.

To coördinate national administration it was voted, May 27,

1906, that this Union enter into relations with the Canadian Amateur Athletic Union, similar to those between the Intercollegiate American Association of Amateur Athletes and the Amateur Athletic Union of United States. This alliance was consummated in 1907 and harmonious coöperation has contributed much to national promotion and control.

THE STRATHCONA TRUST.

Lord Strathcona, Sir Donald A. Smith, a Canadian statesman and High Commissioner for Canada, became much interested in a proposal for physical and military training in the schools of the nation. So, to supplement the work of the Dominion and Provincial Governments, he donated by 1910 $500,000 to be placed in Trust for this purpose. The returns from this Strathcona Fund, invested in government securities at a guaranteed interest of 4 per cent became available to such provinces as entered into the agreement provided, and its distribution was on the basis of school attendance in the respective provinces participating.

The administration of the Fund was placed in an Executive Council composed as follows: The minister of Militia and Defence, the members of the Militia Council, the officers commanding the Military Districts and representatives of each province named by the respective Ministers of Education. Each province was entitled to its Local Committee composed of the District Officer Commanding, three military officers named by the Minister of Militia and Defence, three civilians named by the Provincial Minister of Education and the Deputy Minister or Superintendent of Education of the Province.

The aims or purposes may be stated as follows:
   1. The improvement of the physical and intellectual capabilities of the children while at school, by means of a proper system of physical training.
   2. The fostering of a spirit of patriotism in the boys, leading them to realize that the first duty of a free citizen is to be prepared to defend his country, to which end all boys should, so far as possible, be given an opportunity of acquaintance while at school with military drill and rifle shooting.

Participation by provinces was optional, but those taking advantage of the Trust's provisions agreed:

To incorporate physical training as an integral part of the curriculum in all public schools except those of the lower grades; to offer each teacher in such schools instruction in physical training, to issue certificates of qualification from the Educational Department of the Province and to encourage the formation of Cadet Corps among the older boys.

The Militia Department agreed with participating provinces:

To provide teachers of both sexes facilities for competent instruction in physical training, to instruct teachers in military drill to qualify them as officers of Cadet Corps, and to provide necessary equipment and supplies.

By way of stimulus, awards such as medals, cups, shields, etc., were provided.

From the stated Aims and the Administrative Organization it would appear that the objectives of the Trust were primarily military. This is further evidenced by details contained in the Constitution (p. 10, Sec. 12), *viz.:* "The system of physical training adopted should be such as to lead on naturally, without change, to the system of drill in force for the Canadian Militia." The issuance of Grade B certificates to teachers who have qualified on the basis of a brief (45 clock hours) course usually taken at some Normal School might easily be misinterpreted as qualifying the holder as an "expert" in the field. There is another significant fact in the claim in the Constitution (p. 9, Sec. 7). "No school of higher grade than the third class need be without a teacher competent to give the prescribed drill effectively in all departments of the school."

Formalized drills can scarcely be regarded as the best form of physical activity for children. Little provision is made for PLAY.

ARMY SPORTS.

For years the Canadian Army has been experimenting with a plan of mass sports in the hope of developing the play spirit as well as efficient skills in the various games practiced. Major Beaumont, Army Sports Officer, Division of National Defense, reports that the program has failed to produce either of the above objectives, since many soldiers hesitate to enter a game or sport in which they lack skill, realizing that to join in a game with others having established skills, spoils the game. Who wants to play with a "Dub?"

In order ro correct this situation, Major Beaumont proposes for 1946 the introduction in the regular physical and recreation training period of a "Posture and Play" program, the purpose of which is similar to that of English training, *viz.*, giving ALL an opportunity to develop some skill and to really enjoy the sport itself. By this plan the sports coaches are required to give individual instruction as well as team coaching in the games and sports popular in Canada.

Each fifty-minute period begins with a few minutes of general warming up activities, followed by chalk talks or lantern slides on the fundamentals of the specific game for the day. The squad is then divided into small groups in which these fundamentals are explained and practiced; then follows an explanation of the rules of that particular sport, short group scrimmages are held and the period ends with emphasis on posture.

After 12 of these periods on any given sport, each soldier is given an examination on rules and fundamentals of that sport. Passing this, each may enter voluntarily, on off-duty hours, a series of 6 test games with players of approximately equal skills in the endeavor to qualify for the Army Sports Crest, awarded in each sport and worn on the sports clothes. Sports selected are those popular in the season in which the training is offered.

THE CANADIAN PHYSICAL EDUCATION ASSOCIATION.

At the suggestion of Dr. A. S. Lamb, Director of Physical Education at McGill University, Alma Mater of Dr. James Naismith and Dr. R. Tait McKenzie, the organization of the Canadian Physical Education Association by the Quebec Association was begun in 1931 and completed in 1933. Dr. Lamb served as president until 1938, Miss Florence A. Somers 1939–41, J. G. Lang 1942–43, and Mr. R. Jarman, 1944–.

Mr. Jarman shortly after his appointment ascribed much of the success of the national association to "Dr. Lamb, the Father of Physical Education in Canada, whose profound wisdom, scholarly advice, expert guidance and genial friendliness will never be forgotten." For his outstanding contributions, Dr. Lamb was voted, in 1933, the Honor Award of the American Association for Health, Physical Education and Recreation. Miss Somers was given similar recognition in 1940.

Aims.

According to the constitution, the aims of the Canadian Physical Education Association are:

To stimulate universal, intelligent and active interest in Health and Physical Education.

To acquire and disseminate knowledge concerning same.

To promote interest and strive for the establishment of educative programs under the direction of adequately trained teachers.

To set the standards of the profession.

To coöperate with kindred interests and organizations in the furtherance of these aims.

Membership, Organization, Administration.

Active, voting membership is open to directors and teachers who are graduates of accredited professional schools, teachers and administrators in educational institutions, directors and teachers in playgrounds and recreation associations and those trained in related fields such as Medicine, Social Agencies, Education, Nursing, etc. By 1946 the membership numbered 320.

The strength of the Association lies in its local and branch organizations, scattered over the vast area of the Dominion. In general, the various provinces have their local associations and branches within districts or larger cities.

The Legislative Council which administers the affairs of the Association consists of the officers of the Association, the branch presidents, 1 to 3 members elected from each province on basis of enrolled members and "Members at Large" appointed at the discretion of the President. This last group permits the utilization of persons of prominence whose experience, influence and counsel would contribute to the effectiveness of the National Association.

Resolutions and Research.

During the thirteen years of its history, the Association has adopted many significant resolutions. Among them are: That a National Fitness Program be instituted by Provincial and Federal Governments; that Provincial Governments issue certificates to graduates of recognized schools of Physical Education; that each Province create scholarships in Physical Education for deserving persons; that all colleges and universities require a thorough medical examination of entering students and require a program of Physical Education for at least the first two years of undergraduate life; that Provincial Departments of Physical Education replace the instructors supplied to the Normal Schools by the National Department of Defense by better qualified instructors.

Committee projects sponsored officially by the National Association include: investigation of the special problems of girls and women; preparation of a Badminton Guide on women's athletics; survey of Physical Education in Canada; investigation of forming a Canadian Life Saving Association; at the request of the National Council on Physical Fitness, to investigate, compile and promote a scientific program of Tests and Measurements; to prepare National Standards for teaching and testing swimming and life saving, also to investigate the problem of teacher and leadership training and to make recommendation for its solution.

The C.P.E.A., now an affiliate of the American Association for Health, Physical Education and Recreation, has had a steady, wholesome growth and has every expectation of continued efficiency.

THE NATIONAL PHYSICAL FITNESS ACT.

Being satisfied that the greatest asset of any country is the health of its citizens, the Dominion Government on October 1, 1943, proclaimed the above act. Its stated objectives were:

To assist in the extension of physical education in all educational and other establishments; to encourage, develop and correlate all activities relating to physical development of the people through sports, athletics and other similar pursuits; to train teachers, lecturers and instructors in the principles of physical education and physical fitness; to organize activities designed to promote physical fitness and provide facilities therefor; and to coöperate with organizations such as are engaged in development of physical fitness in the amelioration of physical defects through physical exercise.

To administer the provisions of the above act a National Council on Physical Fitness was appointed February 15, 1944, consisting of a director and 9 other persons, each of whom will represent one of the Provinces of Canada participating in the National Physical Fitness Plan. This Council with Major Ian Eisenhardt appointed its Director (the only paid member) met May 23, 1944, organized committees and adopted resolutions of which the following are examples:

That the National Physical Fitness Act be understood to apply to all Canadian citizens, boys and girls, men and women, old and young, crippled children and disabled veterans; that the Council coöperate with and assist all agencies interested in physical education, recreation, cultural activities (art, music and drama) and sports; that the Council endorse the Report of the British Medical Association which says: "The aim of physical education is to obtain and maintain the best possible development and functioning of the body, and thereby aid the development of mental capacity and character. The mind and body are so essentially ONE that the divorce between them in what is commonly called education appears as unscientific as it is pronounced. However brilliant the intellect, a neglected body hinders the attainment of the highest capacity possible to an individual and, conversely, the maintenance of the best possible functioning of the body must react as a beneficial mental stimulus.

The Council further resolved that special opportunities for recreation be provided for rural areas and industrial plants, that every university should conduct a required Physical Fitness program for every student and that a degree course be established in physical education, that Youth Hostels, hiking and camping be stimulated; that the establishment of a College of Physical Education be considered.

Available to the National Council to operate its program is a Government appropriation of $225,000 to be divided among the provinces, also a fund of $25,000 for expenses of the Council.

TEACHER TRAINING.

The Provincial Normal Schools have been the source of professional training in physical education for teachers in the public schools of the Dominion. Since 1910 these Normal Schools, in the provinces accepting the conditions of the Strathcona Trust, have been supplied with military men with brief special training in physical training. As stated above, the emphasis was upon such activities as related primarily to preparation for Cadet Corps.

University of Toronto, McGill University and the Margaret Eaton School for Girls have for years given independent professional training courses in this field. In 1945, Toronto and McGill agreed upon a four-year curriculum majoring in this field and leading to the baccalaureate degree. It is confidently expected that these University Training Centers will become even more significant as the source of professsional directors and teachers in educational institutions and social agencies.

CADET CORPS.

As early as the Civil War in the United States, the Cadet Corps was organized in many of Canada's high schools with a view of instilling into the boys the claimed benefits of military training, and of providing a citizenry already partially trained for national defense.

Following World War I special emphasis was given to such training, but when, in 1933, the subsidy for Cadet instruction was discontinued, the Cadet Corps was disbanded. The war situation in 1941 called for the reorganization of the Army Cadet Corps, on a voluntary basis, and in 1942, became compulsory. In the fall of 1942 there was a general transfer from the Army Cadet Cadets to the Air Force Cadets. For the next three years certain of the usual high school subjects were dropped to permit the teaching of such courses as Meteorology, Advanced Mathematics, Air Force Navigation, Signalling and Hygiene. During 1943–45 Air Cadets attended summer camps, located on some active service station. For 1945–46 military courses, except Drill and First Aid, were dropped.

BIBLIOGRAPHY.

Beers, W. G.: Lacrosse. Montreal, Dawson Bros., 1867.
———— Lacrosse—National Game of Canada. Montreal, Dawson Bros., 1879, p. 276.
Catlin, G. C.: Report Smithsonian Institution. Washington, Government Printing Office, 1886, p. 939.
Menke, F. G.: Encyclopedia of Sports. New York, A. S. Barnes & Co., 1944, p. 628. (2d edition.)
Miscellaneous Clippings from Montreal and Other Newspapers, University of Toronto, McGill University and Government Publications.

CHAPTER XXXII.

GREAT BRITAIN.*

FOLLOWING the 1936 Olympic Games, with results rather disappointing to Great Britain, there arose a strong insistence that the Government supplement voluntary organizations "to shoulder the task of educating and coaching the people towards greater sports, games and general physical fitness." This demand expressed itself in various ways.

Suggestions were made by "World Sports," official organ of the British Olympic Committee, Woman's A. A. A. and Amateur Fencing Association. "That to every household there be delivered a Government brochure full of useful, simple health and diet rules, and physical exercises, written entertainingly by people who know their subject."

Publicity was given to the claim of Professor Lelean, University of Edinburgh, that: "If diet and exercise were remedied, the national physique would be visibly improved in two years, and remedied in two generations."

Impressed by the further statement of Professor Lelean, "that the physical unfitness is costing Great Britain the stupendous sum of £220,000,000 per year," the Government, realizing that "there shall be a body to train which is capable of profiting by the course of training prepared for it," responded with co-operation and stimulation.

This included a realization that nutrition and exercise combined to constitute a "National Fitness" program so there was voted the following procedure: Funds appropriated, leadership trained, publications issued, publicity promoted, and organizations encouraged.

The National Health Culture Association, a voluntary organization, stated its aims: "To progress only by willing coöperation of members, centralized at headquarters, which advises only, and decentralized by districts and localities, each group retaining control over its own activities, and receiving the fullest sympathy and co-operation from headquarters."

* See also Chapter XIX, p. 219.

Among its guiding principles were, that requiring violent physical exercise of every one, whose sedentary lives have become a habit, is unwise and often dangerous, and that the needs of each section of the community must be given careful study and the right dosage for each determined.

Personal Health Associations were designed to stimulate an active health consciousness in individuals by propagating knowledge of the Public Health Services and health information generally by lectures, film displays, keep fit demonstrations, etc. Gradually it became evident that a central body was essential to guide the work of the local associations, so the "National Federation of Personal Health Associations" was formed and was instrumental in developing many new branches all over the country.

In September 1937, the School of Athletics, Games and Physical Education was opened at Loughborough College, offering to young men of the Public School group an entirely new type of a career. The 1-year course for graduates and certified teachers qualified them as teachers of physical training in Secondary and Senior schools, while the 3-year course, in addition to technical subjects, contained scholastic studies so that those receiving its diploma were qualified to teach also academic subjects and become Games Masters and leaders of clubs for all forms of social and recreative activities.

"The Central Council of Recreative Physical Training," organized 1935–36, has as its avowed purpose the encouragement and development of ALL physical activities, both outdoors and in, for ALL sections of the country. It functions through active coöperation and coördination, without interference with the individual character of any of its more than 100 constituent organizations. More than 300 industrial concerns have been aided in conducting their physical recreation programs, conspicuous among which is the Messrs. Cadbury's of Bournville. To prepare qualified teachers for this specific work, the Council in 1936–37 arranged short courses for 40 persons, this number was trebled in 1937–38 and a continuous supply of leaders has been provided.

In its fourth annual report, the Central Council outlines the efforts of its 115 affiliated organizations in training recreation leaders for adolescents and adults as follows:

	1936	1937	1938	1939
Training courses	10	40	125	247
Lecture—Demonstrations	25	155	350	825
Visits to factories, stores, etc.	10	50	300	533
Talks and lectures	15	52	200	532
Games leadership schemes	..	...	3	25

"The National Fitness Council for England and Wales" is, in a sense, the supreme official organization. It represents the Government, especially in the expenditure of appropriated funds, and shares in the general promotion of the fitness movement. One reason why this Council emphasizes the importance of applying funds for capital equipment and improvement is stated by its press officer, G. Linton-Harris (World Sports, March, 1939), thus:

"The National Fitness Council for England and Wales is faced with the problem of putting over an ideal and arousing enthusiasm in the public. It must 'sell' to the public the idea of physical fitness and the joys and happiness that come with it. . . . . . . In this country we tell our boys and girls, men and women, that the last thing the National Fitness Council wants to do is to prevent them from going to movies or the theatre or to keep them from watching a football match if they feel so inclined. What the Council does say is "Watching is not enough—take an active part." To conclude, it is not yet time to embark upon an intensive scheme of propaganda or publicity. It would be a mistake to work up a tremendous enthusiasm for national fitness until the Council is quite sure that facilities are available for use by those stimulated by the drive."

"The Physical Training and Recreation Act" of 1937, provided for grants-in-aid of capital expenditures for fitness facilities. £2,000,000, limited to the statutory period up to March 31, 1940, and under the supervision of the National Fitness Council. During 1938, 15 organizers were appointed by voluntary organizations with Grant-Aid from the National Fitness Council. Encouragement was also extended to the preparation of teachers. In 1938, from the seven training colleges of the country, were graduated, with three years special study, more than 200 selected women and about 100 men.

The Sports Board of the "Royal Air Force" was set up at the Air Ministry to assist, by grants and otherwise, the playing of games, and generally to raise the standard of sport throughout the service. To accomplish this it was decided to exclude rigorously any taint of professionalism, and to provide facilities for universal participation by officers and men alike. Preference is naturally given to team games as fostering the esprit-de-corps.

All questions of policy are decided by the Sports Board, while the detailed execution of the policy is in the hands of the committees of the various Sports Associations and Unions within the R. A. F. Each officer and airman subscribes a small sum to a fund which is used for the purchase of gear, travelling expenses of away matches, entertaining teams at home, etc. Grants are made to units by the Sports Board for general assistance and improvement of recreation facilities and to R. A. F. Sports Associations where these bodies are not self-supporting; they are also made for improving facilities where the Army, Navy and Air Force are jointly interested. The idea behind the whole organization of sport in the R. A. F. is that the men should never be forced to play games and that sports for every type of physique and temperament should be provided. Every station has its own sports grounds.

An idea of the underlying philosophy of the British plan may be gathered from a statement by G. V. Sibley, Director of Physical Education, Loughborough College. (World Sports, July, 1939.)

"Physical education in England has been built up, in the main, on Swedish gymnastics, except that they have been greatly modified to suit English conditions, and games and athletic exercises are included to meet the temperament of the Englishman.

"Physical education today is a very wide subject and a student of physical education must therefore possess some knowledge of all branches of his work, acquire a catholic outlook on his subject, and study some aspects of his subject to a very high degree. Gymnastics usually take this premier place, although we are making a strong effort to popularize athletics, especially field events, and we are therefore introducing sports-gymnastics into the present day scheme. These exercises, which make the basis of athletic movements, are taught and practiced in a gym lesson—hurdling can be improved by such exercises as sitting on the floor with one leg straight out in front, etc. Similar leading up practices are also included in the teaching of swimming. This is the secret of modern physical education, *viz.*, "leading up practices." Almost every physical training lesson today in a boys school contains some small game which has as its aim the development of tactics, control of a ball, or some other phase of training which produces all-round skill in EVERY boy. There is a much higher standard in boys' games today than there was twenty or thirty years ago.

"This question of leading up exercises is closely linked with style, and this needs a good deal of thought in all our work, for without style one seldom sees a promising young man develop into a first class athlete. People do not realize that by splitting up the movement into its component parts and by practice of those part-strokes we can improve our style."

Sir Henry Pelham, chairman of the National Fitness Grants Committee explains that the purpose of the Government is to enable each individual to attain better physical health, fuller enjoyment of life and added efficiency in work and play.

His expectation is that, in the Universities particularly, grants for a portion only of capital expenditures will enable students to profit from improved facilities and scientific leadership. The Government has no intention of imposing a scheme from the outside, since each institution will determine for itself the amount and form of activities adopted. He does advocate full time lectures on physical education, physical instructors of high academic standing and facilities for medical examinations, the latter to help students themselves to know their physical capacities and weaknesses.

CHAPTER XXXIII.

SOUTH AFRICA*

FIFTY years ago almost the entire South African population consisted of farmers, living on large estates, leading a simple, healthy life and having adequate physical exercise from hunting, walking or horseback riding in supervision of negro laborers. The climate was hot, with the Northern area tropical. During the last quarter of the nineteenth century, the discovery and exploitation of gold in the Transvaal produced an industrial revolution. Foreign capital was invested, immigration began on a large scale, cities sprang up and thousands transferred from the pleasant country life to work in the cities or labor in the mines. The South African war, 1899–1901, accelerated this change.

Today, South Africa is a modern and technically developed country with a cosmopolitan population, great industrial centers, harbors and mines. Thus, has been created the problem of a reorganization of its educational system.

The public had always been interested in games and sports. Some of the schools in the larger cities had introduced gymnastics; and voluntary organizations, such as the South African Gymnastic Union, had promoted swimming, boxing, wrestling and other sports. But it was not until 1936 that, under pressure from both Afrikaans and English, the University of Stellennosch organized the first faculty of Physical Education, with Dr. Ernst Jokl in charge of the new Department. Despite the fact that Stellenbosch, the intellectual center of Afrikaan peoples, was also the seat of the highly orthodox Dutch Reformed Church, the University had the courage to promote this phase of education. The enthusiastic and friendly attitude of the students aided in overcoming the conservatism of the Church so that today the University is the acknowledged center of Physical Education for the Afrikaan speaking population.

Impressed by the success of the above venture, the Government became interested in a National Scheme of Physical Education, and,

* Appreciation is hereby expressed to Dr. Ernst Jokl, Head of the Department of Physical Education, Witwatersrand Technical College, Johannesburg, whose correspondence and publications have been the source of information upon which this article is based.

(423)

in April 1937, the Hon. J. H. Hofmeyer, then minister of education, asked the President of the South African Olympic and Empire Games Association, the late Mr. A. V. Lindberg, to have prepared for the cabinet's consideration, a memorandum on Physical Education. Dr. Jokl was assigned to this task and presented his report to Mr. Hofmeyer, August 13, 1937.

Fig. 104.—Mass instruction in swimming.

On the basis of this report the Government appointed a National Advisory Council on Physical Education, consisting mainly of high administrative officials, under the chairmanship of Professor M. C. Botha, the Secretary for Education. An annual appropriation of £50,000 was voted in support of this new emphasis in education. For the technical and scientific problems, the Government continued its policy of appointing experts to submit reports for its consideration.

TEACHER TRAINING.

One of the imperative needs immediately recognized was that of technical training of teachers for the English speaking population. Approval was given of a Department of Physical Education at the Witwatersrand Technical College, Johannesburg, the largest educational institution in the country. This was organized in 1938 under the Directorship of Dr. Jokl, who, with the hearty coöperation of the Director of the college, Professor John Orr, the "Grand Old

Man" in technical education, was able in 1941 to report an unexpectedly large registration of 3500 students with a strong teaching staff.

It was evident that in the thousands of smaller schools, especially in the country districts, it would be impracticable to employ a full time specialist in physical education. So the National Advisory Council adopted the plan of offering, on a provincial or decentralized basis, a one year specialized course, open to already qualified teachers, who would then be prepared to supervise physical education in addition to teaching academic subjects.

Fig. 105—Dance gymnastics.

For teachers who found it impossible to devote an entire year to special training, the Technical College offered part time courses—six hours per week for one year, to which not only teachers but also the public were eligible. This proved so popular and satisfactory that the National Advisory Council voted to hold each year, beginning in 1940, a central vacation school of four weeks. These courses held at the Technical College, and open to group leaders, teachers and others interested, have attracted students from all parts of the Union and South West Africa. The National Council pays railway fares, and only a small teaching fee is charged registrants.

SYLLABUS.

The National Advisory Council spent much time and thought on the contents of a proposed syllabus. In this case the reports from experts showed various schools of thought. South Africa, fortunately, was free from cramping traditions to both teacher training and program content, in physical training. In addition to a critical review of their own program, representatives, largely graduates of training courses, were brought to the Technical College to explain the basic philosophy and to demonstrate the activities taught or coached in their respective countries. By this plan there was gained an intelligent understanding of the typical physical training in North America, England, Scotland, Denmark, Norway, Sweden, Palestine, Germany, the Netherlands, etc.

FIG. 106.—Indian boys in cross country running in Natal, South Africa. There are about 250,000 Indians living in South Africa.

Dr. Jokl, assisted by Government specialists, conducted much research to ascertain more concerning the effects of various activities on the different groups in his own country and to test out methods of publicity. Selection was made of exercises regarded as most suitable for the several ethnic groups and school grades.

From the standpoint of publicity, Dr. Jokl and his wife produced, in 1938, a sound film on physical training for younger children, in which symbolical activities were represented. This film was first shown at the 1938 meeting of the South African Association for the Advancement of Science. It was received favorably by both the public and the teaching profession and was bought by the Film Bureau of the Union Department of Education and later used in a special pictorial chapter in the textbook.

Perhaps the strongest impression by representatives of foreign countries was that of Niels Bukh who, with a group of his students, toured the country in 1939. Three members of his team remained in South Africa under appointment as specialists in important training centers.

FIG. 107.—Negro (Bantu) girls sprinting

As a result of all these investigations and checks, Dr. Jokl prepared a Syllabus of Physical Exercises for South African Schools, which was published in 1940 by J. L. van Schaik, Pretoria. This exceptionally fine text of 247, 7 x 9, pages sets a new standard for completeness of text and illustrations. It is printed in Afrikaan and English, usually in parallel columns or on facing pages, and every activity, from the simple mimetic plays of children to the complex, competitive events in gymnastics, track and field or swimming, is described in simple, non-technical language and illustrated by sketches, diagrams or photographs. This will prove of special value not only to teachers in South Africa, but also to every specialist in the field.

To aid Dr. Jokl in the administration of this nation-wide program, trained assistants have been appointed including several who have taken post-graduate courses in physical education overseas. From his own home trained men he selected Mr. Jan Botha to secure first hand information concerning the philosophy and practice of physical education in United States. Mr. Botha registered in the graduate

FIG. 108.—Grace hoop exercises.

FIG. 109.—Track team. of high school students of Healdtown College in the Negro (Bantu) Reservation of the Ciskeí (Cape Province, South Africa.)

(428)

department of Springfield College and received his M.Ed. (Master in Education) degree in 1940. Using the college as his headquarters, he for more than a year studied and visited to become personally familiar with the American situation.

CIVIL POPULATION.

The Government Council has also interested itself in keep-fit and recreational activities for the general public. This movement is centralized in the Witwatersrand Technical College of Johannesburg, which has established branches over the entire Trasvaal Gold Reef, and collaborates with the various Municipal Departments of Public Health. Courses are offered for the pre-school age group, apprentices, housewives, professional men and civil servants, all conducted by staff members from the Department of Physical Education of the College, and underwritten by Government funds. Special arrangements have been made with the Railway Employees' Organization as well as with certain gymnastic, jiu jitsu and other clubs. For women, classes in dancing and dramatic art have been introduced with most satisfactory results. The fee is five shillings per month per student; in special cases arrangements are being made to defray this fee by a bursary.

NEGROS POPULATION.

Special interest attaches to physical education for the 8,000,000 negroes of the country for whom three colleges are located in the Eastern Cape. In 1935, Dr. and Mrs. Jokl were asked to make preliminary surveys; and Mr. J. Omond, particularly interested in schools for negroes, has presented valuable memoranda on physical education among these people. Investigations among several native groups have thus far failed to support the reputed superior prowess or first class athletic performances of primitive peoples. However, European teachers are doing excellent work among these groups, and in several institutions are making determined efforts to introduce physical training as a part of the educational syllabus.

THE ARMY.

In 1936, Major A. Barlow of the British Army was asked to reorganize physical training at Roberts Heights, the seat of the Army Headquarters of the South African Defence Force, and has raised that work to a high level. Recently, Captain D. Craven, one of the greatest football players South Africa has produced, has been placed in charge of the physical training of the South African Military

College. He is collaborating with Major Barlow in giving particular attention to the physical training of military instructors.

A unique feature in the physical training work of the army is the special provision made for those recruits, ages 16 to 20, whose physical and general conditions reported by the Medical Officers of Health as "subnormal." Desirous of securing more definite information than the merely "satisfactory results" reported, it was decided to undertake a scientific study of the physiological effects upon this "Special Service Batallion." Supervision of this group was given to Major V. Goedvolk and Dr. Jokl, who have taken a group of 40 hitherto untrained boys, carefully examined, and to be tested at intervals during a six-months' training at Roberts Heights.

RESEARCH.

In 1938 the Union Secretary for Public Health, Dr. H. E. Cluver, asked Dr. Jokl to collaborate in a National Survey, the purpose of which was to collect facts on which further administrative measures for improvement of the nutritional status of the people could be based.

Attention was given not only to the racial differences but also to the economic background in relation to nutrition. All subjects were tested in performances demanding skill, strength and endurance. A provisional evaluation of results from tens of thousands of measurements indicates most interesting and, in many respects, hitherto unknown facts, among which may be mentioned the following:

1. In racial groups examined, the endurance power of girls showed a sharp decline after puberty, except in the Indian girls whose endurance remained constant.

2. Nutritional influences on physical efficiency are not as marked as had been expected.

3. The "critical period" is not so much early childhood as the phases of puberty and postpuberty.

4. Effects of economic environment on efficiency of Europeans do not show themselves with great clarity during the first decade of life.

5. Non-extreme degrees of vitamin C deficiency do not seem to have any influence upon the physical efficiency of Bantu adults.

Further critical assembling and statistical assessment of the data may be expected to manifest additional significant findings.

Research continues in kinesiological and related problems. The central nervous patterns of Negroes are being studied; athletic movements are being analyzed; pictorial presentation of exercises for teaching purposes are being investigated, all for the purpose of compiling a new type of illustrated textbook of physical exercises for children.

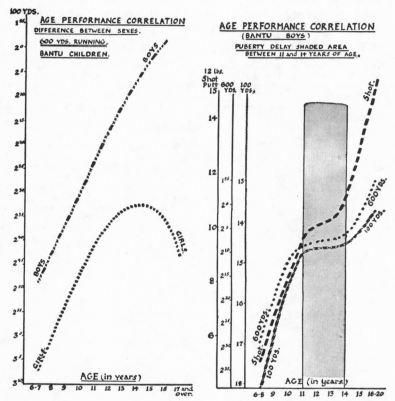

Fig. 110.—Difference between developmental trends of physical endurance of sexes.

Fig. 111.—Pubertal lag in growth of athletes efficiency.

GENERAL SMUTS' PHILOSOPHICAL WORK.

General Smuts, Prime Minister of South Africa, may be regarded as the leading representative of that small but distinguished company of Empire statesmen-philosophers who are contributing so much to the welfare of the country. His book, "Holism and Evolution" presents a critical review of a still popular conception of mind-body relationship. His position may be understood by the following brief quotation:

"The radical mistake made by science and popular opinion is the severance of an individual whole *viz.*, the human personality, into two interlacing entities or substances, the view of life and mind as separate entities of the body."

Stressing the need of a profound revision of existing opinions, he emphasizes the importance of the "holistic" approach to educational and sociological questions.

BIBLIOGRAPHY.

Jokl, Ernst: A Scientific Syllabus of Physical Exercises for Small Children. South African Jour. Sci., **25** (Dec., 1938), 407–411.
——————— On Indisposition After Running. Jour. Phys. Ed. and Sch. Hyg., **93** (July, 1939).
——————— The Medical Aspect of Boxing. South African Jour. Sci., **37** (May, 1940), 561–570.
——————— Congenital Absence of Pectoral Muscle in Athletes. Brit. Med. Jour. (June, 1939), 1156.
——————— Physical Exercises, Syllabus for South African Schools. Pretoria, J. L. van Schaik, 1940, 247 pages (Africans and English).
Jokl, Ernst and Suzmann, M. M.: Aortic Regurgitation and Mitral Stenosis in a Marathon Runner. Jour. Am. Med. Assn., **114** (February, 1940), 467.
Smuts, Right Hon. J. C.: Holism and Evolution, London, Macmillan, 1936.
Suzmann, M. M., and Jokl, Ernst: An Analysis of a Series of Electrocardiograms Taken After Prolonged Intense Muscular Activity. South African Jour. Med. Sci., **1** (June, 1936), 206.
Weiner, J. S.: An Experimental Study of Heat Collapse. Jour. Indus. Hyg. and Toxicol., **20** (June, 1938), 289.

CHAPTER XXXIV

SOUTH AMERICA.*

THE native Indians of South America, in common with other primitive peoples, naturally engaged in certain forms of physical activity incidental to their every day existence. Such exercises as running, jumping, swimming, fishing, canoeing, hunting and the like were practically universal.

Dancing was by far the most widely practised of all what some have termed "non-essential" activities. Many of their dances were symbolic, some commemorating historical or legendary happenings; others were prayers; and certain specially vigorous types were employed to stir up enthusiasm for coming events, e. g., the war dances.

The comparatively modern adoption and adaptation of "folk dances" seems to be a recognition of the values inherent in at least certain forms of these primitive types which have justified their right to be included in a comprehensive program of organized physical education.

The "Zapateo" was a sort of tap dance common among the natives of Andean Brazil. At least certain aspects of this appear to have been retained for Theodore Roosevelt[1] (pp. 200–1) records that in 1914 a village of The Parecis Indians held a tribal dance which he describes as follows:

"The men held a dance in the late afternoon. For this occasion most, but not all of them cast aside their civilized clothing, and appeared doubtless as they would all have appeared had none but themselves been present. They were absolutely naked except for a beaded string around the waist. Most of them were spotted and dashed with red paint, and on one leg wore anklets which rattled. A number carried pipes through which they blew a kind of a deep, stifled whistle in time to the dancing. One of them had his pipe leading into a huge gourd, which gave out a hollow, moaning boom. Many wore two red or green macaw feathers in their hair, and one

* Appreciation is hereby extended to Mr. Alfredo Wood of Buenos Aires and Miss Maria Lenk of the South America Women's Swimming team, whose correspondence has been the main source of information from which this section has been prepared.

[1] Roosevelt, Theodore: Through the Brazilian Wilderness. New York, Scribner's, 1914, 383 pages.

had a macaw feather struck transversely through the septum of
his nose. They circled round and round, chanting and stamping
their feet, while the anklet rattles clattered and the pipes droned.
They advanced to the wall of one of the houses, again and again,
chanting and bowing before it; I was told this was a demand for a
drink. They entered the house and danced in a ring around the
cooking fireplace in the middle of the earth floor; I was told that
they were reciting the deeds of mighty hunters and describing how
they brought in the game. They drank freely from gourds and
pannikins of a fermented drink made from madioc which were
brought out to them."

The same author (p. 235) reports that while his exploring party
was in Nhambiquara land some natives presented several dances
which again impressed his party by the rhythm and weird, haunting
melody of their chanting.

On another occasion the exploring party was entertained by a
group of four men, a boy and two young women[1] p. 219.

. . . "Two of the men and the boy were practically naked, and
the two young women were absolutely so. All of them danced in a
circle, without a touch of embarrassment or impropriety. The
two girls kept hold of each other's hands throughout, dancing among
the men as modestly as possible, and with the occasional interchange of a laugh or jest, in as good taste and temper as in any
dance in civilization. The dance consisted of slowly going round in a
circle, first one way then the other, rhythmically beating time with
the feet the music of the song they were chanting. The chants—
there were three of them—were measured and rather slowly uttered
melodies, varied with an occasional half-subdued shrill cry. The
women continually uttered a kind of long-drawn wailing or dron-
ing; . . . It was a strange and interesting sight to see these utterly
wild, friendly savages, circling in their slow dance, and chanting
their immemorial melodies, in the brilliant tropical moonlight. . . ."

Among contests between individuals, besides those in running,
jumping, swimming, etc., tossing the "caber" was much used. The
"caber" is a fairly straight pole 16 feet or longer. The contestant
stands, feet spread, toeing the line with the light end of the "caber"
cupped in his hands in front of the thighs and with the shaft in a
nearly vertical position balanced against the front of one shoulder.
Tossing consists of bending the knees, arms straight, bringing the
upper, heavier end of the "caber" forward of the perpendicular,
then vigorously straightening the knees and tossing by bringing the
arms upward and forward. The object is to send the "caber" as
far out as possible. Distance is measured from the line to the
nearest point where the pole struck or rests. This event has for
years been popular in Caledonian games.

It was the custom to select leaders or chiefs on the basis of their physical prowess and many traditions exist as to strength and skill or endurance of former chiefs. One of the outstanding stories was of "Tabaré" who was nimble footed and dextrous with bow and lance. Another concerned the famous Caupolican of the Araucanos who was chosen for the leadership of his nation because he held a "caber" on his shoulders for 100 hours and then, handling it as if it were a feather, and with titanic effort drove it into the earth.

Team or rather group games were fairly common, lacking, of course, the refinement of modern rules. Roosevelt[1] (pp. 192–3, 198) gives at length a description of such a game and calls it Headball. The ball used was of soft rubber about 8 inches in diameter and must not be touched by any part of the body other than the head. Even the "kick off" consists of placing the ball on the ground, a player runs forward, throws himself on the ground and butts the ball towards the opponents one of whom meets it with his head until eventually it rises in the air when the skill really comes into play and the modern "soccer" player would envy the dexterity displayed. This game was demonstrated in Rio de Janeiro, 1922, during the celebration of the Centennial festivities.

The Araucano Indians of Chile and part of Argentine played "chueca," somewhat similar to field hockey and after the importation of horses by the Spaniards, these same Indians continued the game on horse back giving a sport similar to the modern polo.

During the transition between the simple life of the natives and the beginnings of the modern movement for physical education, the Gauchos—a mixture of Indians and Spaniards—invented the game "El Pato" to be played on horseback. "The Pato" (the duck) was a ball, about the size of a basketball, made of leather and stuffed with straw. On the outside were three or four handles, stoutly attached to the ball to permit picking it from the ground without dismounting. There appears to have been no limit to the number of players. After the elder had divided the contestants into two groups or teams, and arranged them facing each other at a "prudent" distance, he would throw the "El Pato" up in the air between them. Whenever a player secured possession of it, others would swarm about or over him in the endeavor either to protect him or to steal the "duck." The entire pampas was within bounds and the struggle would continue until one side would surrender on account of exhaustion, of either horses or men.

Another sport of the Gauchos was "la Sortija." From a large frame, the shape of a football (soccer) goal, but with the crossbar high enough to permit a mounted man to pass under, a ring was hung, toward which competitors rode on their horses, one at a time, and tried to remove the ring by sticking a small rod through it.

Horse-racing too was a favorite with these people who practically lived on their horses. Crowds of men and women attended the racing "carreras cuadreras." These occasions also offered the opportunity for social intercourse for those who, during most of the year, lived isolated from each other.

Conquest by the Europeans discouraged the mores of the native peoples. The imposed submission, subjection to domination, initiation into habits of loafing and drinking took a heavy toll from the strong races, formerly owners of the land, and soon physical powers declined and their ideals of physical leadership disappeared.

The need for organized physical education was not fully realized until the growth of cities and their incipient industries made life less active, and sedentary work within doors began to show its effect upon the health of the people. The forms of physical education were influenced largely by the practices of the Europeans themselves, not so much as the result of definite plan but rather by the popularity they gave to certain types of recreation.

The British, while establishing their trade relations, could not forget their love of activity and recreation in the open, and soon made soccer popular outside their own group. Rowing, popular in Brazil during the latter part of the 11th century, was reëmphasized, and such other activities as swimming, sailing, golf, rugby, bicycling, the outdoor picnic idea, etc., began to be adopted.

Through the French immigrants came formal gymnastics, mainly of the German and Swedish schools, though fencing and other military aspects were included. South America had its "war of the systems" even as did United States in the '80's and '90's and the resulting forms in South America represent a selection from several sources.

The revival of the Olympics, national and international congresses, establishment of teacher training courses have all contributed to the growth of South American interest and progress in this field as evidenced by her membership in International Federations.

The growth and present status may be considered under the following topics: (1) Official schools of physical education; (2) private organizations promoting teacher training and leadership courses; (3) the recreation and competitive movement.

OFFICIAL SCHOOL OF PHYSICAL EDUCATION

The first schools of physical education were established in 1906, when Dr. Enrique Romero Brest in Buenos Aires, Argentino, and Don Joaquin Cabezas, in Santiago, de Chile, founded official schools, both on the pattern of the Central Institute of Stockholm, and both available only to school teachers desiring graduation as Professors of Physical Education. Chile's school is a part of the state university, offers a four-year course with 27 major subjects of which there are 95 hours of theory and practice, and a thesis is required. Until 1938, Argentina's school was similar except that it required an additional year, the fourth and fifth years being entirely specialization in physical education. In the new plan, adopted under the "Direccion General de Educacion Fisica"—an office under the Secretary of Public Instruction—there are two courses: (1) One-year course for instructors of gymnastics and recreation; (2) two-year course for Professors of Physical Education. Graduates from either of the above courses are recognized officially all over the country as either "instructors" or "professors" and are eligible to teach in any primary or secondary school.

The public schools (primary) have, for men and women, their own school under the National Council. Diplomas are not granted as the course is considered merely a practical one for teachers graduated from the Normal schools.

Both of the above Argentine schools have had their schedules influenced by the program of the YMCA through two representatives, Mr. Fred. W. Dickens of Springfield College, and Alberto Regina of the Montevideo school.

Argentina's third official school is the "Fencing and Gymnastic School of the Army," also under the National Council of Physical Education. Its program is wider than the title suggests, including Hygiene, History, Pedagogy and Playgrounds. Its strongly Swedish principles have, since the recent visit of Niels Bukh and his gymnastic team, been modified by the inclusion of Danish Basic Gymnastics.

Brazil's national school of physical education, organized in the state of São Paulo, 1934, but was succeeded in 1939 by the "National School of Physical Education and Sports," with its branches in Rio de Janeiro, São Paulo, Porto Alegre, Bahia and Espiritu Santo, all under control of the Secretary of Education and Public Health. This gives Brazil supervision of physical education, teaching in Normal and Secondary schools, Universities and all private institutions. During the last few years this school, from its various branches, has prepared hundreds of teachers of whom 80 per cent are women. Its program includes five different courses to prepare for the various types of positions, one of the most interesting of these is that for physicians, who are required to pursue a one-year course to qualify them as Doctors of Physical Education and Sports.

Peru has its "National School of Physical Education," under supervision of the Military School of Chorrillos, where, in addition to the strictly military courses, there is included a wide variety of calisthenics and related activities, selected from several different sources.

Uruguay is recognized as the outstanding state of South America in the field of physical education and recreation.

In 1906, Mr. Claudio Williman presented to Congress his bill which resulted, in 1911, in the creation of the "Comision Nacional de Education Fisica," instructed to carry out the provisions of the new law, which in part required the Commission: (1) To organize annual competitions; (2) to create associations of rational physical education; (3) to relate existing national associations among themselves and with other foreign countries, unifying the methods; (4) to publish books and magazines for general knowledge and propaganda; (5) to foster the installation of playgrounds, gymnasiums, public baths and shooting stands; (6) to obtainfrom the authorities, corporations and private enterprises the necessary financial help to promote physical education in the country; (7) to prepare conferences and lectures in all national institutions to give parents all possible knowlege about physical education for their children; (8) to organize systematic campaigns against the evils that endanger children and youth in their social relationships; (9) to present a rational plan of compulsory physical education for the primary and secondary schools of the country.

As the Executive to carry out this comprehensive program, the Commission selected Mr. Jess T. Hopkins, a graduate of Springfield College, who had demonstrated marked ability as physical director in the YMCA at Montevideo. His technical training and outstanding ability as a teacher, leader, organizer and administrator, combined with his interest in youth, genial personality and friendly attitude indicated him as "the man" deserving selection for this historically important and nationally significant appointment.

His experience had taught him the need of trained leaders so he organized his "Corps," and from them, selected, among others, Julio J. Rodriguez, Julio Pereyra and H. Chiapella, sent them to his Alma Mater and, upon their graduation, appointed them as his associates to the official positions for which they had been trained. From this center, through its staff, instructors and graduates, the new play emphasis has spread over much of the continent. Mr. Hopkins merits the distinction of the "Father of the Playground Movement in South America."

The various "official" training schools have not been the only agency to be credited with promotion of physical education, in its widest content, over the continent. Clubs, YMCA'S and the Olympic Committee have each contributed.

Business opportunities in South America attracted capital from many European countries as well as from the North America. It appears that wherever these "foreigners" congregated there national community interests resulted in the formation of "clubs" to help keep them mindful of their homelands. A large part of these club programs was physical activity—games and sports. The British were the first to organize them, but they were soon followed by North Americans, Spanish, Germans, Portugese, French, Swedish, Danish, Jewish, Syrian, Czechoslovakian, Italian, Swiss and others.

The capitals of the various countries usually show the greatest number of clubs, but Brazil has a dozen or more cities with exceptionally large organizations, representing enormous investments in buildings, golf links, swimming pools, football and athletic fields, polo grounds, gymnasiums, rowing and sailing equipment, and in some cases, camp and picnic sites.

In Uruguay, Montevideo and Buenos Aires boast of football (soccer) stadia with seating capacities of 120,000. These are used regularly. Some of these clubs have a steady membership of 25,000 members. Frequently the State or Federal government has aided these clubs financially on the basis that they were a real asset to the people.

The "Fundacion Ateneo de la Juventud" of Buenos Aires under the capable leadership of Fred W. Dickens, Springfield College, as its physical director, became one of the outstanding clubs of the country. Mr. Dickens transferred to the "National Institute of Physical Education" at San Fernando, Argentina.

The YMCA, through its physical education department, offered its ideals and wholesome program of physical education over many countries of South America. The significant dates and distributions are: Rio de Janeiro 1911, Buenos Aires and Montevideo 1912, Valparaiso 1916, São Paulo, Lima and Recife 1921, Santiago 1924, Concepcion 1925, Porto Alegre 1928, Rosario and Bahia 1932.

Among the aspects new to South Americans were: Calisthenics with music, mass games, new styles in swimming, track, baseball, basketball and volleyball. All these features spread rapidly and became popular, not only because of their intrinsic merits, but also because the volunteer leaders gave enthusiastically of their time and skills. This program became known as the "New System," was adopted rapidly by many countries.

The need for trained leaders to conduct these activities became urgent, so in 1922, the "International Federation of South American YMCA'S" organized its "Federacion Sudamericana de Associacions Christianas de Jovenes" at Montevideo, Uruguay. As director of its section on Physical Education, known as the Technical Institute (Instituto Technico), selection was made of James S. Summers of Springfield College. This four-year curriculum was fashioned after similar training courses in United States, adapted to local conditions and needs. While designed primarily for training personnel in the

YMCA, graduates of this Technical Institute have accepted appointment in various official government positions. Conditions for admission to this Institute include: Personal character and health; completion of a secondary school course, or a satisfactory examination; and suitable physique and experience.

Each South American country has its own National Olympic Committee, which has a large part in controlling its own physical education activities. This committee represents its country in international contests. Within each country every recognized sport has its own national organization. Argentina has 48 sports, so has 48 associations or leagues, affiliated with its National Committee.

When it became evident that the 12th Olympiad could not be held, the Olympic Committees considered the practicability of organizing a limited championship. So at the invitation of Argentina, a Congress was called at Buenos Aires, August 28–31, 1940, where 16 of the 21 countries in the Pan-American Union, decided to institute a set of Pan-American games every four years, beginning with 1942. The first of these periodic games was held at Buenos Aires offering contests in 16 events with a total of 500 male competitors.

Each country has its official agency in control of its sports. In some cases this is the "official" school, in others the Olympic Committee, but usually it is a combination of these two operating under the supervision of some department of the government.

At the beginning, no special effort was made to sponsor competition among the different promoting agencies, but as sports became more popular it was but natural that members should begin to voice their desire to match their skills against other groups. Soccer, basketball and swimming developed into the most widely accepted sports and were the first to organize for competition.

Soccer, introduced by the British, in the 19th century, has forged ahead until it is now recognized as ranking first with both players and fans. National and international contests are held annually in both amateur and professional leagues. The immense crowds which weekly fill the splendid stadia evidence the popularity of this sport. Uruguay has twice (1924 and 1928) won the Olympic championship, with Argentina in second place. It is common saying that if a South American boy sees a ball rolling on the ground, he will kick it (soccer), whereas in United States the boy would stoop, pick up the ball with his hands to toss or throw it (basketball).

Basketball, introduced by the North American YMCA, must in the country as a whole, be given second place. The climate, in much of the continent, permits the playing of this game during the entire year. In the last 25 years, basketball has made prodigious strides, and even now threatens to challenge soccer as the most popular sport. Agustin Lozano, sports editor of the Buenos Aires newspaper "El Mundo," finds that from 1931 to 1940 the Federation controlling basketball has, in the city of Buenos Aires alone, grown from 52 to 133 affiliated clubs; from 183 to 481 teams and from 1484 to 3848 players with licenses to compete. The tours of two A. A. U. teams proved a strong stimulus to the spread of the game.

Miss Maria Lenk, world champion breast stroker from Brazil, advises that in her country, swimming holds second rank in popularity of sports, while in Equador it is rated first. Cureton in his "How to Teach Swimming and Diving," claims that Trudgeon learned from the South American Indians the style of swimming that he, a sailor, introduced into England in 1869. The Brazilian team holds the championship of South America. The women's team has had outstanding success, capturing fifth place in the Olympic free style and world records in the 200 meter and 400 meter breast stroke.

The visit of the South American swimming team to United States (Dec. 15, 1941 to Jan. 15, 1942) was a decided success. This group not only won its share of events, and established new records, but did much to cement the friendly relations between the countries.

Among the so-called "Minor Sports," tennis, introduced by the French, is played widely for exercise, recreation and competition, both national and international. Other outdoor activities include motoring, gliding, rugby, baseball, rowing, horseback riding and camping, while the indoor forms meeting approval are such as volleyball, handball, fencing, weight lifting, wrestling, jiu jitsu and roller skating.

The plan of organization adopted for most of these sports tends to throw control into the government agencies, under the claim that such a scheme renders these activities of increasing benefit to the people at large. So all forms of organized sport within a given country, are federated into leagues or associations for each sport. These federations are combined into a confederation within each state, and the state confederations in turn are related to the Olympic Committee of that country, which is under the control of Federal authorities.

There is growing up an increasing amount of literature on sports, in the form of newspaper articles, "official" publications, text books, activity programs, pedagogy and philosophy. These are written mostly by men of training and experience in the field.

CHAPTER XXXV

THE BOY SCOUTS OF AMERICA*

Personal Motivation.—In the Scout Oath or Promise the boy engages to keep himself "physically strong, mentally awake and morally straight." The Boy Scout motto is to "Be Prepared." There is thus embodied in the basic idealism of the Movement which the boy takes unto himself when he becomes a Scout a motivating force and a great dynamic leading to the "Will to be Well."

The Chief Scout Executive early expressed this as follows:

"In the Scout Movement we are trying to give each boy a consciousness of his own individual responsibility to make and keep himself physically fit. We are trying to make him believe it is almost an indecent thing to allow an ailment to get the better of him. He must overcome it."

This spiritual motivation of a personal fitness program is deep rooted in the philosophy of Scouting itself. To understand it fully one must understand the significance of the words Scout and Scouting and their historic background. Lord Baden-Powell, founder of the Boy Scout Movement explained that in developing Scouting for boys he drew upon the experiences of the frontiersmen, the backwoodsmen and the oldtime Scout as a basis for his development of the Boy Scout program. He did so because such men were not only self-reliant but were also personally competent as individuals to cope with any emergencies as they confronted life in the primitive. Among other things this involved a high degree of physical fitness, of mental alertness and moral integrity. This was important not only for the man's own preservation but more especially because of the welfare and safety of others frequently dependent upon him. His "Will to be Well" therefore was strengthened by his responsibility for the lives of others who followed his trail.

Upon this philosophy applied to Scouting for boys there was established a program of activities which included achievement in certain skills and the acquisition of certain knowledge as contained, for instance, in the requirements for Tenderfoot, Second

* This contribution of George J. Fisher, M.D., Assistant Chief Scout Executive, is acknowledged herewith.

Class and First Class and in certain merit badges in the process of which the Boy Scout in fulfillment of the Scout motto becomes prepared not only to assist himself but to serve others as well in the spirit of the Scout "good turn." As in the case of the Scout of old, personal fitness played a large part in all of these achievements and activities.

Fig. 112.—Boy scouts—camping.

The romantic appeal of Scouting to the boy constitutes then a powerful leverage for the development of certain attitudes and life habits in the area of personal health and fitness. Because to the boy, Scouting is an adventuresome game he wants to make good as a Scout both in terms of the skills and knowledge which a good Scout should have and in terms of his personal qualifications as embodied in the Scout Oath and Law.

With such spiritual motivation as a foundation and with such specific objectives in terms of fitness before him, there are embodied in the Boy Scout program certain specific means to these ends as follows:

SPECIFIC MEANS TO THE END OF PERSONAL FITNESS.

1. *Growth in Personal Fitness.*—The "Will to be Well" on the part of the Scout might be meaningless if there was not also a program of action for him to follow. This program involves first of all the Scout's knowledge of his fitness as revealed in such procedure as periodical health check-ups and other tests of his personal fitness. It involves in the second place the fulfillment of a personal program of improvement on his part in order to correct any remedial difficulties as revealed in the health check-up. The check-up becomes meaningful principally as it results in such a program of personal improvement.

Fig. 113.—Boy scouts—hiking.

The incentive to such growth in personal fitness is supplied by various forms of counsel which comes to him through individuals, through the Boy Scout Handbook and other basic Scouting texts, as well as through special departments in Scout periodicals such as the "Keeping Physically Fit" page in Boys' Life.

This program of health check-up and personal improvement starts in the Cub program, with boys of 9, 10 and 11. Here. incident

Fig. 114.—Boy scouts—cabin building.

to the Cub's advancement from grade to grade an annual health check-up is required and the Cub is lead to maintain his own health scoreboard in his current Cub handbook.

The health check-up and personal improvement continues in Scouting. It is recommended for application, though not required in every troop and local unit. It is required as a preliminary to participation in the camping program.

A health examination is specifically required in Senior Scouting (ages 15 and upward) as a basis for participation in the Sea Scout Program, the Explorer Scout Program, the Air Scout Program, Rover Scout Program, and the Emergency Service Training Program.

Fig. 115.—Boy scouts egg racing.

For purpose of emphasis let it be said again that the genius of this whole process lies in the opportunity it offers to the Cub, the Scout or the Senior Scout to take active measures in raising the standard of his personal fitness and in correcting any remedial difficulties. The fact that the boy has in his possession an inventory of such difficulties and is motivated to do something about them is a matter of great educational significance.

2. *Personal Achievement of Knowledge and Skills.*—"Health through Knowledge" and "Safety through Skill" are basic slogans in the Boy Scouts of America.

It may be noted that, by and large, these requirements are related to practical life experience especially in the environment of the out-of-doors. This is deemed significant the more so in view of the experience of the training of German youth during the past few decades. There the trend was from the Turn Verein to the open trail and the results of this transition in terms of personal fitness of German youth have been all too apparent.

3. *Group Projects and Activities.*—In addition to the individual program of personal improvement and achievement there are in the Scout program significant opportunities for growth in personal fitness by reason of participation in group projects and activities.

The out-of-doors is the theatre of action for most of these activities in Scouting. Camping, hiking, canoeing and cruising are noteworthy illustrations of this opportunity.

There are obvious values in terms of personal fitness in such participation. There is a certain therapy in the natural environment itself as over against artificial surroundings. There is a powerful motivation that comes from membership in a common group, bent upon certain activities of a healthful nature. There are implicit and potentially available in the activities themselves values which contribute directly to the promotion of personal fitness.

Needless to say these values are conditioned upon the standards maintained in their performance. To this end the Boy Scouts program provides specific standards of health and safety for the protection and the benefit of those who engage in such activities. The program provides such procedures as these for the preservation of health and safety:

(*a*) Inspection of camp sites, meeting places, etc.; (*b*) training of leaders; (*c*) investigation of serious accidents or sickness which occur during these activities in the interest of safeguarding future health and safety.

Thus through the maintenance of health and safety standards the constructive values of these group projects and activities in terms of personal fitness are assured.

It will be observed that in the Boy Scouts program camping, hiking, cruising and the like take the place of formal competitions and athletic meets. A distinctive type of competition is introduced in these Scouting practices against oneself or against a standard.

In such competition every participant can emerge a winner and a winner as well in terms of health and personal fitness.

4. *Service in the Promotion of General Health.*—In the Boy Scout Program service, the capacity to care about others, is a motivating force. As indicated, it underlies the Motto, "Be Prepared" and gives point to the personal fitness program. It follows then that the Scout's interest in public health and the health and safety of those

Fig. 116.—Boy scouts—canoe launching.

'round about him is an important feature of the program. Such interest in public health and safety finds expression in public events: as health rallies, Boy Scout expositions, and the like.

The Emergency Service Training Program, however, is the most dramatic and spectacular feature of such service in behalf of public welfare. While the Emergency Service Program as now carried on in specially trained Emergency Service Corps is an outgrowth of the last several years, the essentials of the program in terms of preparation for service to the community whenever disaster strikes has been a part of Scouting from the earliest day. In floods, hurricanes, forest fires, and earthquakes, Scouts through the years have demonstrated, not only willingness to serve, but preparation for effective service in preserving the health and safety of their respective communities.

It is worthy of note that in all phases of this personal fitness program the "learning by doing" process is involved. The Scouting method is a method of action.

SCOUTING.

TENDERFOOT SCOUT RANK

Learns and subscribes to the Scout Oath and Law with its emphasis on personal fitness.

SECOND CLASS SCOUT RANK

First aid	Use of knife and hatchet
Tracking	Firebuilding
Scout pace	Outdoor cooking
Practice of five rules of safety	

Evidence that he has put into practice in daily life the principles of the Oath and Law.

FIRST CLASS SCOUT RANK

Swimming	Map making
Fourteen mile hike	Axemanship
Advanced first aid	Judging
Advanced outdoor cooking	Nature study

Future evidence that he has put into practice daily the principles of the Oath and Law.

STAR, LIFE AND EAGLE RANKS

Based upon participation in the Merit Badge Program as referred to below, First Class Scouts qualify for Star, Life, or Eagle rank by submitting evidence that they have *first*—actually put into practice in his daily life the ideals and principles of the Scout Oath and Law, the Motto "Be Prepared," and the "Daily Good Turn;" *second*—Maintained an active service relationship to Scouting; *third*—made an effort to develop and demonstrate leadership ability.

The Life Scout status assumes special significance in terms of this Physical Fitness Program in that the following Merit Badges are required for the achievement of the rank:

First aid	Public health
Physical development of athletics	Safety or life saving
Personal health	Pioneering

MERIT BADGE PROGRAM

Direct	Indirect
Archery	Agriculture
Athletics	Angling
Camping	Animal industry
Canoeing	Aviation
Cycling	Beef production
First aid	Bookkeeping
Hiking	Bird study
Horsemanship	Botany
Life saving	Citrus fruit culture
Personal health	Conservation
Physical development	Cooking
Public health	Corn farming
Rowing	Cotton farming
Safety	Dairying
Seamanship	Friendship
Skiing	Forestry
Swimming	Fruit culture
	Gardening
	Grasses, legumes and forage cultiv.
	Hog and pork productions
	Insect life
	Landscape gardening
	Marksmanship
	Nut culture
	Pigeon raising
	Pioneering
	Poultry keeping
	Reptile study
	Rocks and minerals
	Sheep farming
	Small grains and cereal foods
	Stalking
	Surveying
	Zoölogy

CUBBING.

WOLF CUB RANK (9 year olds and up)
Know and practice street and road safety.
Annual health check-up and laws of cleanliness.

BEAR CUB SCOUT (10 years old and up)
More advanced feats of skill and safety.
Know and practice rules for fire safety.

Annual health check-up and show progress in plan for remedying defect.

Eight laws of health and quarantine regulations.

LION CUB RANK (11 year olds)
More advanced feats of skill.
Know and practice rules for water safety.
Annual health check-up and correction of remedial defects.
Morning exercises.

SPECIAL ELECTIVES

Nature	Wrestling
Gardening	Golf
Safety	Tennis
Boxing	Back yard camping

SENIOR SCOUTING
    (*a*) Sea Scouting   (*b*) Explorer Scouting

Here the special skills and knowledge involved are Scoutcraft in wilderness and primitive living.

Life exploration from the standpoint of vocations and avocations is stressed.

(*c*) Air Scouting

Here personal fitness is related to the special skills and knowledge involved in the ground work program of Air Scouting, which involve the following Merit Badges—General Aviation, Airplane Structure, Airplane Design and Engines, and Aerodynamics—and the following ranks in the Senior Air Scout Program—Apprentice Air Scout, Air Scout Observer, Air Scout Craftsman, and Air Scout Ace.

(*d*) Rover Scouting.

This is designated as a brotherhood of service in the out-of-doors for young men eighteen years of age and over.

CHAPTER XXXVI.

BIOGRAPHIES.

ERNEST HERMANN ARNOLD.*

ERNST HERMANN ARNOLD was born in Erfurt, Germany, on February 11, 1865. He became in later years much interested in the subject of heredity and wrote several articles for the Arnold College year book, in which he showed why he might have come to possess certain traits.

His quarterly school reports from his eighth to eighteenth year registered a rate of five, lowest skill grade in physical education, corresponding to between zero and twenty on a hundred percent scale. Dr. Arnold, in one of his articles, attributed his poor grades to the fact that he hated the work, not because of the type but because of the poor teaching done by most of the pupil teachers. When he came into the hands of a master teacher, Karl Kroh, the student learned to love formal gymnastics, a love which proved abiding and he attained such skill as one could at twenty, and with his stature. This lesson in the importance of good teaching remained with him and became the vital principle of his directorship, which was his greatest contribution to physical education, the training of young men and women to be capable teachers.

A lad in his late teens, young Arnold, came to America avowedly to study homeopathy, a school of medicine with no standing in Germany. He had no resources but his own brain and brawn and so the trail to the halls of medicine was a long one, leading through various occupations—cowboy, farm worker, clerk, journalist and finally through a course in the Milwaukee School of Physical Education, later the Normal College of the American Gymnastic Union. He then taught in the Trenton Turngemeinde and in March 1889, married Miss Marie Nagel of that city.

Medicine—no longer specifically homeopathy—was his goal, and a position with the New Haven Turners gave him his opportunity to combine teaching with study at the Yale Medical School. In 1894, he obtained his M. D. and in 1895 took courses in surgery and

---

* Appreciation is hereby expressed to Bertha W. Coburn, Librarian of Arnold College, for this contribution.

(452)

orthopedics at the Universities of Halle and Leipzig. Henceforth, he followed both professions, medicine and the teaching of physical education, with eminent success. He became chief of the New Haven Orthopedic Dispensary, orthopedic surgeon to Griffin Hospital, Derby, Connecticut, and Grace Hospital, New Haven, and in-

FIG. 117.—Dr. E. H. Arnold.

structor of orthopedic surgery at Yale University. His special line of orthopedics contributed much to the development of Arnold College. The students in the earlier classes went to the New Haven dispensary and observed and assisted under his direction. In 1916, he bought property on State Street and remodeled it for a

free orthopedic clinic.   In 1926, he sold this and built one adjoining
the other College buildings on Chapel Street.

Dr. Arnold had become associated with the Anderson Normal
School of Gymnastics on York Street in New Haven as assistant
director and instructor in German gymnastics in 1895.   He became
director in 1897 and in 1900, Dr. William G. Anderson withdrew,
and the school was continued as the New Haven Normal School
of Gymnastics.   A number of men and women had given devoted
service to the institution but it remained for Dr. Arnold to have the
vision, the foresight and the courage to assume the financial obligations necessary for its expansion.

Realizing the demand for well-trained men in the field of physical
education, the Director added a paragraph to the 1905–1906
catalogue ending with this sentence, "This school will make a
special effort to attract men to the field."   Up to this time only
seven men were numbered among its graduates.   Remembering
his own difficulties in securing an education, he always showed
especial consideration for a poor boy who was earnestly working to
succeed.

One of the first objectives the Doctor had in his mind was to
provide a proper home for the women students.   In 1904, he rented
a house for this purpose but it was some distance from the gymnasium, so in 1907, he bought the property at 1452 Chapel Street.
At the opening of school in 1914, the completion of the new gymnasiums placed the class rooms, offices, women's dormitories and
gymnasiums within the same group of buildings at the corner of
Chapel Street and Sherman Avenue.   The purchase of more adjacent
property eventually provided a four-acre campus with fourteen
buildings.

Facilities for sports were developed from a backyard beginning
to a real out-door season in 1909 on rented property at Morris
Cove and, eventually, to eight weeks of camping each year for
all students on owned land at Silver Sands.   This plot consisted
of four hundred acres of farm, meadow, and woodland, a shore
frontage of over five hundred feet, a number of buildings, athletic,
and sport fields.

The two-year normal course was supplanted in 1921 by a three-
year curriculum leading to the degree of Bachelor of Science in
Physical Education and Arnold College for Hygiene and Physical
Education was incorporated under the laws of the State of Connecticut.   Dr. E. H. Arnold became the first president.   In 1929,
by Special Act of the Legislature of the State of Connecticut, a
charter was granted to the College authorizing the organization of
a four-year curriculum leading to the degree of Bachelor of Science.

The first purpose of the school to train students to become

teachers of physical education had been adhered to. The changes in the program had been to improve this preparation and in addition to give the academic training necessary for the granting of a bachelor's degree.

Dr. Arnold was a born teacher and a strict disciplinarian. He gave his graduates not only a thorough knowledge of the subject matter, and practice in the best ways of teaching, but also a training in promptness, obedience to rules, true sense of values, stability in thoughts and actions, and self-assurance to cope with any situation. He was a clear thinker and constantly made use in his lectures of his unusual ability in grasping an idea and developing it. The class would become weak with laughter over his mimicry of someone or something which he wished to portray, and at other times would tremble in sympathy with some individual who had incurred his anger. He kept his students on the alert with keen bits of sarcasm, in the use of which he was a master. He hated parrot recitations and would spend valuable time in helping a student to think out a problem for herself. A pupil might balk at going over a buck. Then, if he thought her honest in her endeavor, would come kindly entreaty, encouraging words, infinite patience and sympathetic understanding, and finally over she would go—much to her own surprise. He would lash unmercifully one who deliberately avoided a difficult task. He expected and demanded that his students live up to his own ideals and standards. His methods of teaching and dealing with them resulted in intense loyalty to him and confidence in his opinions. Letters came to him constantly from graduates asking for advice on personal and family problems. These always received prompt attention.

Regarded as dictatorial by some, Dr. Arnold never interfered in any way with the work of his instructors in their own particular line. He supported his faculty. If they in turn did not support him, his methods and policies, they had to go. One could not often change Dr. Arnold's opinion but one could, without fear, express one's own contradictory ideas honestly and as forcibly as one wished. In the majority of cases, time proved him right.

His love of the arts led him to encourage his pupils to become acquainted with the best. He believed every teacher of physical education should know something about music and so for many years he provided a teacher of piano and required every student who could not play a musical instrument to study for one year. The reward for making the best progress was a ticket to the New Haven Symphony Orchestra concerts. For several years, the College had a box at the Metropolitan Opera House in New York. On Friday evenings the juniors went down in groups to the performances, remaining until Saturday to visit the Metropolitan Museum of Art and the Natural History Museum.

Dr. Arnold was very active in the American Physical Education Association and was a member of the Council from 1894 on, as a representative from the New Haven Society. He was thorough and conscientious in performing the duties he accepted. He was national president for the year 1916. The Council in 1927, emphasizing that no other member had served so long continuously and also the value of his service, elected him to Honorary Membership in the Association with the provision that it should not in any way affect his voting power in the Council.

He was a member of the editorial committee of the magazine *Mind and Body*, from 1900–1907. When a bitter rivalry arose between the different systems in physical education, his articles supporting the German method were widely read and quoted. He belonged to various other organizations, medical, surgical, educational, civic and humanitarian. He was actively interested in every one of them, and his associates marveled that he could carry in his mind and correspondence so many different threads.

Dr. Arnold was a great reader, and his book reviews showed that he grasped fully what he read and, moreover, saw beyond the text to implications not apparent on the surface. He wrote constantly for the *Alumni News* and *Fall In*, the College publications, and for professional journals. All that he wrote embodied much of himself and his philosophy of life. He left in book form only the series of pamphlets on gymnastic topics, *Gymnastic Nomenclature*, *Gymnastic Tactics*, *Elementary Gymnastics on Apparatus* and *Gymnastic Games*. The deep and widespread influence that he exerted on physical education in America came more through his teaching and public speaking than through his writings.

He traveled much to attend conventions and to address bodies of alumni, teachers and other professional groups. He journeyed through Europe several times for both study and pleasure.

Dr. Arnold believed in formal gymnastics as the backbone of the physical education program. He claimed that it had a wholesome and decided influence on posture, furthered all-round development, alertness, obedience and discipline (not the blind variety as demanded by military command). So far as the specific effect of bodily movements upon tissues and organs could be predicted, formal work was far superior to games. On the other hand, he declared that many of the simplest elements of play taught things that could not be developed by formal training. He argued for physical education for the masses at an early age. He showed his belief in playgrounds in a practical way by leaving in his will a sum of money to the City of New Haven to be expended for a playground. The following paragraph from his book, *Gymnastic Games*, expresses best his views:

"We make great demands on inhibition in school and in daily life. The wearing out of this power in its worst forms is well illustrated by the hysterical, the neurasthenic and the choreic person, species ever on the increase in this country. The child must learn to restrain motions and emotions in school life, play knows no such restraint. Nearly all games if well conducted, are good. No restraint of motions should be demanded in playing, nor should we teach those motions necessary for playing too formally. Emotions must be allowed free play, especially joy; shouting is one of the main accompaniments of play; by no means should it be suppressed. School room plays are therefore not even a poor substitute; they must be condemned without condition. Better not rouse joy than rouse it and suppress its manifestations. Lively games with variety of motion in which skill is not a decided element are best."

He disapproved of military training as a type of physical education, and claimed that formal work such as gymnastics, plays, games, hiking, and swimming was begun as an antidote against militarism. He felt that to teach ideas in conjunction with abstract physical-training movements would give new interest in formal gymnastics. He illustrated this by showing the facts of arithmetic, algebra, geometry, trigonometry, physics and psychology that could be taught from a quarter wheel. He continually emphasized the fact that books and expensive apparatus were not necessary for successful teaching. His pamphlet on the jumping rope showed how rhythm, team play, leadership and the overcoming of fear could be taught with this inexpensive piece of equipment. He recommended that all boys of high school age be subjected to training in antagonistics, wrestling, fencing, and boxing, and that this training be especially imposed upon those who displayed rash tempers. He knew that the above training had done much to curb the violent temper which he possessed as a young man. He had no use for the fads that sprang up from time to time and quickly disappeared from the history of physical-education methods.

Dr. Arnold contracted influenza in December 1928, which left him with depleted vitality. An ocean voyage during the Christmas holidays restored him somewhat, so that he attempted to take up his work at the College. Relapses occurred, a hard-driven heart rebelled, and yielding to medical advice, he left for Atlantic City on March 5th. Four days later, he died suddenly. The funeral services were private but on Sunday, May 5th, a memorial service was held in Plymouth Church, New Haven. Relatives, faculty, students, alumni, friends and delegations from various societies assembled to honor their departed teacher and friend.

The editor of the *Alumni News,* who had been associated with the President of the College for many years as student and faculty member, arranged the May issue as a memorial to "Dr. E. H. Arnold, Teacher, Leader, Friend." Much of this material about his life and characteristics has been taken from that source.

The convention of the Eastern District of the American Physical Education Society met in New Haven in April 1929, about a month after Dr. Arnold's death. He had always attended these meetings and usually had an important part on the program. The early plans had included an address by him on the *Futility of Record Chasing.* The committee of arrangements honored him by including in the official program his photograph, resolutions by the New Haven Society and a page history of Arnold College.

To Dr. Arnold were vouchsafed such ability to look and plan far ahead, such faith in one's self and one's ideals, such dogged patience, such refusal to be defeated as few men are granted. He made mistakes, he sometimes inflicted undeserved hurts, he was often himself badly hurt, but his life was a glorious example of a straightforward, unremitting, purposeful march to a goal. A member of the Board of Trustees said of him, "He braved the mountain and died near the top."

_____

JAMES HUFF MCCURDY.*

On December 6, 1866, at Princeton, Maine, was born James Huff McCurdy, destined to become one of the outstanding leaders in the field of Physical Education.

Of English-American ancestry through his mother Augusta Evelyn (Heath), he inherited his Scotch-Irish strain from his father, John, who entered United States from New Brunswick, Canada, and enlisted in the First Maine Cavalry where he served, mostly as a scout for the Army, during three years. At the close of the Civil War, because of his fine service to the country, he was awarded his citizenship.

Returned to civil life he became captain of a lake steamer engaged in the lumber and bark industry. The boy, James, worked on this boat during his high school vacations, not only developing his physique, but also gaining from his father, experience in how to handle men. He was ambitious to become physically skilled, so erected in his back yard a horizontal bar on which he and some high school mates practiced the "stunts" they had seen at the circus.

Graduating from Princeton High School in 1885, James worked

_____

* Appreciation is given herewith for the coöperation by Mrs. Persis B. McCurdy who supplied much of the information on which this article is based.

for a year in a woolen mill, another year on a farm. Neither of these satisfied him, so in 1887 he went to Bangor, Maine, to seek his fortune planning to learn the blacksmith's trade. Mr. Jordan, secretary of the YMCA there, realized the possibilities in this young man and appointed him physical director of the local Association and suggested attendance at the summer session of the School for Christian Workers, Springfield, Massachusetts. Thus was established McCurdy's first contact with Dr. Luther H. Gulick, head of the Physical Education course there, and with other leaders such as Dr. Fred. Leonard of Oberlin College, later to become the historian for the profession of physical education.

FIG. 118.—Dr. J. H. McCurdy

After serving in the Maine YMCA at Lewiston and Auburn, James McCurdy, in the autumn of 1889, entered the School for Christian Workers (later Springfield College), and is recorded as graduating with the class of 1890. He accepted an appointment as physical director of the Twenty-third Street Branch of the YMCA, New York City, and registered in the Medical School of New York University from which he received his M.D. in 1893. His internship was for one and a half years in a dispensary on the lower East Side.

During his connection with the Twenty-third Street YMCA Dr. McCurdy developed an outstanding Leaders' Corps from which went such well-known leaders as Mike Sweeney of high jump fame, who carried his fine ideals to preparatory school youth; George L. Meylan who after graduation from Harvard Medical School, became physical director at the Boston YMCA and, later was Director of the Physical Education Department at Columbia University; also William Skarstrom, who after receiving his medical degree from Harvard, became widely known as an author and Professor of Teacher Training in Physical Training at Wellesley College. Dr. McCurdy played football in medical school and in summers had charge of city-wide athletics and rowing as organized under the YMCA.

This personal experience, together with his medical degree, his demonstrated leadership and Christian ideals, qualified him pre-eminently to accept the offer from Dr. Gulick, in 1895, of a position on the staff at Springfield. After accepting this appointment, Dr. McCurdy, desiring a more comprehensive view of the whole field of physical education, spent the summer as the private pupil of William Skarstrom, who being of Swedish birth and education, was thoroughly grounded in the philosophy of Swedish gymnastics.

Among the objectives which Dr. Gulick had in mind when he selected Dr. McCurdy to be associated with him were:

1. To place the professional course in Physical Education on a more scientific basis. So the agreement contained the proviso that Dr. McCurdy be given leave for graduate study under Dr. Porter, Professor of Physiology at Harvard. The specific field selected was the effect of physical activity upon human functions, especially upon the cardiovascular system. Instruments for measuring and recording blood pressures were devised and constructed, and experiments conducted on volunteer students from the Harvard Medical School. Thus was developed in Dr. McCurdy a dominant interest in Physiology of Exercise, which became a major field for research during his subsequent career.

2. To train students in gymnastics with an understanding of physiological and psychological approaches in order that analysis and selection of activities and teaching methods be scientific. Dr. Gulick held that Springfield graduates should exemplify, in person, the skills which they expected their classes to attain. Dr. McCurdy's gymnastic team from Twenty-third Street had defeated in competition the team of experienced Springfield representatives. This emphasis upon bodily control and skill has continued and the Springfield College exhibition team is well known for its all-round performances. Many individual students have won places in the individual championships of the American Athletic Union.

3. To train students to be scientific TEACHERS of athletic sports, and, through the intimacies with boys and men, to inculcate in them the fundamental social and religious principles of life. The graduate who limits his efforts to merely COACHING athletic techniques fails to measure up to the full opportunities offered by his position.

In this stage of its history the institution was known as the "International Young Men's Christian Training School," because it had been sending its graduates to that Association exclusively. Dr. McCurdy, after an extensive study, discovered that of the college and university physical directors only 41 per cent had special training for their work, of the YMCA only 28 per cent and of the preparatory schools only 12 per cent. Figures for public schools were not available. This led to his statement that the need for qualified leaders in physical education was probably greater than in any other profession. A portion of his concluding claim is:

"We are in the beginnings of great sociological movements for improvement of the race. Physical education in the Associations, educational institutions, clubs, etc., occupies a definite place in these movements. The leaders in this work must be men of earnest Christian character and real ability. They must understand the changed conditions brought about by city life, decrease of muscular work, etc. Men who would enter this profession thoroughly qualified must consecrate heart and head to a life of arduous endeavor."

Dr. McCurdy's conviction and the promotion of his plans paved the way for an extension of the institution's field beyond that of preparing for the YMCA alone, to include other areas where boys and young men were grouped, *e. g.*, schools, colleges, camps, industry, playgrounds, clubs, etc. To entitle graduates to status with other faculty members in schools and colleges, an academic degree was essential, so there had to be added more courses in liberal arts and, for certification to teach in public schools, certain specified courses in Education. These requirements were met gradually as the course was increased from two to three years, then to four years and finally, for graduate degrees, to five years.

In 1905 the Commonwealth of Massachusetts, with the approval of the liberal arts colleges and universities in the state, authorized the "International Young Men's Christian Association College" to confer the degrees: Bachelor and Master of Physical Education (B.P.E. and M.P.E.); also Bachelor and Master of Humanics (B.H. and M.H.). At a later date, there was authorized the additional degrees Bachelor of Science and Master of Education (B.S. and M.Ed.)

Dr. Gulick was so interested in the scientific and philosophical aspects of physical education that he grew impatient over the necessity of administrative details and asked Dr. McCurdy to add to his already heavy duties of teaching and directing, the responsibility of recruiting and selecting students for the department, and also for placing graduates in suitable locations. To gain a more intimate knowledge of the field, Dr. McCurdy accepted appointments on committees and boards of directors of many organizations.

He also withdrew from the Springfield Summer Schools to accept lecture appointments elsewhere, e. g., Harvard (ten years), University of California (Berkeley and Los Angeles), State University of Utah, and many YMCA Conferences and Schools. In this way he had an opportunity to meet alumni and prospective students and to learn details of institutions desiring to employ graduates.

In 1900 Dr. Gulick resigned to accept appointment at Pratt Institute, Brooklyn. In due time Dr. McCurdy succeeded him as Head of the Department, and soon established his reputation as an administrator. He adopted the plan of weekly, evening meetings with his faculty, reporting on trips, conferences and alumni, also sharing plans and proposals for the good of the Department and the college, and asking for free discussion and criticism. Each member had such confidence in Dr. McCurdy that there was no hesitation in offering personal views. In these ways he built up strong friendships and unusual loyalty within his staff.

After many years of membership in the national organization, Dr. McCurdy, in 1906, was appointed editor of its official organ, *The American Physical Education Review.* Two years later he was given the additional duties of secretary and treasurer and carried this triple assignment until his resignation in 1930. During this period the Review developed from a small quarterly to a monthly (ten issues per year) journal of high professional rank.

In August, 1917, he was asked to go overseas to supervise the athletic and recreational work conducted by the YMCA among the American forces in France. Shortly after his arrival he was given the additional responsibility of supervising the health of the "Y" workers in Paris. The Army asked him to develop an adequate program in sex instruction to supplement the recreative attractions offered under the auspices of the "Y." This involved the assembling of a staff of physicians and other experts. After the war he returned to the United States, broken in health from his seventeen months service, and convalescing from an attack of pneumonia. At once he relieved Mrs. McCurdy of the editorial duties of the Review, and after a few weeks rest, he returned to his college duties which had been distributed among his staff.

In his leave of absence, 1900, Dr. McCurdy registered in Clark University to major under Dr. C. Hodge, the biologist, in securing original data on the physiological changes of pubescence, using boys from the Worcester public schools as subjects. Attendance at Dr. G. Stanley Hall's classes gave him a new interest in the genetic point of view as explaining many of the not-too-well understood aspects of youth development. His work earned the degree Master of Arts.

He became even more avid for new truth and its application to physical education. All such were discussed with his staff and criticism invited either at the time or in writing later. In this way he sought to keep them up to date and to educate them in discriminating decisions. As a test of the validity of any new claim, proposal or method, he guarded against too-ready approval by raising the questions: (1) Is it true and worthwhile? and (2) Is it practicable, *i. e.*, can it be applied economically, from the standpoint of cost and time, to large groups of boys or men?

Dr. McCurdy's marked and wholesome influence was exerted not only through his wide acquaintance but also by means of his literary contributions. Many articles appeared over his name in the various professional magazines in his specific field, and in medical or educational periodicals. During his twenty-four years as editor of the Review he gave generous space to researches and discoveries in physical education. Practically all of the editorials were written by him personally. In glancing over these one is impressed by his persistence in promoting ideals and policies in which he believed; his evaluation on proposals under consideration and his comments on new findings in physical education and related fields. Without doubt his matured and sane judgments helped to guide the A. P. E. A. in its success development.

Desiring readily-available references on all phases of physical education, he enlisted the coöperation of his staff, friends and graduate students in its preparation. The Physical Directors Society of the YMCA, at its World's Fair meeting at St. Louis, 1904, appointed a committee, with Dr. McCurdy as chairman, to prepare this material and secure funds for its publication. With a sufficiently large number of advance orders to justify publication, this bibliography of 369 pages was issued by the Society in 1905. It contained thousands of selected titles then available, arranged under a special classification prepared by Dr. McCurdy and J. T. Bowne, librarian at Springfield College.

After years of intensive study, widespread lectures and diligent research, in his special field, Dr. McCurdy prepared copy for his Physiology of Exercise (Lea & Febiger, Philadelphia, 1924). Its 242 pages are crowded with details; its bibliography is extensive, varying from 6 to more than 50 titles per chapter. This renders the text of special value as a source book. A second edition, revised, appeared in 1928 and the third edition, revised and enlarged, in collaboration with Dr. L. A. Larsen in 1939. This edition contains several new chapters making a text of 249 pages.

Among his other publications may be mentioned: A Calisthenic Dictionary, 1916, 34 pages; A Report on 139 Institutions in United States Preparing Teachers in Physical Education, a folio of 45 pages, 1929.

On July 17, 1895, Dr. McCurdy married Miss Persis B. Harlow of Windham, Maine, a student at Mt. Holyoke College. Her constant devotion and able coöperation, especially in administering the office and preparing copy, added much to the quality of the Review. She also contributed several articles, notably the series on the History of the American Physical Education Association.

During his later years at Springfield College, Dr. McCurdy resigned from administrative duties and majored on the problem of devising or discovering a simple test which would indicate organic efficiency in elderly men. Even after his retirement, in 1935, he labored unceasingly on that project. With the endorsement of General Arnold, there was no difficulty in securing adequate men for study, clerical help and suitable facilities. He felt that he was making progress, when ill health interrupted his plans and forced him to discontinue his work. That he did not lose faith in the ultimate solution of the problem on which he had been working, is indicated by a statement to his wife: "The test is so far along that younger or better men can complete it. My work is done." These words were uttered shortly before internal cancer caused his death, September 4, 1940.

Dr. McCurdy labored under certain handicaps. His lack of certain fundamentals in pre-professional education hampered him along literary lines. His ardent willingness to undertake projects, and impatience at delays sometimes involved him in difficulties. His devotion to some new idea or truth sometimes led him to present his views, somewhat indiscriminately, with all the enthusiasm of a young convert. Had it not been for the fine coöperation of students, associates and friends—all of whom appreciated his real worth— much of what he undertook could not have been accomplished. Yet this single-mindedness of purpose and indefatigable industry enabled him to persist in spite of obstacles which would have discouraged one of weaker convictions.

In physique, he was of the "stocky" type which militated against the fine coördinations essential to skilled performance. After watching him on the gymnasium floor, Dr. Gulick, a fine gymnast himself, said, "Mack, you will never make a physical director, you are as graceful as a cow, better pack up and go home." This remark was just the sting that the young McCurdy needed to arouse stubbornness. He would show them. In 1899 Dr. Gulick said to a guest: "See that McCurdy, if he lives he will become a national figure in physical education." Dr. Gulick's second prophecy came true.

Characterized by far-seeing vision, tireless energy, unquestioned honesty, deep sincerity, consuming zeal, friendly attitude, firm convictions and Christian faith, Dr. McCurdy won many real friends and set an example of life and living deserving of emulation by those who would serve humanity.

ROBERT TAIT MCKENZIE.*

In a cultured, Scotch-Presbyterian home at Almonte, Ontario, Robert Tait McKenzie was born, May 26, 1867. When he was but nine years of age his father died, leaving the boy more or less self dependent, yet he spent a happy boyhood. He entered enthusiastically into Canadian winter sports, skating, skiing and tobogganing and enjoyed in other seasons camping, hiking and roaming in the woods. As a result of these outdoor contacts, he developed an unusually strong love and appreciation of Nature. To express his feelings and sense of beauty, he began sketching and, later, painting in water colors.

Sharing his mother's ambition for his career, he decided upon further education, so graduated from the Ottawa Collegiate Institute and entered McGill University in 1885. Securing his A.B. in 1889, he registered in the University Medical School from which he graduated with his M.D. in 1892.

For athletics in college, he elected football, swimming, fencing, gymnastics (in the last he became University champion) and track where he established a high jump record which stood for years.

In 1890 the instructor of the gymnasium died, and James Naismith, a fellow townsman of McKenzie, was selected to fill the vacancy. It was but natural that McKenzie, a senior serving his internship in the University hospital, should be appointed as assistant instructor. At the close of that academic year, Naismith resigned to accept a position on the staff of the Training School (now Springfield College) at Springfield, Mass., where he "invented" basketball, the Jubilee Memorial of which was celebrated in 1942. Dr. McKenzie succeeded James Naismith as instructor of the gymnasium and, to study further the technics of physical education, attended Harvard summer school in 1894. While there he taught a course in anatomy and obtained from Dr. Dudley Sargent a new insight into the significance of tests and measurements on the human body.

In that same year, Dr. McKenzie submitted to McGill University a report setting forth the need for supervision of student health, and accompanied it by a recommendation that physical and medical examination be given to each incoming student. His claims for the advantage of this proposal were:

  1. That students with physical defects or incipient disease might be given needed medical attention.

* Appreciation is expressed, herewith, to Mrs. Ethel McKenzie whose splendid coöperation, through correspondence, has been the chief source of data on which this biographical sketch is based.

2. That students might be advised as to the form of athletics for which they were best qualified, and cautioned against such sports as might be prejudicial to their health.

Despite protests, on the part of some of the faculty, that such procedure would be "unacademic," and of some students that it would be an invasion of their "personal rights," the plan, endorsed by President Sir William Peterson, was adopted. Thus Dr. McKenzie became in Canada the "pioneer" in physical education just as Dr. Sargent at Harvard, Dr. Seaver at Yale and Dr. Hitchcock at Amherst had "pioneered" in the institutions of higher education in the United States.

FIG. 119.—Robert Tait McKenzie. (From a painting by Maurice Malarsky, photo by Chappel.)

He taught gymnastics, gave the medical examinations and served as medical attendant to varsity teams. These duties required his presence on certain afternoons only, so he devoted a portion of his time to private practise, specializing in orthopedics. His original ideas on the treatment of scoliosis attracted patients from all over Canada, and his appointment as House Physician to the Governor General of Canada, the late Marquis of Aberdeen, fostered a life-long friendship.

Upon graduation from Medical School, Dr. McKenzie was appointed demonstrator and, later, lecturer in anatomy, in which capacities he gained much experience in making plaster casts and models. This experience he turned to good account in the making of four life-sized masks to enable students to visualize the changes in facial expression resulting from severe, prolonged activity (dis-

FIG. 120.—The joy of effort.

tance running). Effort, Breathlessness, Fatigue and Exhaustion were so graphically depicted that the masks were pronounced masterpieces by both the artistic and scientific world. These established his reputation as an artist.

His success in this first venture encouraged him to apply the sensitive hand of the surgeon to the equally sensitive but more subtle one of the sculptor. So without any working knowledge of how to set up a figure, he made his own armatures, modeling first from his own image in his office mirror. Then, utilizing measurements of hundreds of college athletes, secured from Dr. Sargent of Harvard and Dr. Phillips of Amherst, he established his "canons" of proportion and produced the one-quarter life sized statuette, The Sprinter, a typical American college track man "on the mark." The first bronze cast was presented by his friend, Captain Munroe Ferguson, to Theodore Roosevelt, who, as President, kept it on his desk in the White House.

Impressed by the beauty and verity of The Sprinter, the Directors of Physical Education in Colleges, of which Dr. McKenzie was a member and several times president, asked him to model a statue of the typical American athlete. Again using judiciously his "canons" of proportion, he unveiled in 1903 his Athlete which, like The Sprinter, showed no trace of "stiltedness."

In 1904 the University of Pennsylvania was planning a new gymnasium and reorganizing its physical education policies. Learning through Dr. J. William Whyte, a trustee and sponsor of their athletics, of the young Canadian physician whose progressive ideas appealed to them, the trustees offered him an appointment with the rating of Professor, and the title of Director of Physical Education, and with full authority to develop his own ideals and plans.

Dr. McKenzie answered this challenge with all the enthusiasm and energy of which he was capable, sleeping in Weightman Hall while supervising its construction, installing equipment, and selecting his staff—that fine group of men whose continued loyalty was the great pride and satisfaction of his life. During the next few years the organization of this new department, its affiliation with the teeming life of a great university, the cementing of his connection with the medical profession, and the many demands of public life taxed his strength to the utmost. Consequently, he welcomed the opportunity for change and rest by accepting invitations to address, in 1907, both the Royal British Medical Society in London and the International Congress of School Hygiene in Paris.

While on this trip, he met and, subsequently, married Ethel O'Neil, the eldest daughter of the late John O'Neil of Hamilton, Ontario.

Upon their return to Philadelphia, Dr. McKenzie renewed his work at University of Pennsylvania. The new department in the University expanded, proving its worth by the improved physical status of the students, as indicated by tests and measurements carefully taken and interpreted during their four years of college life. His interests extended beyond his own department. With his unusual understanding of youth and its problems, he lectured to the students of all departments on hygiene. This led to the founding of the School of Public Health. The summer school in Physical Education was established, and the increased registration of women necessitated the appointment of a dean for them, and, eventually, to the founding of the Bennett College for women as a part of the University of Pennsylvania.

Tireless in his response to requests for coöperation from organizations interested in youth, he promoted such units as the Boys Clubs and the physical education departments of the YMCA. His many years of service to Springfield College, as a member of its Instruction Committee, were noteworthy. Through his interest and advice the Playground Association was formed in Philadelphia, and the first playground opened and equipped. The first local troop of the Boy Scouts of America was organized under his impetus, for he had a great admiration for Sir Robert Baden-Powell, a life-long friend. Dr. McKenzie modeled a figure of the Boy Scout, posed for by a young Scout of Philadelphia, and presented the statue to the Scout organization, with its royalties for all time, as a part of his enduring contribution to the movement.

With his keen appreciation of the ancient Greek ideals, he was intensely interested in the revival of the Olympic Games. His advice was often sought by the founder, Baron de Coubertin and, later, by Count Balliet de LaTour. On every possible occasion he attended these concourses, and, during the games held in Sweden, 1912, he and Mrs. McKenzie were guests of the Prince and Princess at the Royal Palace in Stockholm. On that occasion his large medallion, The Joy of Effort, received the King's medal and, later, was set in the wall of the Stadium to commemorate the Games.

To Dr. McKenzie the Penn Relays offered an exceptional opportunity of observing the varied processions of the best of American youth testing their strength and prowess in athletic contests. His pencil sketches, made on the spot, became a basis for the truly beautiful bronzes regarded as unequalled since the times of ancient Greece. In addition to those already mentioned, the following are among his best known statues: The Competitor, The Boxer, The Relay, The Juggler, The Ice Bird, The Flying Sphere, The Plunger, The Modern Discus Thrower, The Javelin Cast, and The Invictus. His groups most admired include The Onslaught (football) and Brothers of the Wind (skating). Among the colleges and universities housing his bronzes are University of Pennsylvania, Yale University and Springfield College.

On the outbreak of World War I he offered his services to the War Office in London, joining as a recruit the classes in Physical Training in Army headquarters at Aldershot. One day his instructor asked him if he, an American, knew the author of a much-used text in their library by "a fellow named McKenzie" (reference was to Exercise in Education and Medicine, first published in 1912).

"I happen to know him very well," was the answer, "so well that I wrote the book myself."

He was promoted with the rank of Major in the Royal Medical Corps and sent to Heaton Park (Manchester) to organize and command the large depot for disabled men there. Here he devised his special treatments and well-known apparatus and appliances to retrain and rehabilitate disabled men from the wide variety of injuries received on the field of battle. At the request of the Director of Medical Services, Sir Arthur Keogh, he visited the British convalescent hospitals to suggest improvements in their organization and programs. He found his reward in the large percentage of men restored and returned to active service or to useful civilian life.

When United States entered the war Dr. McKenzie returned to the University of Pennsylvania, but continued his work for disabled men, of which he gave the details in his Reclaiming the Maimed. He was appointed consultant to the Walter Reed Hospital where his apparatus was used with marked success. Utilizing his experience as demonstrator in anatomy, he specialized in the treatment of facial wounds. By invitation, he visited the military hospitals of Canada, advising on treatment and equipment.

After the war, Dr. McKenzie held his first exhibition in London. This was received enthusiastically by the English who, after the mutilation so common among them, found joy in the beautiful, unbroken bodies portrayed in all their wholesome grace. One result was a commission to execute for Cambridge a memorial to the men who had returned from the war. This gorgeous statue, for which he made a profound study of the Anglo-Saxon face as represented in the Cambridge students, is known as The Homecoming.

Then followed a series of glorious tributes to the gallant soldier dead: The Volunteer, in his home town, Almonte; The Victor, Woodbury, N. J.; Over the Top, Radnor, Pa.; Altar in the Church of the Saviour, Philadelphia; Col. Harry Baker, the Parliament House, Ottawa; Girard College Memorial, Philadelphia; Captain Guy Drummond, Montreal; Norton Downs, Aviator, Philadelphia; Scottish-American War Memorial, "The Call," Edinburgh.

To his life-sized statue of Young Franklin already on the campus of the University, he added that of George Whitfield and of Provost Edgar Fahs Smith. In Princeton came that of Dean West, and at Harvard, the three football panels to the memory of Percy Haughton. Of international significance were the large relief in the House of Parliament, Ottawa, commemorating the Federation of the Provinces, presented by fellow Canadians residing in United States, also the Statue of General Wolfe in London, unveiled by the Duke of Connaught, and dedicated by a descendant of Wolfe's military foe, the Marquis of Montcalm.

With the increasing demands of his art upon his time and energy, he felt that he should retire from active responsibility for the Department of Physical Education at the University of Pennsylvania, so, in 1930, he tendered his resignation. At the request of the president, he outlined the future policy of the department on what became known as the "Gates" plan. He was retired as Research Professor, but continued to serve in an advisory relationship. Under the terms of his retirement, he assembled the rare collection of athletic bronzes which constitute a lasting record of the athletic life of his time. These are housed in his old office in Weightman Hall.

The breadth of his interests is indicated by his membership and standing in such professional organizations as: American Medical Association, American Academy of Physical Education (Fellow), College of Physicians (Fellow), American Association of Health, Physical Education and Recreation (Fellow), Directors of Physical Education in Colleges (Honorary Life Membership). His name is also found in the membership of such groups as: A.M.P. Medical Fraternity; Franklin Inn, University, Rittenden, and Sketch Clubs; the Century and Charaka Clubs of New York; Royal Canadian Academy; Authors' Club and Athenæum, London.

As an author, Dr. McKenzie is credited with more than one hundred scientific articles in Medical, Educational and Art Journals. He edited a series of textbooks on Anatomy, Physiology of Exercise, History of Physical Education and related subjects, and contributed sections on Physical Therapy to such standard works as Keen, System of Surgery, also Kelly and Musser, Handbook of Practical Treatment.

Among honorary recognitions from educational institutions may be noted: Sargent Summer School, Diploma, 1891; Springfield College, M.P.E.; 1913, McGill University, L.L.D., 1921; University of Pennsylvania, A.E.D., 1928, and St. Andrews University, Scotland, 1938.

On April 28, 1938, Dr. McKenzie spent his usual busy day but later, as he was preparing to take his car to meet Mrs. McKenzie, he died of heart failure. His last race was run, his final trophy won.

On the following Saturday, the great Relay Carnival was held at the hour of his funeral—the flag waved at half mast on Franklin Field during five minutes of silent tribute.

In his removal from active life, Physical Education lost a masterly leader and advisor, while Art was deprived of its outstanding exponent of depicting in statuary the beauties of human physique. Refined in appearance, gentle of speech, delightful in personality, kindly in spirit, logical in thinking, strong in convictions, thorough in research and painstaking in work, Dr. McKenzie by his life and example will continue to be an inspiration to all who knew him.

JAMES NAISMITH.*

Frederick Froebel, a poor, unhappy German boy, gave the world the theory of the kindergarten—education through play. Dr. James Naismith was born in Altmonte, Canada, on November 6, 1861, and eight years later he became an orphan. He gave to youth basketball, a game adapted to youngsters from grade eight to men in maturity. Doubtless the poverty of play in youth's life emphasizes a vital need met by Naismith and Froebel who were able to provide for the world, plays and games that are "necessary for man in order to refresh himself after labor" and to "flee from empty idleness to active recreation in play." This is why the heart of youth goes out into play as into nothing else, as if in it man remembered a lost paradise.

Eight nationally known educators, speaking from the same platform, declared that basketball had all the qualities necessary to teach the educable child: poise, rhythm, grace, coördination, development of skills and of physical vigor. The speakers were not competitive coaches, nor were they athletes.

This game, the only international sport that is the product of one man's brain, stamps Dr. Naismith as a great educator, a kindly humanitarian and a practical Christian. He loved youth. He and his classmate at Springfield, Alonzo Stagg, working together, chose the profession of Physical Education over the ministry, because they felt that in this way they could contribute more to youth. The game of basketball was originated in 1891 by Dr. Naismith at Springfield College to fill the recognized need for a vigorous, indoor winter sport. Two old peach baskets, a soccer ball and thirteen rules were the original equipment of the game which has spread around the world and was introduced as an Olympic event at Berlin in 1936. A photostatic copy of the original rules hangs in my office, while the original copy of the rules is in possession of the Naismith heirs. At the bottom of the original copy, in Dr. Naismith's handwriting is "First draft of basketball rules, posted in the gym that the boys might learn the rules. Feb., 1892. James Naismith."

These original rules have survived the impact of years remarkably well. For the sake of accurate history, a copy is given herewith:

1. The ball may be thrown in any direction with one or both hands.
2. The ball may be batted in any direction with one or both hands, never with the fist.

* Appreciation is hereby expressed for this contribution by Dr. Forrest C. Allen, Director of Physical Education and Varsity Basketball Coach, University of Kansas, Lawrence, Kansas.

3. A player cannot run with the ball; the player must throw it from the spot where he catches it, allowance being made for a man who catches the ball when running at a good speed.

4. The ball must be held in or between the hands; the arms or body must not be used for holding it.

5. No shouldering, holding, pushing, tripping, or striking in any way the person of an opponent is to be allowed. The first infringement of this rule by any person shall count as a foul; the second shall disqualify him until the next goal is made, or if there was evident intent to injure the person, for the whole game; no substitute allowed.

6. A foul is striking the ball with the fist, violation of rules 3 and 4, and such as are described in rule 5.

Fig. 121.—James Naismith.

7. If either side makes three consecutive fouls it shall count for a goal for the opponents. (Consecutive means without the opponents making a foul.)

8. A goal shall be made when the ball is thrown or batted from the grounds into the basket and stays there, providing those defending the goal do not touch or disturb the goal. If the ball rests on the edge and the opponent moves the basket, it shall count as a goal.

9. When the ball goes out of bounds it shall be thrown into the field, and played by the person first touching it. In case of a dispute, the umpire shall throw it straight into the field. The thrower is allowed five seconds; if he holds it longer, it shall go to the opponent. If any side persists in delaying the game, the umpire shall call a foul on them.

10. The umpire shall be the judge of the men, and shall note the fouls, and notify the referee when three consecutive fouls have been made. He shall have power to disqualify men according to rule 5.

11. The referee shall be judge of the ball, and shall decide when the ball is in play, in bounds, and to which side it belongs, and shall keep time. He shall decide when a goal has been made, and keep account of the goals with any other duties that are usually performed by a referee.

12. The time shall be two 15-minute halves, five minutes between.

13. The side making the most goals shall be the winner. In case of a draw, the game may, by agreement of captains, be continued until another goal is made.

The youth of the world lost a great benefactor in Dr. James Naismith. Eighteen million young men all over the world are playing his game of basketball—a game which he originated for eighteen troublesome young men in Springfield College. Dr. Naismith is directly responsible for the large field houses, the large auditoria and gymnasia where basketball is played. Before this game was originated there were few large indoor arenas that were used for any indoor sports. Thickly dotting the middle western states are high school gymnasia that are much larger in size than the entire school buildings were thirty years ago.

From the many press notices after the death of Dr. Naismith, attesting to the wonderful popularity of the sport which he invented, the following may be regarded as representative:

"The game is played today by twenty million persons in seventy-five countries and draws annually ninety million paid admissions in United States."[1]

Dr. Naismith was indirectly responsible for the forward pass in football. Until the popularity of basketball began to spring up in the colleges in America in 1905, the forward pass in football was not thought of. Then the football rules committee incorporated the forward pass, or basketball pass, in football, and immediately the open game became the element that spread the defense. Basketball has become footballized, and football has become basketballized. The forward pass of today is a Naismith innovation, and is the most spectacular of all plays on our gridirons.

"The happiest moment of my life," Dr. Naismith said, "came in 1936," when he attended the Olympic games in Berlin and saw the game of basketball played for the first time in the international Olympic competition. The Father of Basketball was sent to Berlin following a drive for funds sponsored by the National Association of Basketball Coaches among spectators, officials and players who wanted to have Dr. Naismith present when the teams of all nations filed in behind their respective flags. Dr. Naismith addressed the assembled players before the start of the tournament, and admitted that in so doing his eyes were misty.

When Dr. Naismith was appraised of the gratuity and affectionate contribution of his friends toward the Olympic trip, his epic statement was, "Do not be afraid to serve humanity and wait for your reward." The words of Kipling seem most fitting to him:

[1] *Midweek*, December 11, 1939.

"And only the Master shall praise us, and only the Master shall blame,
And no one shall work for money, and no one shall work for fame.
But each for the joy of the working, and each in his separate star,
Shall draw the thing as he sees it for the God of things as they are."

On November 28, 1939, Dr. James Naismith, the inventor of basketball, died at his home in the quiet college town of Lawrence, Kansas. He suffered a critical hemorrhage on November 19, but rallied and returned to his home from the hospital after four days. A few days later he was stricken with a heart attack which resulted in his death.

Dr. Naismith attended McGill University in Montreal, Canada, and graduated with an A.B. degree in 1887. This was the first of his three degrees. In 1890 he graduated from the Presbyterian College, Montreal, in 1891 he completed the work at the Y M C A College at Springfield, and in 1898 he received his Doctor of Medicine degree from the University of Colorado, and was employed by the University of Kansas with the rank of Associated Professor. He was advanced to full Professor in 1907. Honors conferred upon him include: Master of Physical Education, Springfield College; Honorary Diploma in Philosophy, McGill University; Honor Diploma in Hebrew, McGill University; Honor Award of Fellow in Physical Education, American Association of Health, Physicial Education and Recreation. In endorsing him for this Fellowship, Dr. R. G. Clapp wrote:

"Dr. Naismith had a vision, far ahead of his time, of the social values of recreative and competitive athletics. He deserted the ministry, for which he had spent a number of years in preparation, because he saw the great opportunity in recreative physical education for character training of boys and young men."

Dr. Naismith married Miss Maude E. Sherman, Springfield, Mass., in 1894. Three daughters and two sons, all of whom live in the Middle West, were born to this marriage. Mrs. Naismith died in March, 1937.

Four positions in physical education occupied Dr. Naismith's career. From 1887 to 1890 he was Director at McGill University, from 1891 to 1895 he assisted in directing the work at Springfield College, and from 1895 to 1898 he was physical director at the Y M C A, Denver, while studying medicine. Then he began his forty years' service to the University of Kansas.

His military service included that with the First Kansas Regiment, then with Dr. James Huff McCurdy in the Social Hygiene program for the A. E. F. in France. He held membership in many professional organizations, edited the first Basketball Guide, contributed to the section on Athletics in The Modern High School, and, in 1919, published The Basis of Clean Living. The five words of this title characterize the life of this seventy-eight year old Professor Emeritus of the University of Kansas, who retired from active teaching in 1937 after forty years of "building Character in the hearts of young men."

INDEX.

(477)